HOSEA

Zondervan Exegetical Commentary on the Old Testament

HOSEA

God's Reconciliation with His Estranged Household

ZONDERVAN

Exegetical Commentary on the Old Testament

A DISCOURSE ANALYSIS OF THE HEBREW BIBLE

JERRY HWANG

DANIEL I. BLOCK
General Editor

ZONDERVAN ACADEMIC

The Hebrew text is from Deuteronomy 31:11–13, which highlights the importance of "hearing" the voice of Scripture:

> When all Israel comes to appear before יהוה your God at the place he will choose, you shall read this Torah before them in their hearing. Assemble the people—men, women and children, and the foreigners residing in your towns—so they can *listen* and learn to fear יהוה your God and follow carefully all the words of this Torah. Their children, who do not know this Torah, must *hear* it and learn to fear יהוה your God as long as you live in the land you are crossing the Jordan to possess. (NIV, modified)

ZONDERVAN ACADEMIC

Hosea

Published in Grand Rapids, Michigan, by Zondervan. Zondervan is a registered trademark of The Zondervan Corporation, L.L.C., a wholly owned subsidiary of HarperCollins Christian Publishing, Inc.

Requests for information should be addressed to customercare@harpercollins.com.

ISBN 978-0-310-94237-5 (hardcover)

Cover design: Tammy Johnson
Interior design: Beth Shagene

Printed in the United States of America

---

25 26 27 28 29 30 31 32 33 34 35 36 37 38 39 40 /TRM/ 20 19 18 17 16 15 14 13 12 11 10 9 8 7 6 5 4 3 2

To my parents, with love and gratitude

Contents

Series Introduction

Prospectus

Modern audiences are often taken in by the oratorical skill and creativity of preachers and teachers. However, they tend to forget that the authority of proclamation is directly related to the correspondence of the key points of the sermon to the message the biblical authors were trying to communicate. Since we confess that "all Scripture [including the entirety of the OT] is God-breathed and useful for teaching, rebuking, correcting and training in righteousness, so that [all God's people] may be thoroughly equipped for every good work" (2 Tim 3:16–17 NIV), it seems essential that those who proclaim its message should pay close attention to the rhetorical agendas of biblical authors. Too often modern readers, including preachers, are either baffled by OT texts, or they simply get out of them that for which they are looking. Many commentaries available to pastors and teachers try to resolve the dilemma either through word-by-word and verse-by-verse analysis or synthetic theological reflections on the text without careful attention to the flow and argument of that text.

The commentators in this series recognize that too little attention has been paid to biblical authors as rhetoricians, to their larger rhetorical and theological agendas, and especially to the means by which they tried to achieve their goals. Like effective communicators in every age, biblical authors were driven by a passion to communicate a message. So we must inquire not only what that message was but also what strategies they used to impress their message on their hearers' ears. This reference to "hearers" rather than to readers is intentional, since the biblical texts were written to be heard. Not only were the Hebrew and Christian Scriptures composed to be heard in the public gathering of God's people but also before the invention of moveable type, and few would have had access to their own copies of the Scriptures. While the contributors to this series acknowledge with Paul that every Scripture—that is, every passage in the Hebrew Bible—is God-breathed, we also recognize that the inspired authors possessed a vast repertoire of rhetorical and literary strategies. These included not only the special use of words and figures of speech but also the deliberate selection, arrangement, and shaping of ideas.

The primary goal of this commentary series is to help serious students of Scripture, as well as those charged with preaching and teaching the Word of God, to hear the messages of Scripture as biblical authors intended them to be heard. While we recognize the timelessness of the biblical message, the validity of our interpretation and the authority with which we teach the Scriptures are related directly to the extent to which we have grasped the message intended by the author in the first place. Accordingly, when dealing with specific texts, the authors of the commentaries in this series are concerned with three principal questions: (1) What are the principal theological points the biblical writers are making? (2) How do biblical writers make those points? (3) What significance does the message of the present text have for understanding the message of the biblical book within which it is embedded and the message of the Scriptures as a whole? The achievement of these goals requires careful attention to the way ideas are expressed in the OT, including the selection and arrangement of materials and the syntactical shaping of the text.

To most readers syntax operates primarily at the sentence level. But recent developments in biblical study, particularly advances in rhetorical and discourse analysis, have alerted us to the fact that syntax operates also at the levels of the paragraph, the literary unit being analyzed, and the composition as a whole. Discourse analysis, also called macro syntax, studies the text beyond the level of the sentence (sentence syntax), where the paragraph serves as the basic unit of thought. Those contributing to this series recognize that this type of study may be pursued in a variety of ways. Some will prefer a more bottom-up approach, where clause connectors and transitional features play a dominant role in analysis. Others will pursue a more top-down approach, where genre or literary form begins the discussion. However, we all understand that both approaches are required to understand fully the method and the message of the text. For this reason, the ultimate value of discourse analysis is that it allows the text to set the agenda in biblical interpretation.

One of the distinctive goals for this series is to engage the biblical text using some form of discourse analysis to understand not only what the text says but also how it says it. While attention to words or phrases is still essential, contributors to this commentary series will concentrate on the flow of thought in the biblical writings, both at the macroscopic level of entire compositions and at the microscopic level of individual text units. In so doing we hope to help other readers of Scripture grasp both the message and the rhetorical force of OT texts. When we hear the message of Scripture, we gain access to the mind of God.

Format of the Commentary

The format of this series is designed to achieve the goals summarized above. Accordingly, each volume in the series will begin with an introduction to the book being explored. In addition to answering the usual questions of date, authorship, and provenance of the composition, commentators will highlight what they consider to be the main theological themes of the book and then discuss broadly how the style and structure of the book develop those themes. This discussion will include a coherent outline of the contents of the book, demonstrating the contribution each part makes to the development of the principal themes.

The commentaries on individual text units that follow will repeat this process in greater detail. Although complex literary units will be broken down further, the commentators will address the following issues.

1. **Main Idea of the Passage:** A one- or two-sentence summary of the key ideas the biblical author seeks to communicate.
2. **Literary Context:** A brief discussion of the relationship of the specific text to the book as a whole and to its place within the broader arguments.
3. **Translation and Exegetical Outline:** Commentators will provide their own translations of each text, formatted to highlight the discourse structure of the text and accompanied by a coherent outline that reflects the flow and argument of the text.
4. **Structure and Literary Form:** An introductory survey of the literary structure and rhetorical style adopted by the biblical author, highlighting how these features contribute to the communication of the main idea of the passage.
5. **Explanation of the Text:** A detailed commentary on the passage, paying particular attention to how the biblical authors select and arrange their materials and how they work with words, phrases, and syntax to communicate their messages. This will take up the bulk of most commentaries.
6. **Canonical and Theological Significance:** The commentary on each unit will conclude by building bridges between the world of the biblical author and other biblical authors and with reflections on the contribution made by this unit to the development of broader issues in biblical theology—particularly on how later OT and NT authors have adapted and reused the motifs in question. The discussion will also include brief reflections on the significance of the message of the passage for readers today.

The way this series treats biblical books will be uneven. Commentators on smaller books will have sufficient scope to answer fully each of the issues listed above on each unit of text. However, limitations of space preclude full treatment of every text for the larger books. Instead, commentators will guide readers through #1–4 and 6 for every literary unit, but full Explanation of the Text (#5) will be selective, generally limited to twelve to fifteen literary units deemed most critical for hearing the message of the book.

In addition to these general introductory comments, we should alert readers of this series to several conventions that we follow. First, the divine name in the OT is presented as YHWH. The form of the name—represented by the Tetragrammaton, יהוה—is a particular problem for scholars. The practice of rendering the divine name in Greek as κύριος (=Heb. אֲדֹנָי, "Adonay") is carried over into English translations as "LORD," which represents Hebrew יהוה and distinguishes it from "Lord," which represents Hebrew אֲדֹנָי. But this creates interpretive problems, for the connotations and implications of referring to someone by name or by title are quite different. When rendered as a name, English translations have traditionally vocalized יהוה as "Jehovah," which seems to combine the consonants of יהוה with the vowels of אֲדֹנָי. However, today non-Jewish scholars often render the name as "Yahweh," recognizing that "Jehovah" is an artificial construct.

Second, frequently the verse numbers in the Hebrew Bible differ from those in our English translations. Since the commentaries in this series are based on the Hebrew text, the Hebrew numbers will be the default numbers. Where the English numbers differ, they will be provided in square brackets (e.g., Joel 4:12[3:12]).

Third, when discussing specific biblical words or phrases, these will be represented in Hebrew font and in translation, except where the transliterated form is used in place of an English term, either because no single English expression captures the Hebrew word's wide range meaning (e.g., *ḥesed* for חֶסֶד, rather than "lovingkindness"), or when it functions as a title or technical expression not readily captured in English (e.g., *gōʾēl* for גֹּאֵל, rather than "kinsman redeemer").

Daniel I. Block, general editor

Author's Preface and Acknowledgments

Hosea is an amazing book, making this commentary a privilege to write for the ZECOT series. I am thankful for the invitation to do so from Daniel Block, whose lasting faith in me has sometimes been tested ever since I was his PhD student at Wheaton College. He breathed new life into this project when it seemed like it might not see the light of day. I am grateful as well to the ZECOT editors and the editorial team at Zondervan for their patience in tackling the countless minutiae of Hebrew discourse analysis. Nancy Erickson has been a great help both in editing the manuscript and sharpening my thinking.

It has been a distinct pleasure to serve at Singapore Bible College and teach the OT Prophets for a decade. My students have refined my understanding of Hosea in countless ways. A big thank you goes to those courageous and devoted alumni who are now serving faithfully all over Asia and beyond. They have sat through many lectures on the prophetic books that occasionally became sermonic, but as I have tried to remind my students, the prophets were preachers who would have expected no less.

Thanks are also due to the libraries at Singapore Bible College, Biola University and Claremont School of Theology in California, and Tyndale House and Ridley Hall in Cambridge, UK. At different times in the writing process, their facilities have each been a home away from home. Special recognition goes to Jan Shen, the now retired coordinator of the Singapore Bible College library, for cheerfully fulfilling my countless book requests.

My wife Jackie and our three children, Josie, Jacob, and JJ have been companions throughout this journey. Our lives together have been filled with fun, laughter, and forgiveness—God's gifts that keep my call to biblical scholarship in perspective.

Finally, I would like to dedicate this study to my parents, Mr. and Mrs. Ching-Fa Hwang. Their constant support through the years has provided the background and inspiration to study a prophet whose message draws so deeply and passionately upon familial imagery.

Abbreviations

Abbreviations for books of the Bible, pseudepigrapha, rabbinic works, papyri, classical works, and the like are readily available in sources such as the *SBL Handbook of Style* and are not included here.

AB	Anchor Bible
ABCS	Asia Bible Commentary Series
ABR	*Australian Biblical Review*
AJSL	*American Journal of Semitic Languages and Literatures*
AnBib	Analecta Biblica
ANET	*Ancient Near Eastern Texts Relating to the Old Testament*. Edited by James B. Pritchard. 3rd ed. Princeton: Princeton University Press, 1969
ATD	Das Alte Testament Deutsch
AUSS	*Andrews University Seminary Studies*
AYBRL	Anchor Yale Bible Reference Library
BASOR	*Bulletin of the American Schools of Oriental Research*
BBRSup	Bulletin for Biblical Research Supplements
BETL	Bibliotheca Ephemeridum Theologicarum Lovaniensium
BHQ	*Biblia Hebraica Quinta*. Edited by Adrian Schenker et al. Stuttgart: Deutsche Bibelgesellschaft, 2004–
BHRG	*A Biblical Hebrew Reference Grammar*. C. H. J. van der Merwe, J. A. Naudé, and J. H. Kroeze. 2nd ed. London: Bloomsbury T&T Clark, 2017
BHS	*Biblia Hebraica Stuttgartensia*. Edited by Karl Elliger and Wilhelm Rudolph. Stuttgart: Deutsche Bibelgesellschaft, 1983
Bib	*Biblica*
BibInt	*Biblical Interpretation*
BibOr	Biblica et Orientalia
BibSem	The Biblical Seminar
BJS	Brown Judaic Studies
BN	*Biblische Notizen*
BR	*Biblical Research*

BSac	*Bibliotheca Sacra*
BTB	*Biblical Theology Bulletin*
BZ	*Biblische Zeitschrift*
BZAW	Beihefte zur Zeitschrift für die alttestamentliche Wissenschaft
CBQ	*Catholic Biblical Quarterly*
CurBR	*Currents in Biblical Research*
CHANE	Culture and History of the Ancient Near East
ConBOT	Coniectanea Biblica: Old Testament Series
COS	*The Context of Scripture*. Edited by William W. Hallo and K. Lawson Younger. 4 vols. Leiden: Brill, 2003–2016
CTJ	*Calvin Theological Journal*
CTR	*Criswell Theological Review*
CurTM	*Currents in Theology and Mission*
DDD	*Dictionary of Deities and Demons in the Bible*. Edited by Karel van der Toorn, Bob Becking, and Pieter W. van der Horst. Leiden: Brill, 1995. 2nd rev. ed. Grand Rapids: Eerdmans, 1999
EA	El-Amarna tablets. According to the edition of Jørgen A. Knudtzon. *Die el-Amarna-Tafeln*. Leipzig: Hinrichs, 1908–1915. Repr., Aalen: Zeller, 1964. Continued in Anson F. Rainey, *El-Amarna Tablets, 359–379*. 2nd rev. ed. Kevelaer: Butzon & Bercker, 1978
ERT	*Evangelical Review of Theology*
EstBib	*Estudios biblicos*
ESV	English Standard Version
ETL	*Ephemerides Theologicae Lovanienses*
ETSS	Evangelical Theological Society Studies
FAT	Forschungen zum Alten Testament
FRLANT	Forschungen zur Religion und Literatur des Alten und Neuen Testaments
GKC	*Gesenius' Hebrew Grammar*. Edited by Emil Kautzsch. Translated by Arthur E. Cowley. 2nd ed. Oxford: Clarendon, 1910
HBT	*Horizons in Biblical Theology*
HUCA	*Hebrew Union College Annual*
IBHS	*An Introduction to Biblical Hebrew Syntax*. Bruce K. Waltke and Michael O'Connor. Winona Lake, IN: Eisenbrauns, 1990
ICC	International Critical Commentary
IRT	Issues in Religion and Theology
ITC	International Theological Commentary
ITS	*Indian Theological Studies*
JBL	*Journal of Biblical Literature*
JBQ	*Jewish Bible Quarterly*

JETS	*Journal of the Evangelical Theological Society*
JHebS	*Journal of Hebrew Scriptures*
JNES	*Journal of Near Eastern Studies*
Joüon	Joüon, Paul. *A Grammar of Biblical Hebrew.* Translated and revised by T. Muraoka. 2 vols. Rome: Pontifical Biblical Institute, 1991
JSJ	*Journal for the Study of Judaism in the Persian, Hellenistic, and Roman Periods*
JSOT	*Journal for the Study of the Old Testament*
JSOTSup	Journal for the Study of the Old Testament Supplement Series
JTS	*Journal of Theological Studies*
KJV	King James Version
KTU	*Die keilalphabetischen Texte aus Ugarit.* Edited by Manfried Dietrich, Oswald Loretz, and Joaquín Sanmartín. Neukirchen-Vluyn: Neukirchener Verlag, 1976. 2nd enlarged ed. of *KTU: The Cuneiform Alphabetic Texts from Ugarit, Ras Ibn Hani, and Other Places.* Edited by Manfried Dietrich, Oswald Loretz, and Joaquín Sanmartín. Münster: Ugarit-Verlag, 1995 (= *CTU*)
LD	Lectio divina
LDHB	*The Lexham Discourse Hebrew Bible: Introduction.* Steven Runge and Joshua Westbury. Bellingham, WA: Lexham, 2012
LHBOTS	The Library of Hebrew Bible/Old Testament Studies
LTQ	*Lexington Theological Quarterly*
LXX	The Septuagint
MT	Masoretic Text
NAC	The New American Commentary
NASB	New American Standard Bible
NICOT	New International Commentary on the Old Testament
NIDOTTE	*New International Dictionary of Old Testament Theology and Exegesis.* Edited by Willem A. VanGemeren. 5 vols. Grand Rapids: Zondervan, 1997
NIV	New International Version
NLT	New Living Translation
NRSV	New Revised Standard Version
NSBT	New Studies in Biblical Theology
OBO	Orbis Biblicus et Orientalis
OBT	Overtures to Biblical Theology
OTE	*Old Testament Essays*
OTL	Old Testament Library
OTS	Old Testament Studies
OtSt	*Oudtestamentische Studiën*

PEQ	*Palestine Exploration Quarterly*
R&T	*Religion & Theology*
RB	*Revue biblique*
ResQ	*Restoration Quarterly*
RevExp	*Review and Expositor*
RHPR	*Revue d'histoire et de philosophie religieuses*
SAA	State Archives of Assyria
SAOC	Studies in Ancient Oriental Civilizations
SBLAcBib	Society of Biblical Literature Academia Biblica
SBLANEM	Society of Biblical Literature Ancient Near East Monographs
SBLDS	Society of Biblical Literature Dissertation Series
SBLMS	Society of Biblical Literature Monograph Series
SBLSymS	Society of Biblical Literature Symposium Series
SJOT	*Scandinavian Journal of the Old Testament*
SJT	*Scottish Journal of Theology*
SSN	Studia Semitica Neerlandica
StBibLit	Studies in Biblical Literature
TDOT	*Theological Dictionary of the Old Testament.* Edited by G. Johannes Botterweck and Helmer Ringgren. Translated by John T. Willis et al. 16 vols. Grand Rapids: Eerdmans, 1974–2018
Them	*Themelios*
THOTC	The Two Horizons Old Testament Commentary
TLOT	*Theological Lexicon of the Old Testament.* Edited by Ernst Jenni, with assistance from Claus Westermann. Translated by Mark E. Biddle. 3 vols. Peabody, MA: Hendrickson, 1997
TynBul	*Tyndale Bulletin*
UCOP	University of Cambridge Oriental Publications
UF	*Ugarit-Forschungen*
VT	*Vetus Testamentum*
VTSup	Supplements to Vetus Testamentum
WBC	Word Biblical Commentary
WMANT	Wissenschaftliche Monographien zum Alten und Neuen Testament
WTJ	*Westminster Theological Journal*
WW	*Word and World*
WZKM	*Wiener Zeitschrift für die Kunde des Morgenlandes*
ZAW	*Zeitschrift für die alttestamentliche Wissenschaft*

Select Bibliography

Abma, R. *Bonds of Love: Methodic Studies of Prophetic Texts with Marriage Imagery (Isaiah 50:1–3 and 54:1–10, Hosea 1–3, Jeremiah 2–3).* SSN 40. Assen: Van Gorcum, 1999.

Andersen, Francis I., and David Noel Freedman. *Hosea: A New Translation with Introduction and Commentary.* AB 24. Garden City, NY: Doubleday, 1980.

Bechtel, Lyn M. "The Metaphors of 'Canaanite' and 'Baal' in Hosea." Pages 203–15 in *Inspired Speech: Prophecy in the Ancient Near East: Essays in Honor of Herbert B. Huffmon.* Edited by John Kaltner and Louis Stulman. LHBOTS 378. London: T&T Clark, 2008.

Bird, Phyllis A. "To Play the Harlot: An Inquiry into an Old Testament Metaphor." Pages 219–36 in *Missing Persons and Mistaken Identities: Women and Gender in Ancient Israel.* OBT. Minneapolis: Augsburg Fortress, 1997.

Boda, Mark J. *"Return to Me": A Biblical Theology of Repentance.* NSBT 35. Leicester: Apollos, 2015.

Boling, Robert G. "Prodigal Sons on Trial: A Study in the Prophecy of Hosea." Pages 7–25 in *Realia Dei: Essays in Archaeology and Biblical Interpretation in Honor of Edward F. Campbell, Jr. at His Retirement.* Edited by Prescott H. Williams and Theodore Hiebert. Atlanta: Scholars Press, 1999.

Boshoff, Willem S. "Who Let Grain, Grapes and Olives Grow? Hosea's Polemics against the Yahwists of Israel." Pages 265–75 in *Religious Polemics in Context: Papers Presented to the Second International Conference of the Leiden Institute for the Study of Religions (Lisor) Held at Leiden, 27–28 April, 2000.* Edited by Theo L. Hettema and Arie van der Kooij. Studies in Theology and Religion 11. Assen: Royal Van Gorcum, 2004.

Bowman, Craig. "Reading the Twelve as One: Hosea 1–3 as an Introduction to the Book of the Twelve." *Stone-Campbell Journal* 9 (2006): 41–59.

Braaten, Laurie J. "Earth Community in Hosea 2." Pages 185–203 in *The Earth Story in the Psalms and the Prophets.* Edited by Norman C. Habel. The Earth Bible 4. Sheffield: Sheffield Academic, 2001.

———. "God Sows: Hosea's Land Theme in the Book of the Twelve." Pages 104–32 in *Thematic Threads in the Book of the Twelve.* Edited by Paul L. Redditt and Aaron Schart. BZAW 325. Berlin: de Gruyter, 2003.

Brueggemann, Walter. "The Uninflected Therefore of Hosea 4:1–3." Pages 231–49 in *Reading from This Place, Vol. 1: Social Location and Biblical Interpretation in the United States.* Edited by Fernando F. Segovia and Mary Ann Tolbert. Minneapolis: Augsburg Fortress, 1995.

———. *Tradition for Crisis: A Study in Hosea.* Atlanta: John Knox, 1968.

Carew, M. Douglas. "To Know or Not to Know: Hosea's Use of *yd'/d't.*" Pages 73–85 in *The Old Testament in the Life of God's People: Essays in Honor of Elmer A. Martens.* Edited by Jon M. Isaak. Winona Lake, IN: Eisenbrauns, 2009.

Carroll R., M. Daniel. "The Prophetic Denunciation of Religion in Hosea 4–7." *CTR* 7 (1993): 15–38.

Chaney, Marvin L. "Accusing Whom of What? Hosea's Rhetoric of Promiscuity." Pages 97–115 in *Distant Voices Drawing Near: Essays in Honor of Antoinette Clark Wire*. Edited by Marvin L. Chaney and Holly E. Hearon. Collegeville, MN: Liturgical Press, 2004.

Clines, David J. A. "Hosea 2: Structure and Interpretation." Pages 293–313 in *On the Way to the Postmodern: Old Testament Essays, 1967–1998*. JSOTSup 292. Sheffield: Sheffield Academic, 1998.

Day, John. "Hosea and the Baal Cult." Pages 202–19 in *Prophecy and the Prophets in Ancient Israel: Proceedings of the Oxford Old Testament Seminar*. LHBOTS 531. London: T&T Clark, 2010.

Dearman, J. Andrew. "Interpreting the Religious Polemics against Baal and the Baalim in the Book of Hosea." *OTE* 14 (2001): 9–25.

———. *The Book of Hosea*. NICOT. Grand Rapids: Eerdmans, 2010.

Dell, Katharine J. "Hosea, Creation, and Wisdom: An Alternative Tradition." Pages 409–24 in *On Stone and Scroll: Essays in Honour of Graham Ivor Davies*. Edited by J. K. Aitken, Katharine J. Dell, and Brian A. Mastin. BZAW 420. Berlin: de Gruyter, 2011.

Fiddes, Paul S. "The Cross of Hosea Revisited: The Meaning of Suffering in the Book of Hosea." *RevExp* 90 (1993): 175–90.

Haddox, Susan E. "(E)masculinity in Hosea's Political Rhetoric." Pages 174–200 in *Israel's Prophets and Israel's Past: Essays on the Relationship of Prophetic Texts and Israelite History in Honor of John H. Hayes*. Edited by Brad E. Kelle and Megan Bishop Moore. LHBOTS 446. New York: T&T Clark, 2006.

Hwang, Jerry. "The Unholy Trio of Money, Sex, and Power in Israel's 8th-Century BCE Prophets." *Jian Dao* 41 (2014): 181–204.

———. "'I Am Yahweh Your God from the Land of Egypt': Hosea's Use of the Exodus Traditions." Pages 243–53 in *"Did I Not Bring Israel Out of Egypt?": Biblical, Archaeological, and Egyptological Perspectives on the Exodus Narratives*. Edited by James K. Hoffmeier, Alan R. Millard, and Gary A. Rendsburg. *BBRSup* 13. Winona Lake, IN: Eisenbrauns, 2016.

Keefe, Alice A. *Woman's Body and the Social Body in Hosea*. LHBOTS 338. London: Sheffield Academic, 2001.

———. "Hosea's (In)Fertility God." *HBT* 30 (2008): 21–41.

Kelle, Brad E. "Hosea 1–3 in Twentieth-Century Scholarship." *CurBR* 7 (2009): 179–216.

———. "Hosea 4–14 in Twentieth-Century Scholarship." *CurBR* 8 (2010): 314–75.

Kim, Sungjin. "Is the Masoretic Text Still a Reliable Primary Text for the Book of Hosea?" *BBR* 28 (2018): 34–64.

Koch, Klaus. "Is There a Doctrine of Retribution in the Old Testament?" Pages 57–87 in *Theodicy in the Old Testament*. Edited by James L. Crenshaw. Translated by Thomas H. Trapp. IRT 4. Philadelphia: Fortress, 1983.

Kwakkel, Gert. "The Land in the Book of Hosea." Pages 167–81 in *The Land of Israel in Bible, History, and Theology: Studies in Honour of Ed Noort*. Edited by Jacques van Ruiten and J. Cornelis de Vos. VTSup 124. Leiden: Brill, 2009.

Lim, Bo H., and Daniel Castelo. *Hosea*. THOTC. Grand Rapids: Eerdmans, 2015.

Machinist, Peter. "Hosea and the Ambiguity of Kingship in Ancient Israel." Pages 153–81 in *Constituting the Community: Studies on the Polity of Ancient Israel in Honor of S. Dean McBride, Jr.* Edited by John T. Strong and Steven Shawn Tuell. Winona Lake, IN: Eisenbrauns, 2005.

Macintosh, A. A. *Hosea*. ICC. Edinburgh: T&T Clark, 1997.

McComiskey, Thomas E., ed. *The Minor Prophets: An Exegetical and Expository Commentary*. Grand Rapids: Baker Books, 1992.

McConville, J. Gordon. "'I Am Like a Luxuriant Juniper': Language about God in Hosea." Pages 181–92 in *Let Us Go Up to Zion: Essays in Honour of H. G. M. Williamson on the Occasion of His Sixty-Fifth Birthday*. Edited by Iain W. Provan and Mark J. Boda. VTSup 153. Leiden: Brill, 2012.

McKenzie, Steven L. "Exodus Typology in Hosea." *ResQ* 22 (1979): 100–108.

Miller, Patrick D. *Sin and Judgment in the Prophets: A Stylistic and Theological Analysis*. SBLMS 27. Chico, CA: Scholars Press, 1982.

Moberly, R. W. L. "Knowing God and Knowing About God: Martin Buber's Two Types of Faith Revisited." *SJT* 65 (2012): 402–20.

Moon, Joshua. "Honor and Shame in Hosea's Marriages." *JSOT* 39 (2015): 335–51.

Morris, Gerald. *Prophecy, Poetry and Hosea*. JSOTSup 219. Sheffield: Sheffield Academic, 1996.

Munayer, Salim. *Hosea*. ABCS. Manila: Asia Theological Association, 2010.

O'Connor, Michael P. "The Pseudosorites: A Type of Paradox in Hebrew Verse." Pages 161–72 in *Directions in Biblical Hebrew Poetry*. Edited by Elaine R. Follis. JSOTSup 40. Sheffield: JSOT Press, 1987.

Premnath, D. N. "Amos and Hosea: Sociohistorical Background and Prophetic Critique." *WW* 28 (2008): 125–32.

Regt, Lénart J. de. "A Genre Feature in Biblical Prophecy and the Translator: Person Shift in Hosea." Pages 230–50 in *The Elusive Prophet: The Prophet as a Historical Person, Literary Character, and Anonymous Artist*. Edited by Johannes C. de Moor. *OtSt* 45. Atlanta: Society of Biblical Literature, 2001.

Richter, Sandra. "Eighth-Century Issues: The World of Jeroboam II, the Fall of Samaria, and the Reign of Hezekiah." Pages 319–49 in *Ancient Israel's History: An Introduction to Issues and Sources*. Edited by Bill T. Arnold and Richard S. Hess. Grand Rapids: Baker Academic, 2014.

Rooy, H. F. van. "The Names Israel, Ephraim, and Jacob in the Book of Hosea." *OTE* 6 (1993): 135–49.

Stiebert, Johanna. "Shame and Prophecy: Approaches Past and Present." *BibInt* 8 (2000): 255–75.

Stienstra, Nelly. *Yhwh Is the Husband of His People: Analysis of a Biblical Metaphor with Special Reference to Translation*. Kampen: Kok Pharos, 1993.

Tubbs Loya, Melissa. "'Therefore the Earth Mourns': Exploring the Grievance of Earth in Hosea 4:1–3." Pages 53–62 in *Exploring Ecological Hermeneutics*. Edited by Norman C. Habel and Peter L. Trudinger. SBLSymS 46. Atlanta: Society of Biblical Literature, 2008.

Tucker, Gene M. "The Law in the Eighth-Century Prophets." Pages 201–9 in *Canon, Theology, and Old Testament Interpretation: Essays in Honor of Brevard S. Childs*. Edited by Gene M. Tucker, David L. Petersen, and Robert R. Wilson. Philadelphia: Fortress, 1988.

Vang, Carsten. "God's Love According to Hosea and Deuteronomy: A Prophetic Reworking of a Deuteronomic Concept?" *TynBul* 62 (2011): 172–94.

———. "When a Prophet Quotes Moses: On the Relationship between the Book of Hosea and Deuteronomy." Pages 277–304 in *Sepher Torath Mosheh: Studies in the Composition and Interpretation of Deuteronomy*. Edited by Daniel I. Block and Richard L. Schultz. Peabody, MA: Hendrickson, 2017.

Vogels, Walter. "Hosea's Gift to Gomer." *Bib* 69 (1988): 412–21.

Watts, John D. W. "A Frame for the Book of the Twelve: Hosea 1–3 and Malachi." Pages 209–17 in *Reading and Hearing the Book of the Twelve*.

Edited by James Nogalski and Marvin A. Sweeney. SBLSymS 15. Atlanta: Society of Biblical Literature, 2000.

Weinfeld, Moshe. "Appendix B: Hosea and Deuteronomy." Pages 366–70 in *Deuteronomy and the Deuteronomic School*. Oxford: Clarendon, 1972.

Wendland, Ernst R. *The Discourse Analysis of Hebrew Prophetic Literature: Determining the Larger Textual Units of Hosea and Joel*. Mellen Biblical Press Series 40. Lewiston, NY: Mellen, 1995.

Wolff, Hans Walter. *Hosea*. Translated by Gary Stansell. Hermeneia. Philadelphia: Fortress, 1974.

Wu, Daniel Y. *Honor, Shame, and Guilt: Social-Scientific Approaches to the Book of Ezekiel*. *BBRSup* 14. Winona Lake, IN: Eisenbrauns, 2013.

Translation of Hosea[1]

Hosea 1

Superscription (1:1)

1The word of YHWH that happened to Hosea son of Beeri in the days of Uzziah, Jotham, Ahaz, and Hezekiah, kings of Judah, and in the days of Jeroboam son of Joash, king of Israel.

YHWH's Household Estranged and Reconciled: Prophetic Sign-Acts, Part I (1:2–2:3[1])

2When YHWH first spoke through Hosea, YHWH said to Hosea, "Go, take for yourself a wife of harlotry and children of harlotry, for the land commits heinous harlotry in walking away from YHWH."

3So Hosea went and took Gomer daughter of Diblaim as his wife. Then she conceived and bore him a son. 4YHWH said to him, "Name him Jezreel, for soon I will repay the bloodshed of Jezreel upon the household of Jehu, and I will put an end to the kingdom of the household of Israel. 5And on that day, I will break the bow of Israel in the Valley of Jezreel."

6Then Gomer conceived again and bore a daughter. He (YHWH) told him (Hosea), "Name her 'Not-Shown-Mercy,' for I will not continue anymore—[that] I would show mercy to the household of Israel, that/lest I would keep forgiving them. 7Yet to the household of Judah I will show mercy, I will deliver them by YHWH their God, but I will not deliver them by bow, sword, and battle, nor by horses and horsemen."

8Then Gomer weaned Not-Shown-Mercy, and she conceived, and she bore a son. 9Then he (YHWH) said, "Name him 'Not-My-People,' for you are 'Not-My-People,' and I am not your 'I AM.'"

1. When brackets occur in the translation itself, they denote elements implied by the Hebrew but not explicitly present (e.g., 8:1). Parentheses are used for explanations of ambiguous grammatical elements (e.g., 1:6).

Hosea 2

2:1[1:10]"But the number of the children of Israel will be like the sand of the sea, which can be neither measured nor numbered. And in the place where it was said to them, 'You are not my people,' it will be said to them, 'O children of the living God.'
2:2[1:11]Then the children of Judah and the children of Israel will be gathered together, and they will appoint for themselves one leader, and they will go up from the land. Indeed, great will be the day of Jezreel.
3[1]Speak to your brothers, 'O My-People!,' and [speak] to your sisters, 'O Shown-Mercy!'"

YHWH's Quarrel and Restoration with His Household (2:4–25[2–23])

4[2]"Quarrel against your mother, quarrel—
  that she is not my wife,
  and I am not her husband—
so that she would remove her harlotries from her face,
  and her adulteries from between her breasts.
5[3]Lest I strip her naked,
  render her like the day of her birth,
make her like the wilderness,
  set her like a dry land,
and slay her with thirst!
6[4]Nor to her children will I show mercy,
  for they are children of harlotry!
7[5]Indeed, their mother has committed harlotry,
  she has conceived them shamefully,
for she has said,
  'I shall follow after my lovers,
  who give my food and my water,
    my wool and my flax,
    my oil and my drink.'
8[6]Therefore I am blocking your road with thorns,
  I am hedging up her walls,
so that her pathways she will not find.
9[7]Then she will pursue her lovers
  yet not catch up to them.
She will seek them,
  but she will not find.
So she will say,

'Let me go
and return to my first husband,
for it was better for me then than now!'
10[8]On her part, she has not acknowledged
that I myself gave her the grain,
the new wine,
and the olive oil.
The silver I multiplied for her,
but the gold they made for Baal!
11[9]Therefore, I will return,
and I will take my grain in its time,
and my new wine in its season;
and I will remove my wool and my flax,
which cover her nakedness.
12[10]But now, I will uncover her degeneration/folly in the eyes of her lovers,
and nobody will save her from my hand.
13[11]I will put an end to all her rejoicing, her feasts,
her new moon festivals and her Sabbaths,
and all her appointed days!
14[12]I will ransack her vineyard and her fig trees,
of which she said,
'They are a gift to me
that my lovers gave to me!'
But I will make them into a thicket,
and the beast of the field will consume them.
15[13]Then I will repay her for the days of the Baals,
to which she used to burn incense,
and [when] she adorned herself with rings and jewelry,
and walked after her lovers.
But she forgot me!"

—The Declaration of YHWH—

16[14]"Therefore look!
I am coaxing her,
and leading her to the wilderness,
so that I may speak to her heart.
17[15]And I will give to her vineyards from there,
and the valley of Achor as a doorway to hope.
Then she will answer me from there

as in the days of her youth,
and as in the day she came up from the land of Egypt.
18[16]And on that day

—The Declaration of YHWH—

you will call me, 'My husband,'
and no longer call me, 'My Baal.'
19[17]Then I will remove the names of the Baals from her mouth,
and they will not be remembered again by their names.
20[18]Then I will make a covenant for them on that day,
with the beast of the field,
and with the bird of the sky,
and the crawler of the earth.
But as for the bow,
and the sword,
and war,
I will break them from the land,
and I will make them lie down in trust.
21[19]So I will betroth you to myself forever.
I will betroth you to myself with righteousness and justice,
with devotion and mercies;
22[20]I will betroth you to myself in faithfulness,
that you might know YHWH.
23[21]And on that day I will answer . . .

—The Declaration of YHWH—

. . . I will answer the heavens,
and they, in turn, will answer the earth;
24[22]the earth will answer the grain,
the new wine,
and the olive oil,
and they, in turn, will answer Jezreel.
25[23]Then I will sow her for myself in the land.
I will show mercy to Not-Shown-Mercy;
and I will say to Not-My-People,
'You are my people.'
And he will say,
'My God.'"

Hosea 3

Israel's Coming Exile and Restoration: Prophetic Sign-Acts, Part II (3:1–5)

[1]YHWH said to me again, "Go, love a woman loved by a paramour, that is, an adulteress, just as YHWH loves the children of Israel, though they are turning aside to other gods and they are lovers of raisin cakes."

[2]So I bought her for myself with fifteen shekels of silver and a homer-and-a-half
of barley. [3]Then I said to her, "For many days you will dwell as mine. You must not play the harlot, nor may you belong to a man. Yet even on my part, I will be with you."

[4]"Indeed, for many days the children of Israel will dwell without king and without prince, without sacrifice and without sacred pillar, and without ephod and teraphim.
[5]Later the children of Israel will return and they will seek YHWH their God and David their king. So they will tremble before YHWH and his goodness in the latter days."

Hosea 4

YHWH's Contention against Israel's Priestly Failures (4:1–5:7)

[1]"Heed/hear the word of YHWH, O children of Israel!
  For YHWH has a quarrel with the inhabitants of the land/earth:
That there is no truthfulness,
  and no faithfulness,
  and no knowledge of God in the land!
[2][There is] cursing!
  And deceiving!
  And murdering!
  And stealing!
  And committing adultery!
They have burst out upon the land,
  and bloodshed has struck bloodshed!
[3]As a result, the land is mourning,
  and all the inhabitants wither in it.
[As for] the beast of the field,
  the birds of the sky,
  and even the fish of the sea—

they will be taken away!
4Indeed, let nobody contend,
  and may no one rebuke,
because your people are like those who contend with a priest.
5So you will stumble by day,
  and the prophet will also stumble with you by night.
I will destroy your mother;
  6my people are destroyed from lack of knowledge.
Because on your part, you have rejected the knowledge,
  I also will reject you as my priest.
Since you have forgotten the instruction of your God,
  I will forget your children, also on my part.
7As soon as they multiplied
  then they sinned against me.
I will change their honor to dishonor.
8They enjoy the sin of my people,
  and they lift up his soul for their iniquity.
9Thus it shall be—
  like people, like priest!
I will repay his ways upon him,
  and I will bring back his deeds upon him.
10Then they will feast,
  but they will not be satisfied.
They will commit harlotry,
  but not break forth in numbers.
For it is YHWH they have rejected by keeping [harlotry].
11[As for] harlotry, wine, and new wine,
  it will take away a mind.
12My people will ask their stick,
  and their divining rod will tell them.
Because a spirit of harlotries has led astray,
  they have committed harlotry from underneath their God.
13On the tops of mountains they sacrifice,
  on the hills they offer incense,
underneath oak and poplar and terebinth—
  for their shade is pleasant.
As a result your daughters commit harlotry,
  and your daughters-in-law commit adultery.
14I will not repay your daughters
  when they commit harlotry,

nor [will I punish] your daughters-in-law
when they commit adultery.
Because on the men's part,
they keep going off with harlots,
and they offer sacrifices with prostitutes.
But a people who lack understanding will be ruined!
15If you, O Israel, are committing harlotry,
may Judah not become guilty.
Do not enter Gilgal,
neither go up to Beth-Aven,
nor swear,
'As YHWH lives.'
16Since Israel has been stubborn like a stubborn heifer,
now YHWH will drive them like a lamb into a broad place.
17Ephraim is bound to idols—
leave him alone!
18Finishing their liquor,
they intensify their harlotry,
her shields (i.e., leaders) have cherished dishonor.
19A wind has bound her in its wings,
so that they will be ashamed due to their sacrifices."

Hosea 5

1"Heed this, O priests!
Pay attention, O house of Israel!
O house of the king, lend ear,
since to you belongs the justice/judgment!
For you have been a trap at Mizpah,
a net spread out on Tabor,
2and a pit dug deeply at Shittim.
But I am chastisement for them all.
3I myself have known Ephraim,
and Israel has not been concealed from me.
But now, you have committed harlotry, O Ephraim,
Israel has become defiled.
4Their deeds do not allow them
to return to their God.
For a spirit of harlotries is in their midst,

and they do not know YHWH!
[5]So the pride of Israel testifies against him,
Israel and Ephraim stumble in their iniquity;
Judah also has stumbled with them.
[6]With their flocks and their herds they will go to seek YHWH,
but they will not find.
He has withdrawn from them.
[7]Against YHWH they have committed treachery
in that they have borne strange children.
Now a new moon festival will consume them with their portions."

YHWH's Contention against Israel's Political Failures (5:8–7:16)

[8]"Blow a ram's horn in Gibeah,
[blow] a trumpet in Ramah!
Sound the alarm in Beth-Aven—
[sound the alarm,] 'Behind you, O Benjamin!'
[9]Ephraim will become a desolation on a day of rebuke.
Among the tribes of Israel, I hereby make known what is sure—
[10]The princes of Judah have been like those who move a boundary.
Upon them I will pour out my wrath like water.
[11]Ephraim is oppressed,
crushed by judgment,
for he has decided—
he has walked after filth.
[12]Yet I am like a moth to Ephraim,
[and I am] like rot to the house of Judah.
[13]When Ephraim saw his sickness,
and Judah [saw] his wound,
then Ephraim went to Assyria
and [Judah] sent word to the great king.
But on his part, he will not be able to heal you,
nor will he cure your wound.
[14]Indeed, I am like a lion to Ephraim,
like a young lion to the house of Judah.
I, even I, will rip up,
go away,
carry off,
and there will be no one to deliver!
[15]I will go away,

I will return to my place,
until they confess their guilt
and seek my face.
In their distress they will seek me earnestly."

Hosea 6

1"Come,
let us return to YHWH!
Though on his part, he has torn,
yet he will heal us.
He may strike [us],
but he will bind us up.
2He will revive us after two days,
on the third day he will raise us up,
that we might live in his presence.
3So let us know,
let us seek to know YHWH—
His going forth is sure as dawn,
and he will come like the rain to us,
like the latter rain showering earth."
4"What shall I do with you, O Ephraim?
What shall I do with you, O Judah?
Your faithfulness [departs] like a cloud of the morning,
like dew of daybreak going away.
5Therefore I have cut them in pieces with the prophets;
I have slain them with the words of my mouth.
Then your judgments [are the] light [when it] goes forth.
6For I delight in faithfulness and not sacrifice,
in knowledge of God more than burnt offerings.
7But as for them, at Adam they broke a covenant,
there they committed treachery against me.
8Gilead is a city with doers of iniquity,
trampled with bloodstained feet.
9As bandits waiting to ambush a man,
so is the gang of priests who keep murdering on the way to Shechem.
Indeed, they have done lawlessness!
10In the household of Israel I have seen a horrible thing:
Ephraim's harlotry is there,

Israel has been defiled.
[11]Also for Judah, he (YHWH) has appointed a harvest for you."

Hosea 7

[1]"When I would restore the captivity of my people,
as soon as I would heal Israel,
then the iniquity of Ephraim is revealed,
so too the wicked deeds of Samaria!
For they have acted falsely:
A thief enters inside,
a band of robbers dashes outside.
[2]But they do not take to heart
[that] all their evil I have remembered.
Now their wicked deeds surround them,
they are before my face!
[3]In their evil they gladden the king,
and by their wicked acts [they gladden] the princes.
[4]All of them are adulterers,
like an oven burning from a baker,
he will stop stirring and kneading the dough until its leavening.
[5]On the day of our king, the princes have become sick with the heat of wine;
he stretches out his hand with the mockers.
[6]When they approach their plotting with heart like an oven,
all night long their baking [heart] simmers,
in the morning it burns like a flame of fire.
[7]All of them burn like an oven,
and they consume their judges.
All their kings have fallen,
none of them is crying out to me.
[8]Ephraim is mixed among the peoples,
Ephraim has been a flatbread not turned over.
[9]Strangers have consumed his strength,
but on his part, he did not know!
Gray hair is sprinkled on him,
but on his part, he did not know!
[10]So the pride of Israel will testify against his own face,
yet they have not returned to YHWH their God,
nor have they have sought him despite all this.

[11]Ephraim has become like a dove,
naïve, lacking a mind:
They have summoned Egypt,
they have gone to Assyria.
[12]As soon as they go,
I will spread out my net over them.
Like birds of the sky I will bring them down,
I will discipline them according to the report to their assembly.
[13]Woe to them,
for they have fled away from me!
Ruin is theirs,
for they have rebelled against me!
Now on my part, I would redeem them;
yet on their part, they have spoken lies against me.
[14]They do not cry out to me with their hearts,
when they howl upon their beds;
On account of grain and new wine
they keep gashing themselves,
they keep turning away from me.
[15]As for me, I disciplined them,
I strengthened their arms;
but they devise harm against me!
[16]They will return to a no-god,
they have been like a slack bow.
Their princes will fall by the sword
due to the gibberish of their speech,
this will be their mockery in the land of Egypt."

Hosea 8

An Announcement of Exile (8:1–9:9)

[1]"[Put] to your lips the ram's horn,
[one] like an eagle is upon the house of YHWH!
Because they have broken my covenant,
and they have rebelled against my instruction.
[2]They keep crying out to me,
'O my God, we—Israel—have known you!'
[3]Israel has rejected good,

an enemy will pursue him.
[4]On their part, they crowned a king but not from me;
they set up princes
but I did not know/choose [them].
With their silver and gold they made idols for themselves,
in order to be cut off.
[5]He has rejected your calf, O Samaria.
My anger is kindled against them,
how long will they be unable to stay innocent?
[6]Indeed, it (the calf) is from Israel,
and as for it, a craftsman made it,
but it is not God.
For the calf of Samaria will be broken to pieces!
[7]When they sow wind,
then they reap a whirlwind.
Standing grain would not produce anything,
a sprout would not make flour.
If it were to yield [something],
strangers would swallow it.
[8]Israel is swallowed!
Now they were among the nations,
like a vessel in which is no delight.
[9]For on their part, they went up to Assyria/Assur,
a wild donkey wandering by itself.
Ephraim hired lovers.
[10]Even when they hire among the nations,
now I will gather them.
Then they will cease for a time from the burden of a king of princes.
[11]If Ephraim multiplies altars for sin-offering,
they would become altars for his sinning.
[12]Should I write for him a multitude of my instruction,
they would consider it something strange.
[13]As for my roasted sacrifices, they keep sacrificing
and then eat the meat.
[But] YHWH is not pleased with them.
Now he will remember their iniquity,
and he will repay their sins.
In their turn, to Egypt they will return.
[14]Israel has forgotten his Maker,
he has built palaces,

Judah has multiplied fortified cities.
So I will send fire against his cities,
that it might consume her citadels.

Hosea 9

1"Do not rejoice, O Israel,
for the sake of shouting for joy like the peoples.
For you have played the harlot away from your God,
you have loved a harlot's wage on every threshing floor of grain.
2Threshing floor and wine vat will not feed/pasture them,
and new wine will deceive her.
3They will not dwell in YHWH's land:
But Ephraim will return to Egypt,
and in Assyria they will eat uncleanness.
4They will not pour out wine to YHWH,
and they will not please him.
Their sacrifices will be like bread of mourning for themselves.
All who eat them will make themselves unclean,
for their bread will be for themselves.
It will not enter the house of YHWH.
5What will you do on the day of assembly,
on the day of the festival of YHWH?
6For look, they have gone away because of destruction—
Egypt will gather them;
Memphis will bury them.
As for their treasures of silver, thistles will possess them,
briars will be in their tents.
7The days of repayment have come;
the days of payback have come—
Let Israel know!
The prophet is a fool,
the spiritual man is mad,
due to the multitude of your iniquity,
and the abundance of your hostility.
8Ephraim was a watchman with my God,
[but] a prophet is the trap of a bird catcher in all his ways.
Hostility is in the house of his god.
9They have deeply corrupted themselves as in the days of Gibeah—

he will remember their iniquity,
he will repay their sins."

Israel's Apostasy from YHWH: General Verdicts from Creation and History (9:10–11:11)

10"Like grapes in the wilderness I found Israel,
like the firstfruit in the fig grove at the beginning of its season
I saw your ancestors.
As for them, they entered Baal-Peor
and they dedicated themselves to the shameful thing;
and they became detestable like what they loved.
11Ephraim is like a bird,
their glory will fly away:
No more childbirth, no more pregnancy, no more conception!
12Although they raise children,
I will bereave them from humanity.
For indeed, woe to them,
when I turn away from them!
13Ephraim, just as I have seen for Tyre,
is planted in a meadow,
but Ephraim will bring out his children to the slayer."
14"Give them, O YHWH—
what will you give?
Give them a miscarrying womb and shriveling breasts."
15"All their evil is in Gilgal,
for there I have hated them.
On account of the evil of their deeds,
from my house I will drive them out.
I will not love them again,
all of their princes are stubborn.
16Ephraim is stricken:
Their root has dried up,
they will not bear any fruit.
Indeed, when they bear children,
I will put to death the delightful ones of their womb."
17"My God will reject them,
for they have not obeyed him.
So they shall be nomads among the nations."

Hosea 10

[1]"Israel is a lush vine,
he sets fruit for himself.
According to the abundance of his fruit he multiplied his altars,
According to the goodness of his land he enriched sacred pillars.
[2]Their heart has become slippery,
now they are guilty!
He himself will break their altars,
he will destroy their sacred pillars.
[3]But now they might say,
'We do not have a King/king!
For we have not feared YHWH!
And as for a King/king, what could he do for us?'
[4]They have spoken words,
with vain oaths they made a covenant.
Judgment sprouts like a poisonous plant in the furrows of a field.
[5]Regarding the heifers of Beth-Aven,
the inhabitants of Samaria will dread it.
For its people will mourn because of it,
and its priests will shriek for it because of its glory,
since it has gone into exile.
[6]Indeed, as for the thing, it will be carried to Assyria,
as a gift to the great king.
Ephraim brings shame upon himself,
and Israel will be ashamed of his counsel.
[7]Samaria is cut off [with] her king,
as a reed on the surface of waters.
[8]The high places of iniquity, the sin of Israel, will be exterminated.
Thorn and thistle will come up on their altars.
They will say to the mountains,
'Cover us!'
And [they will say] to the hills,
'Fall on us!'
[9]Since the days of Gibeah you have sinned, O Israel.
There they stood.
Will not war against the evildoers overtake them in Gibeah?
[10]When I desire, then I will chastise them,

and peoples will be gathered against them,
when they imprison/bind them for their double iniquity.
11Now Ephraim is a trained heifer
who loves to tread.
On my part, I placed a fine yoke on her neck.
I will harness Ephraim;
Judah will plow;
Jacob will break up the soil for himself.
12Sow for yourselves according to righteousness,
reap according to faithfulness,
till a hard ground for your own sake.
It is time to seek YHWH
until he comes
and is raining rightness toward you.
13You have plowed wickedness;
you have reaped lawlessness;
you have consumed the fruit of lying.
For you have trusted in your way, in the greatness of your strength.
14Then an uproar will rise among your people,
and all your fortifications will be devastated,
as when Shalman destroyed Beth-Arbel in the day of battle,
[when] a mother was dashed to pieces in front of her children.
15Thus he has done to you, O Bethel,
because of your extreme wickedness.
At dawn the king of Israel will be completely destroyed."

Hosea 11

1"Because/when Israel was a child,
I loved him,
and from Egypt I called my son.
2They (Israel) called to them (Egypt),
then they (Israel) went away from them [toward Assyria].
To the Baals they kept sacrificing,
and to idols they kept offering incense.
3As for me, I taught Ephraim to walk,
taking them by their arms.
But they have not known

that I healed them.
4 With cords of a man
I will draw them,
with bands of love.
Then I became for them like those
who lift the yoke from their jaws,
and I will bend down to them
and I will feed [them].
5 He will not return to the land of Egypt;
but Assyria will be his king,
since they refused to repent.
6 So a sword will twirl in their cities,
and will put an end to their gate-bars,
and will consume because of their plans.
7 But as for my people, they are stuck on apostasy from me.
Although to one above they will call together,
he will not lift them up.
8 How could I give you over, O Ephraim?
[How could] I hand you up, O Israel?
How could I give you over like [at] Admah?
[How could] I make you like [at] Zeboiim?
My heart is overthrown within me,
my compassions are kindled to warmth.
9 I will not carry out my fiery anger,
nor will I return to destroy Ephraim.
For I am God
and [I am] not a man.
[I am] a Holy One in your midst,
and I will not come in consuming anger.
10 They will follow after YHWH.
Like a lion he will roar.
When on his part, he roars,
then children will tremble from the west,
11 they will tremble like birds from Egypt,
and like doves from the land of Assyria.
So I shall make them dwell in their homes."

—The Declaration of YHWH.

Hosea 12

Israel's Disobedience toward YHWH: Specific Verdicts from History and Creation (12:1–14:1[11:12–13:16])

12:1[11:12] "Ephraim has encircled me with deception;
the household of Israel [has surrounded me] with treachery.
Judah is also roaming against El,
even against the faithful Holy One.
2[1]Ephraim is grazing on wind
and pursuing an east wind all the day.
Falsehood and violence he multiplies.
They make a covenant with Assyria,
and olive oil is carried to Egypt.
3[2]YHWH also has a quarrel with Judah
to repay Jacob according to his ways.
According to his deeds he (YHWH) will recompense him.
4[3]In the womb he grasped his brother,
and in his vigor he strove with God.
5[4]He strove with the angel
and prevailed.
He wept
and was shown favor.
At Bethel he (God) finds him (Jacob),
and there he speaks with us.
6[5]As for YHWH God of Hosts,
YHWH is his memorial name.
7[6]But as for you,
by your God you shall return.
Keep mercy and justice,
and wait for your God continually.
8[7][As a] merchant,
in whose hand are scales of deception,
he loves to oppress.
9[8]So Ephraim says,
'Surely, I have become rich;
I have found vigor for myself.
All my labors will not find in me any iniquity—which is sin.'
10[9]But I am YHWH your God from the land of Egypt,

again I shall make you dwell in tents,
as in the days of assembly.
11[10]I shall speak by means of the prophets.
For on my part, I will multiply a vision,
and by the hand of the prophets I speak similes:
12[11]'If Gilead [has] wickedness/iniquity,
then they are vanity.
In Gilgal they sacrifice bulls,
but their altars are like heaps on the furrows of the field.'
13[12]Then Jacob fled to the field of Aram,
and Israel served for a wife;
for a wife he guarded [sheep].
14[13]But by a prophet YHWH brought Israel up from Egypt,
and by a prophet he was kept watch."
15[14]"Ephraim has provoked to bitter anger,
so his bloodguilt will be left upon him,
and his Lord will bring his reproach back to him!"

Hosea 13

1"As soon as Ephraim spoke,
[there was] trembling!
He exalted himself in Israel.
Then he became guilty by Baal
and he died.
2But now they continue to sin:
They make for themselves a graven image—
idols from their silver according to their skill,
all of it craftsmen's work.
To themselves they are saying,
'As for those who sacrifice people,
they kiss calves!'
3Therefore they will be like a cloud of the morning,
like dew of daybreak going away,
like chaff blown from the threshing floor,
and like smoke from a chimney.
4But I am YHWH your God from the land of Egypt.
You shall know no god besides me,
since there is no other deliverer.

[5]On my part, I have known you in the wilderness,
  in the land of droughts.
[6]According to their pasturage they were satisfied.
They were satisfied
  and their heart became prideful.
As a result they forgot me.
[7]So I will be like a lion to them,
  like a leopard I will pounce on the way.
[8]I will encounter them like a bereaved mother-bear,
  and I will tear open their chest cavity.
I will devour them there like a lioness,
  a beast of the field will tear them to pieces.
[9][It is] your destruction, O Israel,
  for [you are] against me—against your helper!
[10]Where then is your king,
  and [where is] your deliverer in all of your cities?
And [where are] your judges
  of whom you said,
    'Give me a king and princes'?
[11]I would give you a king in my anger,
  but would take [him] in my wrath.
[12]The iniquity of Ephraim is wrapped up,
  his sin is preserved.
[13]The pangs of childbirth will come in for him.
  He is an unwise son,
because at the proper time he does not appear in the birth canal.
[14]Will I ransom them from the hand of Sheol?
  Will I redeem them from death?
Where are your plagues, O Death?
  Where is your pestilence, O Sheol?
Pity will be hidden from my eyes.
[15]Although on his part he hopes to flourish among allies,
  an east wind will come,
  the Spirit of YHWH coming up from the wilderness.
His fountain will dry up,
  his spring will run dry.
It will plunder his treasury of every precious vessel.
[14:1[13:16]]Samaria must bear her guilt,
  for she has rebelled against her God.

By the sword they will fall,
their children will be dashed to pieces,
their pregnant women will be ripped open."

Hosea 14

Hosea's Summons to Repentance (14:2–4[1–3])

2[1]"Do return, O Israel, to YHWH your God,
for you have stumbled in your iniquity.
3[2]Take vows with you,
and return to YHWH.
Speak to him,
'Every iniquity you will forgive.
Accept a good thing.'
Let us repay as bulls our lips:
4[3]'Assyria will not deliver us;
upon horses we will not ride.'
And let us not say again, 'Our gods,'
to the work of our hands,
for in you the orphan will be shown mercy."

The Restorative Love of YHWH (14:5–9[4–8])

5[4]"I will heal their apostasy,
I will love them with abandon,
for my anger has turned away from him.
6[5]I shall be like the dew for Israel.
He will bud like a lily,
and his root will strike like [the cedars of] Lebanon.
7[6]His shoots will sprout forth,
his splendor will be like the olive tree,
and his fragrance like [the cedars of] Lebanon.
8[7]Those who dwell in his shadow shall again revive grain,
they shall sprout forth like the vine.
His remembrance will be like the wine of Lebanon.
9[8]O Ephraim, what do I still have to do with idols?
As for me, I have answered,

and I have watched over him.
  I am like a sprawling cypress tree;
from me your fruit is found."

The Audience's Urgent Need for Wisdom (14:10[9])

10[9] "Who is wise?
  Then let him understand these things.
[Who is] a discerning person?
  And may he know them!
That the ways of YHWH are upright.
  The righteous will walk in them,
  but the rebellious will stumble in them."

Introduction to Hosea

God's Reconciliation with His Estranged Household

Historical Background to Hosea's Prophecy

The superscription attributes the prophecies in the book of Hosea to a certain "Hosea son of Beeri" (1:1b). The OT provides no further information about Hosea beyond the book that bears his name. Nevertheless, the book presupposes a specific historical setting in its opening notice that Hosea ministered "in the days of Uzziah, Jotham, Ahaz, and Hezekiah, kings of Judah, and in the days of Jeroboam son of Joash, king of Israel" (1:1c–d). The reigns of these five kings spanned the chaotic decades of the eighth century BCE (and, for Hezekiah, extended into the early seventh century BCE), so it will be useful to proceed by examining the social and theological history of the two kingdoms of Israel during this period.

The eighth century BCE saw the best and worst of times for Samaria and Judah, the two divided kingdoms of Israel.[1] On the international scene, weakness in the traditional empires of Egypt and Assyria during the first few decades opened a regional power vacuum that the Israelite kings exploited to full advantage. While the surrounding powers had limited the aspirations of Kings David and Solomon, the perpetual vise of the empires of Mesopotamia (to the northeast) and Egypt (to the southwest) opened briefly in the eighth century BCE. This window of opportunity allowed Samaria and Judah to accelerate the political reforms that they had already begun in the eleventh and tenth centuries BCE, during the days of the united monarchy.

In particular, the transition from judges to kings beginning with Saul and David's time had resulted in a societal shift from family plots of land as the center

1. For clarity's sake, this commentary will generally use "Samaria" and "Ephraim" to refer to the Northern Kingdom (since either name may occur in Hosea, depending on the rhetorical context), "Judah" to refer to the Southern Kingdom, and "Israel" to refer to both. At the same time, the commentary will point out how the prophecy of Hosea plays upon variations in these names for rhetorical purposes.

of Israelite life toward larger, fortified cities. Following the adoption of Jerusalem as Israel's capital (2 Sam 5:5), David and Solomon embarked on numerous initiatives to expand Israelite state infrastructure, such as taxation of the twelve tribes (1 Kgs 4:7; 5:7–8[4:27–28]), military buildup (2 Sam 24:9; 1 Kgs 10:26), and conscription of labor (1 Kgs 5:27–29[13–15]; 2 Chr 2:17–18). Israel's entrance into international trade markets (1 Kgs 10:24–29) drove similar political developments in the united monarchy.

This series of upheavals led to spikes in the urban population, notably in Jerusalem. While the division of Israel into the two kingdoms of Samaria and Judah in 930 BCE (1 Kgs 12:16–20) interrupted these developments somewhat, royal consolidation of power soon resumed during the divided monarchy, especially during the Omride dynasty in Samaria (ca. 885–853 BCE) and the reign of King Jehoshaphat in Judah (ca. 872–848 BCE).[2] The increase in social stratification represented an ominous shift in Israel away from the familial society of "fellow citizens" (Heb. אַחִים, "brothers"; e.g., Deut 15:7; 17:15), which God had envisioned for his special people, and back toward the unjust hierarchies that characterized the rest of the ancient Near East.[3]

Political reforms from the monarchical period onwards went together with a shift in economy from subsistence farming of ancestral lands to one that specialized in providing goods and services for the central governments of Samaria and Judah (cf. 1 Sam 8:11–17). Archaeological findings from the eighth century BCE indicate that the lengthy reigns of King Jeroboam II (ca. 793–753 BCE) in Samaria and King Uzziah (ca. 792–740 BCE) in Judah oversaw the development of large commodity markets for agricultural goods.[4] In support of royal policies of expansion, the Israelite kings annexed arable land from familial plots into larger plantations to produce goods such as olive oil, wine, and grain (Isa 5:8–10). This practice directly transgressed pentateuchal laws (e.g., Lev 25:8–34) that had allocated lands inviolably to individual clans.

The commoditization of agricultural products in Israel during the eighth century BCE meant that an agrarian majority no longer worked for themselves, but for the consumer tastes of a growing urban minority who also used these goods for trade in international markets. In this move from a subsistence-based to a commodity-based economy, inevitably land itself soon became a commodity that was controlled by the brokers of economic power in the capital cities of Samaria and Jerusalem.

2. All regnal years in what follows are approximate and are taken from the groundbreaking work of Edwin R. Thiele, *The Mysterious Numbers of the Hebrew Kings*, new and rev. ed. (Grand Rapids: Kregel, 1994). For dates that are generally a decade later, see John Bright, *A History of Israel*, 4th ed. (Louisville: Westminster John Knox, 2000).

3. Joshua Berman, *Created Equal: How the Bible Broke with Ancient Political Thought* (Oxford: Oxford University Press, 2008), 51–80.

4. For example, the Samarian ostraca that have been excavated in the Northern Kingdom's capital city indicate that large quantities of agricultural products were passing through royal hands, though the exact nature of the transactions is disputed. For further discussion see Sandra Richter, "Eighth-Century Issues: The World of Jeroboam II, the Fall of Samaria, and the Reign of Hezekiah," in *Ancient Israel's History: An Introduction to Issues and Sources*, ed. Bill T. Arnold and Richard S. Hess (Grand Rapids: Baker Academic, 2014), 323–24.

This jolting process, known as *latifundialization*, involved the forcible seizure of patrimonial plots from the families that had occupied and farmed them for untold generations. Although often still occupying their ancestral lands, the average Israelite was relegated to being a tenant farmer at best and debt slave at worst. The resulting social crisis prodded the classical prophets to rail against the social injustices of the "haves" of society who confiscated what rightfully belonged to the "have-nots" (Isa 3:13–15; Amos 5:11; Mic 2:1–2, 9).

Class conflict portended the deeper problem of thoroughgoing corruption among Israel's political, economic, and religious leaders. Here a methodological note is in order—rather than following the modern tendency to compartmentalize Israel's problems into the discrete realms of spiritual and secular, it is more accurate to speak of symbiotic clusters of sin given the entwined nature of these spheres in ancient Israel. In a way that has striking resonances with modern society, the eighth-century-BCE prophets criticized Samaria and Judah for collections of vices that I have described elsewhere as the "unholy trio of money, sex, and power."[5] What follows is a brief exploration of how the "three I's" of injustice, immorality, and idolatry became systematically and systemically embedded in Israel's sinful institutions so that the presence of one vice would inevitably give birth to the other two.

Canaanite Nature Religion and "Baal" in Israel during the Eighth Century BCE

At the junction of these "three I's" stood Canaanite nature religion, a comprehensive worldview that focused on ensuring the fertility of the land but also involved religious, political, and economic dimensions. To begin with, it is instructive to observe how Hosea uses the epithet "Baal" to denote more, not less, than the chief god of Canaanite nature religion.[6] Although King Ahab's official cult of Baalism in Samaria (1 Kgs 16:29–33) had already been eradicated by King Jehu in the late ninth century BCE (2 Kgs 10:18–28; cf. Hos 1:4), the figure of "Baal" returns in Hosea as an umbrella term for various kinds of religious rituals such as the cultic use of sacred pillars (3:4; 10:1–2), divining rods (4:12), illicit sexual practices at the "high places" (4:13–14; cf. 10:8), and worship of calf icons (8:5–6; 10:5; 13:2).[7] While scholars continue to debate whether the metaphor of "Baal" retains any connotation of worship

5. Jerry Hwang, "The Unholy Trio of Money, Sex, and Power in Israel's 8th-Century BCE Prophets," *Jian Dao* 41 (2014): 181–204.

6. The false dichotomy between literal and figurative senses in the Hebrew Bible's use of metaphor, especially in the case of idolatry, has been well demonstrated by David H. Aaron, *Biblical Ambiguities: Metaphor, Semantics, and Divine Imagery* (Leiden: Brill, 2002), 125–55.

7. Jörg Jeremias, "Der Begriff 'Baal' im Hoseabuch und seine Wirkungsgeschichte," in *Ein Gott Allein? JHWH-Verehrung und biblischer Monotheismus im Kontext der israelitischen und altorientalischen Religionsgeschichte*, OBO 139 (Göttingen: Vandenhoeck & Ruprecht, 1994), 441–62.

offered specifically to Baal-Hadad, the Canaanite god of the storm,[8] Hosea clearly links these heterodox practices to the fructifying functions of a deity called "Baal."

In addition to worshiping "Baal," Israel trusted in "lovers" whom she mistakenly thought provided her with the products of the land. YHWH condemns such apostasy: "For she has said, 'I shall follow after my lovers, who give me my food and my water, my wool and my flax, my oil and my drink'" (2:7[5]). This list of agricultural goods to be sought from "lovers" not only reflects some of the most valuable commodities sought in Israel from the tenth century BCE onwards (cf. 1 Kgs 5:11; 2 Chr 2:10, 15; Ezek 27:17), but also evokes the Ugaritic depictions of Baal as the guarantor of oil, wine, and grain to those who worship him. Here the linking of "Baal" with "lovers," a term that clearly refers to Israel's alliance partners in later texts that have been influenced by Hosea (e.g., Jer 3:1; Ezek 16:33; 23:5), suggests that the realms of religion and economics were interwoven in the eighth century BCE.

Hosea condemns another dimension of the sinful synergy of religion and economics under the rubric of apostasy with "Baal." In the subsequent verses of chapter 2, the commodities produced in Israel are linked to Baal and the raw material for making graven images: "Then she [Israel] will pursue her lovers yet not catch up to them. She will seek them, but she will not find. So she will say, 'Let me go and return to my first husband, for it was better for me then than now!' On her part, she has not acknowledged that I myself gave her the grain, the new wine, and the olive oil. *The silver I multiplied for her, but the gold they made for Baal!*" (2:9–10[7–8]).

Later in the book, Hosea repeatedly names "silver and gold" as raw materials for manufacturing idols in Samaria (8:4; 13:2). Since the golden calves had been made by Jeroboam I and set up in Dan and Bethel over a century prior (cf. 1 Kgs 12:28–33), Hosea's references to making more idols indicate that the casting of graven images continued at other cultic sites in the kingdom of Samaria during the eighth century BCE. The fact that accruing "silver and gold" occurred in the name of "Baal" indicates that cultic worship of idols served partially to underwrite Israel's participation in international trade. In particular, the oil mentioned in Hosea (e.g., 2:7[5], 10[8]; 12:2[1]) was native to Canaan but rare elsewhere in the ancient Near East.[9] The opposite was the case for the precious metals of gold and silver, which are essential for making images.

The idolatry and injustice associated with veneration of Baal was reinforced in

8. For a negative view, see Lyn M. Bechtel, "The Metaphors of 'Canaanite' and 'Baal' in Hosea," in *Inspired Speech: Prophecy in the Ancient Near East: Essays in Honor of Herbert B. Huffmon*, ed. John Kaltner and Louis Stulman, LHBOTS 378 (London: T&T Clark, 2008), 203–15. For a positive view, see John Day, "Hosea and the Baal Cult," in *Prophecy and the Prophets in Ancient Israel: Proceedings of the Oxford Old Testament Seminar*, LHBOTS 531 (London: T&T Clark, 2010), 202–19.

9. This was particularly the case in Egypt, whose relative proximity to Canaan meant that olive oil from the latter had been a significant import for centuries rather than being cultivated locally (Margaret T. Serpico, "Oils and Fats," in *The Oxford Encyclopedia of Ancient Egypt*, ed. Donald Redford [Oxford: Oxford University Press, 2001], 584).

sins of immorality at the "high places" associated with Canaanite religious practices. While some "high places" may have served more innocuously as alternative (though still forbidden) sites to worship YHWH (e.g., 1 Kgs 3:2–3; 15:14; cf. Deut 12:2), many of them were the site of cultic rituals (e.g., Hos 4:13–14; 2 Kgs 17:9–11) that people thought ensured the fertility of the earth.[10] The older view on Hosea's condemnation of fertility practices may press the extant evidence too far in its assertion that this sexual behavior reflected a formal cult of "sacred prostitution,"[11] yet it remains difficult not to conclude that the "high places" hosted illicit sexual activity under sacred trees such as "oak and poplar and terebinth" (Hos 4:13) that were associated with Canaanite nature religion.

Therefore, it becomes immaterial whether a special class of "temple prostitutes" existed within Israel (cf. Mic 1:7; Deut 23:18–19[17–18]), for those who served as sexual functionaries at the "high places" could simply have been applying a religious veneer over their own utilitarian expression of lust. As Halbertal and Margalit demonstrate in their groundbreaking study of idolatry and fertility religion, "The attraction of idolatry is embedded either in the erotic temptation of idolatry itself, or in the lifestyle accompanying idolatry. The decision to worship idols reflects a way of life rather than a particular metaphysical worldview."[12]

Such a convergence of different sins explains why the Hebrew verbal root זנה ("to commit harlotry, be a harlot") possesses a variety of literal and figurative senses in the book of Hosea. The commentary on the relevant texts in the book will show that the metaphor of "harlotry" can refer variously to the sins of sexual immorality found at the Canaanite "high places," promiscuity as a shameful lifestyle, and the idolatrous worship practiced in the name of Baal, as well as the unfettered pursuit of prosperity via foreign trade with "lovers." For now, it is sufficient to observe that Hosea uses wordplays on the multifaceted character of "harlotry" to encode the urgent message that economic, religious, and political sins had become symbiotic in the eighth century BCE. In other words, sinful structures had been encased in Israel's institutions by its leaders to such a wide-reaching extent that systemic sin unavoidably led to individual sin, and vice versa. The realization that human sinfulness worked at multiple levels in ancient Israel may be counterintuitive for modern readers of Hosea who typically think about sin in individual or compartmentalized terms.

To this toxic mix of Canaanite nature religion, the worldview of imperialist ideology that dominated the ancient Near East proved a potent addition. Most significantly, the empires of Egypt and Mesopotamia combined several strengths that

10. Day, "Hosea and the Baal Cult," 202–3, 214–15.

11. Following an influential study by Herbert May ("The Fertility Cult in Hosea," *AJSL* 48 [1932]: 73–98), the dominant view about Hosea's references to "harlotry" during the second half of the twentieth century was that priestesses of Astarte (i.e., the primary consort of Baal) served male worshipers of the fertility god Baal.

12. Moshe Halbertal and Avishai Margalit, *Idolatry* (Cambridge: Harvard University Press, 1998), 24.

were irresistible from a human perspective—large population, the latest in military technology, and a seemingly limitless supply of natural resources, water most notably among them, due to the presence of the Nile River (in Egypt) and the Tigris and Euphrates Rivers (in Mesopotamia). Canaan possessed none of these advantages. The comparatively small population of Canaan resided within porous borders and needed to rely on the presence of annual rains that were far from reliable. Additionally, Canaan's strategic position between the continents of Europe, Africa, and Asia meant that Egypt and Mesopotamia were constantly vying with each other to influence or occupy Canaan, often by force.

These two factors presented two temptations to the Israelite kingdoms. The first was the annual attraction of Baalism, which supposedly provided a means to overcome scarcity and the natural limitations of Canaan using cultic rituals dedicated to Baal, the god of the land. When this worldview failed, as the less than predictable climate of Canaan ensured that it often did, it was natural to succumb to the second temptation of relying upon one of the great empires for sanctuary or sustenance, a policy that played into the imperial ambitions of Assyria and Egypt to control the main trade routes of the ancient Near East. For each of these empires, the addition of Israel as a vassal would also provide an ally that was conveniently within striking distance of its main opponent. But on Israel's part, making alliances with either of these empires involved the concession that the pagan gods of Assyria or Egypt, who were listed as covenantal witnesses in these suzerain-vassal treaties,[13] were legitimate deities to be reckoned with rather than "impotent nonentities."[14]

Theopolitics in the Ancient Near East during the Eighth Century BCE

These observations on the ancient Near Eastern linkage between heaven and earth, also known as theopolitics, explain why Hosea condemns alliances and vassalage to foreign empires as apostasy against YHWH. Just as Canaanite nature religion was a comprehensive worldview that stood opposed to faith in YHWH, Israel's choice to trust in imperial power represented conversion to a totalizing system of belief that was incompatible with faith in the God who had promised to secure Israel's borders and provide abundance in the land. Particularly in the eighth century BCE,

13. See, for example, the treaty between Assurnirari V of Assyria and Mati'ilu of Arpad that dates from 750 BCE and is nearly contemporaneous with the eighth-century-BCE prophets. The treaty concludes with appeals to a host of gods and goddesses from both Assyria and Babylon as witnesses, including Assur, Enlil, Ea, Marduk, and Ninurta ("Treaty Between Assurnirari V of Assyria and Mati'ilu of Arpad," trans. Erica Reiner [*ANET*, 532–33]).

14. This is the useful coinage of Richard J. Bauckham to summarize Israelite orthodoxy's view of foreign gods ("Biblical Theology and the Problems of Monotheism," in *Out of Egypt: Biblical Theology and Biblical Interpretation*, Scripture and Hermeneutics Series 5 [Grand Rapids: Zondervan, 2004], 196).

Israel's embrace of Assyria (while at times flirting with Egypt) represented a Faustian bargain that meant capitulating to the Assyrian claim that Assur, the patron god of the Assyrian Empire, and not YHWH, was the most powerful deity in the ancient Near East.[15] Beginning already with Shalmaneser III in the ninth century BCE, the tendency of Assyrian propaganda to boast about the empire's victories in the name of Assur struck terror in the hearts of surrounding ancient Near Eastern peoples such as Israel.[16]

Following a period of internal strife, the Assyrian Empire reemerged as the hegemonic empire in the middle of the eighth century BCE. This development set the stage for a confrontation of international, and indeed cosmic, scale between Assur and YHWH. On one side stood a large army that had perfected the arts of siege and psychological warfare in order to proclaim near and far that "Assur [is] the strong King, King of all the four zones of the Sun (and) of multitudes of men, the marcher over the whole world."[17] On the other side stood the divided kingdoms of Israel as they were torn among several choices: (1) to heed the prophets' invitation to believe YHWH's offer of deliverance; (2) to trust Baal and the Canaanite religion's promises of prosperity; (3) to yield to the might of Assur/Assyria;[18] or (4) to seek relatively weak alliance partners such as Egypt. Common to all these choices was an ancient understanding of deity that was grounded in the functional realities of power and fear more than the modern philosophical categories of essence and existence.[19] Within such a pragmatic understanding (which apostate Israel would have largely shared with its neighbors), YHWH would have seemed much weaker than his opponents. Yet the strikingly countercultural message of the Israelite prophets was that the God of Israel not only remained powerful in times of apparent weakness, but that his purposes could be accomplished equally well through such weakness. The commentary below will explore this point further, but here it is noteworthy that the holistic nature of Israel's predicament in the eighth century BCE made faith in

15. In such a polytheistic worldview, Israelite worship of YHWH was not eradicated by Assyria so much as marginalized by the recognition that Assur was more powerful. The Assyrians generally did not impose religious conformity upon vassal peoples like Israel as long as they recognized the superiority of Assur to their gods, or that their gods had turned against them in supporting their defeat by Assur (Mordechai Cogan, *Imperialism and Religion: Assyria, Judah, and Israel in the Eighth and Seventh Centuries B.C.E*, SBLMS 19 [Missoula, MT: Scholars Press, 1974]).

16. Steven W. Holloway describes thus the "religious imperialism" that characterized Assyria's dealings with vassal states: "Religious imperialism is defined as deliberate, coercive involvement in the affairs of a foreign and subordinate polity with the intention of either manipulating the internal affairs of the foreign cult, or of imposing cultic dues or obligations consciously understood by both polities for the support of the cult(s) of the imperial polity" (*Aššur Is King! Aššur Is King!: Religion in the Exercise of Power in the Neo-Assyrian Empire*, CHANE 10 [Leiden: Brill, 2002], 99). Holloway goes on to demonstrate how every Assyrian military victory fits this definition to one degree or another.

17. This is Shalmaneser III's opening paean to Assur on the "Black Obelisk," a votive inscription that lists the kings of the eastern Mediterranean who became his vassals, King Jehu of Samaria among them. The rendering follows A. H. Sayce in *Records of the Past*, vol. 5 (1873).

18. A. Livingstone, "Ashur," *DDD* 108, notes the convergence of deity, capital city, and empire in that all are named "Ashur."

19. Mark S. Smith, *God in Translation: Deities in Cross-Cultural Discourse in the Biblical World* (Grand Rapids: Eerdmans, 2010), 14–15.

YHWH the God of Israel the antithesis of imperialism in both its pro-Assyrian and anti-Assyrian varieties.[20]

The futility of trusting in power politics rather than the God of Israel came to the fore in 745 BCE when the window of political opportunity slammed shut with the advent of Tiglath-pileser III, the famous Assyrian king. The renaissance of Assyria coincided nearly exactly with the passing of Jeroboam II and Uzziah, two longstanding kings in Samaria and Judah, respectively, whose stable reigns of five decades had been the only leadership that an entire generation of God's people in both kingdoms had ever known. The rise of Tiglath-pileser and the demises of Jeroboam II and Uzziah meant that the balance of power in the ancient Near East had shifted radically, or so it seemed to the frightened peoples of the Israelite kingdoms. As Tiglath-pileser restarted the Assyrian war machine and his armies rumbled southwest toward the eastern Mediterranean, the inhabitants of Samaria and Judah stood directly in his path without proven leadership.

The Assyrian threat was heightened in the decade of the 730s and following by a revolving door of bad leaders in both kingdoms of Israel. Political leadership in the Northern Kingdom of Samaria was the first to implode, with the assassinations of King Zechariah by Shallum after a reign of only six months (2 Kgs 15:8–10) and Shallum after only a month as king by Menahem (2 Kgs 15:13–14). Menahem reigned over Israel for ten years, but his kingship was marred by social injustices and payment of a large tribute to Tiglath-pileser in exchange for the survival of his dynasty (2 Kgs 15:19–20). Although the natural death of Menahem led to an orderly transfer of kingship to his son Pekahiah, the latter was assassinated only two years later by his officer Pekah, who became king in his place (2 Kgs 15:25). The reign of Pekah also marked an escalation of direct Assyrian interference in Israelite affairs, for Tiglath-pileser began seizing larger chunks of Israelite territory (2 Kgs 15:29) and eventually conspired with Hoshea to assassinate Pekah and install him as king over Samaria (2 Kgs 15:30).[21]

The rising specter of Assyria in the 730s similarly defined Judah's struggle for national survival. In particular, the accession of King Ahaz in 735 BCE soon confronted a set of choices that were all equally unappealing from a human perspective. With the kingdoms Aram and Samaria already united against the impending threat from the east, Pekah of Samaria and Rezin of Aram tried to compel King Ahaz to join their coalition against Assyria. Hence Ahaz, being already crippled by an earlier defeat at the hands of this same Syro-Ephraimite alliance (2 Chr 28:5–8), was forced to choose between joining the Aramean and Samarian kings or surrendering to the Assyrian Empire.

20. Michael E. W. Thompson, *Situation and Theology: Old Testament Interpretations of the Syro-Ephraimite War*, Prophets and Historians Series 1 (Sheffield: Almond Press, 1982), 67–68.

21. The biblical record only mentions Hoshea as party to "conspiracy against Pekah" (2 Kgs 15:30), while Tiglath-pileser's annals of his western campaigns add the detail of his own involvement in deposing Pekah (cf., "Summary Inscription 9–10," trans. K. Lawson Younger, Jr. [*COS* 2.117F:291–92]).

The prophet Isaiah offered Ahaz a theocentric, third way out of power politics by trusting in YHWH rather than in either the Syro-Ephraimite alliance or yielding to imperial Assyria. But Ahaz declined this offer of salvation and instead placed his trust in the "hard power" of Assyrian military might (Isa 7).[22] In the subsequent conflict, known as the Syro-Ephraimite War (734–732 BCE), Ahaz's submission to Tiglath-pileser as vassal (2 Kgs 16:7–9) resulted in Assyria soundly defeating the Syro-Ephraimite alliance. Further paganization of Judah soon followed. After Ahaz's meeting with Tiglath-pileser in Damascus, the defeated capital of Aram, the Judahite king ordered his priest to replace some of the temple vessels in Jerusalem with an exact replica of an Aramean or Assyrian altar that he had spotted in Damascus (2 Kgs 16:10–18).[23]

The disastrous policies of the Israelite kings, both in looking outwardly to foreign powers as well as yielding inwardly to socio-religious compromise, eventually led to the destruction and exile of Samaria in 722 BCE. However, Judah escaped narrowly from Assyria's grasp in 701 BCE (2 Kgs 18–20) and survived as a semi-independent, but greatly weakened, kingdom for another 115 years after that. In the face of the successive crises that roiled the Israelite kingdoms during the middle of the eighth century BCE, all of which were inescapably theological at their core, the God of Israel spoke to his people through the prophets Hosea and Amos to the Northern Kingdom of Samaria, and Isaiah and Micah to the Southern Kingdom of Judah. Each in their distinct way, these prophets called the people of God away from their syncretism with pagan worldviews to return to pure trust in YHWH. As the only native northerner in this group, the prophet Hosea drew upon his unique background in Samaria to proclaim a distinctive message during the latter half of the eighth century BCE. The distinctiveness of Hosea's message is found especially in his theology and his literary style, to which we now turn.

Hosea's Distinctive Theology in Its Cultural Context

Given the fall of the two kingdoms of Israel into syncretism of various kinds, it is helpful to borrow the missiological concept of contextualization to analyze the distinctive elements of Hosea's theology, which stand in contrast with its surrounding culture.[24] A highly polemical book like Hosea only becomes intelligible to its

22. The contrast between "soft power" and "hard power," the latter defined as coercion by military and/or economic force, has been famously defined by Joseph S. Nye in various publications (e.g., *Soft Power: The Means to Success in World Politics* [New York: Public Affairs, 2004], x).

23. The biblical text is unclear whether this altar was Aramean or Assyrian in origin.

24. The working definition of contextualization given by Dean Gilliland provides a helpful starting point: "The goal of contextualization perhaps best defines what it is. That goal is to enable, insofar as it is humanly possible, an understanding of what it means that Jesus Christ, the Word, is authentically experienced in each and every human situation. Contextualization means that the Word must dwell among all families of

audience when it frames its distinctive message by using concepts that are already familiar, even if only to offer an opposing view.[25] Like all of Scripture, the book of Hosea preserves an enculturated divine revelation that communicates to its human readers by navigating a spectrum of continuity and discontinuity formed by God's timeless truth on the one hand, and time-bound human conventions on the other. The idea of contextualization proves useful to examine this process of cultural filtering that is part of every act of divine communication to a human audience.[26]

The book of Hosea contextualizes its distinctive message of YHWH's sovereignty over every domain by reworking the categories of history and creation that were contemporary to its audience in the eighth century BCE. Before exploring Hosea's contextualization of history and creation in detail, it is important to observe that the Hosea scholarship of recent decades mirrors a broader struggle within OT scholarship to reconcile the seeming contradiction between these categories. As Leo Perdue summarizes the debate, the realm of history is where YHWH supposedly acts in a transcendent manner as a "God of history" who exists outside his creation, whereas the realm of creation is linked to ancient Near Eastern notions of "myth," especially Canaanite nature religion. Thus the Israelite worldview is ostensibly different from its pagan counterpart by virtue of its emphasis on history over creation.[27] In Hosea studies, the prevailing anxiety to safeguard YHWH's uniqueness vis-à-vis other gods by removing him from the realm of creation is captured in a comment by Gerhard von Rad: "Hosea's whole preaching is rooted in the saving history. It might almost be said that he only feels safe when he can base his arguments in history."[28] While von Rad goes on to acknowledge that Canaanite nature religion has provided the background for much of the OT, he ultimately concludes that Hosea's use of such pagan traditions must be passed through the demythologizing sieve of salvation history.[29]

---

humankind today as truly as Jesus lived among his own kin. The gospel is Good News when it provides answers for a particular people living in a particular place at a particular time" (Dean Gilliland, "Contextualization," *Evangelical Dictionary of World Missions*, ed. A. Scott Moreau [Grand Rapids: Baker, 2000], 225). For a full discussion of contextualization, see David J. Hesselgrave and Edward Rommen, *Contextualization: Meanings, Methods, and Models* (Pasadena: William Carey Library, 2000).

25. Willem Boshoff, "Who Let Grain, Grapes and Olives Grow? Hosea's Polemics against the Yahwists of Israel," in *Religious Polemics in Context: Papers Presented to the Second International Conference of the Leiden Institute for the Study of Religions (Lisor) Held at Leiden, 27–28 April, 2000*, ed. Theo L. Hettema and Arie van der Kooij, Studies in Theology and Religion 11 (Assen: Royal Van Gorcum, 2004), 267–70.

26. On the issue of YHWH's uniqueness vis-à-vis the other gods of the ancient Near East, the key issue on which Israel's own uniqueness stands or falls, Werner H. Schmidt has helpfully described contextualization in the OT as "the double process of recognition and rejection [that] cuts across the foreign gods themselves, since he encounters and chooses their properties and their activities one by one. It could not indeed have been otherwise, since no area of divine activity could have been omitted from Yahweh's power" (*The Faith of the Old Testament: A History* [Philadelphia: Westminster, 1983], 180).

27. See the history of interpretation in Leo G. Perdue, *The Collapse of History: Reconstructing Old Testament Theology*, OBT (Minneapolis: Augsburg Fortress, 1994), 113–50.

28. Gerhard von Rad, *Old Testament Theology*, trans. D. M. G. Stalker, OTL (Louisville: Westminster John Knox, 2001), 2:140.

29. Von Rad, *Old Testament Theology*, 2:141: "The idea of marriage between a deity and an earthly partner had long been familiar to him and his contemporaries through the rites of the Canaanite nature religion (the marriage of Baal to the earth is an example). It was, to all appearances, an extremely bold move to transfer this idea that belonged to a religious ideology

Such a theological dichotomy between creation and history sets up a potentially overdrawn contrast between "demythologized" Yahwism and pagan "myths." Since deities in the ancient Near East were commonly understood to act in both creation and history,[30] the argumentative strategy of Hosea largely grants this worldview for the sake of argument for YHWH to dethrone the prevailing powers in all the realms where they were thought to rule. Hosea's defense of Israelite orthodoxy is effective precisely because of its critical engagement with the prevailing worldviews of the eighth century BCE.

Interpreters' concern to highlight the differences between Israelite faith and ancient Near Eastern myths is necessary and commendable.[31] However, this approach can sometimes lead to a sub-biblical understanding of orthodoxy that overlooks Hosea's arresting depiction of YHWH as a deity who is uniquely sovereign over all realms, and not just salvation history. For as Richard Bauckham notes, a proper biblical understanding of monotheism must include the conceptual spheres of both *being* (i.e., ontology) and *acting* (i.e., function) in order for YHWH to be truly incomparable to all other gods.[32] I therefore proceed with a brief exploration of how the book of Hosea contextualizes existing concepts of creation, history, deity, and covenant in the service of proclaiming its distinctive theological message of God's reconciliation with his estranged household. This discussion will pave the way for assessing the issue of Hosea's historical provenance.

The Portrayal of Creation in Hosea

Creation dominates the landscape from the very beginning of Hosea. Following the accusation that "the land commits heinous harlotry in walking away from YHWH" (1:2), chapter 2 argues that Israel has sinned by forgetting that YHWH is the real god of fertility. Because the people of Israel have misattributed the source of agricultural blessings such as wool, flax, and olive oil to the Canaanite god Baal (2:7[5], 10[8]), YHWH will answer in judgment by removing these blessings from them (2:11[9], 14[12]). The God of Israel is not opposed to the riches of creation, for the temporary judgment of barrenness will be followed by his restoration of fertility. All creatures will flourish again (2:20[18]) and creation will produce the grain, wine, and olive oil (2:24[22]) that Israel had wrongly sought through worship of Baal.

absolutely incompatible with Jahwism as Hosea understood it, to the covenant relationship with Jahweh. Yet, the very fact that the partner to whom this relationship was now applied was conceived altogether in historical terms eliminated the mythological element from this range of concepts."

30. Bertil Albrektson, *History and the Gods: An Essay on the Idea of Historical Events as Divine Manifestations in the Ancient Near East and in Israel*, ConBOT 1 (Lund: Gleerup, 1967).

31. E.g., John N. Oswalt, *The Bible among the Myths: Unique Revelation or Just Ancient Literature?* (Grand Rapids: Zondervan, 2009).

32. Bauckham, "Biblical Theology and the Problems of Monotheism," 213–16.

YHWH even declares that "I will sow her for myself in the land" (2:25[23]). This promise draws on the language of sowing a field (e.g., Gen 1:11–12), and perhaps even of sexual insemination,[33] in describing the restoration of Israel to a prosperous land. I will explore more fully below how this provocative metaphor works, but Hosea's introductory description of salvation history using the terminology of fertility is clearly problematic for the usual dichotomy between creation and history.

Hosea 4–14 builds upon the creation imagery of chapters 1–3. Drawing upon the book's opening indictment that "the land commits heinous harlotry" (1:2), chapter 4 links the sins of Israel (4:1–2) with the de-creation of the world/land in which "the land is mourning" (4:3). In the subsequent drama of human sin and divine judgment, it is remarkable that Hosea depicts both Israel and YHWH with images drawn from the physical world. As one might expect, Hosea condemns the apostasy of Israel using the beastly metaphors of a stubborn heifer (4:16; cf. 10:11), silly dove (7:11), and wild donkey (8:9). In addition, the people misunderstand YHWH to be a Baal-like deity who comes to his people as the dawn and rain, as well as raising them up on the third day (6:2–3; cf. 2:18[16]).[34]

However, it is noteworthy that such syncretism on Israel's part does not dissuade Hosea from a retort using creational language. The prophet depicts YHWH's judgment against his people "like a moth to Ephraim, like rot to the house of Judah" (5:12), a "lion" or "young lion" who tears and takes away his prey (5:14), as well as the monstrous fusion of an ambushing "leopard" and "bereaved mother-bear" who will "devour them . . . like a lioness, [as] a beast of the field will tear them to pieces" (13:7–8). This mixture of animal imagery is clearly too multifaceted and kaleidoscopic to take as a literal reality, yet it is no less terrifying for its figurative character as a contextualization of nature.

As in Hos 1–3, chapters 4–14 depict restoration after judgment by using language that could easily apply to Canaanite conceptions of nature gods. YHWH will initiate his salvation by summoning his children from exile like a roaring lion (11:10). Even so, animal imagery is less common in describing restoration than botanical and agricultural metaphors. YHWH promises to "rain rightness" if Israel will "sow for yourselves according to righteousness, reap according to faithfulness, till a hard ground for your own sake" (10:12). YHWH's oracle of restoration in Hos 14:6–9[5–8] is even more polemical for its use of nature imagery:

> [6[5]]I shall be like the dew for Israel.
> He will bud like a lily,
> and his root will strike like [the cedars of] Lebanon.

33. Alice A. Keefe, "Hosea's (In)Fertility God," *HBT* 30 (2008): 24–25.

34. Day, "Hosea and the Baal Cult," 216–19.

7[6]His shoots will sprout forth,
his splendor will be like the olive tree,
and his fragrance like [the cedars of] Lebanon.
8[7]Those who dwell in his [YHWH's] shadow shall again revive grain,
they shall sprout forth like the vine.
His remembrance will be like the wine of Lebanon.
9[8]O Ephraim, what do I still have to do with idols?
As for me, I have answered,
and I have watched over him.
I am like a sprawling cypress tree;
from me your fruit is found."

In this passage, YHWH not only outdoes nature gods as the real giver of "dew" (14:6[5]), but he even adopts terminology about the sacred trees of Canaanized religion from earlier in the book (4:13–14; cf. Deut 12:2; 2 Kgs 17:10) to show how he gives to his worshipers the protection of "shadow/shade" (14:8[7]). The suggestive picture of Israel as a growing plant that nestles securely under God as enveloping tree becomes explicit when YHWH asserts, "I am like a sprawling cypress tree; from me your fruit is found" (14:9[8]).

This depiction of the Creator in terms of creation problematizes the one-sided portrayal of a transcendent YHWH who shows himself unique by holding himself aloof from an immanent creation. The next section's discussion of salvation history will show the extent to which Hosea's use of contextualization also entails discontinuity between Yahwism and its cultural milieu in the eighth century BCE. At the same time, it is clear that Hosea's pointed use of creation adopts some degree of continuity toward Canaanite nature religion in order to portray YHWH's imminent defeat of Baal on his home turf.

The Portrayal of History in Hosea

All this is not to deny that salvation history plays a significant role in Hosea. Allusions to Israel's foundational stories are numerous in the book, for example, the patriarchal period (12:4[3], 13[12]), exodus from Egypt (2:17[15]; 11:1), giving of the law at Sinai (4:1–3; 8:12; 12:10[9]; 13:4), and murmuring in the wilderness (9:10; 13:5). For my purposes, it is noteworthy that Hosea's references to history always represent a creative contextualization of the past to bear upon the present. Against von Rad's idea that the preaching of Hosea is unshakably "rooted" in salvation history, it would be more accurate to say that Hosea transplants salvation history into new contexts so that it may bear fresh fruit to nourish a generation for whom the old stories had gone stale. In lieu of a full examination of Hosea's contextualization of salvation history,[35] I will highlight two transformations of the exodus motif in chapters 11–12. Other contextualizations of history will be discussed in the commentary as they appear in the text of Hosea.

Hosea 11 links the exodus motif with other events of Israel's history in surprising ways. YHWH's poignant recollection of his kindness in "calling" Israel out of Egypt (11:1) leads suddenly to the accusation that this "calling" has led to nothing but rebellion:

> "They [i.e., Israel] *called* to them [i.e., Egypt],
> then they [Israel] went away from them.
> To the Baals they kept sacrificing,
> and to idols they kept offering incense." (11:2)

Israel's foolish reliance on its alliance with Egypt and other empires (7:11; 12:2[1]) will lead to an "anti-exodus" back to the very place from which Israel once came (7:16; 8:13; 9:3; cf. 11:5). Yet exile as an "anti-exodus" will not be the last word in Israel's history, for the same Father who gently loved his children (11:3–4) is also the roaring lion (11:10) who calls his children to return home through a "new exodus": "They will tremble like birds from Egypt, and like doves from the land of Assyria. So I shall make them dwell in their homes" (11:11). In a manner that anticipates the majestic prophecies of Isa 40–55, Hos 11 creatively juxtaposes the original exodus motif with the counter motif of exile as an "anti-exodus" and the counter-counter-motif of restoration from exile as a "new exodus."[36]

The transformation of the exodus motif continues in Hos 12 through the blending of the exodus story with other episodes from Israel's history. This chapter begins by identifying Hosea's audience as "Jacob" (12:3[2]) in order to link them with their ancestor who was similarly treacherous against God (12:4–5[3–4]). Following a declaration that YHWH is the deity of the exodus who threatens that "again I shall make you dwell in tents" (12:10[9]), chapter 12 concludes with a contrast between Jacob and Moses: "Then Jacob fled to the field of Aram, and Israel served for a wife; for a wife *he guarded [sheep]*. But by a prophet YHWH brought Israel up from Egypt, and by a prophet *he was kept watch*" (12:13–14[12–13]).

35. The commentary will address the historical allusions in the order they appear in Hosea. Comprehensive studies of Hosea's uses of history can be found in Else Kragelund Holt, *Prophesying the Past: The Use of Israel's History in the Book of Hosea*, JSOTSup 194 (Sheffield: Sheffield Academic, 1994); Dwight R. Daniels, *Hosea and Salvation History*, BZAW 191 (Berlin: de Gruyter, 1990); and Heinz-Dieter Neef, *Die Heilstraditionen Israels in der Verkündigung des Propheten Hosea*, BZAW 169 (Berlin: de Gruyter, 1987).

36. For a fuller discussion of how Hosea appropriates the exodus from Egypt, see Jerry Hwang, "'I Am Yahweh Your God from the Land of Egypt': Hosea's Use of the Exodus Traditions," in *"Did I Not Bring Israel Out of Egypt?" Biblical, Archaeological, and Egyptological Perspectives on the Exodus Narratives*, ed. James K. Hoffmeier, Alan R. Millard, and Gary A. Rendsburg, *BBRSup* 13 (Winona Lake, IN: Eisenbrauns, 2016), 243–53; and Santiago Silva Retamales, "Tradición del 'Éxodo' en Oseas," *EstBib* 56 (1998): 145–78.

Here the repetition of the Hebrew root "to guard/keep watch" (שׁמר) heralds a contrast between the impotent patriarch who sought only his own interests when "he guarded [sheep]," and the faithful prophet who was God's chosen instrument to "keep watch" over his people by shepherding them out of Egypt. As in Hos 11, this text recalls the deliverance from Egypt not for antiquarian purposes but for the sake of showing how these historical traditions still have relevance for lukewarm Israelites in the eighth century BCE. The prophet's audience would have recognized these historical allusions while also being shocked that these cherished traditions could be redeployed against them so pointedly.

In summary, the book of Hosea emphasizes the uniqueness of YHWH by transforming existing ideas of both creation and history. Rather than being purely separate domains, salvation history in the past includes YHWH's mighty acts within creation, while his mighty acts within creation give birth to new phases of salvation history. The balancing of these theological poles in Hosea shows that YHWH is both transcendent and immanent, thereby making him a comprehensive replacement for both the high gods of the ancient Near East who were thought to be all-powerful but remote from their worshipers, as well as the personal gods who were limited in power but close to their worshipers.

Thus Hosea's approach of contextualization entails YHWH taking over and reworking all the functions that other gods were thought to perform. This hermeneutic toward culture ensures the uniqueness of YHWH, not by removing him from creation and placing him within a demythologized history but by linking these spheres of influence so that his dominion encompasses every realm. In addition, the cascade of nature imagery used to portray YHWH demonstrates that the God of Israel is powerfully present within the created order, even as the incompatible character of these metaphors underscores how YHWH transcends these physical descriptions. Appreciation of Hosea's own hermeneutic of contextualization can therefore enhance understanding of his prophetic message by sharpening the contours of continuity and discontinuity with its cultural milieu.

The Portrayal of YHWH as Israel's Kin in Hosea

Hosea's contextualization of creation and history also draws support from a striking application of kinship imagery to describe the unique relationship of YHWH to Israel. Although kinship also figures largely in other ancient Near Eastern descriptions of deities relating to their people, the notable differences between Israel and its surrounding cultures in Hosea's use of marriage and sonship imagery highlight YHWH's persistence in loving his people even after Israel has continually fallen into sin. This pained love for Israel is so unique that it requires two family metaphors that cannot simultaneously be true of the same relationship. At the same time, kinship connections are relatable and powerful enough to capture something of how much God cares for his people.

For such reasons, this commentary parts ways at this point from the common approach in OT scholarship to explore covenant theology using legal rather than familial categories.[37] It is instead the kinship institutions of marriage and sonship in the ancient Near East that provide the proper background for understanding God's covenantal relationship to his people.[38] Yet as the commentary below will explore, Hosea's depiction of the covenant between YHWH and Israel far surpasses its cultural analogues for the depth of its emotional intimacy and heartbreak. To appreciate better the nature of this contrast, let us consider briefly how kinship language functioned in the rest of the ancient Near East.

The contextualization of familial imagery begins with the use of marital language in Hos 1–3. In contrast to the OT's account of an exclusive relationship between YHWH and Israel, El and Baal (the most important gods of the Canaanite pantheon) each have multiple consorts. The tablets unearthed at Ugarit (Ras Shamra in modern Syria) depict El and Baal as key players in cultic rituals that are geared toward ensuring the fertility of the earth. El impregnates two of his human wives in order to beget the gods of Dawn and Dusk,[39] while the Baal Cycle apparently records at least two consorts for Baal in the goddesses Astarte and Anat,[40] as well as Baal having sexual relations with a heifer (who may represent Anat).[41]

The divine activities of "sacred marriage" (Gk. *hieros gamos*) found expression to some extent through cultic activity in the human realm. This occurred because ancient Near Eastern peoples tended to link these spheres together as macrocosm and microcosm.[42] Evidence for an official cult of sacred prostitution in Ugarit and Israel is somewhat inconclusive,[43] but scholars generally agree that sexual activities were associated with the practice of Canaanite nature religion,

37. E.g., William L. Moran, "The Ancient Near Eastern Background of the Love of God in Deuteronomy," *CBQ* 25 (1963): 77–87; D. J. McCarthy, "Notes on the Love of God in Deuteronomy and the Father-Son Relationship between Yahweh and Israel," *CBQ* 27 (1965): 144–47.

38. Frank Moore Cross, "Kinship and Covenant in Ancient Israel," in *From Epic to Canon: History and Literature in Ancient Israel* (Baltimore: The Johns Hopkins University Press, 1998), 3–21.

39. El's wives in *KTU* 1.23 (the text in question) have often been interpreted as Anat and Asherah, the Canaanite goddesses of fertility (e.g., Sebastian R. Smolarz, *Covenant and the Metaphor of Divine Marriage in Biblical Thought: A Study with Special Reference to the Book of Revelation* [Eugene, OR: Wipf & Stock, 2011], 42–43). However, the Ugaritic term used to describe these wives can only denote human women and not divine goddesses (David Toshio Tsumura, "Kings and Cults in Ancient Ugarit," in *Priests and Officials in the Ancient Near East: Papers of the Second Colloquium on the Ancient Near East—The City and Its Life Held at the Middle Eastern Culture Center in Japan (Mitaka, Tokyo)*, ed. Kazuko Watanabe [Heidelberg: Winter, 1999], 235–36). Thus, the concept of divine-human marriage at Ugarit yields a closer analogy to Hosea 1–3.

40. Mark S. Smith, *The Ugaritic Baal Cycle*, VTSup 55 (Leiden: Brill, 1994), xxiiin63.

41. Mark S. Smith, *The Ugaritic Baal Cycle*, VTSup 114 (Leiden: Brill, 2009), 303n26.

42. On creation theology in the ancient Near East as the relationship between macrocosm and microcosm, see Ronald A. Simkins, *Creator and Creation: Nature in the Worldview of Ancient Israel* (Peabody, MA: Hendrickson, 1994), 75–81.

43. Hennie J. Marsman, *Women in Ugarit and Israel: Their Social and Religious Position in the Context of the Ancient Near East*, *OtSt* 49 (Leiden: Brill, 2003), 528–51.

though perhaps not always ritual in nature.[44] The prevalence of such a mimetic worldview, which linked sex in the divine and human realms, makes it rather amazing that Hosea employs marriage imagery to polemicize against Canaanite nature religion.[45]

The exclusivity of the covenantal relationship between YHWH and Israel marks only the start of Hosea's depiction of the divergence between Yahwism and Baalism. Hosea 2 goes on to upend the traditional dynamics of gender and honor in Mediterranean societies through YHWH's stated intention to reclaim Israel as his bride.[46] Even after punishing Israel justly for her apostasy, YHWH insists on wooing her again despite the cultural expectation for a cuckolded husband to banish a wayward wife who had caused him to "lose face." YHWH does not seek to "save face" but rather to remarry Israel by leading her back to the wilderness in order to "speak to her heart" (2:16[14]). Needless to say, this sort of divine commitment to a single human partner (and a wayward one at that!) is unprecedented in an ancient Near Eastern context where deities were often thought to keep multiple consorts for the utilitarian end of guaranteeing fertility for the land.

Hosea similarly recasts the terminology of the father-son relationship, this time in polemical dialogue with the realm of international diplomacy rather than Canaanite nature religion. Specifically, the use of father-son language is a common feature of ancient Near Eastern treaties in the second millennium BCE.[47] For example, in a cache of letters at Mari dating to the early second millennium BCE, it was common to identify a suzerain as a "father" who was therefore obligated to care for a vassal as his "son."[48] Analogous terminology of "father" and "son" occurs in diplomatic

44. See the balanced discussion by John Day, "Does the Old Testament Refer to Sacred Prostitution and Did It Actually Exist in Ancient Israel?," in *Biblical and Near Eastern Essays: Studies in Honour of Kevin J. Cathcart*, ed. Carmel McCarthy and John F. Healey, LHBOTS 375 (London: T&T Clark, 2004), 2–21.

45. The useful term "homéopathique" is used by Edmond Jacob ("L'Héritage cananéen dans le livre du prophète Osée," *RHPR* 3 [1963]: 251) to describe Hosea's surprising use of Canaanite religion to cure Israel's disease of religious syncretism. See the "Canonical and Theological Significance" sections on Hos 9:10–11:11 for more on homeopathy as a communication strategy in Hosea.

46. On gender relations in Mediterranean societies, see Carol Delaney, "Seeds of Honor, Fields of Shame," in *Honor and Shame and the Unity of the Mediterranean*, ed. David D. Gilmore, A Special Publication of the American Anthropological Association 22 (Washington, DC: American Anthropological Association, 1987), 35–48. See discussion of "Canonical and Theological Significance" on Hos 2:4–25[2–23] for detailed background on the relationships between gender and honor in Mediterranean cultures. For a general exploration of how honor, shame, and guilt are deeply entwined with one another as well as an application of these concepts to an OT book, see the work of Daniel Y. Wu, *Honor, Shame, and Guilt: Social-Scientific Approaches to the Book of Ezekiel*, *BBRSup* 14 (Winona Lake, IN: Eisenbrauns, 2013).

47. Moshe Weinfeld, "The Covenant of Grant in the Old Testament and the Ancient Near East," *JAOS* 90 (1970): 194 (emphasis added): "The use of familial metaphors in order to express relationships belonging to the royal-national sphere should not surprise us, *since the whole diplomatic vocabulary of the second millennium is rooted in the familial sphere.*"

48. E.g., King Zimri-Lim of Mari repeatedly addresses Ibal-pi-el II of Eshnunna as "King of Eshnunna, my father" (Kenneth A. Kitchen and Paul J. N. Lawrence, "Zimri-Lim of Mari and Ibal-pi-el II of Eshnunna," in *Treaty, Law, and Covenant in the Ancient Near East*, 1:211–16). See discussion of the Mari letters by F. Charles Fensham, "Father and Son as Terminology for Treaty and Covenant," in *Near Eastern Studies in Honor of William Foxwell Albright*, ed. Hans Goedicke (Baltimore: Johns Hopkins University Press, 1971), 122–25.

correspondence between Canaanite chieftains and their Egyptian patrons during the Amarna period in the later second millennium.[49]

However, it is important at this juncture not to import anachronistic notions of an involved father doting attentively upon his sons. Any mirage of emotional affection quickly evaporates upon recognizing that there was often little difference between a son and a servant in the ancient Near East, though the former at least had the benefit of an eventual inheritance.[50] Israelite society largely mirrored the rest of the ancient Near East in that "the relationship of a son to his father in the Hebrew family was essentially one of respect and obedience, in which the emotional element seldom played any large role."[51] Hence the language of a father-son relationship proved suitable for describing the somewhat less rigid hierarchy that characterized political relationships between suzerains and vassals in the second millennium BCE.

The hierarchical character of ancient Near Eastern diplomacy increased sharply with the reemergence of Assyria in the first millennium BCE,[52] a trend reflected in the transformation of father-son imagery in treaty documents of this period. In the Neo-Assyrian treaties, a genre whose appearance was nearly contemporaneous with the ministries of Israel's classical prophets (i.e., those whose oracles become books),[53] it became the Neo-Assyrian king who alone possessed the title of the "son" of Assyrian gods and goddesses.[54] This suzerain would leverage his divinely chosen status to coerce obedience from his pitiful human vassals by threatening them before the gods with a litany of curses.

These treaties lack any list of blessings for obedience, a notable difference from second-millennium treaties that could at least claim the trope of familial devotion by promising that a suzerain would guarantee the vassal's safety in exchange for faithfulness. The language of familial devotion, fleeting as such benevolence could be in the second millennium, was replaced in the first millennium by arm-twisting threats that arose from the massive imbalance of power between the empire and its subjects.[55]

49. E.g., EA 73, in which Rib-Hadda appeals to the pharaoh in Egypt as "my father." See discussion of the Amarna letters by Fensham, "Father and Son as Terminology for Treaty and Covenant," 126–27.

50. Paul Kalluveettil, *Declaration and Covenant: A Comprehensive Review of Covenant Formulae from the Old Testament and the Ancient Near East*, AnBib 88 (Rome: Biblical Institute Press, 1982), 131.

51. Ibid., 132.

52. The longstanding tendency of Mesopotamian cultures to use the language of power in diplomatic documents is well observed by Noel Weeks, *Admonition and Curse: The Ancient Near Eastern Treaty/Covenant Form as a Problem in Inter-Cultural Relationships*, LHBOTS 407 (London: T&T Clark, 2004).

53. Hayim Tadmor, "Treaty and Oath in the Ancient Near East: A Historian's Approach," in *Humanizing America's Iconic Book: Society of Biblical Literature Centennial Addresses*, ed. Gene M. Tucker and Douglas A. Knight (Chico, CA: Scholars Press, 1982), 142–49.

54. Bustenay Oded, *War, Peace, and Empire: Justifications for War in Assyrian Royal Inscriptions* (Wiesbaden: Reichert, 1992), 21–24. This development marks the endpoint of a centuries-long trend of elevating the Assyrian king to nearly divine status, on which generally see Peter Machinist, "Kingship and Divinity in Imperial Assyria," in *Text, Artifact, and Image: Revealing Ancient Israelite Religion*, BJS 346 (Providence, RI: Brown Judaic Studies, 2006), 152–88.

55. Cf. Simo Parpola and Kazuko Watanabe, *Neo-Assyrian Treaties and Loyalty Oaths*, SAA II (Helsinki: Helsinki University Press, 1988), xv–xvi.

This elevation of the Neo-Assyrian emperor matched what had always been true of Egypt's pharaohs, who had always been the only beloved "son" of the gods.[56]

Considering these broader cultural trends, the use of father-son language in Hos 11 presents several salient departures from its context. Foremost among these is that Hosea revives the use of sonship terminology, though not in a manner resembling Assyrian or Egyptian kings' appropriation of this special status for themselves, nor even in applying the language to only the leaders of a vassal group as in second-millennium-BCE treaties. Instead Hosea broadens such language to describe an entire people in that the people of Israel are collectively addressed as YHWH's "son" (11:1).[57]

Additionally, Hosea reframes sonship terminology itself in the depiction of YHWH calling after his disobedient son as a tender father (11:1). In another stunning inversion of cultural expectations, Hosea portrays the heart of YHWH as deeply torn between judgment and salvation for his people (11:8–9). The traditional family hierarchy in the ancient Near East has now been transformed in Hos 11 from a relationship that mainly evoked fear and respect from the son toward his father into an intimate one with deep emotional attachment from the father toward his son. From Hos 11, it is only a short hop from the poignancy of an Israelite father who *calls* to a wayward son to Jesus's even more shocking parable of a Jewish father who *runs* to greet his long-lost son (Luke 15:20).[58]

Hosea's Contextualization of Covenantal Ideas

The book of Hosea creatively brings together the foregoing theological distinctives using the category of covenant, specifically the terminology of "knowing YHWH" and "knowledge of God." Although the political terminology of a vassal's "knowledge" of a suzerain is part and parcel of ancient Near Eastern diplomatic language,[59] Hosea redirects this covenant terminology in a distinctively relational direction, most notably by enlarging the concept of "knowing" from its original meaning in the exodus narrative. The book of Exodus pulses with the theme of

56. John Baines, "Ancient Egyptian Kingship: Official Forms, Rhetoric, Context," in *King and Messiah in Israel and the Ancient Near East: Proceedings of the Oxford Old Testament Seminar*, ed. John Day, JSOTSup 270 (Sheffield: Sheffield Academic, 1998), 23.

57. From a canonical perspective, Hosea certainly does not break new ground since the status of Israel as YHWH's "son" was already announced earlier in the OT (Exod 4:22; Deut 14:1). The observation here is simply that Hos 11:1 would have been an unfamiliar and countercultural assertion during a time when syncretism was prevalent in Israel.

58. On the inversion of Mediterranean cultural dynamics in the latter text, much of which applies to the former, see Kenneth E. Bailey, *The Cross and the Prodigal: Luke 15 through the Eyes of Middle Eastern Peasants*, 2nd ed. (Downers Grove, IL: InterVarsity Press, 2005); and idem, *Jacob and the Prodigal: How Jesus Retold Israel's Story* (Downers Grove, IL: InterVarsity Press, 2003), 143–44.

59. Herbert B. Huffmon, "The Treaty Background of Hebrew *YĀDAʿ*," *BASOR* 181 (1966): 31–37; Herbert B. Huffmon and Simon B. Parker, "A Further Note on the Treaty Background of Hebrew *YĀDAʿ*," *BASOR* 184 (1966): 36–38.

making known YHWH's great name and covenantal deeds throughout the nations.[60] Particularly in chapters 6–14, the missional motivation for Israel's deliverance from Egypt is repeatedly emphasized in YHWH's desire "that he/they/you may know [ידע] that I am YHWH" (e.g., Exod 6:7; 7:5; 14:18).[61]

The book of Hosea expands the scope of this "knowledge" to include three additional aspects of the relationship between YHWH and Israel. Besides its original referent of the deliverance from Egypt (13:4; cf. 12:10[9]), the Hebrew verb also denotes Israel's "knowledge of God" in (1) his provision of the law at Sinai (4:6; cf. 4:1; 6:6; 8:2); (2) his gift of the land and satiety therein (2:10[8]); and (3) renewed relationship with God after the punishment of exile (2:22[20]). In summary, Hosea characterizes the covenantal "knowledge of God" required of Israel as *cognitive* with reference to acknowledging YHWH's acts in exodus and conquest, *experiential* with reference to loving God with an exclusive devotion, and *moral-volitional* with reference to obeying the laws revealed at Sinai.[62] Such a holistic relationship with God encompasses all three kinds of "knowledge" in a way greater than the sum of its parts.[63]

Additionally, the renewed covenant between YHWH and Israel intertwines "knowledge of God" with the harmony of creation in an unprecedented manner. In chapter 4, the lack of such covenantal "knowledge" (4:1), as reflected in Israel's failure to observe the Decalogue (4:2), issues forth in the disintegration of the created order: "As a result, the land is mourning, and all the inhabitants wither in it. [As for] the beast of the field, the birds of the sky, and even the fish of the sea—they will be taken away!" (4:3). Here the order given for land, sky, and sea creatures is literally reversed from the Gen 1 account, suggesting that Israel's lack of "knowledge of God" tears the fabric of creation itself.[64] This intersection of ethical and cosmic order in Hosea is not unique to Israel but common to the ancient Near East.[65]

Where the covenant theology of Hosea breaks new ground is in describing the

60. W. Ross Blackburn, *The God Who Makes Himself Known: The Missionary Heart of the Book of Exodus*, NSBT 28 (Leicester: Apollos, 2012).

61. This "recognition formula" becomes a refrain in Exodus through YHWH's repeated declaration about the goal of the exodus from Egypt: "that X may know [ידע] that I am YHWH." The element X varies in the exodus narrative among Pharaoh, Egypt as a whole, or "you" (i.e., Israel). The pioneering work on the so-called *Erkenntnisaussage* is Walther Zimmerli, "I Am Yahweh," in *I Am Yahweh*, trans. Douglas W. Stott (Atlanta: John Knox, 1982), 1–28. For a more recent treatment, see the study of John Frederick Evans, *An Inner-Biblical Interpretation and Intertextual Reading of Ezekiel's Recognition Formulae with the Book of Exodus* (ThD diss., University of Stellenbosch, 2006).

62. M. Douglas Carew, "To Know or Not to Know: Hosea's Use of *yd'*/*d't*," in *The Old Testament in the Life of God's People: Essays in Honor of Elmer A. Martens*, ed. Jon M. Isaak (Winona Lake, IN: Eisenbrauns, 2009), 73–85.

63. In this regard, Hosea reflects the "both-and" complementarity of knowing God and knowing about God that is characteristic of biblical theology. On the theological impossibility of pitting propositional and relational knowledge of God against each other, see R. W. L. Moberly, "Knowing God and Knowing About God: Martin Buber's *Two Types of Faith* Revisited," *SJT* 65 (2012): 402–20.

64. Katherine M. Hayes, *The Earth Mourns: Prophetic Metaphor and Oral Aesthetic*, SBLAcBib 8 (Atlanta: SBL Press, 2002), 54–56.

65. Hans Heinrich Schmid, "Creation, Righteousness, and Salvation: 'Creation Theology' as the Broad Horizon of Biblical Theology," in *Creation in the Old Testament*, ed. Bernhard W. Anderson, IRT 6 (Philadelphia: Fortress, 1984), 102–17.

restoration of ethical and cosmic order in terms akin to remarriage. Although the sin of humanity has damaged God's creation, the divine husband's reconciliation with his human wife (2:18[16]) leads to a renewal of harmony within the animal world: "I [YHWH] will make a covenant for them [Israel] on that day, with the beast of the field, and with the bird of the sky, and the crawler of the earth" (2:20[18]). Reconciliation between humans and the created order undoes the punishment of 2:14[12] in which "the beast of the field will consume them,"[66] the referent of "them" being the agricultural goods that Israel had mistakenly sought from her pagan "lovers." The irony of the situation is that Israel's misguided pursuit of fertility and prosperity has backfired by violating the connection between ethical and cosmic order, a sin that Hosea expresses using the sexual terminology of adultery and harlotry.

Once YHWH betroths Israel to himself again with the virtues of "righteousness and justice, with devotion and mercies" (2:21[19])—the very qualities that YHWH seeks from his people (cf. 4:1)[67]—then creation will regain its stability and vitality through a cosmic covenant that echoes the Noahic covenant (Gen 9:9–16).[68] The Creator and creatures will celebrate their restoration through a sequence of joyful antiphonies (2:23–24[21–22]) when God answers the heavens, which in turn answer the earth, which respond by producing "the grain, the new wine, and the olive oil" (i.e., the very agricultural goods attributed to Baal; 2:10[8]). Just as Israel "answered" (ענה) YHWH's call to remarriage (2:17[15]),[69] heaven and earth will also be rejoined in covenantal relationship through a similar "answer" to YHWH as well as to one another.[70]

This portrayal of YHWH's relationship with creation contrasts sharply with Canaanite mythology in which the polygamy of the deities ensured the fertility of the earth. Hosea instead depicts YHWH as a monogamous husband whose exclusive relationship with an adulterous wife will secure the harmony of creation. Although Hosea characterizes this relationship using various derivatives of the Hebrew verb ידע ("to know"), one of the most common roots in Hebrew for the intimacy of sexual relations,[71] "knowledge of God" in the book involves total covenantal commitment to YHWH rather than any use of mimetic sexual ritual to manipulate the order of the cosmos.[72]

66. Gene M. Tucker, "The Peaceable Kingdom and a Covenant with the Wild Animals," in *God Who Creates: Essays in Honor of W. Sibley Towner*, ed. William P. Brown and S. Dean McBride (Grand Rapids: Eerdmans, 2000), 223.

67. Katharine J. Dell, "Hosea, Creation, and Wisdom: An Alternative Tradition," in *On Stone and Scroll: Essays in Honour of Graham Ivor Davies*, ed. J. K. Aitken, Katharine J. Dell, and Brian A. Mastin, BZAW 420 (Berlin: de Gruyter, 2011), 417.

68. Hayes, *The Earth Mourns*, 60–61.

69. For a convincing case that ענה in Hos 2:17[15] describes the bride's response to the groom's offer of remarriage, see Mordechai A. Friedman, "Israel's Response in Hosea 2:17b: 'You Are My Husband,'" *JBL* 99 (1980): 199–204.

70. Robert Murray, *The Cosmic Covenant: Biblical Themes of Justice, Peace, and the Integrity of Creation* (London: Sheed & Ward, 2007), 29–30.

71. E.g., Gen 4:1; 19:8; 38:26; Num 31:17; Judg 19:25; 1 Sam 1:19; 1 Kgs 1:4.

72. The stark differences between covenantal and mimetic worldviews are outlined by Merold Westphal, *God, Guilt, and Death: An Existential Phenomenology of Religion* (Bloomington: Indiana University Press, 1987), 194–252.

Thus the book of Hosea embarks on a radical reworking of the marriage metaphor in the service of its distinctive theology of covenant. Sacred marriage in the rest of the ancient Near East served the need for fertility and other forms of cosmic order without any connotation of relationship, but the marriage metaphor in Hosea prioritizes the importance of covenantal reconciliation with God, which in turn leads to the restoration of the land of Israel as a microcosm of creation. Accordingly, people and the rest of creation are conceived of as equal partners in the household of YHWH.

Hosea's reconfiguration of the marriage between Creator and creature furnishes the rationale for the final aspect of Israel's distinctiveness among ancient Near Eastern cultures—the prohibition of images in worshiping YHWH, a phenomenon known as aniconism.[73] In this regard, the book of Hosea exhibits a peculiar tension for being one of the OT's most vehement in denouncing Israel's use of man-made icons such as bull statues (e.g., 8:5–6) yet boldly using word pictures drawn from creation to characterize YHWH the Creator of all things (e.g., 14:6–9[5–8]). Many interpreters have thus noted that the book of Hosea evinces the paradox of vigorous opposition to iconographic representations of God on the one hand, but provocative use of creational metaphors to describe God on the other hand. Traditional attempts to resolve this paradox are problematic, as noted earlier, since their conception of YHWH as radically transcendent and detached from creation fails to explain why the OT prophets would undercut their own argument by procuring ideas from the very realms of immanence that were supposedly problematic for Israel.[74]

Once again, Hosea provides a solution to the theological riddle of aniconism by offering inventive variations on the theme of YHWH's covenant with Israel. In contrast with ancient Near Eastern conceptions of the deity as ritually present with his/her earthly idol, Hosea and other prophets assert the opposite notion that YHWH is absent when his worshipers use physical representations of his presence. The mystery of Yahwism deepens upon recognizing the fact that Israel's God only becomes present when his people worship him within the dialogical tension known as "sacred emptiness."[75] At the same time, the countercultural character of YHWH among the gods raises an urgent question—how and where does Israel worship an unseen Creator who resists creational representations of his presence?

73. The seminal treatment of Tryggve N. D. Mettinger, *No Graven Image?: Israelite Aniconism in Its Ancient Near Eastern Context*, ConBOT 42 (Stockholm: Almqvist & Wiksell, 1995), offers detailed support for the view that Israel's strident form of "programmatic aniconism" was unique in the ancient Near East.

74. Nathan MacDonald, "Aniconism in the Old Testament," in *The God of Israel*, ed. Robert P. Gordon, UCOP 64 (Cambridge: Cambridge University Press, 2007), 21–28.

75. This is the helpful coinage of Mettinger, *No Graven Image*, 19. On a related note, the lack of images that characterizes Israelite orthodoxy means that archaeological evidence of aniconism will always be lacking. Since evidence of aniconism tends to be sparse because, by definition, evidence of invisibility is unlikely to exist, the presence of icons in the archaeological record has tended to skew scholarly discussion toward the view that aniconism and monotheism were the minority position or late developments in Israel (e.g., Robert K. Gnuse, *No Other Gods: Emergent Monotheism in Israel*, LHBOTS 241 [Sheffield: Sheffield Academic, 1997]).

Jill Middlemas and Gordon McConville have shown convincingly that the book of Hosea speaks of iconographic absence to propound an alternative theology of divine presence.[76] The characterization of YHWH using a series of pictures from the created order fills the conceptual vacuum created by the prohibition on physical images. Although this succession of verbal imagery may result in contradictions, strictly speaking (e.g., YHWH as father, physician, fowler, leopard, dawn), the hearer's experience of consternation and contemplation are theologically constructive in that "[t]he symbol gives rise to thought," to quote Ricoeur's memorable dictum.[77]

Pondering Hosea's dissonant metaphors and similes yields a renewed apprehension of YHWH as relatable yet incomparable, understandable yet elusive, both transcendent and immanent. Middlemas usefully summarizes Hosea's exchange of physical images for verbal imagery: "YHWH is ultimately unfathomable, totally other, and the full range of language can only begin to provide a partial portrait."[78] Therein lies the genius of Hosea's covenant theology: its ability to disarm idolatrous portrayals of YHWH as being too similar to his creation while at the same time reinforcing the uniqueness of YHWH without losing account of his presence within the world. The distinctiveness of Israel finds reinforcement in Hosea's innovative summons to "know" this God through a covenant relationship that differs radically from how other nations related to their gods.

The Main Theme of Hosea's Prophecy

Hosea's unique presentation of existing concepts propounds its main theme, namely, God's reconciliation with his estranged household. This formulation of Hosea's main theme has two parts. The first is that of reconciliation with YHWH as a passionate deity who stands apart from the apathetic gods and goddesses of the ancient Near East, not to mention how the majority of religious systems across all human cultures have conceived of the divine.[79] YHWH surpasses the transcendence of all other gods in his dominion over creation and history, while his immanence also exceeds theirs, due to his covenantal involvement in human affairs. His emotional pain toward Israel's apostasy is genuine,[80] though the precise way YHWH exhibits such vulnerability without compromising his sovereignty remains something of a

76. Jill Middlemas, "Divine Presence in Absence: Aniconism and Multiple Imaging in the Prophets," in *Divine Presence and Absence in Exilic and Post-Exilic Judaism*, ed. Nathan MacDonald and Izaak J. de Hulster, FAT 61 (Tübingen: Mohr Siebeck, 2013), 183–211; J. Gordon McConville, "'I Am Like a Luxuriant Juniper': Language about God in Hosea," in *Let Us Go Up to Zion: Essays in Honour of H. G. M. Williamson on the Occasion of His Sixty-Fifth Birthday*, ed. Iain W. Provan and Mark J. Boda, VTSup 153 (Leiden: Brill, 2012), 181–92.

77. Paul Ricoeur, *The Symbolism of Evil*, trans. Emerson Buchanan (Boston: Beacon, 1969), 347.

78. Middlemas, "Aniconism and Multiple Imaging in the Prophets," 205.

79. As famously shown by Abraham J. Heschel, *The Prophets* (New York: Harper & Row, 1962), 232–46.

80. Harold Fisch, *Poetry with a Purpose: Biblical Poetics and Interpretation* (Bloomington: Indiana University Press, 1988), 141: "Hosea more than any other book of the Bible . . .

mystery. The second part of Hosea's theme is the estranged household of God. As Andrew Dearman has shown, the anthropological concept of the "household" draws together Hosea's use of husband-wife and parent-child metaphors.[81] The idea of a household also helps to highlight Hosea's preference for kinship language over political terminology to describe YHWH's familial relationship with Israel.

However, I refine Dearman's insights by extending the concept of YHWH's patrimonial household of past and present Israel to include the whole of creation. In chapters 12–14 especially, solidarity with the right set of ancestors (Jacob/Ephraim vs. Moses) is presented to Hosea's audience as the critical decision (12:9[8], 13–15[12–14]; 14:2–4[1–3]) that marks whether or not they and the rest of YHWH's creatures will experience restoration (13:15; 14:5–9[4–8]). The current hearers confront the urgent choice of which future for history and creation they will enact for themselves. Similarly, in chapter 2 Israel's marred relationship with creation serves as a harbinger of estrangement from God (2:14[12]; cf. 1:2; 4:3), while reconciliation also assumes cosmic dimensions when creation rejoices at Israel's return to YHWH (2:20–24[18–22]). This accounts for the scope of YHWH's reconciliation with his estranged household assuming broader dimensions in history and creation than merely the present generation of Israel's people.

The Literary Style of the Book of Hosea

The observation that the book of Hosea contextualizes existing ideas in the service of its unique theological message leads naturally to a discussion of when and where such a distinctive set of prophecies could have been composed and collected into a literary work. Any exploration of the historical provenance of Hosea must address several issues: (1) Hosea is unique among the OT Prophets for being written in the Hebrew dialect of Samaria, thereby suggesting a northern origin; (2) the superscription of Hosea calls attention to how the word of YHWH came to the prophet during the reigns of four Judahite kings (i.e., Uzziah, Jotham, Ahaz, and Hezekiah), thereby hinting at a process of editorial compilation in Judah after the fall of Samaria in 722 BCE; and (3) the covenant theology of Hosea stands close to that of Deuteronomy, a book whose legal core is usually dated by historical critics to the time of King Josiah's reforms in about 622 BCE, a century after the demise of the Northern Kingdom. Depending on which factor receives priority, scholars have proposed dates for Hosea's composition ranging anywhere from the traditional date in the mid-eighth century BCE to the postexilic period in the mid-fifth century BCE.

gives us God's side of the relationship. It is dominated by the first-person mode of address as God himself cries out, cajoles, reprimands, mourns, and debates with himself."

81. J. Andrew Dearman, *The Book of Hosea*, NICOT (Grand Rapids: Eerdmans, 2010), 44–50.

However, such a wide range of dates often reveals more about scholarly presuppositions in balancing these factors than about the biblical text itself.[82] Thus it will be necessary to evaluate the relative importance of each factor before offering a historical reconstruction of how the book of Hosea's prophecies came to be. When all the facts are in, the traditional view that the prophet Hosea ministered in the Northern Kingdom in the mid-eighth century BCE still has the most to commend itself.

The traditional view about Hosea's journey from oral proclamations to prophetic book proceeds as follows. After the fall of Samaria, oracular and narrative traditions associated with Hosea traveled with the refugees from the Northern Kingdom to Judah, perhaps by the hand of the prophet himself. Scribes in Hezekiah's royal court compiled these traditions alongside the eighth-century prophetic books of Amos, Micah, and Isaiah, with which the book of Hosea shares a standard superscription format. This editorial process for Hosea sought to contemporize the circumstances surrounding Samaria's fall for a time when Judah was facing its own version of the Assyrian crisis.[83]

Sometime after Judah's exile to Babylon in 587 BCE, the book of Hosea was joined to two other collections of prophetic literature that deal with the fall of Judah and destruction of Jerusalem. The smaller of these collections was the Book of the Twelve (i.e., the Minor Prophets), while the larger became known as the Latter Prophets (i.e., Isaiah–Malachi), a group that also includes the Twelve. Below I offer a more detailed account of how the missiological category of contextualization again proves helpful, this time for tracing the development of Hosea's oral preaching to the canonical literary composition associated with him.

The Samarian Origins of Hosea's Prophecy

The first consideration in Hosea's provenance is that the Hebrew text of Hosea reflects a distinct Samarian dialect. Scholarly recognition of this dialect in the last few decades has effected a major shift in Hosea studies. As far back as the translation of the LXX in the third century BCE and onwards, the book of Hosea has proven

82. The trend in Hosea studies for a single *tendenz* to outweigh all other factors is evident in the latest study of Hosea's provenance by James M. Bos, *Reconsidering the Date and Provenance of the Book of Hosea: The Case for Persian-Period Yehud*, LHBOTS 580 (New York: Bloomsbury, 2013). Bos begins with the doubtful presupposition that literacy was uncommon in Israel before the exile to Babylon. By excluding all evidence for an early, northern literary text as anachronistic, Bos arrives via circular reasoning at the conclusion that Hosea is a postexilic creation of Jewish scribes in the Persian period, like all of Israel's other sacred texts.

83. Further evidence for the Judahite scribal strategy of recontextualization can be found in 2 Kgs 17, a chapter that regards Samaria's destruction as paradigmatic for Judah as well. Following an explanation of why Samaria fell to Assyria (2 Kgs 17:7–18), the narrator adds the comment: "Also, Judah did not keep the commandments of YHWH their God, but walked in the customs that Israel had introduced" (2 Kgs 17:19). Since Judah's fall is not narrated until 2 Kgs 25 (and there without any theological rationale), 2 Kgs 17 is clearly designed to explain the exiles of both kingdoms. On the Judahite perspective in this chapter as a whole, see Pauline A. Viviano, "2 Kings 17: A Rhetorical and Form-Critical Analysis," *CBQ* 49 (1987): 548–59.

challenging to interpreters for its obscure terms, sudden topical shifts, awkward turns of phrase, and opaque imagery.[84] The notable differences between the MT and LXX versions of Hosea therefore led to the older consensus that Hosea was either a poorly preserved text or that multiple Hebrew manuscript traditions of the book must have existed.

But following the pioneering work of Gary Rendsburg and his students,[85] a consensus has been building that Hosea preserves the best example in the OT of a northern dialect. The language of Hosea is clearly recognizable as Hebrew, but it diverges in some respects from the vocabulary, grammar, and syntax from the Judahite dialect that predominates in the rest of the OT.[86] Rather than having text-critical significance, then, the discrepancies between the MT and other ancient versions of Hosea mostly reflect difficulties in translation due to unfamiliarity with this northern dialect.[87] This linguistic conclusion, along with the observation that Hosea's prophecy focuses almost exclusively on names and places of the Northern Kingdom, raises in turn the question of why a northern book like Hosea has been included within a canonical literary corpus that focuses on the Southern Kingdom.[88] What relevance would a Judahite audience find in prophetic traditions that are clearly based in the historical context of Samaria's fall in 722 BCE?

The Judahite Reception of Hosea's Prophecy

The answer to this question is found in the second factor to consider in Hosea's provenance, namely, that the superscription to his prophecy is so similar to

84. Jerome's famous statement about Hosea has resonated with every commentator on the book: "Osee commaticus est et quasi per sententias loquens ("Hosea is halting, as if speaking in maxims").

85. Most comprehensively in a doctoral thesis supervised by Gary Rendsburg, viz., Yoon Jong Yoo, "Israelian Hebrew in the Book of Hosea" (PhD diss., Cornell University, 1999). For a recent evaluation of Rendsburg and Yoo suggesting that Hosea's Hebrew may be his idiolect as much as a northern dialect, see Sungjin Kim, "Is the Masoretic Text Still a Reliable Primary Text for the Book of Hosea?" *BBR* 28 (2018): 55–63.

86. Dialectal variations within a language family operate along a spectrum of similarity and dissimilarity. Much as British and American English share some terms (e.g., "pocket money"), retain their own characteristic expressions (e.g., "allowance" in American English only), but still influence each other due to ongoing interaction (e.g., British young people using the "like" discourse marker of California English), Israelian and Judahite Hebrew would have been mutually intelligible and influencing but not identical.

87. This scholarly shift is evidenced in the century or so that separates the ICC volumes on Hosea by William R. Harper (1905) and Andrew A. Macintosh (1997). The former often emends the MT based on the ancient witnesses, while the latter usually defends the MT and explains difficult expressions as northernisms. Similarly, the critical apparatus for Hosea in the *BHQ* volume on the Twelve Prophets (2010) often argues for the integrity of the MT against the tendency of *BHS* (Twelve Prophets fascicle from 1970) and *BHK* (final edition from 1937) to emend the text of Hosea.

88. Against minimalists such as Susanne Rudnig-Zelt, *Hoseastudien: Redaktionskritische Untersuchungen zur Genese des Hoseabuches*, FRLANT 213 (Göttingen: Vandenhoeck & Ruprecht, 2006), the differences between Hosea's vocabulary and Judahite Hebrew indicate that his prophecy has roots in preexilic Samaria rather than postexilic Yehud (Macintosh, *Hosea*, lv–lvii, 585–93). It would have been counterproductive for Jewish scribes to create an entire book out of whole cloth in an unfamiliar dialect or literary style.

other eighth-century prophetic books that it is probable that they passed through the same editorial hands at some point.[89] But who would possess an interest in these prophetic books? The superscription of Hosea mentions four Judahite kings who reigned from about 792 BCE onwards, last among them King Hezekiah (ca. 715–686 BCE). Yet only one ruler of Samaria is named, King Jeroboam II (ca. 793–753 BCE).

This discrepancy in cataloguing Samarian and Judahite kings leaves a surprising gap of four decades between the death of Jeroboam II and the accession of Hezekiah. While any attempt to explain this gap will be speculative,[90] the passing reference in Proverbs to the "men of Hezekiah" as the group that compiled and preserved the wisdom sayings of Solomon (Prov 25:1) indicates that scribes in Hezekiah's royal court were involved in preserving older literary traditions.[91] Thus the mention of Hezekiah as the last Judahite king in all the other eighth-century prophetic superscriptions raises the intriguing possibility that his scribes were responsible for preserving prophetic traditions from both kingdoms while also adding the formulaic superscriptions that included their patron's name.

At the same time, it is notable that the diversity in literary expression and theological ideas among these books has remained intact, as in how Hosea uses his distinct brand of Hebrew to communicate his unusual word pictures. This observation suggests that Hezekiah's scribes were more inclined to preserve than to modify the literary traditions entrusted to them. It is therefore unlikely that Hosea's references to the kingdom of Judah, the Davidic monarchy, and the return of both kingdoms from exile were added by later redactors.[92] In any case, Judahites would have recognized the relevance of Hosea's prophecy without wholesale changes, since the prophet's references to an ambiguous "Israel," originally referring to the Northern Kingdom, could easily be reapplied to the other "Israel" in the Southern Kingdom.[93]

The Later Recontextualizations of Hosea's Prophecy

The final and most difficult issue in assessing provenance is Hosea's literary relationship to other OT books that also bear the linguistic and theological stamp

89. See the comprehensive study of eighth-century prophetic superscriptions by David Noel Freedman, "Headings in the Books of the Eighth-Century Prophets," *AUSS* 25 (1987): 9–26. See also the commentary below on Hos 1:1.

90. Ibid., 18, offers the suggestion that the superscription's break in the dual royal chronologies indicates that Hosea left Samaria during the reign of Jeroboam II.

91. William Schniedewind, *How the Bible Became a Book: The Textualization of Ancient Israel* (Cambridge: Cambridge University Press, 2004), 75–77.

92. Cf. Ronald E. Clements, "Understanding the Book of Hosea," *RevExp* 72 (1975): 405–23.

93. The increasing use of the designation "Israel" as a cipher for Judah in eighth-century prophecy is shown by H. G. M. Williamson, "Judah as Israel in Eighth-Century Prophecy," in *A God of Faithfulness: Essays in Honour of J. Gordon McConville on His 60th Birthday*, ed. Jamie A. Grant, Alison Lo, and Gordon J. Wenham, LHBOTS 538 (London: T&T Clark, 2011), 81–95, though he only demonstrates this phenomenon in Isaiah and Micah.

of Deuteronomy, an exceedingly large group that includes numerous books of the Former Prophets (i.e., Joshua–Kings) as well as several prophetic books, Hosea and Jeremiah prominently among them.[94] Any proposal for Hosea's origins therefore needs to explain the historical and literary links among these diverse books that exhibit this "Deuteronomistic"[95] imprint. The book of Hosea shares with Deuteronomy the terminology of covenant love and a strong polemic against icons while at the same time standing closer to Jeremiah and Ezekiel (e.g., Jer 3; Ezek 16; 23) in its use of the marriage and harlotry metaphors to characterize Israel's relationship to YHWH. The canonical form of these books suggests that Hosea provides the literary bridge between Deuteronomy on the one side and Jeremiah and Ezekiel on the other.

However, critical scholars typically hold that Hosea predates Deuteronomy. Since they date the earliest layer of Deuteronomy (*Urdeuteronomium*) to the reforms of King Josiah, a century after the ministry of Hosea, they argue that Hosea or the scribal circles associated with him planted the seeds of a Deuteronomistic movement of scribes during the eighth century. The seeds of this movement would have germinated during the Assyrian crises of the latter half of that century and eventually sprouted into the books of Deuteronomy in the seventh century as well as Jeremiah and Ezekiel in the sixth century. In such revisionist proposals, Hosea's distinctive use of the marriage metaphor would then be a precursor rather than a recontextualization of Deuteronomy's covenant theology.[96]

Whether or not such a Deuteronomistic movement or scribal school ever existed,[97] the weight of available evidence indicates that Hosea presents an eighth-century Samarian recontextualization of the covenant theology already found in Deuteronomy (as well as Exodus before it). Hosea's theology was then recontextualized for a Judahite audience in the books of Jeremiah and Ezekiel during the sixth century BCE. Reversing the literary relationship between Deuteronomy and Hosea, as redaction

94. Besides Hosea and Jeremiah, Amos is the other prophetic book in which scholars usually see a close relationship to Deuteronomy.

95. The term "Deuteronomistic" has been variously used in OT scholarship. According to Christophe Nihan ("'Deutéronomiste' et 'deutéronomisme': quelques remarques de méthode en lien avec le débat actuel," in *Congress Volume Helsinki 2010*, ed. Martti Nissinen, VTSup 148 [Leiden: Brill, 2012], 409), it may refer to (1) a linguistic style that resembles Deuteronomy; (2) a theology or ideology that resembles that of Deuteronomy; or (3) a group of scribes whose writings evince a Deuteronomic stamp.

96. Although details of their arguments vary, those who present arguments for the chronological priority of Hosea's presentation of covenant to that of Deuteronomy include John Day, "Pre-Deuteronomic Allusions to the Covenant in Hosea and Psalm LXXVIII," *VT* 36 (1986): 1–12; Ernest W. Nicholson, *God and His People: Covenant and Theology in the Old Testament* (Oxford: Clarendon, 1986), 187–88; Moshe Weinfeld, "Appendix B: Hosea and Deuteronomy," in *Deuteronomy and the Deuteronomic School* (Oxford: Clarendon, 1972), 366–70; and Lothar Perlitt, *Bundestheologie im alten Testament*, WMANT 36 (Neukirchen-Vluyn: Neukirchener Verlag, 1969), 129–55.

97. Little scholarly consensus exists on the question of whether Deuteronomistic scribes engaged in a systematic redaction of the OT Prophets, as well as whether such a movement even took place. See the differing opinions presented in the essays in Linda S. Schearing and Steven L. McKenzie, eds., *Those Elusive Deuteronomists: The Phenomenon of Pan-Deuteronomism*, JSOTSup 268 (Sheffield: Sheffield Academic, 1999).

critics have proposed, quickly encounters a series of mounting improbabilities: (1) Hosea or pre-Deuteronomistic scribes first introduced the theme of covenant as marriage during the eighth century; (2) Deuteronomistic scribes then downplayed or removed this theme in an early form of Deuteronomy during the seventh century; but (3) the theme of covenant as marriage was reintroduced on a broad scale in late prophets of the exilic and postexilic periods such as Jeremiah, Ezekiel, and Malachi. I will briefly comment on the escalating unlikelihood in each step of such proposals, all of which ultimately reinforces the plausibility of the traditional view.

To begin with, it is simply incorrect that Hosea invents the marriage metaphor to depict YHWH's love for Israel. Sacred marriage was one of the most common ways to depict an ancient Near Eastern deity's relationship to his or her people, as already noted. The fact that Hosea presumes knowledge of sacred marriage in his attack against ancient Near Eastern notions of sacred marriage shows that Israelites were well aware of alternative traditions. The antiquity and familiarity of covenant ideas in Israel is evident in YHWH's frequent offer of an intimate familial relationship: "I will be your God . . . and you will be my people."[98] This "covenant formula," which Hosea employs in both positive and negative forms (1:9; 2:25[23]), is an Israelite variation upon marriage and adoption formulas from surrounding cultures.[99] Since this formula is ubiquitous in all the tradition layers of the OT proposed by critical scholars, covenant ideas and terminology could not simply have been the invention of Hosea or his prophetic circles.[100] The uniqueness of Hosea's portrayal of covenant theology lies not in its use of marriage imagery but in the sign-act of the prophet's marriage to Gomer.

The notion that Deuteronomistic scribes downplayed the marriage imagery first introduced by Hosea strains credibility further. If Deuteronomistic scribes really were the theological heirs of Hosea's prophecy, it would have been inconceivable for them to omit all references to sacred marriage in Deuteronomy even as they compiled a book that so strongly emphasizes God's love for Israel (e.g., Deut 4:37) and the need for Israel to love God (e.g., Deut 6:5).

The absence of marriage references in Deuteronomy, in favor of references to sonship to describe God's care for Israel during the wilderness period (e.g., Deut 1:31;

98. Rolf Rendtorff, *The Covenant Formula: An Exegetical and Theological Investigation*, trans. Margaret Kohl, OTS (Edinburgh: T&T Clark, 1998), 107–11.

99. Seock-Tae Sohn, "'I Will Be Your God and You Will Be My People': The Origin and Background of the Covenant Formula," in *Ki Baruch Hu: Ancient Near Eastern, Biblical, and Judaic Studies in Honor of Baruch A. Levine*, ed. Robert Chazan, William W. Hallo, and Lawrence H. Schiffman (Winona Lake, IN: Eisenbrauns, 1999), 355–72.

100. Contra Perlitt (*Bundestheologie*, 129–55), who focuses on בְּרִית ("covenant") to the exclusion of the covenant formula. Rendtorff (*The Covenant Formula*, 68–69) rightly notes that Deut 29 uses the covenant formula in a way that draws together בְּרִית and the characteristic terminology of covenant in all the literary sources proposed in pentateuchal criticism.

8:5; 14:1), supports the traditional view that Hosea made explicit the Pentateuch's implicit idea of covenant as marriage since it had become distorted during the eighth century BCE, a time of heightened syncretism with Canaanite nature religion. It would have been rather strange for Hosea to play directly into the hands of syncretists by inventing a marriage metaphor instead of picking up a misunderstood idea and seeking to reclaim its original meaning. Carsten Vang has shown in this regard that the similarities and differences between how Deuteronomy and Hosea conceive of God's love point to the likelihood that Deuteronomy predates Hosea rather than the other way around.[101] And in a more recent and detailed article, Vang demonstrates that the nature of the phraseology unique to, but shared by, Hosea and Deuteronomy (e.g., Hos 13:4–6 // Deut 8:12–14; Hos 2:10[8] // Deut 8:13 / 17:16–17; Hos 4:13 // Deut 12:2) supports the view that the direction of literary influence runs from Deuteronomy to Hosea, rather than in the opposite direction as scholars usually propose.[102]

The third and final step in redactional proposals for Hosea's provenance is still more problematic in failing to explain the close literary links between Hosea and later prophets who also describe the divine-human covenant as marriage. Prophets such as Jeremiah, Ezekiel, and Malachi drew deeply from the well of Hosea's marriage imagery, but with modifications in keeping with the exilic and postexilic situations in which these prophets found themselves.[103] Yet if the critical view that Hosea inspired the Deuteronomistic scribes were correct, then the same Deuteronomistic school of scribes that muted Hosea's references to covenant as marriage suddenly reversed course and featured such imagery in the books of Jeremiah, Ezekiel, and Malachi. The literary trajectory from Hosea to later prophetic books becomes difficult to explain if between them stands a Deuteronomistic scribal movement that was rather conflicted in its view of covenant as marriage. The picture of such a movement that emerges is beset by contradictions on the all-important topic of conceiving YHWH's relationship to his people.

Rather than ascribing such conflicting tendencies to a Deuteronomistic scribal school, the traditional view that Deuteronomy preceded Hosea, whose prophecy was then reused by the exilic and postexilic prophets, still provides the best explanation. In short, the prophet Hosea was a native northerner who contextualized older

101. Carsten Vang, "God's Love According to Hosea and Deuteronomy: A Prophetic Reworking of a Deuteronomic Concept?," *TynBul* 62 (2011): 172–94.

102. Carsten Vang, "When a Prophet Quotes Moses: On the Relationship between the Book of Hosea and Deuteronomy," in *Sepher Torath Mosheh: Studies in the Composition and Interpretation of Deuteronomy*, ed. Daniel I. Block and Richard L. Schultz (Peabody, MA: Hendrickson, 2017), 277–304.

103. On the marriage metaphor in Jeremiah and Ezekiel, see Nelly Stienstra, *YHWH Is the Husband of His People: Analysis of a Biblical Metaphor with Special Reference to Translation* (Kampen: Kok Pharos, 1993), 127–77. On Malachi, see Gordon P. Hugenberger, *Marriage as a Covenant: A Study of Biblical Law and Ethics Governing Marriage, Developed from the Perspective of Malachi*, VTSup 52 (Leiden: Brill, 1994).

pentateuchal traditions of covenant theology for his preexilic audience in Samaria during the eighth century BCE. His prophecy was then edited and recontextualized by Judahite scribes after the fall of Samaria to provide a theological model for Judah's own version of the Assyrian crisis two decades later.

As the specter of Babylon rose over Judah in the late sixth century BCE, prophets such as Jeremiah and Ezekiel who ministered in the decades leading up to Judah's exile again recontextualized Hosea's prophecy for a new situation. The missiological category of contextualization thus highlights how the dynamic word of God spoken through Hosea assumed timeless dimensions by first speaking to and through a particular set of historical circumstances. Before outlining some guidelines for how Hosea's own hermeneutic of contextualization provides a model for recontextualizing Hosea today, it will be useful to take a closer look at Hosea's distinctive symbiosis of literature and theology. As with all books of Scripture, the literary medium of Hosea plays a crucial part in communicating its theological message.

The Literary Medium of Hosea's Message

The book of Hosea accomplishes its timeless purposes by joining literary imagination with its theological message in quite an exceptional way. Elsewhere in the OT Prophets, the closest parallel to Hosea's blend of narratives and oracles would be Jeremiah, a book that follows Hosea in juxtaposing first- and third-person prosaic accounts of the prophet's personal life with poetic oracles about YHWH's relationship to his people. Unique to Hosea, however, is how the marriage metaphor transcends figurative dimensions through the prophet literally embodying God's agonized love for his people. Details of Hosea's marriage to Gomer are sparse and thus should not be overly psychologized, but the emotionally charged character of Hosea's poetic oracles likely springs from the turmoil of bearing a message that draws upon his experience as a wounded messenger.

In this regard, the commentary sections will highlight the features of Hosea's tumultuous poetry that slow down the discourse and draw the emotional tension more tightly. While the entire commentary to follow will employ a discourse-analytical approach that assesses macrolevel clause relationships and microlevel discourse markers in their contexts,[104] here it is appropriate to highlight four discourse features that play a special role in conveying the anguish of God's conflict with his people. The first two of these, *shifting grammatical persons* and *broken chiasm*, each entail an

104. This commentary will employ discourse-analytical concepts from Steven Runge and Joshua Westbury's *The Lexham Discourse Hebrew Bible: Introduction* (Bellingham, WA: Logos Bible Software, 2012), hereafter *LDHB*; and Christo H. J. van der Merwe, Jackie A. Naudé, and Jan H. Kroeze's *A Biblical Hebrew Reference Grammar*, 2nd ed. (London: Bloomsbury T&T Clark, 2017), hereafter *BHRG*.

intentional disjunction within the expected logical flow of Hebrew poetry to depict the rupture of God's relationship with Israel. The third and fourth features of *pseudosorites* and *wordplay* usually depict the poignant transition from estrangement to reconciliation on God's part. Once the reader recognizes these discourse features, it will become clear that the legal categories of judgment and salvation are far too antiseptic to capture the deeply personal character of Hosea's prophecy.

The first feature of *shifting grammatical persons* destabilizes the discourse by shifting rapidly among first-, second-, and third-person forms of address. These transitions in discourse topic convey varying conceptions of relational proximity between parties, as when the relative detachment of third-person forms (i.e., "he/she/it/they") appears alongside the relational thrust of first- (i.e., "I/we") and second-person (i.e., "you") forms that speak directly to persons.[105] Hence, a shift from first- and second-person forms to third-person forms can often presage a chasm growing between God and his people. For instance, Hos 5 begins with a second-person summons for "you" to "Heed!" (5:1) that proceeds to a first-person condemnation of Israel's sins (5:2–3a). Following an accusation that "*you* have committed harlotry," (v. 3c), the covenantal intimacy represented by "I" and "you" language evaporates into a third-person mist: "*Israel* has become defiled. *Their* deeds do not allow them to return to *their* God. For a spirit of harlotries is in *their* midst, and *they* do not know YHWH!" (vv. 3d–4). The staccato use of third-person forms in these verses culminates in the declaration that the covenantal relationship has fractured: "With their flocks and their herds they will go to seek YHWH, but they will not find. He has withdrawn from them" (5:6).[106] It is no longer clear that YHWH is even the one speaking.

Shifting grammatical persons can also face off in a direct confrontation between parties when personal pronouns appear in opposing positions. In Hos 7:13, for example, first-person and third-person pronouns in close proximity provide a literal frame around the struggle between YHWH and Israel: "Now on my part [וְאָנֹכִי], I would redeem them; yet on their part [וְהֵמָּה], they have spoken lies against me!" (7:13e–f). These pronouns are *pleonastic*, that is, grammatically unnecessary due to the subsequent verbs that already inflect for grammatical person. They instead serve the pragmatic function of slowing down the discourse, emphasizing that YHWH's devotion is unrequited by Israel, and communicating the increasing distress on the part of YHWH, the speaker.

The second feature of *broken chiasm* undoes a common literary structure that tends to communicate order or completion. Whereas the mirrored structure (ABB′A′) of chiasm is one of the most common verse-patterns in Hebrew poetry, the book of Hosea often delays or splits the elements of the expected chiasm to heighten suspense for the hearer. To list one of many cases, in Hos 8:9–13 the expected pairing

105. Lénart J. de Regt, "A Genre Feature in Biblical Prophecy and the Translator: Person Shift in Hosea," in *The Elusive Prophet: The Prophet as a Historical Person, Literary Character, and Anonymous Artist*, ed. Johannes C. de Moor, *OtSt* 45 (Atlanta: SBL Press, 2001), 230–50.

106. Fisch, *Poetry with a Purpose*, 138–41.

of Assyria with Egypt (e.g., 7:11; 9:3) as symptoms of Israel's pagan malady is postponed by interrupting the chiasm. The larger unit of 8:9–13 is framed by ABB′A′ elements in 8:9 and 8:13, as shown below:

8:9 "they went up [A] to Assyria [B]"
8:13 "to Egypt [B′] they will return [A′]"

However, between these verses is a section detailing God's judgment against the cultic sins of Israel's kings and priests (8:10–12). Thus the first half of the chiasm hangs in the balance while drawing the audience into the rhetoric of the judgment speech, with the delayed arrival of the chiasm's conclusion sealing the fate of Israel in exile.[107] By briefly shifting the discourse away from what the audience expects and adding more sins to the equation, misdirection serves the ultimate purpose of intensifying the polemic against Israel's apostasy. At the same time, Hosea's use of such misdirection can be difficult to categorize in discourse-analytical terms since the logical relationships among adjacent clauses are less explicit, at least initially, than the usual prophetic pattern of pairing statements of indictment against Israel's sins with the Lord's verdict of judgment against them.[108]

The third device of *pseudosorites* similarly magnifies the disorderliness of Hosea's depiction of the world.[109] The pseudosorite represents the paradox of a succession of poetic lines that undermine one another as they unfold in sequence. In Hosea's use of pseudosorites, the unsettling result is the disintegration of YHWH and Israel's commitments to one another. Hosea 9:10–12 provides such an example of how disobedience increases Israel's estrangement from God: (1) Apostasy against God (9:10) will result in "no more childbirth, no more pregnancy, no more conception!" (9:11); (2) the conclusion of 9:11 is immediately challenged by the protasis, "Although they raise children" (9:12a), from which follows the apodosis, "I will bereave them from humanity" (9:12b).

The escalating illogic of these verses leads to another pseudosorite in Hos 9, this time a sarcastic prayer of the prophet: (1) "Give them, O YHWH—what will you give?" (9:14a–b); (2) "Give them a miscarrying womb and shriveling breasts!" (9:14c). Here the irony is that the gift is no gift at all! Michael O'Connor summarizes well the overall "argument" (if it can be called such) about infertility in Hos 9: "The prophet prays that the women of Ephraim be given wombs that miscarry, wombs that

107. Jack R. Lundbom, "Poetic Structure and Prophetic Rhetoric in Hosea," *VT* 29 (1979): 300–308.

108. In this vein, Patrick D. Miller, *Sin and Judgment in the Prophets: A Stylistic and Theological Analysis*, SBLMS 27 (Chico, CA: Scholars Press, 1982), 121–39, concludes that prophetic statements of acts and their consequences exhibit significant variety rather than conforming to a fixed literary pattern.

109. The high concentration of pseudosorites in Hosea is noted by many scholars, most recently Richard D. Patterson, "An Overlooked Scriptural Paradox: The Pseudosorites," *JETS* 53 (2010): 19–36.

do not come to term. But should the miscarrying wombs come to term anyway, he prays that YHWH give those women breasts incapable of providing nurture."[110] The chain of illogic represented by the pseudosorites in Hos 9 signifies YHWH's complete removal of fruitfulness from the people.

At the same time, the pseudosorites in Hosea can also serve as a literary enabler of restoration to God. The function of the pseudosorites in bridging estrangement and reconciliation is evident in Hos 2:8–12[6–10], a passage that contrasts the character of faithful YHWH and faithless Israel. In order to channel Israel's desires back to him, YHWH sets out to frustrate her sinful desires: (1) to hedge in Israel with thorns that block off her lovers (2:8[6]); (2) even if she pursues her lovers (which she cannot), she would never find them (2:9[7]); and (3) even if she were to find them (which she could not), they would not give what she desires (2:10[8]).[111] Once Israel's pursuit of her "lovers" results paradoxically in the disappearance of all the goods that they were thought to provide (2:11–13[9–11]), the stage is set for Israel to reject them and return to YHWH, the deity who outclasses all others (2:14–17[12–15]). Hence the peculiar flow of the pseudosorite embodies the theological message of Hos 2, that Israel's lovers and the Baals are impotent compared to YHWH, the real giver of creation's gifts.

The final feature of Hosea to consider is that of *wordplay*.[112] Before examining the use of wordplay in the book, it is important to distinguish between wordplay in narrative and poetic genres. In narrative, wordplay is typically confined to repetition of a verbal root and its derivatives to drive the plot forward and emphasize thematic continuity.[113] By contrast, a poetic book like Hosea uses wordplay to punctuate thematic discontinuity as well as continuity. Such a use of wordplay can work across either smaller or larger sections of a book. At the smaller end of the scale, chapter 1 introduces a wordplay on the name "Jezreel" ("God/El will sow"), Hosea's first son with Gomer. This son serves as a symbol for the imminent judgment against King Jehu's dynasty for the "bloodshed of Jezreel" (1:4). Moreover, the place in which YHWH will defeat Israel will be "the Valley of Jezreel" (1:5). Yet following the divine judgment of exile, Israel and Judah will become one again on "the day of Jezreel" (2:2[1:11]) when God's people appoint a new king for themselves and return to the land. Thus the name "Jezreel" traces the journey of Israel all the way from estrangement to reconciliation with God.

110. Michael P. O'Connor, "The Pseudosorites: A Type of Paradox in Hebrew Verse," in *Directions in Biblical Hebrew Poetry*, ed. Elaine R. Follis, JSOTSup 40 (Sheffield: JSOT Press, 1987), 168.

111. Michael P. O'Connor, "The Pseudosorites in Hebrew Verse," in *Perspectives on Language and Text: Essays and Poems in Honor of Francis I. Andersen's Sixtieth Birthday, July 28, 1985*, ed. Edgar W. Conrad and Edward G. Newing (Winona Lake, IN: Eisenbrauns, 1987), 243–44.

112. Gerald Morris, *Prophecy, Poetry and Hosea*, JSOTSup 219 (Sheffield: Sheffield Academic, 1996), 74–100, 148–51.

113. Robert Alter, *The Art of Biblical Narrative* (New York: Basic Books, 1981), 95.

At the larger end of the scale, the transformation of "Jezreel" begins in Hos 1 with the book's wordplay on the related Hebrew root זרע ("to sow") to depict both negative and positive dimensions of God's dealings with Israel. The use of this root spans the major divisions and themes of Hosea's prophecy: (1) Israel is commanded to "*sow* for yourselves according to righteousness" (10:12); Israel's failure to do so will bring punishment by means of poetic justice "when they *sow* wind, then they reap a whirlwind" (8:7); but Israel will be saved from exile by YHWH's promise that "I will *sow* her for myself in the land" (2:25[23]).

Studying Hosea's use of poetic wordplay is therefore useful for tracing the dynamic circumstances of the relationship between YHWH and Israel. The fact that this relationship undergoes the fickle vagaries common to all relationships, though with greater passion, means that the prophetic oracles of Hosea can sometimes unfold in a nonlinear way that defy our attempts to understand them. These features lend the book of Hosea its distinctive character as a collection of turbulent literary forms, amplified through a messenger's agonized life, in order to enact a searing theological message.

Literary Outlines of the Book of Hosea

These observations about Hosea's prophecy underscore the difficulty of outlining the book or employing discourse-analytical methods, both of which tend to presuppose more conventional modes of argumentation. Related to this is the question of whether Hosea's prophetic oracles can properly be considered poetry at all, or should instead be categorized as a heightened form of rhetoric. The book of Hosea lacks the more neatly balanced parallelism of other Hebrew poetry (e.g., Psalms, Isa 40–55), yet the cyclical and halting form of its argument, especially in chapters 4–14, also makes the category of persuasive rhetoric somewhat problematic as a characterization of the book. Compounding these challenges in analyzing the book is the fact that Hosea, unlike the book of Amos from the same period, exhibits relatively few of the discourse markers that signal an overarching logic or literary structure. Amos frequently uses the prophetic formula ("Thus says YHWH"; e.g., Amos 1:3, 6, 9, 11, 13), for example, but this forward-pointing device is completely lacking in Hosea. Hence the question of genre—what kind of literature is it?—looms large as a consideration for interpreting Hosea properly.

The way forward in classifying Hosea's oracles lies in broadening the usual understanding of poetry as mainly a catalogue of literary devices.[114] Biblical Hebrew poetry is certainly never less than this but is always more:

114. Compare, for example, the subtitle of Wilfred G. E. Watson, *Classical Hebrew Poetry: A Guide to Its Techniques*, JSOTSup 26 (Sheffield: JSOT Press, 1984).

> Poetry . . . is not just a set of techniques for saying impressively what could be said otherwise. Rather, it is a particular way of imagining the world—particular in the double sense that poetry as such has its own logic, its own ways of making connections and engendering implications, and because each system of poetry has certain distinctive semantic thrusts that follow the momentum of its formal dispositions and habits of expression.[115]

Thus it is essential to understand that poetry represents an imaginative way of doing theology and bringing God's reality to bear on new situations.[116]

Following the pioneering work of Gerald Morris,[117] this commentary categorizes Hosea as a book driven by a tripartite *lyrical plot*. The book of Hosea contains a threefold, though sometimes nonlinear, discourse that moves from a spurned God's indictment against his unfaithful people to God's sudden change of heart and finally the offer of a restored relationship with him. This theological movement from estrangement to reconciliation, with YHWH's agony as the fulcrum between them, both characterizes the broader flow of Hosea, from the charge of harlotry in chapter 1 to the invitation to repent in chapter 14, as well as being developed in microcosm through the two largest sections of the book: (1) Hosea's Family as Prophetic Sign-Act (1:2–3:5); and (2) YHWH's Contentions with Israel (4:1–14:1[13:16].

After Hosea introduces a list of significant topics at the beginning of each section, verbal repetitions and discourse features push forward the poetry of Hosea by fits and starts along this threefold path from estrangement to reconciliation. For example, Hos 2 opens with lists of God's gifts to Israel of food, water, wool, flax, oil, and drink (2:7[5]) as well as grain, new wine, olive oil, silver, and gold (2:10[8]). While this catalogue of gifts will be removed due to Israel's sinful pursuit of her "lovers," remarriage to YHWH will bring them back (2:23–25[21–23]). Key to this transformation is Hosea's creative use of לָכֵן ("therefore"), a discourse marker that earlier serves as the bridge between YHWH's indictment against Israel and his verdict (2:8[6]a, 11[9]a), but then turns into a conjunction (2:16[14]a) that links YHWH's usual indictment (2:11–15[9–13)]) with the surprise that he has resolved to draw Israel back to himself rather than away (2:16–25[14–23]). From a linguistic perspective, semantics and pragmatics work together marvelously to encode Hosea's message that reconciliation arrives at the moment when estrangement seemed most irreversible.

---

115. Robert Alter, *The Art of Biblical Poetry* (New York: Basic Books, 1985), 151.

116. Patrick D. Miller, "The Theological Significance of Biblical Poetry," in *Israelite Religion and Biblical Theology: Collected Essays*, LHBOTS 267 (Sheffield: Sheffield Academic, 2000), 233–49.

117. Morris, *Prophecy, Poetry and Hosea.*

Similar progressions of the lyrical plot of Hosea can be found, for example, in how later passages reuse the virtues from YHWH's betrothal formula (2:21[19]). The promise that YHWH will betroth Israel again "with righteousness and justice, with devotion and mercies" becomes the semantic reservoir in chapters 4–14 that feeds the accusation that Israel lacks these same virtues and needs to cultivate them (e.g., 4:1; 6:6; 10:12; 12:7[6]).[118] Since these lists and their repetitions span both smaller and larger sections of text, yet in a somewhat impressionistic manner as befitting the nature of lyric poetry, the commentary will attempt to strike a balance between tracing the discourse flow of Hosea's argument within individual passages and the broader movements of the book. The eclectic and sometimes elusive forms of Hosea's poetry nonetheless mean that the literary outline of Hosea proposed below is provisional rather than definitive.

Hosea's Contribution to Christian Theology

The striking combination of literary forms and theological message in the book of Hosea provides much fodder for engagement with contemporary Christian theology, most notably the doctrines of God and salvation. Recent years have witnessed scholarly debate over how to strike the proper balance between legal and covenantal ideas in describing a saving God's relationship to his sinful people.[119] The controversy has involved the question of whether God reveals himself to Israel primarily through familial roles as a father and husband, or rather in a juridical role as a judge, prosecutor, or plaintiff.

It is neither necessary nor wise to dichotomize strictly between familial and juridical roles in speaking of God and his salvation. In the final analysis, these human metaphors are more complementary than contradictory. But as indicated above, the book of Hosea gives theological priority to familial ideas of estrangement and reconciliation while occasionally using the legal imagery of the courtroom to depict God's relationship to his people.

Hosea's portrait of YHWH as one who agonizes between judging and saving his people, who undergoes deep anguish even as he must vindicate his justice, has led more than one commentator to speak suggestively of "the cross of Hosea."[120] The

118. Ibid., 112–13.

119. For example, NT scholars can roughly be divided into the "Traditional Perspective" and "New Perspective" on the apostle Paul's view of justification. To oversimplify somewhat a complex debate, the "Traditional Perspective" regards justification as primarily legal in nature, while the "New Perspective" argues for the priority of covenantal ideas (though both positions can sometimes misunderstand this continuum as a false dichotomy).

120. Paul S. Fiddes, "The Cross of Hosea Revisited: The Meaning of Suffering in the Book of Hosea," *RevExp* 90 (1993): 175–90; H. Wheeler Robinson, "The Cross of Hosea," in *Two Hebrew Prophets: Studies in Hosea and Ezekiel* (London: Lutterworth, 1948), 11–61.

notion of a "cross" in the book of Hosea is certainly anachronistic for conflating the prophet's portrait of YHWH with the person and work of Jesus Christ. Yet several elements in Hosea's characterization anticipate the crucified God of whom John Stott famously said, "I could never myself believe in God, if it were not for the cross. The only God I believe in is the One Nietzsche ridiculed as 'God on the cross.' In the real world of pain, how could one worship a God who was immune to it?"[121] Especially in chapter 11, Hosea offers a nearly unparalleled depiction of a God whose tender heart is pained by sin but still eager for reconciliation for his people.[122]

Exile is then not only an impartial legal necessity but also the bracing matter of a covenantal God's emotional involvement with his people. His familial bond with them (11:8) means that Israel can live again after exile, for in an echo of the Noah narrative, God promises three times that he will not destroy his people in the end (11:9). Although the deportation to Assyria still must and did take place in 722 BCE as a vindication of divine justice, God's promise of restoration "is pointing to a new world where destruction is a challenge, death an opportunity, and ends are beginnings and places of hope. . . . Israel's future is grounded in this new world. All unknowing, Hosea is glimpsing the Father not only of Israel but of the one who could say, 'I am the resurrection and the life.'"[123]

Hence the book of Hosea paints a striking picture of a God who would ultimately join perfect love and perfect justice together in the cross of Jesus Christ. Yet from the perspective of the prophet in the eighth century BCE, the wonderfully mysterious relationship of YHWH to Israel eludes categorical description in that Hosea's metaphors of aggrieved husband, impartial judge, passionate prosecutor or plaintiff, and loving father and mother could each describe only a portion of God's agonized heart for his people.

121. John R. W. Stott, *The Cross of Christ* (Downers Grove, IL: InterVarsity Press, 1986), 335.

122. Christian theology has long debated the question of whether God is "passible" (i.e., God is able to suffer) or "impassible" (i.e., God is unable to suffer). For theologians influenced by Hellenistic notions of God as the unmoved and unmovable Mover, it was thought that emotional involvement with the creation would compromise the absolute sovereignty of the Creator. Christian classical theism's modification of Hellenistic divine impassibility does not assert that God is "apathetic" (from Greek *apatheia*) in the sense of being incapable of loving feelings toward his people but rather that his actions are ultimately governed by reason. Yet as I will seek to show, this account of God's emotions as primarily anthropomorphic or anthropopathic remains inadequate to describe the real pain experienced by God in reconciling his justice with his love (on which see Kazoh Kitamori, *Theology of the Pain of God*, trans. M. E. Bratcher [Richmond, VA: John Knox, 1965], 19–25).

On the genuineness of God's emotional suffering as conceived within passibilist and impassibilist frameworks, respectively, see Richard J. Bauckham, "'Only the Suffering God Can Help': Divine Passibility in Modern Theology," *Them* 9 (1984): 6–12; and Thomas G. Weinandy, *Does God Suffer?* (Notre Dame: University of Notre Dame Press, 2000), 40–63.

123. H. D. Beeby, *Hosea: Grace Abounding*, ITC (Grand Rapids: Eerdmans, 1989), 149.

Outline of the Book of Hosea

Theme: God's Reconciliation with His Estranged Household

	Number of Clauses		
I. Superscription: YHWH's Word to Hosea (1:1)			
1:1	1		**A. The Judahite Context & B. The Samarian Context**
II. Hosea's Family as Prophetic Sign-Act (1:2–3:5)			
1:2	31	1. The Estrangement of YHWH's Household: Sign-Acts Implemented (1:2–9)	**A. YHWH's Household Estranged and Reconciled: Prophetic Sign-Acts, Part I (1:2–2:3[1])**
1:3			
1:4			
1:5			
1:6			
1:7			
1:8			
1:9			
2:1[1:10]	13	2. The Reconciliation of YHWH's Household: Sign-Acts Reversed (2:1–3[1:10–2:1])	
2:2[1:11]			
2:3[1]			
2:4[2]	16	1. YHWH's Quarrel with His Household (2:4–7[2–5])	**B. YHWH's Quarrel and Restoration with His Household (2:4–25[2–23])**
2:5[3]			
2:6[4]			
2:7[5]			
2:8[6]	15	2. YHWH's Determination to Frustrate Harlotry (2:8–10[6–8])	
2:9[7]			
2:10[8]			
2:11[9]	19	3. YHWH's Removal of Creational Blessings (2:11–15[9–13])	
2:12[10]			
2:13[11]			
2:14[12]			
2:15[13]			
2:16[14]	30	4. YHWH's Restoration with His Household (2:16–25[14–23])	
2:17[15]			
2:18[16]			
2:19[17]			
2:20[18]			

Continued on next page.

Verse	Count	Subsection	Section
2:21[19]	30 *cont.*	4. YHWH's Restoration with His Household (2:16–25[14–23]) *cont.*	**B. YHWH's Quarrel and Restoration with His Household (2:4–25[2–23]) *cont.***
2:22[20]			
2:23[21]			
2:24[22]			
2:25[23]			
3:1	6	1. YHWH's Command and Explanation: The Sign-Act of Irrational Love (3:1)	**C. Israel's Coming Exile and Restoration: Prophetic Sign-Acts, Part II (3:1–5)**
3:2	12	2. Hosea's Obedience and Explanation: The Sign-Act as Exile and Restoration (3:2–5)	
3:3			
3:4			
3:5			
III. YHWH's Contentions with Israel (4:1–14:1[13:16])			
4:1a–b	2	1. YHWH's Summons to Israel (4:1a–b)	**A. YHWH's Contention Against Israel's Priestly Failures (4:1–5:7)**
4:1c	7	2. YHWH's Initial Accusation of the People (4:1c–3)	
4:2			
4:3			
4:4	11	3. YHWH's Detailed Accusation of the People, Part I: Contention with God (4:4–6)	
4:5			
4:6			
4:7	43	4. YHWH's Detailed Accusation of the People, Part II: Harlotry with Canaanite Religion (4:7–19)	
4:8			
4:9			
4:10			
4:11			
4:12			
4:13			
4:14			
4:15			
4:16			
4:17			
4:18			
4:19			
5:1	23	5. YHWH's Detailed Accusation of the People, Part III: Corrupt Leadership (5:1–7)	
5:1			
5:2			
5:3			
5:4			
5:5			
5:6			
5:7			

Verse	Count	Section	Division
5:8	4	1. YHWH's Battle Summons to All Israel (5:8)	
5:9			
5:10			
5:11			
5:12	27	2. YHWH's Threat of Exile (5:9–15)	
5:13			
5:14			
5:15			
6:1			
6:2	13	3. Israel's Half-Hearted "Repentance" (6:1–3)	
6:3			
6:4	20		
6:5			
6:6			
6:7			
6:8		4. YHWH's Exasperated Response to Israel (6:4–11a)	
6:9			
6:10			**B. YHWH's Contention Against Israel's Political Failures (5:8–7:16)**
6:11a			
6:11b	58		
7:1			
7:2			
7:3			
7:4			
7:5			
7:6			
7:7			
7:8		5. YHWH's Offer of Restoration Rejected (6:11b–7:16)	
7:9			
7:10			
7:11			
7:12			
7:13			
7:14			
7:15			
7:16			

Continued on next page.

Verse		Section	
8:1			
8:2	8	1. The Divine Judge's Indictment and Verdict (8:1–3)	
8:3			
8:4			
8:5			
8:6	19	2. The Sin-Cluster of King and Cult (8:4–8a)	
8:7			
8:8a			
8:8bc			
8:9			
8:10			
8:11	23	3. The Sin-Cluster of Politics and Religion (8:8b–14)	**C. An Announcement of Exile (8:1–9:9)**
8:12			
8:13			
8:14			
9:1			
9:2			
9:3			
9:4			
9:5	32	4. The End of Israel's Life (9:1–9)	
9:6			
9:7			
9:8			
9:9			
9:10			
9:11			
9:12			
9:13	30	1. Creation and History, Part 1: From Wilderness Fruits to Exiled Nomads (9:10–17)	
9:14			
9:15			
9:16			
9:17			**D. Israel's Apostasy from YHWH: General Verdicts from Creation and History (9:10–11:11)**
10:1			
10:2			
10:3			
10:4	29	2. Creation and History, Part 2: From Fruitful Vine to Thorns and Thistles (10:1–8)	
10:5			
10:6			
10:7			
10:8			

10:9			
10:10			
10:11			
10:12	27	3. Creation and History, Part 3: Miscellaneous Images (10:9–15)	
10:13			
10:14			
10:15			
11:1			
11:2			**D. Israel's Apostasy from YHWH: General Verdicts from Creation and History (9:10–11:11)** ***cont.***
11:3			
11:4			
11:5			
11:6	42	4. The Cycles and Metaphors of Salvation History (11:1–11)	
11:7			
11:8			
11:9			
11:10			
11:11			
12:1[11:12]	8	1. A Summary Accusation of Ephraim and Judah (12:1[11:12]–12:2[1])	
12:2[1]			
12:3[2]			
12:4[3]			
12:5[4]			
12:6[5]	20	2. Judah and Israel as a New "Jacob" (12:3–9[2–8])	
12:7[6]			
12:8[7]			
12:9[8]			
12:10[9]			**E. Israel's Disobedience toward YHWH: Specific Verdicts from History and Creation (12:1[11:12]–14:1[13:16])**
12:11[10]			
12:12[11]	14	3. YHWH's Self-Reintroduction as God of the Exodus (12:10–14[9–13])	
12:13[12]			
12:14[13]			
12:15[14]	3	4. Hosea's Lament for Ephraim (12:15[14])	
13:1			
13:2	9	5. A Reflection on Exodus and Wilderness History (13:1–3)	
13:3			

Continued on next page.

13:4	14	6. YHWH's Vindication in Salvation History (13:4–8)	**E. Israel's Disobedience toward YHWH: Specific Verdicts from History and Creation (12:1[11:12]–14:1[13:16])** ***cont.***
13:5			
13:6			
13:7			
13:8			
13:9	9	7. YHWH's Taunt Against Israel (13:9–11)	
13:10			
13:11			
13:12	21	8. Israel's Unavoidable Demise (13:12–14:1[13:16])	
13:13			
13:14			
13:15			
14:1[13:16]			
IV. An Epilogue on Repentance and Restoration (14:2–10[1–9])			
14:2[1]	2	1. The Corporate Need for Repentance: Israel's Iniquity (14:2[1])	**A. Hosea's Summons to Repentance (14:2–4[1–3])**
14:3[2]	11	2. The Individual Means of Repentance: Israel's Vows (14:3–4[2–3])	
14:4[3]			
14:5[4]	3	1. YHWH's Abundant Love (14:5[4])	**B. The Restorative Love of YHWH (14:5–9[4–8])**
14:6[5]	9	2. YHWH's Restoration of Creation (14:6–8[5–7])	
14:7[6]			
14:8[7]			
14:9[8]	5	3. YHWH's Superiority to Other Deities (14:9[8])	
14:10[9]	4	1. A Summons to the Wise (14:10[9]a–d)	**C. The Audience's Urgent Need for Wisdom (14:10[9])**
	3	2. The Knowledge Needed by the Wise (14:10[9]e–g)	

CHAPTER 1

Hosea 1:1

Main Idea of the Passage

The book of Hosea opens by identifying itself as a divine word-event that literally "happened" (הָיָה; 1:1b) to the prophet in space and time. The life and oracles of Hosea are YHWH's urgent message to two audiences in the eighth century BCE—the Southern Kingdom of Judah (1:1c) and the Northern Kingdom of Samaria (1:1d).

Literary Context

The superscription to Hosea's prophecy as the "word of YHWH" (1:1a) is highly significant. In a cultural milieu where the formula "word of *X*" authenticated a messenger as a representative sent from a higher authority (e.g., "word of *the great king, the king of Assyria*"; 2 Kgs 18:28), the "word of YHWH" through Hosea spoke loudly into the cacophonic world around Israel during the eighth century BCE.[1] Multiple parties within Israel vied for the people's allegiance to their own perversions of Yahwistic faith (e.g., Hos 6:1–3), while the invention of Assyrian propaganda as the megaphone of imperial domination sounded a terrifying note throughout the ancient Near East.[2] Into this chaotic setting comes the authoritative "word of YHWH" using a standard formula that would be easily recognized by its audience, yet whose distinctive message would be countercultural for summoning Israel to repent of its compromise with pagan worldviews. Thus the phrase, "word of YHWH," anticipates how the book takes direct aim at Israel's mistaken beliefs and sinful institutions. This rhetorical goal of confrontation leads inevitably to the clashes found in the book between YHWH and his prophet on one side, and the people of YHWH on the other.

1. Samuel A. Meier, *Speaking of Speaking: Marking Direct Discourse in the Hebrew Bible*, VTSup 46 (Leiden: Brill, 1992), 315–19, notes that the phrase "word of *X*" comes to prominence especially in the Neo-Assyrian period.

2. A modern analogue to ancient Assyria's unique combination of brutality and propaganda would be Adolf Hitler's Third Reich (1933–1945).

Translation and Exegetical Outline

(See next page.)

Structure and Literary Form

The superscription to Hosea consists of two parts: the identification of the divine word-event that happened to Hosea (1:1b), followed by a listing of the Judahite kings (1:1c) and Samarian kings (1:1d) who frame the dual historical backgrounds to Hosea's prophecy. Here the use of the "word-event formula" (1:1a) in Hosea differs in two notable ways from other prophetic books of the OT. The first difference is that the "word of YHWH" in Hosea opens not with a poetic oracle spoken by God (e.g., Joel 1:1) nor a visionary experience of the prophet (e.g., Jer 1:4) as found in other books but to a sign-act narrative that depicts Hosea's marriage to an unfaithful wife and the birth of their three children (ch. 1). Following an impassioned discourse by YHWH (ch. 2), the story of Hosea's life resumes (ch. 3), this time with a narrative of Hosea's reconciliation with his wife, in obedience to the Lord's command. The book of Hosea is therefore unique for beginning with the prophet's story of estrangement and reconciliation. By providing literary bookends around YHWH's direct speech, Hosea's experiences are living proof of YHWH's covenantal commitment to his people and the rest of his creation.

The second difference is that Hosea's superscription does not use the word-event formula as a marker for a new oracle, as is common in later prophetic books such as Ezekiel.[3] In contrast, the word-event formula occurs only in Hos 1:1 as an introduction to the entire book. This fact, coupled with the scarcity of chronological and historical references to the contemporary scene beyond the superscription, lends the rest of Hosea's prophecy a timeless quality that transcends chronology and geography. It is thus no exaggeration to say that Hosea portrays YHWH's dealings with the tiny kingdoms of Samaria and Judah as the fulcrum of creation and history. This depiction of YHWH's sovereignty as universal and cosmic in scope challenges both

3. James Robson, *Word and Spirit in Ezekiel*, LHBOTS 447 (New York: Bloomsbury, 2006), 28.

Hosea 1:1

	Hebrew	Translation	Outline
1:1	דְּבַר־יְהוָה	The word of YHWH	**I. Superscription: YHWH's Word to Hosea (1:1)**
	אֲשֶׁר הָיָה אֶל־הוֹשֵׁעַ בֶּן־בְּאֵרִי	that happened to Hosea son of Beeri	
	בִּימֵי עֻזִּיָּה יוֹתָם אָחָז יְחִזְקִיָּה מַלְכֵי יְהוּדָה	in the days of Uzziah, Jotham, Ahaz, and Hezekiah, kings of Judah,	A. The Judahite Context
	וּבִימֵי יָרָבְעָם בֶּן־יוֹאָשׁ מֶלֶךְ יִשְׂרָאֵל׃	and in the days of Jeroboam son of Joash, king of Israel.[1]	B. The Samarian Context

1. For the sake of differentiating voices in the book of Hosea, this commentary formats direct speech in the prophetic oracles with a white background, except when dark grey shading identifies embedded speech (as when YHWH or the prophet cites the words of the people) or formulaic elements within the prophetic oracles (as in the signatory formula, "The Declaration of YHWH"). By contrast, light grey shading denotes indirect speech or a direct-speech response from Hosea or the people to YHWH's word.

Israel's misconceptions about YHWH as well as the regnant worldview of imperialism in the rest of the ancient Near East.

The superscription also emphasizes the wider relevance of Hosea's message beyond the Northern Kingdom of Samaria by containing, rather surprisingly, a more comprehensive listing of Judahite kings (1:1c) than their Samarian counterparts (1:1e). As the introduction to the commentary already notes, Jeroboam II (ca. 793–753 BCE) is the sole Samarian king named in Hosea's superscription, even as Hosea's repeated predictions of the exile of Samaria (which happened in 722 BCE) and the references to Judah's kings who reign later than Jeroboam II (1:1c) show that his prophetic activity clearly extended to the last days of the Northern Kingdom. It is uncertain whether the superscription's gap in Samarian chronology means that the prophet Hosea migrated southward during the time of Jeroboam II (David Noel Freedman's view), or whether he and/or his prophetic oracles traveled to Judah only after Samaria's fall in 722 BCE (the majority view among scholars).[4]

In either case, the prominence of Judah's kings in the superscription to Hosea points to the contemporization of Hosea's prophecy during the reign of Hezekiah, precisely at the time when the kingdom of Judah faced its own troubles with the Assyrian Empire (Isa 36–39; 2 Kgs 18–20). The original Samarian context remains primary for interpretation of the divine word-event that happened to Hosea there. Nevertheless, his prophecy also speaks to a Judahite context owing to its reception and recontextualization later in the eighth century BCE.

Canonical and Theological Significance

The prophet Hosea did not stand alone in proclaiming the "word of YHWH" during the various crises of the latter part of the eighth century BCE. The prophetic books of Isaiah, Amos, and Micah also link closely to Hosea by virtue of beginning in similar ways. Despite the differences already noted between Hosea and other prophetic books, the superscriptions of Hosea, Isaiah, Amos, and Micah share the purpose of speaking God's word to the Northern and Southern Kingdoms of Israel during the eighth century BCE. A comparison of the four superscriptions reveals significant overlaps in form and content:[5]

The similarities among these headings suggest that Judahite scribes compiled Hosea, Isaiah, Amos, and Micah together to offer a unified theological commentary on the tumultuous decades of the Assyrian threat(s) from approximately 750 BCE to 690 BCE. Freedman usefully summarizes the common message of these four books:

4. ee discussion of "The Judahite Reception of Hosea's Prophecy" in the introduction to Hosea for comparison and critique of these views.

5. Freedman, "Headings in the Books of the Eighth-Century Prophets," 9–26.

	Hosea 1:1	Isaiah 1:1	Amos 1:1	Micah 1:1
Heading Proper	The word of YHWH that happened to Hosea, son of Beeri . . .	The vision that Isaiah son of Amoz saw concerning Judah and Jerusalem . . .	The words of Amos, who was among the shepherds of Tekoa, that he saw concerning Israel . . .	The word of YHWH that happened to Micah the Moreshite . . . that he saw concerning Samaria and Jerusalem . . .
Chronological Indicators	. . . in the days of Uzziah, Jotham, Ahaz, and Hezekiah, kings of Judah.	. . . in the days of Uzziah, Jotham, Ahaz, and Hezekiah, kings of Judah, and in the days of Jeroboam, son of Joash, king of Israel.	. . . in the days of Uzziah king of Judah, and in the days of Jeroboam son of Joash, king of Israel.	. . . in the days of Jotham, Ahaz, and Hezekiah kings of Judah

> YHWH is the devoted Lord of his people in both kingdoms. Both are under heavy judgment for deliberate defiance of the deity and persistent violation of the central demands and commands of the Covenant. The only possibility of escape from violent final punishment is genuine repentance on the part of all, king and nobles, priests and prophets, and the people as a whole.[6]

In light of these commonalities of purpose and message, this commentary will engage in a running dialogue with Isaiah, Amos, and Micah when appropriate so as to situate Hosea on a broader canonical canvas.[7]

The beginning of Hosea also encompasses the broader literary horizon of the OT Minor Prophets (Hosea–Malachi). Since ancient times, readers and interpreters of Scripture have recognized Hosea as the head of a collective group known as the "Twelve Prophets."[8] Although the order of the individual books within the Twelve varies somewhat in the extant lists,[9] it is notable that Hosea's prophecy is nearly always first even though his ministry begins historically later than that of Amos. A chronological scheme is therefore inadequate on its own to explain the prominence of Hosea in the Twelve. Instead, it appears that the book of Hosea, and chapters 1–3 in particular, have been placed at the head of the collection to outline the themes that characterize the Twelve as a whole.[10] Even as the books that follow

6. Ibid., 23.

7. Thus this commentary will extend the argument of Jörg Jeremias ("The Interrelationship between Amos and Hosea," in *Forming Prophetic Literature: Essays on Isaiah and the Twelve in Honor of John D. W. Watts*, ed. James W. Watts and Paul R. House, JSOTSup 235 [Sheffield: Sheffield Academic, 1996], 171–86), who demonstrated the necessity of reading Hosea and Amos together.

8. E.g., Sir 49:10.

9. Besides the MT, the two other significant lists are found in LXX and 4QXII[a]. See discussion of the textual witnesses by Marvin A. Sweeney, "Sequence and Interpretation in the Book of the Twelve," in *Form and Intertextuality in Prophetic and Apocalyptic Literature*, FAT 45 (Tübingen: Mohr Siebeck, 2005), 175–88.

10. Craig Bowman, "Reading the Twelve as One: Hosea 1–3 as an Introduction to the Book of the Twelve," *Stone-Campbell Journal* 9 (2006): 41–59; John D. W. Watts, "A Frame for the

Hosea maintain their individuality, the literary collection as a whole develops the themes introduced in Hosea so that the Book of the Twelve stands together as a coherent theological unity.[11]

Book of the Twelve: Hosea 1–3 and Malachi," in *Reading and Hearing the Book of the Twelve*, ed. James Nogalski and Marvin A. Sweeney, SBLSymS 15 (Atlanta: SBL Press, 2000), 209–17.

11. Jason T. LeCureux, *The Thematic Unity of the Book of the Twelve*, Hebrew Bible Monographs 41 (Sheffield: Sheffield Phoenix, 2012).

CHAPTER 2

Hosea 1:2–2:3[1]

A. YHWH's Household Estranged and Reconciled: Prophetic Sign-Acts, Part I

Main Idea of the Passage

In his life Hosea embodies YHWH's agony in the face of betrayal by Israel. Although the sign-acts of Hosea's family symbolize the rupture between YHWH and his people at first, YHWH also promises to transform the names of Hosea's children—Jezreel ("God-Will-Sow"), Lo-Ruhamah ("Not-Shown-Mercy"), and Lo-Ammi ("Not-My-People")—into the negation of negation itself.

Literary Context

Hosea 1:2–2:3[1] is the first of three literary sections (i.e., 1:2–2:3[1]; 2:4–25[2–23]; 3:1–5) that roughly correspond to the chapter divisions in English Bibles, though chapter 2 in the Hebrew Bible begins two verses earlier for reasons that will be discussed in the commentary below. Following the superscription (1:1) discussed above, the first prophetic word to Hosea (1:2–2:3[1]) is a narrative of the sign-acts of his marriage and three children.

The passing reference to the creational dimensions of Israel's sin (1:2) is developed further in the second prophetic word to Hosea (2:4–25[2–23]). This is a quarrel speech in which YHWH accuses Israel of apostasy and vows to thwart the syncretism of his people. Following the removal of creation's blessings through the discipline of exile, YHWH will surprise his people by reconciling them to himself and restoring creation's blessings as their real giver.

The third prophetic word to Hosea is another, briefer sign-act (3:1–5) of his reconciliation with his estranged wife. The troubled couple's journey from estrangement toward reconciliation, yet unfinished in the time of Hosea, mirrors the first section's theme of Davidic kingship between exile and restoration. In chapter 1 YHWH threatens to punish the injustice of Israel's kings "in the Valley of Jezreel" (1:5) as well as promising to restore Israel's leadership on "the day of Jezreel" (2:2[1:11]). Hence 1:2–2:3[1] introduces several motifs that echo in Hosea as well as the rest of the Twelve: the marriage covenant between YHWH and Israel, the solidarity of creation and people in YHWH's household, and the role of human leaders in YHWH's redemptive purposes.

Translation and Exegetical Outline

(See pages 75–77.)

Structure and Literary Form

Beyond serving as YHWH's messenger, the prophet Hosea himself becomes the medium for the message in this narrative passage's sign-acts concerning "a wife of harlotry and children of harlotry" (1:2d). The sign-act is a symbolic action in which YHWH's prophet becomes or embodies his message to an intransigent people who have become numb to conventional methods of communication.[1] In this passage, the first and foremost sign-act is Hosea's marriage with Gomer (1:2–3b), a union that leads to three sign-acts of their children's birth and naming: Jezreel ("God-Will-Sow"; 1:3c–4b), Lo-Ruhamah ("Not-Shown-Mercy"; 1:6a–d), and Lo-Ammi ("Not-My-People"; 1:8–9b). The performance of each sign-act in accordance with YHWH's commands leads to an explanation of its significance (1:4c–5, 6e–7, 9c–d).

1. The most important work on prophetic sign-acts is Kelvin G. Friebel, *Jeremiah's and Ezekiel's Sign-Acts: Rhetorical Nonverbal Communication*, JSOTSup 283 (Sheffield: Sheffield Academic, 1999), though he unfortunately does not treat Hosea in detail. Since Hosea speaks *to* his wife as part of the sign-act (3:3) and not merely in explaining the sign-act to an audience, the book bearing his name falls outside Friebel's focus on *non-verbal* communication accompanied by dramatized actions, the form that dominates in the books of Jeremiah and Ezekiel.

Hosea 1:2–2:3[1]

			II. Hosea's Family as Prophetic Sign-Act (1:2–3:5)
			A. YHWH's Household Estranged and Reconciled: Prophetic Sign-Acts, Part I (1:2–2:3[1])
			1. The Estrangement of YHWH's Household: Sign-Acts Implemented (1:2–9)
			a. The Sign-Act of Marrying Gomer (1:2–3b)
1:2a	תְּחִלַּת דִּבֶּר־יְהוָה בְּהוֹשֵׁעַ	When YHWH first spoke through Hosea,	(1) YHWH's Command (1:2a–d)
2b	וַיֹּאמֶר יְהוָה אֶל־הוֹשֵׁעַ	YHWH said to Hosea,	
2c	לֵךְ	"Go,	
2d	קַח־לְךָ אֵשֶׁת זְנוּנִים וְיַלְדֵי זְנוּנִים	take for yourself a wife of harlotry and children of harlotry,	
2e	כִּי־זָנֹה תִזְנֶה הָאָרֶץ מֵאַחֲרֵי יְהוָה׃	for the land commits heinous harlotry	(2) YHWH's Reason (1:2e–f)
		in walking away from YHWH."	
3a	וַיֵּלֶךְ	So Hosea went	(3) Hosea's Obedience (1:3a–b)
3b	וַיִּקַּח אֶת־גֹּמֶר בַּת־דִּבְלָיִם	and took Gomer, daughter of Diblaim, as his wife.	
3c	וַתַּהַר	Then she conceived	b. The Sign-Act of "God-Will-Sow":
3d	וַתֵּלֶד־לוֹ בֵּן׃	and bore him a son.	Dissipation of Land (1:3c–5)
4a	וַיֹּאמֶר יְהוָה אֵלָיו	YHWH said to him,	(1) The Naming of Jezreel (1:4a–b)
4b	קְרָא שְׁמוֹ יִזְרְעֶאל	"Name him Jezreel,	
4c	כִּי־עוֹד מְעַט וּפָקַדְתִּי אֶת־דְּמֵי יִזְרְעֶאל	for soon I will repay the bloodshed of Jezreel	(2) The Significance of "Jezreel" (1:4c)
	עַל־בֵּית יֵהוּא	upon the household of Jehu,	(a) The End of Samaria's Kings (1:4d)
4d	וְהִשְׁבַּתִּי מַמְלְכוּת בֵּית יִשְׂרָאֵל׃	and I will put an end to the kingdom of the household of Israel.	
5	וְהָיָה בַּיּוֹם הַהוּא	And on that day,	(b) The Destruction of Samaria (1:5)
	וְשָׁבַרְתִּי אֶת־קֶשֶׁת יִשְׂרָאֵל בְּעֵמֶק יִזְרְעֶאל׃	I will break the bow of Israel in the Valley of Jezreel."	

Continued on next page.

Continued from previous page.

6a	וַתַּהַר עוֹד	Then Gomer conceived again	c. The Sign-Act of "Not-Shown-Mercy":
6b	וַתֵּלֶד בַּת	and bore a daughter.	Dissipation of Divine Presence (1:6–7)
6c	וַיֹּאמֶר לוֹ	He (YHWH) told him (Hosea),	(1) The Naming of Not-Shown-Mercy
6d	קְרָא שְׁמָהּ לֹא רֻחָמָה	"Name her 'Not-Shown-Mercy,'	(1:6a–d)
6e	כִּי לֹא אוֹסִיף עוֹד	for I will not continue anymore—	(2) The Significance of "Not-Shown-Mercy"
			(1:6e–7)
6f	אֲרַחֵם אֶת־בֵּית יִשְׂרָאֵל	[that] I would show mercy to the household of Israel,	(a) Israel as "Not-Shown-Mercy"
6g	כִּי־נָשֹׂא אֶשָּׂא לָהֶם׃	that/lest I would keep forgiving them.[1]	(1:6e–g)
7a	וְאֶת־בֵּית יְהוּדָה אֲרַחֵם	Yet to the household of Judah I will show mercy,	(b) Judah as "Shown-Mercy" (1:7)
7b	וְהוֹשַׁעְתִּים בַּיהוָה אֱלֹהֵיהֶם	I will deliver them by YHWH their God,	
7c	וְלֹא אוֹשִׁיעֵם בְּקֶשֶׁת וּבְחֶרֶב וּבְמִלְחָמָה	but I will not deliver them by bow, sword, and battle,	
	בְּסוּסִים וּבְפָרָשִׁים׃	nor by horses and horsemen."	
8a	וַתִּגְמֹל אֶת־לֹא רֻחָמָה	Then Gomer weaned Not-Shown-Mercy,	d. The Sign-Act of "Not-My-People":
8b	וַתַּהַר	and she conceived,	Dissipation of Identity (1:8–9)
8c	וַתֵּלֶד בֵּן׃	and she bore a son.	(1) The Sign-Act and Naming of
9a	וַיֹּאמֶר	Then he (YHWH) said,	Not-My-People (1:8–9b)
9b	קְרָא שְׁמוֹ לֹא עַמִּי	"Name him 'Not-My-People,'	
9c	כִּי אַתֶּם לֹא עַמִּי	for you are 'Not-My-People,'	(2) The Significance of "Not-My-People"
9d	וְאָנֹכִי לֹא־אֶהְיֶה לָכֶם׃	and I am not your 'I AM.'"[2]	(1:9c–d)
			2. The Reconciliation of YHWH's Household:
			Sign-Acts Reversed (2:1–3[1:10–2:1])
2:1[1:10]a	וְהָיָה מִסְפַּר בְּנֵי־יִשְׂרָאֵל כְּחוֹל הַיָּם	"But the number of the children of Israel will be	a. The Revival of the Progeny Blessing
		like the sand of the sea,	(2:1[1:10]a–c)
2:1[1:10]b	אֲשֶׁר לֹא־יִמַּד	which can be neither measured	
2:1[1:10]c	וְלֹא יִסָּפֵר	nor numbered.	
2:1[1:10]d	וְהָיָה בִּמְקוֹם אֲשֶׁר־יֵאָמֵר לָהֶם	And in the place where it was said to them,	b. The Reversal of "Not-My-People"
2:1[1:10]e	אַתֶּם לֹא־עַמִּי	'You are not my people,'	(2:1[1:10]d–g)
2:1[1:10]f	יֵאָמֵר לָהֶם	it will be said to them,	
2:1[1:10]g	בְּנֵי אֵל־חָי׃	'O children of the living God.'	

2:2[1:11]a	וְנִקְבְּצוּ בְּנֵי־יְהוּדָה וּבְנֵי־יִשְׂרָאֵל יַחְדָּו	Then the children of Judah and the children of Israel will be gathered together,	c. The Reunion of Samaria and Judah (2:2[1:11]a)
2:2[1:11]b	וְשָׂמוּ לָהֶם רֹאשׁ אֶחָד	and they will appoint for themselves one leader,	(1) The Reinstatement of Leadership (2:2[1:11]b)
2:2[1:11]c	וְעָלוּ מִן־הָאָרֶץ	and they will go up from the land.	(2) The Return from Exile (2:2[1:11]c)
2:2[1:11]d	כִּי גָדוֹל יוֹם יִזְרְעֶאל׃	Indeed, great will be the Day of Jezreel.	d. The Negation of Negation: From Estrangement to Reconciliation (2:2[1:11]d–2:3[1])
2:3[1]a	אִמְרוּ לַאֲחֵיכֶם	Speak to your brothers,	
	עַמִּי	'O My-People!,'	
2:3[1]b	וְלַאֲחוֹתֵיכֶם	and [speak] to your sisters,	
	רֻחָמָה׃	'O Shown-Mercy!'"	

1. The sense of כִּי־נָשֹׂא אֶשָּׂא לָהֶם (Hos 1:6g) is less than clear, as the diversity among the ancient witnesses and modern versions attests (for example, *BHS* proposes an emendation with the root שׂנא ["to hate"], but the *BHQ* commentary on the critical apparatus rightly rejects this as lacking textual basis). Rather than viewing the initial כִּי as a causal conjunction ("for"; e.g., NRSV, NIV), it seems better to regard it as an emphatic adverb ("indeed"; *IBHS* §39.3.1d) or a complementizer that introduces a hypothetical or impossible condition ("lest/that"). See the detailed case for the latter by R. Abma, *Bonds of Love: Methodic Studies of Prophetic Texts with Marriage Imagery (Isaiah 51–3 and 51–10, Hosea 1–3, Jeremiah 2–3)*, SSN 40 (Assen: Van Gorcum, 1999), 126–27.

2. This rendering of 9d reflects the MT reading (וְאָנֹכִי לֹא־אֶהְיֶה לָכֶם) rather than the proposed emendation in the *BHS* apparatus (וְאָנֹכִי לֹא־אֱלֹהֵיכֶם) that underlies numerous English translations: "I will not be your God" (e.g., NIV, NRSV). The *BHQ* commentary on the critical apparatus, in reversing course from *BHS*, notes the greater difficulty and likely originality of the MT reading.

Whereas Gomer's unfaithfulness is a metaphor for how "the land commits heinous harlotry in walking away from YHWH" (1:2e), the meaning of their children's names symbolize the outcomes of this apostasy, specifically the dissipation of land (Jezreel), divine presence (Lo-Ruhamah), and identity (Lo-Ammi).[2] Hosea 1 contains the typical form of sign-act narratives in which the prophet's symbolic action leads to an explanation of what the action means for the audience.

Following this verdict of estrangement, the passage continues with a new series of wordplays about YHWH's reconciliation with his people (2:1:–3[1:10–2:1]). The opening narrative of Hosea therefore uses a series of symbols to root its theological message in the concrete realities of everyday life more than communicating with abstract propositions, as preferred by many modern readers of the Bible.[3] This observation about the structure and literary form of Hos 1:2–2:3[1] provides the basis for the "Explanation of the Text" that follows.

Explanation of the Text

1. The Estrangement of YHWH's Household: Sign-Acts Implemented (1:2–9)

The sign-act narrative opens with the phrase, "When YHWH first spoke *through* Hosea" (1:2a). It is notable that the entire book is summarized as YHWH speaking "to" (אֶל) Hosea (1:1a), but YHWH's first speech comes not "to" (אֶל; cf. Jer 11:1; Mic 1:1; Zeph 1:1) but "through/by means of" (בְּ) the prophet (1:2a). Elsewhere in the OT, the grammatical construction "speak through" (דִּבֶּר בְּ) refers to YHWH's public speech that he has entrusted to a prophet (e.g., Num 12:2, 6, 8; 1 Kgs 22:28).

Nevertheless, what follows in Hos 1 is a private conversation in which YHWH simply commands the prophet to marry a woman of harlotry and have children of harlotry with her (1:2b–9). In this respect Hos 1:2a serves as a superscription for the entirety of the first chapter's sign-act narrative that communicates *through* the life of the prophet. The narrative does not record the audience's reaction to the sign-acts, but their curiosity would undoubtedly have been piqued at the rather strange circumstances of Hosea.[4] Beginning with him, the OT prophets often embody the persuasive goal of reaching YHWH's people in times when their faith had become too jaded to accept more traditional methods of communication.

a. The Sign-Act of Marrying Gomer (1:2–3b)

The first sign-act begins (1:2a) when YHWH speaks to Hosea (1:2b): "Go, take for yourself a wife of harlotry and children of harlotry" (1:2c–d). Although the instruction for Hosea to "take for yourself" (קַח־לְךָ) a wife is the standard idiom for

2. David M. Morgan, "Land and Temple as Structural and Thematic Marks of Coherence for the Hebrew Edition of the Book of the Twelve," *BN* 145 (2010): 45.

3. On the extent to which concrete metaphors structure one's thinking even among Westerners who supposedly prefer abstractions, see George Lakoff and Mark Johnson, *Metaphors We Live By* (Chicago: University of Chicago Press, 1980).

4. Explicit descriptions of the audience's response of puzzlement are usually not found in sign-act narratives (e.g., Isa 20:1–5; Jer 13:1–11; Ezek 3:22–27; cf. Ezek 24:19).

the process of betrothal and marriage (e.g., Gen 6:2; 24:3), the second part of the clause is unusual for having more than one grammatical object. It is not only "a wife of harlotry" (אֵשֶׁת זְנוּנִים) but also "children of harlotry" (יַלְדֵי זְנוּנִים) whom YHWH directs Hosea to "take."

It is understandable that English translations render this clause by supplying extra words, either to remove the children as an object of "take" (e.g., NASB's "*have* children of harlotry") or to ascribe harlotry to the wife alone (e.g., NIV's "marry a *promiscuous woman* and have *children with her*"). These renderings illustrate the tendency of interpreters to focus on Hosea's marriage,[5] even as the passage devotes more attention to the naming and birth of the children. It thus becomes necessary to revisit the question—who is guilty of what?

Noteworthy here is that both wife and children are anonymous at this point in the story (to be precise, the children are still unborn). Yet the narrative condemns their conduct in advance as being "of harlotry" (i.e., characterized by or associated with harlotry).[6] This paucity of biographical information indicates that Hosea's family members are more important for their symbolic function than for their historical fulfillment as the persons whom the passage names later as Gomer, Jezreel, Lo-Ruhamah, and Lo-Ammi.[7]

Taken on its own terms, the narrative's third-person presentation undercuts modern speculation about the psychology of Hosea or the circumstances of Gomer's unfaithfulness, whether past or future.[8] The narrative simply records Hosea's obedience (1:3a–b) without offering a glimpse into his emotional state and whether Gomer's adultery is a matter of the past, present, or future. Instead, the theological reality to which Hosea's family points is highlighted by repetition of the Hebrew root זנה ("to commit harlotry, fornication"). In the third and fourth occurrences of זנה in this passage, the reason (כִּי) given for the command for Hosea to marry is astonishing: "for [כִּי] the land commits *heinous harlotry* [זָנֹה תִזְנֶה] in walking away from YHWH" (1:2e).

How can nonhuman אֶרֶץ ("land, earth") be the subject of the human verb זנה ("to commit harlotry")? In other passages the root זנה can denote the harlotry of people in both its literal (e.g., Gen 38:24; Deut 22:21) as well as figurative forms (e.g., Exod 34:16; Judg 8:33). This usage indicates that the semantic range of זנה is sufficiently broad to encompass harlotry as an idea with both literal and figurative aspects.

So when "land" (1:2e) appears as the subject of a double זנה construction (which underlies the intensive rendering, "the land commits *heinous* harlotry"),[9] Hosea's innovative use of זנה parodies Israel's practice of Canaanite nature religion that joined the physical and spiritual worlds together.[10] The opening analogy between the "heinous harlotry" of the land and the "wife of harlotry and children of harlotry" previews the rest of the book's

5. See, e.g., the humorous but reductionistic essay of Gillian Cooper and John Goldingay, "Hosea and Gomer Visit the Marriage Counselor," in *First Person: Essays in Biblical Autobiography*, ed. Philip R. Davies, BibSem 81 (New York: Sheffield Academic, 2002), 119–36.

6. Since Biblical Hebrew has relatively few adjectives, adjectival ideas are commonly expressed using Hebrew construct phrases with nouns (e.g., "of harlotry").

7. Willem S. Boshoff, "Sexual Encounters of a Different Kind: Hosea 1:2 as Foreplay to the Message of the Book of Hosea," *R&T* 1 (1994): 329–32.

8. A tendency that has been exhaustively documented by Brad E. Kelle, "Hosea 1–3 in Twentieth-Century Scholarship," *CurBR* 7 (2009): 179–216.

9. The prepending of the adjective "heinous" attempts to capture two features of the Hebrew infinitive absolute: (1) its emphatic function as an intensified verbal action (*LDHB* §2.1; *IBHS* §35.3.1i); and (2) its alliterative function in repeating the root letters of the main verb ("znh" in English, זנה in Hebrew).

10. See the above description of Canaanite nature religion in the introduction to Hosea, pp. 25–28.

description of apostasy against YHWH as the sinful union of the land with its inhabitants. It is thus inadequate to regard land as just a cipher for the people of Israel,[11] or only as a geographical area in which its inhabitants dwell,[12] since a land characterized by harlotry in Hos 1:2 serves as a metaphor for Canaanite nature religion's characteristic fusion of place and people.

In summary, juxtaposition of land and harlotry serves to modify *both* concepts by creating unanticipated new predications for each.[13] Land becomes personified as a harlot in ways that preview the application of זנה terminology to Israel, and harlotry now assumes creational dimensions that anticipate Hosea's attack against Canaanite nature religion. The dialogical character of place and people in Hosea, in that the actions of each have consequences for the other, is reminiscent of Deuteronomy's use of the language of "inheritance" (נַחֲלָה) for both land and people (e.g., Deut 4:20–21).

b. The Sign-Act of "God-Will-Sow": Dissipation of Land (1:3c–5)

The following sign-act of "God-Will-Sow" (1:3c–5) reinforces the close relationship of land and people. The birth and naming of Hosea's first son symbolizes the convergence of people and land in several ways. His name in Hebrew, "Jezreel" (*yizrĕʿeʾl*, יִזְרְעֶאל), sounds quite similar to "Israel" (*yiśrāʾē*, יִשְׂרָאֵל), but has the meaning, "God will sow [seed]."[14] Jezreel was the name of a fertile valley in Samaria, as well as a strategic outpost within this valley that contained one of Ahab's royal palaces (1 Kgs 21:1). The imposing fortifications that have been unearthed at the archaeological site of Tel Jezreel, far out of proportion to any military necessity, served as a visual projection of the Omride dynasty's might for the entire Jezreel Valley to see.[15]

Beyond evoking associations with places named Jezreel, this passage also marks the birth (1:3c–d) and naming (1:4b) of "God-Will-Sow" as a symbol of YHWH's recompense: "For soon I will repay the bloodshed of Jezreel ["God-Will-Sow"] upon the household of Jehu" (1:4c). YHWH's vow to "repay, reckon" (פקד + עַל) is often rendered in English as "punish" (e.g., NRSV), a term that implies retribution or accounting of a primarily legal kind.[16] Rather, the Hebrew idiom פקד + עַל encapsulates Hosea's signature idea that the Creator God offers a reckoning for sinful human actions with consequences that derive from the order of creation itself.[17]

11. Cf. Laurie J. Braaten, "God Sows: Hosea's Land Theme in the Book of the Twelve," in *Thematic Threads in the Book of the Twelve*, ed. Paul L. Redditt and Aaron Schart, BZAW 325 (Berlin: de Gruyter, 2003), 106–8.

12. Cf. Gert Kwakkel, "The Land in the Book of Hosea," in *The Land of Israel in Bible, History, and Theology: Studies in Honour of Ed Noort*, ed. Jacques van Ruiten and J. Cornelis de Vos, VTSup 124 (Leiden: Brill, 2009), 167–81.

13. The reciprocal structure of metaphor in modifying both the literal and the figurative realms is what Janet Martin Soskice (*Metaphor and Religious Language* [Oxford: Clarendon, 1987], 43–51), following I. A. Richards, usefully describes as "interanimation" between two previously unrelated networks of associations.

14. Morris, *Prophecy, Poetry and Hosea*, 89.

15. H. G. M. Williamson, "Tel Jezreel and the Dynasty of Omri," *PEQ* 128 (1996): 41–51.

16. As argued most recently by Joseph Lam, *Patterns of Sin in the Hebrew Bible: Metaphor, Culture, and the Making of a Religious Concept* (New York: Oxford University Press, 2016), 127–43.

17. This "act-consequence" feature of Hosea's theology (e.g., 2:15[13]; 4:9) was influentially noted by Klaus Koch, "Is There a Doctrine of Retribution in the Old Testament?," in *Theodicy in the Old Testament*, ed. James L. Crenshaw, trans. Thomas H. Trapp, IRT 4 (Philadelphia: Fortress, 1983), 64–69. See the important refinements of Koch's views by Miller, *Sin and Judgment in the Prophets*, 7–20, 122–25.

In addition, this translation of *pāqad* (פקד) is indebted to Stuart Creason's groundbreaking observation that "the Qal verb pāqad involves a change in status. The subject of the verb acts upon the direct object of the verb and this change in status is more fully specified by the prepositional phrase . . . the meaning of the verb pāqad . . . can be defined as 'to assign a person or thing to what the subject believes is its proper or appropriate status or position in an organizational order'" (Stuart Creason,

For murder in particular, the unity of sin and consequence in God's creation is reflected in how "bloodshed" and "bloodguilt" both fall within the semantic range of the Hebrew terms דָּם and דָּמִים, so that "bloodshed" from murder will return upon the killer's own head as "bloodguilt" (e.g., 1 Kgs 2:33; Ezek 18:13).[18] Ancient Israelites regarded the land as stained by the pollution of bloodshed/bloodguilt (e.g., Gen 4:10; Num 35:30–34),[19] so that the murder perpetrated by the "household of Jehu" (Hos 1:4c) would lead to "an end to the kingdom of the household of Israel" (1:4d). Nonetheless, the link between King Jehu and the Northern Kingdom's demise is surprising, given that the narrative of 2 Kgs 9–10 clearly identifies him as God's chosen instrument to destroy the Omride dynasty. This raises the question of how Jehu would have been culpable even though the OT elsewhere condemns Omri and Ahab as the most wicked kings that Samaria ever had (1 Kgs 16:25–26, 30–32).

Scholars differ on this issue,[20] but this passage offers a provisional answer in the final reference to "Jezreel" in vv. 4–5. In parallel to the destruction of Israel's kings (1:4c–d), YHWH promises that "on that day, I will break the bow of Israel *in the Valley of Jezreel*" (1:5). This juxtaposition of "the bow of Israel," a figurative expression for the military prowess of the Northern Kingdom,[21] with the verdict of destruction "in the Valley of Jezreel" shows YHWH's determination to overthrow the kingdom of Samaria in precisely the geographical region where the Omride dynasty believed its strength to be the greatest.[22] Here the wordplay on "Jezreel" pushes beyond a historical referent of solely Ahab or Jehu to include the foundational theological principle that God will "sow" (זרע) consequences back upon the heads of sinful kings.[23] Although less evil than Ahab, Jehu's failure to turn decisively from the brutality of his predecessors (2 Kgs 10:31) meant that his dynasty would meet the same bloody fate that he inflicted upon the family of Ahab.[24]

In summary, the wordplay on "God-Will-Sow" uses the imagery of land to link the sins of Samaria's kings in the ninth century BCE with YHWH's response of poetic justice.[25] The sowing of bloodguilt by the royal line of Jehu (1:4c) will reap the end of Samaria's kingship (1:4d) and the destruction of the Northern Kingdom itself (1:5). Later in Hos 1, the significance of the name of Hosea's first son shifts from a symbol of destruction into one of

"PQD Revisited," in *Studies in Semitic and Afro-Asiatic Linguistics Presented to Gene B. Gragg*, ed. Cynthia L. Miller and Charles E. Jones, SAOC 60 [Chicago: Oriental Institute of the University of Chicago, 2007], 29–30). Applying Creason's categories to the context of Hosea, the verbal subject of פקד is the Creator God, the verbal object is Israel, the prepositional phrase with עַל denotes the status change in which Israel now stands in a relationship of curse rather than blessing with creation, which is the "organizational order" at hand.

18. Klaus Koch, "Der Spruch 'Sein Blut bleibe auf seinem Haupt' und die israelitische Auffassung vom vergossenen Blut," *VT* 12 (1962): 396–416. Although Koch goes too far in pressing the semantic distinction between singular דָּם and plural דָּמִים as one's own blood and the blood of others, respectively, his larger argument about the creational order of justice for "bloodguilt/bloodshed" still stands.

19. Tikva Frymer-Kensky, "Pollution, Purification, and Purgation in Biblical Israel," in *The Word of the Lord Shall Go Forth: Essays in Honor of David Noel Freedman in Celebration of His Sixtieth Birthday*, ed. Carol L. Meyers and Michael Patrick O'Connor (Winona Lake, IN: Eisenbrauns, 1983), 407–8.

20. See the survey of proposals by Stuart A. Irvine, "The Threat of Jezreel (Hosea 1:4–5)," *CBQ* 57 (1995): 494–503.

21. The Hebrew noun קֶשֶׁת ("bow") literally refers to the bow of a hunter or warrior (e.g., Gen 27:3; 1 Sam 2:4), thus enabling its use as a metonym for military power (e.g., Hos 2:20[18]; Ps 46:10[9]).

22. Shawn Zelig Aster, "The Function of the City of Jezreel and the Symbolism of Jezreel in Hosea 1–2," *JNES* 71 (2012): 31–46.

23. For a useful catalogue of the variations on זרע ("to sow [seed]") and its derivatives in Hosea, see Dearman, *Hosea*, 95–96.

24. Thomas E. McComiskey, "Prophetic Irony in Hosea 1.4: A Study of the Collocation פקד על and its Implications for the Fall of Jehu's Dynasty," *JSOT* 58 (1993): 93–101.

25. Cf. Morris, *Prophecy, Poetry and Hosea*, 89.

deliverance for his nation on "the day of Jezreel" (2:2[1:11]).

c. The Sign-Act of "Not-Shown-Mercy": Dissipation of Divine Presence (1:6–7)

The next sign-act of "Not-Shown-Mercy" (1:6–7) portends an important shift in the sign-acts of Hosea's children. While the sign-act of "God-Will-Sow" (1:3c–5) heralded the loss of Israel's kingship and particularly of its land, the following sign-acts of Hosea's second and third children (1:6–9) focus on the unraveling of YHWH's covenant with Israel. The birth and naming of Lo-Ruhamah ("Not-Shown-Mercy"; 1:6a–d), Hosea's second child, marks the end of how YHWH had "shown mercy" (רחם) to his people: "for I will not continue anymore—[that] I would show mercy [רחם] to the household of Israel" (1:6e–f).

The next clause explains the withdrawal of mercy as the cessation of YHWH's willingness to overlook his people's sins: "that/lest I would keep forgiving them" (1:6g). To appreciate the devastating force of this sign-act about Israel's loss of the divine presence, it is essential to hear the echoes of YHWH's promises to "show mercy" (רחם) and to "forgive" (נשׂא) as recorded in the covenant narratives of Exodus.

In the aftermath of covenant ratification at Sinai (Exod 19–24), Israel's manufacture and worship of the golden calf (Exod 32) had severely jeopardized the relationship between YHWH and Israel. So grievous was this transgression that Moses condemned Israel as guilty of "a great sin" (Exod 32:21, 30, 31), an expression that denoted adultery in the ancient Near East.[26] The apostasy of a newly married Israel at Sinai was tantamount to a newlywed exiting the bridal chamber, only shortly after consummating the marriage, to seek a different sexual partner. As Israel's future hung in the balance, YHWH renewed his covenant with a wayward people by declaring himself to be "YHWH YHWH, a merciful [from the root רחם] and gracious God" (Exod 34:6). He would remain the enduring covenant partner of Israel as a God "who forgives [נשׂא] iniquity, transgression, and sin" (Exod 34:7b). YHWH's self-introduction as "a merciful God" became one the most beloved creeds in the OT (e.g., Pss 103:8; 145:8), especially in times when Israel was threatened with destruction (e.g., Joel 2:13; Mic 7:18–20).

In light of these echoes of Exodus, Hos 1's sign-act of "Not-Shown-Mercy" (לֹא רֻחָמָה; 1:6d) expresses the unthinkable end of YHWH's commitment to "show mercy" (רחם; 1:6f), for his people have presumed for too long upon YHWH's willingness to forgive. The presence of the negative particle (לֹא; "no, not") in the child's name announces the new reality that YHWH's answer to Israel would now be "No" where it had previously always been "Yes." Without the gifts of mercy and forgiveness that enable YHWH's presence to remain in Israel, estrangement from his people would be irreversible.

Remarkably, YHWH's explanation of the sign-act continues by limiting the negation of covenant relationship to the Northern Kingdom of Samaria. In contrast to his judgment upon "Not-Shown-Mercy," YHWH promises that "yet to the household of Judah I will show mercy" (1:7a).[27]

26. E.g., Gen 20:9; cf. 2 Kgs 17:21. For ancient Near Eastern references to adultery as a "great sin," see William L. Moran, "The Scandal of the 'Great Sin' at Ugarit," *JNES* 18 (1959): 280–81; and Jacob J. Rabinowitz, "The 'Great Sin' in Ancient Egyptian Marriage Contracts," *JNES* 18 (1959): 73.

27. The surprising reference to Judah by the northern prophet Hosea has led to many proposals that Hos 1:7 was added by a later editor who reflects Judah's more optimistic perspective (e.g., Dearman, *Hosea*, 98). However, Alan R. Millard has shown that the progression from woe to weal and back again is part of a standard pattern in ancient Near Eastern prophetic literature ("From Woe to Weal: Completing a Pattern in the Bible and the Ancient Near East," in *Let Us Go Up to Zion*, 193–201). Against the tendency to argue that predictions of

The instrument of Judah's deliverance from enemies will be "by [means of] YHWH their God" (1:7b) rather than the tangible signs of imperial power: "but I will not deliver them by bow, sword, and battle, nor by horses and horsemen" (1:7c).

The array of weaponry that YHWH repudiates as implements of Judah's deliverance is much more substantial than Samaria's "bow" (1:5). While Samaria's trust in the comparatively miniscule power of the "bow" presented by "Jezreel" would result in destruction "in the Valley of Jezreel" (1:5), Judah would survive the Assyrian threat to see a day of salvation "by [means of] YHWH their God." This was a most unconventional weapon (cf. 1 Sam 17:45) whose invisible presence was mightier than any visible empire.[28]

Historically speaking, the prophesied fates of the Israelite kingdoms came to fulfillment when Samaria fell to Assyria in 722 BCE and Judah barely escaped two decades later in 701 BCE. The narrative of Judah's deliverance from Assyrian siege (Isa 36–37; 2 Kgs 18–19) contains two themes that resonate with Hosea: (1) the futility of military resistance; and (2) the prayerful dependence of King Hezekiah on YHWH. Against the profane taunts of the Assyrian envoys (Isa 36:4–13; 2 Kgs 18:19–35), the God of Israel vindicates his own reputation in the sight of the nations (Isa 37:15–20; 2 Kgs 19:15–19) by turning back the Assyrian invaders without any help from the Judahite king or armies of his people. As predicted in Hos 1:4–7, Samaria's sinful trust in military power led to destruction at the hands of the Assyrian Empire, while Judah's trust in the counterintuitive might of YHWH led to deliverance from these same Assyrians.

d. The Sign-Act of "Not-My-People": Dissipation of Identity (1:8–9)

The final sign-act of "Not-My-People" is the briefest but most shocking of the three involving Hosea's children. Following the symbolic loss of land (1:3c–5) and divine presence (1:6–7), the passage characterizes the birth and naming of "Not-My-People" (1:8–9b) as the unraveling of two covenant identities, those of both Israel and YHWH: "For you are 'Not-My-People,' and I am not your 'I AM'" (1:9c–d). Here the rupture between YHWH and Israel employs a reversal of the covenant formula that appears at important junctures in the book of Exodus, "I will be your God, and you will be my people" (e.g., Exod 6:7; cf. 19:4–6).

But by violating the stipulations given at Sinai, Israel in Hosea's time has forfeited its unique identity as a covenant "people" (עַם). This intimate term of kinship contrasts with the socio-political entity known as a "nation" (גּוֹי).[29] The fact that the positive declaration, "you are my people," echoes ancient Near Eastern formulas of marriage (i.e., "you are my wife") or adoption (i.e., "you are my son") makes the estrangement in these verses all the more painful.[30] As Hans Walter Wolff observes about Hos 1:9, the speech of YHWH "possesses the cutting abruptness of a 'final word' spoken face to face with one's partner in the discussion."[31]

salvation are later additions to oracles of judgment, there seems to be no reason to deny that Hosea could have prophesied both about destruction for Samaria as well as salvation for Judah.

28. Contrast the view of Francis I. Andersen and David Noel Freedman (*Hosea: A New Translation with Introduction and Commentary*, AB 24 [Garden City, NY: Doubleday, 1980], 195), that Hos 1:7 contains a *beth-essentiae*, namely, that YHWH is the agent of rescue. The preceding occurrences of the בְּ-preposition instead suggest that this is an instrumental use of the pronoun.

29. A. R. Hulst, "עַם/גּוֹי," *TLOT* 2:898. The chasm between a special "people" and a common "nation" is similarly reflected in Moses's prayer for Israel after the sin of the golden calf: "See that this nation [גּוֹי] is your people [עַם]!" (Exod 33:13b).

30. See discussion of these ANE formulas by Kalluveettil, *Declaration and Covenant*, 93–111.

31. Hans Walter Wolff, *Hosea*, trans. Gary Stansell, Hermeneia (Philadelphia: Fortress, 1974), 22.

The sign-act of "Not-My-People" therefore symbolizes nothing short of YHWH's divorce or disowning of his people. In the patricentric and collectivist world in which Israel lived, the untimely departure of a husband/father who provided for the sustenance and security of the entire household was the greatest crisis an Israelite family could ever face.[32]

However, the cost of a broken covenant is even greater for YHWH. In another reference to the traditions of Exodus, YHWH asserts that he will no longer reveal himself to his people as the God of the covenant: "I am not your 'I AM'" (1:9d). The negation of "I AM" plays upon YHWH's self-introduction to Israel by the name "I AM" (Exod 3:12–14) in the remarkable scene of Moses's calling at the burning bush. The mighty presence of "I AM" brought Israel out of Egypt and catapulted YHWH onto the stage of world history as the victor over the gods of Egypt (Exod 12:12; 15:11; 18:11). Thus, the denial of YHWH's presence as "I AM" to Israel involves more than the anguish of separation from his people, though certainly not less than this. More importantly, the withdrawal of "I AM" from his people (Hos 1:9d) will lead to their destruction among the nations, who would view the fate of Israel as a public shaming of the Tetragrammaton "YHWH," the personal name of the God of Israel (e.g., Deut 29:23[24]; Ezek 20:9).[33] David Noel Freedman and Francis Andersen rightly summarize the dual identities at stake in these verses as "the annihilation of Israel and the total disappearance of Yahweh from history. He had no other people."[34]

2. The Reconciliation of YHWH's Household: Sign-Acts Reversed (2:1–3[1:10–2:1])

Even so, YHWH determines to overcome the estrangement described in 1:2–9. In a microcosm of the rest of the book, Hos 2:1–3[1:10–2:1] pivots abruptly from the grim reality of the present to hopeful promises for the future. This decisive shift is reflected in the Hebrew versification of a new chapter starting after 1:9, though chapter 2 does not begin in English Bibles until two verses later (i.e., after 1:11). The passage also signals the move from Israel's current estrangement to coming reconciliation in Hos 2:1[1:10] by two instances of the deictic marker וְהָיָה ("and/but it will be"), a converted-perfect verbal form that indicates a logical consequence of what precedes and/or the passage of time from past/present to future.[35]

In a prophetic passage such as Hos 2:1–3[1:10–2:1], וְהָיָה typically marks a shift from oracles of God's judgment to the promise of his salvation to come (e.g., Isa 2:2).[36] Following the sign-acts of woe in 1:2–9, YHWH remains the speaker in 2:1–3[1:10–2:1], but his speech shifts from the compact, poetic declaration of "Not-My-People" (1:9) to an expansive discourse (2:1–3[1:10–2:1]) that climaxes by reversing the negative symbolism of the children's names (cf. 1:3c–9).

a. The Revival of the Progeny Blessing (2:1[1:10]a–c)

The first instance of וְהָיָה in this passage introduces the reinstatement of God's promise to multiply his people: "But the number of the children

32. On the cardinal importance of Israelite men's roles as husbands and fathers, see Daniel I. Block, "Marriage and Family in Ancient Israel," in *Marriage and Family in the Biblical World*, ed. Ken M. Campbell (Downers Grove, IL: InterVarsity Press, 2003), 40–61.

33. The theme of YHWH's reputation among the nations is well studied by David A. Glatt-Gilad, "Yahweh's Honor at Stake: A Divine Conundrum," *JSOT* 98 (2002): 63–74.

34. Andersen and Freedman, *Hosea*, 198.

35. *BHRG* §21.3; *IBHS* §32.2.

36. Joüon §119c.

of Israel will be like the sand of the sea, which can be neither measured nor numbered" (2:1[1:10] a–c). Strikingly, the passage employs the language of God's blessing upon the patriarchs and their descendants "like the sand of the sea" (Gen 22:17; 32:13[12]) to reverse the destruction of Israel envisaged by the three sign-acts of Hosea's children (1:3c–9). Israel's growth during the captivity in Egypt represented a preliminary fulfillment of these promises when "the children of Israel were fruitful, swarmed, multiplied, and became exceedingly mighty" (Exod 1:7; cf. Gen 1:26–28; 9:7).

Another significant stage in fulfilling the progeny blessing came in the conquest of Canaan and the people's growth as a nation: "Judah and Israel were abundant *like the sand on the sea* in abundance" (1 Kgs 4:20a). In Hos 1, then, YHWH promises that the rebirth of his people following their destruction in exile will occur along similar lines. But just as Israel grew numerous in Egypt while only vaguely knowing their deity as a generic, remote "god/God" (Exod 2:23–25),[37] the more pressing need for Hosea's audience lies in renewing covenant with the personal God who had once revealed himself as "I AM" (Hos 1:9; cf. Exod 3:14–15).

b. The Reversal of "Not-My-People" (2:1[1:10]d–g)

What ensues is God's initiative in repairing the breach in covenant relationship as symbolized by the name "Not-My-People" (1:9). In 2:1[1:10]d–g, the second instance of the וְהָיָה discourse marker (cf. 2:1[1:10]a) announces a new identity for Israel: "And in the place where it was said to them, 'You are not my people,' it will be said to them, 'O children of the living God.'"[38] The reversal of "Not-My-People" constitutes not merely restoration to Israel's previous identity as "my people" (2:1[1:10] d–e) but an even better identity as "children of the living God" (2:1[1:10]f–g).

It is significant that Hosea describes Israel as a large, abundant group of "children" (lit. "sons," בָּנִים) rather than a collective singular "son" (בֵּן; cf. 11:1) to highlight how the entire community of reborn people is welcomed home to his family. YHWH thus transforms the status of his people from "children of harlotry" (1:2) into "children of the living God" (2:1[1:10]g).[39] In addition, the new title given to YHWH as "the living God" (אֵל־חָי, lit. "the living El") satirizes the Ugaritic mythology of Baal as a fertility god who underwent an annual cycle of life and death in order to bring seasonal rains to Canaan.[40]

אֵל is a synonym for אֱלֹהִים ("God, god") as well as the name of El, the head of the Ugaritic pantheon who outranks Baal (the former being the father of the latter). This lexical datum explains why the OT sometimes uses "El" epithets (e.g., אֵל אֱלֹהֵי יִשְׂרָאֵל, "El the God of Israel"; Gen 33:20) to identify YHWH the God of Israel.[41] By always remaining the highest sovereign within the created order and never needing to die (contrast the deafening silence of Baal as an absentee god in 1 Kgs 18:26–29), YHWH is the "El" of Israel who proves himself superior to Canaanite gods of nature in every respect.

37. It is no accident that Exod 2:23–25 uses אֱלֹהִים, a general term for deity, since the God of Israel does not introduce himself by his personal name יְהוָה until Exod 3:14–15.

38. The fronting of "in the place" before "where it was said to them" (2:1[1:10]d) and "it will be said to them" (2:1[1:10] f) establishes a particular spatial frame for what follows (see *LDHB* §5.3). Emphasis on the same "place" in both estrangement and reconciliation highlights how the divine-human relationship will come full circle.

39. Wolff, *Hosea*, 27.

40. In the narrative of YHWH's confrontation with Baal (1 Kgs 17–18), for example, the oath formula "as YHWH lives" (חַי־יְהוָה) occurs repeatedly to contrast the living God of the Israelites with Baal, the dead/dying god of the Canaanites (1 Kgs 17:1, 12; 18:10, 15).

41. Patrick D. Miller, "Aspects of the Religion of Ugarit," in *Ancient Israelite Religion: Essays in Honor of Frank Moore Cross*, ed. Patrick D. Miller, Paul D. Hanson, and S. Dean McBride (Philadelphia: Fortress, 1987), 54–56.

c. The Reunion of Samaria and Judah (2:2[1:11]a)

The logical consequences of these וְהָיָה statements ("and/but it will be"; 2x in 2:1[1:10]) come to fruition in the first three clauses of Hos 2:2[1:11]. First and most significant among these is the reunion of the kingdoms of Samaria and Judah, in contrast to their divergent destinies announced earlier (cf. 1:6–7). Although Samaria was destroyed by Assyria and Judah was temporarily delivered in the eighth century BCE, YHWH looks past these historical events to predict an eschatological reunion for all of his people: "Then the children of Judah and the children of Israel will be gathered [קבץ] together" (2:2[1:11]a).

In this regard, the verb קבץ ("to gather, assemble") in prophetic texts usually refers to Israel's return from Assyria and/or Babylon (e.g., Isa 11:12; 40:11; Jer 29:14). However, the historical returns from exile in the sixth and fifth centuries BCE could not have fulfilled Hos 2:2[1:11]a. The Jews who left Persia under the leadership of Zerubabbel and Joshua (Ezra 1–6) as well as the subsequent group under Ezra (Ezra 7–10) only constituted a minority of those in exile,[42] and in any case, their replanting back in the land of their ancestors was shallow and unfruitful at best (e.g., Neh 9:36–37; 13:6–28). This raises the controversial question of whether Israel's figurative exile ever truly ended despite several literal returns to the land.[43] Over two centuries prior, the next clause in Hosea's prophecy had addressed precisely this situation in a preemptive manner by outlining the final prerequisite for ending Israel's exile—the need for leadership renewal.

(1) The Reinstatement of Leadership (2:2[1:11]b)

The next aspect of Israel's restoration is the reinstatement of Israel's leadership institutions. The need for YHWH's king from the line of David to arise and restore the people is hinted at both here and in the final chapters of the Book of the Twelve.[44] Here the passage presents this individual as the people's own choice, at a time when "they will appoint for themselves one leader" (Hos 2:2[1:11]b). But rather than being a "king" whom the people seek to "appoint for themselves" (cf. Deut 17:14–15; 1 Sam 8:5), Hosea initially characterizes him as a "head" (ראשׁ) over the people.

Chapter 3 will go on to portray this leader explicitly as a Davidic "king" (מֶלֶךְ; 3:5). But in Hos 1, the term ראשׁ (2:2[1:11]b) downplays the military overtones associated with a מֶלֶךְ ("king"; cf. 1 Sam 8:20; 2 Sam 8:1–20) in favor of denoting a tribal chieftain more like Moses (e.g., Num 14:4).[45] Hosea's description of Israel as a family, much like Israel's leadership structure of "heads of their ancestral households" (רָאשֵׁי בֵית־אֲבֹתָם) during the time of Moses (Exod 6:14; cf. Num 1:16; Deut 1:13), intimates that Israel's restoration from exile will take the form of a clan's deliverance from Egypt. The next clause explicitly introduces this motif of salvation in the mold of a "new exodus."

(2) The Return from Exile (2:2[1:11]c)

Hosea expresses the final consequence of Israel's return from exile in somewhat cryptic language: "They will go up from the land" (2:2[1:11]c). The appearance of "land" (אֶרֶץ) as an absolute noun (i.e., standing alone) rather than in a construct chain (e.g., "land of Egypt"; Hos 2:17[15]) has

42. Eugene H. Merrill, *Kingdom of Priests: A History of Old Testament Israel*, 2nd ed. (Grand Rapids: Baker Academic, 2008), 484.

43. Martien A. Halvorson-Taylor shows that the figure of exile during the sixth–second centuries BCE served as a metaphor for "death, sterility, bodily and emotional pain, and servitude" (*Enduring Exile: The Metaphorization of Exile in the Hebrew Bible*, VTSup 141 [Leiden: Brill, 2011], 203).

44. Anthony R. Petterson, "The Shape of the Davidic Hope across the Book of the Twelve," *JSOT* 35 (2010): 225–46.

45. Cf. J. R. Bartlett, "The Use of the Word ראשׁ as a Title in the Old Testament," *VT* 19 (1969): 1–10.

occasioned the proposal that resurrection from the underworld may be in view,[46] or that the land will sprout its produce again.[47] It is certainly possible that such an ambiguous use of אֶרֶץ reflects Hosea's penchant for wordplay.[48]

However, B. Renaud has shown that the most likely background for this phrase comes from Exod 1:10, the OT's only other occurrence of the phrase "to go up from the land" (עלה מִן־הָאָרֶץ).[49] The broader context of Exod 1 narrates Pharaoh's fear that the Israelite slaves who "are more plentiful and mighty than us" (Exod 1:9) would "fight against us and *go up from the land*" (Exod 1:10). It is striking that Hos 1 records the same logical sequence found in Exodus, namely, the progeny blessing (Hos 2:1[1:10]a–c) followed by the identical phrase, "go up from the land" (Hos 2:2[1:11]c). These links between Exod 1 and Hos 1 indicate that Israel's first exodus from Egypt serves as the paradigm for a "new exodus" from exile.[50] The new-exodus motif will be developed to a much greater extent in Hos 2, since Hos 1 focuses attention on reversing the sign-acts of Hosea's family.

d. The Negation of Negation: From Estrangement to Reconciliation (2:2[1:11]d–2:3[1])

The climax of the passage arrives here as Hosea summarizes the eschatological finality of Israel's restoration. The sign-acts of the prophet's three children return to center stage as the negation of negation itself. Although the name "Jezreel" (יִזְרְעֶאל, "God-Will-Sow") had denoted the unjust imperialism of the Omride dynasty (1:4c) and the place of its destruction in "the Valley of Jezreel" (1:5), the first child's name will be transformed into a "sowing" (זרע) of salvation: "Indeed, great will be the day of Jezreel" (2:2[1:11]d).[51] The destruction of Israel's productive capability, as epitomized by the earlier wordplays on "God-Will-Sow," gives way to God's promise to provide an innumerable people (2:1[1:10]a). The military connotations of the first "day" (1:5) of judgment have likewise subsided in favor of "the day of Jezreel" (2:2[1:11]d) that overflows with agricultural abundance.

The children's names that mean "Not-Shown-Mercy" (1:6–7) and "Not-My-People" (1:8–9) undergo a similar transformation from estrangement to reconciliation, though in reverse order of their appearance earlier in the passage. Following the restoration of "Jezreel" as the firstfruits of salvation, the passage directs the collective group denoted by "Jezreel" to address his siblings, namely, the rest of YHWH's people: "Speak to your brothers, 'O My-People!,' and to your sisters, 'O Shown-Mercy!'" (2:3[1]). Since the term "Jezreel" carries a distinctly Samarian connotation, it is notable that the scope of reconciliation with YHWH expands to include the entire nation as "your brothers" (אֲחֵיכֶם) and "your sisters" (אֲחוֹתֵיכֶם).[52] Thus the estrangement from YHWH symbolized by Hosea's "children of harlotry" (1:2d) has been overturned by reconciliation to their God and one another. The long history of enmity between Samaria and Judah dissipates in their new and equal identity before YHWH as "My-People" and "Shown-Mercy."

46. E.g., Andersen and Freedman, *Hosea*, 208–9.

47. E.g., Wolff, *Hosea*, 28.

48. Dearman, *Hosea*, 106.

49. B. Renaud, "Osée II 2: *'LH MN H'RṢ*: Essai d'interprétation," *VT* 33 (1983): 455–59.

50. Ibid., 498.

51. The כִּי particle in Hos 2:2[1:11]d appears to be more of an asseverative use ("indeed") to introduce what follows rather than a causal use ("for, because") to ground what precedes. "Jezreel" (2:2[1:11]d) is the first of Hosea's three children, the other two being those whose names are reversed into "O My-People" (2:3[1]a) and "O Shown-Mercy" (2:3[1]b). On the asseverative כִּי and its function in intensifying a vow or affirmation, see *BHRG* §40.29.2.4; Joüon §164b.

52. Andersen and Freedman, *Hosea*, 212.

Canonical and Theological Significance

Under the influence of European Romanticism, modern culture has tended to see the prophets of the OT as the apex of passionate individualism. W. Robertson Smith, the great British Semiticist of the late nineteenth century, sounds rather contemporary in describing Amos and Hosea, respectively, as the forerunners of the principled rationalist and hopeless romantic:

> It is a special characteristic of the Hebrew prophets that they identify themselves with Jehovah's word and will so completely that their personality often seems to be lost in His. In no prophet is this characteristic more notable than in Hosea, for in virtue of the peculiar inwardness of his whole argument his very heart seems to throb in unison with the heart of Jehovah. Amos became a prophet when he heard the thunder of Jehovah's voice of judgment; Hosea learned to speak of Jehovah's love, and of that love in chastisement and in grace towards Israel's infidelity, through some experiences of his own life, through a human love spurned but not changed to bitterness, despised yet patient and unselfish to the end, which opened to him the secrets of that Heart whose tenderness is as infinite as its holiness.[53]

If not for this excerpt's references to two eighth-century-BCE prophets and their theological context, one could almost imagine that Robertson Smith were speaking of the "higher consciousness" of a Johann von Goethe or William Wordsworth. But the OT prophets were hardly the rugged individualists or the angry iconoclasts that they have sometimes become in modern culture. Every era flirts with the danger of remaking the Bible in its own image, so it is essential to explore the historical and theological backgrounds of Hos 1 in a manner that offers cultural bridges to our day. Without doing this, the use of modern lenses in examining the themes of judgment and salvation can lead to the anachronism that the supposed extremes of the prophets reflect the "bipolar"[54] character of YHWH their God as first demonstrated in Exod 34:6–7, an important text for Hosea and the rest of the Twelve.

53. W. Robertson Smith, *The Prophets of Israel and Their Place in History to the Close of the Eighth Century B.C.* (Edinburgh: Black, 1882), 178.

54. This term has often been used to describe the theological contrast between justice and mercy in Exod 34:6–7. While "bipolar" in the scientific sense of a magnet's stable tension between north and south poles is sometimes an author's intended meaning (e.g., Raymond C. Van Leeuwen, "Scribal Wisdom and Theodicy in the Book of the Twelve," in *In Search of Wisdom: Essays in Memory of John G. Gammie*, ed. Leo G. Perdue, Bernard Brandon Scott, and William Johnston Wiseman [Louisville: Westminster John Knox, 1993], 31–49), the psychological sense of "bipolar" as oscillating and unstable often overtakes the scientific sense (e.g., J. P. Bosman, "The Paradoxical Presence of Exodus 34:6–7 in the Book of the Twelve," *Scriptura* 87 [2004]: 233–43, passim).

1. YHWH's Message and Messengers

The Romantic tendency to attribute ideological or emotional swings to the prophets stands at odds with the measured pace of the discourse in Hos 1:2–2:3[1].[55] Rather than psychoanalyzing Hosea, it is better to explore the OT traditions that underlie this passage's description and explanation of sign-acts. Most notable among these are the narratives of covenant breaking and renewal in the book of Exodus. Centuries after Israel had venerated the original golden calf at the foot of Mount Sinai (Exod 32), the newly founded Northern Kingdom revived the cult of golden-calf worship in not one, but at least two, places (1 Kgs 12:28–33; cf. Hos 8:5–6; 10:5; 13:2).

Among the many prophets whom YHWH sent to inveigh against idolatry over the course of two more centuries,[56] Amos and Hosea marked the first of the "classical prophets" whose oral proclamations were eventually recorded as books. But in contrast to our stereotype of the inspired loner, the OT prophets ministered as a community that YHWH had entrusted with the formidable task of speaking his word and holding Israel's political and social institutions accountable. The task of a prophet or prophetess in speaking truth to power was difficult, to be sure, but they were not solitary in standing against the tide. Indeed, the entire weight of Israel's covenant traditions stood behind them so that they were stepping into the sandals of Moses (Deut 18:15–18).

The fact that Israel experienced a consistent prophetic witness for hundreds of years after the exodus helps to situate Exod 34:6–7 in a new light. In the aftermath of Israel's original sin with the golden calf, YHWH was not "bipolar" for introducing himself as "a merciful and gracious God" (Exod 34:6c) who also "will not leave the guilty punished" (Exod 34:7c). Modern interpreters have focused attention on this contrast between mercy and justice in speaking about YHWH, as noted above, but usually in the abstract terms of what Walter Brueggemann influentially calls "a credo of adjectives."[57] Brueggemann does mention that this contrast unfolds on the temporal plane of Israel's history, but his focus on "adjectival witness" ultimately yields a conflicted portrait of YHWH as a "God who is self-giving, harshly demanding, and endlessly restless."[58] This is not so far from the Romantic ideal of a brilliant but tortured soul, except projected onto deity.

55. The narrative of Hos 1:2–2:3[1] is notable for its steady chains of *wayyiqtol* forms that comport with normal word order in Hebrew. With only a few exceptions (e.g., 2:1[1:10] d–e), the discourse features of emphasis available in Hebrew (see *LDHB* §3) are absent in this passage. In addition, YHWH is the only one who speaks, never the prophet.

56. The OT identifies this group of preexilic prophets in two different ways. With reference to YHWH, they are "my/your/his servants the prophets" (e.g., 2 Kgs 9:7; 17:13, 23; cf. 2 Kgs 21:20; 24:2; Ezra 9:11; Amos 3:7; Jer 7:25; Ezek 38:17; Zech 1:6; Dan 9:6); otherwise they are "the sons of the prophets" (e.g., 1 Kgs 20:35; 2 Kgs 2:3; 4:1; 5:22; 6:1; 9:1).

57. Walter Brueggemann, *Theology of the Old Testament: Testimony, Dispute, Advocacy* (Minneapolis: Augsburg Fortress, 1997), 215.

58. Ibid., 228.

Between these theological poles of mercy and justice, it is notable that YHWH introduces himself as a God who is "slow to anger" (Exod 34:6d). This oft-neglected description reconciles the supposedly "bipolar" attributes of YHWH by situating them at different stages of Israel's encounters with a holy God who reveals himself, saves his people, and promises to be with them.[59] This means that YHWH's self-revelation as "a merciful and gracious God" (Exod 34:6c) provides a temporary delay in exercising justice so that repentance can occur, while to "not leave the guilty unpunished" (Exod 34:7c) is the result only after his patience has been presumed upon for too long.[60] The response of YHWH's people to his prophets plays a key role in determining how much time is left before judgment must come—a decision made all the more urgent in the eighth century BCE since YHWH's message had already come through his messengers for centuries.

The reluctance of YHWH to speed up his anger also aids in understanding the relevance of prophetic sign-acts for the audiences that witnessed them. In this regard, scholars have long puzzled over why Hosea's sign-acts of estrangement (1:2–9) would be followed immediately by sign-acts of reconciliation (2:1–3[1:10–2:1]).[61] Operating under the assumption that the prophets mainly address their oracles to the future, the usual view that judgment had become inevitable by the time of Hosea and Amos means that these prophets were simply announcing that salvation would come after judgment rather than referring to a present possibility.[62] As Thomas Raitt observes, this position leads to the dubious conclusion that the preexilic prophets were issuing commands, including calls to repentance, without any possibility that their audience would or could respond.[63] If the future were thus predetermined, the book of Hosea would merely be a specimen of metaphorical language that tried, and inevitably failed, to make sense of paradoxes—again approximating the Romantic ideal, but now from the human side.[64]

But upon hearing the Bible's repeated insistence that YHWH has been "slow to anger" (e.g., Exod 34:6; Num 14:18; Ps 103:8; Joel 2:13; Jonah 4:2; Neh 9:17), it becomes clear that every act of God's communication bears the rhetorical purpose of inviting people to return to him. Hosea's sign-acts of judgment sketch a dismal future precisely to persuade the audience that this does *not* need to happen. For even in what appear to be the OT's most categorical statements of doom, there remains the implicit possibility of repentance, just as Jonah's seemingly unconditional declaration, "Forty days and Nineveh is overthrown!" (Jonah 3:4), results in repentance among

59. James E. Robson, "Forgotten Dimensions of Holiness," *HBT* 33 (2011): 131–45.

60. Patrick D. Miller, "'Slow to Anger': The God of the Prophets," in *The Way of the Lord: Essays in Old Testament Theology* (Grand Rapids: Eerdmans, 2007), 270–73.

61. Wolff, *Hosea*, 24–25.

62. E.g., Donald E. Gowan, *Theology of the Prophetic Books: The Death and Resurrection of Israel* (Louisville: Westminster John Knox, 1998), 6–7.

63. Thomas M. Raitt, "The Prophetic Summons to Repentance," *ZAW* 83 (1971): 30–33.

64. E.g., Francis Landy, "In the Wilderness of Speech: Problems of Metaphor in Hosea," *BibInt* 3 (1995): 35–59.

the Ninevites that YHWH accepts (Jonah 3:10; cf. Jer 18:7–8).[65] How much more so is return available for a chosen people who are bound to YHWH in a covenant relationship! The picture that emerges of Israel's God is of a generous deity who is resolutely for his people in his slowness to anger, even when speaking judgment against them through his servants the prophets.

2. Hosea in the Book of the Twelve and the New Testament

Hosea 1:1–2:3[1] is also the first section of the OT Minor Prophets (Hosea–Malachi), as noted in the discussion of Hos 1:1's "Canonical and Theological Significance." Taking a cue from how Jewish literary traditions have grouped these twelve prophets together since about 200 BCE,[66] the grouping of these individual books as the Book of the Twelve reflects their interlocking themes, such as kingship, repentance, and the day of YHWH, that run through the corpus.[67] This book offers a theological commentary on Israel's history from the divided monarchy until the exiles of both kingdoms and beyond, a period of nearly four hundred years from the eighth century (Hosea) till the fifth century BCE (Malachi).[68] Each book in the collection functions like an instrument playing its part in an orchestra, while the sum of the parts is greater than the whole due to the counterpoint that results from blending different voices.[69]

What sort of music results from hearing the book of Hosea as the first movement of a larger work, and especially through the overture of 1:1–2:3[1]? The memorable beginning of Hosea seems to be the reason for its position at the front of the Twelve even though Amos is somewhat earlier, chronologically speaking.[70] The opening notes of Hosea sound the themes upon which the rest of the Twelve will supply many variations—land and creation, kingship, and a restored humanity after God's sanctifying work of exile.[71] What is more, the sign-acts of the prophet's family are a

65. Paul R. Raabe, "Why Prophetic Oracles against the Nations?," in *Fortunate the Eyes That See: Essays in Honor of David Noel Freedman*, ed. A. B. Beck et al. (Grand Rapids: Eerdmans, 1995), 244.

66. Sirach 49:10, for example, presumes that the Minor Prophets were already associated together in the late third century BCE: "May the bones of the Twelve Prophets send forth new life from where they lie, for they comforted the people of Jacob and delivered them with confident hope."

67. E.g., LeCureux, *The Thematic Unity of the Book of the Twelve*; Jean-Daniel Macchi, "Le thème du 'jour de Yhwh' dans les XII petits prophètes," in *Les prophètes de la Bible et la fin des temps: XXIIIe congrès de L'Association Catholique Française pour l'Étude de la Bible (Lille, 24–27 août 2009)*, ed. Jacques Vermeylen, LD 240 (Paris: Cerf, 2010), 147–81; Petterson, "Shape of the Davidic Hope."

68. There are some minor variations in each manuscript tradition's sequencing of the Twelve, but Hosea is the first book in the two most significant traditions, the MT and LXX.

69. Heath Thomas, "Hearing the Minor Prophets: The Book of the Twelve and God's Address," in *Hearing the Old Testament: Listening for God's Address*, ed. Craig G. Bartholomew and David J. H. Beldman (Grand Rapids: Eerdmans, 2012), 359–60.

70. Amos 1:1 mentions only Uzziah among the Judahite kings who span his ministry, while Hos 1:1 also includes the three Judahite kings who followed him, Jotham, Ahaz, and Hezekiah (Marvin A. Sweeney, *The Twelve Prophets, Volume 1*, Berit Olam [Collegeville, MN: Liturgical Press, 2000], 3).

71. For analysis of these themes in the Twelve as a whole, see Jerry Hwang, "'My Name Will Be Great Among the Nations': The *Missio Dei* in the Book of the Twelve," *TynBul* 65 (2014): 161–80.

microcosm of the historical drama of judgment and salvation in which Israel would repeatedly participate for the next few hundred years. Hosea 1:2–2:3[1] functions like a pair of bifocals that provides the ability to see two horizons, one nearer during Samaria's last days in the eighth century BCE, as well as one further than even Judah's survival in 701 BCE and eventual exile in 587 BCE.

By the time of Malachi in the fifth century BCE, it becomes clear that deportations to Assyria and Babylon, several returns from exile, and divinely empowered building projects on Jerusalem's temple and city wall have all failed to cure the heart problem of apostasy. Israel still has not heeded the sign-acts of Hosea's family; estrangement from YHWH is still described in the poignant kinship terms of challenging a father's love (Mal 1:2), a son dishonoring his father (1:6), marriage with foreigners (2:11), and nonchalance toward divorce (2:16). But the hope of reconciliation in YHWH's household persists—the God who promised that the reunited kingdoms would be "children of the living God" (Hos 2:1[1:10]) will be like a father who spares his son (Mal 3:17) and restores the hearts of fathers and children to one another (Mal 3:24[4:6]a).[72] Restoration will also take on cosmic dimensions by withdrawing the curse that afflicts the land and earth as a result of human sin (Hos 1:2; 4:3; Mal 3:11; 3:24[4:6]b).[73] Thus closes the last verse of Malachi and the Twelve, as well as the latest verse in the OT, with a distinctively Hosean accent. Readers of the Twelve who journey with Hos 1:2–2:3[1] as a roadmap of the possibilities in Israel's covenantal history with YHWH must confront the question—which generation will make the final, decisive U-turn from estrangement toward reconciliation?

The NT's references to Hos 1:2–2:3[1] extend its roadmap in two related directions. First and more fundamental is how the apostle Peter identifies Jesus "the Christ, the *Son of the Living God*" (Matt 16:16), the pivotal moment of recognition at Caesarea Philippi that brings the apostles in line with Matthew's repeated characterization of Jesus as God's "son" (Matt 2:15; 4:3, 6; cf. Hos 11:1). These allusions indicate that "the living God, through Jesus, fulfills the Hosean prophecy of establishing a future Israel. More specifically, Jesus, as the Son of the living God, is the representative of that future Israel promised in Hosea."[74]

Romans 9–11 also fleshes out the theological implications of Jesus serving as the firstfruits of a new Israel. After outlining the problem of Israel's unresolved apostasy, Paul declares that God is assembling a faithful people for himself "not from the among Jews only, but also from among Gentiles" (Rom 9:24). The apostle stakes his argument on Hosea's promises of restoration: "As indeed he says in Hosea, 'Those who were not my people I will call "my people," and her who was not beloved I

72. John D. W. Watts, "A Frame for the Book of the Twelve: Hosea 1–3 and Malachi," in *Reading and Hearing the Book of the Twelve*, ed. James Nogalski and Marvin A. Sweeney, SBLSymS 15 (Atlanta: SBL Press, 2000), 210–12.

73. Morgan, "Land and Temple," 45–46.

74. Mark J. Goodwin, "Hosea and 'the Son of the Living God' in Matthew 16:16b," *CBQ* 67 (2005): 266.

will call "beloved." And in the very place where it was said to them, "You are not my people," there they shall be called children of the living God'" (Rom 9:25–26 NRSV). Paul has taken what Hosea envisioned as restoration for Israel and Judah (Hos 2:2[1:11]) and extended it to all nations who will be joined under the banner of Jesus Christ as God's restored people.[75] On its way to becoming a multitude "from every nation, tribe, people, and language, standing before the throne and before the Lamb" (Rev 7:9), the church has been entrusted with the ministry of reconciling sinners to God just as they themselves have been reconciled to God (2 Cor 5:18–20). Nearly 2,800 years after Hosea and 2,000 years after Jesus and Paul, YHWH has been patient to an unfathomable extent with sinners. At the same time, all people must take heed that his being "slow to anger" (Exod 34:6) does not mean that the day of YHWH so frequently emphasized in the Book of the Twelve (e.g., Joel 2:1; Amos 5:18; Obad 15) will never come (2 Pet 3:9–10).

75. Douglas J. Moo, *The Epistle to the Romans*, NICNT (Grand Rapids: Eerdmans, 1996), 613.

CHAPTER 3

Hosea 2:4–25[2–23]

B. YHWH's Quarrel and Restoration with His Household

Main Idea of the Passage

YHWH confronts Israel, his unfaithful wife, for seeking Baals and "lovers" as the source of agricultural blessings from creation. Even as her harlotry with these paramours requires YHWH to strip her of all that she wrongly attributes to their power, he also resolves one day to bring reconciliation among himself, his people, and the land.

Literary Context

The second of three sections in chapters 1–3, Hos 2:4–25[2–23] is a divine address to Israel that is sandwiched between two narratives of prophetic sign-acts (1:2–2:3[1]; 3:1–5). While the third-person narratives communicate mainly through the family of the prophet, the present passage is an extended speech in which YHWH speaks to his people (albeit indirectly at times through intermediaries, as will be shown below). Hosea 2:4–25[2–23] therefore offers a glimpse into YHWH's impassioned heart in dealing with Israel between the reality of present estrangement and the certainty of future reconciliation.

Hosea 2:4–25[2–23] also links to its surrounding narratives by sending their themes in new directions. While Hos 1:2 and 3:1 hint that Israel's harlotry involves Canaanite nature religion, chapter 2 explains Israel's apostasy in broader terms as a cluster of religious, economic, and political sins with "lovers" and "Baal(s)" (2:7[5], 9–10[7–8], 12[10], 15[13], 19[17]). Similarly, restoration after the punishment of exile is briefly mentioned in both chapters 1 and 3, but Hos 2 offers several variations on this theme as a return to the wilderness (2:16[14]), a reenactment of the exodus from Egypt (2:17[15]), a remarriage between God and his people (2:18–19[16–17], 21–22[19–20]), and even a new act of creation (2:20[18], 23–25[21–23]). By expanding the ideas of chapters 1 and 3 as well as blending history and creation in a way characteristic of chapters 4–14, the divine speech in Hos 2:4–25[2–23] provides an apt summation of the entire book of Hosea.

Translation and Exegetical Outline

(See pages 96–99.)

Structure and Literary Form

YHWH's poignant speech in Hos 2:4–25[2–23] is a superlative example of literary and rhetorical form serving theological function. The passage begins with a summons for the children of Hosea to "quarrel" (ריב as a verb; 2:4[2]a) against their mother "that she is not my wife, and I am not her husband" (2:4[2]b–c). YHWH's speech initially appears to be a hybrid of the covenant "lawsuit" (ריב, a noun) and divorce formulas from the ancient Near East. Yet after this hint of both the juridical and familial realms, the speech unfolds not as a divorce proceeding in which YHWH serves as a prosecutor or judge by calling heaven and earth as witnesses against his people (cf. Isa 1:2–4; Mic 6:1–2), but as a plea from an exasperated husband to his wife by speaking to her through their children.[1]

The numerous discourse elements that convey the deeply personal stakes in YHWH's speech will be discussed below in the "Explanation of the Text." However, one important feature for grasping the passage as a whole is its creative use of Hebrew pronouns. Much of the first half of the speech takes the guise of a command for Hosea's symbolic children to protest the sins of "her" (e.g., 2:4–5[2–3]), that is, their mother. David Clines observes rightly that YHWH's speech uses third-person

1. Cf. Kirsten Nielsen, *Yahweh as Prosecutor and Judge: An Investigation of the Prophetic Lawsuit (Rîb-Pattern)*, JSOTSup 9 (Sheffield: JSOT Press, 1978), 34–38, whose overemphasis on the legal imagery results in neglecting the emotional poignancy of YHWH's speech.

Hosea 2:4–25[2–23]

			B. YHWH's Quarrel and Restoration with His Household (2:4–25[2–23])
			1. YHWH's Quarrel with His Household (2:4–7[2-5])
2:4[2]a	רִיבוּ בְאִמְּכֶם רִיבוּ	"Quarrel against your mother, quarrel—	a. The Accusation of Mother's Harlotry (2:4–5[2–3])
4[2]b	כִּי־הִיא לֹא אִשְׁתִּי	that she is not my wife,	(1) The Intention for YHWH's Exasperation: Mother's Repentance (2:4[2])
4[2]c	וְאָנֹכִי לֹא אִישָׁהּ	and I am not her husband—	
4[2]d	וְתָסֵר זְנוּנֶיהָ מִפָּנֶיהָ	so that she would remove her harlotries from her face,	
	וְנַאֲפוּפֶיהָ מִבֵּין שָׁדֶיהָ׃	and her adulteries from between her breasts.	
5[3]a	פֶּן־אַפְשִׁיטֶנָּה עֲרֻמָּה	Lest I strip her naked,	(2) An Undesirable Alternative: Mother's "Shaming" (2:5[3])
5[3]b	וְהִצַּגְתִּיהָ כְּיוֹם הִוָּלְדָהּ	render her like the day of her birth,	
5[3]c	וְשַׂמְתִּיהָ כַמִּדְבָּר	make her like the wilderness,	
5[3]d	וְשַׁתִּהָ כְּאֶרֶץ צִיָּה	set her like a dry land,	
5[3]e	וַהֲמִתִּיהָ בַּצָּמָא׃	and slay her with thirst!	
			b. The Accusation of the Entire Family's Harlotry (2:6–7[4–5])
6[4]a	וְאֶת־בָּנֶיהָ לֹא אֲרַחֵם	Nor to her children will I show mercy,	(1) The Children's Harlotry (2:6[4])
6[4]b	כִּי־בְנֵי זְנוּנִים הֵמָּה׃	for they are children of harlotry!	
7[5]a	כִּי זָנְתָה אִמָּם	Indeed, their mother has committed harlotry,	(2) The Mother's Greater Responsibility in Harlotry (2:7[5])
7[5]b	הֹבִישָׁה הוֹרָתָם	she has conceived them shamefully,	
7[5]c	כִּי אָמְרָה	for she has said,	
7[5]d	אֵלְכָה אַחֲרֵי מְאַהֲבַי	'I shall follow after my lovers,	
7[5]e	נֹתְנֵי לַחְמִי וּמֵימַי	who give my bread and my water,	
	צַמְרִי וּפִשְׁתִּי	my wool and my flax,	
	שַׁמְנִי וְשִׁקּוּיָי׃	my oil and my drink.'	
			2. YHWH's Determination to Frustrate Harlotry (2:8–10[6–8])
8[6]a	לָכֵן הִנְנִי־שָׂךְ אֶת־דַּרְכֵּךְ בַּסִּירִים	"Therefore I am blocking your road with thorns,	a. The Blocking of Israel's Lust (2:8[6])
8[6]b	וְגָדַרְתִּי אֶת־גְּדֵרָהּ	I am hedging up her walls,	
8[6]c	וּנְתִיבוֹתֶיהָ לֹא תִמְצָא׃	so that her pathways she will not find.	
9[7]a	וְרִדְּפָה אֶת־מְאַהֲבֶיהָ	Then she will pursue her lovers	b. The Disappearance of Israel's Lovers (2:9[7]a–d)
9[7]b	וְלֹא־תַשִּׂיג אֹתָם	yet not catch up to them.	
9[7]c	וּבִקְשָׁתַם	She will seek them,	
9[7]d	וְלֹא תִמְצָא	but she will not find.	
9[7]e	וְאָמְרָה	So she will say,	c. Israel's Frustration with Harlotry (2:9[7]e–h)

Ref	Hebrew	English	Outline
9[7]f	אֵלְכָה	'Let me go	(1) The Inferiority of Lovers (2:9[7]et–g)
9[7]g	וְאָשׁוּבָה אֶל־אִישִׁי הָרִאשׁוֹן	and return to my first husband,	
9[7]h	כִּי טוֹב לִי אָז מֵעָתָּה׃	for it was better for me then than now!'	(2) The Superiority of YHWH (2:9[7]h)
			d. Israel's Ongoing Forgetfulness of YHWH the Giver (2:10[8])
10[8]a	וְהִיא לֹא יָדְעָה	On her part, she has not acknowledged	(1) Agricultural Goods (2:10[8]a–b)
10[8]b	כִּי אָנֹכִי נָתַתִּי לָהּ הַדָּגָן	that I myself gave her the grain,	
	וְהַתִּירוֹשׁ	the new wine,	
	וְהַיִּצְהָר	and the olive oil.	
10[8]c	וְכֶסֶף הִרְבֵּיתִי לָהּ	The silver I multiplied for her,	(2) Precious Metals (2:10[8]c–d)
10[8]d	וְזָהָב עָשׂוּ לַבָּעַל׃	but the gold they made for Baal!"	
			3. YHWH's Removal of Creational Blessings (2:11–15[9–13])
11[9]a	לָכֵן אָשׁוּב	"Therefore, I will return,	a. The Stripping of Harlotry's "Blessings" (2:11[9])
11[9]b	וְלָקַחְתִּי דְגָנִי בְּעִתּוֹ	and I will take my grain in its time,	
	וְתִירוֹשִׁי בְּמוֹעֲדוֹ	and my new wine in its season;	
11[9]c	וְהִצַּלְתִּי צַמְרִי וּפִשְׁתִּי	and I will remove my wool and my flax,	
11[9]d	לְכַסּוֹת אֶת־עֶרְוָתָהּ׃	which cover her nakedness.	
12[10]a	וְעַתָּה	But now,	b. The Exposure of Harlotry's Shamefulness (2:12[10])
	אֲגַלֶּה אֶת־נַבְלֻתָהּ לְעֵינֵי מְאַהֲבֶיהָ	I will uncover her degeneration/folly in the eyes of her lovers,	
12[10]b	וְאִישׁ לֹא־יַצִּילֶנָּה מִיָּדִי׃	and nobody will save her from my hand.	
13[11]	וְהִשְׁבַּתִּי כָּל־מְשׂוֹשָׂהּ חַגָּהּ	I will put an end to all her rejoicing, her feasts,	c. The End of Harlotry's Joy (2:13[11])
	חָדְשָׁהּ וְשַׁבַּתָּהּ	her new moon festivals and her Sabbaths,	
	וְכֹל מוֹעֲדָהּ	and all her appointed days!	
14[12]a	וַהֲשִׁמֹּתִי גַּפְנָהּ וּתְאֵנָתָהּ	I will ransack her vineyard and her fig trees,	d. The Destruction of Harlotry's "Blessings" (2:14[12])
14[12]b	אֲשֶׁר אָמְרָה	of which she said,	(1) Israel's Mistaken Attribution of the "Blessings" (2:14[12]a–d)
14[12]c	אֶתְנָה הֵמָּה לִי	'They are a gift to me	
14[12]d	אֲשֶׁר נָתְנוּ־לִי מְאַהֲבָי	that my lovers gave to me!'	
14[12]e	וְשַׂמְתִּים לְיַעַר	But I will make them into a thicket,	(2) God's Destruction of the "Blessings" (2:14[12]e)
14[12]f	וַאֲכָלָתַם חַיַּת הַשָּׂדֶה׃	and the beast of the field will consume them.	(3) Nature's Destruction of the "Blessings" (2:14[12]f)
15[13]a	וּפָקַדְתִּי עָלֶיהָ אֶת־יְמֵי הַבְּעָלִים	Then I will repay her for the days of the Baals,	e. YHWH's Determination to Repay Pagan Practices (2:15[13])
15[13]b	אֲשֶׁר תַּקְטִיר לָהֶם	to which she used to burn incense,	(1) Israel's Pagan Practices with Baals (2:15[13]a–c)
15[13]c	וַתַּעַד נִזְמָהּ וְחֶלְיָתָהּ	and [when] she adorned herself with rings and jewelry,	
15[13]d	וַתֵּלֶךְ אַחֲרֵי מְאַהֲבֶיהָ	and walked after her lovers.	(2) Israel's Pagan Practices with Lovers (2:15[13]d)

Continued on next page.

Continued from previous page.

Verse	Hebrew	Translation	Outline
15[13]e	וְאֹתִי שָׁכְחָה	But she forgot me!"	(3) Israel's Forgetfulness of YHWH (2:15[13]e–f)
15[13]f	נְאֻם־יְהוָה׃	—The Declaration of YHWH—	
			4. YHWH's Restoration with His Household (2:16–25[14–23])
16[14]a	לָכֵן הִנֵּה	"Therefore look!	a. YHWH's Invitation to Recourtship (2:16–19[14–17])
16[14]b	אָנֹכִי מְפַתֶּיהָ	I am coaxing her,	
16[14]c	וְהֹלַכְתִּיהָ הַמִּדְבָּר	and leading her to the wilderness,	(1) A Surprising Journey to the Wilderness (2:16[14]c–d)
16[14]d	וְדִבַּרְתִּי עַל־לִבָּהּ׃	so that I may speak to her heart.	
17[15]a	וְנָתַתִּי לָהּ אֶת־כְּרָמֶיהָ מִשָּׁם	And I will give to her vineyards from there,	(2) YHWH's Promise of Return from Exile (2:17[15]a)
	וְאֶת־עֵמֶק עָכוֹר לְפֶתַח תִּקְוָה	and the valley of Achor as a doorway to hope.	
17[15]b	וְעָנְתָה שָׁמָּה	Then she will answer me from there	(3) Israel's Acceptance of YHWH's Invitation (2:17[15]b)
	כִּימֵי נְעוּרֶיהָ	as in the days of her youth,	
	וּכְיוֹם עֲלֹתָהּ מֵאֶרֶץ־מִצְרָיִם׃	and as in the day she came up from the land of Egypt.	
18[16]a	וְהָיָה בַיּוֹם־הַהוּא	And on that day	(4) Israel's Choice of YHWH as Husband (2:18–19[16–17])
	נְאֻם־יְהוָה	—The Declaration of YHWH—	(a) The Right Title for YHWH (2:18[16]a–c)
18[16]b	תִּקְרְאִי אִישִׁי	you will call me, 'My husband,'	
18[16]c	וְלֹא־תִקְרְאִי־לִי עוֹד בַּעְלִי׃	and no longer call me, 'My Baal.'	(b) The Wrong Title for YHWH (2:18[16]d)
19[17]a	וַהֲסִרֹתִי אֶת־שְׁמוֹת הַבְּעָלִים מִפִּיהָ	Then I will remove the names of the Baals from her mouth,	(c) YHWH's Removal of Baals as Lovers (2:19[17])
19[17]b	וְלֹא־יִזָּכְרוּ עוֹד בִּשְׁמָם׃	and they will not be remembered again by their names.	
20[18]a	וְכָרַתִּי לָהֶם בְּרִית בַּיּוֹם הַהוּא	Then I will make a covenant for them on that day,	b. YHWH's Covenant with Creation (2:20[18])
	עִם־חַיַּת הַשָּׂדֶה	with the beast of the field,	(1) Peace in the Animal Realm (2:20[18]a)
	וְעִם־עוֹף הַשָּׁמַיִם	and with the bird of the sky	
	וְרֶמֶשׂ הָאֲדָמָה	and the crawler of the earth.	
20[18]b	וְקֶשֶׁת	But as for the bow,	(2) Peace in the Human Realm (2:20[18]b–c)
	וְחֶרֶב	and the sword,	
	וּמִלְחָמָה	and war,	
	אֶשְׁבּוֹר מִן־הָאָרֶץ	I will break them from the land,	
20[18]c	וְהִשְׁכַּבְתִּים לָבֶטַח׃	and I will make them lie down in trust.	

Verse	Hebrew	Translation	Outline
21[19]a	וְאֵרַשְׂתִּיךְ לִי לְעוֹלָם	So I will betroth you to myself forever.	c. YHWH's Covenant with "You"—Israel (2:21–22[19–20])
21[19]b	וְאֵרַשְׂתִּיךְ לִי בְּצֶדֶק וּבְמִשְׁפָּט	I will betroth you to myself with righteousness and justice,	(1) The Bride-Price of Covenant Relationship (2:21[19])
	וּבְחֶסֶד וּבְרַחֲמִים׃	with devotion and mercies;	
22[20]a	וְאֵרַשְׂתִּיךְ לִי בֶּאֱמוּנָה	I will betroth you to myself in faithfulness,	(2) The Intimacy of Covenant Relationship (2:22[20])
22[20]b	וְיָדַעַתְּ אֶת־יְהוָה׃	that you might know YHWH.	
23[21]a	וְהָיָה בַּיּוֹם הַהוּא אֶעֱנֶה	And on that day I will answer	d. YHWH's Reconciliation of Nature and Israel (2:23–24[21–22])
23[21]b	נְאֻם־יְהוָה	—The Declaration of YHWH—	(1) YHWH's Answer to Heaven (2:23[21]a–c)
23[21]c	אֶעֱנֶה אֶת־הַשָּׁמָיִם	I will answer the heavens,	
23[21]d	וְהֵם יַעֲנוּ אֶת־הָאָרֶץ׃	and they, in turn, will answer the earth;	(2) Heaven's Answer to Earth (2:23[21]d)
24[22]a	וְהָאָרֶץ תַּעֲנֶה אֶת־הַדָּגָן	the earth will answer the grain,	(3) Earth's Answer to the Fruits of Earth (2:24[22]a)
	וְאֶת־הַתִּירוֹשׁ	the new wine,	
	וְאֶת־הַיִּצְהָר	and the olive oil,	
24[22]b	וְהֵם יַעֲנוּ אֶת־יִזְרְעֶאל׃	and they, in turn, will answer Jezreel.	(4) Nature's Answer to Jezreel/Israel (2:24[22]b)
			e. YHWH's Reconciliation with His People (2:25[23])
25[23]a	וּזְרַעְתִּיהָ לִּי בָּאָרֶץ	Then I will sow her for myself in the land.	(1) YHWH's Rebirth of "Jezreel" (2:25[23]a)
25[23]b	וְרִחַמְתִּי אֶת־לֹא רֻחָמָה	I will show mercy to Not-Shown-Mercy;	(2) YHWH's Renaming of "Not-Shown-Mercy" (2:25[23]b)
25[23]c	וְאָמַרְתִּי לְלֹא־עַמִּי	and I will say to Not-My-People,	(3) YHWH's Renaming of "Not-My-People" (2:25[23]c–f)
25[23]d	עַמִּי־אַתָּה	'You are my people.'	
25[23]e	יֹאמַר	And he will say,	
25[23]f	אֱלֹהָי׃	'My God.'"	

pronouns as "an alienating device, or at least a signal of his own sense of alienation from Israel."[2]

The first such occurrence is found in Hos 2:7–8[5–6]. Following a flurry of first-person pronouns when YHWH cites his wife's loyalty to "*my* lovers who give *my* food and *my* water, *my* wool and *my* flax, *my* oil and *my* drink" (2:7[5]), YHWH interrupts her monologue by determining to oppose "you": "Therefore I am blocking *your* road with thorns" (2:8[6]).[3] The brief and sudden reference to "*your* road" in Hos 2:8[6] momentarily collapses the distinction between *dramatis personae* and audience in a manner anticipating the use of aside in Shakespearean drama (e.g., *Hamlet,* act 2, scene 2, lines 223–25). In stepping outside the world of the text for a short moment, the divine speech labels the primarily male audience of Israel's leaders (cf. 4:13–14; 5:1) using Hebrew's feminine possessive pronoun "your"[4] (the pronominal suffix *-ēk*) to perform a figurative castration of their authority. This unexpected attack on masculinity would have been deeply offensive in a traditional patricentric society like ancient Israel with its emphasis on the public maintenance of male honor.[5]

Unlike their first occurrence in chapter 2, the second appearance of "me" and "you" pronouns in the passage removes Israel's shame. When YHWH promises to remarry his people, he reverses the divorce formula (cf. 2:4[2]) while simultaneously transforming it into a rejection of Baal: "*You* will call me, 'My husband [אִישִׁי],' and [*you* will] no longer call me, 'My Baal [בַּעְלִי]'" (2:18[16]). In this verse, the wordplay on the term בַּעַל reflects its ambiguity as both the proper name of the Canaanite deity as well as a synonym to אִישׁ ("man, husband").

Israel's renunciation of this impotent fertility idol (2:19[17]) sets in motion the restoration of YHWH's covenant with creation (2:20[18]; cf. 2:14[12]), a process that climaxes with YHWH's threefold promise of betrothal between "you" and "myself": So I will betroth *you to myself* forever. I will betroth *you to myself* with righteousness and justice, with devotion and mercies; I will betroth *you to myself* in faithfulness, that you might know YHWH" (2:21–22[19–20]; cf. 2:25[23]). In stark contrast to the expectation in traditional societies for a cuckolded husband to banish a disgraceful wife, YHWH restores her honor by remarrying her and providing again for her needs.

2. David J. A. Clines, "Hosea 2: Structure and Interpretation," in *On the Way to the Postmodern: Old Testament Essays, 1967–1998*, JSOTSup 292 (Sheffield: Sheffield Academic, 1998), 302.

3. Most English versions render the second-person feminine suffix with the third person "her" (e.g., ESV, NASB) for the sake of smoothness, but this obscures the abrupt change in pronoun for rhetoric's sake.

4. Unlike the generic "you" in English, Hebrew differentiates second-person pronouns into masculine and feminine forms.

5. On this shaming tactic in Hosea generally, Susan E. Haddox, "(E)masculinity in Hosea's Political Rhetoric," in *Israel's Prophets and Israel's Past: Essays on the Relationship of Prophetic Texts and Israelite History in Honor of John H. Hayes*, ed. Brad E. Kelle and Megan Bishop Moore, LHBOTS 446 (New York: T&T Clark, 2006), 174–200.

Explanation of the Text

1. YHWH's Quarrel with His Household (2:4–7[2–5])

The quarrel section (2:4–15[2–13]) of YHWH's speech falls into four parts that mix juridical and familial imagery, though the former kind of imagery serves mainly as a springboard to the latter. Following a quasi-legal summons that is actually more of a plea for Gomer/Israel to choose between honor and shame (2:4–5[2–3]), the middle two sections emphasize the sinful solidarity of mother and children (2:6–7[4–5]) and YHWH's determination to frustrate the harlotry of the entire people (2:8–10[6–8]). Finally, YHWH concludes the quarrel section with a threat to remove creation's blessings that Israel had misattributed to pagan deities (2:11–15[9–13]).

Hosea and Gomer are never explicitly named here as the quarreling parties. But chapter 2's repeated use of familial language links the national horizon of YHWH/Israel with the personal horizon of Hosea/Gomer already narrated in chapter 1. As Diane Jacobson notes, the blended referents of the marriage metaphor "take hold of us and drag us kicking and screaming into the experience of divine judgment, forgiveness, and grace."[6]

a. The Accusation of Mother's Harlotry (2:4–5[2–3])

The family reunion in the previous passage (1:2–2:3[1]) concluded on a positive note with the exhortation to Hosea's children, "Speak to your brothers, 'O My-People!,' and [speak] to your sisters, 'O Shown-Mercy!'" (2:3[1]).[7] Following this jubilant command, the mood of Hos 2 darkens abruptly. The family reunion disintegrates into a quarrel that begins with a double imperative: "*Quarrel* against your mother, *quarrel*!" (2:4[2]a). Other OT prophetic texts with the Hebrew root ריב ("to quarrel, contend") typically describe God's covenant lawsuit against his sinful people (e.g., Isa 3:13–15; Jer 2:4–9).[8]

(1) The Intention for YHWH's Exasperation: Mother's Repentance (2:4[2])

Although ריב can have the technical sense of a lawsuit, any semblance of the courtroom quickly returns to the familial scene of children (cf. "your brothers," "your sisters" in 2:3[1]) who quarrel on the husband's behalf against the wife ("your mother"; 2:4[2]). This shift in discourse focus calls the children as witnesses against their own mother, simultaneously distancing the husband from the wife while drawing upon the children's personal stakes in the well-being of the family. Hence the notion of a formal lawsuit with prosecutor, judge, and witnesses is secondary for Hos 2, though the imagery of a cosmic courtroom will reappear occasionally in the rest of the book (e.g., 4:1–3).

Following their summons to the quarrel (2:4[2]a), the children are commissioned as the mouthpiece for the father's frustration with their mother.

6. Diane L. Jacobson, "Hosea? Yes! A God Who Makes Alive," *WW* 28 (2008): 192.

7. Hosea 2:3[1] is a janus that provides a transition between the first two chapters. On the one hand, it concludes Hos 1:2–2:2[1:11] by placing the theme of reversal on the lips of the restored children of Hosea/Israel. On the other, the verse's masculine-plural imperative verb ("Speak!"), which is directed to the children, makes them the implied subject for the following command in Hos 2:4[2] ("Quarrel!").

8. H. Ringgren, "ריב," *TDOT* 13:477–78. The related noun רִיב means "strife" (e.g., Gen 13:7; Exod 17:7; Deut 1:12) or "dispute/lawsuit" (Deut 19:17; 25:1; 2 Sam 15:2).

Their complaint is "that [כִּי] she is not my wife, and I am not her husband" (2:4[2]b–c).[9] This phrase has numerous affinities with ancient Near Eastern divorce formulas that confirm the finality of estrangement between husband and wife, typically as a twofold vow spoken by each party, "she will not be my wife" followed by "I will not be his wife."[10] However, if Hos 2:4[2] does record a formal divorce, the ensuing verses become rather puzzling for describing a husband who initiates a divorce but continues to pursue reconciliation. The difficulty of resolving these tensions has led some scholars to propose that Hos 2:4[2]b–c describes a temporary negation of marriage rather than a divorce.[11] This interpretation still proves unsatisfactory in light of how Israel later identifies YHWH as her "first husband" (2:9[7]) and YHWH anticipates his rebetrothal and remarriage to Israel (2:16–22[14–20]).[12]

The solution to this conundrum lies in recognizing how Hos 2:4[2] modifies the imagery of divorce to portray the depth of YHWH's countercultural, but no less exasperated, love.[13] While Hos 2:4[2]b–c certainly creates the expectation that a divorce will follow, the speech of YHWH then veers from the script for such legal proceedings. The next step of a divorce in the ancient Near East would normally have involved the process of assigning blame to the party who sought the divorce in the first place, finalizing the division of property, and/or arranging for the woman to leave the couple's home.[14]

To signal the break with these cultural conventions, the following clause shifts to a *wĕyiqtōl* form in Hos 2:4[2]d to indicate YHWH's intention for showing such exasperation.[15] The surprise at hand is that YHWH's exasperation leads to an invitation for the wife to repent rather than to effect a divorce: "*so that* [reflecting the *wĕyiqtōl*'s discourse function] she would remove her harlotries from her face, and her adulteries from between her breasts" (2:4[2]d). The bodily locations of "face" and "breasts" are where cosmetics and dress (cf. Jer 3:3; Ezek 23:40; Prov 6:24–25) would have adorned a seductive woman.[16]

Who is this wife/mother, and is she a harlot by trade? In a manner anticipating v. 7[5]'s ambiguous reference to "lovers," the mention of the woman's "harlotries" (זְנוּנִים) and "adulteries" (נַאֲפוּפִים), both plural nouns in Hos 2:4[2], seems to broaden her identity in the marriage metaphor to include both Gomer and Israel,[17] or less probably, ascribes a litany of adulteries to one party or the other. Hosea 1:2 has already linked the harlotry of Hosea's wife and children with that of the land of Israel. And as

9. The conjunction כִּי is often interpreted as causal ("for, since, because"; e.g., NASB, NIV, NRSV), thereby suggesting that the children are voicing their father's grounds for divorce. But as the commentary below will show, Hos 2:4[2] reworks the terminology of divorce to give voice to YHWH's desire for reconciliation. Thus the function of כִּי is best seen in the broader context as a complementary use (i.e., "that") which introduces the substance of the children's quarrel with their mother.

10. See the comprehensive list of ancient Near Eastern divorce formulas in Markham J. Geller, "The Elephantine Papyri and Hosea 2,3: Evidence for the Form of the Early Jewish Divorce Writ," *JSJ* 8 (1977): 139–48.

11. E.g., Maria Dass, "The Divorce (?) Formula in Hosea 2:4a," *ITS* 34 (1997): 56–88; Andersen and Freedman, *Hosea*, 222.

12. Raymond Westbrook, "Adultery in Ancient Near Eastern Law," *RB* 97 (1990): 577–80.

13. Dearman, *Hosea*, 57–58.

14. Paul A. Kruger, "The Marriage Metaphor in Hosea 2:4–17 against Its Ancient Near Eastern Background," *OTE* 5 (1992): 7–25.

15. When a *wĕyiqtōl* has a different subject from the verbal sequence that precedes, as does the third-person *wĕyiqtōl* in Hos 2:4[2]d (compare the second-person imperative in Hos 2:4[2]a, the preceding mainline verb), it will tend to have the sense of purpose or consequence (Elizabeth Robar, *The Verb and the Paragraph in Biblical Hebrew*, Studies in Semitic Language and Linguistics 78 [Leiden: Brill, 2015], 134–37).

16. Paul A. Kruger, "Israel, the Harlot (Hos 2:4–9)," *JNSL* 11 (1983): 109–11.

17. Cf. Andersen and Freedman, *Hosea*, 220.

noted above, the root זנה is used as a metaphor that includes both literal and figurative harlotry.

For the children of both Gomer and Israel, then, the language of divorce in Hos 2:4[2]b–c raises the ugly specter of a wife and mother abandoning her family. But this confrontation takes place to pierce her conscience and draw her home. The husband's desire is for the wife to "remove" (סור*hiphil*; 2:4[2]d) her sinful practices instead of being banished for them. Thus Hos 2:4[2] represents a gracious but pained attempt to avoid separation rather than to finalize it.

(2) An Undesirable Alternative: Mother's Shaming (2:5[3])

All the same, Hos 2:5[3] warns of the undesirable alternative should the wife/mother refuse to return. The potential consequences, still avoidable at this stage in Israel's history (cf. 3:4; 11:5–6), appear as a series of five verbal clauses spoken by YHWH that are governed by a single instance of the conjunction "lest" (פֶּן): "*Lest* I strip her naked, render her like the day of her birth, make her like the wilderness, set her like a dry land, and slay her with thirst!" The first two clauses of the verse (2:5[3]a–b) allude to the ancient Near Eastern practice of publicly shaming an adulterous wife,[18] but with two important modifications. The first is that the threat to "strip her naked" (2:5[3]a) comes only after the husband's plea to stop exhibiting herself publicly (2:4[2]d). Her refusal to cease this behavior of her own accord leaves the husband no other choice.

Second and especially pertinent for the overall flow of 2:4–15[2–13], the threat of punishment is merely an intermediate step in YHWH's pursuit of his wife's repentance (e.g., 2:8–15[6–13]). These differences from cultural practices around Israel mean that the warnings of Hos 2:5[3] ought not to be understood as a chauvinistic display of rage or violence.[19] Instead, the quarrel speech's frequent shifts between the threat of punishment and the hope of restoration reflect YHWH's genuine anguish in his struggle to vindicate his justice while also showing his mercy (cf. 11:1–11).[20] This is not to say that YHWH stands at odds with himself, for as Paul Fiddes perceptively observes,

> Neither wrath nor restoration are [*sic*, "is"] a mechanical process of causation, but is to do with personal relations, and so both mean pain for God. There is then no *conflict* of love and wrath within God; *both* mean suffering for him, in an intricate double movement of pain, a complex experience that can be described poetically but not literally as a struggle with himself.[21]

The second group of "lest" (פֶּן) clauses (2:5[3]c–e) incorporates the land itself into the marriage metaphor. While the similes "like the wilderness" (2:5[3]c) and "like a dry land" (2:5[3]d) could mirror the first two clauses (2:5[3]a–b) in applying figuratively to a human wife, the primary focus of the metaphor shifts to literal places that lack YHWH's gift of fertility.[22] In a preview of later flashbacks in the book to Israel's history (e.g., 2:16–17[14–15]), YHWH's speech invokes the recollection of the "wilderness" (along with its synonym, "dry land")

18. E.g., Samuel Greengus, "A Textbook Case of Adultery in Mesopotamia," *HUCA* 40–41 (1969): 33–44. In two passages that clearly derive from Hos 2, Jer 3–4 and Ezek 16 both describe YHWH bringing reproach upon Jerusalem before her "lovers" (Jer 4:30; Ezek 16:37), who in these contexts are clearly the nations.

19. Cf. Yvonne Sherwood, *The Prostitute and the Prophet: Reading Hosea in the Late Twentieth Century*, JSOTSup 212 (London: T&T Clark, 2004), 211 et passim.

20. Clines, "Hosea 2," 297–98.

21. Fiddes, "The Cross of Hosea Revisited," 185–86, emphasis original.

22. As in 1:2, the fact that "woman/wife" and "land" are grammatically feminine in Hebrew means that the referent of

as the place where Israel received its due for questioning YHWH's provision after delivering them from Egypt (e.g., Exod 16; Num 14; Deut 1–3). The threat of Canaan similarly becoming shamed "like the wilderness" and "like a dry land" reminds hearers that YHWH is the deity who actually controls the fertility of the land. The failure of Israel to remember this fact would lead to a painful reenactment of history when "[I] slay her [i.e., people and/or land] with thirst!" (Hos 2:5[3]e; cf. Exod 17:3; Deut 11:11; 29:18[19]). The "lest" clauses of Hos 2:5[3] therefore emphasize the symbiosis between the inhabitants and fertility of the land by linking people and place as covenant partners in YHWH's household.[23]

b. The Accusation of the Entire Family's Harlotry (2:6–7[4–5])

The children reappear unexpectedly in these verses and redraw the boundaries of YHWH's metaphorical household yet again. But at this point in YHWH's speech, the hearers have been lulled into thinking that they are innocent children (2:3[1]) who do their father's bidding by confronting their guilty mother (2:4–5[2–3]). What comes next will surprise the audience by accusing the children of being just as guilty as their mother.

(1) The Children's Harlotry (2:6[4])

On the children's part, any perceived gap between themselves and their mother vanishes when YHWH suddenly declares that the entire family is equally sinful: "Nor to *her* children will I show mercy, for *they* are children of harlotry! (2:6[4]a–b).[24] YHWH had previously addressed the children in the second person (e.g., "*your* brothers/sisters" [2:3[1]], "*your* mother" [2:4[2]]), but Hos 2:6[4] shifts to third-person pronouns (e.g., "her, they, their, them") to punctuate the shocking news that the children are further from YHWH than they originally believed. Thus the speech's opening summons for the children, "Quarrel against your mother, quarrel—" (2:4[2]) was actually an oblique way of placing the children under the same condemnation when YHWH turns to them and warns, "Nor to her children will I show mercy, for they are children of harlotry" (2:6[4]; cf. 1:2b). Rather than being self-deceived about their innocence, Hosea's audience must realize that a time of judgment is fast approaching when YHWH will no longer "show mercy" (רחם; 2:6[4]a, cf. 1:6–7). The prospect of forgiveness is offered to Israel not as an unconditional promise to be abused but as an urgent opportunity to be embraced so that restoration may follow.

(2) The Mother's Greater Responsibility in Harlotry (2:7[5])

Following the surprise that the hearers themselves are "children of harlotry" (2:6[4]b), the next clause emphasizes the moral solidarity of mother and children: "Indeed, their mother has committed harlotry, she has conceived them shamefully" (2:7[5]a–b).[25] Although the mother bears greater responsibility, the children share in their mother's "harlotry" (2:7[5]a) because they were conceived

"her" can shift fluidly from the human to the agricultural realm (Dearman, *Hosea*, 111).

23. Laurie J. Braaten, "Earth Community in Hosea 2," in *The Earth Story in the Psalms and the Prophets*, ed. Norman C. Habel, The Earth Bible 4 (Sheffield: Sheffield Academic, 2001), 186–89.

24. YHWH's exasperation is evident in this clause's fronted word order, with the direct object ("her children") preceding the verb ("I will not show mercy [to]"). The same fronted word order for the verbal object of רחם ("to show mercy") is found in Hos 1:7a ("*yet to the household of Judah* I will show mercy"). Together, these clauses contain the discourse feature known as main clause emphasis (*LDHB* §4.1).

25. This rendering takes the כִּי particle in Hos 2:7[5]a to be asseverative (on this use, see Joüon §164b). It is also possible to render the particle in a causal manner ("*for* their mother has

by the sinful process of pursuing after her "lovers" (2:7[5]c–d). Whether one identifies the referent of "their mother" as the land of Canaan (cf. Hos 13:13),[26] the personified city/land of Samaria (cf. Isa 51:17–18),[27] or better, as an open-ended metaphorical combination of the previous two (as argued above in the commentary on 1:2), the fact that some form of "harlotry" (זנה) characterizes both children (2:6[4]b) and mother (2:7[5]a) means that the present generation of Israel cannot escape Hosea's condemnation for its sinful syncretism in an abundant land.[28] Since mother (i.e., city or land) and children (i.e., her harvest or people) stand together and at arm's length from YHWH, the rest of chapters 2–3 only address the wife as a corporate figure whose "harlotry" has tainted the entire household and therefore keeps the children from blaming their mother.[29]

The nature of this harlotry comes to the fore when YHWH cites Israel's apostate words: "For she has said, '*I* shall follow after *my* lovers, who give *my* food and *my* water, *my* wool and *my* flax, *my* oil and *my* drink'" (2:7[5]c–e). In this brief monologue, the eight occurrences of first-person forms (i.e., "I, my") underscore the selfish determination of Israel in pursuing liaisons that are offensive to YHWH. Yet who are these "lovers" whom Israel seeks to "follow after" (הָלַךְ אַחֲרֵי)?

Although some have used later biblical references to identify the "lovers" as political allies and/or trading partners (cf. Ezek 16:28–33),[30] the list of goods in Hos 2:7[5]e indicates that they are primarily Canaanite nature gods whom Israel supposed "gave" (נתן; also in vv. 10[8], 14[12], 17[15]) the fruits of the land. The agricultural items listed in Hos 2:7[5]e reflect the main commodities produced in Israel from the tenth century BCE onwards (cf., e.g., 1 Kgs 5:25[11]; 2 Chr 2:9[10], 14[15]), in addition to evoking the Ugaritic depictions of Baal as the guarantor of oil, wine, and grain to those who worship him.[31]

This convergence of economics and religion becomes explicit later in the passage when the "lovers" become a composite figure that includes "Baal" as a metaphor for the international trade of precious metals in exchange for Israelite agricultural commodities (2:10[8]; cf. 8:4; 12:2[1]; Isa 2:6–8). But at this stage of the argument in Hos 2, the paramours are mainly identified as Canaanite nature gods whom Israel believes to control the rain and provide the fruit of the land. This is not to say that idolatry is purely a domestic religious affair, for the following verses begin to develop the imagery of Israel's journeys to far-flung places in pursuit of illicit love.

2. YHWH's Determination to Frustrate Harlotry (2:8–10[6–8])

In response to Israel's stated determination to "follow after" (2:7[5]d) other gods, YHWH resolves to oppose Israel's wayward movements. Here and elsewhere in the chapter (vv. 8[6], 11[9], 16[14]), the conjunction "therefore" (לָכֵן) provides

committed harlotry"), in which case the clause would parallel the preceding כִּי clause ("for they are children of harlotry; 2:6[4] b). For the family metaphor of Hos 2, the asseverative rendering supports the rest of the chapter's emphasis on the culpability of the mother, though without excusing her children. This distinction between mother and children also enables the rhetorical surprise whereby the children at first accuse their mother (2:4–5[2–3]) but end up condemning themselves (2:6[4]).

26. Braaten, "Earth Community in Hosea 2," 190–91.

27. John J. Schmitt, "The Wife of God in Hosea 2," *BR* 34 (1989): 5–18.

28. A. A. Macintosh, *Hosea*, ICC (Edinburgh: T&T Clark, 1997), 46.

29. Clines, "Hosea 2," 302–4.

30. E.g., Brad E. Kelle, *Hosea 2: Metaphor and Rhetoric in Historical Perspective*, Academia Biblica 20 (Atlanta: SBL Press, 2005), 119–22.

31. Day, "Hosea and the Baal Cult," 205–6.

the transition from Israel's action to YHWH's reaction. He determines to block Israel's lust (2:8[6]) and cause Israel's lovers to disappear (2:9[7]a–d) so that this wayward people become frustrated by idolatry's futility and turn back toward YHWH (2:9[7]e–h).

a. The Blocking of Israel's Lust (2:8[6])

YHWH opposes Israel in its pursuit of idols: "Therefore I am blocking your road with thorns, I am hedging up her walls, so that her pathways she will not find" (2:8[6]).[32] In this verse, the temporary use of the second-person "your" (2:8[6] a) surprises the audience with a personal attack, while the subsequent reversion to the usual third-person pronouns ("her, she"; 2:8[6]b–c) bespeaks the growing relational gap between a holy God and his sinful people.[33] The literal dimension of this imagery involves shutting up a harlot in her home so that she will not be able to ply her trade on the streets, but several figurative referents for this harlotry are also possible.[34] In favor of a political or economic interpretation, the inability for Israel to travel on the "road" (דֶּרֶךְ) and "pathways" (נְתִיבוֹת) may be YHWH's response to the pursuit of military and/or trade alliances with foreign empires (Hos 7:11; 8:9; 12:2[1]).

b. The Disappearance of Israel's Lovers (2:9[7]a–d)

However, a religious or cultic interpretation remains plausible in light of how Israel will "pursue her lovers yet not catch up to them. She will seek [בקשׁ] them, but she will not find [מצא]" (2:9[7]; cf. 2:8[6]c). The pairing of the verbs "seek" (בקשׁ; 2:9[7]c) and "find" (מצא; 2:9[7]d) often describes Israel's relationship with God (e.g., Deut 4:29; Isa 65:1). It is not necessary to distinguish completely among these possibilities, for a holistic interpretation that joins the political-economic and religious-cultic realms together soon becomes likely. In the woman's monologue that follows, she expresses befuddlement at being thwarted in pursuing her lusts and lovers (Hos 2:9[7]e–h).

c. Israel's Frustration with Harlotry (2:9[7]e–h)

YHWH's actions to block the woman's lusts (2:8[6]) and cause her lovers to disappear (2:9[7] d) lead to her frustration with harlotry: "So she will say, 'Let me go and return to my first husband, for it was better for me then than now!'" (2:9[7]e–h). Her words contrast the inferiority of "lovers" in the present with the superiority of YHWH in the past when he fulfilled her desires. Such frustration with her paramours is nevertheless not a genuine act of repentance, since her motivation is more pragmatic than remorseful: "For it was *better for me* then than now!" (2:9[7]h). Indeed, the estrangement that remains between husband and wife is exemplified by how Israel speaks only to herself and perhaps also her "lovers" in the monologues of Hos 2, but never to YHWH.

d. Israel's Ongoing Forgetfulness of YHWH the Giver (2:10[8])

YHWH thus highlights the root problem, namely, Israel's forgetfulness of the past: "On her part, she has not acknowledged [ידע] that I myself gave her the grain, the new wine, and the olive oil.

32. The fronting of the object clause ("her pathways") before the verb ("she will not find") is another instance of main clause emphasis (see n24, p. 104).

33. As already noted in the discussion of "The Literary Medium of Hosea's Message" in the introduction to Hosea, pp. 53–57.

34. Paul A. Kruger, "'I Will Hedge Her Way with Thornbushes' (Hosea 2,8): Another Example of Literary Multiplicity?," *BZ* 43 (1999): 92–99.

The silver I multiplied for her, but the gold they made for Baal!" (2:10[8]). This verse contains the first appearance of the verb ידע ("to know, acknowledge") in Hosea, a Hebrew root that is pivotal for the rest of the book (e.g., 2:22[20]; 4:1; 6:6). Although some English translations render this instance of ידע to indicate Israel's naiveté or unawareness of salvation history (e.g., "she has not known"; Hos 2:10[8]a), three features of Hos 2:10[8]a–b indicate that Israel has willfully forgotten her God or put YHWH out of her mind.[35]

The first is that the verse begins with an independent use of the personal pronoun וְהִיא ("on her part/as for her")—a pause in the discourse that foregrounds the verbal subject of Hos 2:10[8]a as the same woman whom Hosea just mentioned as pursuing her "lovers" (2:7[5], 9[7]).[36] Her boldness in apostasy is thus intentional rather than ignorant. Secondly, this verse uses the Hebrew verb נתן ("to give") to draw a stark contrast between YHWH who truly "gives" the blessings of creation and the useless paramours whom Israel believes "give" them (2:7[5]). Third and finally, the use of the first-person pronoun אָנֹכִי ("I") as emphatic verbal subject of נתן ("*I myself* gave"; 2:10[8]b) furnishes a pointed counterpart to the independent feminine pronoun וְהִיא that opens the verse (2:10[8]a). The cumulative force of Hos 2:10[8] suggests that Israel has not only deliberately forgotten YHWH in seeking her lovers but also that she recalls YHWH's past gifts well enough to seek them (though not him) once more. This theme of Israel's forgetfulness in the face of prosperity echoes the warnings of Moses in Deut 8.[37]

Hosea 2:10[8] also explores the synergy of religious and economic factors that impel Israel toward forgetfulness of YHWH. Most strikingly, the agricultural gifts from Israel's lovers have shifted from their everyday, physical terms in Hos 2:7[5] (i.e., "wool, flax, oil") to the rarer forms associated with ancient Near Eastern nature deities, much as in Deuteronomy (e.g., 7:13; 11:14; 33:28). In Hos 2:10[8]b, the term used for "grain" (דָּגָן) is the Hebrew cognate for Dagon, a widely venerated deity in the ancient Near East who was both the national god of the Philistines (Judg 16:23; 1 Sam 5:2–7) as well as the father to Baal in some Ugaritic texts.[38]

Similarly, Hos 2:10[8]b mentions YHWH's gift of "new wine" (*tîrôš*; תִּירוֹשׁ), the Hebrew cognate to *tiršu*/*trt*, a Canaanite deity of wine. Although some interpret the variations between Hos 2:7[5] and 2:10[8]b as differences in agricultural products,[39] the probability of a contemptuous reference to Canaanite gods increases greatly with Hos 7:14's mention of דָּגָן and תִּירוֹשׁ in an attack upon Israel's participation in the Baalistic ritual of gashing oneself (1 Kgs 18:28; cf. Hos 9:2).[40] By potentially alluding to Canaan's nature deities but then transferring their supposed power to the God of Israel, the rhetoric of Hos 2:10[8]b exemplifies how "[w]e are close to the claim of Yahweh to be *the* fertility god."[41]

The pagan overtones continue in Hos 2:10[8]c–d with the inclusion of precious metals among the

35. Carew, "To Know or Not to Know," 76–77.

36. *LDHB* §1.2 notes the role of forward-pointing pronouns in creating anticipation and slowing a discourse. On this characteristic feature of Hosea's prophecy, see discussion of "The Literary Medium of Hosea's Message" in the introduction to Hosea, pp. 53–57.

37. Carsten Vang, "When a Prophet Quotes Moses," 293–97.

38. J. F. Healey, "Dagon," in *DDD* 216–19.

39. E.g., Macintosh, *Hosea*, 56; Shlomo Naeh and Michael P. Weitzman, "*Tīrōš*—Wine or Grape? A Case of Metonymy," *VT* 44 (1994): 115–20.

40. As conceded by J. F. Healey, "Tirash," *DDD* 871–72. Cf. Day, "Hosea and the Baal Cult," 212–14. For a discussion of how the faith of Israel both adapts and rejects ancient Near Eastern religious ideas on a case-by-case basis, see Daniel I. Block, "Other Religions in Old Testament Theology," in *Biblical Faith and Other Religions: An Evangelical Assessment*, ed. David W. Baker (Grand Rapids: Kregel, 2004), 43–78; republished in *The Gospel according to Moses: Theological and Ethical Reflections on the Book of Deuteronomy* (Eugene, OR: Cascade, 2012), 200–36.

41. Andersen and Freedman, *Hosea*, 242, emphasis original.

items that YHWH's people associate with other deities, in this case the Canaanite god Baal: "The silver I multiplied for her, but the gold they made for Baal" (2:10[8]c–d). Whereas the previous lists only contained domestic products (2:7[5], 10[8]a–b), Hosea now broadens to an international scope. Silver and gold were not native to Canaan, which meant that Israel could only obtain them through trading agricultural commodities on the international market.[42] Later in Hosea, it becomes evident that Israel used these precious metals as raw materials for making cultic images (8:4–6; 13:2). In summary, then, Hos 2:10[8] links domestic agronomics and foreign trade in precious metals together under the guise of worshiping "Baal," originally the Canaanite god of fertility, but now also a metaphor for Israel's sinful synergy between economics and religion.[43]

3. YHWH's Removal of Agricultural Blessings (2:11–15[9–13])

Since Israel has still not gotten the message, YHWH must go further than simply making Israel's harlotry fruitless (cf. 2:8–10[8–6]). The persistence of Israel's harlotry (in every sense) necessitates that YHWH strip his apostate people of harlotry's perceived "blessings" (2:11[9]), expose harlotry's shamefulness (2:12[10]), and put an end to harlotry's joy (2:13[11]).

a. The Stripping of Harlotry's "Blessings" (2:11[9])

YHWH's quarrel against his people culminates in his removal of agricultural blessings in creation: "Therefore, I will return, and I will take my grain in its time, and my new wine in its season; and I will remove my wool and my flax, which cover her nakedness" (2:11[9]).[44] Earlier YHWH had sought to invite Israel's repentance and frustrate her harlotry (2:4–9[2–7]d), but these efforts had only led to a half-hearted desire on her part to "go and return [שׁוּב] to my first husband" (2:9[7]f–g).

Against the pragmatism of his estranged wife, YHWH responds pointedly with a "return" (שׁוּב; 2:11[9]a) of his own, not to provide the gifts sought by Israel in her materialism (2:8–9[6–7]) but to "take [away]" (לקח; 2:11[9]b) since she refuses to acknowledge their true source (2:10[8]). Israel had considered these agricultural goods to be hers (as in the monologue's six-fold mention of "my" in 2:7[5]e), but YHWH insists that he is the rightful owner of "*my* grain," "*my* new wine," "*my* wool," and "*my* flax" (2:11[9]b–c). The only thing his wife possesses is "*her* nakedness" (2:11[9]d; cf. Ezek 16:7–8).

b. The Exposure of Harlotry's Shamefulness (2:12[10])

The language of shaming then escalates with a discourse marker that marks the next stage of the argument: "But now [וְעַתָּה], I will uncover her degeneration/folly [נַבְלוּת] in the eyes of her lovers, and nobody will save her from my hand" (2:12[10]). The frequent translation of נַבְלוּת as "lewdness" (e.g., NASB, NIV, NKJV) suggests an act of sexual exposure, but the Hebrew term is unique to this verse and could derive from one of two different נבל roots. One root means "to be foolish" (e.g., Deut

42. John S. Holladay, Jr., "The Kingdoms of Israel and Judah: Political and Economic Centralization in the Iron IIA–B (ca. 1000–750 BCE)," in *The Archaeology of Society in the Holy Land*, ed. Thomas Evan Levy (London: Leicester University Press, 1998), 382.

43. On Hosea's use of "Baal" as a metaphor with both literal and figurative dimensions, see "Canaanite Nature Religion and 'Baal' in Israel during the Eighth Century BCE" in the introduction to Hosea, pp. 25–28.

44. Following Joüon §124d, the prepositional phrase לְכַסּוֹת אֶת־עֶרְוָתָהּ should be rendered as a descriptive genitive, "of covering her nakedness," or more smoothly in English as a relative clause, "which cover her nakedness."

32:6; Ps 14:1), while the other means "to languish/wither" (e.g., Ps 1:3; Isa 24:4).[45]

Since both etymologies are possible, the ambiguity of נַבְלוּת in both the human and natural realm creates an echo chamber of foolish woman and withering land, much like what we observed earlier in Hos 2.[46] And whatever this Hebrew term's precise sense, the key factor in Israel's fate is the shamefulness of public exposure when YHWH will no longer "cover" (כסה; 2:11[9]d) his people but will instead "uncover" (גלה; 2:12[10]a).[47] The irony is that "lovers," who apparently are both other nations and other gods, will witness her disgrace (2:12[10]a) but be powerless or unwilling to intervene since "nobody will save her from my hand" (2:12[10]b).

c. The End of Harlotry's Joy (2:13[11])

In keeping with the public setting of Hos 2:12[10], the following verses picture YHWH's abolition of cultic celebrations in a prosperous land: "I will put an end to all her rejoicing, her feasts, her new moon festivals and her Sabbaths, and all her appointed days!" (2:13[11]). It is difficult to know whether the occasions criticized here are perversions of the ordinances prescribed in pentateuchal law (e.g., Deut 16), but other eighth-century prophets indicate that Israel and Judah engaged in empty rituals that were characterized by misplaced joy. Penitence for sin should have been the order of the day. For instance, Isa 1:11–15 records YHWH's denunciation of new moon festivals and Sabbaths as a "trampling of my courts" (1:12), while Amos 5:21–23 similarly condemns Samaria for lavish offerings and noisy worship music that were not matched by fidelity to YHWH. Thus, the book of Hosea joins these other prophets in confronting a people whose syncretism is so entrenched that they are numb to the contradiction between their distance from YHWH and the extravagance of their religious observance.

d. The Destruction of Harlotry's "Blessings" (2:14[12])

Syncretistic worship in YHWH's name must result in the collapse of the Canaanite worldview that has ensnared Israel. Thus, YHWH vows, "I will ransack her vineyard and her fig trees, of which she said, 'They are a gift *to me* that my lovers gave *to me*!' But I will make them into a thicket, and the beast of the field will consume them" (2:14[12]). The selfishness of the wife's third and final monologue (2:14[12]c–d; cf. 2:7[5]d–e, 9[7]f–h) confirms that the gifts of creation need to disappear before she will realize the futility of pursuing her paramours. Once the land they supposedly nurture becomes a wilderness (2:14[12]e; cf. 2:5[3]), any remaining fruit in the midst of the desolation will be eaten by wild animals (2:14[12]f). From a religious perspective, the collapse of Canaan's harvests would prove definitively that YHWH has defeated the Canaanite nature deities on their home turf (cf. 1 Kgs 18). From an economic perspective, grapevines and fig trees were integral to survival in Canaan to such an extent that destruction of these crops was among the most catastrophic things that could happen.[48]

e. YHWH's Determination to Repay Pagan Practices (2:15[13])

To this point in Hos 2, the somewhat ambiguous character of Israel's idolatry as both religious and

45. Saul M. Olyan, "'In the Sight of Her Lovers': On the Interpretation of *Nablût* in Hos 2,12," *BZ* 36 (1992): 255–61.

46. Alice A. Keefe, *Woman's Body and the Social Body in Hosea*, LHBOTS 338 (London: Sheffield Academic, 2001), 214–16.

47. The NRSV's rendering of נַבְלוּת as "shamefulness" strikes a good balance in this regard between the folly of the action of the woman/land and the revulsion of the onlookers.

48. For example, in Hab 3:17 the impending destruction of "fig trees" (תְּאֵנָה) and "vines" (גְּפָנִים), the two items that

economic in nature has been described variously as liaisons with "lovers" (2:7[5], 14[12]) and "Baal" (2:10[8]). In the summary statement of Hos 2:15[13], the passage finally makes explicit the identity of YHWH's rivals: "Then I will repay her for the *days of the Baals*, to which she used to burn incense, and [when] she adorned herself with rings and jewelry, and walked *after her lovers*" (2:15[13] a–d). As an umbrella label for economic pursuit of "lovers" and religious syncretism with Baal, the polytheistic term "Baals" (בְּעָלִים) appropriately reflects the pluralism and complexity of syncretism in Israel during the eighth century BCE, including but not limited to veneration of YHWH and Baal the Canaanite god the storm.[49]

The penalty for Israel's compromise with pagan worldviews will be that YHWH will "repay, reckon" (פקד + עַל) sinful actions with their creational consequences. As in the case of YHWH's vow to "repay, reckon" (פקד + עַל) the sin of Jezreel (1:4–5), divine judgment against syncretism comes less in the form of legal retribution and more as the poetic justice of Israel's reaping the nonfruit of an infertile land (2:8[6], 11[9]).[50] In addition to Israel's barrenness, the practices of burning incense for Baals (2:15[13] b), self-adornment for cultic festivals (2:15[13]c), and pursuing fertility rituals (2:15[13]d) will yield nothing for Israel and thereby show the superiority of Yahwistic faith to all its competitors. Yet having described how YHWH justly repays Israel for past sins, the passage lingers in the theological uncertainty of what future could possibly remain between a gracious God and his amnesiac people. YHWH's quarrel speech ends with a cry of betrayal: "But she forgot me!" (2:15[13]e).[51] As James Luther Mays rightly notes, this conclusion "mixes anger and anguish, accusation and appeal; it summarizes in a word the guilt of Israel and the problem of Yahweh."[52] The signatory formula of "The Declaration of YHWH" (2:15[13]f) lends an air of finality to the estrangement spoken of in the preceding quarrel (2:4–15[2–13]).

4. YHWH's Restoration with His Household (2:16–25[14–23])

Suddenly and decisively, however, the reversal of estrangement comes in a heartfelt address of YHWH that falls into two parts. Following YHWH's invitation to recourtship that Israel gladly accepts (2:16–19[14–17]), restoration ripples through creation in "a chain reaction of the Lord's grace"[53] where the broken relationships among YHWH, his people, and land are fully healed (2:20–25[18–23]). The speech ends on a high note (2:25[23]) by alluding to the three children of Hosea and Gomer whose names earlier symbolized the turn from judgment to salvation (1:2–2:3[1]). YHWH's intention to "sow her for myself" (2:25[23]a) uses the same root as the name Jezreel ("God-Will-Sow"), while his determination to "show mercy" to Not-Shown-Mercy (2:25[23]b) and reclaim Not-My-People as "my people" (2:25[23]c–d) means that this family will come to embody the reconciliation that YHWH effects in his household.

a. YHWH's Invitation to Recourtship (2:16[14]a–b)

YHWH's restoration with his household begins unexpectedly with a declaration of love for his

headline the list of agricultural goods, is the test that will demand the greatest faith on the prophet's part.

49. J. Andrew Dearman, "Interpreting the Religious Polemics against Baal and the Baalim in the Book of Hosea," *OTE* 14 (2001): 9–25. Cf. Wolff, *Hosea*, 38–40.

50. Miller, *Sin and Judgment in the Prophets*, 8–9.

51. Though ungrammatical in English, the fronted word order in Hebrew could be rendered literally as "*me* she forgot!"

52. James Luther Mays, *Hosea: A Commentary*, OTL (Philadelphia: Westminster, 1969), 43.

53. Mordechai A. Friedman, "Israel's Response in Hosea 2:17b: 'You Are My Husband,'" *JBL* 99 (1980): 202.

estranged wife: "Therefore look! I am coaxing her . . ." (2:16[14]a–b). The discourse markers לָכֵן ("therefore") and הִנֵּה ("look, behold!") come together only here in the book. Previously the Hebrew conjunction לָכֵן had virtually become a refrain of judgment (2:8[6], 11[9]), much like the crash of a gavel in a modern courtroom. But just as estrangement appears irreversible (2:4–15[2–13]), the next occurrence of לָכֵן is brilliantly paired with the interjection הִנֵּה (2:16[14]a) to introduce a "non-judgmental 'judgment' speech" in which YHWH propounds "a delightful reversal of the expected, a bold rejection of the causal nexus between sin and punishment."[54] The ominousness of the preceding family quarrel dissipates into the happy scene of a groom "coaxing" (פתה)[55] his bride to come to him (2:16[14]b).

(1) A Surprising Journey to the Wilderness (2:16[14]c–d)

YHWH's speech also transforms the "wilderness" (מִדְבָּר), earlier a symbol of judgment (2:5[3]). But now it is the locale for an unexpected honeymoon (2:16[14]c; cf. 13:5) during which the divine groom desires that "I may speak to her heart" (וְדִבַּרְתִּי עַל־לִבָּהּ; 2:16[14]d). In a marvelous pun, the juxtaposition of derivatives from homonymic Hebrew roots דבר illustrates how YHWH "speaks" (דִּבֶּר) life-giving words into a lifeless "wilderness" (מִדְבָּר) where Israel once faced extermination due to her sins.[56]

(2) YHWH's Promise of Return from Exile (2:17[15]a)

Following this reversal, the wilderness undergoes its own transformation when YHWH attributes to it the characteristics of an abundant land. YHWH previously "took away" (לקח) the blessings of the land as punishment (2:11[9]), yet the wilderness will become the source of plenty where YHWH "gives" (נתן) to his people: "I will give to her vineyards from there, and the valley of Achor as a doorway to hope" (2:17[15]a). During the conquest era, Achor (עָכוֹר, meaning "trouble") was the place of Israel's first setback in Canaan when Achan was executed along with his household for keeping some of the spoils of Ai for himself (Josh 7:24–26). By reimagining the place of "trouble" as a "doorway to hope" (2:17[15]a), YHWH invites Israel to journey with him back to places of punishment that have now become places of redemption.

(3) Israel's Acceptance of YHWH's Invitation (2:17[15]b)

Israel will respond affirmatively to such a gracious invitation: "Then she will answer me from there as in the days of her youth, and as in the day she came up from the land of Egypt" (2:17[15]b). Here the "answer" (ענה) denotes Israel's positive reply to the previous verse's proposal of remarriage.[57] But then comes a fascinating twist in that the wilderness period joins Israel's exodus "from the land of Egypt" (2:17[15]b) as the beginning of her honeymoon with YHWH (cf. Deut 8:1–20; Hos 2:1–3[1:10–2:1]). In keeping with this tendency to recast salvation history in creative ways, Hosea will later transpose the motif of deliverance from Egypt into a *minor key* so as to depict Israel's "anti-exodus" of exile (e.g., 8:13; 9:3). The book also changes back into a *major key* when speaking of return from exile as the "new exodus" of return to the land (e.g., 11:11).[58]

54. Clines, "Hosea 2," 297.
55. The sexual connotations of enticement in the Hebrew root פתה can be seen in passages such as Judg 14:15; 16:5.
56. Landy, "Problems of Metaphor in Hosea," 51–52.
57. Friedman, "Israel's Response in Hosea 2:17b," 199–204.
58. Steven L. McKenzie, "Exodus Typology in Hosea," *ResQ* 22 (1979): 100–108.

(4) Israel's Choice of YHWH as Husband (2:18–19[16–17])

The day of eschatological remarriage to YHWH ("on that day"; 2:18[16]a)[59] will enable Israel to address her God directly: "You will call me, 'My husband,' and no longer call me, 'My Baal'" (2:18[16]b–c).[60] Israel had previously shown her obliviousness to YHWH's presence through her monologues about "lovers" (2:7[5], 14[12]; cf. 9[7]), but remarriage means that Israel will speak to YHWH personally as "my husband" (2:18[16] b) rather than seeking only his gifts as "my Baal" (2:18[16]c). The Hebrew term בַּעַל typically means "owner, master, lord" (e.g., Exod 21:28; Judg 19:22) but can refer by extension to a husband as leader of his wife and household (e.g., Exod 21:3; Deut 24:4). Baal was also a Canaanite high god of creation, as well as being an appellative for local deities of Canaan that Israel encountered at various places (e.g., Baal of Peor in Num 25:3, Baal-zebub in 2 Kgs 1:2).

For YHWH to replace the title "my Baal/master" (בַּעְלִי) with "my husband" (אִישִׁי) therefore corrects two significant distortions in Israel's understanding of YHWH. The first is that calling YHWH "my Baal/master" mischaracterizes his relationship to the created order as solely a provider of gifts. YHWH certainly outdoes Israel's "lovers" in this regard (e.g., 2:8–9[7–8]), but the fertility of the land must not be sought for its own sake as Israel did in mingling Yahwism with nature religion. This first misunderstanding leads to the second, namely, that the hierarchical epithet "my Baal/master" cannot reflect the kind of covenantal mutuality that YHWH seeks with his people.[61] Israel will instead call upon YHWH as "my husband" as a reflection of the exclusivity *and* intimacy of this relationship.

Prohibition of this pagan epithet goes beyond the need to address YHWH properly, for Israel must never call upon any "Baal" deities again: "Then I will remove the names of the Baals from her mouth, and they will not be remembered again by their names" (2:19[17]). The idiom "to remember by" (זכר + בְּ) alludes to the practice of Baal worshipers to invoke their deity's name loudly (1 Kgs 18:26) while gashing themselves to manipulate him/her into showing favor upon creation (1 Kgs 18:28). As noted in the commentary on Hos 2:10[8]b, Israel's participation in such Canaanite practices seems to lie behind Hosea's later statement that "on account of grain and new wine they keep gashing themselves" (7:14).[62] In contrast, Israel's reliance upon YHWH as creator and provider was intended to be unique in the ancient world for springing from a genuine covenant relationship as opposed to using mimetic ritual to force the deity's hand.[63]

b. YHWH's Covenant with Creation (2:20[18])

Now that Israel has suffered the ironic verdict of fertility upon a land supposedly nourished by fertility deities (cf. 2:11–15[9–13]), YHWH moves to reverse its destruction and confirm that he is the true source of creation's gifts. In what follows, he promises to enact peace in the animal realm (2:20[18]a) and the human realm (2:20[18]b–c).

(1) Peace in the Animal Realm (2:20[18]a)

The scope of reconciliation expands beyond YHWH and his people to include all the animals

59. The phrase "on that day" (בַּיּוֹם הַהוּא) in prophetic literature refers to an eschatological moment previously named, in this case "the day of Jezreel" (2:2[1:11]). In other Minor Prophets, "on that day" is usually synonymous with "the day of YHWH" (e.g., Amos 8:9; cf. 5:18; Joel 2:10–11).

60. The fronting of "on that day" (2:18[16]a) before the mention of words for Israel to speak (2:18[16]b) creates a temporal frame (*LDHB* §5.2), in this case highlighting the concreteness of the time that Israel's restoration will occur.

61. Dearman, *Hosea*, 124.

62. Day, "Hosea and the Baal Cult," 213–14.

63. On the vast gap between covenant in Yahwism and the mimetic worldview of Baalism, see Westphal, *God, Guilt, and Death*, 194–252.

that he has created: "Then I will make a covenant for them on that day, with the beast of the field, and with the bird of the sky and the crawler of the earth" (2:20[18]a). Earlier in Hos 2, creation itself had opposed Israel's syncretism with Canaanite nature religion when its agricultural goods were devoured by "the beast of the field" (חַיַּת הַשָּׂדֶה; 2:14[12]). But now, YHWH promises to restore order by making a covenant between Israel and a threefold list of animals in harmony with Israel which evokes the picture of God's original blessing upon creation (Gen 1:30) as well as its preservation and restoration through the Noahic covenant (Gen 7:14–15; 8:17, 19).[64] Although the exact phrase is not used in Hos 2, other OT prophetic passages texts speak of a similar "covenant of peace" (בְּרִית שָׁלוֹם; Isa 54:10; Ezek 34:25; 37:26) that involves the eschatological renovation of YHWH's creation to resemble the garden of Eden.[65]

(2) Peace in the Human Realm (2:20[18]b–c)

Cessation of hostility in creation also extends to the human realm: "But as for the bow, and the sword, and war, I will break them *from the land*" (2:20[18]b; cf. 1:7).[66] Here it is notable that the weaponry mentioned earlier in Hosea is again linked to the "land" (אֶרֶץ), the very place that had been tainted by Israel's bloodguilt with "Jezreel," that is, "God-Will-Sow" in Hebrew (יִזְרְעֶאל; 1:4–7). Human wars always have destructive consequences for creation,[67] but the end of military conflict and the ensuing renewal of creation will liberate the people of God to "lie down in trust" (2:20[18]c; cf. Ps 4:9[8]).

c. YHWH's Covenant with "You"—Israel (2:21–22[19–20])

YHWH announces his next act of restoration through an unexpected shift in grammatical person. Whereas the previous verse speaks of YHWH accomplishing peace in creation for "them" (2:20[18]), a somewhat ambiguous group that seems to be Israel as a microcosm of all humanity, the God of Israel now turns to speak personally and directly to his people as "you" (compare a similar rhetorical surprise in 2:8[6]).

(1) The Bride-Price of Covenant Relationship (2:21[19])

Turning to address his people directly, YHWH declares that he will heal the rift between himself and Israel through remarriage: "So I will betroth *you* to myself forever. I will betroth *you* to myself with righteousness and justice, with devotion and mercies" (2:21[19]). Compared to other OT references to betrothal (e.g., Exod 22:15[16]; Deut 20:7; 2 Sam 3:14), Hos 2:21[19]'s threefold use of the Hebrew root ארשׂ ("to betroth, become engaged to a woman") contains a rather unusual description of the betrothal gift to the bride's family. The ancient Near Eastern practice of a prospective son-in-law bringing a gift to the bride's father, who accepts the gift on behalf of the family and grants the couple permission to enter a betrothal period,[68] is here replaced by the arresting image of YHWH unilaterally binding Israel to himself "with righteousness and justice, with devotion and mercies" (2:21[19]b). In a manner that anticipates the New Testament, the holiness of YHWH in "righteousness and justice"

64. Dell, "Hosea, Creation, and Wisdom," 416.

65. Bernard F. Batto, "The Covenant of Peace: A Neglected Ancient Near Eastern Motif," in *In the Beginning: Essays on Creation Motifs in the Ancient Near East and the Bible*, Siphrut 9 (Winona Lake, IN: Eisenbrauns, 2013), 175–98.

66. The fronting of the list of weaponry ("bow," "sword," "war") serves to establish a new topical frame (see *LDHB* §5.1). The slowing of the discourse maximizes the rhetorical force of the verb that refers backwards to its direct objects: "I will break them from the land" (2:20[18]b).

67. Hilary Marlow, *Biblical Prophets and Contemporary Environmental Ethics: Re-Reading Amos, Hosea and First Isaiah* (Oxford: Oxford University Press, 2009), 178.

68. Block, "Marriage and Family in Ancient Israel," 57–58.

is perfectly balanced with "devotion and mercies" when YHWH both takes the initiative for, and pays the cost of, redeeming his people. YHWH's use of his own covenant attributes to pay the "bride-price" (if it can even be called such) is highly unique in Israel's cultural context.

(2) The Intimacy of Covenant Relationship (2:22[20])

The result of YHWH taking such countercultural steps (2:21[19]) is the reestablishment of an intimate relationship with his people: "I will betroth you to myself in faithfulness, that you might know YHWH" (2:22[20]). The Hebrew root ידע ("to know") frequently serves as a euphemism for sexual relations (e.g., Gen 4:17; 1 Kgs 1:4), though the OT contrasts with literature from cultures around Israel in that YHWH is never depicted as a gendered being who engages in sexual relations.[69] Even so, it is astounding that Hosea's prophecy draws upon marital imagery to convey the intimacy of YHWH's covenant with Israel at a time of syncretism with Canaanite fertility deities.

d. YHWH's Reconciliation of Nature and Israel (2:23–24[21–22])

After he has reestablished his covenant with the natural world (2:20[18]) and Israel (2:21–22 [19–20]), YHWH announces the final step of reconciling these creatures of his to one another. Through four repetitions of the Hebrew root ענה ("to answer"), the passage records a series of antiphonal responses among YHWH, the natural world, and people: "And on that day I will *answer*— The Declaration of YHWH—I will *answer* the heavens, and they, in turn, will *answer* the earth; the earth will *answer* the grain, the new wine, and the olive oil" (2:23–24[21–22]a).[70] Much like Israel in the wilderness first "answered" (ענה) YHWH's invitation to remarriage (Hos 2:17[15]b), YHWH will reverse creation's desolation through an "answer" (ענה) to the life-giving "heavens" (2:23[21] a, c). And just as the earth had been stripped bare due to Israel's apostasy with Canaanite nature gods (2:9–14[7–12]; cf. 1 Kgs 17:1, 7), the heavenly "answer" (ענה) of rain (2:23[21]d) will cause to sprout forth earth's "answer" (ענה) of "the grain, the new wine, and the olive oil" (2:24[22]a).

Finally, this trio of agricultural gifts that Israel had previously forfeited for seeking them from other deities (cf. 2:10–11[8–9]) join in greeting Israel when "they, in turn, will answer Jezreel" (2:24[22]b). In Hos 1, the sign-act of Jezreel ("God-Will-Sow") had symbolized the reaping of famine as the consequence of Israel's sinful sowing in the land (1:2–5). But here this name is changed into a sign of fruitful reunion between people and land, two of the members of YHWH's household. The superiority of the God of Israel to "lovers" (2:7[5], 9[7]) and "Baal" (2:10[8]), who supposedly guarantee fertility, thus lies in usurping their supposed authority, first by withdrawing the agricultural gifts they were thought to provide, then in restoring these blessings after "God-Will-Sow" (i.e., Israel) acknowledges their true source. The created order will then be fully reconciled to Israel/Jezreel.

e. YHWH's Reconciliation with His People (2:25[23])

Following the restoration of land and its produce (2:23–24[21–22]), the sphere of God's sowing shifts

69. Cf. Keefe, *Woman's Body and the Social Body in Hosea*, 49.

70. Two literary elements are significant for slowing the discourse. First, the fronted word order of "on that day" (2:23[21] a) highlights the temporal frame (*LDHB* §5.2) of YHWH's vow to reconcile nature to Israel (2:23[21]b–24[22]), as well as pointing backwards to two instances of "on that day" (vv. 18[16]a, 20[18]a). Second, each clause effects a pause through repetition of the preceding element of creation just mentioned (e.g., "heavens" in v. 23[21]c–d, "earth" in vv. 23[21]d–24[22] a), a discourse feature known as tail-head linkage (*LDHB* §1.6).

to the people themselves who will dwell in a verdant place: "Then I will sow her for myself in the land" (2:25[23]a). This clause continues the agricultural imagery that underlies the identification of Israel as "Jezreel" (2:24[22]b), yet with the twist that the sowing metaphor undergoes a change in grammatical gender. While "Jezreel" is a masculine noun, the reconciling action of YHWH takes "her" (i.e., a third-person feminine pronoun) as object of the Hebrew verb זרע ("to sow"; 2:25[23]a). The common proposal to harmonize the pronouns misses the rhetorical point of this shift,[71] namely, that the people are once again portrayed as YHWH's wife rather than as children of a motherly land.[72] By drawing again on the marriage metaphor, the first-person expression of YHWH sowing his people "to/for myself [לִי]" (2:25[23]a) represents the consummation of the remarriage that was initiated by the betrothal formula ("I will betroth you *to myself* [לִי]"; 2:21–22[19–20]a).[73]

Similar reversals upon the two names of Hosea's other children accompany the completion of YHWH's reconciliation with "Jezreel." YHWH declares that "I will show mercy to Not-Shown-Mercy; and I will say to Not-My-People, 'You are my people'" (2:25[23]b–c). Earlier in Hosea the trio of names had served as sign-acts of estrangement and divine judgment (1:4, 6, 9) for being "children of harlotry" (2:6[4]). But after YHWH negates the negation of covenant relationship as originally signified by the children's names (2:24b–25d[22b–23d]), the child Lo-Ammi speaks to YHWH on behalf of his siblings: "And he [Not-My-People] will say, 'My God'" (2:25[23]e–f). The children have been silent bystanders to this point in YHWH's speech of reconciliation, so it is especially poignant that the climax should arrive through a verbal affirmation by the child whose name means "Not-My-People." It is fitting, then, that the third and final child of Hosea and Gomer has the last word in confessing on behalf of YHWH's people, "[You are] my God" (2:25[23]f; cf. 1:8–9).

Canonical and Theological Significance

The book of Hosea uses the missiological methods of *contextualization* to engage creatively with the challenging world around Israel. By following this book's example of seeking middle ground between withdrawing fearfully from culture and engaging syncretistically, the people of God today can develop the same posture of discernment in communicating Hosea's prophecy to a new generation. This ability is especially critical in an age that has often found Hosea's means of communicating the message of estrangement leading to reconciliation with God to be irrelevant or offensive. Most notably, some strands of feminist criticism have argued that the sexually charged language of Hos 2 is misogynistic and consequently incompatible with modern views on gender relations.

But much as a robust understanding of contextualization helps the missionary avoid the trap of cultural imperialism, the same tool on the communicator's workbench can aid in overcoming the anachronisms that are sometimes imposed on

71. E.g., the text-critical emendation proposed by *BHS*; compare the dropping of this suggestion in *BHQ*.

72. Cf. Braaten, "Earth Community in Hosea 2," 195–96.

73. Andersen and Freedman, *Hosea*, 288.

Hosea. In what follows, an examination of the prophet's marriage with Gomer within its ancient Near Eastern framework will demonstrate how the culturally specific layers of the book serve its timeless purpose as God's revelation by speaking both *to* and *through* time-bound human cultures.

1. Gendered Language in Hosea and the Feminist Critique

The book of Hosea uses descriptions of sexual shaming that are rightly troubling to modern readers. Following chapter 1's characterization of the prophet Hosea as God's symbol of a wronged husband, chapter 2 proclaims that his wife's sexual promiscuity must result in public humiliation in the form of being stripped naked (2:5[3], 12[10]) and private confinement in her home away from the "lovers" who fornicate with her (2:7–8[5–6]). On the other side of the marriage metaphor, the passage portrays God as the cuckold (2:10[8]) who nonetheless seeks reconciliation despite her waywardness (2:16[14]).

Feminist critics have raised two important objections to this use of gendered language in depicting the tumultuous relationship between YHWH and Israel. On the one hand, the graphic imagery used to condemn the woman's insatiable lust for "lovers" (2:7[5], 9[7]) has led to the charge that the book of Hosea engages in *pornoprophetics*, that is, the obsession with female sexuality as an object to be controlled and used by men.[74] On the other hand, the description of Gomer's punishment of public exposure and private confinement as appropriate to her sexual crimes has raised the protest that Hosea is an androcentric book that views the battering of women by their male partners as inconsequential or even necessary. Renita Weems captures well the abhorrent character of such a conclusion: "What in the image of a naked, mangled female body grips the religious imagination? What can humiliating women and mutilating their bodies have to do with talk about God's love for a people?"[75] In the view of these feminist scholars, the book of Hosea embodies the sort of ancient patriarchal ideology that modern people must actively resist.[76] The prevalence of domestic violence by men against women in today's world, often tragically using the Bible as justification, means that such accusations against the book of Hosea must be taken with utmost seriousness by those who hold that the Scriptures possess authority for today.[77]

74. Athalya Brenner, "Pornoprophetics Revisited: Some Additional Reflections," *JSOT* 70 (1996): 63–86; T. Drorah Setel, "Prophets and Pornography: Female Sexual Imagery in Hosea," in *Feminist Interpretation of the Bible*, ed. Letty M. Russell (Philadelphia: Westminster, 1985), 86–95.

75. Renita J. Weems, *Battered Love: Marriage, Sex, and Violence in the Hebrew Prophets* (Minneapolis: Augsburg Fortress, 1995), xvii.

76. The most sustained critiques of Hosea in this regard are Sherwood, *The Prostitute and the Prophet*; and Rut Törnkvist, *The Use and Abuse of Female Sexual Imagery in the Book of Hosea: A Feminist Critical Approach to Hos 1–3*, Acta Universitatis Upsaliensis 7 (Uppsala: Uppsala Universitet, 1998).

77. For a recent example of a work that takes seriously both the OT as authoritative Scripture as well as feminist objections to the OT, see Andrew Sloane, ed., *Tamar's Tears: Evangelical*

2. Contextualization within and after Hosea

However, it is important to observe that not all feminist scholars take such a dim view of Hosea. While acknowledging the need to expose how the book of Hosea has often been used to justify sexual oppression of women, Alice Keefe is one such feminist scholar who challenges the applicability of the feminist concern for individual liberation in this instance. She observes that a fixation on individual liberation will overlook the dignity afforded to women within the interpersonal web of a collectivist society like ancient Israel:

> When feminist (and other) readers look at the inscription of female sexuality in the book of Hosea and see the female body only as an individual body sexually constrained by the powers of patriarchy, they overlook the corporate and corporeal dimensions of human meaning which were constitutive of the fabric of life in ancient Israel and are at work in Hosea's imagery.[78]

Although Keefe does not use the term "contextualization" in this summary, her observations on the book of Hosea dovetail closely with missiological research on the cultural differences between guilt-based and shame-based approaches to communication.[79] Guilt-based communication places a premium on individual vindication according to an external moral standard, while shame-based communication relies more on the social context of the community and thus looks more to the group for moral guidance. A full survey of these cultural differences is not necessary here,[80] but it is notable that public humiliation of the offender in shame-based communication is the expected norm when the offended party occupies a higher social stratum than the offender.[81] Since the shame of sin matters more in its collective than individual dimensions (again, as a spectrum more than a dichotomy), the entire community restores its honor by dealing publicly with a dishonorable act.

Yet in such societies with a high degree of collective consciousness, this tit-for-tat system of maintaining order in relationships, always at the expense of the offender's

Engagements with Feminist Old Testament Hermeneutics (Eugene, OR: Pickwick, 2012).

78. Keefe, *Woman's Body and the Social Body in Hosea*, 160.

79. E.g., Timothy Tennent, *Theology in the Context of World Christianity: How the Global Church Is Influencing the Way We Think about and Discuss Theology* (Grand Rapids: Zondervan, 2009), 77–101.

80. It is important to note that the usual classification of societies into bifurcated "honor-shame cultures" and "guilt-innocence cultures" is overstated. As Wu observes, "There are no guilt cultures or shame cultures. Or, perhaps more accurately, *all* cultures are shame cultures, and *all* cultures are guilt cultures. Thus, what differs between them (and their individual members) is not which of these dynamics they operate on, but how these concepts are variously configured, related, and articulated" (*Honor, Shame, and Guilt*, 178).

81. Joshua Moon, "Honor and Shame in Hosea's Marriages," *JSOT* 39 (2015): 346–47; Victor H. Matthews, "Honor and Shame in Gender-Related Legal Situations in the Hebrew Bible," in *Gender and Law in the Hebrew Bible and the Ancient Near East*, ed. Victor H. Matthews, Bernard M. Levinson, and Tikva Frymer-Kensky, LHBOTS 226 (Sheffield: Sheffield Academic, 2004), 98–100.

dignity, means that "selfless love" is the "missing middle," as missiologist Alex Toorman notes.[82] Thus the theological concept of grace takes on heightened significance in Hosea's world precisely by defying cultural expectations that find the concept of God's unmerited favor to be incoherent. This observation suggests that, troubling as it might be to modern sensibilities, Hosea uses gendered marital imagery precisely because of its ability to emphasize the strongly relational dimension of YHWH's commitment to Israel in a manner that surpasses the more detached imagery of the legal realm. Put another way, divine grace becomes even more amazing in cultures that understand sin more in public and collective categories than in private and individual categories!

These conclusions find support in the clustering of "shame" language in Hos 2. While the abrupt shift from disgrace to restoration in Hos 2:16–17[14–15] has proven jolting for interpreters, such a logical disjunction actually provides the crux of YHWH's proclamation of grace and forgiveness by asserting that reconciliation will come unexpectedly after public humiliation.[83] In keeping with the frequent usage of "shame" language elsewhere in the OT Prophets,[84] Hos 2 describes Gomer's sin of apostasy as "shameful" (2:7[5]) while also describing her punishment as a public exposure of her "degeneration/folly" (2:12[10]).[85] This punishment is followed not by ostracization, as is the standard in traditional cultures that expect a shamed female to disappear,[86] but an astounding restoration of the relationship when YHWH leads Israel back to the wilderness to "speak to her heart" (2:16[14]) and reenact the honeymoon of the exodus-wilderness period (2:17[15]). Unlike most males in traditional societies, then, YHWH does not go to extremes to "save face" by disassociating from the one who caused him to "lose face."[87] Hosea's selective engagement with culture again underscores how an awareness of contextualization can highlight the unique features of the prophet's message by tracing its continuities and discontinuities with the surrounding environment.

Another area in which moderate feminist studies prove helpful is in elucidating the shock value of Hosea's imagery upon a predominantly male audience.[88] For an audience immersed in traditional expectations of men, it would have

82. Alex Toorman, "Selfless Love: The Missing Middle in Honor/Shame Cultures," *Evangelical Missions Quarterly* 47 (April 2011): 160–67.

83. Clines, "Hosea 2," 297.

84. Johanna Stiebert, "Shame and Prophecy: Approaches Past and Present," *BibInt* 8 (2000): 255–75.

85. See n45 above for this rendering.

86. The most extreme example in modern times being the abomination of "honor killing," in which male relatives banish a female relative who has brought shame upon the family by killing her publicly.

87. See the groundbreaking discussion of "face" as a universal human phenomenon by Christopher L. Flanders, *About Face: Rethinking Face for 21st-Century Mission*, American Society of Missiology Monograph Series 9 (Eugene, OR: Pickwick, 2011).

88. On this tactic in Hosea generally, see Susan E. Haddox, *Metaphor and Masculinity in Hosea*, StBibLit 141 (New York: Lang, 2011).

been deeply offensive to be attacked using the language of female promiscuity (e.g., 1:2). Moreover, the accusation that the leaders of Israel represented illegitimate "children of harlotry" (2:6[4]) would have struck at the heart of an unjust economic system that had itself overturned traditional lines of inheritance from fathers to sons.[89] Hence the rationale for attacking Gomer (and Israel) using such loaded sexual terminology is not to reinforce sexist views, as some feminist scholars have argued, but rather to turn the unjust hierarchies of gender relations in eighth-century Israel on their head using the very stereotypes that empowered their exploitation of women and the poor.[90] As in Hosea's references to Canaanite nature religion, it is crucial to recognize what Hosea grants about gender relations for argument's sake in order to subvert misunderstandings and redirect Israel toward theological orthodoxy.

In a paradoxical way, the interpreter's awareness of contextualization in Hosea also provides the key to recovering transcontextual interpretation of the book. Although modern Western societies on the whole tend toward individualism, there still exist within them collectivistic subcultures that prioritize honor and shame, such as any sphere in which the need to maintain one's reputation exists alongside intense scrutiny (e.g., social media, athletic teams) and/or hierarchical relationships (e.g., the corporate boardroom, the middle-school courtyard). These environments mirror ancient Near Eastern societies like Israel in that "saving face" in the eyes of others is never far from the consciousness of the group's members. Even in modern Western societies, there can be great overlap with ancient Israel in that "losing face" often does such irreparable damage to one's reputation that the social expectation for all parties involved is for the shamed party to vanish.[91]

But it is precisely at this point that the God of Hosea reclaims his people in a countercultural way by restoring them publicly to their original position. The sexual imagery of the book of Hosea therefore needs translation so that modern audiences do not consign its message to the anachronistic extremes of voyeurism on the one hand, or repression on the other. Instead, connecting the dynamics of honor and shame in Hosea to their modern analogues may provide the best

89. Marvin L. Chaney, "Accusing Whom of What? Hosea's Rhetoric of Promiscuity," in *Distant Voices Drawing Near: Essays in Honor of Antoinette Clark Wire*, ed. Marvin L. Chaney and Holly E. Hearon (Collegeville, MN: Liturgical Press, 2004), 106.

90. Phyllis A. Bird, "To Play the Harlot: An Inquiry into an Old Testament Metaphor," in *Missing Persons and Mistaken Identities: Women and Gender in Ancient Israel*, OBT (Minneapolis: Augsburg Fortress, 1997), 236. I would register two minor disagreements with Bird's position, however. First, the use of the Hebrew root זנה as a metaphor for political and economic apostasy does not rule out the multivalency of the metaphor in serving also as a literal indictment against sexual activity at cultic sites. Second, Hosea's use of gendered language does not presume approval but rather critical engagement.

91. The Western tendency to misunderstand "face" as a primarily Eastern phenomenon is well discussed by Flanders, *About Face*, 44–74. For a comprehensive study of honor, shame, and guilt as universal human phenomena, see Wu, *Honor, Shame, and Guilt*.

avenue to communicate the timeless truths of this book. By vindicating the ancient book from the modern charges of obsolescence and misogyny, the voice of Hosea's prophecy can then speak afresh to the people of God in an age of globalization and social media where the cultural values of honor and shame are making a rapid comeback.[92]

92. On which see David Brooks, "The Shame Culture," *The New York Times*, March 15, 2016.

Hosea 3:1–5

CHAPTER 4

C. Israel's Coming Exile and Restoration: Prophetic Sign-Acts, Part II

Main Idea of the Passage

Hosea's irrational love for his wife, who became the lover of another, will bring reunion following a temporary separation between them. His life symbolizes how YHWH's chastening love toward his estranged people will reconcile them to himself following the temporary deprivations of exile.

Literary Context

The prose narrative in Hos 3 offers a brief respite after the emotional intensity of the poetic speeches in chapter 2. The prophet's life again takes center stage, as in chapter 1, but the children of Hosea and Gomer have now dropped out of the picture. Such an omission appears to reflect the modification of the marriage metaphor in Hos 2:6–7[4–5] so that the woman now refers to YHWH's entire household of people and land (see commentary above). Therefore, chapter 3 furnishes an appropriate conclusion to the various relational metaphors found in the previous chapters.

In addition, the mention of YHWH's loving discipline for his people as a time of abstention from their sinful loves for corrupt societal institutions such as kingship and cult (3:4) anticipates the covenant lawsuits against different pillars of Israelite society that feature in Hos 4–10. The concluding turn from judgment to salvation in Hos 3:5 also sets the stage for the longer presentation of this important motif in Hos 11. By linking thematically to what precedes and follows, the five compact verses of chapter 3 provide an important transition between chapters 1–3 and 4–11, the first two literary units of the book.[1]

1. Rainer Kessler, "Hosea 3—Entzug oder Hinwendung Gottes?," *ZAW* 120 (2008): 575–81.

Translation and Exegetical Outline

(See next page.)

Structure and Literary Form

Although Hos 3's opening reference to "again" (עוֹד; 3:1a) represents a continuation of the sign-act narrative from Hos 1, these two chapters exhibit several notable differences in their structure and literary form. First, whereas chapter 1 is an extended account of the harlotry that characterizes Hosea's wife and children, in which the prophet never speaks, chapter 3 records a shorter account of Hosea's marriage and speech to an adulterous woman without any mention of the prophet's children.

Second, each sign-act of the prophet's family in Hos 1 is completed before YHWH offers an explanation of its symbolism. This reflects the usual pattern in other prophetic sign-acts (e.g., the potter/clay sign-act in Jer 18:1–10). But in chapter 3, the command for Hosea to love a woman (3:1b–c) leads immediately to YHWH's explanation of how this marriage symbolizes his love for the Israelites (3:1d). The sign-act itself does not begin (3:2) until part of the explanation has been given (3:1b–f).

Third and related to this, Hosea's obedience to the command (3:2) is followed by his own elaboration upon the sign-act (3:3–5), rather than YHWH's address to the people, as in chapter 1. Taken together, these three modifications in chapter 3 highlight Hosea's personal stake in the larger drama of judgment and salvation while also simplifying the marriage metaphor considerably.

This sign-act narrative's message of salvation that follows judgment, along with the passing reference to "David their king" (3:5b), has spawned the theory that Hos 3 has been reworked by a Judahite editor in Hezekiah's time, several decades after the fall of the Northern Kingdom of Samaria.[2] In such redactional proposals, the operative presupposition is that any reference to eschatological salvation and/or the

2. E.g., Brevard S. Childs, *Introduction to the Old Testament as Scripture* (Philadelphia: Fortress, 1979), 378–79.

Hosea 3:1–5

	Hebrew	English	Outline
			C. Israel's Coming Exile and Restoration: Prophetic Sign-Acts, Part II (3:1–5)
3:1a	וַיֹּאמֶר יְהוָה אֵלַי עוֹד	YHWH said to me again,	1. YHWH's Command and Explanation: The Sign-Act of Irrational Love (3:1)
1b	לֵךְ	"Go,	a. The Command: Love Another's Lover (3:1a–c)
1c	אֱהַב־אִשָּׁה אֲהֻבַת רֵעַ	love a woman loved by a paramour,	
	וּמְנָאָפֶת	that is, an adulteress,	
1d	כְּאַהֲבַת יְהוָה אֶת־בְּנֵי יִשְׂרָאֵל	just as YHWH loves the children of Israel,	b. The Explanation: YHWH's Irrational Love for the Unlovable (3:1d–f)
1e	וְהֵם פֹּנִים אֶל־אֱלֹהִים אֲחֵרִים	though they are turning aside to other gods	
1f	וְאֹהֲבֵי אֲשִׁישֵׁי עֲנָבִים׃	and they are lovers of raisin cakes."	
			2. Hosea's Obedience and Explanation: The Sign-Act as Exile and Restoration (3:2–3)
2	וָאֶכְּרֶהָ לִּי בַּחֲמִשָּׁה עָשָׂר כָּסֶף וְחֹמֶר שְׂעֹרִים וְלֶתֶךְ שְׂעֹרִים׃	So I bought her for myself with fifteen shekels of silver and a homer-and-a-half of barley.	a. Hosea's Obedience: Paying the Bride-Price (3:2)
3a	וָאֹמַר אֵלֶיהָ	Then I said to her,	b. Hosea's Explanation to his Wife: Separation and Reunion (3:3)
3b	יָמִים רַבִּים תֵּשְׁבִי לִי	"For many days you will dwell as mine.	(1) A Temporary Separation (3:3a–d)
3c	לֹא תִזְנִי	You must not play the harlot,	
3d	וְלֹא תִהְיִי לְאִישׁ	nor may you belong to a man.	
3e	וְגַם־אֲנִי אֵלָיִךְ׃	Yet even on my part, I will be with you."	(2) The Certainty of Reunion (3:3e)
			c. Hosea's Explanation to Israel: Exile and Restoration (3:4–5)
4a	כִּי יָמִים רַבִּים יֵשְׁבוּ בְּנֵי יִשְׂרָאֵל	"Indeed, for many days the children of Israel will dwell	(1) Temporary Deprivations of Exile (3:4)
	אֵין מֶלֶךְ וְאֵין שָׂר	without king and without prince,	(a) No More Leaders (3:4a)
4b	וְאֵין זֶבַח וְאֵין מַצֵּבָה	without sacrifice and without sacred pillar,	(b) No More Rituals (3:4b)
4c	וְאֵין אֵפוֹד וּתְרָפִים׃	and without ephod and teraphim.	(c) No More Guidance (3:4c)
5a	אַחַר יָשֻׁבוּ בְּנֵי יִשְׂרָאֵל	Later the children of Israel will return	(2) The Coming Restoration of the Exiles (3:5)
5b	וּבִקְשׁוּ אֶת־יְהוָה אֱלֹהֵיהֶם וְאֵת דָּוִד מַלְכָּם	and they will seek YHWH their God and David their king.	(a) Sincere Repentance (3:5a–b)
5c	וּפָחֲדוּ אֶל־יְהוָה וְאֶל־טוּבוֹ	So they will tremble before YHWH and his goodness	(b) Lasting Reverence (3:5c)
	בְּאַחֲרִית הַיָּמִים׃	in the latter days."	

Southern Kingdom of Judah must be a secondary development in a prophetic book that originally focused on God's judgment against Samaria.

While insertions of this sort are certainly possible within the context of ancient Near Eastern scribal culture,[3] the confidence with which redaction critics identify later additions in Hos 3:5 is questionable.[4] As Grace Emmerson has shown, the logic of the chapter demands that the provisional suspension of Israel's institutions (3:4) be followed by their restoration (3:5),[5] much as do the antecedent predictions in Lev 26; Deut 4:25–31; 29–30. The fourfold repetition of the keyword "to love" (אהב; 3:1c–f) also binds the chapter together, so that removing Hos 3:5 as secondary is to miss the passage's integral point that YHWH's discipline is part of a longer process of loving his people and drawing them back to him.

Thus, the elements in this chapter that redaction critics have attributed to the hindsight of a later Judahite scribe are more likely due to a theological emphasis on the sovereignty of YHWH that overrides the historical sins of Samaria and Judah. By offering the promise of salvation before judgment has even begun, Hos 3:5 and 14:2[1] preemptively offer an invitation to "repent/return" (שׁוב) that reverberates into the exilic period and through the rest of the Book of the Twelve.[6]

Explanation of the Text

The sign-act narrative of Hos 3 is structured as two halves. The first and shorter part involves YHWH's command and explanation of the sign-act to Hosea (3:1). The second and longer part concerns Hosea's obedience (3:2) and explanation of the sign-act, first to his wife (3:3) and then to Israel (3:4–5). As in chapter 1, the family life of the prophet is a means to the end of portraying the irrational love that YHWH shows toward his unlovable people. The human party in the marriage metaphor shifts almost imperceptibly in the passage from Hosea's wife (3:2–3) to the people as a whole (3:4–5), thereby indicating that she is a corporate symbol for all Israel.

1. YHWH's Command and Explanation: The Sign-Act of Irrational Love (3:1)

Interpreters of Hos 3 often wonder about the identity of the prophet's unnamed wife. If she is not Gomer, as some have suggested, then the marriage metaphor of chapters 1–3 quickly implodes. The substitution of another woman for Gomer as Hosea's wife would contradict the persistence of YHWH's love for Israel as depicted in chapters 1–2. Yet if Hosea's wife is Gomer, as most interpreters have held, there remains the problem of when a divorce took place so that God could command Hosea to marry her again. Both possibilities for

3. John H. Walton and D. Brent Sandy, *The Lost World of Scripture: Ancient Literary Culture and Biblical Authority* (Downers Grove, IL: IVP Academic, 2013), 72.

4. Cf. Clements, "Understanding the Book of Hosea," 410.

5. Grace I. Emmerson, *Hosea: An Israelite Prophet in Judean Perspective*, JSOTSup 28 (Sheffield: Sheffield Academic, 1984), 12.

6. LeCureux, *The Thematic Unity of the Book of the Twelve*, 77–80.

the woman's identity thus encounter numerous difficulties.

Related to this, could some degree of harmonization be achieved by regarding the events of chapter 3 as a parallel account to chapter 1? Or should Hos 3 still be interpreted as subsequent to Hos 1, but with some passage of time during which Gomer might have fallen into adultery? These questions defy easy answers. But the desire to resolve these issues often reflects a concern for the human side of the metaphor to the neglect of the divine side, in contrast to how the passage presents itself. What follows, then, is a brief case for interpreting chapter 3 as Hosea's remarriage to Gomer, but paying greater attention to the theme of God's unthinkable love for an obstinate people. In fact, it is precisely the irrationality of YHWH's dealings with Israel that causes any attempt to impose logical coherence on the marriage metaphor to break down. The grace of Israel's God surpasses human categories so that every humanly comprehensible metaphor and sign-act will remain inadequate to portray the tenacity of his devotion.

a. The Command: Love Another's Lover (3:1a–c)

The story begins with a command to the prophet: "YHWH said to me *again*, 'Go, love a woman loved by a paramour, that is, an adulteress'" (3:1a–c). Here the adverb "again" (עוֹד) could pair grammatically with either the preceding verb "said" (3:1a) or the subsequent command for Hosea to "go, love a woman" (3:1b–c). Whichever rendering is chosen,[7] the reference to "again" (3:1a) likely describes a time later than chapter 1's description of "when YHWH first spoke through Hosea" (1:2a). What is more, both chapters portray Hosea joining himself to a woman of questionable reputation, earlier a "wife of harlotry" (1:2d) and now "a woman loved by a paramour, that is, an adulteress" (3:1c).

Thus the present command to "love" (3:1) such a woman is no more or no less an interpretive problem than in Hos 1, a chapter that similarly focuses on the symbolism of Hosea's family more than their historical referent. Nevertheless, YHWH surprisingly commands Hosea to remarry an unfaithful wife (cf. Deut 24:1–4), who is explicitly also called an "adulteress" (a participle from the root נאף; cf. Exod 20:14; Hos 4:2). In contrast to the general verb זנה ("to commit harlotry"; cf. Hos 1:2), which denotes any sexual activity outside of marriage, the sin denoted by the verb נאף refers more specifically to the liaisons of husbands or wives with someone not their spouse (e.g., Prov 6:32; Jer 23:14).

At face value, the use of נאף and the narrative sequence of Hos 1–3 suggest that Gomer violated her marriage vows to Hosea sometime after the events of chapter 1. However, details about her sins are neither forthcoming nor relevant for interpreting the metaphor. Like Hos 1, chapter 3 does not dwell on the metaphor's human dimension but instead portrays the strangeness of Hosea being told to "love" an adulteress who is already "loved" by another man (3:1c). Adultery was punishable by death in ancient Israel (e.g., Deut 22:22), but what YHWH desires for Israel is not punishment but their restoration after a time of purification.

b. The Explanation: YHWH's Irrational Love for the Unlovable (3:1d–f)

The passage then applies the asymmetry of Hosea's marital "love" (אהב) to God's relationship with his people. The story of the prophet and his wife is a pale shadow of something deeper: "just as YHWH *loves* the children of Israel, though they are turning aside to other gods and they are *lovers* of raisin cakes"

7. The masoretic accentuation is ambiguous at this point.

(3:1d–f). The comparison in view (from the opening preposition כְּ; "like, just as") highlights a contrast between unequal kinds of "love" that reaches back to the earliest days of Israel's history. Despite YHWH's persistent care in the centuries since the exodus and conquest, the people were nearly always ungrateful, reaching back to their grumbling in the wilderness (Exod 16–17) and idolatry with the golden calf prior to leaving Mount Sinai (Exod 32). Apostasy with "other gods" became a constant refrain of Israel's life in the land (e.g., Josh 23:16; 1 Sam 8:8; 1 Kgs 9:6).

Hosea 3 links Israel's pattern of disobedience to the present generation by identifying their sin as "turning aside to other gods" (3:1e), an idiom drawn from Deuteronomy's motif of journey as an expression of one's relationship with God. More than being Israel's literal trip to Canaan, faithfulness in Deuteronomic terms is the figurative journey of "walking in YHWH's ways" (Deut 5:33; 8:6; 10:12) without "turning aside to the right or the left" (Deut 5:32; 17:11), while apostasy is departing from YHWH by "going after other gods" (Deut 8:19; 28:14) or "turning aside to other gods" (Deut 31:18, 20). This last Deuteronomic expression matches exactly the one found in this passage, "turning aside to other gods" (פנה אֶל־אֱלֹהִים אֲחֵרִים; Hos 3:1e).

The passage does not specify the identity of these "other gods," though chapter 2 has already mentioned Israel's consorting with "lovers" and "Baal[s]" (2:7[5], 9[7], 15[13]) whom the people wrongly thought to provide the fruit of the land. In addition to the synergy of religious, political, and economic sins already mentioned in the previous chapter, Hos 3 adds the information that the Israelites are "lovers of raisin cakes" (3:1f). Other OT references to these pastries indicate that they are not inherently sinful (cf. 2 Sam 6:19; 1 Chr 16:3). However, the pastries mentioned here are clearly pagan since they are part of Israel's veneration of "other gods" (3:1e). The identity of these baked goods may anticipate those offered in Jeremiah's time to the Queen of Heaven, a pagan fertility goddess. But since the Hebrew word for "cake" (כַּוָּן) used in the book of Jeremiah (cf. Jer 7:18; 44:19) differs from that used in Hosea (אֲשִׁישָׁה), the question of what kind of syncretistic "raisin cakes" Hos 3:1f envisions remains open.

2. Hosea's Obedience and Explanation: The Sign-Act as Exile and Restoration (3:2–5)

In contrast to other prophetic figures who protest their difficult call from God (cf. Exod 4:10; Jer 1:6), Hosea does not object to YHWH's instructions. He dutifully obeys the command to marry an adulterous woman (3:2) and then explains his actions to her (3:3). In fact, the narrative portions of the book (i.e., chs. 1, 3) never explicitly record Hosea speaking to God but have him speaking only to his wife (3:3) or explaining to Israel the theological significance of his sign-act (3:4–5).

a. Hosea's Obedience: Paying the Bride-Price (3:2)

The ceremony of remarriage begins with Hosea paying what appears to be the bride-price. Although the Hebrew verb describing the prophet's act of purchase or redemption in Hos 3:2 is somewhat obscure,[8] the action of Hosea is clearly related to YHWH's earlier promise to betroth his people by paying the bride-price of covenant relationship himself (see commentary on 2:21[19]b–22[20]a). The table below outlines the three similarities between these passages:[9]

8. The form וָאֶכְּרֶהָ could derive from the Hebrew root כרה ("to get by trade"; Deut 2:6; Job 6:27) or נכר/ מכר ("to purchase for marriage"; perhaps 1 Sam 23:7). See the discussion in Andersen and Freedman, *Hosea*, 298–99.

9. Walter Vogels, "Hosea's Gift to Gomer," *Bib* 69 (1988): 418–21.

	Hos 2:21[19]b–22[20]a		Hos 3:2	
1. Verb of relationship + feminine-singular personal suffix	וְאֵרַשְׂתִּיךְ	Then I will betroth you	וָאֶכְּרֶהָ	Then I purchased (?) her
2. 1st-person prepositional phrase (לְ) of belonging	לִי	to/for myself	לִי	to/for myself
3. Bride-price (?) paid by YHWH/Hosea to his wife	בְּצֶדֶק וּבְמִשְׁפָּט וּבְחֶסֶד וּבְרַחֲמִים	with righteousness and justice, with devotion and mercies	בַּחֲמִשָּׁה עָשָׂר כָּסֶף וְחֹמֶר שְׂעֹרִים וְלֵתֶךְ שְׂעֹרִים	with fifteen shekels of silver and a homer and a *lethek* of barley

The third element of the comparison is controversial and deserves special comment. For this transaction in Hos 3:2, some commentators have suggested that the monetary amount of the silver (i.e., fifteen silver pieces) and barley (i.e., one-and-a-half homers of barley) adds up to thirty shekels and thereby reflects the price for redeeming a slave (cf. Exod 21:32).[10] To interpret the financial transaction as the redemption of a slave or prostitute is possible, but the surrounding literary context of v. 2 points in another direction.

Instead, the correspondences between Hos 2 and 3 make it more likely that the bride-price of money and grain represents a marriage gift to the bride herself. Much like the promise of betrothal in Hos 2 involves YHWH's gifts of "righteousness and justice" as well as "devotion and mercies" (2:21[19]b) to bind Israel to himself in relationship, the provision of money and food (3:2) reverses the divine husband's earlier threat to punish his human wife's harlotry by stripping her of the same categories of items—money (i.e., silver and gold; 2:10[8]c–d) and food (i.e., grain, wine, and olive oil; 2:10[8]b, 11[9]b–c). Admittedly, the references to silver and barley in Hos 3:2 are not an exact match with the longer lists of items in chapter 2, but the prophecy of Hosea often varies its lists so that mentioning a subset of items intends to evoke the entire list. As Gerald Morris has shown, the literary feature of partial repetition is especially common in the opening chapters of the book.[11] These allusions to previous passages indicate that Hosea is bringing back the same woman whom he married in chapter 1 and whose harlotry symbolized Israel's apostasy in chapter 2. The provision of money and food in Hos 3 restores the sustenance that YHWH had stripped away. The likelihood of Gomer reappearing as Hosea's wife (3:1–2) also finds support in the prophet's explanation of the sign-act in the next three verses (3:3–5).

10. Tradition holds that the *lethek* is half of a homer, the latter being a dry measure of approximately 394 liters (although estimates vary). Since a homer of barley apparently costs ten shekels (2 Kgs 7:1), the amount of barley that Hos 3:2 mentions as costing fifteen shekels, the monetary amount of this barley plus the fifteen pieces of silver (shekels being the unstated measure) would total thirty shekels, the amount that Exod 21:32 legislates as payment to the master whose servant has been gored to death by an ox. Thus Wolff (*Hosea*, 61) proposes that Gomer had become a slave or prostitute who needed redemption. Although possible, this interpretation goes far beyond what the text explicitly says. Also, Wolff's view rests upon two problematic assumptions: (1) the price of barley was fixed in ancient Israel, even though the price named in 2 Kgs 7:1 was inflated because of the ongoing siege of Samaria; and (2) the price of redeeming a slave was fixed, yet Lev 27:2–7 assumes the variability of pricing for redeeming a slave (Vogels, "Hosea's Gift to Gomer," 414).

11. Morris, *Prophecy, Poetry and Hosea*, 69–70.

b. Hosea's Explanation to His Wife: Separation and Reunion (3:3)

The beginning of Hosea's explanation of the sign-act (3:3) is one of the most disputed verses in the entire book, especially the difficult final clause (3:3e) concerning the prophet's disposition toward his wife after their remarriage.[12] The numerous renderings available reflect indecision over how far to press the sign-act of Hosea's remarriage (3:2–3) as a symbol for Israel's exile and restoration (3:4–5). As we will explore below, the prophet envisions a temporary separation that paves the way for the certain reunion of God with his people. The necessity of chastening as a precursor to reconciliation applies both to Hosea's marriage and YHWH's covenant with Israel, since the former serves as an imperfect mirror to reflect the perfect love of the latter.

(1) A Temporary Separation (3:3a–d)

For the first and only time in the book, Hosea speaks directly to his wife (3:3a) with an explanation of what their shared future will entail (3:3b–d). Although the remarriage is now official (3:1–2), their life together cannot return immediately to its original state of intimacy that produced children (cf. ch. 1). There must first be a separation "for many days" (3:3b).[13] This chronological expression, which is also used in the next verse to characterize YHWH's separation from Israel (3:4a), designates an extended but finite span of time.[14] The relationship between Hosea and his wife will remain that of a legal marriage in that "you will dwell as mine" (תֵּשְׁבִי לִי; 3:3b).

Whichever rendering one chooses for this cryptic Hebrew phrase,[15] the next two clauses explain the reality of partial estrangement that will characterize their marriage. Hosea directs his wife not only to abstain from harlotry (3:3c) but also to refrain from intimacy with *any* man (3:3d), possibly including Hosea as well (3:3e). But why the truism that a wife ought to be faithful to her husband? The opaqueness of this paragraph has led to an abundance of speculation far out of proportion to the terseness of Hosea's words. We will explore the meaning of Hos 3:3e further in the next section, but for now the reader must remember that the prophet's unusual life is always a means to communicating "when YHWH first spoke *through* [בְּ] Hosea" (1:2a) rather than being an end in itself.

(2) The Certainty of Reunion (3:3e)

The key to coherence in this chapter lies in Hosea's final statement to his wife (3:3e), literally in Hebrew, "and also/even I to you" (וְגַם־אֲנִי אֵלָיִךְ). The additive adverb גַּם ("also, even") makes his wife's abstinence (3:3c–d) analogous in some way to his behavior toward her, though the narrative leaves unspecified the character of Hosea's action since the nominal clause lacks a finite verb. In contrast to this bare syntax, the tendency among commentators has been to expand this clause by inserting a negative particle לֹא and/or a verb of motion (typically בוא, "to come in/enter") so that

12. The challenges are well summarized by Andersen and Freedman, *Hosea*, 300–5.

13. The fronted position of this phrase in Hos 3:3b speaks to its importance in offering a new temporal frame for what follows (see *LDHB* §5.2). Taking v. 2 and v. 3 together, the discourse category of time itself receives greater prominence than the actions that Gomer and Israel will undertake during that period. Hosea 3:4a uses the same phrase in a deictic כִּי clause that similarly foregrounds the category of time.

14. E.g., Gen 21:34; Josh 22:3; 1 Chr 7:22. Contrarily, Wolff (*Hosea*, 61–62) notes that לְעוֹלָם ("forever, to everlasting"; Hos 2:21[19]) is Hosea's way of referring to indefinite and/or eschatological time.

15. Andersen and Freedman, *Hosea*, 291: "you will wait for me"; Macintosh (*Hosea*, 103) and Wolff (*Hosea*, 56): "you shall remain at home as mine"; R. Abma, *Bonds of Love: Methodic Studies of Prophetic Texts with Marriage Imagery (Isaiah 50:1–3 and 54:1–10, Hosea 1–3, Jeremiah 2–3)*, SSN 40 (Assen: Van Gorcum, 1999), 208: "you will sit down for me," with emphasis on Israel's loneliness in exile.

the reading is along the lines of "and I also *will not come in* to you" (i.e., the proposed emendation of *BHS*). The textual basis for such additions is lacking. More significantly, textual emendations do not satisfactorily resolve the logical problems in attempts to draw parallels between the wife's abstinence (3:3c–d) and that of Hosea (3:3e).

In this regard, Rainer Kessler has perceptively noted that interpreting the time limit of "many days" (3:3b) as the duration of the wife's abstinence (3:3c–d), but without the hope of any further reconciliation with Hosea in 3:3e, leads to the unsavory conclusion that her harlotry could resume after this temporary separation from her husband.[16] Since Hos 3:3e is the hinge between the "Gomer" and "Israel" portions of the marriage metaphor, any strictly disjunctive reading of וְגַם־אֲנִי אֵלָיִךְ (3:3e) risks undermining the comparison between Gomer's abstinence (3:3) and Israel's deprivation (3:4) as provisional steps toward full reunion with God (3:5). The unresolved estrangement in Hosea's family would render the marriage metaphor illogical as an anticipation of YHWH's reconciliation with Israel.

Therefore, it is better to understand this ambiguous clause in a concessive but emphatic manner (i.e., "*yet even* on my part, I will be with you"; 3:3e) as the surprising conclusion of the wife's chastisement during "many days." The possibility of such a contrastive function for the focus particle גַּם when followed immediately by a personal pronoun is well attested in other OT texts (e.g., Gen 20:6; Neh 5:8).[17] To reinforce this function for גַּם, the fronted position of the emphatic first-person pronoun אֲנִי ("I, on my part") draws a marked contrast in the discourse between the actions of Gomer as "you" (3:3b–d) and Hosea as "I" (3:3e).[18] So to summarize the discussion, Hosea will *nonetheless* (i.e., disjunctive גַּם) remain "to/with" (אֶל) his wife after the awkward necessity of estrangement despite remarriage. In the larger flow of the chapter, for Hosea to insist counterintuitively on the certainty of reunion (3:3e), notwithstanding a time of separation (3:3b–d), provides a powerful symbol of YHWH's coming reconciliation with Israel. This rendering also offers a more intelligible comparison between Hosea's family life (3:3) and Israel's future (3:4–5). The commentary on the following verses will outline the lexical links among these verses that frame such a comparison.

c. Hosea's Explanation to Israel: Exile and Restoration (3:4–5)

YHWH now seeks to discipline his people for their sinful devotion to corrupt politics and religion (3:4). Following YHWH's removal of these gangrenous institutions, YHWH will reconstitute the entire family of Israel and Judah as a people who return to their God and receive his gift of a Davidic king once again (3:5).

(1) Temporary Deprivations of Exile (3:4)

The narrative marks the transition between Hosea's sign-act with his wife (3:3) and its symbolic meaning for Israel (3:4–5) using the explanatory conjunction כִּי ("because/for"; 3:4a; cf. 1:2e, 4c, 6e). The personal horizon of Hosea now begins to recede from view, though his explanation of Israel's

16. Kessler, "Hosea 3," 567–68.

17. Ibid., 569, notes that the possibility of either conjunctive or disjunctive syntax for the Hebrew adverbial conjunction גַּם resembles the German adverb *auch* (compare similarly the adverb "even" in English, though its conjunctive sense as a synonym to "also" is becoming archaic in modern usage). In Neh 5:8–10, for example, the grammatical construction of גַּם + personal pronoun can play both a disjunctive (5:8) and conjunctive (5:10) role. For a fuller discussion of גַּם as a focus particle that can convey repetition, addition, or contrast, see *BHRG* §40.20.

18. To be specific, the pronoun אֲנִי (3:3e) introduces a topical frame (*LDHB* §5.1) that shifts attention to Hosea's posture toward Gomer.

exile (3:4) and subsequent restoration to YHWH (3:5) continues to draw upon the moving portrait of estrangement and reconciliation of v. 3. Just as Hos 3:3b delineates "many days" (יָמִים רַבִּים) as Gomer's period of discipline when she nonetheless continues to "dwell" (ישׁב) as Hosea's wife, Hos 3:4a foresees a similar period of "many days" (יָמִים רַבִּים) when the children of Israel will "dwell" (ישׁב) in exile after being stripped of their cherished institutions. Thereafter, five instances of the adverb "without" (אֵין) introduce the three diseased areas of Israel's life to be excised: (1) human leadership (3:4a); (2) cultic rituals (3:4b); and (3) divine guidance (3:4c).[19]

(a) No More Leaders (3:4a)

The first and most influential institution that Israel will lose is human leadership (3:4a). Beginning with Saul the first king (1 Sam 9), the kings of Israel and Judah mostly drove a vulnerable people down paths of apostasy. The Pentateuch had predicted that kings from Israel would play a key role in YHWH's plan to redeem the world (Gen 17:6; 35:11; Num 24:7, 17) while also warning that the powerful institution of kingship needed always to yield to divine rule (Deut 17:14–20). Like the sexual intimacy that is temporarily forbidden in Hosea's marriage (3:3), kingship is a normal part of Israel's life that YHWH must remove due to its role as an enabler of various idolatries.

With the exception of the next verse's positive mention of "David their king" (3:5), Hosea's subsequent references to monarchy are all negative, placing responsibility at the feet of kings for Israel's many sins (e.g., 5:1; 7:3). This is not to deny the solidarity of the people with their kings (e.g., 8:4; 10:3; 13:10), but rather highlights the unique authority that Israelite kings possessed to immerse their people in idolatrous worldviews such as imperialism and Canaanite nature religion (e.g., 7:1–16).

In fact, Hos 3:4a envisages the overthrow of the entire political system and not merely the "king" (מֶלֶךְ). Following the reference to the "king" is the companion term "prince" (שַׂר). This is a more general word that returns later in Hosea to identify regional leaders who can move boundary stones between ancestral plots of land (5:10), join the king's drunken festivals in Samaria (7:5), and manage the cultic apparatus of Canaanite nature religion in Gilgal (9:15). This variety of roles accords with the OT's depiction of the שַׂר in the monarchical period as officials in the royal court (2 Sam 3:38), religious functionaries (1 Kgs 4:2), military chieftains (1 Kgs 11:24), or even as an umbrella term for "leader" (1 Chr 22:17). Thus the punishment of subsisting "without king and without prince" (3:4a) means that Israel would lack human leaders at precisely the same time in the eighth century BCE when the "great king" (5:13; 10:6) of Assyria was conniving to expand his borders. Other eighth-century prophets go even further than Hosea in declaring that YHWH has personally commissioned the Assyrian king to punish Israel (e.g., Isa 7:17–20; 8:7).

(b) No More Rituals (3:4b)

The next fixture to disappear will be Israel's religious rituals that involve "sacrifice and sacred pillar" (3:4b). While "sacrifice" (זֶבַח) is the regular term for an offering in OT law (e.g., Exod 23:18; Lev 3:1), the Israelite sacrificial system had mutated by the time of the eighth century BCE into forms of pointless ritualism. Thus, the prophets of YHWH during this time repeatedly exposed the charade of using diligent religious observance as

19. Paul A. Kruger, "The Fact of Disorder: A Note on Hos 3,4a," *ZAW* 124 (2012): 249–54.

a way to excuse the immorality and injustice of the people (e.g., Isa 1:11; Hos 4:13–14; Amos 4:4). For example, in Hosea's other reference to זֶבַח (6:6), the prophet attacks the false assurance of "sacrifice" and "burnt offerings" that lacks the true reverence for YHWH as shown in "faithfulness" and "knowledge of God" (cf. 4:1). The hypocrisy of the sacrificial system must be destroyed so that Israel can no longer use lavish religion as a cover for moral bankruptcy.

The threat of destruction extends to the "sacred pillar" (מַצֵּבָה), one of the most prominent carryovers from Canaanite religion in the period following Israel's conquest of the land (cf. Exod 23:24; Deut 7:5). Unlike the "sacrifice" (זֶבַח) that was typically offered at cultic sites such as Dan or Bethel (cf. 1 Kgs 12:28–33), rituals with the "sacred pillar" were not always tied to the cult and could take place anywhere.[20]

The מַצֵּבָה could serve as a "memorial stone" (Gen 35:14; Isa 19:19) of pilgrimage to YHWH, but it more commonly refers to pagan stone pillars used in veneration of Baal (e.g., 2 Kgs 3:2; 10:27), often at the "high places" (1 Kgs 14:23; 2 Kgs 17:9–10). Since these standing stones were often adjacent to wooden poles of the fertility goddess Asherah (e.g., Exod 34:13; 2 Kgs 17:10, 16; Mic 5:12–14), the מַצֵּבָה likely represented the phallic presence of Baal in Canaanite fertility rituals. By condemning both "sacrifice" at official sites and "sacred pillars" at the popular level, Hos 3:4b foresees the collapse of Israel's entire religious life, both orthodox and otherwise.

(c) No More Guidance (3:4c)

The final foundation to collapse in Israelite society will be the provision of divine guidance through the ephod and teraphim (3:4c). The "ephod" (אֵפוֹד) was a costly priestly garment that contained the Urim and Thummim (Exod 28:28–30; Lev 8:7–8), two items of unknown shape and material.[21] These were used in an unknown way for determining the will of God (Num 27:21; 1 Sam 23:6, 9; Ezra 2:63). Unlike the role that YHWH ordained for the ephod and the articles within it, the "teraphim" (תְּרָפִים) also mentioned in Hos 3:4c were objects of pagan origin, perhaps from the Hittites.[22] They seem to have been portable figurines of gods (Gen 31:19) that were typically kept in the home (Judg 18:14–20) and used in divination (2 Kgs 23:24; Ezek 21:26; Zech 10:2).

Hosea's mention of the pair "ephod and teraphim" recalls the sordid episodes in the late chapters of Judges (e.g., 17:5; 18:5), when the Israelites used these two cultic items together to seek YHWH's guidance with no designs on obedience.[23] The irony thickens upon hearing the echoes of Judges's description of a rudderless society in which "Israel had no king [אֵין מֶלֶךְ]; each would do right in his own eyes" (Judg 17:6; 21:25; cf. 18:1; 19:1). This anarchistic history was repeating itself in Hosea's time because kings had erected sinful economic, political, and religious structures in Israelite society. What hope would remain for Israel considering this nearly unbroken history of apostasy, with and without kings?

20. Ziony Zevit, *The Religions of Ancient Israel: A Synthesis of Parallactic Approaches* (London: Continuum, 2001), 256–65, catalogues the various archaeological and textual evidence that links stones, Asherah, and high places.

21. However, the Hebrew term for ephod is cognate to the Hittite word *ipantu*, which in one text appears to be a garment of silver or have silver designs (Harry A. Hoffner, "Hittite Equivalents of Old Assyrian *Kumrum* and *Epattum*," *WZKM* 86 [1996]: 155–56).

22. On which see Harry A. Hoffner, Jr., "Hittite *Tarpiš* and Hebrew *Terāphîm*," *JNES* 27 (1968): 61–68. For a recent argument that teraphim resemble mantic figurines from Mesopotamia and Egypt, see Shawn W. Flynn, "The Teraphim in Light of Mesopotamian and Egyptian Evidence," *CBQ* 74 (2012): 694–711.

23. Kruger, "A Note on Hos 3,4a," 251–52.

(2) The Coming Restoration of the Exiles (3:5)

The prophet answers with the promise of a better future "later/afterwards" (אַחַר; 3:5a), following the impending ruin of Israel (3:4). The verse also concludes with anticipation of new hope "in the latter days" (בְּאַחֲרִית הַיָּמִים; 3:5c). Between these chronological markers, vv. 4–5 preview the salvation that cures the heart problem of Israel's apostasy. More than a physical return to the land, Hos 3 outlines a comprehensive restoration (3:5a) of sincere repentance (3:5b) and lasting reverence (3:5c) that will characterize Israel's restoration after a time of discipline.

(a) Sincere Repentance (3:5a–b)

Hosea 3 does not explicitly mention exile to a foreign land, unlike other OT prophetic passages about Israel's punishment that date from the Neo-Assyrian period (e.g., Hos 9:3; Isa 8:4; Amos 4:2–3; Mic 1:5–6). Instead, this chapter offers a sedentary picture of Israel's time of discipline, as noted in the earlier discussion of the verb ישׁב ("to sit, dwell"; 3:4a). For after this period of immobility (in an unspecified place), YHWH promises that his people will be on the move again when "they will return" (3:5a), a form of the verb שׁוב ("to return, repent").

YHWH powerfully communicates this breakthrough from stagnation to movement by a wordplay on two verbal forms that have the same Hebrew consonants (ישׁבו) and differ in only two vowels (יֵשְׁבוּ ["they will dwell"; 3:4a] vs. יָשֻׁבוּ ["they will return/repent"; 3:5a]).[24] Since no destination is named as an adverbial modifier for the שׁוב form found here, the idea of restoration in 3:5 is less a literal return from exile and more a figurative return to YHWH's paths that leaves behind the false gods to whom Israel had "turned aside" (פנה; 3:1e). Thus Hos 3:5 envisions a radical transformation of the heart that contrasts with Israel's half-hearted attempts to "return" (e.g., 6:1) in the rest of the book.[25] In this vein, Hosea joins Deuteronomy in prioritizing the inner dimension of restoration as the process of "seeking YHWH" (בקשׁ + יְהוָה; Hos 3:5b; Deut 4:29–31), perhaps through spiritual pilgrimage (cf. Deut 12:5),[26] over the outer dimension of returning to the land.

Given the unmistakable theocentrism of this passage, that the figure of "David their king" is also one whom Israel will "seek" (בקשׁ; 3:5b) is surprising. Other passages in Hosea mainly use בקשׁ to speak of Israel's pursuit of YHWH himself (5:6, 15; cf. 2:9[7]). Therefore, for Israel to "seek" such a king is not a sentimental pining for monarchy but rather a prediction that Israel will venerate a descendant of David who is so closely identified with YHWH that he receives the honor usually reserved for God (e.g., Deut 4:29; 2 Chr 7:14). The remarkable convergence of YHWH and David in Hos 3 provides the seed for the messianic hope that sprouts in later prophetic passages (e.g., Isa 9:6–7; Jer 23:5–6; Ezek 34:23–31), not to mention the NT.

(b) Lasting Reverence (3:5c)

The fruit of repentance (3:5a–b) will be lasting reverence toward God that will never turn back toward apostasy: "So they will tremble before YHWH and his goodness in the latter days" (3:5c). Although the verb "tremble" (פחד) often refers to dread of enemies (e.g., Deut 28:67; Isa 19:16; Ps 27:1), the context provided by pairing this with YHWH's "goodness" (טוּב) points to a positive understanding of trembling. Much like the "fear of YHWH" (e.g., Ps 19:9; Prov 1:7) in the OT denotes glad submission to God without the

24. Cf. Andersen and Freedman, *Hosea*, 307.

25. See the extended discussion of שׁוב in Hosea by LeCureux, *Thematic Unity of the Book of the Twelve*, 63–110.

26. Cf. Jeffrey H. Tigay, *Deuteronomy*, The JPS Torah Commentary (Philadelphia: Jewish Publication Society of America, 1996), 120.

extremes of unbridled terror and casual flippancy, the "goodness" of God is his moral perfection that nonetheless draws penitent sinners back to him. As Andrew Dearman observes, this verse recalls the self-introduction of YHWH's name as "goodness" (Exod 33:19–20; cf. 34:6–7) that is free to show mercy and compassion to an idolatrous people.[27]

However, these important lessons about YHWH's character following the sin with the golden calf at Mount Sinai (Exod 32) went tragically unheeded for later generations. Hosea will later condemn Samaria for worshiping the same kinds of golden-calf idols (8:5–6; 10:5; 13:2; cf. 1 Kgs 12:28–30). Thus the literary unit of Hos 1–3 closes by anticipating salvation as the final stage of Israel's history, whereas the rest of the book concerns a nearer time when the people still struggle between the prophet's call to "repent" (e.g., 12:7[6]; 14:2[1]) and their failure to do so (e.g., 2:9[7]; 5:4).

Therefore, it is inevitable that divine judgment come first (3:4) as a prerequisite to Israel's salvation "in the latter days" (3:5c). This phrase marks an indeterminate point in the future (e.g., Gen 49:1; Deut 4:30) but is not necessarily eschatological. In the broader context of Hosea, the "latter days" (lit. "the end of the days," אַחֲרִית הַיָּמִים) anticipate an end within history as signaled by Israel's sincere return to God rather than the end of history itself, as apocalyptic passages tend to view the "latter days" (e.g., Dan 10:14).

Canonical and Theological Significance

Hosea 3's focus on the love of God, as echoed in the familiar declaration that "God is love" (1 John 4:8, 16), is both the easiest and hardest of theological truths to grasp. Christian clichés such as "God's love is unconditional" or "He loves you just as you are" run aground on the reality that this loving God requires obedience (John 14:15) and directs his beloved people to repent when they sin (Rev 3:19). But how can loving God—which many take to be mainly a feeling or experience—also be something that Jesus *commands* (Matt 22:37–38)? D. A. Carson observes that part of the problem is that the banality of love in popular culture has distorted our ways of talking about our love for God and his love for us.[28] What we need, then, is to recover the biblical way of thinking about love in *covenantal* rather than only contractual or emotional terms.

A sidelong glance at divine love in the ancient Near Eastern societies surrounding Israel helps to illuminate the distinctive contours of YHWH's love for Israel. Although modern people instinctively understand the Bible's teaching on a loving God (e.g., Deut 7:9; Neh 13:26; 1 John 4:8, 16) in terms of a singular deity, this idea sounds quite different in cultures where people believe in many deities. Not only were some deities venerated as patrons or patronesses of love itself (e.g., Inanna in Sumer, Ishtar in Babylon), the idea that worshipers were "beloved" by their god or

27. Dearman, *Hosea*, 142.

28. D. A. Carson, *The Difficult Doctrine of the Love of God* (Wheaton, IL: Crossway, 2000), 9–27.

goddess was extremely common.[29] Diplomatic correspondence also speaks of the language of a superior's "love" for an inferior as well as the patron demanding the loyalty of the client's "love."[30] Thus, on one level, it is hardly unique in Israel's cultural environment to say that a god or goddess loves a person or that the worshiper ought to return the favor.

Rather, the key question in polytheistic cultures is one of pragmatism and hierarchy—*which* deity or patron is most generous and therefore most deserving of such love? And on the flip side, when a follower of a deity breaches their contract with the deity through neglect or disobedience, what sort of "love" remains? In diplomatic documents from the rest of the ancient Near East, the fickleness of such "love" is evident in that a vassal's disobedience quickly results in the suzerain's removal of protection through "divine abandonment" (by a god/goddess) or the imposition of treaty curses (by a patron).[31] If not destroyed in the process, the vassal would survive only to be left scrambling to find a new divine or human patron.

These cultural observations place Hos 3 in fresh perspective. Coming immediately after the numerous references to Israel's illicit "lovers" in Hos 2 (vv. 7[5], 9[7], 12[10], 14[12], 15[13]), chapter 3 offers a covenantal understanding of YHWH's love that perseveres beyond the disobedience of Israel. In fact, the four references to "love" in v. 1 make this the Bible's densest cluster of "love" language, more so than any verse in Song of Songs or the "love hymn" of 1 Cor 13. As noted in the commentary above, Hosea is enjoined to "love" a woman who is already "loved" by another—an absurd act that would bring public shame. No respectable man in the Israelite community would identify fully with a woman who did not share the same commitment to him.[32] But as the divine side of the metaphor fleshes out this asymmetric "love," YHWH wills to "love" Israel despite this people's shamelessness in associating with other deities and being "lovers of raisin cakes" (3:1e–f). In other words, the love of YHWH is deeply countercultural for seeking his unlovable people despite the disgrace that this brings to his reputation.[33]

Having thus identified himself with a shameful people, this God who is willing to suffer reproach will also work to restore his honor among the nations as well as among his people.[34] With this missional end in mind, Israel's exile and restoration to

29. E.g., Gilgamesh is identified as the one "whom divine Shamash loves" in the Epic of Gilgamesh (Andrew George, *The Epic of Gilgamesh: The Babylonian Epic Poem and Other Texts in Akkadian and Sumerian* [New York: The Penguin Press, 2003], 9).

30. E.g., Esarhaddon the Neo-Assyrian emperor directs his subjects to love his son Assurbanipal, the crown-prince designate, as they do themselves ("The Vassal-Treaties of Esarhaddon," trans. D. J. Wiseman, *ANET*, 537).

31. In one of the Amarna Letters (i.e., EA 114), for example, Rib-Hadda the governor of Byblos expresses his relationship to both Pharaoh (his suzerain) and his own vassals in terms of "love" (William L. Moran, "The Ancient Near Eastern Background of the Love of God in Deuteronomy," *CBQ* 25 [1963]: 79–80).

32. Moon, "Honor and Shame in Hosea's Marriages," 342–43.

33. Ibid., 348–49.

34. Glatt-Gilad, "Yahweh's Honor at Stake," 63–74. At the same time, it is critically important that YHWH's honor has an objective dimension that is grounded in his faithful character and not merely the subjective dimension of what people

come (Hos 3:4–5) serve as YHWH's discipline of imposing temporary deprivation upon Israel. Rather than being an impersonal punishment, the loss of political and religious institutions (3:4a–c) is the most loving thing that could happen to Israel due to the self-destructive idolatry that has metastasized in them.

The covenantal love of God is therefore a *persisting* and *purifying* love that is more than adequate to meet the challenges posed by human sin. To live in covenant with God is far better than clichés about his love being "unconditional" or "loving people as they are," much like an overdose of freedom from parents actually serves to plunge children into misery rather than setting them free. This misunderstanding of love as unrestricted "freedom" distorts what should be a warm and mutual relationship into an unfeeling contract devoid of emotional stakes, as Israel also sought to do in seeking Canaanized religion for what it would offer in terms of creational blessings.

However, such a transactional notion fails to apprehend how our God's love is incomparable for its peculiar willingness to do what does not come easily in a relationship, in contrast to lesser deities and human patrons who quickly abandon those who disappoint them. Such an irrational commitment to shameful people like us is also why the Bible commands our love for God as an act of the will and not merely the emotions. Thus, in Hos 3 and 11, the moving portrayal of God's love anticipates the even greater overturning of relational expectations in the parable of the lost son in Luke 15.[35]

attribute to him. For this reason, Wu is correct to assert that "YHWH can never truly be shamed in the OT" (*Honor, Shame, and Guilt*, 172).

35. Bailey, *The Cross and the Prodigal*, 143–44.

CHAPTER 5

Hosea 4:1–5:7

A. YHWH's Contention against Israel's Priestly Failures

Main Idea of the Passage

Israel has failed to hear and heed the covenant stipulations that YHWH made with them at Mount Sinai. As spiritual pollution from the sins of Israel spreads and a defiled land/earth revolts against its sinful inhabitants, YHWH warns that the various harlotries of his people will result in the removal of fertility rather than a realization of the fertility they seek.

Literary Context

Hosea 4:1–5:7 opens the second major section of the book found in chapters 4–14. This unit of eight chapters is enclosed by an opening reference to "the word of YHWH" (4:1a) that marks the beginning of a new section (cf. 1:1) and a concluding caption for the speeches within as "The Declaration of YHWH" (11:11). Between these literary bookends, YHWH indicts Israel for numerous violations of the covenant that he gave to his people at Mount Sinai.

Although the present chapter's legal terminology of a "lawsuit" (one possible rendering for רִיב; 4:1b) seems initially to supersede the marriage metaphor of chapters 1–3, it would be mistaken to view YHWH's accusations against Israel as a strictly legal matter. Not only does Hosea use similar terminology in the marriage metaphor (רִיב in 2:4[2] translated above as "quarrel"), the disputations of chapters 4–14 also portray YHWH flexibly as judge, prosecutor, and plaintiff in a series of increasingly urgent appeals for his estranged people to repent. Family imagery for God then returns explicitly in chapter 11 with the portrayal of YHWH as a pained father who longs for his prodigal son (11:8–9). However, this chapter also describes the God of Israel as a fierce lion whose roar summons his children from exile like migratory birds returning to roost (11:10–11; cf. 5:14). Following the mingling of kinship and creational metaphors with which Hos 4–11 concludes, chapters 12–14 begin another round of covenant contentions, but with more of a focus on Israel's salvation history.

Translation and Exegetical Outline

(See pages 138–41.)

Structure and Literary Form

Structurally, Hos 4:1–5:7 appears to involve a series of interlocking chiasms. At the level of the overall passage, a somewhat unbalanced chiastic structure highlights the central theme (i.e., the "D" element) of Israel's spiritual harlotry against YHWH:[1]

A Indictment of Israel (4:1–3): People Must "Hear/Heed" (שׁמע; 4:1) God's Accusation

B Coming Judgment (4:4–6): People and Leaders Will "Stumble" (כשׁל; 4:5) in Sin

C Condemnation and Warning (4:7–11): "Dishonor" (קָלוֹן; 4:7) through Drunkenness and Sex

D The Sin of Harlotry (4:12–14): Condemnation of Idols and Canaanite Fertility Practices

C′ Condemnation and Warning (4:15–19): "Dishonor" (קָלוֹן; 4:18) through Drunkenness and Sex

A′ Indictment of Israel (5:1): Leaders Must "Hear/Heed" (שׁמע) God's Accusation

B′ Coming Judgment (5:2–7): Leaders and People Will "Stumble" (כשׁל; 5:5) in Sin

1. This diagram slightly modifies the influential work on chiasmus in the OT by David A. Dorsey, *The Literary Structure of the Old Testament: A Commentary on Genesis–Malachi* (Grand Rapids: Baker Academic, 2004), 267–68.

Hosea 4:1–5:7

Verse	Hebrew	Translation	Outline
			III. YHWH's Contentions with Israel (4:1–14:1[13:16])
			A. YHWH's Contention against Israel's Priestly Failures (4:1–5:7)
4:1a	שִׁמְעוּ דְבַר־יְהוָה בְּנֵי יִשְׂרָאֵל	"Heed/Hear the word of YHWH, O children of Israel!	1. YHWH's Summons to Israel (4:1a–b)
1b	כִּי רִיב לַיהוָה עִם־יוֹשְׁבֵי הָאָרֶץ	For YHWH has a quarrel with the inhabitants of the land/earth:	
			2. YHWH's Initial Accusation of the People (4:1c–3)
1c	כִּי אֵין־אֱמֶת	That there is no truthfulness,	a. The Absence of Covenant Fidelity (4:1c)
	וְאֵין־חֶסֶד	and no faithfulness,	
	וְאֵין־דַּעַת אֱלֹהִים בָּאָרֶץ׃	and no knowledge of God in the land!	
2a	אָלֹה	[There is] cursing!	b. The Presence of Decalogue Violations (4:2a)
	וְכַחֵשׁ	And deceiving!	
	וְרָצֹחַ	And murdering!	
	וְגָנֹב	And stealing!	
	וְנָאֹף	And committing adultery!	
2b	פָּרָצוּ בָּאָרֶץ[1]	They have burst out upon the land,	c. Sin's Deflement of the Land/Earth (4:2b–c)
2c	וְדָמִים בְּדָמִים נָגָעוּ׃	and bloodshed has struck bloodshed!	
3a	עַל־כֵּן תֶּאֱבַל הָאָרֶץ	As a result, the land is mourning,	(1) The Poisoning of Land and People (4:3a–b)
3b	וְאֻמְלַל כָּל־יוֹשֵׁב בָּהּ	and all the inhabitants wither in it.	
3c	בְּחַיַּת הַשָּׂדֶה	[As for] the beast of the field,	(2) The Dissipation of Earth's Creatures (4:3c)
	וּבְעוֹף הַשָּׁמָיִם	the birds of the sky,	
	וְגַם־דְּגֵי הַיָּם	and even the fish of the sea—	
	יֵאָסֵפוּ׃	they will be taken away!"	
			3. YHWH's Detailed Accusation of the People, Part I: Contention with God (4:4–6)
4a	אַךְ אִישׁ אַל־יָרֵב	"Indeed, let nobody contend,	a. Censure: Contention with God and Priest (4:4)
4b	וְאַל־יוֹכַח אִישׁ	and may no one rebuke,	
4c	וְעַמְּךָ כִּמְרִיבֵי כֹהֵן׃	because your people are like those who contend with a priest.	
5a	וְכָשַׁלְתָּ הַיּוֹם	So you will stumble by day,	b. Sentencing: Four Wordplays of Poetic Justice (4:5–6)
5b	וְכָשַׁל גַּם־נָבִיא עִמְּךָ לָיְלָה	and the prophet will also stumble with you by night.	(1) Stumbling & Stumbled (4:5a–b)
5c	וְדָמִיתִי אִמֶּךָ׃	I will destroy your mother;	(2) Destroying & Destroyed (4:5c–6a)
6a	נִדְמוּ עַמִּי מִבְּלִי הַדָּעַת	my people are destroyed from lack of knowledge.	

6b	↓ כִּי־אַתָּה הַדַּעַת מָאַסְתָּ	↓ Because on your part, you have rejected the knowledge,	(3) Rejecting & Rejected (4:6b–c)
6c	וְאֶמְאָסְאךָ מִכַּהֵן לִי	I also will reject you as my priest.	
6d	↓ וַתִּשְׁכַּח תּוֹרַת אֱלֹהֶיךָ	↓ Since you have forgotten the instruction of your God,	(4) Forgetting & Forgotten (4:6d–e)
6e	אֶשְׁכַּח בָּנֶיךָ גַּם־אָנִי׃	I will forget your children, also on my part."	
			4. YHWH's Detailed Accusation of the People, Part II: Harlotry with Canaanite Religion (4:7–19)
7a	↓ כְּרֻבָּם	↓ "As soon as they multiplied	a. Cultic Sins as Harlotry (4:7–10)
	כֵּן חָטְאוּ־לִי	then they sinned against me.	(1) People's Fertility and Sin (4:7)
7b	כְּבוֹדָם בְּקָלוֹן אָמִיר׃	I will change their honor to dishonor.	
8a	חַטַּאת עַמִּי יֹאכֵלוּ	They enjoy the sin of my people,	(2) The Priest's Feasting on People's Sin (4:8)
8b	וְאֶל־עֲוֹנָם יִשְׂאוּ נַפְשׁוֹ׃	and they lift up his soul for their iniquity.	
9a	וְהָיָה כָעָם כַּכֹּהֵן	Thus it shall be—like people, like priest!	(3) Solidarity of People and Priesthood (4:9a)
9b	וּפָקַדְתִּי עָלָיו דְּרָכָיו	I will repay his ways upon him,	(3´) Solidarity of Act as Consequence (4:9b–c)
9c	וּמַעֲלָלָיו אָשִׁיב לוֹ׃	and I will bring back his deeds upon him.	
10a	וְאָכְלוּ	Then they will feast,	(2´) The Priests' Dissatisfaction with Feasting (4:10a–b)
10b	וְלֹא יִשְׂבָּעוּ	but they will not be satisfied.	
10c	הִזְנוּ	They will commit harlotry,	(1´) People's Harlotry and De-Fertility (4:10c–d)
10d	וְלֹא יִפְרֹצוּ	but not break forth in numbers.	
10e/11a	כִּי־אֶת־יְהוָה עָזְבוּ לִשְׁמֹר׃ [זְנוּת]	For it is YHWH they have rejected by keeping [harlotry].	b. Drunken Divination as Harlotry (4:10e–12) (1) Harlotry and Disorientation (4:10e–11b)
11b	↓ זְנוּת וְיַיִן וְתִירוֹשׁ	↓ [As for] harlotry, wine, and new wine,	
	יִקַּח־לֵב׃	it will take away a mind.	
12a	עַמִּי בְּעֵצוֹ יִשְׁאָל	My people will ask their stick,	(2) Divination's Dumb Question (4:12a)
12b	וּמַקְלוֹ יַגִּיד לוֹ	and their divining rod will tell them.	(2´) Divination's Mute Answer (4:12b)
12c	↓ כִּי רוּחַ זְנוּנִים הִתְעָה	↓ Because a spirit of harlotries has led astray,	(1´) Harlotry and Wandering (4:12c–d)
12d	וַיִּזְנוּ מִתַּחַת אֱלֹהֵיהֶם׃	they have committed harlotry from underneath their God.	
			c. Fertility Rituals as Harlotry (4:13–14g)
13a	עַל־רָאשֵׁי הֶהָרִים יְזַבֵּחוּ	On the tops of mountains they sacrifice,	(1) Older Men's Roles: Canaanite Sites and Practices (4:13a–c)
13b	וְעַל־הַגְּבָעוֹת יְקַטֵּרוּ	on the hills they offer incense,	
13c	תַּחַת אַלּוֹן וְלִבְנֶה וְאֵלָה	underneath oak and poplar and terebinth—	
	כִּי טוֹב צִלָּהּ	for their shade is pleasant.	

Continued on next page.

1. Here the inclusion of the prepositional phrase בָּאָרֶץ ("in the land") reflects the *Vorlage* of the LXX (which adds ἐπὶ τῆς γῆς). The MT for Hos 4:2b simply reads פָּרָצוּ ("they burst out"). As noted by Douglas Stuart (*Hosea-Jonah*, WBC 31 [Waco, TX: Word, 1987], 72) and Hans Walter Wolff (*Hosea*, trans. Gary Stansell, Hermeneia [Minneapolis: Fortress, 1974], 65), the MT probably lost the prepositional phrase בָּאָרֶץ due to haplography with the similar ending פָּרָצוּ.

Continued from previous page.

13d	עַל־כֵּן תִּזְנֶינָה בְּנוֹתֵיכֶם	As a result your daughters commit harlotry,	(2) Younger Women's Roles: Sexual Promiscuity (4:13d–e)
13e	וְכַלּוֹתֵיכֶם תְּנָאַפְנָה׃	and your daughters-in-law commit adultery.	
14a	לֹא־אֶפְקוֹד עַל־בְּנוֹתֵיכֶם	I will not repay your daughters	(2′) Younger Women's Roles: Lesser Responsibility for Harlotry (4:14a–d)
14b	כִּי תִזְנֶינָה	when they commit harlotry,	
14c	וְעַל־כַּלּוֹתֵיכֶם	nor [will I punish] your daughters-in-law	
14d	כִּי תְנָאַפְנָה	when they commit adultery.	
14e	כִּי־הֵם	Because on the men's part,	(1′) Older Men's Roles: Greater Responsibility for Harlotry (4:14e–g)
	עִם־הַזֹּנוֹת יְפָרֵדוּ	they keep going off with harlots,	
14f	וְעִם־הַקְּדֵשׁוֹת יְזַבֵּחוּ	and they offer sacrifices with prostitutes.	
14g	וְעָם לֹא־יָבִין יִלָּבֵט׃	But a people who lack understanding will be ruined!	d. The Spread of Israel's Harlotry (4:14g–16)
15a	אִם־זֹנֶה אַתָּה יִשְׂרָאֵל	If you, O Israel, are committing harlotry,	(1) YHWH's Warning to Judah about the Harlotry of Israel (4:15)
15b	אַל־יֶאְשַׁם יְהוּדָה	may Judah not become guilty.	
15c	וְאַל־תָּבֹאוּ הַגִּלְגָּל	Do not enter Gilgal,	
15d	וְאַל־תַּעֲלוּ בֵּית אָוֶן	neither go up to Beth-Aven,	
15e	וְאַל־תִּשָּׁבְעוּ	nor swear,	
	חַי־יְהוָה׃	'As YHWH lives.'	
16a	כִּי כְּפָרָה סֹרֵרָה סָרַר יִשְׂרָאֵל	Since Israel has been stubborn like a stubborn heifer,	(2) YHWH's Exposé of Israel's Stupidity (4:16)
16b	עַתָּה יִרְעֵם יְהוָה כְּכֶבֶשׂ בַּמֶּרְחָב׃	now YHWH will drive them like a lamb into a broad place.	
17a	חֲבוּר עֲצַבִּים אֶפְרָיִם	Ephraim is bound to idols—	e. The Self-Destruction of Israel's Harlotry (4:17–19)
17b	הַנַּח־לוֹ׃	leave him alone!	
18a	סָר סָבְאָם	Finishing their liquor,[2]	(1) Increasing Harlotry and Dishonor (4:18)
18b	הַזְנֵה הִזְנוּ	they intensify their harlotry,	
18c	אָהֲבוּ הֵבוּ קָלוֹן מָגִנֶּיהָ׃	her shields (i.e., leaders)[3] have cherished dishonor.	
19a	צָרַר רוּחַ אוֹתָהּ בִּכְנָפֶיהָ	A wind has bound her in its wings,	(2) Shameful Departure for Exile (4:19)
19b	וְיֵבֹשׁוּ מִזִּבְחוֹתָם׃	so that they will be ashamed due to their sacrifices."	
			5. YHWH's Detailed Accusation of the People, Part III: Corrupt Leadership (5:1–7)
5:1a	שִׁמְעוּ־זֹאת הַכֹּהֲנִים	"Heed this, O priests!	a. YHWH's Summons to the Leaders (5:1a–c)
1b	וְהַקְשִׁיבוּ בֵּית יִשְׂרָאֵל	Pay attention, O house of Israel!	
1c	וּבֵית הַמֶּלֶךְ הַאֲזִינוּ	O house of the king, lend ear,	
1d	כִּי לָכֶם הַמִּשְׁפָּט	since to you belongs the justice/judgment!	(1) Their Duty to Keep "Justice" (5:1d)

1e	כִּי־פַח הֱיִיתֶם לְמִצְפָּה	For you have been a trap at Mizpah,	(2) The Reasons and Places for Their "Judgment" (5:1e–2)
	וְרֶשֶׁת פְּרוּשָׂה עַל־תָּבוֹר׃	a net spread out on Tabor,	
2a	שַׁחַת הַשִּׁטִּים הֶעְמִיקוּ	and a pit dug deeply at Shittim.[4]	
2b	וַאֲנִי מוּסָר לְכֻלָּם׃	But I am chastisement for them all.	
3a	אֲנִי יָדַעְתִּי אֶפְרַיִם	I myself have known Ephraim,	b. Grammatical Distancing as Covenantal Estrangement (5:3–4)
3b	וְיִשְׂרָאֵל לֹא־נִכְחַד מִמֶּנִּי	and Israel has not been concealed from me.	(1) YHWH's First-Person "Knowledge" of Ephraim (5:3a–b)
3c	כִּי עַתָּה הִזְנֵיתָ אֶפְרַיִם	But now, you have committed harlotry, O Ephraim,	(2) YHWH's Second-Person Confrontation of Ephraim's Harlotry (5:3c)
3d	נִטְמָא יִשְׂרָאֵל׃	Israel has become defiled.	(3) A Third-Person Verdict on Israel's Corruption (5:3d–4)
4a	לֹא יִתְּנוּ מַעַלְלֵיהֶם	Their deeds do not allow them	
	לָשׁוּב אֶל־אֱלֹהֵיהֶם	to return to their God.	
4b	כִּי רוּחַ זְנוּנִים בְּקִרְבָּם	For a spirit of harlotries is in their midst,	
4c	וְאֶת־יְהוָה לֹא יָדָעוּ׃	and they do not know YHWH!	
5a	וְעָנָה גְאוֹן־יִשְׂרָאֵל בְּפָנָיו	So the pride of Israel testifies against him,	c. The Shared Futility of Forsaking YHWH (5:5)
5b	וְיִשְׂרָאֵל וְאֶפְרַיִם יִכָּשְׁלוּ בַּעֲוֹנָם	Israel and Ephraim stumble in their iniquity;	
5c	כָּשַׁל גַּם־יְהוּדָה עִמָּם׃	Judah also has stumbled with them.	
6a	בְּצֹאנָם וּבִבְקָרָם יֵלְכוּ לְבַקֵּשׁ אֶת־	With their flocks and their herds they will go to seek	(1) Belated Rituals (5:6)
	יְהוָה	YHWH,	
6b	וְלֹא יִמְצָאוּ	but they will not find.	
6c	חָלַץ מֵהֶם׃	He has withdrawn from them.	
7a	בַּיהוָה בָּגָדוּ	Against YHWH they have committed treachery	(2) Rejected Offerings (5:7)
7b	כִּי־בָנִים זָרִים יָלָדוּ	in that they have borne strange children.	
7c	עַתָּה יֹאכְלֵם חֹדֶשׁ אֶת־חֶלְקֵיהֶם׃	Now a new moon festival will consume them with their portions."	

2. The renderings of Hos 4:17b and 4:18a follow the MT. Although *BHS* proposes several emendations (e.g., relocating the clause סָר סָבְאָם ["finishing their liquor"] from v. 18a to v. 17b), the decision of *BHQ* to refrain from recommending any emendations indicates that the MT is coherent.

3. As with the previous two verses, this rendering follows the MT. NASB and NIV apparently interpret "shields" as a metonym for the people who bear such shields, that is, Israel's "leaders" (NASB) or "rulers" (NIV). By contrast, LXX seems to read מִגְּאוֹנָהּ ("her pride/honor") instead of the MT's מָגִנֶּיהָ ("her shields"). This interpretive suggestion is followed by NRSV ("glory") and NLT ("honor"). However, the basic soundness of the MT reading is reflected in the fact that *BHQ* makes no proposals for emending the text (cf. *BHS*).

4. The Hebrew text and English translation of Hos 5:2a reflect the frequently suggested emendation [וְשַׁחַת הַשִּׁטִּים] of the difficult MT reading וְשַׁחֲטָה שֵׂטִים (Wolff, *Hosea*, 94; J. Andrew Dearman, *The Book of Hosea*, NICOT [Grand Rapids: Eerdmans, 2010], 169, n. 38.; cf. LXX). The emendation thus continues the metaphor of animal trapping with mention of the specific place of "Shittim." Alternatively, Hos 5:2a MT has been rendered as "the rebels are deep in slaughter" (Francis I. Andersen and David Noel Freedman, *Hosea: A New Translation with Introduction and Commentary*, AB 24 [Garden City, NY: Doubleday, 1980], 386) or "these perverse men have delved deep into corruption" (A. A. Macintosh, *Hosea*, ICC [Edinburgh: T&T Clark, 1997], 178).

The ending sequence of A′ (5:1) followed by B′ (5:2–7) unfolds the A/B elements in consecutive order rather than reversing them as in a traditional chiasm. This asymmetry leads some scholars to propose that Hos 4:1–19 constitutes a discrete section independent from 5:1–7.[2] More likely, the slightly uneven shape of Hos 4:1–5:7 is due to a combination of two factors. The first is that each of the individual sections often contain chiasms of their own (each to be explored below in the "Explanation of the Text"). Since the smaller chiasms furnish building blocks that are not identical in size and shape, stacking them to form a larger structure inevitably causes some mismatches at higher levels. A second reason for the unevenness is that the speaker's promotion of the A′ element ahead of the B′ element surprises the addressees of priests and royal house with an unexpected verbal assault. In Hos 5:1, the sudden command for these two groups of complacent leaders to "hear/heed!" rouses them from apathy.

As for literary form, Hos 4:1–5:7 displays a more poetic quality than the preceding chapters.[3] Parallelism between adjacent lines sometimes exhibits a paradoxical tension between orderly repetition of terms and disorderly shifts in grammatical person, gender, and number. The effect of these competing poetic tendencies can be illustrated briefly in Hos 4:4–6. On the one hand, this section exhibits repetition of Hebrew roots from one line to the text, as in the successive use of the five verbs ריב ("to contend"; 4:4a, 4c), כשׁל ("to stumble"; 4:5a, 5b), דמה ("to destroy"; 4:5c, 6a), מאס ("to reject"; 4:6b, 6c), and שׁכח ("to forget"; 4:6d, 6e). This kind of tail-head linkage[4] slows down the discourse and draws attention to the causal relationship between sins and consequences.

On the other hand, the phenomenon of rapid grammatical shifts within the same passage (often with the same verse) creates dissonance amidst the harmony conveyed by verbal repetition. For example, Hos 4:4 begins with the third-person prohibition, "let nobody *contend*" (4:4a), but the verse concludes with a sudden topic shift into the second person, "*your people* are like those who contend with a priest" (4:4c).[5] In concert with this shift, the verbal root ריב ("to contend") appears in this verse first as a jussive form addressed to a general audience but then changes to a participle that describes the actions of the second-person entity "your people." The directness of such a confrontation seems to reflect Hosea's heightened emotions at this juncture.

Similarly abrupt shifts in topic between second and third person, masculine and feminine, and singular and plural forms dot the passage. This is not to say that Hos 4:1–5:7 breaks the rules of Hebrew grammar, only that the chaotic parallelism

2. E.g., Matthieu Richelle, "Structure littéraire et interprétation en Osée 4," *RB* 121 (2014): 5–20, though he concedes that the numerous lexical and thematic links between 4:1–19 and 5:1–7 may point to a larger structure encompassing both parts (8n14).

3. Andersen and Freedman, *Hosea*, 317–26.

4. This useful label comes from *LDHB* §1.6.

5. This is the discourse feature of changed reference (*LDHB* §2.6) in which a text uses new forms of address to reconfigure the relationship among participants in the discourse.

found in Hos 4:1–5:7 explores the full spectrum of similarity and difference between adjacent lines to a much greater degree than is typical in biblical poetry.[6] The literary tension between order and disorder reflects the turbulence of Hosea's prophecies on behalf of an impassioned God.

Explanation of the Text

1. YHWH's Summons to Israel (4:1a–b)

The first cycle of covenant contentions in Hosea begins with a summons to Israel: "Heed/Hear the word of YHWH, O children of Israel!" (4:1a). The specter of the prophet's personal life disappears as the emphasis now turns fully to the prophetic word as divinely given speech. For this reason, interpreters have usually understood the command to "heed, hear" (שׁמע) as a legal summons to witness YHWH's lawsuit against his people (cf. Isa 1:2, 10; Amos 3:1; Mic 1:2).[7]

The terminology of the law court is certainly present in chapters 4–14, as noted above. But the ties of kinship remain primary in that the speech begins in Hos 4:1 with an emotionally charged, vocative form of address to the people, "O children of Israel" (בְּנֵי יִשְׂרָאֵל; cf. "Israelites" in NIV, an English designation that is more ethnopolitical than familial).[8] This title occurs several times in the sign-acts of Hosea's family (e.g., 2:1[1:10]; 3:1, 4, 5; cf. 2:4–7[2–5]), so the section of 4:1–5:7 is mainly a family "contention/quarrel" (רִיב) rather than an impersonal "charge" (NIV) or "controversy" (ESV).

However, it remains surprising that the passage then identifies the accused party in YHWH's "quarrel" (רִיב; 4:1b) as "the inhabitants of the land/earth [אֶרֶץ]" (4:1b). This topic shift to the third person creates relational distance from the previous clause's second-person summons to "heed/hear" (שִׁמְעוּ) that was directed at the "children of Israel" (4:1a). By briefly recasting the Israelites as outsiders with reference to YHWH's speech, v. 1 intimates what becomes explicit later in v. 3—the conduct of the particular nation of Israel in the "land" plays a pivotal role in God's dealings with the universal horizon of the "earth."[9] This theme of Israel's priesthood in creation will be developed further through several occurrences of אֶרֶץ in Hos 4:1–3.

2. YHWH's Initial Accusation of the People (4:1c–3)

The next paragraph marshals the evidence of the sins of omission and commission by a priestly people.[10] Due to the absence of covenant fidelity (4:1c) but the presence of Decalogue violations

6. On the characteristic tension between similarity and difference in Hebrew poetry, see Adele Berlin, *The Dynamics of Biblical Parallelism*, 2nd ed. (Grand Rapids: Eerdmans, 2008).

7. E.g., Gene M. Tucker, "The Law in the Eighth-Century Prophets," in *Canon, Theology, and Old Testament Interpretation: Essays in Honor of Brevard S. Childs*, ed. Gene M. Tucker, David L. Petersen, and Robert R. Wilson (Philadelphia: Fortress, 1988), 204.

8. On the vocative as a form of redundant address that calls the hearer to heightened attention, see *LDHB* §2.3.

9. Cf. Paul R. Raabe ("The Particularizing of Universal Judgment in Prophetic Discourse," *CBQ* 64 [2002]: 664–65) and Patrick Miller (*Sin and Judgment in the Prophets*, 10), who rightly see the universal dimensions of אֶרֶץ but overlook the distancing shift in grammatical person that creates a part-to-whole relationship between the vocative, "O children of Israel!" (4:1a), and third-person address to the "inhabitants of the land/earth" (4:1b). Hence these two groups are related but not synonymous.

10. Miller, *Sin and Judgment in the Prophets*, 10.

(4:2a), defilement will emanate from Israel's sin to infect the land/earth and inflict pain upon its living creatures (4:2b–3c). Apostasy therefore jeopardizes Israel's mission in the world to be "a kingdom of priests" who safeguard the order of creation by being "a holy nation" (Exod 19:6).

a. The Absence of Covenant Fidelity (4:1c)

The content of YHWH's indictment is "that there is no truthfulness, *and* no faithfulness, *and* no knowledge of God in the land!" (4:1c).[11] Among these three virtues of covenant fidelity that are missing in Israel, the word pair of "truthfulness" (אֱמֶת) and "faithfulness" (חֶסֶד) is especially significant in the OT for characterizing YHWH as the unfailingly loyal God of his people (e.g., Gen 24:27; 2 Sam 2:6; Ps 26:3). אֱמֶת is the quality of relational fidelity and moral integrity, while חֶסֶד is the quality of steadfastness in fulfilling a prior commitment and promise. Taken together, they express the essence of YHWH's nature as a faithful God who has irrevocably committed himself to his people (e.g., Exod 34:6; 1 Kgs 3;6; Ps 89:15[14]).[12] During the eighth century BCE, the failure of Israel to imitate YHWH in these paramount covenant virtues (cf. Hos 2:21[19]), both in showing loyalty to their God (6:4, 6) and other people (10:12; 12:7[6]), has come to symptomize the deeper problem of lacking "knowledge of God" (דַּעַת אֱלֹהִים).

Regarding this third virtue mentioned in Hos 4:1c, the nominal term דַּעַת reflects both an objective body of "knowledge" (as in NASB) as well as a subjective act of "acknowledgment" (as in NIV). Indeed, the holistic nature of such "knowledge of God" makes it an apt conclusion for the covenant virtues mentioned in Hos 4:1c. The unique combination of cognition and volition in דַּעַת reflects the all-encompassing nature of covenantal "knowledge" in Hosea's characteristic uses of the verbal root ידע ("to know").[13]

This sort of "knowledge" is both deeply personal (e.g., 2:22[20]) and includes propositional "knowledge" about God and his statutes, for the next few clauses (v. 2a; cf. 4:6; 6:6–7; 8:1) allude to the Decalogue, suggesting Israel's awareness of an authoritative body of teaching. Against the common tendency to force an *either-or* choice between "knowing God" and "knowing about God," biblical faith always links them together as the *both-and* complementarity of "knowing who God is and what he expects."[14] By virtue of capturing these many dimensions of covenant relationship in a single phrase, the "knowledge of God" is a central theme in Hosea's theology.[15]

11. The presence of redundant conjunctions וְ ("and") in Hos 4:1c, a communicative device called *polysyndeton*, has the effect of slowing down the pace of the contention and thereby prolonging the agony of the audience. As shown below, polysyndeton is even more pronounced in Hos 4:2a.

12. For further discussion, see R. W. L. Moberly, "אמן," *NIDOTTE* 1:428–29; and D. A. Baer and R. P. Gordon, "חסד," *NIDOTTE* 2:213–18.

13. Nominal and verbal forms of ידע occur 14x in Hosea, beginning notably with the marriage metaphor in chs. 1–3 (e.g., 2:10[8], 22[20]). Cf. Wolff (*Hosea*, 67), who takes the parallel in Hos 4:6 between "the knowledge [of God]" (הַדַּעַת) and "the instruction of your God" (תּוֹרַת אֱלֹהֶיךָ) to indicate that "knowledge" refers to Israel's awareness of divine revelation, i.e., the Torah.

14. Robert C. Dentan, *The Knowledge of God in Ancient Israel* (New York: Seabury, 1968), 36, cited in Gregory Vall, "An Epistemology of Faith: The Knowledge of God in Israel's Prophetic Literature," in *The Bible and Epistemology: Biblical Soundings on the Knowledge of God*, ed. Mary Healy and Robin A. Parry (Milton Keynes: Paternoster, 2007), 31. As Walter Moberly has noted, OT scholarship has long struggled with a false dichotomy between "Hebrew" (i.e., subjective) and "Greek" (i.e., objective) ideas of knowing God ("Knowing God and Knowing About God," 402–20).

15. Carew, "To Know or Not to Know," 73–85.

b. The Presence of Decalogue Violations (4:2a)

Thus Israel is not ignorant but rather willfully disobedient toward God. In place of YHWH's covenant virtues, Israel exhibits the vices of breaking that ancient and familiar code of conduct, the Decalogue. Notably, Hosea depicts the sinful behavior of the audience in v. 2a using five instances of the Hebrew infinitive absolute, in contrast to the preponderance of finite verbs in the Decalogic prohibitions of Exod 20 and Deut 5. As verbal nouns in the active voice, these infinitives underscore the present and persistent character of Israel's rebellion against YHWH.[16] In addition, the use of more Hebrew conjunctions than necessary to link the infinitives has the effect of drawing out the pace of the accusations.[17] These two features of Hebrew grammar bring the discourse to a halt with agonizing and shattering force: "[There is] Cursing! *And* deceiving! *And* murdering! *And* stealing! *And* committing adultery!" (4:2a, emphasis added).[18]

The first two verbs listed in Hos 4:2a, אלה ("cursing") and כחש ("deceiving"), do not appear in the original Decalogues nor in the subsequent case laws that explain the "Ten Words" (e.g., Exod 21–23; Deut 12–26).[19] Each of them nonetheless has similarities to individual items in the Decalogue. אלה ("cursing") refers not so much to the specific sin of profanity but generally to foolish speech and false oaths (Hos 10:4; cf. Judg 17:2), much like the commandment against taking YHWH's name in vain (Exod 20:7; Deut 5:11). כחש ("deceiving") can denote both lying words as well as the intention to defraud others (Hos 7:3; 10:13; 12:1[11:12]; cf. Nah 3:1), making this transgression somewhat broader than the commandment's prohibition on perjury (Exod 20:16; Deut 5:20).

Following these two offenses, the last three in Hos 4:2a use the same verbal roots as the Decalogues in the Pentateuch, though in a slightly different order from Exod 20 and Deut 5: גנב ("stealing"; cf. Exod 20:15; Deut 5:19), רצח ("murdering"; cf. Exod 20:13; Deut 5:17), and נאף ("committing adultery"; cf. Exod 20:14; Deut 5:18). These three condemnations reflect the sorts of real-life scenarios that the Pentateuch addresses in its case laws: גנב involves taking property that belongs to someone else (Exod 22:1[2]) or the act of kidnapping a person (Deut 24:7); רצח refers to the unauthorized killing of another person (e.g., Num 35:30; Deut 22:26);[20] and נאף refers to sexual relations with someone other than one's spouse

16. GKC §113ff; Carew, "To Know or Not to Know," 79n32.

17. See n11 above on polysyndeton in Hos 4:1c as well.

18. For this translation and its rationale, see Carl J. Bosma, "Creation in Jeopardy: A Warning to Priests (Hosea 4:1–3)," *CTJ* 34 (1999): 72–73.

19. The differences between the OT's versions of the Decalogue (i.e., Exod 20:2–17; Deut 5:6–21) have led to revisionist proposals that Hosea (as well as Jeremiah after him; cf. Jer 7:9) knew a different literary form of the Decalogue or that the various lists of covenant stipulations were in flux and did not reach their canonical form until late in Israel's history (e.g., Erhard Blum, "The Decalogue and the Composition History of the Pentateuch," in *The Pentateuch: International Perspectives on Current Research*, ed. Thomas B. Dozeman, Konrad Schmid, and Baruch J. Schwartz, FAT 78 (Tübingen: Mohr Siebeck, 2011), 289–301; Bernhard Lang, "Twelve Commandments—Three Stages: A New Theory on the Formation of the Decalogue," in *Reading from Right to Left: Essays on the Hebrew Bible in Honour of David J. A. Clines*, ed. J. Cheryl Exum and H. G. M. Williamson, JSOTSup 373 (London: Sheffield Academic, 2003), 290–300).

But rather than taking these variations in wording or order as evidence of an unstable literary tradition, it is more plausible that such variations reflect a predominantly oral culture's disposition to mix and match aspects of the Decalogue for rhetorical effect to highlight the sins of which Israel was guilty at a particular moment. Indeed, the five verbal roots of Hos 4:2a often appear elsewhere in the book to condemn Israel's sins in the eighth century BCE, sometimes in a cluster that indicates that their inextricable links (e.g., 7:1–4). For a more detailed argument along these lines, see the excursus on Hosea and the Decalogue in Dearman, *Hosea*, 150–52.

20. Thus the KJV's traditional rendering of the commandment as "Thou shalt not kill" is too broad.

(e.g., Lev 20:10[4x]; Prov 6:32). It is nevertheless significant that the semantic range of adultery in Hosea includes the figurative act of "committing harlotry" (זנה and its derivatives) associated with Canaanite nature religion (e.g., Hos 3:1; 4:13–14).

c. Sin's Defilement of the Land/Earth (4:2b–c)

The opening verse of Hos 4 has already mentioned אֶרֶץ ("land/earth") twice as the place of Israel's disobedience (4:1b, c). In what follows, the symbiosis of place and people becomes explicit through the declaration that human transgressions have a negative impact on creation itself: "They [i.e., the five sins in 4:2a] have burst out [פרץ] upon the land, and bloodshed has struck [נגע] bloodshed" (4:2b–c).[21] The passage does not identify an explicit subject for פרץ (4:2b), but the nearest nouns are the five infinitives (i.e., verbal nouns) in Hos 4:2a. This accumulation of nouns (4:2a), which is grammatically dependent on the main verb that does not appear until later (4:2b), draws intense attention to Israel's sins before describing their effect.[22]

The verbs פרץ and נגע in these parallel clauses both come from the realm of physical touch. On the one hand, Hos 4:2b describes the defilement of the land using פרץ ("to break forth, burst out"). This vivid verb refers to the transgression of physical boundaries, as when an enemy penetrates a battle line (e.g., 2 Sam 5:20) or a baby begins to emerge from the birth canal (e.g., the wordplay on פֶּרֶץ/פרץ ["Perez"]; Gen 38:29). The sins listed in Hos 4:2a are therefore depicted as a contagion that breaks out and infects the land/earth. On the other hand, Hos 4:2c uses the verb נגע ("to touch, reach, strike") to portray the infection worsening through the spread of "bloodshed/bloodguilt" (דָּמִים). The painful repetition of דָּמִים as both subject and object of נגע (4:2c) is powerful for "illustrating the way that violence breeds violence and heightening the sense of Israel [and likely creation as well] as a war zone."[23]

The term דָּמִים (an unusual plural form of דָּם, "blood") deserves special comment since it lacks an English equivalent. This single word encapsulates Israel's priestly worldview in which literal "bloodshed" causes figurative defilement of the land through "bloodguilt" (e.g., Gen 4:10–11; Num 35:33; Ps 106:38; Ezek 36:18). So taking Hos 4:2 as a whole, the blight introduced by Israel's vices (4:2a–b) has now assumed a life of its own through an escalating cycle of violence (4:2c).[24] The poetic justice of "bloodshed" for the sin of "bloodguilt" mirrors the portrayal in Hos 1 of the violent end of Jehu's kingdom as repayment for its brutality (1:4). Later passages in Hosea will return to this unnerving picture of Israel as a toxic people who have toxified their land (e.g., 6:8–10; 12:15[14]).[25]

(1) The Poisoning of Land and People (4:3a–b)

The rest of creation cannot stay mute when force-fed such poison: "As a result, the land is mourning [אבל], and all the inhabitants wither [אמל] in it" (4:3a–b). The fourth and final reference to אֶרֶץ (4:3a) in this passage (cf. 4:1b–c, 2b) portrays land/earth not as an inert object, as scientifically inclined moderns tend to expect, but as a living subject who laments the iniquity foisted upon it by the sin of the people (4:2). In the next clause, the imagery shifts from a personified אֶרֶץ to its human inhabitants who "wither" (4:3b), a verb

21. On the text-critical decision to restore this clause as "they have burst out upon the land" (cf. MT's shorter "they have burst out"), see the translation note on Hos 4:2b above.

22. See *LDHB* §4.3 on the discourse feature of fronting a subordinate clause for emphasis's sake.

23. Hayes, *The Earth Mourns*, 49.

24. Koch, "Doctrine of Retribution," 67.

25. Frymer-Kensky, "Pollution, Purification, and Purgation in Biblical Israel," 409–10.

that elsewhere in the OT denotes the loss of fertility (e.g., 1 Sam 2:5; Joel 1:10).

How should interpreters understand the poetic parallelism of land/earth (4:3a) and people (4:3b)? The tendency is to muzzle the land's own voice by classifying the literary unit of Hos 4:1–3 as a prophetic oracle of judgment against people.[26] In Western scholarship land is typically demythologized into the place and means of Israel's punishment due to the perception of "difficulty in ascribing mourning to *inanimate objects*"[27] rather than being a covenant partner in YHWH's household.[28] Interpreters adduce further support for viewing the land as the impersonal counterpart to the people from the suggestion that אבל in Hos 4:3a has a homonym that means "to be/become dry" rather than "to mourn."[29]

Nonetheless, regarding land as a synonym for people or cipher for God's punishment overlooks an important detail of the passage. Hosea 4:3 begins with the conjunctive phrase עַל־כֵּן ("as a result") to introduce the consequences that follow inevitably from the preceding list of sins (4:1–2).[30] Hosea 4:1–3 differs in this regard from chapter 2's threefold use of the conjunction לָכֵן ("therefore") to explain YHWH's direct intervention in repaying his sinful people.[31] The differing contexts of these two passages illustrate how עַל־כֵּן emphasizes the organic link between human actions and their intrinsic consequences for YHWH's order of creation,[32] whereas לָכֵן points to the juridical relationship between human sin and divine retribution.[33] Katherine Hayes summarizes well the poisonous and poisoned relationships at work in the passage: "[T]he bloodshed in the land, as well as the other harmful acts that break out within it, cause the earth to mourn, and this mourning is expressed as a drought. It is as if the blood physically alters and sickens the earth."[34]

(2) The Dissipation of the Earth's Creatures (4:3c)

The hint that אֶרֶץ refers to the entire world and not merely the particular land of Israel comes to explicit expression in the paragraph's final clause:

26. E.g., Wolff, *Hosea*, 65–66.

27. David J. A. Clines, "Was There An *'ABL* II 'Be Dry' In Classical Hebrew?," *VT* 42 (1992): 8n19; emphasis added. Although Clines is summarizing the view of others, he retains the Western modernist distinction between animate and inanimate things that inevitably places land in the latter category. Compare the non-Western reading of the Palestinian scholar Salim Munayer (*Hosea*, ABCS [Manila: Asia Theological Association, 2010], 87), who recognizes that the land is mourning as a reaction to the death of its people as well as the pollution of blood.

28. On which see the important work of Christopher J. H. Wright, *Old Testament Ethics for the People of God* (Downers Grove, IL: InterVarsity Press, 2004), 76–99.

29. Following the influential proposal of Godfrey R. Driver, "Confused Hebrew Roots," in *Occident and Orient, Being Studies in Semitic Philology and Literature, Jewish History and Philosophy and Folklore in the Widest Sense, in Honour of Haham Dr. M. Gaster's 80th Birthday. Gaster Anniversary Volume*, ed. Bruno Schindler (London: Taylor, 1936), 73–83. Those who cite Driver with varying levels of agreement include Macintosh, *Hosea*, 131–33; Clines, "Was There An *'ABL* II 'Be Dry' In Classical Hebrew?," 1–2; and Wolff, *Hosea*, 65, 68.

30. Hayes, *The Earth Mourns*, 45; Bosma, "Creation in Jeopardy," 89, 108–9.

31. Clines, "Hosea 2," 296–97.

32. Compare the incisive article on Hos 4:3 by Walter Brueggemann ("The Uninflected Therefore of Hosea 4:1–3," in *Reading From This Place, Vol. 1: Social Location and Biblical Interpretation in the United States*, ed. Fernando F. Segovia and Mary Ann Tolbert [Minneapolis: Augsburg Fortress, 1995], 231–49), who unfortunately overlooks the priestly image of pollution in Hos 4:2 and thereby concludes that "the poem carefully and deliberately mumbles over the relation between Decalogue and creation. It does not want to reduce this connection to a formula, and it does not want to identify an agent" (242).

33. Thus Klaus Koch is half-right that "Hosea is not compelled by the idea that God requites sin" ("Doctrine of Retribution," 66). This assertion is true for the creational causality of עַל־כֵּן (4:3), but less so for the divine intervention announced by לָכֵן (2:8[6], 11[9], 16[14]).

34. Hayes, *The Earth Mourns*, 51.

"[As for] the beast of the field, the birds of the sky, and even the fish of the sea—they will be taken away!" (4:3c). The trio of beasts, birds, and fish represents a reversal of the narrative sequence of creation found in Gen 1.[35] The reference to fish in particular shows that אֶרֶץ in Hos 4:3 can no longer be limited to the drought of the "land" in the specific sense but must be understood in the wider sense of "earth."[36] All the creatures of land, sky, and sea will "be taken away" (אסף *niphal*), a passive verb that, in contexts of death, refers to the ritual act of gathering the bones of the deceased for burial (cf. Gen 25:8; 49:33; Num 20:24). Considering the manifold picture of destruction painted by this passage's four references to אֶרֶץ and the creatures who live upon it, Walter Brueggemann rightly concludes that "the abuse of אֶרֶץ locally leads to the death of אֶרֶץ cosmically."[37]

3. YHWH's Detailed Accusation of the People, Part I: Contention with God (4:4–6)

Hosea 4:4–6 unpacks the preceding verses by moving to a detailed accusation of the people. Although many scholars have held that 4:4 begins a new section that is independent from 4:1–3,[38] it is noteworthy that two Hebrew terms are repeated across both sections: (1) the root ריב, both as a noun meaning "quarrel/contention" (רִיב; 4:1b) and a verb meaning "to contend" (ריב *qal* [4:4a], *hiphil* [4:4c]); and (2) "knowledge" (דַּעַת), first in the construct chain "knowledge of God" (דַּעַת אֱלֹהִים; 4:1c) and twice later in an allusive form as "the knowledge" (הַדָּעַת; 4:6a, b) that Israel rejects. These links indicate that the specific explanations of Hos 4:4–6 explain the general accusation of Israel's sins found in 4:1–3.

As noted above in the discussion on "Structure and Literary Form," Hos 4:4–6 creatively mingles the literary phenomena of repetition and variation. Following a twofold prohibition on "contention" (4:4) that summarizes YHWH's accusation against the people, the verdict and punishment against them unfolds in a series of four wordplays (4:5–6). The repetition of verbal roots lends a measure of predictability to Hos 4:4–6, even amidst the rapid topic shifts that the passage communicates through modulations in grammatical subject, object, voice, and tense for these same verbs.

These verbal variations have led commentators to disagree over whether this passage addresses an individual priest and his children,[39] Israel as a corporate priesthood,[40] the people without reference to the priesthood,[41] or perhaps even the king of Israel.[42] The last of these options is unlikely since the passage contains no references whatsoever to a king, but some combination of the first three is probable since the immediate context does refer to the audience as both people and priest(s). The commentary below will show that the fluidity of address seems to be a rhetorical device to emphasize the solidarity of the official priesthood with the people as a priestly nation.[43] The open-endedness of this presentation paves the way for explicitly linking the destiny of these two groups later in the chapter: "Thus it shall be—like people, like priest!" (4:9a).

35. Michael Deroche, "The Reversal of Creation in Hosea," *VT* 31 (1981): 400–409.

36. Hayes, *The Earth Mourns*, 41; Bosma, "Creation in Jeopardy," 106–07.

37. Brueggemann, "The Uninflected Therefore of Hosea 4:1–3," 241.

38. E.g., Wolff, *Hosea*, 73–74.

39. Andersen and Freedman, *Hosea*, 342–43.

40. Bosma, "Creation in Jeopardy," 110–11.

41. Michael Deroche, "Structure, Rhetoric, and Meaning in Hosea IV 4–10," *VT* 33 (1983): 187–89.

42. Jack R. Lundbom, "Contentious Priests and Contentious People in Hosea IV 1–10," *VT* 36 (1986): 52–70.

43. M. Daniel Carroll R., "The Prophetic Denunciation of Religion in Hosea 4–7," *CTR* 7 (1993): 25–27.

a. Censure: Contention with God and Priest (4:4)

Hosea 4:4 begins with two clauses that issue a categorical prohibition on belligerence: "Indeed, let nobody contend [רִיב], and may no one rebuke" (4:4a–b).[44] Here it is striking that YHWH forbids exactly the action that he has himself undertaken in his "quarrel/contention [רִיב] with the inhabitants of the land/earth" (4:1b). The God of Israel (and his authoritative prophets, by extension; cf. 6:5; 12:11[10]) alone has authority to challenge the conduct of his people. The placement of the verb ריב ("to contend") in poetic parallel with יכח ("to rebuke"), a verb that signifies relational strife more than legal wrangling (e.g., Gen 31:37; Lev 19:17), underlines the interpersonal stakes in Israel's conflicts with various parties, including God.

Which group within Israel is YHWH censuring in Hos 4:4a–b? The next clause supplies an answer by implying the identity of the audience: "because *your people* are like those who contend with a priest" (4:4c).[45] The condemnation of "those who contend with a priest" (a *hiphil* participle from ריב) rules out the priests themselves as Hosea's audience, at least at this juncture of the speech. Instead, Hosea's prophecy links the nation as a corporate whole (i.e., "your people") with the case law of Deut 17:12–13 that pronounces the death sentence upon any Israelite who quarrels with a priest or judge.[46]

b. Sentencing: Four Wordplays of Poetic Justice (4:5–6)

Capital punishment for Israel will nevertheless not occur in a merely judicial sphere. Four wordplays on Hebrew verbs in Hos 4:5–6 instead depict the creational principle that sinful acts will carry their own consequences. This is not so much a legal sentence directly imposed by a transcendent God from without as it is the poetic justice that is divinely ordained as a kind of death from within creation itself. In the tightly argued logic of Hos 4:6d–e, for example, a wordplay on the root שׁכח ("to forget") carries the verdict that Israel's act of "forgetting" God (4:6d) will lead to being "forgotten" by God (4:6e). The six clauses of Hos 4:5–6 thus contain a rapid-fire wordplay on verbs of act (A) and consequence (B) which leads to a threefold alternation of elements (i.e., an A-B-A′-B′-A″-B″ structure), in contrast to the chiastic structures that follow in Hos 4:11–5:7.

The first of these wordplays in v. 5a–b centers on repetition of כשׁל ("to stumble"), a verb that here signifies figurative weakness (e.g., Neh 4:4[10]; Ps 31:11[10]) rather than the literal act of tripping over something. The act of "stumbling" later becomes a summary for all of Israel's sins (14:2[1]). In Hos 4:5, the nature of the parallelism between "you will stumble by day" (4:5a) and "the prophet will also stumble with you by night" (4:5b) is somewhat unclear, but the merism "by day and . . . by night" indicates that Israel's stumbling will be unceasing.[47]

44. Since the following verses expand the terminology of Hos 4:1–3, our translation takes the particle אַךְ that opens Hos 4:4 to be asseverative (i.e., "indeed") rather than contrastive (i.e., "but, however").

45. *Pace* Andersen and Freedman (*Hosea*, 346–50), the number of emendations required to turn Hos 4:4b into a clear censure against the priest (i.e., "My contention is indeed with you, priest") speaks to its unlikelihood. The MT of Hos 4:4b is coherent as it stands.

46. Deroche, "Structure, Rhetoric, and Meaning in Hosea IV 4–10," 190.

47. Merism is the literary device of using two contrasting parts to denote the whole of something, as when the phrase "heaven and earth" (e.g., Gen 1:1; Matt 5:18) refers to the whole of creation.

Since the four other occurrences of כשׁל in Hosea refer to the consequences wrought by sin (14:2[1]), particularly those of pride (5:5[2x]) and rebellion (14:10[9]), Hosea may have in mind the ongoing refusal of the people and their false prophets to submit to his ministry of speaking YHWH's word (9:7–9).[48]

The second wordplay not only falls across two verses (vv. 5, 6), but the grammatical forms of דמה ("to destroy") also alternate between a first-person active ("*I will destroy* your mother"; 4:5c) and a third-person passive ("*my people are destroyed* from lack of knowledge"; 4:6a). The first line's mention of "your mother" as object of destruction recalls the figurative description of "your mother" in chapter 2 (cf. 2:4[2]) as the embodiment of Israel's land and perhaps also the capital of the Northern Kingdom (i.e., the city of Samaria).[49] YHWH asserts that the mother's destruction will also lead to the destruction of "*my* people." Here the shift to the first person offers a moment of soliloquy in which YHWH reasserts sovereignty over the same Israel whom Hosea had just identified as "*your* people" (4:4c). The verdict that Israel will perish for "lack of *knowledge*" (4:6a; cf. 4:1c) anticipates the next wordplay's punishment for a priestly nation that rejects "knowledge" (4:6b–c).

The following two wordplays are so closely entwined in v. 6 that we need to examine them together. YHWH frames his verdict and punishment using contrasting pronominal phrases: "Because *on your part*" (כִּי־אַתָּה; 4:6b) and "also *on my part*" (גַּם־אֲנִי; 4:6e).[50] Between these outer clauses that highlight the opposing actors, four poetic lines trace the connection between sinful act and inevitable consequence. The third wordplay uses two clauses with מאס ("to reject"; 4:6b–c), while the fourth uses two instances of שׁכח ("to forget"; 4:6d–e). Parallel to how Israel's rejecting "the knowledge [of God]" (4:6b) will result in their rejection by YHWH as "*my* priest" (4:6c), Israel's forgetting "the instruction of *your* God" (4:6d) will lead to YHWH's forgetfulness toward "*your* children" (4:6e). The deep entanglements between first- and second-person grammatical forms capture the emotional intensity of YHWH's struggle for Israel.

Intriguingly, the wordplays on מאס ("to reject"; 4:6b–c) and שׁכח ("to forget"; 4:6d–e) are also bracketed by parallel clauses about priestly rejection of "the knowledge [of God]" (דַּעַת; 4:6b) and forgetfulness of "the instruction of your God" (תּוֹרַת אֱלֹהֶיךָ; 4:6d). The term דַּעַת links back to the Decalogue (4:2a), while the mention of תּוֹרָה ("instruction/law") looks ahead to Hosea's references to a written body of teaching that derives from the covenant at Sinai (8:1, 12). Since the Pentateuch narrates the commissioning of Israel as "a kingdom of priests" (Exod 19:6) directly before YHWH's speaking of the Decalogue (Exod 20:1–17), it is probable that YHWH's rejection of "you as my priest" (4:6c) also refers to neglect of the Decalogue (4:2) by a priestly nation rather than only an individual priest or group of priests.[51]

4. YHWH's Detailed Accusation of the People, Part II: Harlotry with Canaanite Religion (4:7–19)

Following YHWH's accusation regarding the absence of covenant virtues (4:4–6; cf. 4:1c), the

48. For this interpretation of Hos 9:7–9, see Margaret S. Odell, "Who Were the Prophets in Hosea?," *HBT* 18 (1996): 83–87.

49. Dearman, *Hosea*, 158.

50. Although pleonastic pronouns of this sort are usually forward pointing (*LDHB* §1.2), it is notable that the pleonasm in Hos 4:6e ("also on my part") is unusual for coming *after* the verbal clause in Hos 4:6e ("I will forget your children"). The rhetorical effect of this clause order becomes one of rueful reinforcement instead of building anticipation.

51. Cf. Andersen and Freedman, *Hosea*, 342–43.

next major section elaborates upon the presence of covenant vices (4:7–19; cf. 4:2–3a). As noted in the introduction to the commentary, Hosea frequently uses the language of "committing harlotry" (זנה) to condemn Canaanite religion in its various social, economic, and cultic aspects. This is especially so in Hos 4:7–19, the portion of the book with the densest cluster of זנה instances (10x in just thirteen verses). The rubric of "committing harlotry" in this passage joins together several different kinds of syncretism with Canaanite ideas. These practices are initially described in Hos 4:7–19 as debauchery involving cultic sins (4:7–10) before Hosea moves to a more detailed condemnation of fertility rituals (4:11–19). In short, the passage reflects the symbiosis of idolatry and immorality in how the interpreter struggles to identify clear boundaries between paragraphs concerning these sins. The commentary below will demonstrate how one literary structure seems to crash haphazardly into the next, with previously treated themes often making an unexpected reappearance later in the passage.

a. Cultic Sins as Harlotry (4:7–10)

Hosea 4:7–10 extends the preceding attack on the nation's priestly identity (4:4–6) by taking aim at the debauchery of both common people and official priesthood. Two features mark this section as the beginning of a new literary unit (though not completely detached from what precedes). The first transition is signaled by the grammatical shifts back into the third person as a harbinger of increasing estrangement between YHWH and Israel. While the previous section concludes with an exasperated reference to "*your* children" whom YHWH will forget (4:6e), the next clause stoically names the same group as "they" (4:7a). The second transition in Hos 4:7–11 is that the connection between act and punishment develops across the entire section in a chiasm with three pairs of elements (A-B-C-C′-B′-A′) instead of the staccato-like repetition of adjacent lines in Hos 4:4–6.

At the center of Hos 4:7–11 lie two clauses that draw parallels between people and priests (C) as well as their sins and consequences (C′). The priestly sins (A) have infected the official priesthood of Israel (B) so that the two groups share the same fate (C), that is, punishment from within God's creation (C′). But unlike the logical succession of act and consequence in Hos 4:4–6, the lustful sins of feasting (B′) and harlotry (A′) will *fail* to achieve the satisfaction desired by Israel.[52] Although the lexical pairs in the chiasm are not exact (apart from אכל ["to eat"] in B/B′), the paired concepts in this passage work together to show that Israel will experience punishment as a reversal of fortunes:

A The People's Fertility (4:7): Multiplication (רבב) and Sinful Cultic Acts (חטא)
  B The Priests' Feasting (4:8): Enjoyment (אכל) of Sin (חטאת)
    C Solidarity of People and Priesthood (4:9a): Comparison of Parties (Double כְּ-Prep)
    C′ Solidarity of Act as Consequence (4:9b–c): Repayment (פקד) and Rebound (שׁוב)
  B′ The Priests' Feasting (4:10a–b): Eating (אכל) but No-Satisfaction (שׂבע לא)
A′ The People's Defertility (4:10c–d): Harlotry (זנה) but No Breakthrough (לא פרץ)

52. Here we identify the chiasm using conventional A-B-C-C′-B′-A′ terminology, in contrast to the numbered structure given above (1-2-3-3′-2′-1′), which uses an outlining schema to situate Hos 4:7–10 within the book as a whole.

(1) The People's Fertility and Sin (4:7)

The sinful interaction between people and priest in the chiastic structure above deserves special comment. Hosea 4:7 continues the preceding topic of "your children" (i.e., Israel; 4:6e) and accuses them of misusing the Abrahamic promise of multiplication: "*as soon as* [כְּ] they multiplied then they sinned against me" (4:7a).[53] The connection between "multiply/increase" (רבב) and "sin" (חטא), the latter probably ritual in nature (cf. Hos 10:8), also hints at Israel's participation in Canaanite nature ceremonies that are mentioned later in chapter 4.

YHWH will respond to syncretism with fertility religion (4:7a) by bringing disgrace upon "their honor" (4:7b). The term "honor/glory" (כָּבוֹד) appears to be a proverbial way of referring to the progeny blessing of Genesis, as when Hosea later mentions "glory" in connection with the people's ability to procreate (9:11) and Samaria's state-sponsored worship of the golden calf (10:5). This was a cultic symbol that drew upon Egyptian and Canaanite fertility icons. In an implicit manner that becomes explicit as the chiasm progresses, the people are passing their contagion to Israel's priests, the leaders who handle the rituals thought to ensure fertility.

(2) The Priests' Feasting on People's Sin (4:8)

Beginning in Hos 4:8, spiritual contagion begins its spread even at the semantic level through repetition of the Hebrew root חטא ("to sin"). While the previous verse condemns the common people's cultic actions using the verb חטא (4:7a), Hos 4:8 introduces the official priesthood as gluttonous participants in "the sin [חַטַּאת] of my people" (4:8a). Here the people's role as *sin producers* (4:7a) who feed the desires of priests as *sin consumers* is highlighted by the verb אכל ("to eat"; 4:8a). The nature of the cultic sins that pass from people to priests is not specified here, but the upcoming complement in the chiasm (i.e., 4:10, where אכל also occurs) reveals that the hedonism of the people involves a wretched combination of offerings and debauchery. At this point in the chiasm, the emphasis remains on the spread of sin from one group to another within Israel.

(3) Solidarity of People and Priesthood (4:9a)

It is nevertheless notable that the passage has not yet overtly named the priests as the next group to be infected within Israel. Rather, Hos 4:8–9 brilliantly conveys the spread of the people's contagion by another Hebrew wordplay that, unlike the obvious repetition of sin terminology, is difficult to reproduce in English. Almost imperceptibly, the referent of "they" moves away from Israel (4:6–7) and toward another group whose identity hangs in the balance until Hos 4:9a. The italics in the table below track the destabilization of the pronouns and their referents:

Negotiating Pronouns (4:8a–b)	"*They* enjoy the sin of *my people*, and *they* lift up *his* soul for *their* iniquity.
Disambiguating Summary (4:9a)	"Thus it shall be—like people, like priest!"

Who are "they" and "he" in these verses? The blending of plural and singular third-person pronouns in the two clauses of Hos 4:8 has occasioned many proposals for emendations that collapse one of the two parties into the other.[54] Yet the verse

53. The eagerness to sin as soon as receiving the blessing of offspring is highlighted by the fronted subordinate clause of כְּ-preposition + infinitive construct. *IBHS* §36.2.2b observes that this kind of כְּ-preposition clause expresses immediacy of action, in contrast to the general proximity in time as expressed by בְּ-preposition + infinitive construct.

54. E.g., Wolff, *Hosea*, 71, who uses the evidence of the textual witnesses to argue for the reading נַפְשָׁם ("their soul/life")

remains coherent when the hearer of this text pays closer attention to the interplay of plural and singular forms in Hos 4:8.

In the first clause, the ambiguous plural group "they" is distinct from "my people" (4:8a), while in the next clause the same group of "they" is the subject of the verb נשא ("to lift") who will bring "his soul" (4:8b) before God. The parallelism of similarity between "my *people*" (4:8a) and "*his* soul" (4:8b) indicates that the people are now to be identified with the collective-singular pronoun "his." In support of this shift in discourse focus, the verbal phrase נֶפֶשׁ + נשא ("to lift up a soul") is an idiom for coming to cultic worship (e.g., Pss 24:4; 25:1; 143:8), indicating that the priests are performing their regular duties on behalf of someone else.

Putting all these pieces together, the differing possessive pronouns for "*his* soul" (3rd masc. sg.) and "*their* iniquity" (3rd masc. pl.) suggest that the priests enjoy the people's sinful conduct to such an extent that they assist the people in making lavish offerings that in turn enrich themselves. This is an outbreak of spiritual contagion in which the priests consume and internalize "the sin of my people" (4:8a) so that it becomes "their iniquity" (4:8b). The infected parties finally become explicit through the arrival of the chiasm's pivot: "Thus it shall be—like people, like priest!" (4:9a). The two groups stand in sinful solidarity because the disease that originated with the common people has now spread to the official priesthood.[55]

(3′) Solidarity of Act as Consequence (4:9b–c)

The people and priest not only share in their sins (4:9a), but they will also similarly reap the fate of actions that have sown their own consequences: "I will repay his ways upon him, and I will bring back his deeds upon him" (4:9b–c). As noted above, the opening indictment of Hos 4 introduces the creational principle that YHWH deals with sin through creation's rebellion against the pollution wrought by its human stewards. The verdict of act-*as*-consequence becomes explicit in Hos 4:9 by the use of שׁוב ("to return") and פקד ("to repay, reckon"). These two verbs of cyclical motion describe the theological axiom that sin eventually rebounds upon the sinner, though using the creational images of a bottomless hunger (4:10a–b) and a barren womb (4:10c–d) instead of a sickening poison (cf. 4:2–3).

(2′) The Priests' Dissatisfaction with Feasting (4:10a–b); (1′) The People's Harlotry and Defertility (4:10c–d)

Hosea 4:10 begins to offer a mirror image of vv. 7–9, though the compactness of the next two chiastic elements within the confines of a single verse means that we need to examine them together. These verses also contrast to Hos 4:7–9 in that sin is no longer itself the agent of the sinner's suffering (cf. Hos 4:5–6), for Hos 4:10 presents sin as an exercise in futility. The chiastic structure that pairs together Hos 4:8 and 4:10 (see diagram above) condemns Israel's sins in the opposite order (B′-A′) of their initial appearance (A-B) to depict how YHWH has turned Israel's hedonistic world upside down. Feasting will lead to dissatisfaction (4:10a–b) rather than satisfaction on the part of the priests (cf. 4:8), while the sexual activity of harlotry (4:10c) will lead to defertility (4:10d) rather than

rather than נַפְשׁוֹ ("his soul/life"). This emendation makes all the third-person pronouns of Hos 4:8a into plurals and thereby obscures the connection between the priests' gluttony and their role in receiving sacrifices from the people.

55. This account of sin's outbreak in Israel is greatly indebted to Richelle, "Osée 4," though he posits a reverse order of infection from the priests to the people. This conclusion reverses the order of the comparison in Hos 4:9a, which seems to make the people a template for what happens to the priests.

the Abrahamic blessing of fertility for the people (cf. 4:7). A summary statement captures the syncretism of Israel with Canaanite practices: "For it is YHWH they have rejected by keeping [harlotry]" (4:10e).

b. Drunken Divination as Harlotry (4:10e–12)

The end of Hos 4:10 flows into the beginning of Hos 4:11 using the literary device of enjambment.[56] This is a poetic technique where one line concludes with an incomplete thought that is not resolved until the next line.[57] In Hos 4:10, the concluding verb שׁמר ("to keep") is briefly lacking a direct object. This tension only attains resolution via the next verse's first word זְנוּת ("harlotry"; 4:11), a denominative form of the root זנה ("to commit harlotry"). זְנוּת goes on to perform double duty by introducing a mini-chiasm about harlotry and drunken divination (4:11–12). The boundary between the chiasms in Hos 4:7–10 and 4:11–12 disappears by means of a Hebrew run-on sentence that explains apostasy from YHWH as both physical and spiritual harlotry:

> "For it is YHWH they have rejected by keeping [harlotry].
>
> [As for] ***harlotry***, wine, and new wine, it will take away a mind." (4:10e–11)[58]

The mini-chiasm that begins in Hos 4:11b is developed using the verb זנה and two nominal derivatives. It is difficult in English translation to capture this Hebrew root's versatility in linking the inward disposition of "promiscuity/harlotry" (זְנוּת; 4:11) with the physical sin of "harlotries/fornications" (זְנוּנִים; 4:12c) and spiritual sin of apostasy as "committing harlotry" (זנה; 4:12d). The chiasm proceeds as follows:

(A) Harlotry and Disorientation (4:11b): "[As for] harlotry [זְנוּת], wine, and new wine, it will take away a mind"

  (B) Divination's Dumb Question (4:12a): "My people will ask their stick. . . ."

  (B′) Divination's Mute Answer (4:12b): ". . . and their divining rod will tell them"

(A′) Harlotry and Wandering (4:12c–d): "Because a spirit of harlotries [זְנוּנִים] has led astray, they have committed harlotry [זְנוּנִים] from underneath their God."

The outer A/A′ clauses portray Israel's disorientation brought on by various kinds of harlotry, firstly that of wanton drunkenness through "harlotry, wine, and new wine [תִּירוֹשׁ]" (4:11). As in Hos 2:10[8], the mention of תִּירוֹשׁ hints at Israel's apostasy with other gods through the Hebrew term being cognate to Ugaritic *tiršu/trt*, one of the Canaanite gods of wine. This collaboration between immorality and idolatry becomes overt in the two A′ clauses (4:12c–d). The presence of a spiritual being that entices Israel into physical sins appears to be the referent of "a spirit [רוּחַ] of harlotries" (4:12c).[59] The profligacy of these literal

56. See discussion of enjambment in Watson, *Classical Hebrew Poetry*, 332–36.

57. It is somewhat debatable whether Hos 4:10 is poetic to begin with, given the presence of the prosaic direct object marker אֶת־ in Hos 4:10e. As Watson notes, the effect of enjambment in poetry is "to bring verse closer to everyday speech rhythms" (ibid., 335).

58. In favor of grouping זְנוּת with both what precedes and follows is the resulting three-beat rhythm of "promiscuity, wine, and new wine" (4:10e–11). The prophecy of Hosea often uses lists of three (e.g., 2:10[8], 20[18]; 4:13; 5:1). On the possibility that Hos 4:11 concludes with an implicit relative clause (i.e., the inferred "which"), see Macintosh, *Hosea*, 149.

59. Christopher J. H. Wright, *The Mission of God: Unlocking the Bible's Grand Narrative* (Downers Grove, IL: InterVarsity Press, 2006), 146; Andersen and Freedman, *Hosea*, 325.

"harlotries/fornications" (זְנוּנִים; 4:12c) leads to the second A′ clause that condemns the figurative act of "committing harlotry from underneath [מִתַּחַת] their God" (4:12d). Although the compound preposition מִתַּחַת may also be translated "in place of" (cf. Gen 30:2; 50:19), the sexual pun on Israel's participation in spiritual harlotry "from underneath" is unmistakable.[60]

Between this A/A′ frame, the two B/B′ clauses in Hos 4:12 stress the thoroughly pagan character of the proceedings. Despite being "my people" (i.e., YHWH's; cf. 2:25[23]), YHWH exposes the depravity of Israel as exemplified in the foolishness of talking to a wooden stick (B). The people are apparently so drunk with wine that they expect this inanimate object to answer them (B′). This seems to refer to a cultic instrument of divination that the people could "ask" (שׁאל) and that would "tell" (נגד) in response. At the same time, the sexual innuendo of Hos 4:11 may continue into this verse through the phallic imagery of "stick" (עֵץ, lit. "tree"; 4:12a) and "rod" (מַקֵּל; 4:12b).[61] This wordplay would underscore the crass reality that "wine has taken away the men's minds and they are thinking with another part of their anatomy."[62] The fact that Ugaritic literature euphemistically describes ritual sexual activity in terms of rods and staffs speaks in favor of the latter interpretation.[63]

c. Fertility Rituals as Harlotry (4:13–14g)

The insinuations of the previous verses spill into the open through the detailed account of sexual and cultic sins in vv. 13–14g. The diversity of participants, places, and activities in the rituals described makes it unlikely that Hosea's references to harlotry are merely a metaphor for breaking covenant with YHWH, as some commentators have argued.[64] The all-encompassing nature of harlotry as both spiritual and physical contagion that spreads uncontrollably from one group and one activity to another can be seen in the chiastic structure of these verses:[65]

(A) Older Men's Roles (4:13a–c): Canaanite Sites and Practices (sacrifice [זבח], incense [קטר])
 (B) Younger Women's Roles (4:13d–e): Sexual Promiscuity (harlotry [זנה], adultery [נאף])
 (B′) Younger Women's Roles (4:14a–d): Lesser Responsibility for Harlotry (harlotry [זנה], adultery [נאף])
(A′) Older Men's Roles (4:14e–f): Greater Responsibility for Harlotry (sacrifice [זבח] with prostitutes, going off with harlots [זנות])

Hosea identifies the epicenter of Israel's harlotry epidemic as the ancient cultic sites "on the tops of mountains" (4:13a) and "on the hills" (4:13b). These places were populated by "oak and poplar and terebinth" (4:13cα). These verses leave unstated the identity of the god venerated by Israel at these sites where "their shade is pleasant" (4:13cβ), likely a reference to the sexual pleasure of the worshipers. Although earlier OT texts mention some

60. Dearman, *Hosea*, 163.

61. Phyllis A. Bird, "Prostitution in Ancient Israel," in *Prostitutes and Courtesans in the Ancient World*, ed. Christopher A. Faraone and Laura McClure, Wisconsin Studies in Classics (Madison: University of Wisconsin Press, 2006), 50.

62. Haddox, "(E)masculinity," 193.

63. Ibid.

64. E.g., Stephanie Lynn Budin, *The Myth of Sacred Prostitution in Antiquity* (Cambridge: Cambridge University Press, 2010); Karin Adams, "Metaphor and Dissonance: A Reinterpretation of Hosea 4:13–14," *JBL* 127 (2008): 291–305; Kristel Nyberg, "Sacred Prostitution in the Biblical World?," in *Sacred Marriages: The Divine-Human Sexual Metaphor from Sumer to Early Christianity*, ed. Martti Nissinen and Risto Uro (Winona Lake, IN: Eisenbrauns, 2008), 312–13.

65. Richelle, "Osée 4," 16.

of the trees in Hos 4:13b as places where YHWH appears to his people (cf. Gen 12:6; 35:4; Judg 6:11), this verse's references to "mountains" (הָרִים) and "hills" (גְּבָעוֹת) tip the scales toward the forbidden "high places" (בָּמוֹת; cf. Hos 10:8) of Canaanite origin. Israel should have destroyed these shrines in the conquest (Deut 12:2),[66] but a victorious people redeployed them as syncretistic cultic sites to worship both YHWH and other gods (e.g., 1 Kgs 3:2–3; 11:7; 12:31–32; 2 Kgs 17:29–32).

The deity (or deities) venerated in Hos 4:13 remains ambiguous (unlike the mention of Baal[s] and "lovers" in chapter 2). Even so, the initiators of rituals on the mountains and hills clearly are Israelite men, who are the masculine-plural subjects of the roots זבח ("to engage in sacrificial feasting"; 4:13a) and קטר ("to offer incense"; 4:13b). Sacrifices and incense offerings are paired together in the pentateuchal laws (e.g., the confluence of זבח and קטר in Lev 4), so it is possible that some form of Yahwistic practice is in view.

Given the immediate context, it is more likely that Hos 4:13–14 describes the ongoing "Canaanization of Israel"[67] that began after the conquest of the promised land and continued into the monarchical period. The fact that the syncretism of cultic worship with illicit sex only worsened in the divided monarchy, and especially in the Northern Kingdom of Samaria, becomes explicit as Hos 4 shifts attention from the older men of the Israelite community to its younger women for the first time.

The next two clauses portray the younger women's involvement in syncretism as the outcome of the older men's lechery: "*As a result* [עַל־כֵּן] your daughters commit harlotry, and your daughters-in-law commit adultery" (4:13d–e; cf. 4:3a). As a discourse marker that links a statement of grounds with the facts that result,[68] the conjunction עַל־כֵּן in Hos 4:13d recalls the chapter's exposition of the principle that sin sows its own consequences (4:3a). In this case the older men's sin of syncretistic worship leads somehow to the consequence of promiscuous younger women.

In what manner does this cause-effect relationship work? The full answer is not forthcoming until the rest of the chiasm unfolds in v. 14 with its condemnation of sexualized rituals. For now, it is more important that Hos 4:13d–e does not introduce the younger Israelite women as sex workers in "sacred prostitution" or "ritual prostitution" (both terms being notoriously imprecise),[69] but as "*your* daughters" (בְּנוֹתֵיכֶם) and "*your* daughters-in-law" (כַּלּוֹתֵיכֶם; "brides" is also possible).

Here it is notable that the mention of impersonal sexual functionaries is postponed until Hos 4:14e–f, in favor of pricking the predominantly male audience's conscience to realize that these women are their own daughters and daughters-in-law. By failing to honor the family ties that bind, older Israelite men are guilty of spreading harlotry's contagion to younger women. As Macintosh pointedly observes,

> From the older generation to the younger the corruption is passed on; the example of the former prompts the excesses of the latter. Those [Israelite men] who partake in such worship fail to appreciate . . . that it is their own young who are tainted by corruption and not merely impersonal whores whom, they suppose, may be used as the objects of their lust.[70]

66. Carsten Vang traces the verbal parallels between Hos 4:13 and Deut 12:2 indicating that the former text probably borrows from the latter ("When a Prophet Quotes Moses," 297–302).

67. Daniel I. Block, *Judges, Ruth*, NAC 6 (Nashville: Broadman & Holman, 1999), 57–59.

68. *BHRG* §40.38.

69. See discussion in Introduction to Hosea, pp. 25–28.

70. Macintosh, *Hosea*, 154.

Primary responsibility for starting the contagion of Israel's harlotry thus falls at the feet of Israelite patriarchs. Instead of being the leaders of their homes these men erect the predatory societal systems that debase the daughters and daughters-in-law among them.[71]

This is not to excuse the women in Israel as blameless victims, since Hosea does enumerate their sins in "committing harlotry" (זנה; 4:13d) and "committing adultery" (נאף; 4:13e). Both verbs have already appeared several times in this chapter. While "harlotry" possesses a broad range of meaning in Hos 4, the mention of "committing adultery" refers specifically to sexual sins and occurs in Hosea's earlier allusion to the Decalogue (4:2a). It is therefore both men and women who are guilty of polluting Israel's worship and creation as a whole through sexual transgressions.

Given the emphasis on the complicity of both sexes in 4:13, surprisingly the beginning of the next verse apparently exonerates Israelite women from their share of responsibility: "I will not repay your daughters when they commit harlotry, nor [will I punish] your daughters-in-law when they commit adultery" (4:14a–d). To "commit harlotry" (זנה) and "commit adultery" (נאף) were just named in v. 13 as the sins of Israel's younger women. Thus many interpreters have questioned the assertion at face value that YHWH will not punish the women for their promiscuity (4:14a–d), especially since the broader context highlights the sins of all Israel that he promises to "repay" (4:9; cf. 1:4; 2:15[13]).[72]

The next two clauses of v. 14 indicate that the preceding negation of the women's guilt (4:14a–d) should likely be interpreted in a relative instead of absolute sense. That is to say, the women bear lesser responsibility than the men who are the leaders of the Israelite community.[73] Hosea 4:14 thus concludes by shifting attention back to older Israelite men and their lewd behavior by means of an emphatic grammatical construction: "*Because on the men's part* [כִּי־הֵם], they keep going off with harlots and they offer sacrifices with prostitutes" (4:14e–f, emphasis added).[74]

While deriving from the root זנה ("to commit harlotry"), which can be applied broadly to both men and women (e.g., Hos 1:2; 2:7[5]; 4:10), the reference to the nominal term זֹנָה ("harlot") in v. 14, along with its frequent parallel קְדֵשָׁה ("prostitute"), refers in particular to a woman who offers sexual services for payment (e.g., Gen 38:21–22; Deut 23:18–19[17–18]).[75] These repetitions of זנה-forms join the figurative disposition toward "harlotry" (זְנוּת; 4:11) to the literal sin of fornicating with the "harlot" (זֹנָה), thereby showing that the language of prostitution in Hos 4:13–14 cannot be merely a metaphorical description of apostasy.[76] The fact that the men "go off" (פרד; 4:14e) with harlots refers to pairing off and going to a private place for the purpose of sex, while the poetically parallel clause about men offering "sacrifice" (זבח; 4:14f) with prostitutes links syncretistic rituals with sex for hire, though how these practices are mingled is not stated.

71. Christl M. Maier, "Myth and Truth in Socio-Historical Reconstruction of Ancient Societies: Hosea 4:11–14 as a Test Case," in *Thus Says the Lord: Essays on the Former and Latter Prophets in Honor of Robert R. Wilson*, ed. John J. Ahn and Stephen L. Cook, LHBOTS 502 (New York: T&T Clark, 2009), 260–61.

72. E.g., Andersen and Freedman (*Hosea*, 369) propose either to read Hos 4:14a as a rhetorical question (i.e., "Shall I not . . . ?") or that the particle לֹא takes an unusual asseverative ("surely") rather than negative sense ("not").

73. Macintosh, *Hosea*, 159–60.

74. Andersen and Freedman (*Hosea*, 370) note a similarly emphatic use of the pronoun occurs in Hos 4:6b, "because on your part" (כִּי־אַתָּה). On this use of pronouns that are grammatically unnecessary and thereby draw extra attention to the "target," see *LDHB* §1.2.

75. James E. Miller, "A Critical Response to Karin Adams's Reinterpretation of Hosea 4:13–14," *JBL* 128 (2009): 503–4.

76. Cf. Adams, "Metaphor and Dissonance: A Reinterpretation of Hosea 4:13–14."

More important than these prurient details, it is instructive to compare these A′ clauses (4:14e–f) with their counterparts in the A portion of the chiasm (4:13a–b) to see the rhetorical trap that surprises the hearer with the assertion that Israelite males bear greater responsibility. The older men in both A/A′ sections are guilty of syncretistic worship through habitual rather than one-time rituals (imperfective יְזַבֵּחוּ; 4:13a/14f, lit. "they keep sacrificing"),[77] but confirmation that cultic ritual somehow involves sexual predation (i.e., the resultative mention of young women's promiscuity in the B/B′ clauses) does not occur until the A′ clause, which accuses the men of sexualized offerings with impersonal functionaries known as "harlots" (זֹנוֹת) and "prostitutes" (קְדֵשׁוֹת). The passage might appear to segregate the sexes so that men are guilty of ritual sins (4:13a–c) and women of sexual sins (4:13d–14d), only for the chiasm to end with the shocking revelation that the men's rituals are not only lecherous. Even worse than this, they may also be incestuous in nature because the "harlots" (4:14e) and "prostitutes" (4:14f) are mirrored in the B/B′ section by their own "daughters" (4:13d) and "daughters-in-law" (4:13e)!

To summarize the chiasm, this passage offers an unmistakable echo of the Judah-Tamar narrative in Gen 38. The identity of the "daughters" and "daughters-in-law" (i.e., the B/B′ sections of the chiasm in vv. 13–14) who sinned "as a result" (עַל־כֵּן; 4:13d) of their patriarchs' actions (4:13a–c) is specified in the concluding A′ section as the "harlots" and "prostitutes" (4:14e–f). Or reading the chiasm from bottom to top, it becomes likely that these women service their fathers and fathers-in-law in sacrificial rituals on mountains and hills (4:13a–c).

As Hos 8–10 also describes later, such a combination of cultic sacrifices with sexual promiscuity in Hos 4:13–14 forms part of a larger societal web of sin in which religion, economics, and politics symbiotically intertwine. However, one must be cautious not to read into Hos 4:13–14 the famous description of Herodotus the Greek historian about the lurid fertility religion of Babylonia.[78] As noted above and in the introduction to Hosea, the fragmentary extrabiblical evidence indicates that Hosea's references to sexual activity at religious shrines may amount to something less than a formal sex cult in Israel.[79]

With this important caveat in mind, two lines of extrabiblical evidence from Syro-Palestinian archaeology indicate that Israel incorporated into worship of YHWH a pervasively sexual dimension of the Canaanite nature religion. The first is the archaeological evidence of fertility icons from the time of the divided monarchy that has been unearthed at multiple Canaanite sites.[80] The second

77. The verbs in Hos 4:14e–f are imperfective forms, which means that the men's practice of sexual exploitation was repeated rather than isolated in nature. On this customary or habitual sense for the Hebrew imperfect, see *BHRG* §19.3.3; *IBHS* §31.2a.

78. Cf. May, "The Fertility Cult in Hosea," *AJSL* 48 (1932): 73–98.

79. Compare the overstatement to the other extreme by Stephanie Lynn Budin that "[s]acred prostitution never existed in the ancient Near East or Mediterranean" (*The Myth of Sacred Prostitution in Antiquity*, 1). This conclusion can only be achieved by dismissing the testimony of the biblical authors, who would have little to gain by inventing references to sexual cultic activity in the name of YHWH and then attributing it to a supposedly special people.

80. Othmar Keel and Christoph Uehlinger (*Gods, Goddesses, and Images of God in Ancient Israel* [Minneapolis: Augsburg Fortress, 1998], 133–281) show that Israelite iconography exhibits considerable diversity during Iron Age IIB-C (ca. 1000–700 BCE) due to various Mesopotamian, Egyptian, and Canaanite influences. However, consistently prominent throughout this period of divided monarchy is the motif of fertility, whether expressed through human figurines with exaggerated sexual features or other ancient Near Eastern fertility symbols such as bulls, pillars, and trees.

is that of Ugaritic mythic poetry that describes the Canaanite gods El and Baal as engaged in sexual relations with an assortment of women.[81] Given that ancient Near Eastern peoples tended to trace close links between the divine and human worlds, the vigorous promiscuity of the gods served as an object of imitation through rituals that their human followers also performed. Against this cultural norm, Hosea warns Israel of the dire consequences of venerating the fickle, lustful deities of nature: "But a people who lack understanding will be ruined!" (4:14g).

d. The Spread of Israel's Harlotry (4:14g–16)

Hosea 4:14g not only closes the preceding chiasm (vv. 13–14); it also carries the threat of contagion beyond Israel's borders. Then in Hos 4:15 the return of singular, second-person address (אַתָּה; "you"; cf. 4:4–6) marks the beginning of new sections about the spread of Israel's harlotry within the corporate body (4:15–16) and the self-destruction wrought by such behavior (4:17–19). In the first part of this progression (4:14g–16), the prophet focuses on the negative example of Israel/Samaria and its implications for the Southern Kingdom of Judah.

(1) YHWH's Warning to Judah about the Harlotry of Israel (4:15)

This section opens with an emphatic, conditional sentence that warns that the harlotry of the Northern Kingdom must not migrate southward to Judah: "If you [אַתָּה], O Israel, are committing harlotry [זנה], may Judah not become guilty [אשׁם]" (4:15a–b). Scholars tend to regard the mention of Judah in a northern prophetic book to Samaria as secondary,[82] but such a conclusion overlooks the rhetorical continuity in Hosea's theme of spiritual contagion that respects no borders. Previously the outbreak of harlotry was confined to smaller groups such as transmission between fathers and daughters (4:13–14).[83] But in Hos 4:15b, the verb אשׁם ("to be/become guilty") previews the possibility that guilt can spread, either when Samaria exports its syncretism to Judah or when Judah desires to imitate Samaria's characteristic sin of "committing harlotry" (זֹנֶה, a durative participle; 4:15a).[84] Whichever direction of travel is in view, Hos 4:15 offers a variation on the previously mentioned theme of imitation that foreshadows a larger chiasm in Hos 4:11–19. The overarching literary structure of this section only becomes visible at the end when vv. 18–19 reuse and intensify terminology that first appeared in vv. 11–12.[85]

For the Judahite hearer of this prophecy (cf. Hos 1:1b), Hosea outlines the prohibition on imitating Samaria (4:15b) as three forbidden practices: "Do not enter Gilgal, neither go up to Beth-Aven, nor swear, 'As YHWH lives'" (4:15c–e). Gilgal (גִּלְגָּל, lit. "circle [of stones]") was the site of the first Yahwistic shrine upon entering Canaan (Josh 4:19–20; 5:9–10) and remained an important cultic center in Samuel's time (1 Sam 7:16; 10:8). But by the eighth century BCE, the cultic rituals practiced at Gilgal had already degenerated into syncretism (Hos 9:15; 12:12[11]); Amos 4:4; 5:5).

Much the same is true of "Beth-Aven" (בֵּית אָוֶן, lit. "house of iniquity"; 4:15d), a sarcastic reference to "Bethel" (בֵּית־אֵל, lit., "house of God"; cf. 10:15). This place in central Canaan was where Abraham built his second altar to YHWH (Gen 12:8) as well where Jacob encountered YHWH several times

81. For references and discussion, see Introduction to Hosea, pp. 25–28.

82. E.g., *BHS*; Macintosh, *Hosea*, 162; Emmerson, *Hosea*, 77–83.

83. Richelle, "Osée 4," 18–19.

84. On the function of the durative participle in communicating repeated or ongoing action, see *IBHS* §37.6d.

85. Richelle, "Osée 4," 19.

(Gen 28:19; 35:1; cf. Hos 12:5[4]). Bethel also achieved notoriety in the latter part of the tenth century BCE when Jeroboam I, the first king of the Northern Kingdom after the division of the monarchy, chose to erect a golden calf there (and in the far northern city of Dan) as a substitute for worshiping YHWH at the temple that Solomon built in Jerusalem (1 Kgs 12:28–33).

In sum, the locations of Gilgal and Bethel in the southern hill country of Samaria were close enough to the border between the two kingdoms to tempt Judahites across for illicit pilgrimages. Ironically, the sanctuary at Bethel had been established almost two hundred years prior because of Jeroboam's desire to sever ties with Solomon's family and cult in Jerusalem, yet the Northern Kingdom now possessed the religious shrine that Judahites found attractive in the eighth century BCE. For a people of wavering loyalty to YHWH, it would therefore be blasphemy to invoke the ancient vow, "As YHWH lives" (4:15e). This oath formula is forbidden to Judahites who lack the requisite devotion to YHWH for swearing in his name (cf. Deut 6:13; Ruth 3:13; 1 Kgs 17:1).

(2) YHWH's Exposé of Israel's Stupidity (4:16)

The kingdom of Judah remains the implied audience in Hos 4:16. The prophet goes on to declare that imitating Israel is nothing short of stupid. Beastly stupidity has become the lot of the Northern Kingdom as they venerate worthless images of animals: "Since Israel has been stubborn like a stubborn heifer, now YHWH will drive them like a lamb in a broad place" (4:16a–b).[86] The feminization of Israel as a "heifer" (סֹרֵרָה) insults the masculinity of a people who prided themselves on worshiping a male "calf" (8:5–6; 10:11; 13:2). The uselessness of this beast of burden is therefore reproduced in its worshipers who are similarly "stubborn" (סרר).

YHWH degrades Israel further before Judah's eyes when the pastoral metaphor shifts in the second half of Hos 4:16 from a powerful bovine (i.e., cow) to a helpless ovine (i.e., sheep). The heifer is strong enough to stand its ground and resist its owner's commands (4:16a), but this image is replaced by that of a pliable lamb that is "driven [from behind]" (רעה) by its master (4:16b).[87] The irony of this verse culminates with the assertion that Israel's reluctant journey will take it "into a broad place" (בַּמֶּרְחָב), usually the place of safety in the Psalms for human Israel away from encroaching enemies (Pss 18:20[19]; 31:9[9]; 118:5), but here a vulnerable place for animal Israel to be set upon by predators. Hosea 4:16's act of shaming men not only as females but as helpless animals to boot would have been deeply insulting in a Mediterranean society like ancient Israel with its relational dynamics of honor and shame.[88]

e. The Self-Destruction of Israel's Harlotry (4:17)

Hosea returns to third-person address (cf. 4:7–14) with another attack against Israel's harlotry, this time highlighting its self-destructive character. The following verse opens with the raw lexical material for two withering puns in the present literary context: "Ephraim [אֶפְרָיִם] is bound to idols [עֲצַבִּים]" (4:17a). This clause contains the first of Hosea's many references to "Ephraim," one of the largest

86. The particle כִּי ("for, since, because") may also be asseverative ("indeed") since Hos 4:16a has two features of a concluding statement: (1) a shift back to a perfective verb, in contrast to the four instances of volitive imperfective verbs that precede (4:15b–e); and (2) the introduction of bovine imagery as a summary of Israel's history of stubbornness.

87. On this translation and its rationale, see Pierre J. P. Hecke, "Conceptual Blending: A Recent Approach to Metaphor. Illustrated with the Pastoral Metaphor in Hos 4,16," in *Metaphor in the Hebrew Bible*, ed. Pierre J. P. van Hecke, BETL 187 (Leuven: Peeters, 2005), 223–28.

88. Haddox, "(E)masculinity," offers a perceptive study of feminization as a shaming strategy in Hosea, but not animalization.

tribes of the Northern Kingdom and the tribe from which its first king, Jeroboam I, came. For this reason, it often functions as an alternative name for the Northern Kingdom of Israel. But where the patriarch Joseph gave his newborn son a name that means "double fruitfulness" (a noun deriving from the root פרה, "to bear fruit"; Gen 41:52), Hosea has already paved the way for mocking this cherished etymology by identifying Israel as an incorrigible "heifer" (פָּרָה; 4:16a). The pronunciation of this Hebrew term borrowed from the previous verse is jarringly close to "Ephraim" (אֶפְרָיִם; 4:17a). Thus Hos 4:16–17 begins a trend of transmuting the three consonants of the common fertility verb פרה (cf. Gen 1:22, 28; 9:1) into puns about Ephraim's infertility, as in the motifs of terminal illness (5:13), sexual impotence and dissatisfaction (7:4–8), and fruitlessness of different kinds (9:16; 13:15).[89]

Another accent on the infertility of Ephraim's fertility practices comes through naming its object of worship as עֲצַבִּים. This rare term can mean "idols" (e.g., Isa 46:1; cf. 48:5), but its three root consonants (עצב) typically refer to a different verb that means "to hurt, grieve, be distressed" (e.g., Gen 45:5; Isa 54:6; Neh 8:10–11). As Macintosh summarizes, the poignant pun on the root עצב captures how Ephraim is "enslaved by the toil and pain of their idolatry."[90] The severity and contagiousness of Ephraim's self-inflicted suffering are why Judah must step back and "leave him alone!" (4:17b) rather than imitating or intervening in the self-destructive affairs of their northern relatives.

(1) Increasing Harlotry and Dishonor (4:18)

Hosea 4:18 follows by revisiting the theme of Israel/Ephraim's harlotry in still more intense terms. Although certain aspects of this brief verse remain obscure, words and ideas from earlier in the passage reappear and apparently bind up a larger chiasm that began in v. 11 and concludes in v. 19.[91] Hosea had previously described Israel as carousing in "harlotry, wine, and new wine" (4:11bα). This drunken orgy results in Israel losing its "mind/heart" (לֵב; 4:11bβ) and being led astray by "a spirit of harlotries" (רוּחַ זְנוּנִים; 4:12c). Following the chiasm's middle section about the spiritual contamination that spreads from group to group (4:13–17), the final section in vv. 18–19 traces the downward spiral of Ephraim's self-inflicted wounds. The milder, grape-based alcoholic drinks mentioned before (4:11) have given way to stronger "liquor" (סֹבֶא, some sort of malt drink; 4:18a).

Verse 18 narrates how Israel's party should have concluded when the people "finish" (lit. "turn aside," from סור; 4:18a) their drinks, but the onset of sobriety brings neither regret nor hangover. Instead, a now-sober people plunge into even greater hedonism: "They intensify their harlotry [הַזְנֵה הִזְנוּ], her shields have cherished dishonor" (4:18b–c).[92] This double use of זנה forms (i.e., indicative + infinitive absolute) recalls the book's opening reference to "heinous harlotry" (Hos 1:2), but with the causative dimension of the *hiphil* verbal stem rather than the simple action denoted by the *qal* stem.[93]

89. Morris, *Prophecy, Poetry and Hosea*, 125–26.

90. Macintosh, *Hosea*, 168.

91. The commentary below will argue that the apparent end of a chiasm in 4:19 only prepares the way for the surprise of another chiasm (5:1–7) that is overlaid on top of the first one (4:1–19), this time through an unexpected attack against the priests.

92. The term "shields" appears to be a metonym for those who bear them, i.e., Israel's "leaders" (so also NIV, NASB).

93. For Hos 4:18c, the puzzle of referent of the comparison between loving honor "more than her pride" (מְגִנֶּיהָ) remains, especially since the next verse also refers to "her" (i.e., third-feminine singular object pronoun). No clear feminine antecedent for these pronouns appears in the immediate context. Dearman (*Hosea*, 169) plausibly suggests that the two instances of feminine pronouns "her" (4:18c, 19a) could refer back to the land (4:1–3), Israel as "mother" (4:5c), or the heifer (4:16a).

(2) Shameful Departure for Exile (4:19)

Against such a sin-infested people, a wordplay on רוּחַ ("wind, spirit") arrives bearing the creational truth that sin of such shameful extremes will have inescapable consequences. The "spirit [רוּחַ] of harlotries" that led Israel into immorality (4:12c) will be overtaken by a stormy "wind" (רוּחַ) that wraps the people in its wings and carries them into judgment (4:19a). The "wind" is probably a metaphorical reference to exile, so that its blowing takes Israel to a faraway place where "they will be ashamed due to their sacrifices" (4:19b; cf. Deut 4:27–28). Only in a place far away from the syncretistic shrines of Canaan will the Israelites come to regret their apostasy that involves a nauseating combination of alcohol, sex, and fertility rituals beneath sacred trees (4:13–14). Since chapter 2 had described Israel as committing "harlotry" (זנה) of various kinds with nary a sense of "shame" (בוש; 2:7[5]), Hos 4:19 adds the verdict of "being/becoming ashamed" (בוש) in exile, far away from the influences toward harlotry (cf. 4:13–14, 18) that drew Israel into sin.

5. YHWH's Detailed Accusation of the People, Part III: Corrupt Leadership (5:1–7)

The allusive nature of YHWH's first (4:4–6) and second accusations (4:7–19) become an overt quarrel in the third accusation against Israel (5:1–7). Compared to the previous chapter, the bluntness of a legal verdict (5:1–7) dissipates the indirectness that tends to characterize chiastic structures (4:7–19). The people at large were the main targets in the first two accusations, but YHWH now takes aim specifically at the leaders of Israel for their myriad failures in governance. As the commentary will show, the surprising rhetorical turns in Hos 5:1–2 mean that YHWH's indictment in chapters 4–5 grows in emotional intensity just as the audience might have expected it to end.

The divine speech opens with a confrontation against particular sins of the leaders at well-known places in the Northern Kingdom (5:1–2). Following this, Hosea asserts the inevitability of Israel's judgment (5:3) using the counterintuitive "logic" of the pseudosorite (5:4–7). As in chapter 2, the pseudosorite in Hos 5 is a literary device of illogic that heaps layer upon layer of absurdity. In vv. 3–7, a series of pseudosorites traces the meandering and ultimately hopeless steps of a people who have determined to walk in the ways of the nations and their gods.[94] The motif of futile journeys in these verses serves as a preview for the next passage's polemic against Israel's pursuit of foreign alliances (5:8–6:6).

a. YHWH's Summons to the Leaders (5:1a–c)

Chapter 5 begins abruptly with a summons to attention: "Heed this, O priests! Pay attention, O house of Israel! O house of the king, lend ear . . . !" (5:1a–c).[95] This trio of plural imperatives comes as an unexpected coda since the audience would have just heard Hos 4:19 as a conclusion for the interlocking chiasms of chapter 4 (e.g., starting in vv. 7, 11). But YHWH's indictment is far from over, since the command for the priests to "heed/hear" (שׁמע; 5:1a) recalls the same command directed to Israel as a whole (4:1).

94. Compare this proposal of a larger structure in vv. 4–7 with those of Patterson, "The Pseudosorites," 33; and Michael P. O'Connor, "The Pseudo-Sorites in Hebrew Verse," 242. Patterson and O'Connor identify pseudosorite sequences only in 5:4–5 and 5:4–6, respectively.

95. Hosea 5:1a is significant for being one of only two examples in the book (cf. 7:10) of "this" serving as a forward-pointing reference (it is relatively common in Amos, as in 2:11; 7:3, 6; 8:4). This discourse feature involves a special use of the demonstrative pronoun to draw attention to a target that has not yet been introduced (*LDHB* §1.2). In this case, the forward-pointing reference conveys the special urgency of how Israel must "heed/hear" what follows.

On this note, several reuses of familiar terminology strengthen the integral links of Hos 5:1–7 to the previous chapter: זנה ("to commit harlotry," 5:3c; cf. 4:13–14); רוּחַ זְנוּנִים ("a spirit of harlotries," 5:4b; cf. 4:12); יְהוָה לֹא ידע ("to not know YHWH," 5:4c; cf. 4:1); כשׁל ("to stumble," 5:5[2x]; cf. 4:5), and בָּנִים ("children," 5:7b; cf. 4:1, 6). These echoes do not mean that Hos 5:1–7 simply repeats chapter 4. As noted earlier, in Hos 5, the repetition of the summons to Israel (vv. 1–3) before presenting God's verdict (vv. 4–7) rearranges the expected B′/A′ order for the broader chiasm that spans Hos 4:1–5:7. So just as the priests might have wondered if they were off the hook due to the emphasis upon the nation's sins in chapter 4, and at the very moment when Hos 4:19 seems to have signaled the end of YHWH's accusations, the prophetic word in chapter 5 suddenly turns against the priests as first among the leaders whom YHWH will judge.

Why, then, do the targets of YHWH's indictment in Hos 5:1 also include "the house of Israel" (בֵּית יִשְׂרָאֵל; 5:1b)? In addition, the medial position of "the house of Israel" between the narrower leadership groups of "the priests" (5:1a) and "the house of the king" (5:1c) is rather unexpected. On this note, it is significant that Micah, prophesying in the same period, also juxtaposes "the rulers of the house of Israel" (קְצִינֵי בֵּית יִשְׂרָאֵל) with "the heads of Jacob" (רָאשֵׁי יַעֲקֹב; Mic 3:1).[96] This comparison with Micah suggests that the phrase "the house of Israel" (Hos 5:1b) directs attention to the royal establishment (i.e., the dynastic sense of בַּיִת, "house") as a parallel to "the house of the king" (בֵּית־הַמֶּלֶךְ; Hos 5:1c), without excluding the familial dimension in the phrase's wider denotation as "the *household* of Israel" (e.g., 1:4, 6; 12:1[11:12]).[97] This understanding of the paired references to "house" in Hos 5:1 also offers continuity with the theme of spiritual contagion in Hos 4. The contagion spreads between groups in Israel, much like an illness tends to spread first between members of an immediate family.

(1) Their Duty to Keep "Justice" (5:1d)

A pointed wordplay emphasizes the reason (כִּי) for summoning leaders to their God-given responsibility to their people: "since [כִּי] to you belongs the judgment/justice [מִשְׁפָּט]!" (5:1d; cf. 10:4). The Hebrew word מִשְׁפָּט means both "justice" as a leader's duty to uphold moral standards (e.g., Deut 16:18–19; 1 Sam 8:3) as well as the verdict of "judgment" for moral faults (e.g., Deut 17:11; Hos 6:5). Although Hos 5:1d is momentarily ambiguous, the subsequent clauses expose Israel's perversion of "justice" and confirm the punishment of "judgment" that is explained in the next verse.[98] Much like the use of דָּמִים ("bloodshed, bloodguilt") in chapter 4, Hosea again uses a pun to describe the sinner's act as the seed of its own consequence. This verdict in Hos 5:1d is directed "to you [all]" (לָכֶם), a second-person plural in Hebrew that addresses the entire group of leaders just mentioned. The fronted position of this prepositional phrase heightens the tension—is it "justice" or "judgment" that is predicated of Israel's priests and royal officials?

96. Macintosh, *Hosea*, 176.

97. This combination of royal and familial aspects mirrors the situation in King Shalmaneser's mention of Jehu as a member of "the house of Omri" ("Black Obelisk," trans. K. Lawson Younger, Jr. [*COS* 2.113F:269–70]), the Tell Dan inscription's reference to "the house of David" ("The Tell Dan Stele," trans. Alan Millard [*COS* 2.39:162–62]), and Amos's warning against "the house of Hazael" (Amos 1:4). If this last epithet refers to the Aramean state of Damascus, it may well be a case of local coloring. In all instances of using "the house of RN" to designate a nation, "RN" refers to the founder of the royal dynasty. The OT never uses "house of RN" to denote either the northern or Southern Kingdom; it always refers to the royal household/dynasty.

98. Dearman, *Hosea*, 171.

(2) The Reasons and Places for Their "Judgment" (5:1e–2)

Another instance of כִּי ("for, since, because") introduces the three lines of evidence that tilt the meaning of מִשְׁפָּט (5:1d) from "justice" to "judgment": "For [כִּי] you [all] have been a trap at Mizpah, a net spread out on Tabor, and a pit dug deeply at Shittim" (5:1e–2a). Mizpah and Tabor were in the forested heights of the Northern Kingdom where hunters would set traps, nets, and pits to ensnare animals.[99] The threefold imagery of hunting is applied to the leaders' entrapment of their people in sin, though here the metaphorical language precludes an identification of specific transgressions. Similar imagery of traps, nets, and pits occurs in the Psalms to describe the schemes of enemies against the righteous (e.g., Pss 9:16[15]; 35:7), making it ironic that Israel's enemies who trap people like animals are actually their own leaders.

More challenging to interpret is the phrase, "a pit dug deeply at Shittim" (5:2a). References to Shittim in Hosea's time are lacking, other than the proverbial link with the ancient site of Israel's harlotry with Moabite women (Num 25:1–9). Hosea 5 is therefore vague about the nature of the leaders' sins. Even so, later passages in Hosea (e.g., 8:1–9:9) and other eighth-century prophetic books (e.g., Isa 5:8–10; Amos 2:6–8; Mic 2:1–2; 3:1–9) illustrate how royal and priestly leaders in Israel colluded with local landowners to enslave poor tenant farmers in a sinful system of idolatry, immorality, and injustice. As discussed in the introduction to Hosea, the agricultural commodities produced by Israelite farmers were offered at syncretistic shrines—probably with sexual rites involved—and then taken by the central government in Samaria to buy precious metals and military protection from allies.

The preceding trio of places (5:1e–2a) where Israel's leaders perverted "justice" (the first sense of מִשְׁפָּט) confirms that "judgment" (the second sense of מִשְׁפָּט) must come. The first-person voice of YHWH returns (its last appearance being in 4:14) to confirm this verdict: "But I am chastisement for them all" (5:2b). More than being the judge of Israel's sins, as a primarily legal reading of Hos 5 would suggest,[100] YHWH reintroduces himself on more personal terms as "chastisement" (מוּסָר; 5:2b). מוּסָר signifies the wise father's dual goal in imparting "instruction" for an obedient son but "chastisement" for a disobedient son (30x in Proverbs, e.g., 1:2; 3:11; 4:1; 5:12; 13:24). The legal language of indictment (5:1–2a) now shifts to a familial image (5:2b) in preparation for the picture of relational estrangement that follows.

b. Grammatical Distancing as Covenantal Estrangement (5:3–4)

As in chapter 2, Hos 5:3–4 employs changes in grammatical person to communicate varying of relational proximity or distance. YHWH's first-person vow (5:3a–b) becomes a direct second-person confrontation (5:3c) before the emotional intensity dissipates in a third-person verdict against Ephraim (5:3d–4).

(1) YHWH's First-Person "Knowledge" of Ephraim (5:3a–b)

YHWH continues the previous verse's sudden shift to "I"-speech (אֲנִי; 5:2b) with two more solemn references to himself: "I myself have known [אֲנִי יָדַעְתִּי] Ephraim, and Israel has not been concealed from me [מִמֶּנִּי]" (5:2b–3b). Like the familial language of מוּסָר ("chastisement"; 5:2b), ידע ("to know"; 5:3a) is the usual root for the intimacy of husband-wife relations (e.g., Gen 4:1; 1 Sam 1:19). The first-person description of YHWH who "knows" (ידע)

99. Macintosh, *Hosea*, 176.

100. E.g., Wolff (*Hosea*, 95–96) regards Hos 5:1–7 as a combination of the legal genres of messenger speech (vv. 1–3) and prophetic disputation (vv. 4–7).

his covenant partner recalls chapters 1–3 (e.g., 2:22[20]), while the parental picture of God as one who wisely but firmly "chastises" (יסר, the verbal root for מוּסָר) in Hos 5:2 awaits fuller development in later passages (e.g., 7:12, 15; 10:10).

(2) YHWH's Second-Person Confrontation of Ephraim's Harlotry (5:3c)

Hosea 5:3–4 begins to modulate the use of grammatical person to express the growing estrangement between YHWH and Israel. Following the first-person speech of YHWH (i.e., "I, myself, me"), which exposes the pointlessness of Israel's attempts to hide (5:2b–3b), YHWH turns directly to his people to warn them, addressing them directly with "you."[101] This omniscient God exposes the sins of his people: "But now, you have committed harlotry, O Ephraim, Israel has become defiled" (5:3c–d). The discourse marker, "But now" (כִּי עַתָּה), marks a change in topic from Israel's past inability to hide sin (cf. 5:3a–b) to YHWH's present ability to confront sin (5:3c).[102] And as already seen in 4:16–17, God used "Ephraim" (i.e., "double fruitfulness") as an ironic title to criticize the people for their fertility rituals (compare a similar link in Hos 5:3a), but "Israel" is a broader term that can refer to people, land, or both at the same time.

The parallel epithets in Hos 5:3c–d raise the question—which nuance for "Israel" is in view? It is probable that the contamination wrought by the harlotry (זנה) of "Ephraim" (5:3c; cf. 4:10–14) results in "Israel" as land "being/becoming defiled" (טמא; 5:3d).[103] The cultic rituals associated with "committing harlotry" (זנה; 5:3c; cf. 4:13–14) backfire so that what ensues causes damage to the land rather than its flourishing (cf. 9:13–16).[104] In this regard the stative verb טמא denotes ritual defilement that stands at the extreme opposite end of the spectrum from the superlative holiness of YHWH (e.g., Lev 10:10; 11:44).[105] The priests who headline YHWH's indictment (5:1a) would have been horrified by Hosea's redeployment of familiar concepts to attack them as destroyers of the order of creation rather than its preservers.

(3) A Third-Person Verdict on Israel's Corruption (5:3d–4)

The widening relational chasm between YHWH and his people is also evident in the change from an impassioned second-person vocative, "O Ephraim" (5:3c), to YHWH's complete disappearance from the next clause (5:3d). It appears that the emotional turbulence of condemning "you" for harlotry (5:3c) leads to a detached account of Israel's defilement using a third-person, passive verb of "being/becoming defiled" (טמא *niphal*; 5:3d) without so much as mentioning YHWH as subject or object. It is even unclear whether Hosea is now the one speaking or if YHWH is referring to himself in the third person. In any case, grammar and theology converge in vv. 2–3 to show that polluted Israel is now alone and as far from YHWH as can be.

101. See n. 5 above on the discourse feature of changed reference (*LDHB* §2.6).

102. In discourse terms, עַתָּה is serving in this context more as a discourse marker that links the *premise* of Israel's sin to the *logical conclusion* that YHWH must confront sin (i.e., "therefore"; *BHRG* §40.39.1) than as an adverb that shifts the focus to the speaker's present frame of reference (*BHRG* §40.39.2).

103. The root טמא ("to be/become unclean") can denote the ritual defilement of both people (e.g., Gen 34:5; Lev 7:21; Num 19:11–12; cf. Isa 6:5; Ezek 14:11) and land (e.g., Lev 18:25–28; Num 35:34; Josh 22:19; cf. Amos 7:17; Jer 2:7).

104. The case for viewing Hos 5:3c as a case of spiritual contamination finds support in the unusual use of the *hiphil* stem for the root זנה (cf. Hos 4:10, 18). This yields the sense of "to draw into committing harlotry, to make into a harlot," since the causative stem tends to be transitive and requires a direct object to be acted upon, in this case "Israel" as land in the next clause.

105. Philip P. Jenson, *Graded Holiness: A Key to the Priestly Conception of the World*, JSOTSup 106 (Sheffield: JSOT Press, 1992), 43–54.

Apostasy has become so pervasive that any possibility of repentance is paralyzed by Israel's deep investments in sin: "Their deeds do not allow them to return [שׁוּב] to their God" (5:4a). Other Hosean uses of שׁוּב ("to repent, turn, return") summon Israel to return to YHWH (e.g., 12:7[6]; 14:2[1]) or speak of restoration in the future after judgment has passed (2:9[7]; 3:5). But at the present juncture in the eighth century BCE, the possibility of journeying back to YHWH has been obviated by Israel's sinful entanglements in economics, religion, and politics—themes that will especially come to the fore in Hosea 7–8.

Hosea asserts that this inability to turn away from danger is due to Israel's inner corruption rather than any external constraints from YHWH: "For a spirit of harlotries is in their midst, and they do not know YHWH!" (5:4b–c). In Hos 5:4b, the "spirit of harlotries" (רוּחַ זְנוּנִים) that previously enticed Israel from a distance and "led them astray" (4:12) has now been ushered into the body politic as an honored guest "in their midst" (בְּקִרְבָּם, lit. "in their inner part[s]").[106] The corollary of YHWH's expulsion from among his people is accentuated by a hideous contrast between the God who asserts, "I myself have known Ephraim" (5:3a) and his people who "do not know YHWH" (5:4c).

c. The Shared Futility of Forsaking YHWH (5:5)

Despite being unwelcome among his people, the God of Israel will not remain silent. In this regard, the first clause of v. 5, "So the pride of Israel testifies against him" (5:5a; cf. 7:10), needs comment. Although "testify against him" (עָנָה בְּפָנָיו, lit. "to answer/respond against his face") refers to a confrontation and is clearly negative, the meaning of "the pride of Israel" (גְּאוֹן־יִשְׂרָאֵל) is ambiguous. This Hebrew construct chain that begins with "pride" (גְּאוֹן) could refer either to Israel's sinful self-confidence (e.g., Isa 23:9; Amos 6:8) or to YHWH himself as Israel's object of exultation (e.g., Exod 15:7; Mic 5:3[4]). The negative interpretation is more likely here considering the next clause's prediction that, in lieu of repentance toward YHWH, Israel will instead journey in unstable places: "Israel and Ephraim stumble [כשׁל] in their iniquity" (5:5b). However, the positive interpretation of "the pride of Israel" is also possible if YHWH remains present in Israel as a witness to "testify against him" (5:5a) and as the enforcer of creational order who causes his people to "stumble in their iniquity" (5:5b; cf. 4:5a–b).

Whichever interpretation of Hos 5:5a–b one chooses, the final clause of the verses makes clear that those who stumble are not only Israel as a whole—the verb כשׁל occurs again with the Southern Kingdom as its grammatical subject: "Judah also has stumbled with them" (5:5c). Many have excised this reference to the Southern Kingdom as an intrusive addition.[107] But just as partners in a three-legged race will collapse in a heap should only one of them lose their balance, the fates of the kingdoms of Israel and Judah are closely linked. What Israel is prone to do (the habitual *yiqtōl* forms of 5:5a–b), Judah has already determined to join in doing (the past perfective *qātal* of 5:5c). The stumbling of one unavoidably drags down the other given the shared history, adjacent geography, and common spiritual heritage that join these nations.

(1) Belated Rituals (5:6)

The pseudosorites of wayward journeys that have been limping through the present passage

106. קֶרֶב ("inward part, midst") is a collective term for a person's literal and figurative internal organs that are "the bearer of man's spiritual and ethical impulses" (Hans Walter Wolff, *Anthropology of the Old Testament* [Philadelphia: Fortress, 1974], 66).

107. E.g., Emmerson, *Hosea*, 65–67.

specify the nature of this stumbling. Although sin has paralyzed the people of God and made them unable to return to YHWH (5:4), and they have set out on pilgrimage but stumble into sin (5:5), they persist in setting out on a futile journey to worship YHWH: "With their flocks and their herds they will go to seek YHWH, but they will not find" (5:6a–b). Here the livestock are probably sacrificial animals to be taken to Israelite cultic shrines, perhaps at Mizpah, Tabor, and Shittim (cf. 5:1e–2a). The likelihood of a religious pilgrimage to these sites finds support in the mention of Israel's God as subject of the verbs "seek" (בקשׁ) and "find" (מצא), a conceptual pair that often occurs in the context of prayer and worship (e.g., Deut 4:29; 2 Chr 15:4; Jer 29:13). Nonetheless, the religious sphere is still tied to politics and economics, since these two verbs also appear earlier with reference to Israel's dealings with "lovers" (2:8–9[6–7]) who are both foreign alliance partners and Canaanite deities. Parallel to the seeking of paramours in chapter 2, the people's seeking of YHWH will fail because "he [YHWH] has withdrawn from them" (5:6c).

(2) Rejected Offerings (5:7)

The momentum of illogic staggers toward a conclusion in Hos 5:7. For even if a spiritually immobile people (5:4) manage to plod their way toward YHWH (5:5) and perform syncretistic rites at their local shrines (5:6a), and despite the unlikelihood that they find YHWH there (5:6b–c), such a flurry of religious activity would still not gain the favor of their God: "Against YHWH they have committed treachery in that they have borne strange children" (5:7a–b). The "treachery" [בגד] of covenant faithlessness (cf. 6:7) results in bearing "strange children" (בָּנִים זָרִים; 5:7b), a phrase that recalls the "children of harlotry" (יַלְדֵי זְנוּנִים) born to Hosea and Gomer (1:2). Since the adjective זָר ("strange") connotes something pagan and dangerous (e.g., Lev 10:1; Deut 25:5), the children mentioned here are likely the illegitimate offspring of fertility rites (cf. 4:13–14). The impressionistic language makes certainty impossible, of course, but the likelihood of a ritual interpretation increases in light of the next clause.

Hosea expresses the conclusion of the pseudosorite in a bizarre reversal of the usual relationship between worshipers and their gatherings: "Now a new moon festival will consume them with their portions" (5:7c). In ancient Israel, the "new moon festival" (חֹדֶשׁ, sometimes translated "month") was a monthly event that heralded major events on the festal calendar (e.g., Num 10:10; 28:11; Isa 1:14). But where the new moon was traditionally a time of joyful feasting (1 Sam 20:5), Hosea personifies the feast as a glutton with an insatiable appetite to devour both the worshipers and "their portions" (חֶלְקֵיהֶם). This noun from the root חלק ("to apportion, divide, share") is probably a reference to the priests' share of the offerings (Lev 6:10[17]; Deut 18:8), or perhaps the tribal lands that produced these agricultural goods (Deut 10:9; Amos 7:4). Both possibilities fall within the semantic range of חֵלֶק ("share, portion").

In either case, what should have been a celebration of creation's bounty becomes creation's rebellion against its unrighteous priests. The pilgrimage on which Israel set out to worship YHWH (5:4–6) has accomplished nothing less than the destruction of the land and people (5:7). In summary, the act-as-consequence wordplay on אכל ("to eat, consume"; 5:7c) not only develops the theme of futile feasting from the middle of the chiasm in chapter 4 (Hos 4:8, 10), but the portrayal of an unruly and ravenous creation also closes the larger section of Hos 4:1–5:7 by providing an *inclusio* to the mourning of creation after a priestly people have sinned (4:1–3).

Canonical and Theological Significance

1. Creation, Covenant, and Priesthood

"The world is charged with the grandeur of God." The stirring introduction of Gerald Manley Hopkins's poem, "God's Grandeur" (1877), challenges the dominant view in modernity that the land beneath our feet is simply an *it*. But as this Victorian poet recognized, regarding God's creative handiwork as an inert object ultimately leads to polluting creation and its denizens to the utmost. A few lines later, Hopkins laments the consequences of people mistreating the land that has nurtured and sustained them: "Generations have trod, have trod, have trod; And all is seared with trade; bleared, smeared with toil; And wears man's smudge and shares man's smell: the soil is bare now, nor can foot feel, being shod."[108]

In the act of severing our primeval connection to the ground, the shoes on our feet serve as microcosm of a larger tragedy. Modern humanity has mostly forgotten that it does not stand in a subject-object relationship to an impersonal thing called *nature* but as smaller subjects enveloped by a personal creation, behind which stands the greatest subject who is the Creator himself.[109] The environmental crises of our time—shrinking biodiversity, growing scarcity of clean water, and the buildup of untreated industrial waste, to name just a few—are not simply consequences of modernization and consumerism gone awry, but come from the deeper issue of estrangement from the world that God has made.[110] Reconciliation between humanity and the rest of creation, and even more with the Creator whose electric presence infuses everything, is the urgent need for our time.[111]

While Hos 2 and 14 describe this cosmic reconciliation to come, the passage at hand in chapters 4–5 highlights the estrangement between people and land (as well as humanity and world) when sin enters God's creation. The various transgressions of Israel that this passage lists are familiar enough from the Decalogue—cursing, deceiving, murdering, stealing, and adultery (4:2). But as noted above, what is unexpected for contemporary readers is the following assertion (4:3) that covenantal rupture and creational chaos are closely linked.[112] God has ordained that the lives of humanity and the rest of creation are entwined so that they share their welfare in a symbiotic relationship.

The notion that creation is alive is not Eastern pantheism, the worldview in which

108. Text taken from Gerard Manley Hopkins, *"God's Grandeur" and Other Poems* (New York: Dover, 1995), 15.

109. Simkins, *Creator and Creation*, 34–40.

110. Noah Toly and Daniel I. Block, eds., *Keeping God's Earth: The Global Environment in Biblical Perspective* (Downers Grove, IL: IVP Academic, 2010).

111. Fred Bahnson and Norman Wirzba, *Making Peace with the Land: God's Call to Reconcile with Creation* (Downers Grove, IL: InterVarsity Press, 2012), 28–35.

112. Brueggemann, "The Uninflected Therefore of Hosea 4:1–3."

only a single, sacred, and absolute reality exists. Nor is this to be confused with the animist's view that every nonhuman creature possesses a spiritual essence whose power can often surpass that of humans. Rather, the biblical perspective reflected in Hos 4:1–5:7 understands that humanity is commissioned to reflect the *imago Dei* (Gen 1:26–28) in the priestly task of "serving" (עבד) and "guarding" (שׁמר) creation (Gen 2:15; compare the same pair of verbs which describe the Levites' responsibilities in Num 3:7–8). The entirety of the world is conceived in the biblical storyline as sacred space to be managed by humanity as YHWH's vice-regents.[113] But as Hosea and other passages in the OT Prophets outline (e.g., Amos 1:2; Isa 24:4; Jer 12:4), the tragedy is that creation mourns and withers when the people of God, who should have been priests for all humanity (Exod 19:5–6), instead become purveyors of pollution, both spiritual and physical.[114]

The wailing of creation against covenant violations can at first be difficult for us to hear, given that the shape of covenant and creation's interlinkages in our time is not identical to ancient Israel. It is safe to say that Christians in the twenty-first century do not share the priestly and theocratic framework in which obedience to the covenant made at Mount Sinai links directly to ancient Israel's ability to remain in its land (cf. Lev 26; Deut 27–28). Part of the reason for losing one's organic connection to land, of course, is that mass migration has led to the majority of the world's inhabitants dwelling in urban centers for the first time in human history.[115] Although a crowded world now tends to stack people vertically in cities, the nexus between human obedience to God and creational flourishing remains today because the world reflects, above all, the Creator's moral order in which acts have consequences.[116] Creation still speaks to those who have ears to hear (Hos 4:1–3; cf. Ps 19:1–4).[117] It thus remains possible to draw contemporary analogies with priestly Israel's failures that allow us to hear creation's voice anew.

The first bridge with our world lies in how Hos 4:2–3 traces Israel's downward spiral from the sins of depersonalizing others in the community (4:2a) to escalating violence between people (4:2b–c), and finally to the dire consequences suffered by all God's creatures (4:3). The history of industrial farming's growth in the twentieth

113. Daniel I. Block, "To Serve and to Keep: Toward a Biblical Understanding of Humanity's Responsibility in the Face of the Biodiversity Crisis," in *Keeping God's Earth*, 126–32.

114. For a convincing case that the personification of creation cannot be reduced to a figure of speech, see The Earth Bible Team, "The Voice of Earth: More than Metaphor?," in *The Earth Story in the Psalms and the Prophets*, ed. Norman C. Habel, The Earth Bible 4 (Sheffield: Sheffield Academic, 2001), 23–28.

115. According to the World Health Organization's website, the second decade of the twenty-first century marks the turning point in history when more people will live in cities than in rural areas ("Urban Population Growth: Situation," http://www.who.int/gho/urban_health/situation_trends/urban_population_growth_text/en/).

116. On the role of Israel's covenantal relationship to God as a model of how all peoples were to relate to God, see Wright, *Old Testament Ethics for the People of God*, 62–74.

117. Melissa Tubbs Loya, "'Therefore the Earth Mourns': Exploring the Grievance of Earth in Hosea 4:1–3," in *Exploring Ecological Hermeneutics*, ed. Norman C. Habel and Peter L. Trudinger, SBLSymS 46 (Atlanta: SBL Press, 2008), 53–62, shows that the earth is the main actor and speaker in Hos 4:1–3.

century, for instance, reads in many ways like the threefold act of de-creation mentioned in these verses. Much like latifundialization was an instrument of the elite to maximize agricultural production and enrich themselves during the eighth century BCE,[118] today farmers the world over, who used to work their own land, have often become migrant tenants or indentured servants of large enterprises that control the entire farming process. The agronomic push to maximize efficiency and year-round consumer choice impels the use of nonnatural means of farming to counter decreasing returns from the land.[119] Yet this strategy succeeds only in jeopardizing further and irreversibly the long-term sustainability of the land's production.[120]

Industrial farming and other commodity-driven macroeconomics often begin a vicious cycle in which the spiritual pollution of objectifying resources (i.e., people, land, water, and harvest) begins to eat into profits due to the obstacle of physical pollution. As famously narrated in John Steinbeck's novel *The Grapes of Wrath*, sinful corporations inevitably resort to violence to safeguard their interests and maintain expedient walls separating the "haves" from the "have-nots." This approach sows further seeds of violence among the beleaguered "have-nots," who tend to turn against one another while coping with the stress of living under such oppressive systems. Sin's very nature is to beget further sin so that the question of the first sinner in the chain becomes irrelevant, for all practical purposes.[121]

The Dust Bowl's ageless narrative of economic migrancy colliding with social unrest, both of which spring from and propagate creational trauma, continues to repeat itself. To mention just a few examples in recent history—the lucrative trade in African "blood diamonds" that funds and fuels regional conflicts; the toxic legacy of California's 1849 Gold Rush in that mercury used for mining continues to poison water and river/ocean life over a century later; and the overfishing of southeast Asia's oceans that favors the rise of oppressive fishing conglomerates which employ slave labor from developing countries.

In short, the sinful synergy of economics, religion, and politics in eighth-century-BCE Israel is not so different from the modern chain of production, nearly every step of which is tainted by depersonalizing people and the rest of creation—all toward the end of supplying goods to the unsuspecting consumer. Yet for all their product choices, consumers can end up just as dehumanized as producers by settling for greater affinity with things than with people. Walter Brueggemann observes that frantic modern people may as well be living in ancient Egypt where "Pharaoh's *system*

118. See "Historical Background to Hosea's Prophecy" in the introduction to Hosea, pp. 25–28.

119. Bahnson and Wirzba, *Making Peace*, 95–97.

120. Calvin B. DeWitt, "Unsustainable Agriculture and Land Use: Restoring Stewardship for Biospheric Sustainability," in *Creation in Crisis: Christian Perspectives on Sustainability*, ed. Robert S. White (London: The Society for Promoting Christian Knowledge, 2009), 137–56.

121. Cornelius Plantinga, *Not the Way It's Supposed to Be: A Breviary of Sin* (Grand Rapids: Eerdmans, 1999), 52–77.

of production and consumption had, as its major output, systemic anxiety that pervaded every level of society."[122]

How should we then live amidst the unrootedness and contamination of our world? Our passage addresses this question by narrowing its focus from the cosmos to the ethical responsibilities of God's priestly people. Hosea 4:4–6 asserts that the people of YHWH cannot blame their institutions since they are a corporate priesthood who have themselves fallen into sin.[123] To cast the entire nation as priests evokes how YHWH calls the newly redeemed community of Israel "a kingdom of priests and a holy nation" (Exod 19:6). The God who owns the whole earth (Exod 19:5) hereby commissions his mediators to a distinctive way of life that will serve as a model for the world to watch, seek, and imitate (cf. Deut 4:5–8),[124] an idea that is the OT mirror of Jesus's command that his disciples should live as "the light of the world" (Matt 5:14). This is perhaps why the apostle Peter combines the images of priesthood and light (1 Pet 2:9–10) at the beginning of his exposition about how Christians ought to remain consecrated to God in a hostile society, no matter how great the obstacles they face (1 Pet 2:11–25).

To live as a priestly people among the nations therefore brings great privileges and responsibilities. But when the leaders among this priestly people go astray, devastating consequences follow due to the overturning of God's moral order by those who ought to have maintained it. The next passage details the prophet's role in holding accountable this priestly people and the official priesthood at their shared point of weakness—the constant temptation of syncretism that uses cultic rituals as a means for satisfying their fleshly desires.

2. Spiritual Harlotry, "Rape/Porn Culture," and Whistleblowing

The other bridge to the present comes in the timeless truth that worldliness often spreads like an infection between people and their leaders (Hos 4:7–10). Other passages in Hosea describe sin mainly as a figurative journey from leaders down to people (e.g., 8:1–9:9). In this passage, however, the spiritual harlotry of pursuing fertility, food, and debauchery is a contaminant that both pollutes priests with the people's sins, as well as travels in the opposite direction when the leaders retransmit their transgressions back to the people through sins in the political realm (5:1–7).

122. Walter Brueggemann, "Sabbath as Antidote to Anxiety," in *Disruptive Grace: Reflections on God, Scripture, and the Church* (Minneapolis: Augsburg Fortress, 2011), 55, emphasis original. See also the insightful discussion of "Leaving Egypt Behind: Embracing the Wilderness Economy" in Ellen F. Davis, *Scripture, Culture, and Agriculture: An Agrarian Reading of the Bible* (Cambridge: Cambridge University Press, 2009), 66–79.

123. See the commentary above on taking the mention of "priest" (4:6) as referring to Israel as a corporate priesthood.

124. Wright, *Old Testament Ethics for the People of God*, 64–65.

On the one hand, the chiasm in Hos 4:7–10 interweaves sins of sex, cult, and gluttony in a manner exemplifying how human desires and religious syncretism frequently work together. More than the outward act of venerating a deity, the twin inward impulses for the sacred and pleasurable become tightly enmeshed. In their insightful book on idolatry, Halbertal and Margalit note that "first, idolatry itself is described as a sin akin to adultery; second, the worshipers of idols do so in order to permit adultery. According to the internal logic of the biblical metaphor, if sexual sins in the sphere of the family are permitted, then idolatry in the sphere of the relationship between human beings and God will also be permitted, and vice versa."[125] That is to say, sexual immorality is symbiotic with many other kinds of sins.

On the other hand, Hos 4:11–5:7 goes on to detail the ways in which "harlotry" in Israel acts in synergy with cultic violations and social injustice. To be specific, Hosea exposes the older men of the covenant community for sexual predation against the younger women in their midst. Then and now, sinful males in positions of influence tend to exercise their power over others, especially women, by letting their "stick" (4:12) direct the course of their lives rather than their "mind" that they have lost (4:11). Unhesitatingly, the prophet speaks against such depersonalization of sex with the reminder that these women were "your daughters" and "your daughters-in-law" (4:13d–14c) long before they became "harlots" and "prostitutes" (4:14e–f). The historical particulars behind these lewd rituals are difficult to reconstruct, but it is clear that the male spiritual leaders of Israel have abused their position to enrich themselves, both with food/drink and sex (4:11–12, 17–18). This is not to excuse the women from their share of blame for participating in these rituals, but Hosea lays primary responsibility at the feet of men who should have protected the shalom of their community by realizing that the women they objectified were their own flesh and blood.

Unfortunately, it remains a truism today that powerful men exploit the weak who are under them, both figuratively through oppression and literally through sex. So although Hosea is sometimes accused of being a misogynistic prophetic book (on which see commentary on Hos 2), we should observe that Hos 4:1–5:7 passes over the assumption of the prophet's brothers in Israel being the stronger (physical) sex on the way to leveling a broadside against the leading men of his community for being sexual predators (4:13–14). Particularly against the priesthood and elders (cf. 5:1–2), Hosea took a bold stand against "rape culture" in the eighth century BCE long before this term was popularized by the modern feminist movement to describe the chauvinistic idea that the vulnerable somehow deserve to be violated.[126]

This means that Hosea's attack on harlotry, far from being anti-women or sexually repressive, is feminist for his time and place. Male leaders need to learn from this

125. Halbertal and Margalit, *Idolatry*, 23–24.

126. E.g., Emilie Buchwald, Pamela R. Fletcher, and Martha Roth, eds., *Transforming a Rape Culture*, rev. ed. (Minneapolis: Milkweed, 2005).

prophet's example of shaming their brothers for their oppression of the weaker members of the community, especially in the form of lechery toward younger women and girls. This condemnation of "harlotry" includes but is not limited to the sex act itself, since ancient and modern cultures have deeper interconnections among sex, religion, politics, and economics than people typically realize. This principle underlies the statement attributed to the Irish poet Oscar Wilde: "Everything in the world is about sex except sex. Sex is power."

Depersonalization of humans and creation by the powerful continues in our time through the less obviously exploitative but no less dangerous complex of harlotries in "porn culture." This umbrella term refers to more than the existence of explicit images, including cottage industries and macroscopic systems that have made sex ubiquitous in the modern world.[127] The factors undergirding "porn culture" would include, to name just a few, the idealization of women's bodies in mass media, women and child trafficking, the drug trade that is part and parcel of prostitution, and the social and economic inequities that can leave women few options for survival except to sell themselves for sex (e.g., Fantine in Victor Hugo's *Les Misérables*).

The Christian tradition has tended to individualize sexual sin of this nature, often in ways that disproportionately shame the female party.[128] In contrast, Hos 4:1–5:7 places sexual sin within a larger societal matrix of literal and figurative "harlotry"—the lusts of economic, political, and religious institutions that serve themselves rather than the people and the God they should be serving. Knowingly or not, the quest of institutions to maintain order or propagate themselves can come at the expense of commoditizing people and the rest of creation. Bahnson and Wirzba aptly summarize the moral disaster of making life a means to the ends of progress and productivity: "Our growing separation from the land and our lack of understanding of the land's integrity result in a growing separation from people. Just as we view land abstractly—as a pile of natural resources—we also come to see people abstractly—as fodder for the growing economy. *People cease to matter except if they contribute to a business plan.*"[129]

Institutions, systems, and organizations remain a necessary part of human existence, to be sure. But our generation demands whistleblowers and prophets such as Hosea who oppose pragmatic institutions when they depersonalize life and trample the weak and vulnerable in the process. As difficult as it was for Hosea to be a prophet who opposed kings and priests—the other two main leadership offices in ancient Israel—the history of God's people preserved in Scripture reveals that the

127. Carmine Sarracino and Kevin M. Scott, *The Porning of America: The Rise of Porn Culture, What It Means, and Where We Go from Here* (Boston: Beacon, 2008).

128. As exemplified in Nathaniel Hawthorne's 1850 novel, *The Scarlet Letter*.

129. Bahnson and Wirzba, *Making Peace*, 33; emphasis added.

whistleblowing ministry of the prophets had the last word. Unlike the Assyrians, whose imperial "spin machine" refused to tell the whole truth about the foibles of their kings and the defeats of the empire, the book of Hosea is part of a prophetic history that does not shrink from explaining that Israel's sinful institutions led to its downfall. And in a time when Christians are finally coming to terms with the enormous cost of sheltering or otherwise failing to expose the predators among them,[130] the whistleblower who asks tough questions and challenges the "culture of silence" in our institutions occupies an integral (though still uncomfortable) place in holding them accountable. This peculiar willingness of Israel to critique its institutions, rather than to excuse their behavior or defend their reputation at all costs, will come up again in the book's exposition of faulty leadership (8:1–9:9) and final call for Israel to repent (14:2–10[1–9]).

130. While working on just this section of the commentary, for example, I happened upon countless news reports about sexual abuse of women and children by those working under the auspices of churches and parachurch organizations. In each instance the consequences of whistleblowers being absent or silenced were catastrophic for everyone involved. The welcome fact that such abuse is starting to be widely investigated represents a sea change in the twenty-first century.

CHAPTER 6

Hosea 5:8–7:16

B. YHWH's Contention against Israel's Political Failures

Main Idea of the Passage

Hosea joins other eighth-century-BCE prophets who present a vision of countercultural rest in YHWH's sovereignty despite foreign threats, and in so doing he calls for a distinctive theopolitics that contrasts to the prevailing realpolitik of imperialism and intrigue.

Literary Context

Hosea 5:8–7:16 is the second of five covenant discourses in chapters 4–14. While the first discourse (4:1–5:7) contends against Israel's sins as a priestly people, the present section focuses on political failures in the face of the external menace of Assyrian imperialism and the internal drama of royal intrigue. As in Hos 4:1 and 5:1, the beginning of a new section in Hos 5:8 is marked by a string of plural commands, though this time cast as a war oracle to the peoples of both kingdoms (5:8) rather than as instructions to leaders in Samaria (cf. 5:1). Also, the topic in chapter 5 shifts from Israel's participation in Canaanite fertility rituals (5:1–7) to a different kind of pagan compromise—the seesaw battle to control the borders between Samaria and Judah that seemingly hold the key to stability and power like other nations possess (5:8–11). After the ensuing disputations in 5:12–7:16 about the proper relationship between divine and human power, Hosea returns in the next section (8:1–9:9) to more explicitly religious matters such as Israelite kings' sponsorship of calf worship (8:4–8).

Translation and Exegetical Outline

(See pages 177–81.)

Structure and Literary Form

YHWH's exposition of faithful theopolitics is framed by two sections (5:8–15; 7:8–13) that target Israel's sins on the international scene.[1] Between these bookends he offers an extended disputation about domestic affairs (6:1–7:7). This contentious passage opens with a half-hearted call to repent (6:1–3) that an unnamed leader issues to the Israelite community. Because this confused "repentance" mixes YHWH's own words from Hos 5:8–15 with Canaanite ideas and terminology for Baal as a nature deity, YHWH rebukes the syncretism of his people by pointing out their religious hypocrisy (6:4–5) and social injustices (6:7–10). Following this is another heartfelt speech by YHWH against Israel's failures despite his gracious offer of restoration (6:11–7:1b), in particular Israel's sins of intrigue in the domestic (7:1c–7) and foreign (7:8–13) realms. In the conclusion to this second covenant discourse (5:8–7:16), YHWH offers another round of variations on the metaphor of Israel's wayward journeys (7:14–16; cf. 5:13–15).[2] Exile will be the final destination of a rebellious people who persistently "turn away/aside" (סור; 7:14d) and "return/turn to a no-god" (שׁוּב; 7:16a).

The literary approach just outlined for Hos 5:8–7:16 parts ways from the scholarly predilection to focus on historical reconstruction. Following the seminal work of Albrecht Alt,[3] the smaller section in Hos 5:8–6:6 has often been identified as a prophetic commentary to the events of the Syro-Ephraimite War (734–732 BCE).[4]

1. Carroll R., "The Prophetic Denunciation of Religion in Hosea 4–7," 34.

2. Found in 5:15; 6:1, 11; 7:10, 16.

3. Albrecht Alt, "Hosea 5,8–6,6. Ein Krieg und seine Folgen in prophetischer Beleuchtung," in *Kleine Schriften zur Geschichte des Volkes Israel*, 2 vols. (Munich: Beck, 1959), 163–87.

4. See the Introduction to Hosea, pp. 28–31.

Hosea 5:8–7:16

			B. YHWH's Contention Against Israel's Political Failures (5:8–7:16)
5:8a	תִּקְעוּ שׁוֹפָר בַּגִּבְעָה	"Blow a ram's horn in Gibeah,	1. YHWH's Battle Summons to All Israel (5:8)
8b	חֲצֹצְרָה בָּרָמָה	[blow] a trumpet in Ramah!	
8c	הָרִיעוּ בֵּית אָוֶן	Sound the alarm in Beth-Aven—	
8d	אַחֲרֶיךָ בִּנְיָמִין׃	[sound the alarm,] 'Behind you, O Benjamin!'	
9a	אֶפְרַיִם לְשַׁמָּה תִהְיֶה בְּיוֹם תּוֹכֵחָה	Ephraim will become a desolation on a day of rebuke.	2. YHWH's Threat of Exile (5:9–15)
9b	בְּשִׁבְטֵי יִשְׂרָאֵל הוֹדַעְתִּי נֶאֱמָנָה׃	Among the tribes of Israel, I hereby make known what is sure—	
10a	הָיוּ שָׂרֵי יְהוּדָה כְּמַסִּיגֵי גְּבוּל	The princes of Judah have been like those who move a boundary.	a. The Declaration of Judah's Guilt (5:10)
10b	עֲלֵיהֶם אֶשְׁפּוֹךְ כַּמַּיִם עֶבְרָתִי׃	Upon them I will pour out my wrath like water.	
11a	עָשׁוּק אֶפְרַיִם	Ephraim is oppressed,	b. A Lament for Ephraim's Guilt (5:11)
11b	רְצוּץ מִשְׁפָּט	crushed by judgment,	
11c	כִּי הוֹאִיל	for he has decided—	
11d	הָלַךְ אַחֲרֵי־צָו׃	he has walked after filth.	
12a	וַאֲנִי כָעָשׁ לְאֶפְרָיִם	Yet I am like a moth to Ephraim,	c. YHWH as Pest to Ephraim and Judah (5:12–13)
12b	וְכָרָקָב לְבֵית יְהוּדָה׃	[and I am] like rot to the house of Judah.	(1) YHWH as Moth and Rot (5:12)
13a	וַיַּרְא אֶפְרַיִם אֶת־חָלְיוֹ	When Ephraim saw his sickness,	(2) The Faulty Self-Diagnosis of Israel (5:13a–d)
13b	וִיהוּדָה אֶת־מְזֹרוֹ	and Judah [saw] his wound,	
13c	וַיֵּלֶךְ אֶפְרַיִם אֶל־אַשּׁוּר	then Ephraim went to Assyria	
13d	וַיִּשְׁלַח אֶל־מֶלֶךְ יָרֵב	and [Judah] sent word to the great king.	
13e	וְהוּא לֹא יוּכַל לִרְפֹּא לָכֶם	But on his part, he will not be able to heal you,	(3) The Futile Remedy of Assyria (5:13e–f)
13f	וְלֹא־יִגְהֶה מִכֶּם מָזוֹר׃	nor will he cure your wound.	
14a	כִּי אָנֹכִי כַשַּׁחַל לְאֶפְרַיִם	Indeed, I am like a lion to Ephraim,	d. YHWH as Predator against Ephraim and Judah (5:14)
14b	וְכַכְּפִיר לְבֵית יְהוּדָה	like a young lion to the house of Judah.	(1) YHWH as Israel's Predator (5:14a–b)
14c	אֲנִי אֲנִי אֶטְרֹף	I, even I, will rip up,	
14d	וְאֵלֵךְ	go away,	
14e	אֶשָּׂא	carry off,	(2) Israel as YHWH's Prey (5:14c–f)
14f	וְאֵין מַצִּיל׃	and there will be no one to deliver!	

Continued on next page.

Continued from previous page.

	Hebrew	Translation	Outline
15a	אֵלֵךְ	I will go away,	e. A Hope for Israel's Repentance (5:15)
15b	אָשׁוּבָה אֶל־מְקוֹמִי	I will return to my place,	(1) The Sting of YHWH's Departure (5:15a–b)
15c	עַד אֲשֶׁר־יֶאְשְׁמוּ	until they confess their guilt	(2) The Goal of YHWH's Departure (5:15c–e)
15d	וּבִקְשׁוּ פָנָי	and seek my face.	
15e	בַּצַּר לָהֶם יְשַׁחֲרֻנְנִי׃	In their distress they will seek me earnestly."	
6:1a	לְכוּ	"Come,	3. Israel's Half-Hearted "Repentance" (6:1–2)
1b	וְנָשׁוּבָה אֶל־יְהוָה	let us return to YHWH!	a. A Call to Repentance (6:1a-b)
1c	כִּי הוּא טָרָף	Though on his part, he has torn,	b. Faulty Reasons for Seeking YHWH (6:1c–2)
1d	וְיִרְפָּאֵנוּ	yet he will heal us.	
1e	יַךְ	He may strike [us],	(1) Misunderstandings of YHWH's Discipline (6:1e–f)
1f	וְיַחְבְּשֵׁנוּ׃	but he will bind us up.	
2a	יְחַיֵּנוּ מִיֹּמָיִם	He will revive us after two days,	(2) Misunderstandings of YHWH's Deliverance (6:2)
2b	בַּיּוֹם הַשְּׁלִישִׁי יְקִמֵנוּ	on the third day he will raise us up,	
2c	וְנִחְיֶה לְפָנָיו׃	that we might live in his presence.	
3a	וְנֵדְעָה	So let us know,	c. A Syncretistic Summons to Know YHWH (6:3)
3b	נִרְדְּפָה לָדַעַת אֶת־יְהוָה	let us seek to know YHWH—	
3c	כְּשַׁחַר נָכוֹן מוֹצָאוֹ	His going forth is sure as dawn,	(1) Confusion with Canaanite Deities (6:3c)
3d	וְיָבוֹא כַגֶּשֶׁם לָנוּ	and he will come like the rain to us,	(2) Confusion with Creation (6:3d)
	כְּמַלְקוֹשׁ יוֹרֶה אָרֶץ׃	like the latter rain showering earth."	
4a	מָה אֶעֱשֶׂה־לְּךָ אֶפְרַיִם	"What shall I do with you, O Ephraim?	4. YHWH's Exasperated Response to Israel (6:4a–b)
4b	מָה אֶעֱשֶׂה־לְּךָ יְהוּדָה	What shall I do with you, O Judah?	
4c	וְחַסְדְּכֶם כַּעֲנַן־בֹּקֶר	Your faithfulness [departs] like a cloud of the morning,	a. Their Fleeting Devotion (6:4c–d)
4d	וְכַטַּל מַשְׁכִּים הֹלֵךְ׃	like dew of daybreak going away.	
5a	עַל־כֵּן חָצַבְתִּי בַּנְּבִיאִים	Therefore I have cut them in pieces with the prophets;	b. His Purpose for the Prophetic Word (6:5)
5b	הֲרַגְתִּים בְּאִמְרֵי־פִי	I have slain them with the words of my mouth.	
5c	וּמִשְׁפָּטֶיךָ אוֹר יֵצֵא׃	Then your judgments [are the] light [when it] goes forth.	
6a	כִּי חֶסֶד חָפַצְתִּי וְלֹא־זָבַח	For I delight in faithfulness and not sacrifice,	c. The Real Definition of "Knowing YHWH" (6:6)
6b	וְדַעַת אֱלֹהִים מֵעֹלוֹת	in knowledge of God more than burnt offerings.	

7a	וְהֵמָּה כְּאָדָם עָבְרוּ בְרִית	But as for them, at Adam they broke a covenant,	d. Three Places of "Not-Knowing YHWH" (6:7–9)
7b	שָׁם בָּגְדוּ בִי׃	there they committed treachery against me.	(1) At Adam: Breaking Covenant (6:7)
8a	גִּלְעָד קִרְיַת פֹּעֲלֵי אָוֶן	Gilead is a city with doers of iniquity,	(2) At Gilead: Trampling the Weak (6:8)
8b	עֲקֻבָּה מִדָּם׃	trampled with bloodstained feet.	
9a	וּכְחַכֵּי אִישׁ גְּדוּדִים	As bandits waiting to ambush a man,	(3) On the Way to Shechem: Murderous Priests (6:9)
9b	חֶבֶר כֹּהֲנִים דֶּרֶךְ יְרַצְּחוּ־שֶׁכְמָה	so is the gang of priests who keep murdering on the way to Shechem.	
9c	כִּי זִמָּה עָשׂוּ׃	Indeed, they have done lawlessness!	
10a	בְּבֵית יִשְׂרָאֵל רָאִיתִי (שַׁעֲרִירִיָּה) [שַׁעֲרוּרִיָּה]	In the household of Israel I have seen a horrible thing:	e. A Final Warning to Ephraim and Judah (6:10–11a)
10b	שָׁם זְנוּת לְאֶפְרַיִם	Ephraim's harlotry is there,	
10c	נִטְמָא יִשְׂרָאֵל׃	Israel has been defiled.	
11a	גַּם־יְהוּדָה שָׁת קָצִיר לָךְ	Also for Judah, he (YHWH) has appointed a harvest for you."	
11b	בְּשׁוּבִי שְׁבוּת עַמִּי׃	"When I would restore the captivity of my people,	5. YHWH's Offer of Restoration Rejected (6:11b–7:16) a. Another Offer of YHWH's Restoration (6:11b–7:1b)
7:1a	כְּרָפְאִי לְיִשְׂרָאֵל	as soon as I would heal Israel,	
1b	וְנִגְלָה עֲוֹן אֶפְרַיִם וְרָעוֹת שֹׁמְרוֹן	then the iniquity of Ephraim is revealed, so too the wicked deeds of Samaria!	
1c	כִּי פָעֲלוּ שָׁקֶר	For they have acted falsely:	b. Ephraim's Rejection of Restoration, Part I: Domestic Intrigue (7:1c–7)
1d	וְגַנָּב יָבוֹא	A thief enters inside,	
1e	פָּשַׁט גְּדוּד בַּחוּץ׃	a band of robbers dashes outside.	(1) Summarizing a Coup (7:1c–2)
2a	וּבַל־יֹאמְרוּ לִלְבָבָם	But they do not take to heart	(a) Evil Remembered by God (7:2a–c)
2b	כָּל־רָעָתָם זָכָרְתִּי	[that] all their evil I have remembered.	
2c	עַתָּה סְבָבוּם מַעַלְלֵיהֶם	Now their wicked deeds surround them,	(b) Wickedness Reaped by Sinners (7:2c–d)
2d	נֶגֶד פָּנַי הָיוּ׃	they are before my face!	
3a	בְּרָעָתָם יְשַׂמְּחוּ־מֶלֶךְ	In their evil they gladden the king,	(2) Executing a Coup (7:3–7)
3b	וּבְכַחֲשֵׁיהֶם שָׂרִים׃	and by their wicked acts [they gladden] the princes.	(a) Flattery (7:3)
4a	כֻּלָּם מְנָאֲפִים	All of them are adulterers,	(b) Treachery (7:4)
4b	כְּמוֹ תַנּוּר בֹּעֵרָה מֵאֹפֶה	like an oven burning from a baker,	
4c	יִשְׁבּוֹת מֵעִיר מִלּוּשׁ בָּצֵק עַד־חֻמְצָתוֹ׃	he will stop stirring and kneading the dough until its leavening.	
5a	יוֹם מַלְכֵּנוּ הֶחֱלוּ שָׂרִים חֲמַת מִיָּיִן	On the day of our king, the princes have become sick with the heat of wine;	(c) Drunkenness (7:5)
5b	מָשַׁךְ יָדוֹ אֶת־לֹצְצִים׃	he stretches out his hand with the mockers.	

Continued on next page.

Continued from previous page.

6a	כִּי־קֵרְבוּ כַתַּנּוּר לִבָּם בְּאָרְבָּם	When they approach[1] their plotting with heart like an oven,	(d) Assassination (7:6–7)
6b	כָּל־הַלַּיְלָה יָשֵׁן אֹפֵהֶם	all night long their baking [heart] simmers,	
6c	בֹּקֶר הוּא בֹעֵר כְּאֵשׁ לֶהָבָה׃	in the morning it burns like a flame of fire.	
7a	כֻּלָּם יֵחַמּוּ כַּתַּנּוּר	All of them burn like an oven,	
7b	וְאָכְלוּ אֶת־שֹׁפְטֵיהֶם	and they consume their judges.	
7c	כָּל־מַלְכֵיהֶם נָפָלוּ	All their kings have fallen,	
7d	אֵין־קֹרֵא בָהֶם אֵלָי׃	none of them is crying out to me.	
8a	אֶפְרַיִם בָּעַמִּים הוּא יִתְבּוֹלָל	Ephraim is mixed among the peoples,	c. Ephraim's Rejection of Restoration, Part II: International Intrigue (7:8–12)
8b	אֶפְרַיִם הָיָה עֻגָה בְּלִי הֲפוּכָה׃	Ephraim has been a flatbread not turned over.	
9a	אָכְלוּ זָרִים כֹּחוֹ	Strangers have consumed his strength,	(1) Ignorance of Weakness (7:8–9)
9b	וְהוּא לֹא יָדָע	but on his part, he did not know!	
9c	גַּם־שֵׂיבָה זָרְקָה בּוֹ	Grey hair is sprinkled on him,	
9d	וְהוּא לֹא יָדָע׃	but on his part, he did not know!	
10a	וְעָנָה גְאוֹן־יִשְׂרָאֵל בְּפָנָיו	So the pride of Israel will testify against his own face,	(2) Vulnerability Due to Pride (7:10)
10b	וְלֹא־שָׁבוּ אֶל־יְהוָה אֱלֹהֵיהֶם	yet they have not returned to YHWH their God,	
10c	וְלֹא בִקְשֻׁהוּ בְּכָל־זֹאת׃	nor have they have sought him despite all this.	
11a	וַיְהִי אֶפְרַיִם כְּיוֹנָה	Ephraim has become like a dove,	(3) Dumbness with Imperialism (7:11)
	פוֹתָה אֵין לֵב	naïve, lacking a mind:	
11b	מִצְרַיִם קָרָאוּ	They have summoned Egypt,	
11c	אַשּׁוּר הָלָכוּ׃	they have gone to Assyria.	
12a	כַּאֲשֶׁר יֵלֵכוּ	As soon as they go,	(4) Discipline from YHWH (7:12)
12b	אֶפְרוֹשׂ עֲלֵיהֶם רִשְׁתִּי	I will spread out my net over them.	
12c	כְּעוֹף הַשָּׁמַיִם אוֹרִידֵם	Like birds of the sky I will bring them down,	
12d	אַיְסִרֵם כְּשֵׁמַע לַעֲדָתָם׃	I will discipline them according to the report to their assembly.	
13a	אוֹי לָהֶם	Woe to them,	d. YHWH's Final Verdict of Woe (7:13–16)
13b	כִּי־נָדְדוּ מִמֶּנִּי	for they have fled away from me!	(1) The Indictment: Rebellion Leading to Ruin (7:13a–d)
13c	שֹׁד לָהֶם	Ruin is theirs,	
13d	כִּי־פָשְׁעוּ בִי	for they have rebelled against me!	

13e	וְאָנֹכִי אֶפְדֵּם	Now on my part, I would redeem them;	(2) The Evidence: Ephraim's Foolish Exchanges (7:13e–15)
13f	וְהֵמָּה דִּבְּרוּ עָלַי כְּזָבִים׃	yet on their part, they have spoken lies against me.	(a) *Realpolitik* instead of Theopolitics (7:13e–f)
14a	וְלֹא־זָעֲקוּ אֵלַי בְּלִבָּם	They do not cry out to me with their hearts,	(b) Baal instead of YHWH (7:14)
14b	כִּי יְיֵלִילוּ עַל־מִשְׁכְּבוֹתָם	when they howl upon their beds;	
14c	עַל־דָּגָן וְתִירוֹשׁ	On account of grain and new wine	
	יִתְגּוֹדָדוּ	they keep gashing themselves,[2]	
14d	יָסוּרוּ בִי׃	they keep turning away from me.	
15a	וַאֲנִי יִסַּרְתִּי	As for me, I disciplined them,	(c) Harm instead of Love (7:15)
15b	חִזַּקְתִּי זְרוֹעֹתָם	I strengthened their arms;	
15c	וְאֵלַי יְחַשְּׁבוּ־רָע׃	but they devise harm against me!	
16a	יָשׁוּבוּ לֹא עָל	They will return to a no-god,	(3) The Result: A Turn Toward Exile (7:16)
16b	הָיוּ כְּקֶשֶׁת רְמִיָּה	they have been like a slack bow.	
16c	יִפְּלוּ בַחֶרֶב שָׂרֵיהֶם	Their princes will fall by the sword	
16d	מִזַּעַם לְשׁוֹנָם	due to the gibberish of their speech,	
16e	זוֹ לַעְגָּם בְּאֶרֶץ מִצְרָיִם׃	this will be their mockery in the land of Egypt."	

1. This rendering keeps to MT, as opposed to English versions that follow the LXX (e.g., NRSV, NLT) in substituting בער ("to burn"; cf. v. 4b) for קרב ("to approach").

2. This rendering accepts *BHQ*'s proposed emendation of יִתְגּוֹרָרוּ ("they keep gathering") to יִתְגּוֹדָדוּ ("they keep gashing themselves"), as also the LXX and some English versions (e.g., NIV, ESV, NRSV; cf. NASB).

For all its merits and influence, Alt's view suffers from the circularity of proposing drastic emendations to the text that accord with his understanding of the two Israelite kingdoms during the 730s BCE.[5] As such, Alt's strategy necessitates interpreting vague historical references in Hos 5:8–6:6 as a detailed account of tit-for-tat actions by specific rulers. Under the influence of Isa 7 and 2 Kgs 16, for instance, Alt holds that Ephraim's general call to arms (Hos 5:8–9) alludes specifically to the defensive campaign of Ephraim against the Assyrian king Tiglath-pileser, who responded in 733 BCE with a massive show of force to the request of King Ahaz of Judah for help against the northern coalition of Aram and Ephraim.[6]

Given the historical and text-critical speculation that lies behind Alt's view, we are on more solid ground in examining this passage's main theme as YHWH's repeated castigation of both Israelite kingdoms for relying on imperial power (e.g., 5:12–14). The sweeping condemnation of imperialism in both pro- and anti-Assyrian manifestations, without mentioning specific rulers or events associated with any kingdom, indicates that Hos 5:8–6:6 is a topically organized section that addresses the theological issues common to a slate of Assyrian crises during the eighth century BCE. Since Hos 6:7–7:16 develops similar anti-imperialist ideas (e.g., condemning Israel's dependence on Assyria and Egypt in 7:11, 16), it is best to interpret all of Hos 5:8–7:16 as a literary unity.[7]

The inability to reconstruct the history of this text is no great hindrance considering the superb act of communication preserved in the text's literary forms. In this regard the metaphors, similes, and other literary devices in Hos 5:8–7:16 are remarkable for their number and creativity. On the divine side, YHWH characterizes himself with an array of images: moth and rot that invade his people (5:12); a ravenous lion (5:14) that nonetheless returns to its lair and waits for its prey to show penitence (5:15); a fowler who captures his wandering people like birds (7:12); and a frustrated father whose child repays tenderness with vindictiveness (7:15).

On the human side, the portrayal of Israel is equally colorful: an individual boxed in by judgment and oppression yet somehow able to walk (5:11); a sick patient with oozing wounds (5:13); a lopsided pancake that is contaminated and burnt (7:8), though still appetizing enough to be eaten by others (7:9a); an aged man who is clueless about his frailty (7:9c); a silly dove that flies aimlessly in search of a home (7:11); and an ungrateful child who commits treachery (7:15).

Three extended metaphors in these chapters deserve particular attention. First, the sphere of medicine appears when YHWH is, incredibly enough, both the source of his people's infection and decay (5:12) as well as the only one who can cure Israel

5. Frédéric Gangloff, "La 'guerre syro-éphraïmite' en Osée 5:8–14? Quelques observations critique brèves," *BN* 118 (2003): 74–84.

6. Alt, "Hosea 5,8–6,6," 164–70.

7. Thompson (*Situation and Theology*, 63–78) and Wolff (*Hosea*, 108–12) follow the same procedure by extending the section to 7:16.

(7:1). Both kingdoms of Israel incorrectly diagnose their wounds from YHWH as requiring the treatment of a faraway doctor, sarcastically identified here as the "great king" of Assyria (5:13).[8] This depiction of seeking Assyria to "heal" (רפא) relates closely to the passage's second extended metaphor of traveling to and fro, since both YHWH and Israel are the subject of numerous verbs of motion (e.g., הלך; "to go, walk").[9]

Third and most strikingly, Hos 7:4–6 stretches the thermal image of "bread oven/ furnace" (תַּנּוּר) to the breaking point so as to convey, in successive verses, Ephraim's bloodlust as heat (7:4), the physical warmth of drunkenness (7:5), and a nocturnal conspirator's smoldering excitement (7:6) about a *coup d'état* to be carried out in the morning (7:7). As literary forms serving theological functions, this potpourri of military, political, sexual, culinary, cultic, medical, and military images in this passage gives another outstanding example of Hosea's mediation on behalf of an earnest and passionate God who uses every conceivable device of communication to reach his people.

Explanation of the Text

1. YHWH's Battle Summons to All Israel (5:8)

Much like previous transitions in the book (cf. 4:1; 5:1), Hos 5:8 introduces a literary unit with a sequence of Hebrew imperatives: "Blow [תקע] a ram's horn in Gibeah, [blow] a trumpet in Ramah! Sound [רוע] the alarm in Beth-Aven!" (5:8). The verbs תקע ("to blow a horn/trumpet") and רוע ("to raise a cry"), when appearing in contexts with שׁוֹפָר ("ram's horn") and חֲצֹצְרָה ("trumpet"), denote a summons to battle (e.g., Num 10:9; Judg 7:20). But are the three Benjamite towns that Hos 5:8 lists being mobilized to defend against invasion or to conduct offensive warfare? The direction of the impending battle is momentarily ambiguous and thus stokes the curiosity of the audience, perhaps in a manner anticipating YHWH's similar commission to the watchman in Ezek 33:1–9.

The beginning of an answer comes in observing this verse's northward geographical progression from Gibeah (5:8a) to Ramah (5:8b) and Beth-Aven (5:8c). These three villages were hotly contested as part of the territory allocated to Benjamin, a buffer zone between Ephraim's hill country to the north and Judah's steppe plateau to the south. The rump tribe of Benjamin that lay between these areas exhibited split loyalties ever since the ten northern tribes rebelled against the Davidic kingdom of Judah in approximately 930 BCE, following Solomon's death (1 Kgs 12:20–21).

In the ensuing conflicts between Samaria and

8. Although Assyria identified its kings with this bombastic title (e.g., Isa 36:4, 13), the one speaking in Hos 5:13 is YHWH, whom the OT prophets repeatedly assert is the real King of the world (Isa 6:5; 33:17; Jer 10:7; Zech 14:16–17).

9. Forms of הלך occur in Hos 5:11, 13, 14, 15; 6:1, 4; 7:11, 12. See discussion by Göran Eidevall, *Grapes in the Desert: Metaphors, Models and Themes in Hosea 4–14*, ConBOT 43 (Stockholm: Almqvist & Wiksell, 1996), 100.

Judah for these strategic outposts, the successful military campaign of the northern king Jehoash against Jerusalem around 788 BCE (2 Kgs 14:11–14) brought Benjamin under Samarian control in the early eighth century BCE. Assuming the situation in Benjamin remained similar until the time of Hosea (the OT does not mention any intervening conflicts between the divided kingdoms), the battle summons to the three Benjamite towns (5:8), each slightly farther north than the previous, seems to picture a defensive struggle by Samaria against an invasion from a Judahite army traveling north on the main road between Jerusalem and Bethel.[10]

These towns in Benjamin were also important for evoking some of the most troubling events in Israel's history. In the village of Gibeah (Hos 5:8a) a Levitical priest had horrified Israel by dismembering his concubine and sending her body parts to all the tribes (Judg 19–20). Gibeah later was also King Saul's hometown (1 Sam 10:26; 15:34). Related to Saul and his myriad failures, Ramah (Hos 5:8b) was the ancestral home of Samuel where Israel's mostly disastrous quest for kings began (1 Sam 8:4). Beth-Aven ("house of wickedness"; Hos 5:8c) is Hosea's pejorative name (4:15; 10:5; cf. 12:5[4]) for the ancient pilgrimage site of Bethel ("house of God"; Gen 12:8; 13:3–4). But the passage purposely mangles the name to condemn Bethel as one of the hosts for King Jeroboam's syncretistic cult of calf worship (cf. Hos 10:5; 1 Kgs 12:28–33). By singling out three of Benjamin's infamous towns, Hos 5:8 heralds that this tribe's time of reckoning has arrived.

The martial terminology of Hos 5:8a–b suggests the prophet is summoning Benjamin to defend against frontal attack, yet the spatial orientation then flips to entrapment from the rear. Abruptly, a voice sounds the alarm (5:8c), "Behind you, O Benjamin!" (5:8d). Especially devastating is how Hos 5:8d announces an attack using the identical Hebrew phrase (אַחֲרֶיךָ בִּנְיָמִין) that Judg 5:14 uses to describe Benjamin's privileged place near the head of a victory procession. Benjamin no longer marches triumphantly with other tribes in tow—the enemies of Israel now pursue "behind you, O Benjamin" (5:8d) and will ambush Benjamin and/or force a retreat to friendly territory. The form of rhetorical surprise unmistakably mirrors the function of military surprise.

2. YHWH's Threat of Exile (5:9–15)

The fall of Benjamin will eventually lead to the fall of the whole nation when "Ephraim will become a desolation on a day of rebuke" (5:9a). This reference to the destruction of Ephraim does not merely identify this tribe as the next stop in the southern aggressor's path (cf. 5:8), since the figure of "Ephraim" has already served in Hos 5 as part-for-whole symbol (i.e., synecdoche) of the Northern Kingdom (e.g., Hos 5:3, 5). Thus, all of Samaria will be the victim of "desolation" (שַׁמָּה), a term picturing both the destruction of war (e.g., Isa 5:9) as well as its psychological trauma upon people (e.g., Deut 28:37).

However, at this juncture the audience of Hosea's prophecy faces a nagging question—who is this unstoppable power in a campaign that begins with Benjamite towns, proceeds to the rest of Benjamin's territory, and then swallows the whole nation? Hosea's presentation of war is tantalizing for identifying the nemesis of Israel as a personal agent who has chosen a particular "day of rebuke" (יוֹם תּוֹכֵחָה; 5:9a). Hosea 1 has already predicted a "day" (יוֹם; 1:5) of YHWH's repayment against Israel on the battlefield, while the only other reference to the Hebrew root יכח in the book comes when

10. Cf. Patrick M. Arnold, "Hosea and the Sin of Gibeah," *CBQ* 51 (1989): 447–60.

YHWH explicitly forbids others to "rebuke" (4:4). In the space of a few clauses, Hosea will provide unsettling confirmation that YHWH himself is Israel's most threatening opponent, not the mighty Assyrian Empire. Although the outline entitles these sections as "YHWH's Battle Summons to All Israel" (5:8) and "YHWH's Threat of Exile" (5:9), it is not until the latter part of Hos 5:9b that YHWH explicitly introduces himself as the one who summons.

To this point Hosea has directed the diatribe exclusively against the northern tribes. But just when their southern kin might feel smug, YHWH introduces himself as the "I"-speaker, and at precisely that moment the audience broadens to include the entire family of Jacob: "Among the tribes of Israel, I hereby make known what is sure" (5:9b). The phrase "tribes of Israel" (שִׁבְטֵי יִשְׂרָאֵל; 5:9bα) recalls the ailing patriarch's farewell to his sons on his deathbed (Gen 49:28). However, Hosea surprisingly follows up this statement with a formula of indictment rather than a pronouncement of blessing. The first-person perfect verb, "I *hereby* make known" (הוֹדַעְתִּי; 5:9bβ) signifies a performative utterance that enacts the very reality being described,[11] in this case the punishment of all God's people. This verdict is irreversible because it is "sure" or "[the] truth" (נֶאֱמָנָה; 5:9bβ), a passive participle (a *niphal* form of אמן, "to be faithful/reliable") that may function either as an adjective ("sure") or a noun ("truth"). But what is the wrongdoing that YHWH condemns? From the perspective of the hearer, the northbound itinerary of Hos 5:8–9 might imply that Judah is on the warpath as YHWH's instrument against Samaria for the sins associated with Gibeah, Ramah, and Bethel.

a. The Declaration of Judah's Guilt (5:9–10)

Any misconception that YHWH stands on Judah's side (5:9) dissipates in the following verse: "The princes of Judah have been like those who move a boundary" (5:10a). Guilty as Samaria has historically been, Judah must not imagine itself to be YHWH's friend simply by virtue of being the enemy of YHWH's enemy. Most interpret the condemnation of Judah's leaders as "those who move a boundary" (מַסִּיגֵי גְּבוּל; 5:10a) as a criticism of Judah's opportunism in invading Samaria after enlisting the help of Assyria against the Syro-Ephraimite alliance.[12] This reconstruction of events is not impossible,[13] though the literary focus of Hos 5 lies elsewhere in placing Judah under Deuteronomy's curse of exile for those who move ancient territorial markers (סוג גְּבוּל; Deut 19:14; 27:17).[14] Exile from the land was tantamount to a death sentence for the nation of Judah, for life in Canaan was the most visible symbol of YHWH's covenant with his people.[15]

A distressing metaphor from creation seals the inescapability of judgment upon Judah: "Upon them I will pour out my wrath like water" (Hos 5:10b). In the ancient Near East water evoked the mythological forces of chaos,[16] but here YHWH will "pour out" (שפך) these cosmic forces like a torrent against his own people (cf. Amos 5:8; 9:6)

11. See discussion of performatives in *IBHS* §30.5.1d.

12. E.g., Thompson, *Situation and Theology*, 67; Alt, "Hosea 5,8–6,6," 169, 172.

13. However, eighth-century-BCE narratives and prophetic books never record offensive warfare by Ahaz. The OT consistently portrays Judah as the helpless kingdom that is sandwiched between the Syro-Ephraimite alliance and the Assyrian Empire.

14. Dearman, *Hosea*, 184–85.

15. Harry M. Orlinsky, "The Biblical Concept of the Land of Israel: Cornerstone of the Covenant between God and Israel," in *The Land of Israel: Jewish Perspectives*, ed. Lawrence A. Hoffman, University of Notre Dame Center for the Study of Judaism and Christianity in Antiquity 6 (Notre Dame: University of Notre Dame Press, 1986), 27–64.

16. In the theogonic literature of both Mesopotamia (e.g., Enuma Elish) and Ugarit (e.g., the Baal Cycle), for example, the sea embodies the cosmic forces of chaos that must be brought under control.

rather than subdue them as he usually does (cf. Gen 1:2; Isa 27:1; Ps 29:3). The expansive flow of water (Hos 5:10b) contrasts sharply with Judah's localized motion of "moving a boundary" (5:10a). Also, the "cool" image of water as a vehicle for YHWH's anger clashes with the usual use of metaphorical "heat" (e.g., חרה, "to be hot/burn with anger"; cf. Exod 4:14; Num 12:9) to express the emotional intensity of wrath.[17] Hosea 11:8 will nevertheless return to a "hot" image to depict the rekindling of YHWH's compassion upon his people.

b. A Lament for Ephraim's Guilt (5:11)

Compared to the impassioned, first-person exposé of Judah's guilt (5:10), the lament for Ephraim that follows in Hos 5:11 is strangely muted for its third-person description of Ephraim's lot using passive verbs: "Ephraim is oppressed, crushed by judgment" (5:11a–b). Earlier in chapter 5, a sudden shift from YHWH's direct address to third-person passive forms had heralded the growing estrangement between Israel and its God (5:3c–d). What is more, the same pair of passive participles in Hos 5:11, "oppressed" (עָשׁוּק) and "crushed" (רָצוּץ), occurs in Deut 28:33 to describe the horror of Israel being abused by enemies in wartime. Given the frequency with which Deuteronomy undergirds Hosea's prophecy,[18] the present reference to "judgment" (מִשְׁפָּט; 5:11b) likely denotes the rightness of God's verdict of exile for Ephraim. Already in the previous verse, Judah has been declared guilty using a similar allusion to the covenant curses of Deuteronomy.

Hosea then condemns the sort of apostasy that requires exile for Ephraim using a scatological reference: "For he has decided—he has walked after filth" (5:11c–d). The immobile picture of Israel as "oppressed" (5:11a) and "crushed" (5:11b) shifts to Deuteronomy's idiom of "walking after other gods" (e.g., Deut 6:14; 28:14), but with the provocative substitution of these foreign deities with "filth" (צָו; cf. Isa 28:10, 13).[19] Idols are so disgusting to YHWH that he condemns them using a profane Hebrew word that signifies vomit or excrement.[20]

c. YHWH as Pest to Ephraim and Judah (5:12–13)

Another twist of Hosea's kaleidoscope brings an unexpected picture of YHWH: "Yet I am like a moth to Ephraim, [and I am] like rot to the house of Judah" (5:12). A "moth" (עָשׁ; 5:12a) is the airborne insect that consumes what is valuable but perishable (Ps 39:12[11]; Isa 50:9), while "rot" (רָקָב; 5:12b) is the decay of a living creature's internal organs (Prov 12:4; Hab 3:16). Taken together, the poetic parallelism of Hos 5:12a–b portrays YHWH

17. Eidevall (*Grapes in the Desert*, 81) suggests that the move to a "cool" metaphor may point to the depth of God's pain involved.

18. Against the scholarly consensus that Hosea's prophecy in the eighth century BCE is the precursor to the Deuteronomistic movement in the seventh century (e.g., Nicholson, *God and His People*, 187–88; Weinfeld, *Deuteronomy and the Deuteronomic School*, 366–70), there are numerous thematic developments between Deuteronomy and Hosea that make better sense if the latter is dependent on the former. One such theme is the love of God, since it becomes difficult to see why a post-Hosean Deuteronomy would remove all traces of Hosea's marriage metaphor in describing something as profound and important as covenant relationship (Carsten Vang, "God's Love According to Hosea and Deuteronomy," 172–94).

19. Although Hebrew lexicons differ on the possible meaning of צָו (and whether it is a by-form of צֵאָה, "human excrement"), it is notable that several ancient witnesses (e.g., LXX, Vulgate, Peshitta) render the term as "filth" or a similarly derogatory reference to idols (Myrto Theocharous, *Lexical Dependence and Intertextual Allusion in the Septuagint of the Twelve Prophets: Studies in Hosea, Amos and Micah* [New York: T&T Clark, 2012], 85–87, 92–94).

20. Andersen and Freedman, *Hosea*, 410. This use of a vulgarity echoes other passages that refer to idols as גִּלּוּלִים ("round feces"; e.g., Lev 26:30; Deut 29:16[17]; 1 Kgs 15:12; Jer 50:2; Ezek 6:4, 5, 9, 13[2x]). For a detailed argument along these lines, see Daniel Bodi, "Les *gillûlîm* chez Ézéchiel et dans l'Ancien Testament et les différentes pratiques cultuelles associées à ce terme," *Revue Biblique* 100 (1993): 481–510.

as a pest who degrades the two Israelite kingdoms in both physical and spiritual ways (cf. Job 13:28). However, these afflictions from YHWH are not retributive in a strict legal sense. YHWH is only responding to Israel's determination to pursue idols (5:11) with the sort of creational curses that should prick the conscience of his people and induce their repentance (cf. Joel 2:1–13; Amos 4:6–11). To use a similar English idiom from the insect realm, YHWH determines to introduce a fly in the ointment of Israel's self-sufficiency.

The simile of YHWH as pest in Hos 5:12 also links closely with the complex medical/political/religious metaphor that follows: "When Ephraim saw his sickness and Judah [saw] his wound, then Ephraim went to Assyria and [Judah] sent word to the great king" (5:13a–d).[21] In this rather motley picture, the Israelite kingdoms correctly "see" (ראה; i.e., perceive/diagnose) their "sickness/wound" (חֳלִי; i.e., military vulnerability) but incorrectly cast Assyria in the role of a doctor who is able to help. More than mere pragmatism is in view, since Samaria and Judah's pursuit of Assyria (5:13c) and its ruler (5:13d) represents nothing less than a form of conversion to an ideology that might be called "Assyrianism." "Assyria" (אַשּׁוּר) is the name of the empire's national god as well as its capital city,[22] while the "great king"[23] incarnates the god Assur's reign over all the earth.[24] Thus the Israelite kingdoms' faith in Assyrianism (5:13c–d) involves a renunciation of YHWH and his apparent weakness in favor of the strength of Assyria/Assur.

YHWH warns that converts to Assyrianism will be sorely disappointed: "But on his part [וְהוּא], he will not be able to heal you, nor will he cure your wound" (5:13e–f). The passage foregrounds the chasm between Israel's expectations and the reality of Assyria's cruelty by using the pleonastic pronoun הוּא ("on his part"). This shift in topical frame draws a tight contrast between Judah's faulty self-diagnosis of its woes (5:13a–d) with Assyria's response as futile remedy (5:13e–f).[25] To anyone familiar with the self-serving brutality of Assyria, it is quite laughable to imagine the empire and its despotic rulers to be a physician with good intentions.

Self-deception in eighth-century Samaria and Judah has taken hold to such an extent that the people thought that Assyrian power politics could never rebound against them to their hurt. Simply put, the Assyrians were like the Nazis of the ancient Near East for their unprecedented ability to wage war and deport captive peoples for their own purposes, all while using the visual medium of imperial iconography to strike fear into the hearts of surrounding nations. But the two kingdoms of Israel believed Assyrianism to be their salvation and thereby missed all the warning signs that Assyria was an executioner-in-waiting rather than a doctor.

d. YHWH as Predator against Ephraim and Judah (5:14)

For Ephraim and Judah, in fact, the problem runs deeper than the reality that converts to Assyrianism will both live and die by the sword. More importantly, the people of YHWH have failed to respond to his gentler method of being a pest to them (5:12) by their choosing Assyrian strength

21. In this section's exposition of how Ephraim/Samaria and Judah approached the Assyrian crisis, "Judah" is sometimes omitted as an implied subject, as in Hos 5:13d (Macintosh, *Hosea*, 209; Andersen and Freedman, *Hosea*, 413).

22. A. Livingstone, "Ashur," *DDD* 108.

23. Literally "King Jareb" (מֶלֶךְ יָרֵב), a Hebrew pun that means both "may a king contend" as well as being a partial transliteration of the common Akkadian title for Assyrian potentates, "great king" (*šarru rabû*; e.g., "Adad-Nirari III: Antakya Stela," trans. K. Lawson Younger, Jr. [*COS* 2.114A:272]).

24. Machinist, "Kingship and Divinity in Imperial Assyria," 152–88.

25. On the use of topical frames that shift a discourse and its participants to a new set of interrelationships, see *LDHB* §5.1.

(5:13) rather than accepting their God-given weakness. Since the Israelite kingdoms apparently only understood the language of power, the mild simile of YHWH as pest mutates into the severe simile of YHWH as predator: "Indeed [כִּי], I am like a lion to Ephraim, like a young lion to the house of Judah" (5:14a–b).[26] Although the OT sometimes portrays Assyria as a lion (e.g., Isa 5:29–30; Nah 2:12–14[11–13]),[27] Hosea asserts that the sole lion that Israel is to fear is YHWH. Indeed, this passage insists that YHWH is the ultimate predator by using an agonizing series of two first-person pronouns and three first-person verbs: "*I* [אֲנִי], *even I* [אֲנִי], will rip up, go away, carry off, and there will be no one to deliver!" (5:14c–f; cf. Deut 32:39). Andrew Dearman rightly observes that this confluence of grammatical forms depicts a predator's total domination of its prey: "The poetry is exquisite, the content frightful."[28]

e. A Hope for Israel's Repentance (5:15)

The image of lion then takes an extraordinary turn. After picturing YHWH as a predator who has captured and dismembered its meal (5:14), the passage describes the divine lion experiencing a sudden change of heart: "I will go away, I will return to my place" (5:15a–b). Abruptly, the predator who had been standing guard over its dead victim leaves to its "place" (מָקוֹם), a generic term for location that can denote both the lion's lair (cf. Jer 4:7) within the leonine image of 5:14 as well as Israel's cultic "place" of worship (cf. Deut 12:5, 11). The following verse implies the latter sense of מָקוֹם since the "place" is where YHWH will wait for his people "until they confess their guilt and seek my face" (5:15c–d).

To join the leonine and cultic sides of the metaphor, the purpose of YHWH in mauling his people has never been to inflict a fatal wound, as if abandoning their corpses to carrion birds were the ultimate goal. As already evident in the covenant curses, he has instead sought to instill the kind of desperation for his presence that could only come from extreme hardship when "in their distress they will seek me earnestly" (5:15e). Given this poignant shift from pest to predator to a God who eagerly awaits Israel, the prospect of restoration remains for an estranged people if they are willing to acknowledge their sins and return to YHWH.[29]

3. Israel's Half-Hearted "Repentance" (6:1–2)

a. A Call to Repentance (6:1a–b)

A voice from the people responds to YHWH with a corporate call to repentance: "Come, let us return to YHWH" (6:1a–b). The plural summons to "come" (לְכוּ; 6:1a), followed by the first-person cohortative, "let us return to YHWH" (וְנָשׁוּבָה אֶל־יְהוָה; 6:1b), recalls the opening call to worship in Ps 95: "Come [לְכוּ], let us shout aloud to YHWH [נְרַנְּנָה לַיהוָה]" (Ps 95:1). Such an echo of Israel's corporate worship has led to the proposal that Hos 6:1–3 is part of a liturgical text,[30] in contrast to Albrecht Alt's influential reading of Hos 5:8–6:6

26. Hosea 5:14a represents another shift in topical frame (see n25 above) from the "great king of Assyria (5:13c–f) to YHWH as a first-person "I am" (אָנֹכִי). This suggests that the כִּי particle in Hos 5:14a serves an asseverative function ("indeed") rather than introducing a causal clause (i.e., "for," "since," "because') that is subordinate to what precedes. The confluence of solemn, first-person verbs in what follows (Hos 5:14c–f, 5:15a–b) reinforces this shift to YHWH as the main actor.

27. Brent A. Strawn, *What Is Stronger than a Lion?: Leonine Image and Metaphor in the Hebrew Bible and the Ancient Near East*, OBO 212 (Göttingen: Vandenhoeck & Ruprecht, 2005), 52.

28. Dearman, *Hosea*, 186.

29. Cf. Dennis T. Olson, "The Lion, the Itch and the Wardrobe: Hosea 5:8–6:6 as a Case Study in the Contemporary Interpretation and Authority of Scripture," *CurTM* 23 (1996): 178–79.

30. Edwin M. Good, "Hosea 5:8–6:6: An Alternative to Alt," *JBL* 85 (1966): 273–86.

as a stricture against Samaria and Judah's political entanglements during the Syro-Ephraimite War (734–732 BCE). Both political and liturgical frameworks can illuminate certain features of the passage, though an exclusive focus on one realm or the other neglects how the larger section of Hos 5:8–7:16 joins them together in a holistic vision of Israel's journeys before YHWH. Political sins involving Israel's abuse of power (5:8–14; 6:7–7:16) require national repentance (6:1–3; cf. Isa 2:5–11), since imperialism and injustice are both expressions of syncretism that must never characterize YHWH's distinctive people.

However, who is the worship leader speaking for Israel in these verses? The passage does not give this individual's identity, but such an omission has not stopped speculation that he may be Hosea himself,[31] a priest or priests who intercede(s) for the people,[32] or perhaps the people themselves.[33] Here it becomes crucial to assess the content of the prayer for clues about the credibility of its speaker(s). The initial call for Israel to "come" (הלך; 6:1a) is quite orthodox for contravening Israel's attempts to "go" (הלך; 5:11, 13) toward other nations and choosing instead the figurative footsteps of where YHWH will "go" (הלך; 5:14, 15).

The next summons to "return" (שׁוב; 6:1b) likewise takes up an important Hebrew root in the prophecy of Hosea (e.g., 3:5; 5:4; 6:11; 11:5). But as the rest of the prayer unfolds, the faulty reasoning given for seeking YHWH (6:1c–2c) that motivates a syncretistic call to know him (6:3), coupled with an exasperated response from YHWH (6:4–6), make it unlikely that his authoritative prophet is speaking.[34] The commentary below will demonstrate that Hosea records either the people or their representative who adopts the customary form of repentance (6:1a–b) but misses its true heart (6:1c–3).

b. Faulty Reasons for Seeking YHWH (6:1c–2)

The prayer begins to go awry upon exploring a misleading contrast between YHWH's past and future actions: "Though on his part [כִּי הוּא], he has torn [טרף], yet he will heal [רפא] us" (6:1c–d). The combination of the כִּי particle (concessive "although" in this context) and the pleonastic pronoun הוּא ("he, him") draws attention to the supposed actions of YHWH that follow. On their face, the two verbal clauses in Hos 6:1c–d seem to agree with YHWH's earlier assertions that he is the predator who "tears" (טרף; 5:14c) Israel as well as the denial that Assyria is a doctor who can "heal" (רפא; 5:13f). The problem at hand, however, lies not in YHWH's *willingness* to forgive (cf. 11:8–9) but in Israel's misunderstandings about the *timing* of YHWH's discipline and deliverance. The right idea at the wrong time is still the wrong idea—the people mistakenly expect woe to be quickly followed by weal: "He may strike [us], but he will bind us up. He will revive us after two days, on the third day he will raise us up, that we might live in his presence" (6:1e–2c).[35]

Indeed, it is telling how disproportionately the prayer leader emphasizes YHWH's role as healing doctor. The use of five positive verbs (i.e., heal, bind, revive, raise, live) but only two negative verbs (i.e., tear, strike) contrasts notably from YHWH's last metaphorical description of himself as a ferocious beast (5:14). In place of misplaced faith that

31. E.g., Macintosh, *Hosea*, 217–19.

32. E.g., Wolff, *Hosea*, 116–17.

33. E.g., Dearman, *Hosea*, 189.

34. For a detailed argument along these lines, see Ernst R. Wendland, *The Discourse Analysis of Hebrew Prophetic Literature: Determining the Larger Textual Units of Hosea and Joel*, Mellen Biblical Press Series 40 (Lewiston, NY: Mellen, 1995), 172–77, 204–18.

35. Macintosh (*Hosea*, 221) notes that the number 2 is often a symbol for shortness (e.g., 1 Kgs 17:12; Isa 7:21).

Assyria/Assur could "heal" (5:13), Israel has fallen into the more subtle error of domesticating YHWH into a deity who will quickly and unconditionally "heal" (6:1d) the wounds he has inflicted upon the people. In light of how death and resurrection in the context of Hosea's theology refer to exile and restoration, respectively,[36] it is apparent that Israel wrongly envisions YHWH's punishment of exile from the land to be of short duration. Judah would make the same mistake 150 years later in expecting that Babylon's deportation of exiles from Jerusalem would be short-lived (cf. Jer 28–29).

c. A Syncretistic Summons to Know YHWH (6:3)

The syncretism of seeking YHWH's answer to prayer as if he were merely a nature god compounds the error of expecting YHWH to provide immediate deliverance: "So let us know, let us seek to know YHWH—His going forth is sure as dawn, and he will come like the rain to us, like the latter rain showering earth" (6:3). This corporate summons for Israel to "know" twice uses the root ידע, thereby echoing Hosea's many references to covenant knowledge of YHWH (e.g., 2:22[20]; 4:1, 6). But in Hos 6:3, attributes of other deities blend with YHWH as the object of Israel's knowledge. The portrayal of YHWH's appearance as "dawn" (שַׁחַר; 6:3c) may allude to Shahar,[37] the Ugaritic deity of the morning star.[38]

Even more explicit in drawing upon pagan ideas are the statements of Hos 6:3d that YHWH will arrive like "rain" (גֶּשֶׁם) and "latter rain" (מַלְקוֹשׁ). The former term refers generally to moisture from heaven and evokes apostate Israel's expectation that Baal, as the Canaanite god of the storm, would be able to bring rain on the earth; the latter term for precipitation refers specifically to the rain that would fall in Israel's spring season.[39] Orthodox Yahwism typically usurps the functions of Baal as a polemical form of contextualization that is designed to highlight the God of Israel's uniqueness among the gods, as when YHWH causes rain to fall on drought-ridden Israel only after he defeats Baal on Mt. Carmel (e.g., 1 Kgs 17–18). But when Israel misunderstands YHWH to be merely another form of Baal (cf. Hos 2:10[8]), the result is a dangerous form of syncretism that mixes Yahwistic and pagan ideas. In summary, the Israelites have confused the uniqueness of their God with both Canaanite deities (6:3c) and the created order that they were thought to govern (6:3d).

4. YHWH's Exasperated Response to Israel (6:4a–b)

YHWH responds sharply to the muddled prayer of Israel: "What shall I do with you, O Ephraim? What shall I do with you, O Judah?" (6:4a–b). These two poetic lines are rhetorical questions that are nearly identical, their only difference being the change of vocative address from "Ephraim" (6:4a) to "Judah" (6:4b). The almost-verbatim repetition reflects the common guilt of the two kingdoms as well as a growing frustration on YHWH's part toward his people. What will follow in vv. 4c–6 is YHWH's exasperated response to Israel that builds on these rhetorical questions.

36. Day, "Hosea and the Baal Cult," 216.

37. Interestingly, שַׁחַר in Hos 6:3c lacks the article (cf. Josh 6:15; Hos 10:15), unlike what is implied by the typical rendering "the dawn" (e.g., ESV) or "the morning" (e.g., KJV). This suggests that שַׁחַר may serve here as a proper name (though note that "earth" in 6:3d also lacks the article).

38. S. B. Parker, "Shahar," *DDD* 754–55.

39. The unmistakable reference to Baal in Hos 6:3 may indicate that the preceding verse's reference to death and resurrection alludes to the Ugaritic legend of Baal's annual demise and return to life (Day, "Hosea and the Baal Cult," 216–17), though the referents for death and resurrection in the metaphor would have changed from the god himself to his worshiper.

a. Their Fleeting Devotion (6:4c–d)

The stridency of tone increases in the rest of Hos 6:4 with YHWH's own pointed references to creation. Rather than depicting creation as a symbol of predictability, as Israel does (6:3), YHWH sets forth a different parallel between the transience of creation and the fleeting devotion of Israel: "Your faithfulness [departs] like a cloud of the morning, like dew of daybreak going away" (6:4c–d).[40] "Faithfulness/devotion/lovingkindness" (חֶסֶד) is the covenantal virtue of loyalty that YHWH exemplifies in seeking after and reconciling an estranged people to himself (2:21[19]; cf. Exod 34:6–7), but which Israel has repeatedly lacked toward God and neighbor as part of its apostasy "in the land" (4:1). Here in chapter 6, Hosea goes a step further by expressing the absence of חֶסֶד in the creational language of the heavens rather than the earth. The certitude of the sun arriving each day, as Israel expected of YHWH's return (6:3), now serves to expose the fickleness of the people's loyalty, much like the Mediterranean sun quickly burns off the "cloud of the morning" (עֲנַן־בֹּקֶר; 6:4c) and "dew of daybreak" (טַל מַשְׁכִּים; 6:4d).

Later in the book, Hosea joins the same Hebrew expressions about evaporating moisture with the images of chaff and smoke in a description of YHWH's punishment for Israel's idolatry (13:3). We should not take these polemical references to creation to mean that YHWH is a god only of history and not of creation,[41] since reconciliation between YHWH and his people will one day bring his presence like "dew" (טַל; 14:6[5]) to enrich the land of Israel with fertility once again (cf. Gen 27:28; Deut 33:28). Instead, creation is the primary stage on which YHWH works out his purposes in discipline and deliverance for Israel.

b. His Purpose for the Prophetic Word (6:5)

However, Hosea has predicted elsewhere that restoration of creational blessings will not occur until YHWH punishes the sins of his people (e.g., 2:20–25[18–23]). The agent of punishment will be the word of YHWH's prophets: "Therefore I have cut them in pieces with the prophets; I have slain them with the words of my mouth" (6:5a–b). The preceding image of a dissipating fog (6:4) changes to the violent picture of Israel as a rock that must be "cut in pieces" (חצב; 6:5a). This stonemasonry metaphor (cf. Deut 6:11; 1 Kgs 5:29[15]) identifies the mallet that strikes with destructive force as the "prophets" (נְבִיאִים; 6:5a). This is a general term for God's spokespersons that includes nonwriting prophets like Nathan (e.g., 2 Sam 12:25) as well as those like Amos and Hosea whose oracles were eventually written down.

Against these chosen servants, false prophets were also propounding their oracles in YHWH's name during the eighth century BCE (e.g., Hos 4:5; Mic 3:5–6; Isa 29:10). Amidst such mixed messages, YHWH has specifically commissioned a group of authoritative messengers who speak only "the words of my mouth" (Hos 6:5b). The words emanating from them are lethal projectiles with power to destroy those who remain unresponsive and thereby bring the threatened punishment upon themselves. To emphasize the imminence of such a judgment, the grammatical person of YHWH's speech shifts from the intimacy of the second-person "you" (6:4) to the estrangement of speaking of his people as the third-person "them" (6:5). In the immediate context, the danger that Israel fails to take seriously seems to be the preceding depiction of YHWH as pest and predator (5:12–14).

40. In this poetic technique called gapping, the verb in Hos 6:4d ("it departs") does double duty as the delayed verb for Hos 6:4c.

41. Compare the famous overstatement of von Rad on history's superiority to creation in Hosea: "Hosea's whole preaching is rooted in the saving history. It might almost be said that he only feels safe when he can base his arguments in history" (*Old Testament Theology*, 2:140).

Neither of these threatening images ultimately aims at destruction, but to bring the people of YHWH to sincere repentance (5:15; cf. 6:1–3).

In Hos 6:5c creation reappears briefly in a simile, but a series of difficulties in the syntax of this clause has led to different renderings. A literal translation could read, "then your judgments [are the] light [when it] goes forth," the brackets here reflecting the possible syntactical relationships between elements. Based on which of several proposed emendations translators choose and whether "light" (אוֹר) is a positive or negative image, several renderings are possible:

1. "Then my judgments go forth like the sun" (NIV; cf. "as the light" in NRSV)

   However, this rendering is unlikely since "go forth" is a singular verb in Hebrew (יֵצֵא, lit. "he/it will go forth"). Thus it should take "the sun" rather than plural "judgments" as object.
2. "With judgments as inescapable as light" (NLT)

   This rendering takes "judgments" as an explanation of the previous clause's divine "words." But this supplies a comparative or adverbial "as" where the usual Hebrew preposition (כְּ) for such a function is missing.
3. "Can judgment in your favor be a shining light?"

   This is Macintosh's proposal of a rhetorical question with an optimistic expectation.[42] However, the emendations required by Macintosh render this reading unlikely.

Certainty is elusive for Hos 6:5c, but the earlier wordplays on "justice/judgment" (מִשְׁפָּט; 5:1, 11), along with Israel's misunderstandings about YHWH's deliverance as dawn (6:3), may hint at the irony that judgment against Israel has now become as inevitable as the sunrise.

c. The Real Definition of "Knowing YHWH" (6:6)

The passage attains a climax when YHWH cuts through the fog of syncretism with a declaration of what true worship ought to be: "For I delight in faithfulness and not sacrifice, in knowledge of God more than burnt offerings" (6:6a–b). Echoing the plea that opens this covenant contention (4:1–3), Hosea now sets the frequently mentioned virtues of "faithfulness" (חֶסֶד; 6:6a) and "knowledge of God" (דַּעַת אֱלֹהִים; 6:6b) against Israel's religious observances of "sacrifice" (זֶבַח) and "burnt offerings" (עֹלוֹת), respectively.

There is a long history of interpreters taking this verse as an absolute contrast between covenantal virtue and cultic activity. Prophets like Hosea were supposedly the pioneers for a new "ethical monotheism" that pits universal morality over Israelite ritual (e.g., Isa 1:11–15; Mic 6:6–8; cf. Matt 12:7).[43] But given the combination of priestly and covenantal ideas that undergirds Hos 4–11,[44] it is better to understand this as a relative contrast of unequals, namely, that "sacrifice" and "burnt offerings" are not *as* pleasing to YHWH as faithfulness and knowledge of God. In Hos 6:6b, the use of the preposition מִן, which functions here in a comparative way to assert how YHWH "delights" (חפץ; cf. 8:8) in covenantal knowledge *more than* cultic observance, reinforces the likelihood of such a relative contrast. God-directed "knowledge" (דַּעַת; cf. 4:1, 6) is rather different from the self-centered

42. Macintosh, *Hosea*, 230–31.

43. Julius Wellhausen most prominently among them (*Prolegomena to the History of Israel* [Eugene, OR: Wipf & Stock, 2003], 398–99, 470–77).

44. See the commentary on Hos 4:1–5:7 on pp. 143–67.

pragmatism that seeks YHWH mainly for the sake of what he can do, as Israel expressed in its stated desire to "know" (ידע) him for the sake of receiving his benefits (6:1–3).

d. Three Places of "Not-Knowing YHWH" (6:7–9)

Wrong ideas about YHWH lead to wrong conduct of various kinds. The emphatic contrasting pronoun, "but as for them" (וְהֵמָּה; 6:7a), highlights the chasm between the covenantal obedience that YHWH seeks (6:6) and the transgressions of which Israel is guilty (6:7–9).[45] Hosea recalls three historical episodes of "not-knowing YHWH" to illustrate the ways in which Israel in the eighth century BCE was walking the sinful paths of its forebears.

(1) At Adam: Breaking Covenant (6:7)

The first example of apostasy happened near the Jordan River: "But as for them, at Adam they broke a covenant, there they committed treachery against me" (6:7a–b). Many have interpreted this reference to "Adam" (אָדָם) as a reference to the first human (e.g., NASB, ESV), but the parallelism with the adverb "there" (שָׁם; 6:7b) suggests a geographical reference to the town near Zarethan where the waters of the Jordan River were stopped up for Israel to cross on dry ground (Josh 3:16). The כְּ preposition affixed to "Adam" usually means "like, as" (e.g., 3:1; 4:9) but can mean "as at/in" when preceding a place name (e.g., 11:8).[46] Therefore, it is unnecessary to take אָדָם to be the primeval ancestor or to emend the attached preposition to בְּ ("in").[47]

Furthermore, the following mention of Israel's wickedness at Gilead (6:8) and Shechem (6:9) makes it more likely that in Hos 6:6 "Adam" is a toponym rather than a personal name. While the Bible does not record how Adam was the place where Israel "broke a covenant" (6:7a) and "committed treachery against me" (6:7b), the historical allusion would have been understood by Hosea's original audience. The occasion when Israel "broke a covenant" (עבר בְּרִית) employs an idiom for sinning against YHWH by making idols (Hos 8:1; cf. Deut 17:2; Judg 2:20), while "to commit treachery" (בגד) reflects the language of interpersonal betrayal (e.g., Judg 9:23; Ps 78:57) such as adultery (e.g., Jer 3:8, 20; 9:1[2]). Accordingly, Hosea's only other use of the root בגד refers to the Canaanite fertility rites that result in illegitimate children (5:7).

(2) At Gilead: Trampling the Weak (6:8)

The next sin in the list took place in the neighboring region of the Transjordan: "Gilead is a city with doers of iniquity, trampled with bloodstained feet" (6:8). The reminiscence of Gilead as containing "wickedness, trouble, iniquity" (אָוֶן; 6:8a) draws a link between Israel's past and the Northern Kingdom's present syncretism with the calf cult of "Beth-Aven" (בֵּית אָוֶן, lit. "house of wickedness"; 5:8). Moreover, the graphic description of Gilead as "trampled with bloodstained feet" (6:8b) may recall the war of opportunity that occurred in Jabesh-Gilead (e.g., Judg 21:8–12), especially since the beginning of this section (Hos 5:8) already alludes to the vile story of Judg 20 in Gibeah. "Gilead" might then be a shorthand reference to the city of Jabesh-Gilead. Whether cultic sins or war crimes are in view, Israel is foolishly repeating the mistakes of its past in Hosea's day.

(3) On the Way to Shechem: Murderous Priests (6:9)

The third and final historical reference takes aim at Israel's religious leaders: "As bandits waiting to ambush a man, so is the gang of priests who

45. See nn. 25–26 above on the discourse function in Hos 5's similar use of distancing pronouns.

46. Joüon §133h; BDB 455a.

47. Cf. *BHS*. *BHQ* rightly observes the soundness of MT.

keep murdering on the way to Shechem" (6:9a–b). Here the scene shifts from the nether regions east of the Jordan River to Israel's central hill country in Shechem, a centrally located city where Abram had once built an altar (Gen 12:6–7) and all the tribes of Israel would convene for important meetings (e.g., Josh 24:1; 1 Kgs 12:1). Tragically, Shechem had become infamous for its homicidal priests who lurk "as bandits waiting to ambush a man" (6:9a). Earlier Hosea had accused the priests of Israel of being neglectful of YHWH's statutes and abusers of his sacrificial system (4:8–9; cf. 5:1), but to this litany of sins Hosea now adds that of violence against their own people. In Hos 6:9b, the habitual imperfective verb יְרַצְּחוּ (i.e., "they [the priests] *keep* murdering") indicates that Hosea has moved from historical flashbacks (6:7–8) to sins in the present. The fact that Shechem was once a city of refuge for the unjustly targeted fugitive (Josh 20:7) makes it doubly ironic that the priests who should have mediated blessing to Israel (e.g., Num 6:24–26) instead bring a curse by "committing murder" (רצח). This verbal root also alludes to the Decalogue (Hos 4:2; cf. Exod 20:13; Deut 5:17).

Hosea therefore condemns the murderous priests of Israel who bring chaos rather than order into YHWH's world: "Indeed [כִּי], they have done lawlessness" (6:9c).[48] "Lawlessness" (זִמָּה) accurately summarizes their conduct, for this broad term can signify sins of lewdness (e.g., Lev 18:17; Ezek 16:27) or wicked scheming (e.g., Isa 32:7; Prov 24:9). Not only were the priests guilty of both kinds of "lawlessness," but chapter 4 has also shown the numerous links between a negligent priesthood and a priestly nation's rejection of "knowledge of God" (4:1, 6–9).

e. A Final Warning to Ephraim and Judah (6:10–11a)

Following these references to specific places, YHWH levels an indictment against the whole of his people and not merely the priests: "In the house of Israel I have seen a horrible thing: Ephraim's harlotry is there, Israel has been defiled. Also for Judah, he [YHWH] has appointed a harvest for you" (6:10–11a). In these four clauses, "the household of Israel" (בֵּית יִשְׂרָאֵל; 6:10a) seems to be an umbrella term that includes the constituent parts of the northern tribe of "Ephraim" (6:10b), the rest of the kingdom of Samaria as "Israel" (6:10c), and the Southern Kingdom of "Judah" (6:11a).[49] Hosea's earlier designation "the tribes of Israel" (5:9) emphasized the familial bond of Jacob's descendants, while "the household of Israel" (6:10a) highlights its royal character in the present passage.

The accusation that "I have seen a horrible thing" (6:10a) applies slightly differently to each member of the "household." Ephraim has engaged in "harlotry" (זְנוּת; 6:10b), the nominal form of Hosea's most frequent verb (זנה, "to commit harlotry") for the syncretism of Canaanite nature religion (e.g., 1:2; 4:10–13). "Israel" at large is guilty of "defiling oneself" (טמא *niphal*; 6:10c), a priestly word for impurity (e.g., Lev 11:43). This use of ritual terminology echoes the innovation of Hos 5:3d ("Israel has become defiled [טמא *niphal*]") in applying the concept of individual uncleanness before God to the entire people (cf. Jer 2:23; Ezek 20:30–31).

Nevertheless, Hosea names no particular sin of Judah's that underlies the somewhat cryptic assertion that "he has appointed a harvest for you" (6:11a). The paragraph division of Hebrew and English Bibles understands Hos 6:11a as the

48. This rendering takes the particle כִּי to be asseverative ("indeed, surely") rather than causal or evidential ("for, since"). The likelihood of a summary asseverative clause in Hos 6:9c is supported by the fact that the description of sin at Shechem in Hos 6:9 would then be two clauses long (6:9a–b), just as in the preceding descriptions of Adam (6:7a–b) and Gilead (6:8a–b).

49. Andersen and Freedman, *Hosea*, 442.

introduction to YHWH's following promise of salvation, "when I would restore the captivity of my people" (6:11b). While a positive interpretation of Hos 6:11a is not out of the question,[50] the parallelism of these clauses suggests that we should interpret the agricultural image of "harvest" (קָצִיר) for Judah negatively as a reference to sins that reap a harvest of judgment (e.g., Isa 17:5; Jer 51:33). The commentary below will argue that Hos 6:11b belongs with 7:1 as the start of a new section.

5. YHWH's Offer of Restoration Rejected (6:11b–7:16)

Hosea 6:11b commences a monologue of YHWH that never addresses Israel directly (cf. 6:4–11a). Rather than speaking to Israel as "you," YHWH stops pleading with his intransigent people and steps back to expose their motives in continuing to resist him (6:11b–7:1b). As an omniscient God, he knows perfectly how committed they are to political intrigue, both domestic (7:1c–7) and international (7:8–12). YHWH therefore pronounces woe upon his people for embracing the pagan theopolitics of nature religion and imperialism (7:13–16). Even so, Hos 6:11b–7:16 is not a judgment oracle in the usual sense—instead YHWH offers a plaintive take on his rebellious people, sometimes even assuming the dispassion of a bystander in referring to himself in the third person (7:10).

a. Another Offer of YHWH's Restoration (6:11b–7:1b)

Having already summoned his people in vain (e.g., 6:4–11a), YHWH delves further into the reasons why his people remain so unresponsive. He starts with a flourish that heaps up descriptions of his past attempts at reconciliation: "*When* I would restore the captivity of my people, *as soon as* I would heal Israel . . ." (6:11b–7:1a). The two Hebrew prepositions introducing these clauses reflect increasing urgency, from a general "when" (בְּ) to the immediacy of "as soon as" (כְּ) in YHWH's desire to help his people.[51] The God of Israel has sought to "restore the captivity" (6:11b) of Israel, the usual idiom for reversal of judgment (e.g., Deut 30:3),[52] including (though not limited to) return from exile (e.g., Amos 9:14–15; Job 42:10). What is more, YHWH's resolve to "heal" (רפא; 7:1a) his people brings the potential for restoring a relationship that was lost when Israel pursued Assyria/Assur (5:13) and a Baalized picture of YHWH (6:1) even though these kinds of syncretism could never "heal" (רפא).

Even as YHWH is willing to extend such grace to his people, a full return to him remains on hold because of the depth of his people's sinful entanglements. The temporal clauses asserting YHWH's love meets the reality of his people's rebellion: ". . . then the iniquity of Ephraim is revealed, so too the wicked deeds of Samaria!" (7:1c). "Iniquity" (עָוֹן) previously described the guilt of gluttonous priests who feasted on the offerings of the people (4:8) as well as the sins of both kingdoms (5:5). Here the people's "wicked deeds" (רָעוֹת; 7:1c) manifest outwardly the term's additional nuance of inward corruption (7:1b). The rest of Hos 7 unveils these actions as the power politics of Ephraim's royal court. For all their attempts at concealment, the people of YHWH cannot escape the theological

50. This assertion usually comes with the caveat that Hos 6:11a is a positive gloss in an otherwise negative section (e.g., Emmerson, *Hosea*, 86–87). Contrast the methodological circularity of Macintosh (*Hosea*, 247–48), who argues that because Hosea's references to Judah are late, 6:11a must be a secondary addition.

51. When introducing temporal clauses, the בְּ-preposition refers to the general time frame for subsequent ideas (*BHRG* §39.6.2), while the כְּ-preposition conveys a specific and immediate point in time (*BHRG* §39.10.4). In context, this combination results in the rhetorical progression of "when (6:11b) to "as soon as . . ." (7:1a).

52. John M. Bracke, "*Šûb Šebût*: A Reappraisal," *ZAW* 97 (1985): 233–44.

reality that all their conspiracies will yet be "revealed" (גלה *niphal*; 7:1b) by their omniscient God.

b. Ephraim's Rejection of Restoration, Part I: Domestic Intrigue (7:1c–7)

Hosea exposes the first of Ephraim's conspiracies as the domestic intrigue of the royal court (7:1c–7). Following YHWH's mocking exposé of an internal coup that its conspirators would undoubtedly have wanted to keep hidden, Hosea moves similarly to unveil the presence of international intrigue (7:8–12) as another form of Ephraim's rejection of restoration.

(1) Summarizing a Coup (7:1c–2)

YHWH's uncovering of domestic intrigue begins by identifying the connivers at work: "For they have acted falsely: A thief enters inside, a band of robbers dashes outside" (7:1c–e). The strategy of "falsehood/deception" (שֶׁקֶר; 7:1c) seeks to cloak the marauding quickness of "thief" (גַּנָּב; 7:1d) and "a band of robbers" (גְּדוּד; 7:1e). Related forms of the latter two terms have already occurred in Hosea to portray the violent chaos that threatens to envelop creation through "stealing" (גָּנֹב; 4:2) and Israel through a "gang [of bandits]" (גְּדוּדִים; 6:9). In vv. 2–7, this threat to God's order takes the form of a coup against the royal house of Ephraim.

Nonetheless, the stealth of sinners and their schemes cannot escape the notice of YHWH: "But they do not take to heart [that] all their evil I have remembered" (7:2a–b). For an all-knowing God to "remember" (זכר; 7:2b) is to hold his people accountable for their sins (cf. 8:13; 9:9), but their obliviousness has reached such an extreme that "Israel does not remember that God remembers."[53]

However, YHWH's perfectly photographic memory (cf. 7:2a–b) means that the conspirators can never outrun their own sins: "Now their wicked deeds surround them" (7:2c). Here the image shifts from a remembering God (7:2b) to evil actions that are personified as opponents who "surround" (סבב) like encircling enemies (cf. Gen 19:4; Amos 3:11; Ps 22:17[16]). In this reference to Hosea's frequent theme of sin that ensnares the sinner (cf. 4:5–6), the Creator who always sees ("they are before my face!" [7:2d]) enforces the link between act and consequence. The plural verbal subject "they" is ambiguous in this clause and could refer to sins or the sinners themselves; either way, the declaration of YHWH's lordship over creation and omniscience remains valid. The assassins are badly mistaken for imagining God to be blind to their plots.

(2) Executing a Coup (7:3–7)

The preceding summary of intrigue's motivations and futility (7:1d–2) leads to a blow-by-blow account of the Ephraimite coup(s?) in vv. 3–7. The allusive language makes it difficult to determine which of several possible incidents from his time the prophet was describing, especially since the related passage in 2 Kgs 15 records four assassinations of northern kings (i.e., Zechariah, Shallum, Pekahiah, Pekah) during the tumultuous period in Israel from about 750–730 BCE, just as the Assyrian Empire was regaining its strength. However, Hos 7:3–7 not only never mentions any Samarian kings by name, but the concluding comment that "*all their kings* have fallen, none of them is crying out to me" (7:7c–d) also appears to sum up an entire era of Samaria's royal intrigue in response to the pressures of Assyrian imperialism. In keeping with YHWH's indignation with which the passage

53. Dearman, *Hosea*, 200.

opens (7:1–2), the following verses aim less at historical specificity and more at the corrupt heart underlying the actions of the conspirators.

YHWH's exposé of the conspiracy begins by highlighting the sycophantic practices that characterize the plotters: "In their evil they gladden the king, and by their wicked acts [they gladden] the princes" (7:3). The God of Israel has already asserted that he knows "their evil" (רָעָתָם; 7:2b), even as the schemers nonetheless exercise "their evil" (רָעָתָם; 7:3a) by their plot to "gladden" (שׂמח) the members of the royal house (7:3a–b). This use of שׂמח may anticipate the mention of drunkenness in v. 5 as an accomplice to committing treason. Before uncovering this plot in vv. 5–6, the text's focus in vv. 3–4 remains on the twisted heart of the schemers.

The next verse combines word pictures from the bedroom and kitchen. The first two clauses of v. 4 highlight the gap between the action of flattery (7:3) and the attitude of treachery (7:4): "All of them are adulterers, like an oven burning from a baker" (7:4a–b). Since nothing in the immediate context points to "adulterers" (מְנָאֲפִים; 7:4a) being a literal act of "committing adultery" (נאף; cf. 3:1; 4:2, 13–14), this may be another case of Hosea's tendency to use the idea of sexual sin in a summary sense (e.g., 1:2). A trace of sexual innuendo may remain, in that the top of the Mediterranean "bread oven/furnace" (תַּנּוּר; 7:4b) had a cylindrical hole through which a pancake would be placed on the flame below.[54]

The תַּנּוּר itself will become the focus in v. 6. But here it functions mainly as a prop to describe the baker's skillfulness both in keeping the oven from becoming too hot, too early (7:4b), as well as in knowing when to stop stirring and kneading the dough so that it will rise optimally (7:4c). Synchronizing the readiness of oven's temperature and dough's rising allows the baker to finish baking quickly when mealtime draws near, much like plotters against the royal house are ready to set their elaborate plans in motion as soon as the right opportunity arises.[55] To use a culinary expression more native to English, one might say that the conspiracy is already brewing and ready to boil over at a moment's notice.

Hosea 7:5 records the preparation of the opportune time for assassination. Compared to what precedes, the metaphor of heat briefly goes in a different direction by portraying the sensation of warmth experienced by the king's drunken protectors: "On the day of our king, the princes have become sick with the heat of wine" (7:5a). The phrase, "day of our king" (יוֹם מַלְכֵּנוּ) that fronts the clause seems to be a religious festival or royal banquet when the "princes" (שָׂרִים; cf. v. 3) would have been present. While "the heat of wine" (7:5a) clearly refers to drunkenness on this festal occasion, the referent of "he stretches out his hand with the mockers" (7:5b) is unclear. The closest "he" in this context is the previous mention of "our king" (7:5a). The expression "to stretch out the hand" (משׁך יָד) might then describe how the king deploys an assault against the members of his court.[56]

However, the problem with this interpretation is that v. 3 has already named king and princes as naïve victims of violence. Therefore, an unnamed "he," probably refers to a conspiring royal official who has stayed sober to seize the moment, and then gives a hand signal to his co-conspirators to assassinate the king and his princes. These accomplices would then be the "mockers" (לֹצְצִים; 7:5b) whose meticulous plans reflect their open defiance of God's righteousness (e.g., Ps 1:1; Prov 3:34). The

54. Haddox, "(E)masculinity," 194.

55. Shalom M. Paul, "The Image of the Oven and Cake in Hosea VII 4–10," *VT* 18 (1968): 114–20.

56. This military sense for משׁך can be seen in Judg 4:6; 20:37.

conspiracy of Pekah against King Pekahiah and his officers fits this profile (2 Kgs 15:23–25),[57] though the passage's scarcity of detail leaves open the question of which assassination of an Israelite king is in view. The tragic pattern of Israel's history means that several different assassinations are possible.

Even as the assassins strive to conceal their activities, their intentions are laid bare before YHWH at a particular time "when they approach their plotting with heart like an oven" (7:6a). Here the earlier picture of the baker's restraint in tending the oven (7:4) has shifted to the oven itself as a symbol of the conspirator's excitement on the eve of the *coup d'état*. The "heart/mind" (לֵבָב; 7:6a; cf. v. 2) is the smoldering nerve center of the assassins from which "their baking [heart] simmers [ישׁן, lit. "to sleep"]" (7:6b) with anticipation during the night and erupts in "a flame of fire" (7:6c) when morning comes. Fire thus depicts both the motives and emotions of sedition against the king.

The word picture of intense heat, already stretched to its figurative limits, concludes by leaping yet another gap from devious attitude to murderous action: "All of them burn like an oven, and they consume their judges" (7:7a–b). While the figurative language in this section has been opaque at times, the conclusion leaves no doubt about the literal outcome of the conspiracy: "All their kings have fallen, none of them is crying out to me" (7:7c–d). In Hos 7:3–7, then, the pursuit of domestic intrigue has not installed the conspirators' king of choice and strengthened Ephraim's hand against Assyria, as they had sought. It has accomplished exactly the opposite by sealing the downfall of Ephraim's royal house. The politics of internal intrigue will ultimately impale those who live by this pagan worldview.

c. Ephraim's Rejection of Restoration, Part II: International Intrigue (7:8–12)

(1) Ignorance of Weakness (7:8–9)

Then YHWH's gaze turns outward from the domestic realm to international intrigue in Ephraim's dealings with other nations. This section about the perils of ancient Near Eastern imperialism divides into two panels. The first concerns the vulnerability of Ephraim in the face of its greedy neighbors (7:8–10), while the second goes a step further in warning that courtship of imperial power will bring downfall (7:11–12). Both sections refer often to "Ephraim" (7:8a, 8b, 11a) and thereby offer creational images on the inability of "double fertility" to live up to his name. Instead, rejecting the offer of YHWH's restoration will lead to infertility and impotence.

Ephraim's draw toward the power politics of intrigue is turned on its head by rearranging the baking metaphor of the preceding verses. Rather than being like the baker and oven (7:4, 6–7), the children of God will become like the bread: "Ephraim is mixed among the peoples, Ephraim has been a flatbread not turned over" (7:8).[58] In an echo of Hos 4:17, the twice-repeated name "Ephraim" (lit. "double fruitfulness") in Hos 7:8 underscores the reversal of fortunes from blessing to curse. Ephraim as active participant in imperialism will suffer as its helpless victim when a syncretistic people experiences the further syncretism of being "mixed" (בלל *hithpael*; 7:8a) with the impurities of foreign "peoples" (עַמִּים; cf. 9:1; 10:10).

In fact, the only possible strength to stand before the Assyrian threats of the eighth century BCE comes from the counterintuitive theopolitics of pure dependence upon YHWH (cf. Isa 36–37). But

57. Macintosh, *Hosea*, 261.

58. Paul ("Hosea VII 4–10," 117–18) suggests that the culinary image is found in the entire verse since the Hebrew root בלל ("mixed"; 7:8a) has an Akkadian cognate *balālu*, which means "kneading [bread]." On this point, it is notable that Ezek 11:1–10 and 24:1–14 also use culinary metaphors to challenge people's thinking.

Ephraim has sabotaged itself by diluting its uniqueness (7:8a). To add insult to injury in this culinary image, Hosea then likens the weakness of Israel to a burnt pancake (7:8b) that is as unappetizing as it is useless. The "flatbread" (עֻגָה) was the handheld bread cake that provided everyday sustenance for the Israelites (e.g., Gen 18:6; 1 Kgs 17:13). To use similar English idioms, the people of Ephraim will be used and burned by greedy "friends" who exploit the weakness of their "ally."

The next verse contrasts the opportunism of the surrounding empires with the cluelessness of Ephraim about its weakness: "Strangers have consumed his strength, but on his part, he did not know! Gray hair is sprinkled on him, but on his part, he did not know!" (7:9). "Strangers" (זָרִים; cf. Isa 1:7; Jer 2:25) are foreign invaders who will come and pillage Ephraim's "strength" (כֹּחַ; 7:9a), a term that often denotes military power (e.g., Isa 10:13; Hab 1:11) or physical ability (e.g., Amos 2:14; Isa 37:3). Given the prophet's use of culinary images to describe both strength and weakness, one might say that Ephraim is rotten to the point that his bread and butter have spoiled, yet he will still be devoured by others.

Being violated by foreign powers will cause Ephraim to age prematurely, like a once-vibrant youth who experiences the sudden onset of "gray hair" (שֵׂיבָה; cf. Gen 15:15; 1 Kgs 2:6). However, most tragic among Ephraim's flaws is his utter unawareness of being abused at the hand of others. YHWH twice laments the numbness of his people using two pleonastic pronouns: "But on his part [וְהוּא], he did not know!" (7:9b, d).[59] Israel's persistent refusal to "know (ידע) or display "knowledge" (דַעַת) directed toward God has surfaced as an important theme in Hosea (e.g., 2:10[8]; 4:1; 5:4). To Ephraim's ignorance of God and his ways, the passage now adds the plight of self-ignorance.

(2) Vulnerability Due to Pride (7:10)

Because of Israel's willful ignorance, YHWH determines to prick the conscience of his people from within: "So the pride of Israel will testify against his own face" (7:10a). The expression "pride of Israel" (גְּאוֹן־יִשְׂרָאֵל) has already denoted the arrogance of Israel's attitudes and actions against God (cf. 5:5). The shift from "Ephraim" (7:8) back to "Israel" (7:10) suggests either that "pride of Israel" is a stock phrase in Hosea's time or that that all of God's people are in view. Less ambiguous in this clause is how Israel's sinful behavior will "testify against his own face" (ענה בְּפָנָיו) rather than YHWH himself (cf. 5:8–15). The people of YHWH have become deaf to his voice in misunderstanding his threats as exaggerated and his promises as unconditional (cf. 6:1–3).

Be that as it may, the strategy of indirect rather than direct confrontation, though frustrating at times for YHWH (cf. 6:4–6), has become necessary toward an unresponsive people who "have not returned to YHWH their God, nor have they sought him despite all this" (7:10b–c). As in Hos 4:1–5:7, suffering at the hands of the created order has not produced the intended result of bringing Israel back to YHWH, so the next step in correcting this recalcitrant people is to give them over to the consequences of their imperialism. The continual rejection of YHWH's offer of restoration (cf. 6:11–7:1), first through domestic intrigue (7:1c–7) and now through international intrigue (7:8–12), simply leaves YHWH no other recourse to deal with Ephraim but to allow the nations to have their way with this people.

59. These pleonastic pronouns employ the discourse feature of forward-pointing reference (*LDHB* §1.2) to focus attention on Ephraim as an impotent actor.

(3) Dumbness with Imperialism (7:11)

The stupidity of Ephraim is the action that sets in motion the consequences of embracing imperialism. YHWH exposes his people's foolish attempt to manipulate powerful empires by using an avian image: "Ephraim has become like a dove, naïve, lacking a mind: They have summoned Egypt, they have gone to Assyria" (7:11). The "dove" (יוֹנָה) is the second bird that Noah sends out from the ark and that brings back good news of peace (Gen 8:8–12). But in seeking allies for war rather than peace, Israel descends to the level of the senseless creature itself that is described in 7:11a as "naïve" (an adjectival participle from פתה, "to be simple/ ignorant") and "lacking a mind" (אֵין לֵב).

In OT wisdom literature, for a person to be "naïve, simple-minded" (פֶּתִי, an adjective also derived from פתה; 7:11a) is to be vulnerable to deception (e.g., Prov 1:22; 9:16). A parallel description of Israel's intellectual limitations in "lacking a mind" (אֵין לֵב; 7:11a) reinforces this age-old problem of spiritual ignorance. Israel exemplifies both kinds of dimwittedness (cf. Prov 7:7; 8:5) in the eighth century BCE through foolhardy pursuit of alliances with Egypt (7:11b) and/or Assyria (7:11c), two superpowers whose self-interest always meant taking far more from the kingdoms of Israel than they would ever give. As Shalom Paul rightly observes of these empires and their relationship to unreliable Israel, "Who would want to be associated or allied with such a faithless, fickle flirt!"[60] It is therefore apt that Hos 7:11 describes the absurdity of Ephraim's choices in terms of a senseless bird that seeks refuge by flying directly to its predators rather than fleeing away (cf. 5:13).

(4) Discipline from YHWH (7:12)

Despite the threat of these predators, the greatest opponent at hand is not the surrounding nations. Rather, YHWH will personally thwart his people's flirtations with imperialism, much like a fowler captures a bird in a trap before it can escape: "As soon as they go, I will spread out my net over them" (7:12a–b). The wandering bird of 7:11 that flits indecisively between empires will be caught in a "net" (רֶשֶׁת) that YHWH will "spread" (פרשׂ; 7:12b). This form of poetic justice befits Israel's leaders who ensnare their countrymen like "a net [רֶשֶׁת] spread out [פרשׂ passive] on Tabor" (5:1e). Not only will Israel trap itself by its own sins,[61] but those who imagine themselves to have eluded YHWH's reach will soon also find that "like birds of the sky I will bring them down" (7:12c). Thus Hosea's kaleidoscope of similes transforms the earlier picture of Israel as lion's prey (5:14) into a depiction of the people as a trapper's prize (7:11–12c).

Whatever animal simile Hosea uses, the Lord of all the earth simply cannot tolerate another master over his people. He must therefore rebuke them in the sight of others: "I will discipline them according to the report to their assembly" (7:12d). Here the prophet does not specify the occasion and participants of the "assembly" (עֵדָה), but the public nature of a "report" (שֵׁמַע; cf. Isa 23:5; Hab 3:2) suggests that Israel will suffer disgrace before its allies (cf. 2:12[10]; Lam 1:2). Shaming his people is never YHWH's ultimate goal, since he always seeks to "discipline" (יסר; cf. 7:15; 10:10) so that they might "repent/return" (שׁוב; 7:10b; cf. 2:8–9[6–7]). In this way Hos 7:12 hints at a restored future for Israel beyond its long history of rejecting YHWH's ways (e.g., 3:1–5; 11:1–11).

60. Shalom M. Paul, "Hosea 7:16: Gibberish Jabber," in *Pomegranates and Golden Bells: Studies in Biblical, Jewish, and Near Eastern Ritual, Law, and Literature in Honor of Jacob Milgrom*, ed. David P. Wright, David Noel Freedman, and Avi Hurvitz (Winona Lake, IN: Eisenbrauns, 1995), 707–8.

61. Cf. Paul A. Kruger, "The Divine Net in Hosea 7,12," *ETL* 68 (1992): 132–36, who overlooks the echoes of Hos 5:1 in the description of Israel falling into its own net, thereby leading to the interpretation that YHWH himself is the net.

d. YHWH's Final Verdict of Woe (7:13–16)

Yet before restoration can happen, the judgment of exile must come. A woe oracle in three parts introduces the inevitability of what must follow Israel's apostasy: (1) the indictment that Israel has rebelled (7:13a–d); (2) the evidence of such rebellion (7:13e–15); and (3) the tragic result of exile (7:16).

(1) The Indictment: Rebellion Leading to Ruin (7:13a–d)

The oracle begins with YHWH's pronouncement that destruction stands on the near horizon: "Woe to them, for they have fled away from me! Ruin is theirs, for they have rebelled against me!" (7:13a–d). The exclamation "woe!" (אוֹי; 7:13a) usually marks a move from indictment to condemnation in OT prophetic literature (e.g., Isa 3:9; Jer 10:19). But in this passage, the preceding image of Israel's bird-like movements away from YHWH (7:11), though briefly arrested by his net (7:12), hardens into the accusation that Israel has "fled away" (נדד; 7:13b).

Rather than escaping danger, as uses of the root נדד connote (e.g., Isa 10:31; 21:15), Israel's rebellious flight leads not to safety but to "ruin" (שֹׁד; Hos 7:13c; cf. Isa 13:6). Yet in the next clause, the imagery changes again when Israel is no longer the naive bird but a seditious band of fugitives who deserve a guilty verdict for the time when "they rebelled [פשׁע] against me" (7:13d). The explicitly political undertones of the verb פשׁע ("to rebel"; e.g., 1 Kgs 12:19; 2 Kgs 3:5) frame Israel's conversion to the ancient Near Eastern worldview of imperialism, and its particular expression as "Assyrianism" (see commentary on 5:13), as nothing less than treason against YHWH.

(2) The Evidence: Ephraim's Foolish Exchanges (7:13e–15)

Ephraim's departure from orthodox Yahwism entails several foolish exchanges that trade what is valuable for what is worthless: (a) realpolitik instead of theopolitics (7:13e–f); (b) Baal instead of YHWH (7:14); and (c) harm instead of love (7:15). These three unwise transactions provide supporting evidence for YHWH' s indictment against his people (7:14).

(a) Realpolitik instead of Theopolitics (7:13e–f)

YHWH's theopolitics and the realpolitik of Assyrianism are mutually exclusive, for the God of Israel asserts that he has always been able, available, and willing to save his people from their enemies: "Now on my part, I would redeem them" (7:13e). The direct conflict in this verse between YHWH's willingness to "redeem" (פדה) and Israel's apostasy to trust other redeemers is framed by two opposing discourse elements, the pleonastic pronouns, "now on my part" (וְאָנֹכִי; 7:13e) and "yet on their part" (וְהֵמָּה; 7:13f). In the clause referring to YHWH's side of the conflict, the root פדה ("to redeem"; 7:13e) echoes several key OT texts that characterize YHWH's mighty acts of deliverance in the exodus (e.g., Deut 7:8; 2 Sam 7:23[2x]; Ps 78:42). The God who defeated Egypt while Israel simply watched (Exod 14:13, 30–31) extended his people the offer of protection as long as they lived by this distinctive worldview of divine power amidst human weakness.

However, as had been the case for centuries, in Hosea's time Israel had chosen to go the seditious route of seeking other powers for help: "Yet on their part, they have spoken lies against me" (7:13f). The passage does not explicitly state the content of these "lies" (כְּזָבִים) against YHWH, though vv. 14–16 go on to condemn the syncretistic use of Canaanite rituals intended for Baal to procure creational blessings from YHWH. Later in Hosea, the underlying root כזב ("to lie") also describes two-faced Israel pitting Assyria and Egypt against each other (12:2[1]). Thus, it appears that Israel's lies about

YHWH relate to the false ancient Near Eastern worldviews of imperialism and nature religion.

(b) Baal instead of YHWH (7:14)

Hosea supplies further evidence for the verdict of woe (7:13a–d) in Ephraim's choice of Baal instead of YHWH, specifically in borrowing two rituals from the Baal cult. As a reflection of their insincerity in worship (7:14a), the people pray to YHWH with loud howling (7:14b) and cutting themselves (7:14c). Both actions had characterized Israel's futile veneration of Baal on Mount Carmel (1 Kgs 18:28). The location of Israel's howling on "their couches/beds" (מִשְׁכְּבוֹת; 7:14b) may refer to cultic sexual activity on the Canaanite high places (cf. Isa 57:7–8), though the verb (ילל, "to howl") usually denotes a cry of sadness rather than pleasure (Isa 15:3; Amos 8:3). On a less ambiguous note, this verse clearly outlines the purpose of these ascetic rituals in seeking "grain and new wine" (דָּגָן וְתִירוֹשׁ). Hosea had used the first appearance of this word pair to condemn Israel's pursuit of Baal as fertility god as well as the lesser Canaanite deities of grain and wine, Dagon and Tirosh (see commentary on 2:10[8]). Indeed, this people are guilty of persistent apostasy in that "they keep turning away from me" (7:14d).

(c) Harm instead of Love (7:15)

YHWH responds to Israel's intransigence with a deeply moving assertion of his parental care. The next three words are a poignant, concise rhyme: "As for me [וַאֲנִי], I disciplined them [יִסַּרְתִּי], I strengthened [חִזַּקְתִּי] their arms" (7:15a–b). The opening pleonastic pronoun, "as for me" (וַאֲנִי), looks back to this section's numerous uses of this discourse feature to draw out the conflict between YHWH and his people (5:13e, 14c; 6:7a; 7:9b, d; 13e, f). Along similar lines of foregrounding the relational stakes, the verbs יסר ("to chasten, teach, discipline") and חזק ("to strengthen") anticipate the portrayal of YHWH as Israel's father in Hos 11:3–4. But in an appalling twist on the murderous schemes described earlier (7:4–7), YHWH laments that the object of Israel's "evil [deeds]" (רָעָה/רָעוֹת; 7:1–3) has turned from other people toward him: "But they devise harm [רָע] against me!" (7:15c). Unthinkably, Israel the son has turned against YHWH his father by plotting against the very one who has sought his good (7:15a–b). In the next verse, the final exchange of repaying love with harm will be the most foolish mistake of all.

(3) The Result: A Turn toward Exile (7:16)

The incorrigibility of such children can only be fixed by the extreme measure of giving them over to another master: "They will return [שׁוב] to a no-god" (7:16a; cf. Deut 32:17, 21). The root שׁוב ("to repent/return") has consistently denoted in Hosea what YHWH seeks from Israel (e.g., 3:5; 7:10). However, the object of the verb here is not YHWH but "a no-god" (לֹא עָל). While the first part of this appellation is straightforward as the negative particle לֹא (e.g., 7:9b, 10b, 14a), the more cryptic second part is a Hebrew preposition that usually means "on, upon, over" (e.g., 7:12b, 14c). In favor of a divine referent, this preposition refers later to a heavenly dwelling of "the Most High" (עַל; 11:7).[62]

The immediate literary context also reiterates Israel's preference for earthly things as a self-destructing people who have been "like a slack bow" (כְּקֶשֶׁת רְמִיָּה; 7:16b). This probably denotes Israel's longstanding tendency to live and die by the disproportionate killing effected by the "bow" (קֶשֶׁת; 1:5, 7). Poetic justice for such violence will

62. Many emend the text to readings such as "Most High" (Andersen and Freedman, *Hosea*, 477) or "No Profit" (Dearman, *Hosea*, 207n6).

arrive soon when "their princes will fall by the sword" (7:16c). The "prince" (שַׂר) is a shorthand way of referring to all of Israel's leaders (cf. 3:5; 5:10), as when Hosea previously declared that kings will "fall" (נפל; 7:7), that is, suffer a violent and untimely death.

However, in Hos 7:16 the summary of the manifold sins of these leaders as "the gibberish of their speech" (7:16d) is puzzling, specifically on the occasion of their death (7:16c). This passage quotes no words spoken by Israel,[63] but the many references to diplomatic intrigue in chapter 7 suggest that treacherous speech about YHWH (7:13), perhaps the wrong kind of self-talk about sin which has displaced the right kind of self-talk about repentance (7:2),[64] is mirrored by Israel's attempts to curry favor with the surrounding empires (e.g., 7:11).

In addition to being the cause of death (7:16c), apostasy of words (7:16d) will also lead to Israel becoming the butt of jokes in a foreign land: "this will be their mockery in the land of Egypt" (7:16e). Other passages refer to Israel's "mockery" (לַעַג) in exile (e.g., Ps 44:14[13]; Isa 28:11), though it is unclear whether the people of Ephraim at this point are actually in Egypt or this is simply where ridicule originates against Ephraim. The exile of both Israelite kingdoms occurred at the hands of the Mesopotamian empires of Assyria (2 Kgs 17) and Babylon (2 Kgs 24–25). In any case, the book of Hosea goes on to speak of a figurative return to Egypt as an overturning of the great deliverance accomplished by YHWH (e.g., 8:13; 9:3; cf. Deut 17:16; 28:68). The "anti-exodus" of returning to Egypt (7:16) will one day go in the reverse direction when YHWH brings a "new exodus" of restoration back to the land of Canaan (2:17[15]; 11:11).[65]

Canonical and Theological Significance

1. God, War, and Politics

The Jewish philosopher Martin Buber offers an incisive summary of prophetic paradoxes in the eighth century BCE: "He who has dealings with the powers renounces the power of powers, that which bestows and withholds power, and loses its help; whereas he who confides and keeps still thereby gains the very political strength and understanding to hold his ground."[66] As Hosea and his contemporaries assert, the people of YHWH must exercise the distinctive theopolitics of waiting

63. Shalom Paul notes that the usual sense of Hebrew זַעַם (7:16) as "wrath, imprecation" does not fit the context. Thus via comparison with an Arabic cognate, he proposes translating זַעַם in 7:16 not as "insolence" (as with the English versions) but as "gibberish" intended to mock the vain attempts of Ephraim to negotiate with the Egyptians in their own language ("Hosea 7:16," 711–12). This is the rendering adopted here.

64. The English versions render Hos 7:2a idiomatically as "they do not realize" (NIV, NLT) or "they do not consider" (NASB, NRSV), but the literal Hebrew idiom involves talking to oneself: "but they do not speak to their heart" (וּבַל־יֹאמְרוּ לִלְבָבָם).

65. On Hosea's creative transformation of exodus motifs, see Hwang, "Hosea's Use of the Exodus Traditions," 243–53; Silva Retamales, "Tradición del 'Éxodo' en Oseas," 145–78.

66. Martin Buber, *The Prophetic Faith* (New York: Harper & Row, 1949), 137. Similarly, Michael Walzer summarizes the cultural oddity of the prophets' political theology: "*Do nothing:* this is the prophetic idea of a religious foreign policy, and this is the prophetic challenge to the kings of Israel and Judah, who were as likely as Assyrian kings to rely on the 'strength' of their hands and the 'wisdom' of their counselors" ("Prophecy and International Politics," *Hebraic Political Studies* 4 [2009]: 324, emphasis original.).

and trusting, even when the sabers of superpowers begin rattling and lesser powers scramble to find stronger friends. Vulnerable Israel will thrive the less it tries to survive using the standard tools of ancient Near Eastern statecraft. But it will suffer destruction the moment it tries to escape destruction through arming itself with weapons and allies like other nations.

The notion that might makes wrong, and not right, is as foreign in the contemporary world of realpolitik as it was Hos 5:8–7:16. Perhaps surprisingly for modern audiences who typically associate the OT with violence, the prophets of the eighth century BCE (i.e., Hosea, Isaiah, Amos, Micah) stood out in their world for propounding an ethic of nonviolence. In a passage like Hos 5:8–7:16, which begins with martial language, military conquest is not the end in itself that other ancient Near Eastern kingdoms pursued by fighting battles in the names of their deities. Unlike the gods and goddesses of the nations, the God of Israel had no need to enlarge his fame or territory through successful wars by his kings.[67]

YHWH already ruled the whole world, whether his people were strong or weak. This contrasted starkly with Assyria's national god, who needed his earthly empire to validate the expansionist claim that "Assur is king! Assur is king!."[68] This means that in Hos 5:8–15, YHWH summons the kingdoms of Samaria and Judah to battle, not as a war of conquest but as punishment for their wars of conquest against each other.[69] Even so, the prophet Isaiah also asserts that YHWH will later fight for his people and against Assyria (Isa 10:5–19; cf. Nahum), along with one day saving both Assyria and Egypt (Isa 19:24–25)—the mighty empires between which the tiny Israelite kingdoms took turns being squeezed.

The distinctive many-sidedness in YHWH's theopolitics becomes evident through a comparison with the height of human political wisdom in Abraham Lincoln's "Meditation on the Divine Will" (1862). This American president famously mused about divine providence at the height of the American Civil War, a conflict between two sides that each claimed God's support for their respective causes. To quote the relevant sentences from Lincoln that illustrate the contrast with Hosea:

> The will of God prevails. In great contests each party claims to act in accordance with the will of God. Both may be, and one must be, wrong. God cannot be for and against the same thing at the same time. In the present civil war it is quite possible that God's purpose is something different from the purpose of either party; and yet

67. One might object, however, that the kings of Israel did seek to expand their territory, beginning with David and his various conquests. Yet the OT remains distinct in its cultural context for problematizing the usual one-to-one connection between an empire's success in expansion with the power and reputation of its national deity. More on this below.

68. For more on the "religious imperialism" of the Neo-Assyrian Empire, see Holloway, *Aššur Is King!*, 99.

69. Thompson, *Situation and Theology*, 67.

> the human instrumentalities, working just as they do, are of the best adaptation to effect his purpose.[70]

Although describing a different civil war between north and south, Lincoln's observation that "each party claims to act in accordance with the will of God" could apply equally to the Syro-Ephraimite War (734–732 BCE) in which the two Yahwistic kingdoms of Israel squabbled in the growing shadow of the Assyrian Empire. Hosea would also resonate with Lincoln's wisdom that opposing sides of God's people can both be wrong in waging conflicts against one another in his name. But speaking under divine guidance, the prophet Hosea would object to Lincoln's binary logic that "God cannot be for and against the same thing at the same time." In the book of Hosea, YHWH is both for and against his people in the two Israelite kingdoms. The corollary to this is that victory in battle is no more guarantee of God's blessing than defeat provides a sure sign of his curse. But in his Second Inaugural Address (1865) that was influenced by the "Meditation," Lincoln could only hint at such a mystery that transcends how people typically understand Providence's relationship to victory and defeat: "The prayers of both could not be answered positively. That of neither has been answered fully. The Almighty has his own purposes."[71]

Hosea unveils the Almighty's own purposes in the eighth century BCE as the desire to "heal" (7:1; cf. 5:13; 6:1) his people from their disease of apostasy, whether because of, in, or despite their wars with one another. While human depravity does not negate the possibility of just wars, the Soviet dissident Aleksandr Solzhenitsyn echoes the OT Prophets in his reminder that supposedly higher causes tend to deconstruct themselves through the lower conduct of their participants. The human predicament is irreducibly spiritual rather than political in nature, as Solzhenitsyn warned in *The Gulag Archipelago*, the memoirs of his time in Soviet prisons:

> So let the reader who expects this book to be a political exposé slam its covers shut right now. If only it were so simple! If only there were evil people somewhere insidiously committing evil deeds, and it were necessary only to separate them from the rest of us and destroy them. *But the line dividing good and evil cuts through the heart of every human being. And who is willing to destroy a piece of his own heart?*[72]

Hosea 5:8–7:16 performs this very act of detonating human sensibilities, since the facile claim of God's support in war, as both Samaria and Judah were prone to make, reflects the apostasy of YHWH's people that needs healing. I will address this topic further below in the discussion of nominal faith, contextualization, and syncretism.

70. Text taken from Robert R. Mathisen, ed., *The Routledge Sourcebook of Religion and the American Civil War: A History in Documents* (New York: Routledge, 2014), 176.

71. Ibid., 427.

72. Aleksandr Solzhenitsyn, *The Gulag Archipelago* (London: Vintage Books, 2003), 75; emphasis added.

However, the inscrutable ways of God and the nearly infinite human capacity for self-deception do not invalidate all attempts to apply the Bible in politics. Against modern secularists who claim that religion is the impetus for all wars,[73] the OT Prophets would counter that the unique theopolitics of the Bible enable human flourishing by relativizing the centers of institutional power and challenging simplistic claims of God's unilateral support for them.[74] Augustine later reinforced this perspective in his influential tractate on the fall of Rome, *The City of God*, in arguing that every human institution cannot escape its contingent and imperfect nature.[75]

Within such an Augustinian framework of chastened politics,[76] modern interpreters can still bridge the vast differences between ancient Israel and modern nations by applying the timeless principles of a passage. Richard Bauckham offers a useful guideline for how to proceed:

> [W]hile the law and the prophets cannot be instructions for our political life, they can be instructive for our political life. We cannot apply their teaching directly to ourselves, but from the way in which God expressed his character and purposes in the political life of Israel we may learn something of how they should be expressed in political life today.[77]

So while the theopolitical principle of nonviolence in Hos 5:8–7:16 is impracticable in today's world of geopolitics, this can still be the distinctive way that individual believers effect change in a violent world by embracing weakness and suffering, practicing thoughtful civil disobedience, and trusting their God for vindication as people who serve him from the margins more than the centers of power.[78]

Indeed, all the basic elements of the NT's cruciform spirituality are present in the OT's countercultural view of what strength really is. Centuries before the person and work of Christ, the portrait of the sovereign and longsuffering God of Israel in Hos 11 had already exemplified how "cruciformity is the character of God."[79] However, faith in this unique God is not fatalism or resignation in the face of defeat. As the Japanese theologian Kosuke Koyama notes, "Christ's mutilated hands, seemingly so

73. E.g., Christopher Hitchens, *God Is Not Great: How Religion Poisons Everything* (London: Atlantic Books, 2008).

74. J. G. McConville, *God and Earthly Power: An Old Testament Political Theology, Genesis–Kings*, LHBOTS 454 (London: T&T Clark, 2006), 19–28.

75. Available online at http://www.ccel.org/ccel/schaff/npnf102.iv.html.

76. On which see Paul Weithman, "Augustine's Political Philosophy," in *The Cambridge Companion to Augustine*, ed. Eleonore Stump and Norman Kretzmann (Cambridge: Cambridge University Press, 2001), 234–52.

77. Richard Bauckham, *The Bible in Politics: How to Read the Bible Politically*, 2nd ed. (Louisville: Westminster John Knox, 2011), 6, emphasis original.

78. Walter Wink, *Engaging the Powers: Discernment and Resistance in a World of Domination* (Minneapolis: Augsburg Fortress, 1992), 169–257.

79. Michael J. Gorman, *Cruciformity: Paul's Narrative Spirituality of the Cross* (Grand Rapids: Eerdmans, 2001), 18.

weak, appear over against our world that is replete with 'strong,' oppressive fists. Yet, Christ's hands are more 'truthful,' therefore more healing, of human ills than all our fists put together."[80]

2. Contextualization, Nominalism, and Syncretism

While Israelite faith is distinctive in its cultural context, this distinctiveness takes on a relative rather than absolute character. The geographical realities of Canaan meant that YHWH's sovereignty over this often-arid place would always overlap with the spheres that formerly belonged to the nature deities of the land. Both Egypt and Mesopotamia had massive rivers to irrigate their crops. By contrast, agriculture in Canaan depended on an annual cycle of spring and autumn rains, separated by a long dry spell during the summer.

This climatological given brought YHWH into direct conflict with Baal, the Canaanite god of the storm. And as YHWH took over all of Baal's functions, the historical God of the exodus and conquest also became for Israel the creator God who annually provided rain. YHWH would always be more than a nature deity of Canaan, of course, but Hosea's many references to YHWH as the usurper of Baal's realm of nature show that he could never be less than this.[81] By contextualizing his message and methods so that his people can know him in familiar categories, the God of Israel employs contextualization as his strategy in communicating with humanity, much like what missionaries do in communicating the Bible's truth across cultures.

Nonetheless, Israel's prayer of "repentance" in Hos 6:1–3 illustrates how hearers may still misunderstand the missionary's best efforts in the service of translating God's unchanging message. This is the missiological dilemma known as *syncretism*, that is, a mixture of right and wrong theological ideas. The very actions that YHWH undertook to replace Canaanite deities also meant that his people were always prone to misunderstand him as merely a nature deity. Over time, this kind of pragmatism can devolve into *nominalism*—the exchange of a living covenant relationship for dead rituals of a transactional nature. The nominal believer seeks God only insofar as he continues to provide his blessings, yet the animistic worldview of seeking blessings or deliverance from fear remains essentially intact.

Overt apostasy and doctrinal error are easier to recognize than nominal faith that seeks the right God, but for the wrong reasons. The latter typically cloaks itself in the

80. Kosuke Koyama, "The Hand Painfully Open," *LTQ* 22 (1987): 34.

81. Willem S. Boshoff, "Yahweh as God of Nature: Elements of the Concept of God in the Book of Hosea," *JNSL* 18 (1992): 13–24.

external forms of orthodoxy, as when Israel prays to YHWH (6:1–3) using several terms of repentance that he has just used in warning his people (5:13–15). Ironically, the insincere words of Israel have sometimes been convincing enough for Christian worship traditions to adopt Hos 6:1–3 as a prayer of sincere penitence.[82] But YHWH is not deceived nor mocked—his cutting answer to Israel exposes the inward charade of the heart that the outward piety of words cannot conceal (6:4–6). The truth of the matter is that nominalism's apathy toward God works closely in concert with syncretism's distortion of God into (merely) the one who fulfills human desires.

Although nominalism and syncretism are dangerous, YHWH amazes by continuing to speak with the devices of anthropomorphism and anthropopathism—the use of human forms and feelings—even at the risk of being misunderstood. And when his nominal and syncretistic people misunderstand him, as they often do, Hosea illustrates how their God does not reject them outright but keeps on communicating through the prophets using concepts they can understand. Hosea's message in the present passage is harsh, but this God persists in speaking through his prophet so that the bad news of judgment may pave the way for good news of deliverance to come (e.g., Hos 11:1–11). Thus, in both his message and methods, it is resoundingly true that "the living God is a missionary God."[83] May his missionary people imitate this posture of discerning engagement for the sake of bringing God's truth to a confused world.

---

82. For example, Hos 6:1–3 provides the basis for an Anglican canticle of penitence in "Canticle H," in *Enriching Our Worship 1: Morning and Evening Prayer, The Great Litany, and The Holy Eucharist* (New York: Church, 1998), 34.

83. John R. W. Stott, "The Living God Is a Missionary God," in *Perspectives on the World Christian Movement: A Reader*, ed. Ralph D. Winter and Steven C. Hawthorne, 3rd ed. (Pasadena, CA: William Carey Library, 1999), 3–9.

CHAPTER 7

Hosea 8:1–9:9

C. An Announcement of Exile

Main Idea of the Passage

YHWH announces the verdict of exile against his syncretistic people who attempt to "make" (עשׂה) and "multiply" (רבה)—two key verbs in this passage—their own way in imitation of other nations. Their "Maker" (עֹשֵׂה; 8:14) brooks no man-made idols and will level the punishment of exile as a homeopathic remedy to expunge Israel's pagan tendencies.[1]

Literary Context

Hosea 8:1–9:9 is the third of five covenant discourses in chapters 4–14. Following divine speeches against Israel's priestly (4:1–5:7) and political transgressions (5:8–7:16), this passage develops ideas introduced earlier by exposing the sinful synergies at work among Israelite kingship, cultic worship, and foreign policy. The "ram's horn" (שׁוֹפָר) had previously sounded an urgent call to response (5:8), but this same instrument now announces divine judgment (8:1), imaginatively transposing a battle cry into a funeral dirge for Israel's impending death.

At a more granular level, the creative use of images to describe Ephraim's syncretism and its consequences (e.g., spoiled cake [7:8], wandering donkey [8:9]) binds chapters 7–8 closely together.[2] Even as Hos 8:1–9:9 describes exile for this syncretism as a foregone conclusion of sorts, the subsequent section in 9:10–11:11 sets this

1. Edmond Jacob was the first to note the homeopathic posture of Hosea toward his syncretistic culture ("L'Héritage cananéen dans le livre du prophète Osée," 250–59), though he unfortunately limited his treatment of this form of contextualization to Canaanite nature religion.

2. Emmanuel O. Nwaoru, "The Role of Images in the Literary Structure of Hosea VII 8–VIII 14," *VT* 54 (2004): 216–22.

miserable episode to come in the bigger context of YHWH's covenantal history with Israel. His ultimate purpose for these disobedient children is not to abandon them in exile (11:1–7), since this covenantal God of deep affections (11:8–9) will bring a chastened people back to himself and his land (11:10–11).

Translation and Exegetical Outline

(See pages 211–13.)

Structure and Literary Form

This discourse joins many of the covenantal motifs found in the literary units of Hos 4:1–5:7 and 5:8–7:16. As Walter Brueggemann has observed, the prophecy of Hosea ingeniously mixes and matches the formal literary elements of the "covenant lawsuit" (רִיב; 2:4[2]; 4:1) rather than arranging them in any fixed order.[3] Hosea 8:1–9:9 is no exception, especially in YHWH's accusations that seem at first to meander between condemnations of king and cult (8:4–8a) as well as politics and religion (8:8b–14). The opaque relationships among these sin-clusters have led to numerous attempts to simplify Hos 8:1–9:9 by reducing the real-life background of the passage to a single *Sitz im Leben* that scholars usually hold to be either cultic or political.[4]

Upon closer examination, the somewhat unpredictable juxtaposition of economics, religion, and politics reflects the holistic character of Israel's faith in YHWH. The way these realms spill over into one another defies modern attempts at discrete classification, for Hosea's vision of Israel as a distinctive people among the nations

3. Walter Brueggemann, *Tradition for Crisis: A Study in Hosea* (Atlanta: John Knox, 1968), 55–56.

4. For the view that Hos 8:1–3 presupposes a cultic situation, see the representative article by Grace I. Emmerson, "The Structure and Meaning of Hosea 8:1–3," *VT* 25 (1975): 700–710. For the contrasting proposal that Hos 8 mainly has a political background, see Wolff, *Hosea*, 133–47.

Hosea 8:1–9:9

			C. An Announcement of Exile (8:1–9:9)
8:1a	אֶל־חִכְּךָ שֹׁפָר	"[Put] to your lips the ram's horn,	1. The Divine Judge's Indictment and Verdict (8:1a–3)
1b	כַּנֶּשֶׁר עַל־בֵּית יְהוָה	[one] like an eagle is upon the house of YHWH!	
1c	יַעַן עָבְרוּ בְרִיתִי	Because they have broken my covenant,	a. Broken Covenant with YHWH (8:1)
1d	וְעַל־תּוֹרָתִי פָּשָׁעוּ׃	and they have rebelled against my instruction.	
2a	לִי יִזְעָקוּ	They keep crying out to me,	b. Insincere "Knowledge" of YHWH (8:2)
2b	אֱלֹהַי יְדַעֲנוּךָ יִשְׂרָאֵל׃	'O my God, we—Israel—have known you!'	
3a	זָנַח יִשְׂרָאֵל טוֹב	Israel has rejected good,	c. YHWH's Summary and Verdict (8:3)
3b	אוֹיֵב יִרְדְּפוֹ׃	an enemy will pursue him.	
4a	הֵם הִמְלִיכוּ וְלֹא מִמֶּנִּי	On their part, they crowned a king but not from me;	2. The Sin-Cluster of King and Cult (8:4–8a)
4b	הֵשִׂירוּ	they set up princes	a. Israel's Idolatrous Kings (8:4)
4c	וְלֹא יָדָעְתִּי	but I did not know/choose [them].	
4d	כַּסְפָּם וּזְהָבָם עָשׂוּ לָהֶם עֲצַבִּים	With their silver and gold they made idols for themselves,	
4e	לְמַעַן יִכָּרֵת׃	in order to be cut off.	
5a	זָנַח עֶגְלֵךְ שֹׁמְרוֹן	He has rejected your calf, O Samaria.	b. YHWH's Rejection of Israel's Idolatry (8:5)
5b	חָרָה אַפִּי בָּם	My anger is kindled against them,	
5c	עַד־מָתַי לֹא יוּכְלוּ נִקָּיֹן׃	how long will they be unable to stay innocent?	
6a	כִּי מִיִּשְׂרָאֵל	Indeed, it (the calf) is from Israel,	(1) The Deadness of the Calf-Idol (8:6)
6b	וְהוּא חָרָשׁ עָשָׂהוּ	and as for it, a craftsman made it,	
6c	וְלֹא אֱלֹהִים הוּא	but it is not God.	
6d	כִּי־שְׁבָבִים יִהְיֶה עֵגֶל שֹׁמְרוֹן׃	For the calf of Samaria will be broken to pieces!	
7a	כִּי רוּחַ יִזְרָעוּ	When they sow wind,	(2) The Creational Consequences of Idolatry (8:7–8a)
7b	וְסוּפָתָה יִקְצֹרוּ	then they reap a whirlwind.	
7c	קָמָה אֵין־לוֹ	Standing grain would not produce anything,	(a) The Land's Goods Destroyed (8:7)
7d	צֶמַח בְּלִי יַעֲשֶׂה־קֶּמַח	a sprout would not make flour.	
7e	אוּלַי יַעֲשֶׂה	If it were to yield [something],	
7f	זָרִים יִבְלָעֻהוּ׃	strangers would swallow it.	
8a	נִבְלַע יִשְׂרָאֵל	Israel is swallowed!	(b) Israel Itself Swallowed (8:8a)

Continued on next page.

Continued from previous page.

8b	עַתָּה הָיוּ בַגּוֹיִם	Now they were among the nations,	3. The Sin-Cluster of Politics and Religion (8:8b–c)
8c	כִּכְלִי אֵין־חֵפֶץ בּוֹ׃	like a vessel in which is no delight.	
9a	כִּי־הֵמָּה עָלוּ אַשּׁוּר	For on their part, they went up to Assyria/Assur,	a. The Folly of Imperial Politics (8:9–10)
9b	פֶּרֶא בּוֹדֵד לוֹ	a wild donkey wandering by itself.	(1) Israel's Dumbness About Imperialism (8:9)
9c	אֶפְרַיִם הִתְנוּ אֲהָבִים׃	Ephraim hired lovers.	
10a	גַּם כִּי־יִתְנוּ בַגּוֹיִם	Even when they hire among the nations,	(2) YHWH's Thwarting of Israel's Politics (8:10)
10b	עַתָּה אֲקַבְּצֵם	now I will gather them.	
10c	וַיָּחֵלּוּ מְּעָט מִמַּשָּׂא מֶלֶךְ שָׂרִים׃	Then they will cease[1] for a time from the burden of a king of princes.	
11a	כִּי־הִרְבָּה אֶפְרַיִם מִזְבְּחֹת לַחֲטֹא	If Ephraim multiplies altars for sin-offering,	b. The Folly of Idolatrous Religion (8:11)
11b	הָיוּ־לוֹ מִזְבְּחוֹת לַחֲטֹא׃	they would become altars for his sinning.	
12a	(אֶכְתּוֹב־)[אֶכְתָּב־]לוֹ (רֻבּוֹ) [רֻבֵּי] תּוֹרָתִי	Should I write for him a multitude of my instruction,[2]	(1) Israel's Rejection of YHWH's Instruction (8:12)
12b	כְּמוֹ־זָר נֶחְשָׁבוּ׃	they would consider it something strange.	
13a	זִבְחֵי הַבְהָבַי יִזְבְּחוּ	As for my roasted sacrifices,[3] they keep sacrificing	(2) YHWH's Rejection of Israel's Sacrifices (8:13a–c)
13b	בָשָׂר וַיֹּאכֵלוּ	and then eat the meat.	
13c	יְהוָה לֹא רָצָם	[But] YHWH is not pleased with them.	
13d	עַתָּה יִזְכֹּר עֲוֹנָם	Now he will remember their iniquity,	c. The Punishment of Anti-Exodus (8:13d–f)
13e	וְיִפְקֹד חַטֹּאותָם	and he will repay their sins.	
13f	הֵמָּה מִצְרַיִם יָשׁוּבוּ׃	In their turn, to Egypt they will return.	
14a	וַיִּשְׁכַּח יִשְׂרָאֵל אֶת־עֹשֵׂהוּ	Israel has forgotten his Maker,	(1) Idolatrous Forgetfulness of the Creator (8:14a–c)
14b	וַיִּבֶן הֵיכָלוֹת	he has built palaces,	
14c	וִיהוּדָה הִרְבָּה עָרִים בְּצֻרוֹת	Judah has multiplied fortified cities.	
14d	וְשִׁלַּחְתִּי־אֵשׁ בְּעָרָיו	So I will send fire against his cities,	(2) The Creator's Response to Forgetfulness (8:14d–e)
14e	וְאָכְלָה אַרְמְנֹתֶיהָ׃	that it might consume her citadels.	
			4. The End of Israel's Life (9:1–9)
			a. The Forms of Syncretistic Worship (9:1)
9:1a	אַל־תִּשְׂמַח יִשְׂרָאֵל	"Do not rejoice, O Israel,	(1) A Prohibition on Pagan Rejoicing (9:1a)
	אֶל־גִּיל כָּעַמִּים	for the sake of shouting for joy like the peoples.[4]	
1b	כִּי זָנִיתָ מֵעַל אֱלֹהֶיךָ	For you have played the harlot away from your God,	(2) The Means of Pagan Rejoicing (9:1b–c)
1c	אָהַבְתָּ אֶתְנָן עַל כָּל־גָּרְנוֹת דָּגָן׃	you have loved a harlot's wage on every threshing floor of grain.	
2a	גֹּרֶן וָיֶקֶב לֹא יִרְעֵם	Threshing floor and wine vat will not feed/pasture them,	b. The Punishments for Syncretistic Worship (9:2–5)
2b	וְתִירוֹשׁ יְכַחֶשׁ בָּהּ׃	and new wine will deceive her.	(1) The End of Life in a Fertile Land (9:2–3)
3a	לֹא יֵשְׁבוּ בְּאֶרֶץ יְהוָה	They will not dwell in YHWH's land:	

3b	וְשָׁב אֶפְרַיִם מִצְרַיִם	But Ephraim will return to Egypt,	
3c	וּבְאַשּׁוּר טָמֵא יֹאכֵלוּ׃	and in Assyria they will eat uncleanness.	
4a	לֹא־יִסְּכוּ לַיהוָה יַיִן	They will not pour out wine to YHWH,	(2) The End of Rituals (9:4–5)
4b	וְלֹא יֶעֶרְבוּ־לוֹ	and they will not please him.[5]	(a) Rejected Liquid Offerings (9:4a–b)
4c	זִבְחֵיהֶם כְּלֶחֶם אוֹנִים לָהֶם	Their sacrifices will be like bread of mourning for themselves.	(b) Defiled and Defiling Bread/Food (9:4c–f)
4d	כָּל־אֹכְלָיו יִטַּמָּאוּ	All who eat them will make themselves unclean,	
4e	כִּי־לַחְמָם לְנַפְשָׁם	for their bread will be for themselves.	
4f	לֹא יָבוֹא בֵּית יְהוָה׃	It will not enter the house of YHWH.	
5a	מַה־תַּעֲשׂוּ לְיוֹם מוֹעֵד	What will you do on the day of assembly,	(c) The End of Festal Days (9:5)
5b	וּלְיוֹם חַג־יְהוָה׃	on the day of the festival of YHWH?	
6a	כִּי־הִנֵּה הָלְכוּ מִשֹּׁד	For look, they have gone away because of destruction—	(3) Israel's Departure from the Land (9:6)
6b	מִצְרַיִם תְּקַבְּצֵם	Egypt will gather them;	(a) Israel's Death in Exile (9:6a–c)
6c	מֹף תְּקַבְּרֵם	Memphis will bury them.	
6d	מַחְמַד לְכַסְפָּם קִמּוֹשׂ יִירָשֵׁם	As for their treasures of silver, thistles will possess them,	(b) The Victory of Canaan's Plants (9:6d–e)
6e	חוֹחַ בְּאָהֳלֵיהֶם׃	briars will be in their tents.	
7a	בָּאוּ יְמֵי הַפְּקֻדָּה	The days of repayment have come;	(4) The Arrival of YHWH's Days of Retribution (9:7–9)
7b	בָּאוּ יְמֵי הַשִּׁלֻּם	the days of payback have come—	
7c	יֵדְעוּ יִשְׂרָאֵל	Let Israel know!	(a) The Object of Punishment: Religious Leaders (9:7)
7d	אֱוִיל הַנָּבִיא	The prophet is a fool,	
7e	מְשֻׁגָּע אִישׁ הָרוּחַ	the spiritual man is mad,	
	עַל רֹב עֲוֺנְךָ	due to the multitude of your iniquity,	
	וְרַבָּה מַשְׂטֵמָה׃	and the abundance of [your] hostility.	
8a	צֹפֶה אֶפְרַיִם עִם־אֱלֹהָי	Ephraim was a watchman with my God,	(b) The Reason for Punishment: Israel's Iniquity (9:8)
8b	נָבִיא פַּח יָקוֹשׁ עַל־כָּל־דְּרָכָיו	[But] a prophet is the trap of a bird catcher in all his ways.	
8c	מַשְׂטֵמָה בְּבֵית אֱלֹהָיו׃	Hostility is in the house of his god.	
9a	הֶעְמִיקוּ־שִׁחֵתוּ כִּימֵי הַגִּבְעָה	They have deeply corrupted themselves as in the days of Gibeah—	(c) The Certainty of Punishment: YHWH's Justice (9:9)
9b	יִזְכּוֹר עֲוֺנָם	he will remember their iniquity,	
9c	יִפְקוֹד חַטֹּאותָם׃	he will repay their sins."	

1. This rendering accepts LXX's rendering from the Hebrew root חדל ("to end, cease") rather than the MT's reading from חלל ("to defile"). For reference's sake, the MT reading is retained in the lefthand column since the LXX's *Vorlage* is not found in any extant Hebrew manuscript.

2. Here the Hebrew reading (רַבֵּי) and the English rendering given ("multitude[s] of") follow the *qere* of the MT.

3. Though the term הַבְהָבַי is a *hapax legomenon*, it appears to be a northern Hebrew term which means "to roast, singe" (Yoon Jong Yoo, "Israelian Hebrew in the Book of Hosea" [Ph.D. diss., Cornell University, 1999], 102–4).

4. As recommended by the *BHQ* commentary on the critical apparatus, this rendering keeps the MT rather than following the suggestion of *BHS* to emend the preposition אֶל ("to" in the sense of motivation or grounds [*BHRG* §39.3.4]) to the negative adverb אַל ("not…"). The latter reading is attested in LXX, Vulgate, and modern translations such as NIV ("do not be jubilant like the other nations"). 5. For the rationale behind rendering this instance of the homonymic ערב root as "to please" (e.g., Jer 6:20; Prov 3:24, see Yoo, "Israelian Hebrew," 110.

5. For the rationale behind rendering this instance of the homonymic ערב root as "to please" (e.g., Jer 6:20; Prov 3:24), see Yoo, "Israelian Hebrew," 110.

encompasses all areas of life and therefore serves as a comprehensive alternative to the worldviews of the ancient Near East. The commentary below will demonstrate that YHWH simultaneously addresses a variety of issues due to their mutually reinforcing nature. In particular, the Israelite king's official cult of the golden calf and other idols (8:4–6) serves as a means to gather agricultural commodities (9:1–2), these being used in turn for international trade with "lovers" (2:7[5], 10[8]) that brings in precious metals for making more idols.

The interconnectedness of Israel's life is recognizable in the use of keywords to bridge the causes and effects of apostasy. As noted above, the idea of misguided human effort in constructing (עשׂה, "to do/make"; בנה, "to build") and multiplying (רבה, "to be/make many") is especially prominent: the forging of idols (8:4, 6), the practice of futile agriculture (8:7), the propagation of syncretistic altars (8:11), and the construction of fortified cities (8:14). An incessantly busy people will find that forgetting their "Maker" (עֹשֶׂה; 8:14) leads only to the helplessness of being unable to "do" (עשׂה) anything on a day of divine reckoning (9:5). The harder Israel tries to control its destiny by worldly means, the more Israel will lose its grip and recognize the futility of these means.

Another devastating example of wordplay comes from the semantic field of food and ritual, since Israel's "eating" (אכל; 8:13) of pagan sacrifices will result in God-sent fire "consuming" (אכל; 8:14) its cities. He will sentence this people in exile to "eat" (אכל) what is "defiled" (טָמֵא adjective; 9:3) and "defiling" (טָמֵא verb; 9:4). Such a holistic perspective on Israel's life appears even at the grammatical level of the passage through the unusual frequency of the particle כִּי ("for, if, indeed, when"). For instance, Hos 8:6–11 contains six adjacent כִּי clauses about economics, politics, and religion that embody the sinful synergies in Israel.[5]

Although the use of keywords lends some predictability to Hos 8:1–9:9, other literary devices in the passage epitomize the disorderly world that Israel has made for itself. Most effectively in this regard, this passage develops the theme of chaos through abrupt changes in grammatical person and number, each of which reorients the focus of the discourse even when the topic remains the same. To name one example, the grammatical relationships between subject (YHWH) and object (Israel) in Hos 8:5 shift rapidly in the two opening clauses:[6] "He [i.e., YHWH; third-person masculine singular] has rejected your [second-person feminine singular] calf, O Samaria [second-person vocative]. My [i.e., YHWH's; first-person common singular] anger

5. Robert K. Gnuse, "Calf, Cult, and King: The Unity of Hosea 8:1–13," *BZ* 26 (1982): 85–86.

6. This feature of Hosea combines the interrelated discourse elements of thematic address (*LDHB* §2.3) and changed reference (*LDHB* §2.6). The former denotes the use of vocatives in highlighting a particular relationship between speaker and hearer, while the latter is the appearance of different epithets or pronouns to reconfigure the relationship between speaker and hearer.

is kindled against them [i.e., Samaria; third-person masculine plural]" (8:5a–b).[7] The commentary on Hos 8:1–9:9 that follows will discuss how these discourse features convey a sense of disorder.

Explanation of the Text

1. The Divine Judge's Indictment and Verdict (8:1–3)

a. Broken Covenant with YHWH (8:1)

The first section of Hos 8:1–9:9 begins with a strangely truncated announcement: "[Put] to your lips the ram's horn, [one] like an eagle is upon the house of YHWH!" (8:1a–b). No verb appears in these parallel clauses, only two prepositional phrases describing the upward movements of a "ram's horn" (שׁוֹפָר; 8:1a) and a swooping creature that resembles an "eagle/vulture" (נֶשֶׁר; 8:1b).[8] Whereas the earlier blowing of the שׁוֹפָר (5:8) had summoned to prepare for battle, this loud instrument in chapter 8 announces that the threat has already arrived "upon/against [עַל] the house[hold] of YHWH [בֵּית יְהוָה]!"

Which sense of "house/household" is in view? The Hebrew construct phrase בֵּית יְהוָה refers to Jerusalem's temple in Judahite prophetic books of the eighth century BCE (e.g., Isa 2:2 // Mic 4:1; Isa 37:1; 38:20). But for Hosea as a prophet to the Northern Kingdom, this kinship term would be too approving to denote the aberrant sanctuaries of YHWH located in Bethel and Samaria, the places where syncretistic Israel venerated golden calves as icons for YHWH (8:5–6; cf. 13:2; 1 Kgs 12:28–33). It is more likely that Hosea's familial language denotes the entire household of Israel's God, both land and its people (e.g., 1:6; cf. 5:12).[9]

Yet who is the fearsome enemy who threatens the covenant community of YHWH? The Neo-Assyrian kings were fond of styling themselves as birds on the attack, leading some to suggest that Assyria is in view.[10] However, the use of predator imagery for YHWH in Hos 5 suggests that the main opponent at hand in chapter 8 is none other than the God of Israel. This referent gains support through the OT's other depictions of YHWH as a swift and powerful bird with no boundaries to its dominion.[11] Much like Hos 5:8–14 hints at the menace from Assyria while then identifying YHWH as the real foe, chapter 8 also opens ambiguously but portrays the God of Israel as the judge over his household, against whom Israel has committed apostasy.

This identification becomes explicit in subsequent clauses when YHWH speaks in the first person and summarizes the reasons for his indictment: "Because they have broken my

7. Compare the common proposal (e.g., Douglas Stuart, *Hosea–Jonah*, WBC 31 [Waco, TX: Word, 1987], 128) to revocalize the third-person finite verb זָנַח ("he has rejected") as either an infinitive absolute זָנֹחַ ("to reject"; cf. LXX ἀπότριψαι) or participle זֹנֵחַ ("[I am] rejecting"). While such readings are undeniably smoother for making the pronouns consistent, they neglect the oddness of the MT that defies the usual explanations from scribal error. The *lectio difficilior* represented by the MT reading is likely original.

8. The species denoted by נֶשֶׁר is ambiguous and could refer to both birds. In the rest of the OT, נֶשֶׁר usually denotes the swift eagle that swoops down on its prey (e.g., Deut 28:49; 2 Sam 1:23), less commonly the carrion-eating vulture (Mic 1:16).

9. Dearman, *Hosea*, 217.

10. Eidevall, *Grapes in the Desert*, 127–28.

11. E.g., Exod 19:4; Deut 32:11. Both these passages describe YHWH as a נֶשֶׁר ("eagle/vulture"), the same term found in Hos 8:1.

covenant, and they have rebelled against my instruction" (8:1c–d). The idiom עבר בְּרִית ("to break a covenant"; 8:1c) elsewhere denotes the sin of making and/or worshiping idols (Deut 17:2; Judg 2:19–20), a transgression that the next clause of Hos 8:1 explains as a violation of the literary collection known as "my instruction/Torah" (8:1d). This is a reference to the opening and most important words of the Decalogue that prohibit Israel from making idols to replace YHWH (Exod 20:3–4; Deut 5:7–8). Already in Hos 4:1–3, the prophet has presumed that his audience knows an ancient tradition of YHWH's revelation at Mount Sinai.[12]

b. Insincere "Knowledge" of YHWH (8:2)

Ironically, it appears to be this personal experience of a saving history (8:1; cf. 2:17[15]) that emboldens Israel: "They keep crying out to me, 'O my God, we—Israel—have known [ידע] you!'" (8:2). That the people of YHWH would "know" (ידע) him as a covenant-keeping God was one of the main goals of salvation from Egypt (e.g., Exod 6:3, 7; Deut 4:32–39). What is more, Hosea consistently uses the root ידע to summarize the covenantal ethics of YHWH as "knowledge of God" (דַּעַת אֱלֹהִים; 4:1; 6:6; cf. 4:6). Much like the people of YHWH had already expressed overconfidence in "knowing" him (6:3), the God of Israel quotes his people in Hos 8:2 as claiming to "know" YHWH without having any intention to follow his statutes (cf. Deut 4:39–40). Israel's persistent claims to be sincere (i.e., the habitual imperfective verb יִזְעָקוּ, "they *keep* crying out"; 8:2a) cannot fool the God who sees through such hypocrisy.

c. YHWH's Summary and Verdict (8:3)

YHWH must therefore expose the self-deception of this people who pretend to be his: "Israel has rejected good" (8:3a). The verb זנח ("to reject") will reappear momentarily in an assertion that YHWH will also "reject" (8:5a) the pagan rituals of his people, specifically the calf cult. This cause-and-effect wordplay on זנח helps to specify the meaning of the טוֹב ("good, goodness"; 8:3a) that Israel is said to "reject." The virtue of "good/goodness" in the OT broadly characterizes the nature of YHWH (Pss 34:9[8]; 136:1) and his creative works (Gen 1:4, 10, 12), as well as the benefits enjoyed by those who walk in his covenantal revelation to Israel (Deut 6:24; Jer 5:25; Ps 84:12[11]).[13]

Hosea 8:3 foregrounds this third sense of טוֹב as what Israel has rejected. As one who has just been depicted as a transgressor of "my covenant" (8:1c) and "my instruction/Torah" (8:1d), Israel will suffer the covenant curse of being chased by adversaries: "an enemy will pursue him" (8:3b; cf. Lev 26:17, 36; Deut 28:22, 45). Combined with Israel's rejection of "goodness" (טוֹב) in Hos 8:2, for Israel to be "pursued" (רדף) by an adversary upends the famous depiction of life under YHWH's protection described in Ps 23:6. This figurative sanctuary from enemies is where only the personified virtue of "goodness" (טוֹב) will "follow/pursue" (רדף). Yet in Hos 8:3, the agent in pursuit will not only be a human superpower, since the sovereign force behind Israel's death in exile will ultimately be YHWH.

2. The Sin-Cluster of King and Cult (8:4–8a)

The general description of apostasy (8:1c–3) then leads to a specific listing of sins (8:4–8a).

12. Tucker, "The Law in the Eighth-Century Prophets," 204–5, 210–11.

13. In fact, טוֹב often becomes a summary term for "covenant benefactions" of all kinds (e.g., 2 Sam 7:28), particularly Deuteronomy's characteristic connection between the "good" (e.g., Deut 6:18; 12:28) that Israel must do as a condition of receiving "good" from YHWH (e.g., Deut 26:11; 30:15).

First among these is Israel's choice of bad leaders: "On their part, they crowned a king but not from me; they set up princes, but I did not know/choose [them]" (8:4a–c). The opening clauses of this verse are introduced by a pleonastic pronoun, "on their part/as for them" (הֵם).[14] This emphatic construction highlights the estrangement between YHWH and a people who have erred by selecting kings and princes on their own initiative (cf. 1 Sam 8:5–8).[15]

Although kingship as an institution was always part of YHWH's design for Israel (e.g., Gen 17:6; Num 24:17; Deut 17:14–20), the problem throughout history has been that the kings of Israel were "not from me" (8:4a). Israel's previous claim to "know" (ידע) YHWH and his will (8:2b) hereby meets the latter's rebuttal that these leaders are those whom "I did not know/choose [ידע]" (8:4c).[16] The most important qualification of Israel's future kings was instead that they be those whom YHWH should "choose" (בחר; Deut 17:15).

a. Israel's Idolatrous Kings (8:4)

Lacking this essential prerequisite of God's choice (Hos 8:4a–b; cf. 13:10–11), it is unsurprising that kings in Israel behaved in precisely the aggrandizing and idolatrous ways that Deuteronomy prohibited (Deut 17:14–20), in particular violating the ban on stockpiling precious metals (Deut 17:17). Hosea 8 exposes how the kings of Hosea's time linked this form of wealth with idolatry: "With their silver and gold they made idols for themselves" (8:4d). The next two verses identify the most notorious of Israel's graven images as the "calf of Samaria" (8:5–6).

The manufacture of idols links the realms of government, economics, and religion in Israel. Silver and gold were not native to the land of Canaan and could only be obtained via the Israelite king's sponsorship of international trade.[17] Dating back to King Solomon's time, Israel obtained silver and gold from surrounding empires in exchange for agricultural commodities (e.g., 1 Kgs 5:25[11]; 9:14; 10:10, 22). These precious metals furnished raw material for making images in the eighth century BCE, as Hosea and other prophets of the same period attest (e.g., Hos 13:2; Isa 2:7–8, 20).

The disobedience of kings in cultic matters will eventually result in an unnamed subject being "cut off" (8:4e). The passive verb in this cryptic clause represents a sudden change to the singular (cf. 8:4d), possibly referring to an anonymous king, kingship as an institution, or Israel as a whole. To be "cut off" (כרת *niphal*) refers to estrangement from a people or community (e.g., Exod 30:38; Lev 7:25; Num 19:13). This relational nuance makes it unlikely that Hos 8:4e points forward to the (grammatically singular) idol that the following verses describe, as some have suggested.[18]

Verses 5–6 focus on the kings' sponsorship of the foremost idol in Israel during the eighth century BCE. Hosea's mention of only one "calf" (עֵגֶל; 8:5a) evokes the single bovine image that Aaron made to depict YHWH several centuries prior (Exod 32:2–4). By contrast, King Jeroboam erected two "calves of gold" (עֶגְלֵי זָהָב) in the cities of Dan and Bethel (1 Kgs 12:28–33) two hundred years before Hosea. King Jehu had apparently left these calves intact in his crusade against Baalism in Samaria

14. Brueggemann (*Tradition for Crisis*, 60) notes that this is a distancing pronoun.

15. In discourse terms, this is a topical frame (*LDHB* §5.1) that shifts the characterization of Israel from a verbal object who is a victim (i.e., the preceding clause in which "an enemy will pursue *him*"; 8:3b) to a verbal subject who is a perpetrator (8:4–8a).

16. Passages such as Gen 18:19 and Amos 3:2 use ידע as a synonym to בחר ("to choose").

17. Holladay, Jr., "The Kingdoms of Israel and Judah," 382.

18. E.g., Andersen and Freedman, *Hosea*, 493.

during the ninth century BCE (2 Kgs 10:29). Thus, Hos 8 may be using the singular phrase "calf of Samaria" (8:6d) for a different calf cult in the Northern Kingdom's capital city of Samaria, or possibly describing the entirety of Jeroboam's calf cult in "Samaria" (whether kingdom or capital city) as a collective singular.

In either case, there is an obvious wordplay between Israel's decision to "reject" (זנח; 8:3a) YHWH and the punishment that "he [YHWH] has rejected [זנח] your calf, O Samaria" (8:5a). It is also possible to take "my [YHWH's] anger" in the subsequent clause (8:5b) as a delayed, elliptical subject, "[my anger] has rejected your calf";[19] or one could understand the calf itself as the subject of a homonymous זנח root that means "to stink," yielding the translation, "your calf stinks, O Samaria."[20] The last rendering is perhaps less likely for downplaying the זנח wordplay of a tit-for-tat rejection on God's part (or that of his anger) against the idolatry of his people.[21]

b. YHWH's Rejection of Israel's Idolatry (8:5)

As noted above, the stridency of YHWH's polemic increases through two unexpected shifts of grammatical person: "*My* anger is kindled against *them*" (8:5b). YHWH now speaks personally and directly against every inhabitant of the Northern Kingdom, and not merely its leaders, for all are complicit in the guilt of idolatry: "How long will *they* be unable to stay innocent?" (8:5c). To be "innocent" (נִקָּיוֹן) denotes those qualities of ritual purity (e.g., Ps 26:6) and moral uprightness (e.g., Gen 20:5) that Israel lacks for having repeatedly polluted itself and its world (cf. Hos 4:1–3).

Consequently, it is the height of irony that YHWH asserts his justice using the very same rhetorical question—"How long?" (עַד־מָתַי; 8:5c)—that Israel uses in the lament psalms to complain about perceived divine injustice (e.g., Pss 6:4[3]; 80:5[4]). Unlike its use in the lament psalms, YHWH's insistent question to Israel is not merely rhetorical. He determines to carry out the destruction of the golden-calf cult and those who participate in it, as the following verses outline.

(1) The Deadness of the Calf-Idol (8:6)

Hosea 8:6–7 intensifies the exasperation of v. 5 in two attacks against Israel's idols, most notably the golden calf. The first of these is the common OT refrain that idols are nothing but impotent human creations: "Indeed, it [the calf] is from Israel, and as for it, a craftsman made it, but it is not God" (8:6a–c; cf. 13:2; Deut 4:28; 32:17, 21; Ps 115:4; Isa 37:19; Jer 10:3–5). The passage withholds the referent for two instances of "it" (הוּא; 8:6b, c) until the verse's concluding clause when YHWH predicts the destruction of the idol: "For the calf of Samaria will be broken to pieces" (8:6d).

(2) The Creational Consequences of Idolatry (8:7–8a)

The initial verdict of deadness against a bovine (8:6), the genus that is the most common icon of fertility in the ancient Near East,[22] leads to another attack against the worshipers of such fertility deities. In what follows, YHWH vows that Israel's fertility will be destroyed (8:7) before the nation itself is swallowed (8:8a) by its enemies.

YHWH begins his attack with a proverbial warning that Israel's attempts to manipulate the fertility of the land will backfire badly: "When they

19. Jack R. Lundbom, "Double-Duty Subject in Hosea VIII 5," *VT* 25 (1975): 228–30.

20. Dearman, *Hosea*, 222.

21. Andersen and Freedman, *Hosea*, 493–94.

22. See the overview of ancient Near Eastern bovine imagery and Israel's original golden calf in J. Gerald Janzen, "The Character of the Calf and Its Cult in Exodus 32," *CBQ* 52 (1990): 597–607.

sow [זרע] wind, then they reap [קצר] a whirlwind" (8:7a–b). The agricultural verb pair זרע ("to sow") and קצר ("to reap") expresses Hosea's signature link between sinful act and creational consequence. As elsewhere in this prophetic book, the justice of YHWH plays out in the realm of creation's inbuilt mechanisms of morality more than through a juridical act of retribution (cf. 1:4; 4:9).[23]

The seeds of fertility religion will not only reap infertility of some kind. The futility of trying to sow an elusive entity like "wind" (רוּחַ; 8:7a) will also result in creation's heightened reply of "whirlwind" (סוּפָתָה; 8:7b). סוּפָתָה is a by-form of סוּפָה, the Hebrew term for a severe gale that brings devastation (e.g., Job 37:9; Isa 21:1). It can also bear the figurative sense of destruction wrought by an invading army of chariots and/or troops (e.g., Isa 5:28; Jer 4:13). Natural and human forms of destruction are not mutually exclusive, as their complementary depiction in the book of Joel abundantly demonstrates.[24]

Indeed, Hosea taps both sides of the wind metaphor in a biting pseudosorite that asserts that any harvest (which the wind makes impossible to begin with) would quickly be swept away by foreigners anyway. The wind's first act of destruction is that "standing grain would not produce anything" (8:7c), that is, it cannot even grow to maturity. Were this plant to grow somehow, futility persists in that "a sprout would not make flour" (8:7d). But even "if it were to yield [something]" (8:7e), against all the aforementioned odds, the result is that "strangers [זָרִים] would swallow [בלע] it" (8:7f). Hosea has already described "strangers" (זָרִים) as the pagan invaders sent by YHWH from afar to take Israel into exile (7:9). In these tightly packed clauses, the spiraling illogic of the pseudosorite underscores the pointlessness of Israel's attempts to manipulate the created order in opposition to a sovereign Creator. This is a frequent theme elsewhere in the book of Hosea (e.g., 5:4–7; 9:10–14).

Futility will climax with Israel itself being swallowed (8:8a). This clause combines the reference to "strangers" (8:7f) with the stormy image that opens this section (8:7a–d) to depict the total collapse of Israel's economics, politics, and religion. In concert with how "the victims of the catastrophe are pictured as agents,"[25] repetition of the verb בלע ("to swallow") completes the metaphor's movement from windy infertility in Canaan to immobile death—the hungry foreigners who had come to "swallow" (בלע) the land's goods (8:7f) ensure an even more dire result when "Israel is swallowed [בלע *niphal*]" (8:8a). The idol-driven agronomics of Israel's nature rituals (cf. 8:7) has led to the demise of the nation itself.

3. The Sin-Cluster of Politics and Religion (8:8b–c)

The target of YHWH's polemic then shifts from pagan agronomics to the syncretism of Israel's foreign policy. Much like other abrupt transitions in the book (cf. 4:10–11), the passing mention of "strangers" (זָרִים) who will come and "swallow" (בלע) the land and people (8:7f–8a) becomes an expansive discourse about the distinctive theopolitics that YHWH desires but Israel fails to exhibit (8:8b–14). Hosea had just pictured the nations as invaders (8:7f), but here they become the superpowers from which scattered and vulnerable Israel seeks favor: "Now they were among the nations,

23. Koch, "Doctrine of Retribution," 64–65; Miller, *Sin and Judgment in the Prophets*, 123.

24. Ronald A. Simkins, "God, History, and the Natural World in the Book of Joel," *CBQ* 55 (1993): 435–52.

25. Eidevall, *Grapes in the Desert*, 131.

like a vessel [כְּלִי] in which is no delight [חֵפֶץ]" (8:8b–c).

Israel is struggling for footing among the nations from a precarious position, not only as a dehumanized "vessel" (כְּלִי; cf. 13:15) but also as an objectified people with none of the qualities that other nations would consider a "delight" (חֵפֶץ; cf. 6:6). As a penalty for forsaking their distinctive theopolitics, the people of God come to the negotiating table of the ancient Near East without any real bargaining power. The following verses describe the utter folly of this realpolitik.

a. The Folly of Imperial Politics (8:9–10)

Hosea adduces evidence for the idiocy of Israel's diplomacy in a striking blend of travel and animal imagery: "For on their part, they went up to Assyria/Assur" (8:9a). The clause's pleonastic pronoun הֵם ("on their part") links the present sin-cluster of politics and religion (8:8b–14) with Hosea's exposition of the sin-cluster of king and cult (8:4a). Similarly, Hosea has named Assyria twice previously (5:13; 7:11) as the opportunistic empire that welcomes Israel's clueless overtures (cf. 2 Kgs 15–16). The present verse adds the polemical nuance that Israel's "going up" (עלה) to "Assyria" (אַשּׁוּר) may also be a religious pilgrimage to venerate "Assur" (אַשּׁוּר), the national god who bears the same name as his empire.[26] The various connections between Hos 8:9a and other texts hint at the broader synergy between politics and religion that the rest of this passage will highlight.

(1) Israel's Dumbness about Imperialism (8:9)

In the rest of 8:9, the metaphorical journey into apostasy continues as a satire against Israel as a "wild donkey" (פֶּרֶא; 8:9b), an equine creature that is naturally friendly, not to mention promiscuous. Yet this passage depicts the donkey as "wandering by itself" (בּוֹדֵד לוֹ; 8:9b).[27] As if losing YHWH's presence through paganized politics were not enough, this stupid people will also suffer the disorientation of being put out to pasture, figuratively speaking, by the very powers that they thought could help them.

Hosea also captures the victimization of Israel in a sexual pun on "Ephraim" (אֶפְרַיִם; 8:9c). On the one hand, this favorite name for the Northern Kingdom (e.g., 4:17; 5:5, 9; 6:4; 7:8) sounds like the "wild donkey" (פֶּרֶא; 8:9b) that the passage has just mentioned.[28] On the other, Hosea ironically feminizes the people of "double fruitfulness" (i.e., the meaning of "Ephraim") as a bankrupt harlot: "Ephraim has hired lovers" (8:9c).[29] In this anticipation of Ezek 16, Ephraim has strangely become a harlot who pays rather than receives fees for her services!

Taken as a whole, the hybrid imagery of Hos 8:9 indicates that this *creature* has plenty of potential mates in its own herd.[30] However, here we also see a *human victim* who experiences the indignity of being ostracized to such an extent that payment becomes necessary to find sexual/political consorts. The multiple layers of Hosea's reference to "lovers" (8:9c) mirror how those whom Israel

26. Religious pilgrimages to deity typically go upward (עלה) in the OT, as in Moses's repeated climbs up Mount Sinai (e.g., Exod 19:3; 24:18), the psalmists' invitations to "go up" to Zion, as in Ps 24:3 ("Who will ascend [עלה] the hill of YHWH?"), and the individual titles for Pss 120–134 as "A Song of Ascent" (שִׁיר הַמַּעֲלוֹת).

27. Eidevall, *Grapes in the Desert*, 134.

28. Morris, *Prophecy, Poetry and Hosea*, 89.

29. "Ephraim" is the third name that Hosea uses for YHWH's people in this passage, "Israel" (8:2b, 3a, 8a) and "Samaria" (8:5a, 6d) having appeared already. This discourse feature of changed reference (*LDHB* §2.6) involves using a different title for a participant who is already in view, thereby describing them in new terms. Here and elsewhere in Hosea, the name "Ephraim" paves the way to mock the infertility of "double fruitfulness."

30. Dearman, *Hosea*, 229.

"loves" (אהב) have already denoted both other gods as well as economic allies (2:7[5], 9[7], 12[10], 14[12], 15[13]; 3:1). Compared to these earlier descriptions, the present language of "hire" (תנה; 8:9c) evokes the prostitute's occupation of trading sex for money (cf. 2:14[12]; 9:1). But the tragedy of the mixed picture in Hos 8:9, as later in Ezek 16, is that Israel cedes not just her body but her money as well. This harlot's bankruptcy is complete—both moral and financial.

(2) YHWH's Thwarting of Israel's Politics (8:10)

Hosea 8:10 marks a return to the literal realm of politics (cf. v. 8) from a figurative play on harlotry (cf. 8:9). Picking up on the description of how "Ephraim hired [תנה] lovers" (8:9c) the verb תנה ("to hire") reappears in portraying Israel's futility among the superpowers: "Even when they hire [תנה] among the nations, now I will gather them" (8:10a–b).[31] The causal relationship between Israel's action to "hire" itself or "bargain" (i.e., the NRSV's rendering of תנה) and YHWH's response to "gather [קבץ] them" is difficult to interpret. If the metaphor of Israel as a wandering donkey/harlot (8:9) continues into this verse, as the repetition of תנה suggests, YHWH's reaction to "gather" (קבץ) may be an act of sabotage against Israel's attempts to develop political and economic allies.[32]

In such an understanding, the Hebrew object pronoun "them" (8:10b) would then refer to the "nations" (cf. 8:8) that YHWH commissions for his disciplinary purposes of exile rather than referring to Israel itself.[33] In support of this view, Hosea later uses the root קבץ in a context of Israel's death in exile and the subsequent "gathering" (9:6) of bones by foreign invaders. It is therefore likely that Hos 8:10a–b expresses the collapse of Israel's syncretistic diplomacy, which in turn leads to the implosion of Israel's syncretistic monarchy.

Hosea 8 expresses this kind of political causality several times (vv. 10, 13, 14) by the appearance of a *wayyiqtōl* form, unusual in Hebrew poetry, to indicate a progression from act to consequence: "*Then* they will cease for a time from the burden of a king of princes" (8:10c). As hinted already in Hos 3:4–5, YHWH intends for the temporary moratorium on a "king" (מֶלֶךְ) who reigns over "princes" (שָׂרִים) to lift a heavy "burden" (מַשָּׂא) from Israel (8:10c)—the injustices and idolatries that were inherent to ancient Near Eastern models of hierarchical governance.[34] Exile among the nations thus does not serve only as punishment for Israel but also as a homeopathic treatment to excise Israel's self-destructive inclinations. Only this extreme remedy can prepare Israel to receive again the gift of a king from David's line.

b. The Folly of Idolatrous Religion (8:11)

Since Israel's faith in YHWH should have been a countercultural blend of politics and religion, YHWH's words in Hos 8:11 move from the folly of imperial politics (cf. 8:9–10) to the folly of Israel's idolatrous rituals. The cult, like Israel's other institutions, fell under the sinful influence of Israel's kings who served their own interests rather than God's (cf. 8:4–6). Yet the focus in the present verse lies not on the destruction of the cult in exile (cf. 3:4–5) but on its utter futility in blessing the worshiper whose name ironically means "double fruitfulness": "If Ephraim multiplies altars for sin

31. The repetition of a preceding element is the discourse feature known as tail-head linkage (*LDHB* §1.6), which serves to slow the discourse and call attention to the logical relationship between the two clauses.

32. Dearman, *Hosea*, 230.

33. Cf. Stuart A. Irvine, "Politics and Prophetic Commentary in Hosea 8:8–10," *JBL* 114 (1995): 293.

34. On the countercultural character of Israel's political models, see the important work of Berman, *Created Equal.*

offering [חטא], they would become altars for his sinning [חטא]" (8:11).

This pun on חטא, a Hebrew root that can flexibly mean both "sin offering" (e.g., Exod 29:14) as well as an act of "sin" (e.g., Exod 32:31),[35] illustrates the surprise that multiplying cultic worship leads to the opposite of its intended effect. Israel will experience destruction due to greater "sin" rather than receiving deliverance through a "sin offering." As Robert Gnuse observes: "Moral corruption only brings greater damnation when it attempts to offer holy sacrifice."[36]

(1) Israel's Rejection of YHWH's Instruction (8:12)

Hosea proceeds to unpack the general polemic against idolatrous religion (8:11) in two parts (vv. 12–13). First, the terminology of Israel's cultic fervency becomes the object of ironic parody. The attempt to "multiply" (רבה *hiphil*; 8:11a) places of worship actually means that Israel cares nothing for the "multitude" (רֹב) of his instruction: "Should I write for him a multitude [רֹב] of my instruction [תּוֹרָה], they would consider it something strange [זָר]" (8:12). Attentiveness to the outward forms of worship does not reliably indicate depth of inward devotion to God.

Equally caustic is the accusation that Israel considers YHWH's "instruction/Torah" (תּוֹרָה) to be "strange" (זָר), that is, foreign or illegitimate (cf. 5:7). But how could this charge ever be true of YHWH's familiar revelation that he has already insisted is "my instruction/Torah" (תּוֹרָתִי; 8:1d)? The personal reference to "*my* instruction/Torah" indicates that YHWH's authoritative body of teaching at Sinai and as proclaimed by Moses on the plains of Moab is in view. The religiosity of Israel flies in the face of its unconscionable rejection of the Torah—the distinctive possession of a missional people whom YHWH intended to be a blessing among the nations (Exod 19:5–6; Deut 4:5–8). For Israel to denigrate this spiritual lifeblood as something "strange" (זָר) leads to the homeopathic necessity that a covenant curse of "strangers" (זָרִים) will come to devour Israel (8:7).

(2) YHWH's Rejection of Israel's Sacrifices (8:13a–c)

Striking a similar note of useless religiosity, the tables turn when YHWH rejects Israel's sacrifices (8:13) just as Israel has rejected YHWH's instruction (8:12). The earlier reference to "altars" (מִזְבְּחֹת; 8:11a) becomes an occasion for mockery through several wordplays on its verbal root זבח ("to sacrifice"). YHWH cannot accept the ritual offerings of this self-serving people: "As for my roasted sacrifices [זִבְחֵי הַבְהָבַי], they keep sacrificing [יִזְבְּחוּ] and then eat the meat" (8:13a–b). As in Hos 8:2a, the use of a imperfective verb (יִזְבְּחוּ, likely with the habitual sense, "they *keep* sacrificing") characterizes Israel's apostasy as a longtime pattern rather than a one-time occurrence. These religious routines of Israel will prove useless since they serve the worshiper's appetite instead of being sincerely given to YHWH. It is thus no surprise that "YHWH is not pleased with them" (8:13c).

c. The Punishment of Anti-Exodus (8:13d–f)

The inescapable verdict of YHWH's rejection leads to an elaboration of what the punishment of exile will be like: "Now he [YHWH] will remember their iniquity, and he will repay their sins [חַטָּאת]" (8:13d–e). The people who thought that their "sin-offering" could atone for their "sin" (8:11) will instead find that "he will remember their iniquity" (יִזְכֹּר עֲוֹנָם) and "he will repay their sins" (יִפְקֹד חַטֹּאותָם). These statements involve

35. Alex Luc ("חטא," *NIDOTTE* 2:90) similarly notes the presence of both senses of the nominal form חַטָּאת in Lev 4:3.

36. Gnuse, "Calf, Cult, and King," 91.

two phrases that spring from Israel's foundational creed about the goodness and justice of YHWH as "one who forgives iniquity, transgression, and sin" (Exod 34:7).[37] The people have presumed too many times upon this God who is "slow to anger" (Exod 34:6), so his immense patience through the centuries is finally running out.

The use of an impersonal pronoun of estrangement serves as the final nail in Israel's coffin: "In their turn [הֵמָּה], to Egypt they will return" (8:13f).[38] YHWH conjures up Israel's ancient folly in rejecting the exodus and seeking to return to Egypt (cf. Num 14; 20) and transposes it into a future punishment of "anti-exodus." Although Hos 8:13 depicts judgment as the reversal of Israel's deliverance from enslavement (cf. 7:16; 9:3), other passages also recast the exodus motif as a future deliverance from exile, a "new exodus" (e.g., 2:17[15]; 11:11).[39]

(1) Idolatrous Forgetfulness of the Creator (8:14a–c)

These clauses depict Israel as the subject of a final litany of sins leading to the punishment of exile. Hosea summarizes the sins that precede anti-exodus and new exodus using artisan terminology: "Israel has forgotten his *Maker*, he has *built* palaces, Judah has *multiplied fortified cities*" (8:14a–c). Hosea expresses the spiritual amnesia of Israel as a bracing contrast between worshiping YHWH as "Maker" (עֹשֶׂה; 8:14a) on the one hand, and the idolatry of trying to "build" (בנה; 8:14b) and "multiply" (רבה; 8:14c) on the other. In addition, the explicit mention of Judah's ambitions (8:14c; cf. 5:5, 10; 6:4) means that the Israelite kingdoms share responsibility for constructing symbols of defiance toward YHWH. Ephraim and Judah are equally guilty of idolatrous forgetfulness of the Creator.

(2) The Creator's Response to Forgetfulness (8:14d–e)

God will "remember" (זכר; 8:13d) the iniquity of a nation that "has forgotten [שכח] his Maker" (8:14b). The final two clauses of the verse expand on this contrast between remembrance and forgetfulness. Israel's selfish misuse of creativity (cf. 8:4, 6) will meet a bitter end when YHWH destroys the lesser creator's work: "So I will send fire against his cities, that it might consume her citadels" (8:14d–e).[40] Those who "consumed" (אכל; 8:13b) half-hearted sacrifices to YHWH will experience the poetic justice of seeing their precious fortresses "consumed" (אכל; 8:14e).

These "palaces" (הֵיכָלוֹת; 14b), "fortified cities" (עָרִים בְּצֻרוֹת; 14c), and "citadels" (אַרְמְנוֹת; 14e) were

37. Dearman, *Hosea*, 232.

38. See a similar use of הֵמָּה/הֵם ("they") in Hos 6:7; 7:13; 8:4, 9 (Brueggemann, *Tradition for Crisis*, 60).

39. Silva Retamales, "Tradición del 'Éxodo' en Oseas," 145–78. However, Hosea uses the figure of Egypt in both literal and figurative ways to symbolize the reversal of salvation history. As Gert Kwakkel demonstrates ("Exile in Hosea 9:3–6," in *Exile and Suffering: A Selection of Papers Read at the 50th Anniversary Meeting of the Old Testament Society of South Africa OTWSA/OTSSA, Pretoria, August 2007*, ed. Bob Becking and Dirk J. Human, *OtSt* 50 [Leiden: Brill, 2009], 125–31), the final form of Hosea's prophecy conceives of the exile as a paradoxical combination of literal return to Egypt (e.g., 8:13; 9:3) as well as a figurative return to the "Egypt" represented by Assyria (e.g., 11:5). Regarding Hosea's typological references to Egypt, see Norman K. Gottwald, *All the Kingdoms of the Earth: Israelite Prophecy and International Relations in the Ancient Near East* (Minneapolis: Augsburg Fortress, 2007), 132–35.

40. This verdict against the Israelite kingdoms has the unusual literary feature of mixing masculine and feminine pronouns together, viz., both "*his* cities" (8:14d) and "*her* citadels" (8:14e). The masculine pronoun for a patronymic nation is no surprise, but using the feminine pronoun with reference to the machismo of having "citadels" may be a way of shaming the mostly male audience (cf. 2:8[6]). It is also possible that the Northern Kingdom's capital city of Samaria is in view, which, like Jerusalem, is grammatically feminine (e.g., Isa 10:11; Hos 8:5; Amos 3:9). On Hosea's rhetorical strategy of figurative castration, see Haddox, "(E)masculinity," 174–200.

the pride of both Ephraim and Judah (cf. Isa 32:14; Amos 6:8). As before, the foreign nations that apparently come of their own initiative to destroy and deport the Israelite kingdoms are ultimately sent by the God of Israel himself. Although Hos 8 primarily concerns the Northern Kingdom, the closing reference to "Judah" (8:14c) warns the Southern Kingdom that it will suffer the same fate as its neighbor unless it learns crucial theological lessons about economics, politics, and religion in the eighth century BCE (cf. 1:1; 12:2[1]).[41]

4. The End of Israel's Life (9:1–9)

The final part (9:1–9) of this extended announcement of Israel's exile (8:1–9:9) signals the end of Israel in all its unholy syncretism. The people of YHWH will no longer rejoice as other nations do (9:1a–b) through their fertility rituals (9:1c–2) and other cultic practices (9:4–5), for the blessings of life in their own land will come to an end (9:3, 6–7). The punishment of exile has now become inevitable (9:8–9), though Hos 9:1–9 is now noticeably more resigned in addressing Israel compared to the previous three sections about exile (i.e., 8:1–3; 8:4–8a; 8:8b–14).

In fact, the numerous third-person references to "YHWH" (9:3, 4[2x], 5), who is also named as "your God" (9:1) and "my God" (9:8), raise the possibility that Hosea himself may now be speaking rather than YHWH. Earlier in the book, abrupt changes from intimate (i.e., first- and second-person) to aloof (i.e., third-person) forms of address often indicate that YHWH has withdrawn momentarily from his apostate children, even as he remains the speaker (e.g., 4:1, 5:3). By way of contrast, the emotional tenor of Hos 9:1–9 is subdued in lacking the rapid shifts between intimate and aloof grammatical forms that signal YHWH's growing exasperation with his people.

However, Hos 9:1–6 will take up several themes and terms from the preceding chapter (e.g., harlotry's wages, sacrifices), while then issuing a biting critique of prophets in Israel (9:7–8). This may indicate that YHWH continues to be the speaker in Hos 9:1–9. It would be especially odd for Hosea to condemn the office of prophet when he was among their number.[42] Certainty is elusive since this passage never identifies the speaker explicitly. But if YHWH is still addressing Israel, he does so with the eerily mournful tone of one speaking about his people as if they are already dead.

a. The Forms of Syncretistic Worship (9:1)

The somber tone of Hos 9:1–9 begins immediately with a prohibition on pagan rejoicing: "Do not rejoice, O Israel, for the sake of shouting for joy like the peoples" (9:1a). This is the only place in the OT that prohibits Israel from being glad (cf. Prov 24:17; Luke 10:20), for the references to "rejoice" (שׂמח) and "exult in joy" (גיל) in Hos 9:1a are usually proper for a people blessed by God (e.g., Pss 14:7; 16:9; 97:8). But Israel's problem is the *manner* of rejoicing "like the peoples." This comparison (כְּ, "like, as") is explained in the following clause's reference to fertility rituals as the *means* (כִּי) of pagan rejoicing: "For you have played the harlot [זנה] away from your God" (9:1b). The root זנה ("to commit harlotry") is Hosea's characteristic verb for summarizing Israel's literal sins of sexual immorality (e.g., 4:13–14) as well as figurative sins of Baal worship and pursuing alliances with foreign paramours (e.g., 2:9[7]; 5:3).

This whole network of associations for זנה prepares for what follows—an exposé of nature religion's international and domestic scope: "You

41. Emmerson, *Hosea*, 74–77.

42. Cf. Odell, "Who Were the Prophets in Hosea?," 78–95.

have loved a harlot's wage on every threshing floor of grain" (9:1c). On the foreign front, the "harlot's wage" (אֶתְנָן; cf. Mic 1:7; Deut 23:19[18]) denotes Israel's flirtations in the diplomatic realm by seeking to "hire [תנה] lovers" (8:9c). On the home front, the mention of "grain" (דָּגָן; 9:1c) recalls the commodities that Israel sought from the Canaanite god Baal (2:7[5], 10[8]) listed in chapter 2. Moreover, this verse identifies "every threshing floor [כָּל־גָּרְנוֹת]" (9:1c) as the place of Israel's harlotry. Threshing floors are agricultural places that had long served as cultic sites (e.g., 2 Sam 6:6; 24:21) where farm commodities were collected from the people in the name of "Baal" (2:10[8]) to trade for precious metals (8:4; 13:2).[43] In short, the Israelite kings oversaw an intertwined network of economic, religious, and political harlotries that, to one extent or another, all had their roots in Canaanite nature religion.

b. The Punishments for Syncretistic Worship (9:2–5)

(1) The End of Life in a Fertile Land (9:2–3)

The cardinal importance of Israel's land explains why Hosea presents the punishment of exile first and foremost as an agricultural fiasco: "Threshing floor and wine vat will not feed/pasture [רעה] them, and new wine will deceive her" (9:2). Here the passage personifies the storage basins for two of Israel's main products, grain and wine, as unable either to "feed" or "pasture" the people. The Hebrew root in Hos 9:2a could have either definition. Whichever is chosen (most English versions render the verb as "feed"), the force of the warning to a syncretistic people is essentially the same—the enablers of nature religion in which Israel unwisely trusts will fail.

What is more, Hos 9:2b adds the sarcastic illogic of the pseudosorites. Even if any wine were produced, its utility would suffer from its tendency to "deceive" (כחש). The root כחש appears in other lists of Israel's sins (4:2; 7:3; 10:13; 12:1[11:12]), but its unique usage in Hos 9:2 lies in personifying "new wine" (תִּירוֹשׁ) as yet another deceiver who will mislead rather than nurture Israel.[44] The unexpected and poignant shift to characterizing Israel as "her" (9:2b) completes the previous clause's metaphor of drought as infertility (9:2a; cf. ch. 2).

Verses 3–4 expand the preceding negation (לֹא) of Israel's feeding/pasturing (9:2) with four more negations (לֹא) that describe several other endings in Israel's life. First and most important among these is the end of life in a fertile land: "They will not dwell in YHWH's land: But Ephraim will return to Egypt, and in Assyria they will eat uncleanness" (9:3). The fact that Canaan is "YHWH's land" (9:3a; cf. Amos 4:13; 5:8; 9:6), an appellation that in the next verse forms an *inclusio* with "the house of YHWH" (9:4f), asserts that the God of Israel owns this land. This counters Israel's mistaken notion that Canaanite deities hold its title and are thus worthy of veneration.[45] Ironically, however, pursuing the deities of Canaan will result in their worshipers losing the land that those gods supposedly govern.

Hosea explains such an inability to live in "YHWH's land" (9:3a) as a twofold geographical movement. First comes a southwesterly banishment of anti-exodus to Egypt (9:3b; cf. 8:13), followed by a northeasterly shift to defilement in Assyria (9:3c). It is difficult to understand the parallel references to "Egypt" and "Assyria" in these clauses. Eighth-century prophetic poetry (both in Hosea and other

43. D. N. Premnath, "Amos and Hosea: Sociohistorical Background and Prophetic Critique," *WW* 28 (2008): 129; Marvin L. Chaney, "Hosea's Rhetoric of Promiscuity," 112.

44. Other verses mention that Israel's pursuit of "new wine" is vain or harmful (cf. 2:10[8]; 4:11; 7:14), but do not personify "new wine" itself as the enemy.

45. Kwakkel, "The Land in the Book of Hosea," 179.

books) sometimes views these two empires as a merism for the entire Mediterranean region, all the way from the southwest to the northeast (e.g., Hos 11:11; Isa 7:18; Mic 7:12).

A symbolic interpretation of this nature would see exile in more general terms as a reversal of salvation history and defilement among pagan peoples. Yet the twofold fact that Egypt was a regional force in Hosea's time and that imperial Assyria did eventually take its vassal Samaria into captivity indicates that the fulfillment of Hos 9:3 may be both literal as well as figurative. The scales will shortly tip toward a more literal interpretation when Hos 9:6 details Egypt's role in ransacking the exiled refugees from Samaria.

(2) The End of Rituals (9:4–5)

The brief mention of ritual "uncleanness" (טָמֵא; 9:3c) in Assyria leads in vv. 4–5 to a catalogue of ritual observances to YHWH that exiled Israel will no longer engage in: liquid offerings (9:4a–b), bread/food offerings (9:4c–f), and festal days (9:5). The first two of these go together due to their interwoven roles in presenting a pseudosorite, the paradox of illogic that is one of Hosea's favorite communicative devices (e.g., 8:7; 9:2).

Liquid offerings are the first of the three items that YHWH rejects. At the start of this sequence, Hos 9:4 uses the negative particle (לֹא) twice more (cf. 9:2a, 3a) to turn back Israel's attempt to bring liquid offerings: "They will *not* pour out wine to YHWH, and they will *not* please him" (9:4a–b). Yet were Israel, against all likelihood, to have any such sacrifices to present while in exile (i.e., the mounting illogic of the pseudosorite), these would both harm the worshiper and be rejected by YHWH (cf. Deut 4:27–28).

Hosea then makes a cryptic comparison between these (nonexistent) liquid offerings and bread/food that is both defiled and defiling (9:4c–e). Some form of ritual pollution involving "bread of mourning" (9:4c) and "bread . . . for themselves" (9:4e) appears likely since the intervening clause envisions a cultic setting: "All who eat them will make themselves unclean [טמא *piel*]" (9:4d; cf. 5:3; 6:10; 9:3c). That the Hebrew term לֶחֶם (2x in Hos 9:4) also means "food" (e.g., Hos 2:7[5]; Lev 3:11; Ps 147:9) suggests that Hos 9:4 may allude to offerings of foodstuffs intended for YHWH that Israel's priests defiled (cf. 4:8) and the people at large (cf. 8:13) greedily "consumed/ate" (אכל). If this understanding is correct, Hosea is warning that gluttony toward YHWH's sacred food will bring the exile as an occasion of "mourning" (אוֹנִים; Hos 9:4c) as for the dead (cf. Deut 26:14). The inevitability of starving in exile, where the only alternative will be nourishment from defiled food, is perhaps another reason this passage opens by forbidding Israel from rejoicing (Hos 9:1).

The last of five negations in Hos 9:2–4 is enigmatic and deserves brief comment: "It will not [לֹא] enter the house of YHWH" (9:4f). The verb "to enter/come" (בוֹא) must take a singular masculine subject, but the only suitable candidate for a named subject in the vicinity is "bread/food" (9:4e). Although it is possible that Hosea personifies "bread/food" as unable to worship YHWH, it is more likely that defilement of this people has led to their bread offerings being similarly defiled and unusable in worshiping YHWH.

Therefore, what is worse even than losing a distinctively blessed way of life in "YHWH's land" (9:3a) will be losing access to YHWH himself through his "house/temple" (בַּיִת; 9:4f). The phrase בֵּית יְהוָה functions flexibly in Hosea, having referred in an earlier passage to the family of God's people (8:1). Here also in chapter 9, the intended sense is probably the figurative "household" (another rendering of בַּיִת; cf. 1:2–9) that YHWH leads as father/husband and to whom he avails himself.

The literal referent of the temple in Jerusalem would make little sense for Hosea as a prophet to the northern rather than Southern Kingdom, though a cultic locale remains possible if "house of YHWH" is a pejorative reference to a syncretistic temple in Samaria (see commentary below for this possibility from Hos 9:8).

The third and final disaster for Israel's ritual life is the cessation of festal days (9:5). YHWH's rejection of liquid offerings (9:4a–b) and Israel's defiled/defiling sacrifices (9:4c–f) leaves the people with nothing to celebrate: "What will you do [עשׂה] on the day of assembly, on the day of the festival of YHWH?" (9:5). Building on five previous occurrences of the verb עשׂה ("to do, make") that expose Israel's futile attempts at self-actualization (8:4, 6, 7[2x], 14), the stinging rhetorical question in Hos 9:5 mocks Israel's helplessness in the face of self-inflicted disaster.

This passage describes this nation's time of reckoning as "the day of assembly" (9:5a) and "the festival of YHWH" (9:5b). Hosea has already listed the "assembly" (מוֹעֵד) as a joyful occasion of enjoying God's bounty (2:13[11]), perhaps in connection with venerating Baal(s) (2:15[13]). However, later in Hosea the term מוֹעֵד refers to the Feast of Tabernacles (12:10[9]]; cf. Lev 23:34–43). This latter interpretation gains support from the identical phrase "the festival of YHWH" (חַג־יְהוָה; 9:5b) appearing in the description of the Feast of Tabernacles/Booths (Lev 23:39). The phrase can nevertheless refer generally to any feast/festival in honor of YHWH (e.g., Exod 10:9; Judg 21:19).

(3) Israel's Departure from the Land (9:6)

In contrast to their powerlessness to "enter" (בוא) the safe presence and family of YHWH (9:4f), the religious tracks of this people will reverse course and go to dangerous places: "For look, they have gone away [הלך] because of destruction" (9:6a).[46] Israel's access (בוא) to a privileged place has not only dissipated into "destruction/ruin" [שֹׁד]" (cf. 7:13; 10:14)—instead Israel will "go away" (הלך) to a place of certain death: "Egypt will gather them; Memphis will bury them" (9:6b–c).

Hosea 9:6 supplements the previous mention of Egypt as the destination of the anti-exodus (7:16; 8:13; 9:3) with further details about Israel's fate there. In this verse, the verbal pair of "gather" (קבץ; 9:6b) and "bury" (קבר; 9:6c) refers to an undertaker's actions in preparing a corpse for interment (cf. Gen 35:29; Jer 25:33). In this case, Egypt would be the undertaker who collects Israel's bones (Hos 9:6b) to place in a cemetery at Memphis (9:6c), the capital during the glory days of ancient Egypt and the site of numerous cemeteries (e.g., the flat pyramids known as mastabas). Hans Walter Wolff rightly observes that burial in Egyptian graves will be the ironic fate of those who thought Egypt would be a sanctuary from harm (cf. 7:11).[47]

The land that the exiles leave behind will suffer the same fate as the decomposing bodies of the exiles in Egypt (cf. 9:6a–c). But amazingly, what withers in Canaan will not be its living things but the inert objects that formerly symbolized Israel's strength: "As for their treasures of silver, thistles will possess them, briars will be in their tents" (9:6d–e). In this echo of the fall narrative, the cosmos will exact its retribution like "thorns and thistles" (Gen 3:18) on those worshipers who tried to manipulate creation through a Baalistic nature cult of silver and gold images (cf. Hos 2:10[8]; 8:4).

Hosea's employment of the imagery of conquest to explain how Canaan's wild thistles will

46. The verse's opening interjection, "For look" (כִּי־הִנֵּה), interrupts the discourse and heightens the urgency of what follows (see *LDHB* §1.4; *BHRG* §40.22), in this case Israel's change of direction from life in YHWH's presence (9:3–5) to death in exile (9:6).

47. Wolff, *Hosea*, 156.

"possess" (ירשׁ; cf. Deut 1:8; Josh 23:5) the silver of its former inhabitants (Hos 9:6d) is equally striking. To this counterintuitive picture of weeds on the warpath, the passage adds that briars will penetrate even Israel's "tent[s]" (אֹהֶל; 9:6e). This place is either the warrior's sanctum of rest (Judg 4:17–22; 1 Sam 17:54) or the cultic site where Israelite pilgrims celebrated the Feast of Tabernacles that Hosea mentions elsewhere (12:10[9]; cf. 9:5). In sum, the plant overgrowth of Canaan will emerge from the ground as victor over Israel's rotting vainglories.

(4) The Arrival of YHWH's Days of Retribution (9:7–9)

The physical departure of Israel to exile (9:6) coincides with a weightier arrival of a temporal kind—the arrival of YHWH's days of retribution (9:7). In contrast to Israel's sinful paralysis to "enter/ come [to]" (בוא) the presence of YHWH (9:4), the time of judgment appointed by YHWH has already "come" (בוא) to Israel: "The days of repayment have come [בוא]; the days of payback have come [בוא]" (9:7a–b). The unusual grammatical parallelism of these two clauses, coupled with Hosea's first use of perfective verb forms to denote judgment (בָּאוּ; "they have come"), signals a major and emphatic transition in the book.

The discourse has now moved from an approaching threat of destruction (cf. 8:1–14) to a present and urgent moment of "repayment" (פְּקֻדָּה; 9:7a) and "payback" (שִׁלֻּם; 9:7b). Hosea frequently uses the verbal root from which the first of these nouns is derived, פקד ("to intervene, reckon, repay"), to convey the theological principle that God responds to human sins with consequences that spring up within the created order (e.g., 1:4; 2:15[13]; 4:9). Adding to this repetition of פקד, Hosea uses the root שׁלם ("to pay back") for the first time, a verb that denotes making amends and restoring harmony in God's moral order (e.g., Exod 21:34; Lev 5:16; 1 Sam 24:20[19]).[48] Taken together, the nominal forms of these verbs portray the arrival of YHWH's retribution as a matter of restoring the shalom of God's creation through cleansing judgment more than a legal act of God's recompense.[49] The people of YHWH, who often claim to "know" (ידע) YHWH and his truth (e.g., 6:3; 8:2; cf. 4:6), must instead take to heart that their punishment is coming: "Let Israel know!" (9:7c).

The specter of destruction in exile arrives with an unexpected shift of topic. Hosea suddenly names the people's religious leaders as the object of punishment: "The prophet is a fool, the spiritual man is mad, due to the multitude of your iniquity, and the abundance of [your] hostility" (9:7d–e). However, it is unclear whether the singular pronoun "your" in Hos 9:7e (which appears only once in Hebrew but modifies both "iniquity" and "hostility") attributes sinful opposition to Israel as a whole or to a particular individual.

Related to this question, some have proposed that the speaker is neither YHWH nor Hosea but rather the people themselves who attack Hosea as a religious leader marred by "iniquity" and "hostility" (v. 9:7e).[50] This interpretation is possible since the book of Hosea elsewhere cites the people's intransigent speech against YHWH and his prophet (e.g., 6:1–3). However, the typical changes in grammatical person, tone, and theme that signal shifts of speaker in such disputation speeches are absent from this passage.

48. Schmid, "Creation, Righteousness, and Salvation," 105–6.

49. Koch, "Doctrine of Retribution," 67.

50. E.g., Wolff (*Hosea*, 150, 156–57) supports this view with an emendation of Hos 9:7c to "Israel may cry."

For these reasons, it appears that Hos 9:7 records YHWH or Hosea attacking the false prophets whom Hos 4:5 mentioned. In chapter 4 the prophet had attributed the legal status of "iniquity/guilt" (עָוֹן) to priests (4:8). The priestly leaders whom Hosea earlier condemned now expand to include the prophetic group who are epitomized by "the spiritual man" (אִישׁ הָרוּחַ; 9:7e).[51] While the religious inspiration attributed to the "spirit/Spirit" (רוּחַ) was a feature of both prophets and priests (e.g., 1 Kgs 22:21–24; Mic 3:8; Ezek 2:2), Hosea's previous references to רוּחַ as "spirit of harlotry" (רוּחַ זְנוּנִים; 4:12; 5:14) suggest that it is not the divine "Spirit" who controls these leaders in the Northern Kingdom but a more sinister "spirit" of idolatrous hedonism.[52]

Hosea 9:8 appears to expound the reason for punishment. This extremely challenging verse repeats the terms "prophet" (נָבִיא) and "hostility" (מַשְׂטֵמָה) from what precedes (9:7d–e),[53] but these are perhaps its only clear features. To begin with, while the first clause refers to "my God" (אֱלֹהָי; 9:8a), the verse as a whole concludes with "his god/God" (אֱלֹהָיו; 9:8c). Although any interpretation must be considered tentative, it seems that the prophetic task of the "watchman [צֹפֶה] . . . with my God" (9:8a) applies to Ephraim as a whole,[54] but this people lacked the integrity and vigilance that the "watchman" should exhibit (compare the ideal צֹפֶה of Ezek 3:16–22). Instead, they were tricky: "a prophet is the trap of a bird catcher" (9:8b). Hosea has already confronted Israel's priests at Mizpah for being a "trap" (פַּח) that lies in wait for their own people (5:1). To that description the prophet now adds that the people are perpetrators and not just victims—they have imitated the deceptive and predatory leaders among them in their own conduct (cf. 4:7–10).

By this interpretation, Hos 9:8a–b contrasts between a true prophet (Hosea himself? Corporate Ephraim in his intended mission?), who stands "with my God" (9:8a), and the false prophet, whose treachery is like a fowler's snare "in all his ways" (9:8b). If this contrast between Hos 9:8a and 9:8b is correct, then the final clause's statement, "Hostility is in the house of his god" (9:8c) would refer to Ephraim's loyalty to a rival deity and his rival temple (Hos 8:1; 9:4), perhaps the cult of calf worship located at Samaria or Bethel (8:1–6).[55]

Whatever the condemned practices in v. 8, v. 9 announces the certainty of Israel's punishment for these sins. Hosea emphasizes the seriousness of such apostasy a final time by shifting to the third-person plural: "They have deeply corrupted themselves as in the days of Gibeah" (9:9a; cf. 10:9). Previous shifts in Hosea from singular to plural forms have highlighted the culpability of the entire people and not merely their representatives (e.g., 8:5). Moreover, the sordid events of rape and murder that occurred at the Benjamite village of Gibeah (Judg 19–20) have already been alluded to in Hos 5:8 as the forerunner to Ephraim's impending destruction. This pattern now reappears in Israel's sins "as in the days of Gibeah" (9:9a), a phrase parallel to, and theological justification for, the arrival of "the days of repayment" and "the days of payback" (9:7).

51. An attributive genitive; see *IBHS* §9.5.3a.

52. Odell, "Prophets in Hosea," 85. By contrast, the term רוּחַ ("wind/spirit/Spirit") has positive associations with God and/or empowerment for ministry in eighth-century prophetic books associated with Judah (e.g., Isa 11:2; Mic 3:8).

53. Here is another instance of tail-head linkage (cf. Hos 8:10a–b and 114n70 and 221n31 above).

54. Paul A. Kruger ("The Prophet 'with' God: The Prophetic Image in Hosea 9:7b–8 and the Colometry," *UF* 25 [1993]: 219–26) argues that Ephraim is the watcher who is being criticized by Hosea. Compare the less likely view that the prophet himself is the watcher (e.g., David Greenspoon, "The Prophet as Watcher," *JBQ* 27 [1999]: 29–35).

55. Odell, "Prophets in Hosea," 84.

The cyclical nature of Israel's history also appears at the clause level of the passage. Hosea 9:9 takes up the exact wording of Hos 8:13 to declare the certainty of punishment from YHWH: "He will remember their iniquity, he will repay their sins" (9:9b–c). Thus YHWH's last announcement of exile concludes on a surprisingly terse and withdrawn note; Israel is running out of time to avoid it (8:1–9:9). The book will offer only one more opportunity to heed the call to "sow for yourselves according to righteousness, reap according to faithfulness, till a hard ground for your own sake" (10:12). These will be Hosea's last directives to an apostate people on this side of exile.

Canonical and Theological Significance

1. Leadership

This passage's critique against Israelite kingship and its related institutions occurs against the theological backdrop of the book of Exodus and the first leaders among YHWH's people. Centuries earlier, Israel's exodus from Egypt had birthed a nation unlike any other through the relativizing of the main strongholds of power in ancient Near Eastern societies—kingship and cult.

On the one hand, leaving Egypt behind undermined a model of deified human leadership in which "the king (= pharaoh) had an absolute status as head of state and representative of the gods, exercising the divine rule of the cosmos and upholding the cosmic order that sustained the world and Egypt."[56] YHWH's defeat of the demigod Pharaoh overthrew a totalizing way of life in which the Egyptian king was literally in control of everything—politics, economics, and religion. In place of a royal ideology that recognized Pharaoh alone as the beloved son of the gods,[57] the entire nation of Israel was elevated by their God to a new status as "my son" (Exod 4:22–23; cf. Deut 14:1). And in place of Pharaoh's vast state apparatus that required labor without end to maintain, as the Hebrew slaves could attest, the people of Moses received a lifestyle of meaningful work punctuated with Sabbath rest. As Walter Brueggemann summarizes the deliverance of Israel, "The program of Moses is not the freeing of a little band of slaves as an escape from the empire . . . his work is nothing less than an assault on the consciousness of the empire, aimed at nothing less than the dismantling of the empire both in its social practices and in its mythical pretensions."[58]

On the other hand, YHWH instituted a unique form of cultic worship in which

56. Knut M. Heim, "Kings and Kingship," in *Dictionary of the Old Testament: Historical Books*, ed. Bill T. Arnold and H. G. M. Williamson (Downers Grove, IL: InterVarsity Press, 2005), 610.

57. Baines, "Ancient Egyptian Kingship," 23.

58. Walter Brueggemann, *The Prophetic Imagination*, 2nd ed. (Minneapolis: Augsburg Fortress, 2001), 9.

he would be present with his people but remain invisible to their eyes. The prohibition on using images to represent YHWH (Exod 20:3–4), known as *aniconism*, bypassed the elaborate and costly process of image making in favor of a theological paradox that Tryggve Mettinger has evocatively described as "sacred emptiness."[59] In addition, oversight of the ritual system passed from the king, who in Egypt was charged by the gods with this priestly task,[60] to a separate class of priests in Israel (Exod 28–30). Priesthood in Israel also gained stature from how this role, along with the prophetic office (Deut 18:15–18), had the important responsibility of holding the king accountable (Deut 17:18–20). The restrictions that YHWH placed on Israel's kings (Deut 17:14–20) were unparalleled in the ancient world. Leadership in Israel was therefore a matter of divesting power to a familial polity of "brothers" (e.g., Deut 10:9; 17:15; 18:15) who would worship and serve their unseen God together.[61]

The countercultural diminution of king and cult made Israel vulnerable to seduction by visible and outsized forms of power.[62] With YHWH having denied his people the trappings of empire (for reasons made explicit in Hos 14; see commentary), the temptation for Israel to seek strength through other means, such as military alliances, increased markedly due also to the vulnerability of Canaan's relatively porous borders. Herein lay Israel's constantly nagging question—was YHWH still the strong God of the exodus, considering his people's weakness after the conquest?

Such were the theopolitical factors that drove Israel to take an initial step toward autocracy when asking YHWH for a "king to judge us like all the nations" (1 Sam 8:5 ESV) during the time of the judges. To this request, Samuel responded that such a self-serving ruler would prey upon the community by taking their best people and things (1 Sam 8:10–17). The pain inflicted by this king would be so acute that Israel would "cry out" (זעק; 1 Sam 8:18). The book of Exodus uses the same verb to describe the effects of suffering under Pharaoh's oppression (Exod 2:23; cf. Ezek 34:10).

Having demanded essentially a pharaoh for themselves, in Israel kings soon also brought the cult under royal control. The trend of kings taking over cultic roles was less nocuous during the reigns of David and Solomon (e.g., 2 Sam 6:13–14; 1 Kgs 8:2, 22, 54, 63–64), but it took an ominous turn with the division of the kingdom when Jeroboam established the veneration of the golden calf/calves as Samaria's official religion (1 Kgs 12:28–33). Having sojourned in Egypt (1 Kgs 11:40; 12:2); these Egypt-inspired measures as a new king were not surprising. Indeed, the refrain

59. Mettinger, *No Graven Image?*, 19.

60. Baines, "Ancient Egyptian Kingship," 41–46.

61. On the cultural uniqueness of the OT's leadership models, see Daniel I. Block, "The Burden of Leadership: The Mosaic Paradigm on Kingship (Deut 17:14–20)," *BSac* 162 (2005): 259–78; republished in idem, *How I Love Your Torah, O Lord!"* (Eugene, OR: Cascade, 2011), 118–39.

62. Jacques Ellul, *The Politics of God and the Politics of Man*, trans. Geoffrey W. Bromiley (Grand Rapids: Eerdmans, 1972), 125–26.

in 1–2 Kings condemning the northern kings who walked in "the sin of Jeroboam, son of Nebat"[63] indicates that the pharaonic model of consolidating power under the king continued for centuries.

The long preference of God's people for autocratic leadership, whether indigenous or foreign, stands in the background of Hos 8:1–9:9. Each in their own way, the political, economic, and religious sins mentioned in Hos 8:4–9:9 represent an outgrowth of Israel's original sin upon entering the land, namely, that of picking leaders who violated YHWH's special design for their society by their obsession with human power (8:4). Whereas these worldly models prioritize strength and victory, God has often accomplished his purposes through weakness and defeat. Long before secular management theory established that "servant leadership" was more transformative than traditional leadership models,[64] and prior also to Jesus's and Paul's embodiment of leading from weakness rather than strength,[65] the OT set forth a distinctive model of leadership as divesting rather than consolidating authority.[66]

Nevertheless, the people of God have tended to walk in the opposite direction of choosing pharaohs for themselves—to their hurt. The sacralizing mindset of leadership that drives imperialism is alive and well today. This is the case not just in political systems but in any predilection for greater strength and control as a response to weakness. Hosea reminds us that much of what is regarded today as "visionary leadership" may represent a figurative return to Egypt. But in handing over authority to a gifted and/or powerful individual in the hope of receiving otherwise unattainable benefits, the typical result is a "scorched-earth" existence in which the achievement of predetermined goals comes at the expense of people's God-given dignity.

2. Poetic Justice and Violent Judgment

Israel's preference for the theopolitical pattern of anti-exodus also illuminates this passage's three references to a "return to Egypt" (8:13; 9:3, 6). In the OT the figure of "Egypt" often functions as a symbol for the worldview (more than just the place) to which Israel was forbidden to return (e.g., Deut 17:16; 28:68; cf. Num 14:1–4).[67] Since the kingdoms of Israel actually went to exile in Mesopotamia (cf. 2 Kgs 17; 24–25; Neh 9:32), the figurative verdict of a "return to Egypt" becomes an alternative way of portraying exile as the confirmation of Israel's refusal to live an exodus-shaped life.[68] Human weakness provides an opportunity to trust God, in contrast to self-centered doubt that envies natural or superhuman strength.

63. 1 Kgs 14:16; 15:30, 34; 16:2, 19, 26, 31; 21:22; 22:53[52]; 2 Kgs 3:3; 10:29, 31; 13:2, 6, 11; 14:24; 15:9, 18, 24, 28; 17:21, 22; 23:15.

64. Dirk van Dierendonck, "Servant Leadership: A Review and Synthesis," *Journal of Management* 37 (2011): 1228–61.

65. Efrain Agosto, *Servant Leadership: Jesus and Paul* (Atlanta: Chalice, 2005).

66. Berman, *Created Equal*, 51–80.

67. McConville, *God and Earthly Power*, 23, 151.

68. Gottwald, *All the Kingdoms of the Earth*, 132–35.

In allowing the direction of pagan theopolitics to reach its ultimate end in exile, God ordains the creative form of discipline known as *poetic justice*—the use of an action's intrinsic consequences to teach an unforgettable lesson rather than imposing an extrinsic and less-relevant punishment.[69] Or, as C. S. Lewis inimitably described the nature of final judgment as the outworking of a life that rejects God, "There are only two kinds of people in the end: those who say to God, 'Thy will be done,' and those to whom God says in the end, 'Thy will be done.' . . . No soul that seriously and constantly desires joy will ever miss it. Those who seek find. To those who knock it is opened."[70]

The nature of poetic justice sheds new light on the references to violent judgment in Hos 8:1–3. While the arrival of a figurative bird of prey against his people (8:1) appears initially like YHWH's unilateral act of violence (cf. Exod 19:4; Deut 32:11), this is another case of the creational principle that "they sow wind, then they reap a whirlwind" (8:7). Israel had long ago sown the seeds of violent judgment by its decision to realign itself with the worldview of realpolitik, an ailment of the heart to which YHWH offers the remedy known as "return to Egypt" (8:13; 9:3, 6). Yet the mode of this violent judgment is not so much YHWH's initiation or endorsement of violence but rather allowing a people who choose to live by the sword to die by the sword.

As the commentary above notes, Hos 8:1–9:9 repeatedly describes divine intervention to come using the Hebrew verb פקד (8:13; 9:8, 9; cf. 1:4; 2:15[13]; 4:9, 14; 12:3[2]). It is better to render this root as "repayment" or "reckoning" in enforcing the creational link between act and consequence rather than as the strictly legal sentence of "punishment." Because these two levels of causality intersect, YHWH can speak in the same breath of coming against his people like a predator as a secondary cause (8:1) even while the primary cause and literal reality remain that "an enemy [Assyria] will pursue him" (8:3). We will need to say more about the violence of Israel's judgment in exile, given other passages in the book that describe the violence of exile in even starker terms than Hos 8:1–9:9. The description of divine judgment as war crimes against Israel (14:1[13:16]), for example, raises ethical dilemmas that distinguishing between primary and secondary causality will not be able to resolve.[71]

Even so, Hos 8:1–9:9 clearly portrays YHWH's intention to work *through* the (mistaken) desires of his people rather than *against* them. As the pursuit of power ends in weakness and the desire for fertility ends with barrenness, YHWH allows Israel's freely chosen decisions to work themselves out so that this empty worldview of imperialism will hollow itself out from within. In God's economy, it is sometimes

69. M. H. Abrams, "Poetic Justice," in *A Glossary of Literary Terms*, 9th ed. (Boston: Wadsworth, 2008), 270.

70. C. S. Lewis, *The Great Divorce: A Dream* (London: Geoffrey Bles, 1956), 66–67.

71. Cf. Yairah Amit, "The Dual Causality Principle and Its Effects on Biblical Literature," *VT* 37 (1987): 385–400.

the counterintuitive decision to allow the stubborn to have exactly what they want, while determining ahead of time not to rescue from the attendant consequences, that becomes the most effective form of discipline.[72] Hosea 8:1–9:9 therefore presents one of several aspects of a broader strategy with which YHWH seeks to change the recalcitrance of his people. But much like a wise parent knows when the gentler approach of "reality discipline"[73] has run its course, our God will not be endlessly patient with his children to their detriment.

72. Many parents of headstrong children attest that the homeopathic methods of "reality discipline" are uniquely effective. The seminal work on "reality discipline" is Kevin Leman, *Making Children Mind Without Losing Yours*, 2nd ed. (Grand Rapids: Revell, 2005).

73. Ibid.

CHAPTER 8

Hosea 9:10–11:11

D. Israel's Apostasy from YHWH: General Verdicts from Creation and History

Main Idea of the Passage

Most poignantly in the entire OT, Hos 9:10–11:11 traces the relationship between divine wrath and mercy. YHWH must discipline but cannot abandon his wayward people, a theological tension that captures all the key thematic intersections in Hosea—the interplay between creation and history in YHWH's dealings with Israel, the relationship between judgment and salvation, and the outworking of these mysteries on the temporal planes of past, present, and future.[1]

Literary Context

Hosea 9:10–11:11 is the fourth of five covenant discourses in chapters 4–14. All that falls between the initial reference to "the word of YHWH" in chapter 4 (4:1; cf. 1:1) and the signatory formula that closes this larger section—"The Declaration of YHWH" (11:11c)—is a divinely given word. In its nearer context, Hos 9:10–11:11 contains a series of first-person speeches *to* Israel by YHWH himself that contrast markedly in tone from the previous discourse's dispassionate, third-person addresses *about* Israel, by an unnamed speaker who may be either YHWH or his prophet Hosea (8:1–9:9).

Although not the conclusion of Hosea's prophetic oracles, in many ways Hos 9:10–11:11 represents the theological climax of this prophetic book, particularly the bracing monologue by YHWH in chapter 11. In addition, the book weaves important

1. J. P. Siebert-Hommes, "Hosea 11 as 'Recapitulation' of the Basic Themes in the Book of Hosea," in *Unless Some One Guide Me—: Festschrift for Karel A. Deurloo*, ed. J. W. Dyk, Amsterdamse cahiers voor exegese van de Bijbel en zijn tradities 2 (Maastricht: Shaker, 2001), 167–73.

themes of creation and history even more tightly in Hos 9:10–11:11 than the earlier discourses (i.e., 4:1–5:7; 5:8–7:16; 8:1–9:9). Hosea then applies these themes to the entire sweep of YHWH's covenant with his people, from before the exodus until after the exile. The present discourse in 9:10–11:11 concludes with an exposition of new beginnings after judgment in Israel's life with YHWH (11:8–11). Chapters 12–13 will flesh out this general presentation of creation and history in more specific ways, such as several allusions to Jacob and Moses.

III. YHWH's Contentions with Israel (4:1–14:1[13:16])
- A. YHWH's Contention against Israel's Priestly Failures (4:1–5:7)
- B. YHWH's Contention against Israel's Political Failures (5:8–7:16)
- C. An Announcement of Exile (8:1–9:9)
- ➡ **D. Israel's Apostasy from YHWH: General Verdicts from Creation and History (9:10–11:11)**
- E. Israel's Disobedience toward YHWH: Specific Verdicts from History and Creation (12:1–14:1[11:12–13:16])

Translation and Exegetical Outline

(See pages 238–43.)

Structure and Literary Form

The image of YHWH's troubling family that opens the book of Hosea comes full circle as chapter 11 approaches. While Hos 1–3 had described the relationship between YHWH and his entire household (i.e., Israel and its land) primarily in marital terms, and chapters 4–10 set YHWH's covenant lawsuits against his people in the whole of creation or a heavenly courtroom, Hos 11 recasts the family metaphor with Israel as a child and returns to everyday Israelite scenes in the home and village gate. A familial setting appears in that chapter's reminiscence of the pentateuchal case law for a rebellious son (Deut 21:18–21) but with the innovation that Israel then becomes the intransigent child who is deserving of death for his persistent ingratitude and disobedience (11:1–5).[2] Just as the capital sentence (of exile) is about

2. Robert G. Boling, "Prodigal Sons on Trial: A Study in the Prophecy of Hosea," in *Realia Dei: Essays in Archaeology and Biblical Interpretation in Honor of Edward F. Campbell, Jr. at His Retirement*, ed. Prescott H. Williams and Theodore Hiebert (Atlanta: Scholars Press, 1999), 19–20.

to be handed down (11:6–7), Hosea portrays YHWH as a tender parent who experiences a change of heart, stops the trial, and reasserts his unbreakable commitment to his stubborn children (11:8–9). This unexpected turn of events comes after several cycles of covenant lawsuits (Hosea 4–10) that have characterized YHWH flexibly as a judge, prosecutor, plaintiff, witness, and creator. Yet in the final analysis, it will be the relational depth of the parent-child metaphor that expresses most memorably the essence of covenant between YHWH and his people.

Hosea's kaleidoscope for this multifaceted picture of God concludes with another surprising twist. Having presented YHWH as a distressed parent who longs for his son "Ephraim/Israel" (11:8–9; cf. v. 1), Hos 11 also depicts him as a terrifying lion (11:10–11; cf. 5:14; Amos 1:2; 3:8) whose roar will summon home his trembling children from their exile. In short, Hos 11 blends concepts from the realms of kinship and animals to portray God in a manner that simultaneously amazes and unsettles.[3]

An array of other references to history and creation drive the buildup to this rhetorical peak in chapter 11. Most notably, an allusion to Israel's salvation history using creational concepts introduces each of the three major sections of Hos 9:10–11:11. The first beginning in 9:10 compares the early days of YHWH's relationship with Israel to a hungry traveler's joyful discovery of food: "Like grapes in the wilderness I found Israel, like the firstfruit in the fig grove at the beginning of its season I saw your ancestors" (9:10a–b). The second section in Hos 10 fleshes out the viticultural side of the agricultural image in Hos 9:10 when YHWH condemns Israel's syncretism with fertility-cult practices as "a lush vine" (10:1). Third and most significantly, chapter 11 reaches into the distant past by describing Israel's historical beginnings in the divine parent's adoption and nurture for a son while also drawing on creational ideas to depict Ephraim/Israel as a domesticated animal (cf. 8:9; 10:11) that YHWH leads with "cords" and "bands" (11:4a). The versatility of Hosea's imagery is particularly evident when the figure of YHWH lifting Israel's "yoke" (11:4b) denotes both the burdens of the heifer in the creational metaphor (10:11) as well as the historical "yoke" of exile (cf. Isa 9:3[4]; 10:27; Lam 1:14).

In summary, the general progression among past, present, and future in Hos 9:10–11:11, with unexpected references to creation and history dotting the way, provides a characteristic instance of what Gerald Morris has called the "lyrical plot" of Hosea.[4] This term refers to Hosea's tripartite but often nonlinear movement of themes—from a scorned God's judgment against an ungrateful people, to his heart's turn from justice to mercy, and finally the offer of healing his people's estrangement from him. The structure of individual poetic sections in Hosea can be difficult to outline, as the "Explanation of the Text" will attest.

But at the broader level, the three phases of YHWH's vexed relationship with

3. Merryl Blair, "'God Is an Earthquake': Destabilising Metaphor in Hosea 11," *ABR* 55 (2007): 1–12.

4. Morris, *Prophecy, Poetry and Hosea*, 101–31.

Hosea 9:10–11:11

Verse	Hebrew	Translation	Outline
			D. Israel's Apostasy from YHWH: General Verdicts from Creation and History (9:10–11:11)
			1. Creation and History, Part 1: From Wilderness Fruits to Exiled Nomads (9:10–17)
9:10a	כַּעֲנָבִים בַּמִּדְבָּר מָצָאתִי יִשְׂרָאֵל	"Like grapes in the wilderness I found Israel,	a. Israel's Apostasy in History, Cycle 1: Joy and Shame in the Wilderness (9:10)
10b	↓ כְּבִכּוּרָה בִתְאֵנָה בְּרֵאשִׁיתָהּ	↓ like the firstfruit in the fig grove at the beginning of its season	(1) YHWH's Joyful Discovery of Israel (9:10a–b)
	רָאִיתִי אֲבוֹתֵיכֶם	I saw your ancestors.	
10c	הֵמָּה בָּאוּ בַעַל־פְּעוֹר	As for them, they entered Baal-Peor	(2) Israel's Shameful Worship of Baal (9:10c–e)
10d	וַיִּנָּזְרוּ לַבֹּשֶׁת	and they dedicated themselves to the shameful thing;	
10e	וַיִּהְיוּ שִׁקּוּצִים כְּאָהֳבָם׃	and they became detestable like what they loved.	
11a	אֶפְרַיִם כָּעוֹף	Ephraim is like a bird,	b. Creation as Agent of Judgment, Cycle 1: Infertility (9:11–13)
11b	יִתְעוֹפֵף כְּבוֹדָם	their glory will fly away:	
11c	מִלֵּדָה וּמִבֶּטֶן וּמֵהֵרָיוֹן׃	No more childbirth, no more pregnancy, no more conception!	(1) The Departure of Fertility (9:11)
12a	↓ כִּי אִם־יְגַדְּלוּ אֶת־בְּנֵיהֶם	↓ Although they raise children,	(2) The Curse of Childlessness (9:12)
12b	וְשִׁכַּלְתִּים מֵאָדָם	I will bereave them from humanity.	
12c	כִּי־גַם־אוֹי לָהֶם	For indeed, woe to them,	
12d	בְּשׂוּרִי מֵהֶם׃	when I turn away from them!	
13a	אֶפְרַיִם	Ephraim,	(3) The Cruelty of Parents (9:13)
	↑ כַּאֲשֶׁר־רָאִיתִי לְצוֹר	↑ just as I have seen for Tyre,	
	שְׁתוּלָה בְנָוֶה	is planted in a meadow,[1]	
13b	וְאֶפְרַיִם לְהוֹצִיא אֶל־הֹרֵג בָּנָיו׃	but Ephraim will bring out his children to the slayer."	
14a	תֵּן־לָהֶם יְהוָה	"Give them, O YHWH—	c. Hosea's Lament for Ephraim (9:14)
14b	מַה־תִּתֵּן	what will you give?	
14c	תֵּן־לָהֶם רֶחֶם מַשְׁכִּיל וְשָׁדַיִם צֹמְקִים׃	Give them a miscarrying womb and shriveling breasts."	
15a	כָּל־רָעָתָם בַּגִּלְגָּל	"All their evil is in Gilgal,	a′.[2] Israel's Apostasy in History, Cycle 2: Evil at Gilgal (9:15)
15b	כִּי־שָׁם שְׂנֵאתִים	for there I have hated them.	(1) Broken Covenant at Gilgal (9:15a–b)
15c	↓ עַל רֹעַ מַעַלְלֵיהֶם	↓ On account of the evil of their deeds,	(2) Banishment from YHWH's Family (9:15c)
	מִבֵּיתִי אֲגָרְשֵׁם	from my house I will drive them out.	

15d	לֹא אוֹסֵף אַהֲבָתָם	I will not love them again,	(3) YHWH's Angry Vow (9:15d–e)
15e	כָּל־שָׂרֵיהֶם סֹרְרִים׃	all of their princes are stubborn.	
16a	הֻכָּה אֶפְרַיִם	Ephraim is stricken:	b´. Creation as Agent of Judgment, Cycle 2: Infertility (9:16)
16b	שָׁרְשָׁם יָבֵשׁ	Their root has dried up,	
16c	פְּרִי (בְלִי־)[בַל־]יַעֲשׂוּן	they will not bear any fruit.	(1) "Fruitful One" as Dried Plant (9:16a–c)
16d	↓ גַּם כִּי יֵלֵדוּן	↓ Indeed, when they bear children,	(2) "Fruitful One" as Bereaved Parent (9:16d–e)
16e	וְהֵמַתִּי מַחֲמַדֵּי בִטְנָם׃	I will put to death the delightful ones of their womb."	
17a	יִמְאָסֵם אֱלֹהַי	"My God will reject them,	c´. Hosea's Prayer of Agreement (9:17)
17b	כִּי לֹא שָׁמְעוּ לוֹ	for they have not obeyed him.	
17c	וְיִהְיוּ נֹדְדִים בַּגּוֹיִם׃	So they shall be nomads among the nations."	
10:1a	גֶּפֶן בּוֹקֵק יִשְׂרָאֵל	"Israel is a lush vine,	2. Creation and History, Part 2: From Fruitful Vine to Thorns and Thistles (10:1–8)
1b	פְּרִי יְשַׁוֶּה־לּוֹ	he sets fruit for himself.	a. Israel's Doomed Syncretism (10:1–2)
1c	כְּרֹב לְפִרְיוֹ הִרְבָּה לַמִּזְבְּחוֹת	According to the abundance of his fruit he multiplied [his] altars,	(1) Excess "Fruit" and Illicit Altars (10:1a–c)
1d	כְּטוֹב לְאַרְצוֹ הֵיטִיבוּ מַצֵּבוֹת׃	According to the goodness of his land he enriched sacred pillars.	(2) Good Land and Sacred Pillars (10:1d)
2a	חָלַק לִבָּם	Their heart has become slippery,	(3) Broken Altars and Destroyed Pillars (10:2)
2b	עַתָּה יֶאְשָׁמוּ	now they are guilty!	
2c	הוּא יַעֲרֹף מִזְבְּחוֹתָם	He himself will break their altars,	
2d	יְשֹׁדֵד מַצֵּבוֹתָם׃	he will destroy their sacred pillars.	
3a	כִּי עַתָּה יֹאמְרוּ	But now they might say,	b. Israel's Seditious Words (10:3–4)
3b	אֵין מֶלֶךְ לָנוּ	'We do not have a King/king!	(1) Rejection of YHWH as King (10:3)
3c	כִּי לֹא יָרֵאנוּ אֶת־יְהוָה	For we have not feared YHWH!	
3d	וְהַמֶּלֶךְ מַה־יַּעֲשֶׂה־לָּנוּ׃	And as for a King/king, what could he do for us?'	
4a	דִּבְּרוּ דְבָרִים	They have spoken words,	(2) Embrace of Foreign Alliances (10:4a–b)
4b	אָלוֹת שָׁוְא כָּרֹת בְּרִית	with vain oaths they made a covenant.	
4c	וּפָרַח כָּרֹאשׁ מִשְׁפָּט עַל תַּלְמֵי שָׂדָי׃	Judgment sprouts like a poisonous plant in the furrows of a field.	(3) Corruption in the Legal System (10:4c)
			c. YHWH's Reversals upon Israel's Syncretism (10:5–8)
5a	↓ לְעֶגְלוֹת בֵּית אָוֶן	↓ Regarding the heifers of Beth-Aven,	(1) Calf Cult: From Delight to Dread (10:5a–c)
	יָגוּרוּ שְׁכַן שֹׁמְרוֹן	the inhabitants of Samaria will dread it.	
5b	כִּי־אָבַל עָלָיו עַמּוֹ	For its people will mourn because of it,	
5c	וּכְמָרָיו עָלָיו יָגִילוּ עַל־כְּבוֹדוֹ	and its priests will shriek for it because of its glory,	

Continued on next page.

1. Here and similarly to Hos 12:8[7], dotted lines are used to link a predicate phrase ("is planted in a meadow") back to its suspended subject ("Ephraim"). An intervening adverbial clause ("just as I have seen for Tyre") has separated them. This convention with dotted lines differs from the use of solid lines to mark clausal subordination.

2. As explained in the commentary, the nomenclature of a´-b´-c´ (9:15–17) seeks to show that these verses are a mirror image of the preceding a-b-c section (9:10–14).

Continued from previous page.

5d	כִּי־גָלָה מִמֶּנּוּ׃	since it has gone into exile.	(2) Calf Cult: From Glory to Shame (10:5d–6)
6a	גַּם־אוֹתוֹ לְאַשּׁוּר יוּבָל	Indeed, as for the thing, it will be carried to Assyria,	
	מִנְחָה לְמֶלֶךְ יָרֵב	as a gift to the great king.	
6b	בָּשְׁנָה אֶפְרַיִם יִקָּח	Ephraim brings shame upon himself,	
6c	וְיֵבוֹשׁ יִשְׂרָאֵל מֵעֲצָתוֹ׃	and Israel will be ashamed of his counsel.	
7a	נִדְמֶה שֹׁמְרוֹן מַלְכָּהּ	Samaria is cut off [with] her king,	(3) Kingship: From Ruler to Flotsam (10:7)
	כְּקֶצֶף עַל־פְּנֵי־מָיִם׃	as a reed on the surface of waters.	
8a	וְנִשְׁמְדוּ בָּמוֹת אָוֶן חַטַּאת יִשְׂרָאֵל	The high places of iniquity, the sin of Israel, will be exterminated.	(4) Fertility Religion: From Blessing to Curse (10:8a–b)
8b	קוֹץ וְדַרְדַּר יַעֲלֶה עַל־מִזְבְּחוֹתָם	Thorn and thistle will come up on their altars.	
8c	וְאָמְרוּ לֶהָרִים	They will say to the mountains,	(5) Fertility Religion: From Pleasure to Pain (10:8c–f)
8d	כַּסּוּנוּ	'Cover us!'	
8e	וְלַגְּבָעוֹת	And [they will say] to the hills,	
8f	נִפְלוּ עָלֵינוּ׃	'Fall on us!'	
			3. Creation and History, Part 3: Miscellaneous Images (10:9–15)
9a	מִימֵי הַגִּבְעָה חָטָאתָ יִשְׂרָאֵל	Since the days of Gibeah you have sinned, O Israel.	a. Examples of Judgment in History, Part I (10:9–10)
9b	שָׁם עָמָדוּ	There they stood.	(1) Judgment in the Past: War in Gibeah (10:9)
9c	לֹא־תַשִּׂיגֵם בַּגִּבְעָה מִלְחָמָה עַל־בְּנֵי עַלְוָה׃	Will not war against the evildoers overtake them in Gibeah?	
10a	בְּאַוָּתִי וְאֶסֳּרֵם	When I desire, then I will chastise them,	(2) Judgment in the Future: YHWH's Use of the Nations (10:10)
10b	וְאֻסְּפוּ עֲלֵיהֶם עַמִּים	and peoples will be gathered against them,	
10c	בְּאָסְרָם לִשְׁתֵּי (עֵינֹתָם) [עוֹנֹתָם]	when they imprison/bind them for their double iniquity.	
11a	וְאֶפְרַיִם עֶגְלָה מְלֻמָּדָה	Now Ephraim is a trained heifer	b. Examples of Judgment through Creation (10:11–13)
11b	אֹהַבְתִּי לָדוּשׁ	who loves to tread.	(1) Israel as a Trained Heifer (10:11)
11c	וַאֲנִי עָבַרְתִּי עַל־טוּב צַוָּארָהּ	On my part, I placed a fine yoke[3] on her neck.	(a) A Fine Yoke (10:11a–c)
11d	אַרְכִּיב אֶפְרַיִם	I will harness Ephraim;	(b) A Calling to Serve (10:11d–e)
11e	יַחֲרוֹשׁ יְהוּדָה	Judah will plow;	
11f	יְשַׂדֶּד־לוֹ יַעֲקֹב׃	Jacob will break up the soil for himself.	
			(2) Israel as a Negligent Farmer (10:12–13)
12a	זִרְעוּ לָכֶם לִצְדָקָה	Sow for yourselves according to righteousness,	(a) Israel's Duty to Sow Faithfully (10:12a–c)
12b	קִצְרוּ לְפִי־חֶסֶד	reap according to faithfulness,	
12c	נִירוּ לָכֶם נִיר	till a hard ground for your own sake.	

Verse	Hebrew	Translation	Outline
12d	וְעֵת לִדְרוֹשׁ אֶת־יְהוָה	It is time to seek YHWH	(b) YHWH's Warning about Raining Judgment (10:12d–e)
12e	עַד־יָבוֹא	until he comes	
	וְיֹרֶה צֶדֶק לָכֶם׃	and is raining rightness toward you.	
13a	חֲרַשְׁתֶּם־רֶשַׁע	You have plowed wickedness;	(c) Israel's Neglect of Sowing Faithfully (10:13)
13b	עַוְלָתָה קְצַרְתֶּם	you have reaped lawlessness;	
13c	אֲכַלְתֶּם פְּרִי־כָחַשׁ	you have consumed the fruit of lying.	
13d	כִּי־בָטַחְתָּ בְדַרְכְּךָ בְּרֹב גִּבּוֹרֶיךָ׃	For you have trusted in your way, in the greatness of your strength.	
14a	וְקָאם שָׁאוֹן בְּעַמֶּךָ	Then an uproar will rise among your people,	c. Examples of Judgment in History, Part II (10:14–15) (1) The Verdict of Judgment (10:14a-b)
14b	וְכָל־מִבְצָרֶיךָ יוּשַּׁד	and all your fortifications will be devastated,	
14c	כְּשֹׁד שַׁלְמַן בֵּית אַרְבֵאל בְּיוֹם מִלְחָמָה	as when Shalman destroyed Beth-Arbel in the day of battle,	(2) The Past Case of Shalman and Beth-Arbel (10:14c–d)
14d	אֵם עַל־בָּנִים רֻטָּשָׁה׃	[when] a mother was dashed to pieces in front of her children.	
15a	כָּכָה עָשָׂה לָכֶם בֵּית־אֵל	Thus he has done to you, O Bethel,	(3) The Present Case of Bethel/Israel (10:15)
	מִפְּנֵי רָעַת רָעַתְכֶם	because of your extreme wickedness.	
15b	בַּשַּׁחַר נִדְמֹה נִדְמָה מֶלֶךְ יִשְׂרָאֵל׃	At dawn the king of Israel will be completely destroyed."	
			4. The Cycles and Metaphors of Salvation History (11:1–11) a. The Events of Salvation History (11:1–2)
11:1a	כִּי נַעַר יִשְׂרָאֵל	"Because/when Israel was a child,	(1) Adoption in the Exodus (11:1)
	וָאֹהֲבֵהוּ	I loved him,	
1b	וּמִמִּצְרַיִם קָרָאתִי לִבְנִי׃	and from Egypt I called my son.	
			(2) Apostasy in the Land (11:2)
2a	קָרְאוּ לָהֶם	They (Israel) called to them (Egypt),	(a) Political Sins (11:2a–b)
2b	כֵּן הָלְכוּ מִפְּנֵיהֶם	then they (Israel) went away from them (toward Assyria).	
2c	לַבְּעָלִים יְזַבֵּחוּ	To the Baals they kept sacrificing,	(b) Cultic Sins (11:2c–d)
2d	וְלַפְּסִלִים יְקַטֵּרוּן׃	and to idols they kept offering incense.	
3a	וְאָנֹכִי תִרְגַּלְתִּי לְאֶפְרַיִם	As for me, I taught Ephraim to walk,	b. The Metaphors of Salvation History (11:3–4)
3b	קָחָם עַל־זְרוֹעֹתָיו	taking them by their arms.	(1) A Parent's Tenderness (11:3a–b)
3c	וְלֹא יָדְעוּ	But they have not known	(2) A Child's Ignorance (11:3c–d)
3d	כִּי רְפָאתִים׃	that I healed them.	

Continued on next page.

3. This translation accepts the emendation of the preposition עַל ("on, upon, over") to the noun עֹל ("yoke"), as suggested by Stuart, *Hosea-Jonah*, 166; Andersen and Freedman, *Hosea*, 567. A few English versions follow the MT rather than the emendation for Hos 11:1c which is adopted by this commentary, NIV, and ESV. This decision yields the unusual rendering "I will come over her fair neck [with a yoke?]" (NASB) or "I spared her fair neck" (NRSV).

Continued from previous page.

Verse	Hebrew	Translation	Structure
4a	בְּחַבְלֵי אָדָם ↓	↓ With cords of a man	(3) A Parent's/Farmer's Provision (11:4)
	אֶמְשְׁכֵם	I will draw them,	
	בַּעֲבֹתוֹת אַהֲבָה ↑	↑ with bands of love.	
4b	וָאֶהְיֶה לָהֶם	Then I became for them like those	
	כִּמְרִימֵי עֹל עַל לְחֵיהֶם	who lift the yoke from their jaws,	
4c	וְאַט אֵלָיו	and I will bend down to them	
4d	אוֹכִיל׃	and I will feed [them].	
5a	לֹא יָשׁוּב אֶל־אֶרֶץ מִצְרַיִם	He will not return to the land of Egypt;	c. The Reversals of Salvation History (11:5–7)
5b	וְאַשּׁוּר הוּא מַלְכּוֹ	but Assyria will be his king,	(1) The Journey of Exile: From Exodus to Anti-Exodus (11:5)
5c	כִּי מֵאֲנוּ לָשׁוּב׃	since they refused to repent.	
6a	וְחָלָה חֶרֶב בְּעָרָיו	So a sword will twirl in their cities,	(2) The Punishment of Exile: Two Kinds of Ruin (11:6–7)
6b	וְכִלְּתָה בַדָּיו	and will put an end to their gate-bars,	(a) Physical Ruin (11:6)
6c	וְאָכָלָה מִמֹּעֲצוֹתֵיהֶם׃	and will consume because of their plans.	
7a	וְעַמִּי תְלוּאִים לִמְשׁוּבָתִי	But as for my people, they are stuck on apostasy from me.	(b) Spiritual Ruin (11:7)
7b	וְאֶל־עַל יִקְרָאֻהוּ יַחַד ↓	↓ Although to one above they will call together,	
7c	לֹא יְרוֹמֵם׃	he will not lift them up."	
			d. A New Beginning to Salvation History: The Rekindling of YHWH's Compassion (11:8–11)
			(1) YHWH's Turn from Anger to Compassion (11:8–9)
8a	אֵיךְ אֶתֶּנְךָ אֶפְרַיִם	"How could I give you over, O Ephraim?	(a) Introspection: YHWH's Resolve Tested (11:8a–d)
8b	אֲמַגֶּנְךָ יִשְׂרָאֵל	[How could] I hand you up, O Israel?	
8c	אֵיךְ אֶתֶּנְךָ כְאַדְמָה	How could I give you over like [at] Admah?	
8d	אֲשִׂימְךָ כִּצְבֹאיִם	[How could] I make you like [at] Zeboiim?	
8e	נֶהְפַּךְ עָלַי לִבִּי	My heart is overthrown within me,	(b) Struggle: YHWH's Heart Turned (11:8e–f)
8f	יַחַד נִכְמְרוּ נִחוּמָי׃	my compassions are kindled to warmth.	
9a	לֹא אֶעֱשֶׂה חֲרוֹן אַפִּי	I will not carry out my fiery anger,	(c) Reversal: YHWH's Anger Extinguished (11:9a–b)
9b	לֹא אָשׁוּב לְשַׁחֵת אֶפְרָיִם	nor will I return to destroy Ephraim.	
9c	כִּי אֵל אָנֹכִי	For I am God	(d) Reasoning: YHWH's Incomparable Holiness (11:9c–f)
9d	וְלֹא־אִישׁ	and [I am] not a man.	
9e	בְּקִרְבְּךָ קָדוֹשׁ	[I am] a Holy One in your midst,	
9f	וְלֹא אָבוֹא בְּעִיר׃	and I will not come in consuming anger.	

10a	אַחֲרֵי יְהוָה יֵלְכוּ	They will follow after YHWH.	(2) Israel's New Salvation History (11:10–11)
10b	כְּאַרְיֵה יִשְׁאָג	Like a lion he will roar.	(a) A Lion's Summons from Exile (11:10a–c)
10c	כִּי־הוּא יִשְׁאַג	When on his part, he roars,	
10d	וְיֶחֶרְדוּ בָנִים מִיָּם׃	then children will tremble from the west,	(b) The Birds' Trembling Response (11:10d–11a)
11a	יֶחֶרְדוּ כְצִפּוֹר מִמִּצְרַיִם	they will tremble like birds from Egypt,	
	וּכְיוֹנָה מֵאֶרֶץ אַשּׁוּר	and like doves from the land of Assyria.	
11b	וְהוֹשַׁבְתִּים עַל־בָּתֵּיהֶם	So I shall make them dwell in their homes"	(c) YHWH's Promise to Regather Israel (11:11b–c)
11c	נְאֻם־יְהוָה׃	—The Declaration of YHWH.	

Israel are roughly discernible through repeated wordplays on the title "Ephraim" (אֶפְרַיִם). In chapters 4–14, Hosea's puns on the name "double fruitfulness" undergo a transition from mostly negative in chapters 4–10, to Ephraim as the unexpected recipient of YHWH's mercy in 11:9, and then finally to "double fruitfulness" (אֶפְרַיִם) bearing "fruit" (פְּרִי) of praise (14:3[2]) and creational bounty (14:9[8]) once the God of history and creation has saved his people again.[5] As noted in the introduction to Hosea, the theological program of estrangement that YHWH transforms into reconciliation is also descriptive of the book of Hosea as a whole.

Explanation of the Text

1. Creation and History, Part 1: From Wilderness Fruits to Exiled Nomads (9:10–17)

The divine speech in Hos 9:10–17 takes the form of two parallel panels (9:10–13, 15–16) about apostasy in history (9:10, 15) and judgment against "Ephraim" ("double fruitfulness") from the realm of creation (9:11–13, 16). Each part concludes with a prayer by the prophet (9:14, 17) that responds to YHWH's strident declaration that Israel/Ephraim must be punished by infertility. Occasionally the tripartite panels can be somewhat unbalanced between (abc) and (a′b′c′), as the commentary below will note.

a. Israel's Apostasy in History, Cycle 1: Joy and Shame in the Wilderness (9:10)

The section begins in Hos 9:10 by recalling the first encounter between YHWH and his people. He discovered them in an unlikely place: "Like grapes in the wilderness I found Israel" (9:10a).[6] This positive simile of the "wilderness" (מִדְבָּר; cf. 13:5; Deut 8:2–3) echoes the earlier reference to YHWH's honeymoon with Israel (2:16[14]), though in Hos 9 the desert serves a different function as the setting for a traveler's surprising discovery of food (cf. Exod 16:2–3; Num 21:5). What YHWH finds there are "grapes" (עֲנָבִים), the main fruit that the Israelite spies brought back to symbolize the bounty of Canaan (Num 13:20–23). Whereas the vehicle of the metaphor eventually becomes the grapevine itself as a symbol for Israel (Hos 10:1; cf. Isa 5:1–7), the grape cluster in Hos 9:10a represents YHWH's joy at finding Israel.

The parallel comparison in the next clause adds the dimension of long-awaited sweetness by changing the fruit to a first-ripe fig: "Like the firstfruit in the fig grove at the beginning of its season I saw your ancestors" (Hos 9:10b). Compared to the relative brevity of Hos 9:10a, the heaping up of three prepositional phrases in 9:10b—"Like the firstfruit/in the fig grove/at the beginning of its season"—slows the discourse and expresses the fullness and freshness of YHWH's delight toward his people.[7] Likewise, the reference to the "firstfruit" (בִּכּוּרָה;

5. Cf. ibid., 125–26.

6. Hosea 9:10 marks the only section in the book that opens with a comparative frame (*LDHB* §5.5). This is significant since the section it introduces (9:10–11:11) contains some of the most creative similes and metaphors found in Hosea (e.g., Israel as both dried plant and bereaved parent [e.g., 9:16], Israel as negligent farmer [10:12–13], YHWH as both parent and farmer [11:1–4]).

7. To be specific, the fronted prepositional phrases in Hos 9:10b involve comparison ("like the firstfruit"), identifying

9:10b) mirrors the familial privileges extended to Israel in the exodus period when YHWH calls Israel "my firstborn son" (בְּנִי בְכֹרִי; Exod 4:22), though for the moment Hosea's historical referent remains the plural group of "your ancestors" (אֲבוֹתֵיכֶם; Hos 9:10b). Chapter 11 will characterize Israel as a singular "youth" (נַעַר) and "son" (בֵּן) when recalling the exodus from Egypt.

However, the primeval sweetness described in Hos 9:10a–b sours abruptly in the rest of v. 10 (cf. Isa 5:2). In response to creational plenty in salvation history, these same ancestors committed apostasy against YHWH: "As for them, they entered Baal-Peor and they dedicated themselves to the shameful thing; and they became detestable like what they loved" (9:10c–e). As in previous passages (e.g., 8:4, 9, 13), the pleonastic pronoun "as for them" (הֵמָּה; 9:10c) is Hosea's characteristic transition to YHWH's judgment against his people.[8] The transgression at hand is the episode recorded in Num 25, when Israelite men consorted with Moabite women and their deities, most notably a local manifestation of Baal called "Baal [of] Peor" (Num 25:3, 5). Israel's veneration of this "shameful thing" (בֹּשֶׁת; Hos 9:10d) and thereby becoming "detestable" (שִׁקּוּצִים; Hos 9:10e) lies centuries in the past, but Hosea views that ancient episode as paradigmatic for Israel's present idolatry.

The sinful history of the book of Numbers also repeats itself in the ironic terms of becoming "dedicated" (נזר *niphal*; Hos 9:10d), much like a "Nazirite" (נָזִיר, e.g., Num 6:1–21). But the object of such devotion is not YHWH but rather בֹּשֶׁת (lit. "shame," in 9:10d as a substantive that means "shameful thing"). In other OT passages that condemn Israel's syncretism, בֹּשֶׁת is both a derogatory term for Baal (e.g., אִישׁ בֹּשֶׁת/"Ish-Bosheth" [i.e., "man of shame"] as substitute for "man of Baal"; 2 Sam 2:8) as well as denoting the reproach that comes from worshiping idols such as him (Isa 42:17; Jer 3:24–25).

Moreover, Israel's choice to view these shameful deities with "love" (אהב; 9:10e) evokes Hosea's earlier descriptions of misplaced "love" (e.g., 2:7[5]; 4:18; 8:9) for various paramours from Canaanite nature religion, including but not limited to the deity Baal. In Hosea, every instance when Israel is the verbal subject of the Hebrew root אהב refers to illicit love.[9] Israel literally looked for love in all the wrong places! The abundant gifts of YHWH in creation (9:10a–b) have led to Israel forgetting him as the sole God of creation (9:10c–e). Like other dalliances with Canaanite nature religion (e.g., 2:10[8], 15[13]), the sin of forgetfulness sows the seeds of its own punishment when shameful worship (9:10d) gives rise to shamed worshipers (9:10e).

b. Creation as Agent of Judgment, Cycle 1: Infertility (9:11–13)

Israel's syncretism with nature deities makes it necessary for YHWH to deploy creation as his agent of judgment (9:11–14). In a biting pseudosorite, Hosea outlines how fertility will flee Israel like a bird (9:11), children that are born will nonetheless die (9:12), and any children who somehow survive will be handed over to death by cruel parents (9:13). These themes echo the maledictions in the ancient Near Eastern genre known as *futility curses*,[10] though the book of Hosea remains unique for employing the pseudosorite as the literary means of conveying the verdict of infertility.

space ("in the fig grove"), and specifying time ("at the beginning of its season"), thereby creating three frames of reference for YHWH's delight in the ancestors. These clauses correspond to frames of reference in the comparative (*LDHB* §5.5), spatial (*LDHB* §5.3), and temporal (*LDHB* §5.2) realms.

8. For other topical frames (*LDHB* §5.1) that effect a new frame of reference and shift the discourse toward a new topic (e.g., divine judgment), see passages such as Hos 6:7 and 8:4.

9. Only in Hos 3:1 is the root אהב used in any other sense, since here YHWH is the subject.

10. The most familiar examples from the OT are the covenant curses of Lev 26 and Deut 28. Outside the OT, most

Hosea presents the first kind of creational judgment (9:11) upon syncretism that follows the historical pattern at Baal-Peor. Fertility will flee from "double fruitfulness": "Ephraim is like a bird, their glory will fly away: No more childbirth, no more pregnancy, no more conception!" (9:11). The first clause's portrait of Israel as a bird (9:11a) recalls Israel's dove-like pursuit of Assyria (7:11), but the next clause's reference to the departure of "their glory" (9:11b) brings the image from the international sphere of diplomacy back to the domestic spheres of childrearing and divine presence. Earlier the Hebrew term for "glory/honor" (כָּבוֹד) denoted the procreative capacity of Israel (4:7), which the OT uses elsewhere for the splendorous presence of God (e.g., Exod 33:18; Lev 9:6; Ezek 10:18) or, by way of metonymic extension, the ark of the covenant (e.g., 1 Sam 4:21–22). The senses of childbearing and divine presence are both present in Hos 9:11, as Göran Eidevall notes: "Far from just being juxtaposed, the motifs of divine withdrawal and childlessness are closely interconnected in this passage. As YHWH abandons the people, fertility is reversed into sterility."[11]

A pseudosorite about infertility begins in the following verses through a chain of illogic that escalates from one clause to the next.[12] No realm of Israel can escape YHWH's curse of childlessness—should Israelite women be able to conceive (though they cannot; cf. 9:11c), the children whom they bear would not live anyway: "Although they raise children, I will bereave them from humanity" (9:12a–b). And were these children not to die (though they will), they would grow up only to lament the unthinkable reality that YHWH is totally absent from them: "For indeed, woe to them, when I turn away from them!" (9:12c–d). The exclamation "woe" (אוֹי; 9:12c) both pronounces the advent of trouble (e.g., Hos 7:13; Isa 3:9, 11) as well as sounding the cry of mourning of those who are under curse by YHWH (e.g., Isa 24:16; Lam 5:16).

But if these children somehow survive this woe (which they cannot; cf. 9:12a–d), and even more improbably, were "Ephraim" to enjoy life like a flourishing plant (9:13a; cf. 9:10; 10:1), then this people named "double fruitfulness" would quickly destroy their own flesh and blood by becoming filicidal parents who consign their children to a cruel death: "Ephraim will bring out his children to the slayer" (9:13b).[13] By spreading the curse of childlessness even to impossible places, the pseudosorite cuts off every remaining prospect of fertility for Israel and thereby asserts that the life of "double fruitfulness" has come to an untimely end. Any illusion of present security (9:13a) dissipates before the reality of future slaughter (9:13b). Other statements in chapters 9–10 describe Israel's punishment as the historical punishment of exile in a foreign land (e.g., 9:1–9, 17), but 9:10–13 expresses similar ideas using the terminology of a total collapse in creation's usual functions.

c. Hosea's Lament for Ephraim (9:14)

The scope and intensity of Ephraim's self-inflicted disaster induce a halting prayer from the prophet: "Give them, O YHWH—what will you give?" (9:14a–b). In prayers, imperative forms of נתן ("to give") typically express the boldness

notable is the bilingual Akkadian-Aramaic statue inscription from Tell Fekheriye in modern Syria ("Hadad-yith'i," trans. Alan Millard [*COS* 2.34:153–54]), in which an Aramean king invokes the curses of infertility and plague upon anyone who dares to efface his name from the statue.

11. Eidevall, *Grapes in the Desert*, 152.

12. See the discussion of Hosea's characteristic use of pseudosorites in the introduction to Hosea, pp. 53–57.

13. Hosea 9:13 is difficult. See Thomas E. McComiskey, "Hos 9:13 and the Integrity of the Masoretic Tradition in the Prophecy of Hosea," *JETS* 33 (1990): 155–60, for the rationale behind this translation and understanding of the MT reading.

of the supplicant in requesting something from God (e.g., Pss 28:4; 72:1; 115:1). However, in the present context, an imperatival form of נתן (9:14a) leads immediately to a rhetorical question with נתן (9:14b) to indicate the prophet's hesitation rather than confidence.

This reluctance carries over to the third clause of Hosea's prayer, which makes a sorrowful observation that YHWH now gives nongifts to his people: "Give [נתן] them a miscarrying womb and shriveling breasts" (9:14c). As Deborah Krause rightly notes, the various uses of נתן in the book of Hosea emphasize the sovereign authority of YHWH to "give" but also to take away when Israel fails to recognize him as the source of gifts (e.g., 2:7[5], 14[12]; 13:10).[14]

Since the prophet knows that fertility is no longer forthcoming from YHWH (9:10–13), this request for "miscarrying womb" and "shriveling breasts" (9:14c) is certainly ironic and perhaps also frustrated in tone. The word-pair "womb" (רֶחֶם) and "breasts" (שָׁדַיִם) recalls the covenant blessings of fertility bestowed on Joseph by a dying Jacob (Gen 49:25) but now reversed into the curse of infertility against the people of Ephraim, the descendants of Joseph.[15] Consequently, the visceral wording of Hos 9:14 is a lament rather than a positive and/or polite request to YHWH, as some versions of the Bible imply.[16]

a′. Israel's Apostasy in History, Cycle 2: Evil at Gilgal (9:15)

As noted above, Hos 9:15–17 appears to be a mirror image of the previous section (9:10–14): (1) Israel's historical sin (9:15a–b; cf. 9:10); (2) the link between past and present apostasy (9:15c–d; cf. 9:11a, 13a); (3) a pseudosorite of God's judgment in creation (9:16; cf. 9:11b–12, 13b); and (4) a prayer of response from the prophet (9:17; cf. 9:14).[17]

(1) Broken Covenant at Gilgal (9:15a–b)

In this second exposition of Israel's apostasy in history (cf. 9:10–14), the focus shifts from Baal-Peor (cf. 9:10) to Israel's sin at "Gilgal" (lit. "circle [of stones]"; Hos 9:15a). Gilgal was an ancient cultic site, the scene of Israel's first Yahwistic shrine upon entering Canaan (Josh 4:19–20; 5:9–10), but which had become syncretistic by the eighth century BCE (cf. Hos 4:15). Thus YHWH identifies Gilgal as a paradigmatic case of "all their evil" (כָּל־רָעָתָם; 9:15a), רָעָה being Hebrew's most general term for moral corruption of all kinds (e.g., Hos 7:1–3[3x]; 10:15[2x]).

YHWH indicates the reason for his revulsion toward sins in the Gilgal mold through a causal כִּי clause: "For there I have hated them" (9:15b). This assertion of "hate" (שׂנא) toward his people hints at the relational language of divorce (cf. 2:4–7[2–5]; Deut 24:1–4). The verb שׂנא also appears in the realm of ancient Near Eastern diplomacy and thus has political connotations as well.[18] This semantic flexibility in שׂנא comes from its being a covenantal term—the opposite of אהב ("to love"). The latter is also a covenantal term that in theological contexts refers to God's commitment to act in the interests of his people as the weaker party.[19] Thus the use of שׂנא denotes a rejection from covenant relationship and the end of YHWH's care as the stronger party.

14. Deborah Krause, "A Blessing Cursed: The Prophet's Prayer for Barren Womb and Dry Breasts in Hosea 9," in *Reading Between Texts: Intertextuality and the Hebrew Bible*, ed. Danna Nolan Fewell, Literary Currents in Biblical Interpretation (Louisville: Westminster John Knox, 1992), 195–96.

15. Keefe, "Hosea's (In)Fertility God," 39.

16. For example, the NLT renders Hos 9:14b as follows: "What should I request for your people?"

17. Cf. Andersen and Freedman, *Hosea*, 539.

18. Norbert Lohfink, "Hate and Love in Osee 9,15," *CBQ* 25 (1963): 417.

19. Susan Ackerman, "The Personal Is Political: Covenantal and Affectionate Love (*ʾĀHĒB, ʾAHĂBÂ*) in the Hebrew Bible," *VT* 52 (2002): 437–58.

(2) Banishment from YHWH's Family (9:15c)

Hosea does not describe precisely what transpires at Gilgal (9:15a–b), but Amos his contemporary links Gilgal with Israel's excessive attention to the forms, but not the heart, of cultic devotion to YHWH (Amos 4:4; cf. Isa 1:11–15). It may therefore be a cultic context that lies behind YHWH's subsequent vow to expel his people: "On account of the evil of their deeds, from my house I will drive them out" (9:15c). Once again Hosea describes Israel's deeds as רֹעַ ("evil/wickedness," a variant of רָעָה; cf. v. 15a). However, it is unlikely that the specific reference to expulsion out of "my house[hold]" (בֵּיתִי; 9:15c) in a northern prophetic book involves a literal connection between YHWH and Samaria's illicit sanctuaries and rituals (cf. 4:13–14; 8:4–6). The בַּיִת in Hos 9:15c is more likely YHWH's figurative "household" of land and people from which Israel will be driven out rather than a cultic place.[20]

(3) YHWH's Angry Vow (9:15d–e)

The holistic character of Israel's sins becomes explicit when YHWH declares that his covenant stands in antithesis to Israel's politics: "I will not love [אהב] them again, all of their princes are stubborn" (9:15d–e). The root אהב in Hosea has repeatedly denoted Israel's determination to "love" its paramours, both Baal and foreign trading partners (e.g., 2:9[7]; 8:9; 9:1, 10). But YHWH determines no longer to "love" this people (9:15d) because the exclusiveness of covenant relationship is incompatible with the syncretistic politics of this people (9:15e).

YHWH reinforces this angry vow against his people with a jarring Hebrew pun. The group of leaders known as "their princes" (שָׂרֵיהֶם), whom the book linked earlier to the dogged pursuit of injustice (5:10) and intrigue (7:3, 5), come under censure in Hos 9:15e as "stubborn" (סֹרְרִים).[21] As in Hos 7–8, covenant relationship with YHWH should have resulted in a theopolitics that was distinctive among the nations but sadly went missing in syncretistic Israel.

b′. Creation as Agent of Judgment, Cycle 2: Infertility (9:16)

In closing this section (9:10–17), the next two verses blend the realms of creation and history to describe complementary aspects of Israel's fate as an abandoned people. On the one hand, exile as figurative fruitlessness *in* the land draws upon the realm of creation when "double fruitfulness" (i.e., the meaning of Ephraim's name) becomes a dried plant (9:16a–c) and bereaved parent (9:16d–e). On the other hand, exile as literal expulsion *from* the land draws upon the realm of history (9:17). Both kinds of exile share the feature that the land is refusing to fulfill its normal function within the tripartite covenant relationship among God, land, and people.[22]

This passage opens with creation as YHWH's primary agent of judgment. As in Hos 9:11–14, the escalating illogic of the pseudosorite cuts deeply: "Ephraim is stricken: Their root has dried up, they will not bear any fruit. Indeed, when they bear children, I will put to death the delightful ones of their womb" (9:16). The apostate named "double fruitfulness" will lose his reproductive capacity (9:16a–b) so that no "fruit" (i.e., children) can result from this dried "tree" (9:16c).[23] Yet if Israel were somehow able to bear children (9:16d), this

20. Compare Hosea's other references to "the house of Israel/Judah" (1:6–7; 6:10) which denote only the people.

21. Morris, *Prophecy, Poetry and Hosea*, 123.

22. For more on this topic, see Hos 2:11–25[9–23] and 4:1–3 as well as the commentary on these passages.

23. O'Connor ("The Pseudosorites in Hebrew Verse," 251) notes that the "dried" (יָבֵשׁ) plant is a symbol for the eunuch's infertility in Isa 56:3. However, the appearance of a "tree" (עֵץ) in that passage contrasts with the reference to a "root" (שֹׁרֶשׁ) in Hos 9:15.

newfound fertility would all remain pointless since YHWH would put these children to death (9:16e).

The pseudosorite thus covers every scenario in YHWH's creation, both possible and impossible, ensuring that "Ephraim" (אֶפְרַיִם; 9:16a) will never bear any "fruit" (פְּרִי; 9:16c). This verse is not a literal statement about YHWH as a "baby-killer"[24] but a literary expression of the figurative outcome for a people planted in a land that is "stricken" (הֻכָּה; 9:16a) and "dried up" (יָבֵשׁ; 9:16b). The parallel section in Hos 9:11–14 had similarly asserted that responsibility for bringing the next generation to slaughter ultimately lies with a guilty people themselves rather than with YHWH.

c′. Hosea's Prayer of Agreement (9:17)

The passage shifts from a figurative depiction of exile as sedentary fruitlessness in the land (9:16) to the literal reality of forced deportation from the land (9:17). As in Hos 9:14, the dismayed prophet prays in response to what YHWH has just spoken through him: "My God will reject them, for they have not obeyed him. So they shall be nomads among the nations" (9:17; cf. Deut 4:25–28). For YHWH to "reject" (מאס; 9:17a) his people is not a first move but a reaction to how they have already "rejected" (מאס; 4:6) him. The prophet can still call YHWH "my God" (אֱלֹהַי; 9:17a, cf. 9:8), in contrast to Ephraim who cannot because he has "not obeyed/listened" (לֹא שָׁמְעוּ; 9:17b) to the repeated calls of YHWH/Hosea to "listen" (שמע; cf. 4:1; 5:1).

Since YHWH's people have not met his conditions to live in the land, no recourse remains but for them to become "nomads" (נֹדְדִים; 9:17c). Back in Hos 7:13b, the same root נדד ("to flee") had portrayed Israel as a foolish bird seeking refuge with Assyria their predator, even as YHWH thwarted their imperialist designs like a fowler casting his net (7:12). But in Hos 9:17, the completion of this figurative journey is at hand when YHWH's people finally receive their sinful wish to "flee" from their God. In summary, exile from the land is both a freely chosen decision of God's people to become wanderers (Hos 9:17) as well as a reversal of the conquest when YHWH personally "drives away" (גרשׁ; Hos 9:15) Israel from Canaan (cf. Deut 33:27; Josh 24:18). Hosea concludes this section (9:10–17) by praying in agreement with YHWH that Israel must suffer the consequences of its wrong choices (cf. 9:14).

2. Creation and History, Part 2: From Fruitful Vine to Thorns and Thistles (10:1–8)

Hosea 10 is a longer section than 9:10–17, consisting of two subsections (10:1–8, 9–15) with disparate ways of interweaving the motifs of creation and history. As in Hos 9:10–17, chapter 10 charges Israel with falling into syncretism with Canaanite nature deities after YHWH had provided blessings of creational abundance. The persistence of Israel's apostasy will predictably bring judgment against Israel in the realms of both creation and history—infertility in the land and exile from the land.

This chapter's two sections utilize the imaginative rhetorical strategy of joining the themes of infertility and exile. The first section moves from Israel's syncretism with creation and calf cult (10:1–5) to the historical judgment of exile (10:6–8); the second begins with sins in Israel's history (10:9–10) before using agricultural language (10:11–13) as a cipher for sin and judgment in the military sphere.[25]

24. Cf. Walter Brueggemann, "The Recovering God of Hosea," *HBT* 30 (2008): 10.

25. The somewhat erratic way in which Hos 10 joins together creation and history has led to the proposal that this chapter may represent a single, discrete section. The commentary on vv. 9–15 below will discuss this and other views on the passage's literary structure.

a. Israel's Doomed Syncretism (10:1–2)

Hosea 10:1–8 opens with a positive image of creation just as Hos 9:10–17 does. But the picture has changed here from Israel as grapes (9:10): "Israel is a lush vine" (10:1a). Whereas the grapes were the passive object of YHWH's delight in the earlier picture, Israel as the personified "vine/vineyard" (גֶּפֶן; cf. 2:14[12]; 14:8[7]) will assume a surprisingly active role in vv. 1–2 by doing two tasks more characteristic of farmers than their crops. However, the failure of these agricultural activities to produce anything will again prove that Israel's syncretism with Canaanite nature religion is doomed from the start.

(1) Excess "Fruit" and Illicit Altars (10:1a–c)

The first unusual action of the "lush vine" (10:1a) lies in displaying its own fruit: "He sets [שׁוה *piel*] fruit for himself" (10:1b). The verb שׁוה involves a rare root found only in poetry (e.g., Pss 16:8; 119:30) and typically takes as its subject a person rather than a thing (e.g., Pss 18:34[33]; 21:6[5]). Hosea hereby recasts an inert vine as a moving object that can present itself to others.

Second, this vine on the move takes advantage of an increase in "fruit" (פְּרִי; 10:1b) to capitalize on the Canaanite synergy between agriculture and religion: "According to the abundance of his fruit [פְּרִי] he multiplied his altars" (10:1c). These two references to "fruit" begin to redraw the word picture from a personified farm product to a harvesting farmer who brings agricultural offerings for cultic worship.

(2) Good Land and Sacred Pillars (10:1d)

The metaphor completes its journey from the agricultural to the religious realm in this verse's second instance of a clause beginning with "according to" (כְּ-preposition): "According to [כְּ] the goodness of his land he enriched sacred pillars" (10:1d). In Hos 10:1, Hosea's wordplays on פְּרִי and the two כְּ-clauses bridge the conceptual gaps between Israel as personified plant (10:1a), fruit producer (10:1b), and fruit offerer (10:1c–d).

Along similar lines to Hos 8:1–13,[26] the second action of Israel in "multiplying altars" (הִרְבָּה לַמִּזְבְּחוֹת; 10:1c) and "enriching sacred pillars" (הֵיטִיבוּ מַצֵּבוֹת; 10:1d) represents a sinful response to the land's "abundance" (רֹב; 10:1c). Israel has twisted YHWH's gift of a land full of "good[ness]" (טוֹב; Hos 10:1d, cf. Exod 3:8; Deut 1:25) into an opportunity to "enrich/make good" (יטב *hiphil*; Hos 10:1d) the nature rituals that the land's original inhabitants had associated with it. These passages in Hosea demonstrate how Israel's syncretism took full advantage of the Canaanite symbiosis between cultic rituals *for* the land and agricultural prosperity *in* the land. As "fruit" (פְּרִי) of all kinds increased during the boom decades of the mid-eighth century BCE, both in the form of children (9:16) and farm commodities (10:1), Israel's devotion to the cultic practices and deities that supposedly supplied excess "fruit" in a prosperous land increased as well.

(3) Broken Altars and Destroyed Pillars (10:2)

Despite such outer devotion to ritual, the inner waywardness of YHWH's people cannot be hidden from him: "Their heart [לֵב] has become slippery, now they are guilty" (10:2a–b). In Hebrew, the "heart" (לֵבָב/לֵב) encompasses both thought and emotion as the innermost part of a person (cf. Deut 6:5).[27] For the figurative insides of Israel to become "slippery/smooth" (חלק; cf. Ps 55:22[21]) leads to ritual pollution that cannot help but drive YHWH away: "Now [עַתָּה] they are guilty [אשׁם]!" (Hos 10:2b; cf. 4:15; 5:15). Here the adverb עַתָּה

26. See discussion of symbiotic sins in Hos 8:1–13 by Gnuse, "Calf, Cult, and King," 83–92.

27. Wolff, *Anthropology of the Old Testament*, 40–55.

("now") announces an inescapable verdict from YHWH (cf. 4:16; 7:2; 8:8), namely, that Israel's greater religious activity only leads to greater degrees of "guilt" (אשם). The root אשם denotes either the objective reality of sin ("to become guilty," e.g., Lev 5:17, 19) or, less likely in this passage, the subjective recognition of sin ("to accept guilt," e.g., Lev 5:23[6:4]).

In both senses of אשם, the judicial portrait is that of a widening gap between a holy God and sinful people (Hos 10:2a–b). At the same time, Hosea warns that YHWH is not absent but unmistakably present to judge Israel's syncretism: "He himself [הוא] will break [ערף] their altars, he will destroy their sacred pillars" (10:2c–d). The pleonastic pronoun הוא ("he himself/as for him"; 10:2c) emphasizes how YHWH will personally come to smash the cultic rituals and instruments in which Israel exults (10:1). As the sole Creator, YHWH cannot tolerate the heresy that Israel could manipulate him with sacrifices as if he were merely a nature deity.

This passage underscores the futility of using sacrifices to guarantee creation's plenitude through an ironic reference to ערף ("to break the neck," a denominative verb from עֹרֶף, "neck") in the act of destroying Israel's altars (10:2c). By Hosea's use of a verb that everywhere else in the OT refers to breaking the neck of a sacrificial animal (e.g., Exod 13:13; Deut 21:4), the terminology of ritual is turned against itself when YHWH "breaks [the neck]" of altars (10:2c). Altars (cf. 10:1) are raised but flat platforms, thereby distinguishing them from the wood or stone pillars protruding visibly above the ground which YHWH also determines to destroy (10:2d).

b. Israel's Seditious Words (10:3–4)

Not surprisingly in Hosea, YHWH anticipates that recalcitrant Israel will mount another protest. In this regard Hos 10:3–4 takes the literary form of a disputation (cf. 6:1–6; 9:7–9) in which YHWH quotes the objections of Israel before offering a rebuttal. The people directly challenge the rule of the heavenly King over them, and perhaps that of YHWH's earthly king as well: "But now they might say, 'We do not have a King/king [מֶלֶךְ]! For we have not feared YHWH! And as for a King/king [מֶלֶךְ], what could he do for us?'" (10:3).

It is unclear whether the two occurrences of מֶלֶךְ (10:3b, d) refer to a divine "King" or human "king."[28] The Hebrew language does not explicitly signal references to God (as English Bibles typically do by using capital letters). While both "King" and "king" are possible, a brief exploration of historical and theological background will suggest that YHWH is the primary ruler in view whom Israel has rejected.

(1) Rejection of YHWH as King (10:3)

To this point Hosea has portrayed the rulers of the Northern Kingdom in overwhelmingly negative ways (5:1; 7:7), as well as emphasizing the flawed foundations of Israelite kingship itself (8:4; 13:9–11).[29] The people's confident assertion that "we do not have a King" (אֵין מֶלֶךְ לָנוּ; Hos 10:3b) echoes the refrain of Judg 17–21, the darkest era in Israel's past that the narrator chillingly summarizes four times, "In those days there was no king [אֵין מֶלֶךְ] in Israel" (17:6; 18:1; 21:25; the variant phrase מֶלֶךְ אֵין is found in 19:1)—not even YHWH! These factors indicate that Hos 10:3 is citing Israel's

28. E.g., Andersen and Freedman (*Hosea*, 553) argue for a divine "King," Wolff (*Hosea*, 174) for a human "king."

29. On which see Peter Machinist, "Hosea and the Ambiguity of Kingship in Ancient Israel," in *Constituting the Community: Studies on the Polity of Ancient Israel in Honor of S. Dean McBride, Jr.*, ed. John T. Strong and Steven Shawn Tuell (Winona Lake, IN: Eisenbrauns, 2005), 153–81.

rejection of YHWH more than any human king (cf. 1 Sam 8:6–7).

As in the book of Judges, the presence or absence of human kings in the eighth century BCE becomes irrelevant when a rebellious people possess the chutzpah to state so baldly: "For [כִּי] we have not feared YHWH!" (10:3c).[30] Unlike in the book of Judges, the people themselves rather than the narrator express such apostasy with their own lips. More important than the ambiguities with מֶלֶךְ (10:3b, d) and two instances of the particle כִּי ("indeed, for"; 3a, c), the extreme willfulness of Israel's speech betrays the cantankerous heart of a people who would reject any and every leader. They are concerned only with themselves: "And as for a King/king, what could he [i.e., a divine or human king] do for us?'" (10:3d).

(2) Embrace of Foreign Alliances (10:4a–b)

As if this were not argumentative enough, the seditious words of Israel are just getting started. Here the disputation shifts from Israel's words to YHWH's, but the topic of sinful speech continues when YHWH condemns his people's duplicitous words in their foreign policy: "They have spoken words, with vain oaths they made a covenant" (10:4a–b). Earlier passages in Hosea have mentioned the deceitful use of speech in the context of Israel's domestic affairs (e.g., 4:2; 7:13). It is now the international scene that comes to the fore in Israel's act of "making a covenant" (כרת בְּרִית), an idiom that Hosea later uses to describe Israel taking initiative to make a treaty or alliance with Assyria (12:2[1]).

While this idiom in Hos 10:4b can also refer to covenant-making between YHWH and his people (e.g., 6:7; 8:1), it is more likely that the "words" (דְּבָרִים) and "oaths" (אָלוֹת) mentioned here are part of the diplomatic ceremonies involved in ratifying treaties and agreements in the predominantly oral world of the ancient Near East.[31] In addition, a political understanding of Hos 10:4a–b as an embrace of foreign alliances accords best with Hos 5:8–7:16, a passage that roundly criticizes Israel's inclination toward the syncretistic politics of injustice and intrigue.

(3) Corruption in the Legal System (10:4c)

The holism of YHWH's distinctive theopolitics for Israel remains the topic in the rest of Hos 10:4. Moving briefly to the topic of corruption in the legal system, the themes of history and creation recur together in a condemnation of Israel's perversion of "justice" (מִשְׁפָּט). This is the same Hebrew term for the covenantally motivated "justice" that YHWH seeks from his people (e.g., 5:1; 12:7[6]) but that now signifies "judgment" that "sprouts [פרח] like a poisonous plant [ראשׁ] in the furrows of a field" (10:4c). Since ראשׁ refers to something toxic (Deut 32:33; Jer 8:14), the species in question is likely a strangling plant with the ability to "sprout/blossom" (פרח; cf. Isa 17:11) and undermine a farmer's neatly plowed rows of crops (i.e., the context and image of 10:4c).

This depiction of social injustice as a plant that damages other plants seems to operate also on an economic level. Hosea and other prophets condemn kings and priests for conspiring in an

30. The כִּי conjunction in Hos 10:3c could be either causal/evidential ("for, since"; *BHRG* §40.29.2.2) or asseverative ("indeed"; *BHRG* §40.29.2.4). Although the former is more common, the latter is possible since the bluntness of the preceding clause ("We do not have a King!"; 10:3b) functions as a virtual oath, the usual context in which an asseverative כִּי would follow (e.g., Gen 42:16).

31. On the binding nature of oral agreements in the ancient Near East, see Kalluveettil, *Declaration and Covenant*, 92–106.

oppressive system of land tenure (Isa 3:13–15; Amos 5:11; Mic 2:1–2, 9). The leaders of Israel forced individual farmers, who should have worked their ancestral plots of land for themselves (cf. Lev 25; Deut 26), to produce agricultural goods that enriched the upper class (Amos 2:8; 5:11; 6:6) and provided commodities for international trade (Hos 2:7[5], 10[8]; 12:2[1]). Corruption in Israel's legal system is doubly like a poisonous plant, for it both contaminates the land as well as strangling the people who work it.

In what follows, the synergistic links among politics, economics, and religion (10:1–4) drive the prophecy of Hosea toward another extended condemnation of the cult of golden-calf worship (10:5–8). As in Hos 8:4–14, the king's sponsorship of this syncretistic institution draws together the various political and economic threads of Israel's life in the eighth century BCE.

c. YHWH's Reversals upon Israel's Syncretism (10:5–8)

Israel defies YHWH's unique theopolitics through syncretistic veneration of calf images. As other passages describe, the king's golden calf (or calves, see below on Hos 10:5) and other idols are forged from gold and silver (Hos 8:4–6; 13:2) that Israel had obtained through trading agricultural commodities on the international market (Hos 2:7[5], 10[8]). Israelite farmers would have produced these commodities and brought them as offerings to cultic sites that Israel's exploitative leaders controlled, such as high places (4:13–14) and threshing floors (9:1). YHWH therefore determines to respond to the syncretistic calf cult that is Israel's pride and joy (8:5–6; 10:5–8) with a series of ironic reversals.

(1) Calf Cult: From Delight to Dread (10:5a–c)

The first reversal involves turning Israel's delight in bovine images to dread: "Regarding the heifers [עֶגְלוֹת] of Beth-Aven, the inhabitants of Samaria will dread [גור] it. For its people will mourn [אבל] because of it, and its priests will shriek [גיל] for it because of its glory" (10:5a–c). Before exploring the three verbs denoting fear and sadness, it is important to note the discrepancies in grammatical gender and number between the singular male "calf" (עֵגֶל), which Hosea had earlier condemned (8:5–6), and this passage's feminine plural "heifers" (עֶגְלוֹת; 10:5a).[32] In addition, a final reference to masculine plural "calves" (עֲגָלִים; 13:2) combines grammatical elements from both depictions.

On this note, the circumstances of Israel's calf cults in each of their locations are somewhat uncertain. Clearly there were calf cults in Bethel, Samaria, and Dan (Hos 8:6; 1 Kgs 12:28–33), but how many golden calves did Israel venerate in each place? It is difficult to resolve these discrepancies of grammatical number,[33] but the surprising change of masculine "calf" (8:4–6) into feminine "heifers" (10:5a) most likely intends to emasculate a bovine image that the people venerate for its "glory" (כָּבוֹד; 10:5c).[34] The use of כָּבוֹד also connects this icon of fertility to Israel's pride in its virility (4:7; 9:11). The rhetorical strategy of feminizing and/or figuratively castrating the largely male audience of Hosea has appeared numerous times in the book (e.g., 1:5; 2:8[6]; 7:4–8).[35]

32. English versions tend to follow the LXX's strategy to harmonize Hosea's references to bovines of different gender and number as a singular, male "calf" (μόσχος). However, it is difficult to explain the MT's variations as scribal or translational issues. Thus, this commentary's English rendering of Hos 10:5 reflects the MT.

33. To name just one difficulty, the mention of plural "heifers" (10:5a) shifts immediately to the masculine pronoun "him/it" (10:5b–c) without any indication that the object in view has changed.

34. Dearman, *Hosea*, 224.

35. Haddox, "(E)masculinity," 174–200.

In a Mediterranean cultural setting where the community hashes out honor and shame in the "Public Court of Reputation,"[36] the ritual actions of mourning recorded in Hos 10:5 gain special poignancy. On the one hand, the Canaanized worship of Israel in the eighth century BCE was characterized by public and noisy displays (Hos 9:1; cf. Amos 5:23). On the other hand, Hos 10:5a–b reverses the calf cult's fortunes into an object of public embarrassment (גור, "to dread"; 10:5a) and sadness (אבל, "to mourn"; 10:5b).

The next clause (10:5c) strengthens this reversal upon Hos 9:1 by the reappearance of גיל. The range of meaning for this Hebrew root includes happy gyrations of "rejoicing" or "celebration" (9:1) as well as the traumatized movements of "shrieking" or "trembling" (10:5c).[37] Verbal repetition across these chapters thus highlights Israel's tragic twist of fate. In addition, every subgroup among "the inhabitant[s] of Samaria" (10:5a) will experience the overturning of delight to dread—both the "people" (עַם) at large (10:5b) as well as their "[pagan] priests" (כְּמָרִים; 10:5c; cf. 2 Kgs 23:5; Zeph 1:4).

(2) Calf Cult: From Glory to Shame (10:5d–6)

The domestic humiliation of Israel (10:5a–c) culminates in a fiasco of international proportions with the "departing/exile" (גלה; 10:5d) of the calf/calves to Assyria. There they will become tribute to the "great king" (10:6a), a favorite self-appellation of the kings of Assyria.[38] In the process of this very public event, the final stage in Israel's loss of "glory" (cf. 10:5c–d) will be humiliation in the eyes of a watching world: "Ephraim brings shame [בָּשְׁנָה] upon himself, and Israel will be ashamed [בוש] of his counsel" (10:6b–c). As anthropological studies of traditional cultures have recognized, the communal orientation of Mediterranean societies means that shaming always includes a loss of status in the public arena.[39] In this text, the people of YHWH suffer reproach before the nations in losing their golden calf/calves (10:5d–6b), as well as experiencing the failure of their diplomatic "counsel" (עֵצָה; 10:6c) that vacillates unwisely between pro-Assyria and anti-Assyria policies (cf. 5:8–7:16).

(3) Kingship: From Ruler to Flotsam (10:7)

The next reversal in Hos 10:7–8 confronts kings as the architects of sinful bridges that join economics, religion, and politics in Israel. Hosea has already addressed the sinful connections between king and cult (8:4–8a) as well as politics and religion (8:8b–14), so this passage focuses on the fate of the kings themselves: "Samaria is cut off [with] her king, as a reed [קֶצֶף] on the surface of the waters" (10:7). Other passages depict the end of kingship in the historical language of exile (3:4–5) or death (7:7), but Hos 10:7 uses the natural object קֶצֶף to portray kings dissipating like flotsam of some kind, either a "splinter/reed" of plant debris or "foam" that will soon sink into the water.[40] For both meanings of קֶצֶף, the import of this vivid picture from creation is unmistakably clear—kings in Israel are worthless and destined to be flotsam.

36. On the all-important role of the "Public Court of Reputation," see Zeba Crook, "Honor, Shame, and Social Status Revisited," *JBL* 128 (2009): 591–611.

37. Andersen and Freedman, *Hosea*, 556.

38. On a similar use of the title "great king," see the commentary above on Hos 5:13.

39. Saul M. Olyan, "Honor, Shame, and Covenant Relations in Ancient Israel and Its Environment," *JBL* 115 (1996): 203–4; Lyn M. Bechtel, "Shame as a Sanction of Social Control in Biblical Israel: Judicial, Political, and Social Shaming," *JSOT* 49 (1991): 54–55. Compare the work of Wu, who is rightly critical of anthropology's oft-used and simplistic category of "honor-shame society" but concurs that the relational dynamics of "face-to-face communities" in Mediterranean cultures (such as ancient Israel) require a public reckoning for honorable and shameful behavior (*Honor, Shame, and Guilt*, 163–65).

40. Macintosh, *Hosea*, 406–7.

(4) Fertility Religion: From Blessing to Curse (10:8a–b)

Hosea 10:8a–b follows the creational picture of Hos 10:7 with a brief foray into historical language. Exile now becomes the destruction of the cultic system masterminded by Israel's kings: "The high places of iniquity, the sin of Israel, will be exterminated [שׁמד *niphal*]" (10:8a). The root שׁמד comes from the conceptual field of military destruction (e.g., Gen 34:30; Deut 7:23; 2 Sam 21:5). However, why is the particular object to be destroyed the "high places of iniquity" (בָּמוֹת אָוֶן) rather than Samaria or its fortresses? The term "wickedness, trouble, iniquity" (אָוֶן) probably serves as an abbreviated form for "house of wickedness" (בֵּית אָוֶן; Hos 4:15; 5:8; 10:5), the pejorative name for "Bethel" (Hebrew for "house of God"). This city where Israel's patriarchs encountered God (e.g., Gen 12:8; 28:19; 35:1) eventually hosted one of several syncretistic cults of YHWH throughout Israel's monarchical era (e.g., 1 Kgs 12:29; 13:4; 2 Kgs 23:15).

Being located on the hills and mountains of Israel, "high places" at sites like Bethel differed from the threshing floors located in agricultural areas where leaders collected usurious offerings from the people (Hos 9:1). The high places served instead as sites of illicit sexual rituals associated with nature religion (4:13–14).[41] But in a shift back to creational language, Hosea warns that the natural world will itself rise against the high places and Israel's attempts there to manipulate it: "Thorn and thistle will come up on their altars" (10:8b). This reference to "thorn" and "thistle" alludes to Gen 3:18, suggesting the cultic rituals of Israel are inviting the fall's curse upon creation rather than its blessing.

(5) Fertility Religion: From Pleasure to Pain (10:8c–f)

In addition, the imagery of backfiring nature rituals takes an even darker turn when Hosea personifies the high places themselves as traumatized victims of Israel's actions: "They [i.e., the high places] will say to the mountains, 'Cover us!' And [they will say] to the hills, 'Fall on us!'" (10:8c–f). Hosea 4:13–14 has already named the "mountains" and "hills" as the location of Israel's sexualized worship. But these elevated geographical features, which used to host the high places and witness the pleasurable rituals there, will now collapse upon the high places at their own request to end their misery. In short, this section warns that Israel's rituals of calf worship (10:5–6; cf. 8:4–5), perhaps located at the high places (10:8a; cf. 2 Kgs 16:4), will turn creational blessing into curse (10:8b) and sexual pleasure into pain (10:8c–f). The fruitful vine (10:1) has morphed into thorns and thistles. These will both destroy Israel's fertility as well as calling down even greater destroyers against nature religion (10:8).

3. Creation and History, Part 3: Miscellaneous Images (10:9–15)

Hosea 10:9 marks a new stage of the argument by changing the mode of speaking to the heightened urgency of second-person singular (i.e., "you have sinned") and vocative address (i.e., "O Israel").[42] Compared to the two previous cycles about creation and history (9:10–17; 10:1–8), the third cycle in Hos 10:9–15 leaves behind the circuitousness of YHWH's speech *about* Israel in favor of his blunt speech *against* Israel. The growing

41. Andersen and Freedman, *Hosea*, 559.

42. These grammatical shifts are two examples of changed reference (*LDHB* §2.6), a discourse feature in which new titles or descriptors recharacterize existing participants in the discourse. The purpose is to highlight a changing relationship between parties, in this case YHWH's increasing exasperation toward Israel.

emotional intensity in this passage prepares the way for the outpouring of divine agony in Hos 11. Before that chapter's final turn from estrangement to reconciliation in YHWH's household, judgment against Israel plays out comprehensively in the rest of Hos 10 on both human and cosmic stages—the complementary realms of history and creation.

a. Examples of Judgment in History, Part I (10:9–10)

Hosea 10:9–10 initiates the first of two cycles (cf. 10:14–15) of YHWH's judgment in the realm of history. Judgment in the past at Gibeah (10:9) and Beth-Arbel (10:14) furnishes the template for how Israel will suffer exile in the future (10:10, 15). Nevertheless, between these passages about destruction that seems inevitable, the prophet employs the realm of creation to issue one final opportunity for Israel to repent (10:11–13).

(1) Judgment in the Past: War in Gibeah (10:9)

Condemnation of Israel's high places both closes the previous section (10:8) and carries over to the present reference to Israel's hill country (10:9). But at the beginning of Hos 10:9–15, an elevated geographical setting connects not to sins in the creational realm (cf. 10:7–8) but to Israel's transgressions in history: "Since the days of Gibeah [גִּבְעָה] you have sinned, O Israel" (10:9a). Related to a noun that means "hill" (גִּבְעָה; e.g., Hos 4:13; 1 Kgs 14:23; cf. Josh 18:28), Gibeah was a Benjamite town in the hilly area between Samaria and Judah that Hosea has already mentioned twice (5:8; 9:9).

In keeping with earlier passages, YHWH charges Israel in Hos 10:9a with a historical pattern of "having sinned" (a perfective form of חטא; cf. 4:7; 8:11) in the pattern or vicinity of Gibeah. חטא is the most general of Hebrew's roots for sin (e.g., Gen 13:13; 39:9) and likely alludes to the reprehensible events of rape, murder, and internecine warfare narrated in Judg 19–21. Whatever the subsequent and obscure sentence "there they stood" (Hos 10:9b) might mean with reference to these events in or near Gibeah,[43] the verse's condemnation of "evildoers" (בְּנֵי עַלְוָה) confirms that the detestable history in Judges is the pattern in question. In Hos 10:9c, the group identified as בְּנֵי עַלְוָה (lit. "children of lawlessness") recalls the בְּנֵי־בְלִיַּעַל ("children of worthlessness"; Judg 19:22; 20:13) who spearheaded sexual and cultic sins in Gibeah of an earlier generation.[44]

This background from Judg 19–21 also helps to unravel the difficult Hebrew syntax of the dual historical references in Hos 10:9c. For though the usual interrogative particle (הֲ) is missing in Hos 10:9c,[45] its use of the adverb לֹא ("no, not") appears to introduce a negative rhetorical question (cf. 1 Sam 20:14; 2 Sam 23:5) that expresses the certainty that Gibeah must surely be destroyed.[46] This yields the following rendering (as with most English versions): "Will not [לֹא] war against the evildoers overtake them in Gibeah?" (10:9c). Interpreting this verbal clause as a question that demands a positive answer rather than an assertion (i.e., "war *will not* overtake the evildoers") also makes better sense of the following context about YHWH's pained reaction to this history of apostasy.

43. The reason for the sudden shift from second-person singular ("you have sinned"; 10:9a) to third-person plural ("there they stood"; 10:9b) is unclear. In Judg 19–21 the only mention of the verb עמד ("to stand") is Phinehas's priestly ministry (20:28; cf. Ps 106:30), but this is a singular reference that does not accord with Hos 10:9b.

44. Bo H. Lim and Daniel Castelo, *Hosea*, THOTC (Grand Rapids: Eerdmans, 2015), 165.

45. The interrogative particle הֲ does not occur in the book of Hosea, but *IBHS* §18.1c, n. 1, notes that interrogative particles are not necessary to mark questions in Hebrew.

46. On this use of the negative particle, see BDB 519a.

(2) Judgment in the Future: YHWH's Use of the Nations (10:10)

Hosea 10:10 links the past with the future in that YHWH's judgment against Gibeah furnishes the pattern for Israel's coming exile. The insistent "I" of first-person divine speech returns (cf. 9:15–16) in a vow to punish this wayward people: "When I desire, then I will chastise them, and peoples will be gathered against them, when they [i.e., the peoples] imprison/bind them [i.e., Israel] for their double iniquity" (10:10). The timing of Israel's coming exile is neither arbitrary nor automatic but hinges upon the impassioned "desire" (אַוָּה; 10:10aα) of a sovereign God who must "chastise" (יסר; 10:10aβ) his people. אַוָּה is the usual language for the immanence of human "desire" (e.g., Deut 12:15; 1 Sam 23:20), but it is only God in his transcendence who has authority to thwart the wayward wants of an entire nation (e.g., Hos 7:12; Ps 94:10). In this regard, the verb יסר usually refers to a parent's discipline toward children (Prov 19:18; 29:17), but here describes YHWH's discipline toward an entire people (as in Hos 7:15).

Indeed, this picture of divine sovereignty takes on international dimensions in the next two clauses which portray other nations as YHWH's instruments who will "be gathered" (אסף *niphal*; 10:10b) against and "imprison" (אסר; 10:10c) YHWH's people (cf. 8:8; 9:17). These non-Israelite nations will ultimately answer to the God of Israel for their imperialist policies of deportation and torture (cf. Isa 10:5–11; Amos 1:3–2:3). But before then, the mystery is that their freely chosen actions are also YHWH's sovereign plan to use sinful nations to punish his people. The pronouncement of YHWH's verdict against "their double iniquity" (שְׁתֵּי עוֹנֹתָם; 10:10c) refers to an additional measure of guilt after Israel still refuses to repent in the face of being confronted with various kinds of "iniquity" (עָוֹן; 4:8; 7:1; 9:7). As in the realm of creation lapsing into infertility as a result of syncretism (cf. 9:10–17), Israel's long history in following the ways of the nations will meet with a homeopathic remedy—these same powers will come to impose their brutal will upon Israel.

b. Examples of Judgment through Creation (10:11–13)

The theme of divinely sanctioned discipline continues in the next three verses, but with the theme of judgment in the realm of creation making a cameo reappearance (10:11–13; cf. 10:8) between two discourses about judgment in history (cf. 10:9–10, 14–15). The image of exile moves from Israel as a people to be deported and imprisoned (10:10) to a beast of burden being sent to work the fields (10:11).

(1) Israel as a Trained Heifer (10:11)

The first creaturely image about Israel's figurative downgrading from human to animal occurs by way of the semantic flexibility of אסר (10:10c; "to imprison, tie, bind"). This verbal root bridges the domains of *binding* human captives (e.g., Gen 42:24; Isa 22:3) as well as *harnessing* domestic animals (e.g., 1 Sam 6:7; Jer 46:4). So, where the simile had just portrayed the nations as a warden who dictates his prisoners' movements (10:10c), YHWH will also act like a farmer who controls his beast: "Ephraim is a trained heifer who loves to tread (10:11a–b). This "heifer" (עֶגְלָה) is of the same class of animals as the "heifers" (עֶגְלוֹת) of the syncretistic calf cult (10:5), making it unlikely that Hosea's characterization of Israel as a bovine is a complimentary picture, as some scholars have proposed.[47] For this heifer to be "trained" (10:11a;

47. E.g., Dearman, *Hosea*, 270; Wolff, *Hosea*, 185.

cf. Jer 31:18) and "love to tread" (10:11b) highlights positively its compliance with the farmer's will but does not mitigate the insulting reality that it is still a beast.

The following clauses explicate the image of a trained heifer with an allusion to the pervasive biblical motif that worshipers of idols will become stupid like them: "On my part, I placed a fine yoke on her neck" (10:11c). As previously in Hosea (9:10c; 10:2c), this clause begins with a pleonastic pronoun (וַאֲנִי, "on my part") to focus attention on YHWH's speech in contrast to Israel's actions. In this case, he pronounces the poetic justice of dehumanization upon those who venerate lifeless gods (cf. Pss 115:2–8; 135:15–18). Israel's decision to worship golden calf/calves (cf. Hos 8:4–6; 1 Kgs 12:28–33) will result in Israel becoming beasts/slaves under a harsh burden which is ironically pictured as "a fine/good yoke" (cf. Deut 28:48; 1 Kgs 12:4).[48] The figure of the "yoke" (עֹל) is usually a symbol in eighth-century prophetic discourse for deportation and victimization by Assyria, as in the following chapter of Hosea (11:4; cf. Isa 10:27; 14:25).

Yet in this passage the prophet declares that the fitter of the "yoke" and the farmer who drives Israel the heifer (10:11c) is none other than YHWH himself: "I will harness Ephraim; Judah will plow; Jacob will break up the soil for himself" (10:11d–f). To "harness/put out to ride" (רכב *hiphil*), "plow" (חרשׁ *qal*), and "harrow a field" (שׂדד *piel*) evidently picture a farmer's work of plowing which uses a beast of burden. However, the creational simile in Hos 10:11 is challenging to interpret since it journeys one step further—from Ephraim as farm animal under YHWH's direction (10:11d) to Judah and Jacob who apparently remain free to plow land for themselves (10:11e–f). But do all three entities wear "a fine yoke on her neck" (10:11c)?

Earlier Hosea had often paired Judah with Ephraim as Israelite peoples who are both estranged from YHWH and must return to him (e.g., 5:5, 12–14). But not only is Hos 10:11 the first clear reference in the book to the two kingdoms having divergent fates, but "Judah" is also now linked to "Jacob" in being subjects (10:11e–f) rather than objects (cf. 10:11d) of verbs about farming. The Southern Kingdom and a heretofore-unmentioned entity called "Jacob" (cf. 12:3[2], 13[12]) may still choose to be a farmer "for himself" (לוֹ; 10:11f) in YHWH's household rather than a domestic animal.

This difference in the simile indicates that Ephraim's estrangement from YHWH must inevitably lead to the yoke of Assyrian exile. By contrast, Judah and Jacob still have an opportunity to reconcile themselves with the head of this figurative household by choosing the path of repentance.[49] In a manner anticipating chapter 12, the figure of Jacob represents an open-ended future for estranged people of YHWH who can still chose reconciliation with him—in this case, the Southern Kingdom of Judah.

(2) Israel as a Negligent Farmer (10:12–13)

The image of judgment against Israel then changes from an animal (10:11) back to the human picture of a negligent farmer (10:12–13). The theme of sowing provides an outer frame in these two verses, both in enjoining Israel to sow faithfully (10:12a–c) and confronting its failure to do so (10:13). A more ominous depiction of the Creator appears between these pastoral depictions of Israel—YHWH who comes like a driving rain and threatens to shower his people with judgment (10:12d–e).

48. G. K. Beale, *We Become What We Worship: A Biblical Theology of Idolatry* (Downers Grove, IL: IVP Academic, 2008), 99–101.

49. Alternatively, Wolff (*Hosea*, 185) proposes that the threefold reference to Ephraim, Judah, and Jacob emphasizes the unity of God's people. This interpretation takes the bovine characterization of Ephraim to be positive. However, the "calf" has earlier appeared to be negative in Hos 10.

(a) Israel's Duty to Sow Faithfully (10:12a–c)

Although exile now seems inevitable for Ephraim (cf. 10:11d), Hosea explicates the possibility of return for Judah and Jacob (10:11e–f) in v. 12 as a better kind of farming. Of the three imperatives in this verse, the first two involve positive uses of agricultural language to summon Israel to covenantal obedience: "Sow [זרע] for yourselves according to righteousness, reap [קצר] according to faithfulness" (10:12a–b). The injunction to "sow" (זרע; 10:12a) and "reap" (קצר; 10:12b) contrasts notably with Ephraim's unwise moves described earlier to "sow" sinful seeds and "reap" the corresponding consequences (8:7).

Similarly, the audience of Hosea must also sow "righteousness" (צְדָקָה) to reap "faithfulness" (חֶסֶד). In Hebrew, צְדָקָה is less the abstract legal quality of "righteousness" and more the concrete interpersonal action of "right behavior or status in relation to some standard of behavior accepted in the community."[50] While this term can describe fidelity in human relationships (e.g., Gen 18:19; 30:33; 2 Sam 8:15; Job 27:6; Prov 21:3), its most tangible exemplar is YHWH himself in remembering his covenant and delivering Israel from Egypt (e.g., 1 Sam 12:7; Ps 103:6; cf. Judg 5:11). Following YHWH's lead, Israel must keep faith in relationships (10:12a), most notably with YHWH himself (cf. Gen 18:19; 1 Kgs 3:6; Ps 106:3), as the seed that bears fruit of חֶסֶד ("mercy/devotion/lovingkindness"; 10:12b). This virtue is the sort of steadfast relational commitment that YHWH both exhibits himself as well as seeks from his people (Hos 4:1; 6:4, 6). The commands of Hos 10:12a–b encompass covenant loyalty in every dimension, both to God and to other people.

However, the agricultural metaphor of Hos 10:12 does not remain positive. The third command differs from the first two by hinting that Hosea's audience still hangs in the balance between estrangement and reconciliation with YHWH: "Till [נִיר] a hard ground [נִיר] for your own sake" (10:12c). Logically, plowing the soil (10:12c) ought to occur before the farmer sows (10:12a) and reaps (10:12b). But by concluding three imperatives in Hos 10:12 with the first and most taxing step in farming, and then pairing this final imperative verb נִירוּ ("till!") with its cognate-accusative noun נִיר ("a hard ground"; cf. Jer 4:3; Prov 13:23), Hosea emphatically warns that his hearers are still resistant toward YHWH's covenant demands. This description of apostasy resembles other OT passages that use the material properties of hardness or stiffness to describe human stubbornness (e.g., Exod 13:15; Deut 10:16). In sum, this verse confronts Israel's failure in its duty to sow faithfully but issues Judah and Jacob an urgent invitation to do so.

(b) YHWH's Warning about Raining Judgment (10:12d–e)

The pessimistic turn in Hos 10:12c follows with an urgent warning that Israel's window for repentance will soon close: "It is time to seek YHWH until he comes and is raining rightness toward you" (10:12d–e). The "time" (עֵת; 10:12d) of YHWH coming to his people is the same historical event as the arrival of the "day of rebuke" (5:9) and the "days of repayment/payback" (9:7a–b) that Hosea has mentioned earlier, namely, the pouring out of divine judgment through the Assyrian Empire. But even amidst this depiction of judgment in the realm of history, the land remains a prominent player when the rest of the verse takes the word pictures of Hos 10:12 in a different direction.

The last two clauses in Hos 10:12 literally turn the metaphor of farming upside down. In the initial

50. David J. Reimer, "צדק," *NIDOTTE* 3:750.

metaphor, the rainy season would have separated the periods of reaping (10:12a) and sowing (10:12b). But the present clause indicates that YHWH will postpone precipitation until he "comes" (בוֹא; 10:12eα), an ironic allusion to Israel's mistaken expectation that "he [YHWH] will come [בוֹא] like the rain to us" (6:3d). Alluding once more to Hos 6:3, the contrast with Israel's syncretistic nature religion intensifies when the substance that YHWH will "rain/throw" (ירה; 6:3d) down on Israel is revealed, not as creational bounty (cf. Hos 6:3) but as "rightness [צֶדֶק] for you" (10:12eβ).

What kind of strange farming is this? And what is the nature of this figurative rain? The difference between the two nominal derivatives of the root צדק ("to be righteous") that occur in Hos 10:12 (צְדָקָה in 10:12a, צֶדֶק in 10:12e) is notable. Most English Bibles render these terms identically (e.g., KJV, NIV, ESV) in that Israel's sowing of "righteousness" (10:12a) becomes a precursor to YHWH's coming to rain "righteousness" (10:12e), as if the underlying Hebrew terms are identical. However, the second term in this verse, צֶדֶק (10:12e), communicates English's abstract notion of "righteousness" (e.g., Isa 1:21; 11:5; Hos 2:21[19]) better than the concreteness of צְדָקָה as "right relating/a righteous act" (10:12a) that Israel can and must do. An idiomatic English translation is difficult, so I distinguish them by using the terms "righteousness" (10:12a) and "rightness" (10:12e). During the eighth century BCE, Israel should have worked out both relational צְדָקָה and legal צֶדֶק through practicing social justice (e.g., Isa 5:7; Amos 5:7, 24).[51]

In short, only a limited amount of time remains for Israel to do צְדָקָה before YHWH arrives as a judge. He will not only uphold his creation's צֶדֶק (Pss 89:15[14]; 97:2; cf. Deut 1:16; 16:20) but also "rain/throw [it] down" (ירה *hiphil*; 10:12e), perhaps in the manner of projectiles (cf. 1 Sam 20:20).[52] The menacing prospect of being in the moral crosshairs of creation and the Creator, as divine rains of justice prepare to fall (cf. 6:3), illustrates the urgent need for God's people to "seek YHWH" (10:12d; cf. 5:15; 7:10) in prayerful repentance.[53]

(c) Israel's Neglect of Sowing Faithfully (10:13)

In verse 13 the image shifts from YHWH as Creator and sovereign over the weather back to his people as earth's inhabitants, once again as farmers (compare a similar image of people "cultivating" faithfulness in Ps 37:3). Despite the preceding exhortations to cultivate wisely (10:11–12), the people of YHWH have done the exact opposite: "You have plowed [חרשׁ] wickedness; you have reaped [קצר] lawlessness; you have consumed [אכל] the fruit [פְּרִי] of lying" (10:13a–c). Hosea redeploys the verbs for plowing (חרשׁ) and reaping (קצר) used in Hos 10:11–12 to expose Israel's determination to pursue "wickedness" (רֶשַׁע; 10:13a) and "lawlessness" (עַוְלָתָה; 10:13b).

Hosea 10:13c supplements these general terms for sin with a reference to the "eating" (אכל) of

51. Moshe Weinfeld, "Justice and Righteousness—מִשְׁפָּט וּצְדָקָה—The Expression and Its Meaning," in *Justice and Righteousness: Biblical Themes and Their Influence*, ed. Henning Graf Reventlow and Yair Hoffman, JSOTSup 137 (Sheffield: JSOT Press, 1992), 236. On a broader note, Hosea's synergy between abstract and concrete ideas of rightness/righteousness reflects the influence of Deuteronomy, where the Hebrew root צדק ("to be right, righteous") involves both actions and dispositions relating to one's inner self, relating to deity, and relating to the family, as well as relating to others (e.g., Deut 1:16; 6:25; 9:4; 16:18, 20; 24:13; 25:15).

52. The ירה root has three homonyms: "to throw" (ירה I), "to make drenched/saturated" (ירה II), and "to teach" (ירה III). Although ירה I is nearly always in the *qal* stem (e.g., Exod 15:4; Ps 11:2), the presence of ירה *hiphil* in 1 Sam 20:20 with a clear sense of "throw" hints that the first two homonyms may overlap in meaning or even be the same root (so also BDB 434d–435b).

53. The verb for "seeking" used in Hos 10:12d (דרשׁ) and Hos 5:15; 7:10 (בקשׁ) are virtual synonyms (e.g., Deut 4:29; Judg 6:29; Ps 38:13[12]).

deceptive "fruit" (פְּרִי), a clear allusion to the account of the fall in Gen 3. Nearer to this literary context, Hosea has also attacked Israel's sins using the words אכל and פְּרִי—defilement by "eating" impure food and sacrifices (4:8; 8:13), "consuming" Israel's leaders by way of political sedition (7:7), exile as the punishment of being "consumed" by fire (8:13–14), and the illicit "fruit" of sexualized nature rituals (9:16; 10:1–2). Therefore, Hos 10:13a–c is a summary statement that the people of YHWH have failed to heed the many warnings given through his prophet.

But abruptly at the end of Hos 10:13, the scene shifts from the farm back to history, coinciding with the discourse's shift in grammar from plural (10:13a–c) back to singular: "For [כִּי] you [2nd masc. sg.] have trusted in your [2nd masc. sg.] way, in the greatness of your [2nd masc. sg.] strength" (10:13d). The two features noted in brackets clarify an otherwise opaque relationship between creation and history in this verse. First, an explanatory use of the conjunction כִּי ("for, since, because"; 10:13d) links the just-named sins of farming and feasting (10:13a–c) to their ultimate expression in the historical sphere of imperialism (10:13d).

Second, these verses borrow a notable rhetorical device from Deuteronomy, where changing the grammatical person from second-person plural to singular marks a climax in the argument—Hosea no longer addresses the audience as plural individuals but corporately as a singular nation (e.g., Deut 1:20–21).[54] The preceding clauses about creation (10:13a–c) involve second-person plural forms and speak more to individuals, but the present section about history (10:13d) shifts to the grammatical singular so as to attack the nation as a whole for its tendency to "trust" (בטח; cf. Isa 30:12; 31:1; Amos 6:1) in realpolitik (cf. 5:18–7:16).[55]

To summarize and unpack the tightly crafted poetry of Hos 10:12–13, which serves as a virtual microcosm of the book—the seeds of Israel's syncretism with Canaanite ideas, as sown by individual Israelites, eventually blossom and yield the fruit of the nation's systemic sins of imperialism, with its many interdependencies among economics, religion, and politics.

c. Examples of Judgment in History, Part II (10:14–15)

(1) The Verdict of Judgment (10:14a–b)

YHWH responds to his people's sins (cf. 10:12–13) with the determination that Israelite imperialism will become its own undoing. The hint of history's reappearance on the scene (10:13d) becomes explicit in a prediction of imminent invasion: "Then an uproar will rise among your people, and all your fortifications will be devastated" (10:14a–b). The noisy panic of "uproar" (שָׁאוֹן; 10:14a, cf. Isa 17:12) will accompany the destruction of Israel's "fortifications" (מִבְצָרִים; 10:14b), formerly a cause for pride in guarding Israel's "fortified cities" (עָרִים בְּצֻרוֹת; Hos 8:14) but now the source of terrifying noise when they crash to the ground. As elsewhere in Hosea, YHWH's reckoning for apostasy in the future (10:14a–b) and present (10:15) will follow the historical pattern of the past (10:14c–d).

(2) The Past Case of Shalman and Beth-Arbel (10:14c–d)

Hosea reinforces the verdict that Israel's apostasy will lead to destruction (9:9; 10:9) by recalling an event not mentioned elsewhere in the OT: "As

54. Timothy A. Lenchak, *Choose Life!: A Rhetorical-Critical Investigation of Deuteronomy 28,69–30,20*, AnBib 129 (Rome: Pontifical Biblical Institute, 1993), 12–16.

55. Machinist, "Hosea and the Ambiguity of Kingship in Ancient Israel," 178.

when Shalman destroyed Beth-Arbel in the day of battle, [when] a mother was dashed to pieces in front of her children" (10:14c–d). Here the "day of battle" (יוֹם מִלְחָמָה; 10:14c, cf. 1 Sam 13:22; Amos 1:14) refers to a military confrontation about which the audience would have known and therefore required no explanation.[56] To this general allusion, Hosea adds the terrifying specificity of a mother being "dashed to pieces" (רטשׁ *pual*) in the presence of her little ones. The past trauma of witnessing this brutality will soon recur when Israel's children themselves suffer the same war crime of being "dashed to pieces" (14:1[13:16]).

(3) The Present Case of Bethel/Israel (10:15)

Lest this ghastly picture (cf. 10:14) cause misgivings about YHWH's justice, Hosea again declares that ultimate responsibility lies with the people of Israel. The past case of Beth-Arbel (i.e., "the house of Arbel") is replicating itself in the current case of Bethel (i.e., "the house of God"): "Thus he has done to you [2nd masc. pl.], O Bethel, because of your extreme wickedness" (10:15a). Here the prophet shifts back to plural address (cf. 10:13a–b) to emphasize the culpability of "Bethel" (בֵּית־אֵל, "house of God"), by now a familiar target in Hosea due to Bethel's calf cult and syncretistic rituals (10:5–6; cf. 8:5–6).

According to Hos 10:15a, the inhabitants of Bethel are guilty of "extreme wickedness" (רָעַת רָעַתְכֶם, lit. "the wickedness of your wickedness"), a superlative Hebrew expression that escalates the prophet's earlier attacks on Israel's "wickedness" (רָעָה; e.g., 7:1–3; 9:15).[57] Given this conceptual bridge through forms of רָעָה, the manifold sins of Bethel appear to symbolize the apostasy of the entire Northern Kingdom. Hosea supports this argument by announcing that the historical sins of this city will lead to the collapse of the monarchy itself: "At dawn the king of Israel will be completely destroyed" (10:15b). Israel's fate of "being destroyed" (דמה *niphal*; 10:15b) by exile in Assyria is like an infestation that grows irrepressibly—a pestilence that rises in Israel's hierarchy from the people (4:5–6), to the whole nation, and finally to the king himself (10:15). What hope remains for a nation that is rotting upward from its roots?

4. The Cycles and Metaphors of Salvation History (11:1–11)

Hosea 11:1–11 offers a sublime answer to this question by retracing the events of salvation history. This exceptional divine monologue combines recital of events in salvation history with word pictures from the spheres of family (e.g., parent, child) and animals (e.g., shepherd/heifer and lion) to offer a remarkable portrayal of the covenant between God and his people.

The many intricacies of chapter 11 are difficult to capture in a literary outline. On the one hand, it exhibits signs of a rough chronological progression from past (11:1–4) to near future (11:5–6) and eschatological future (11:10–11), with rhetorical questions and their answers (vv. 89) that signal the turning point between these horizons. On the other hand, a geographical movement is evident in the reversal of the exodus from Egypt (11:1) to an "anti-exodus" from the land to exile (11:5–7). Israel's return from exile becomes a "new exodus" (11:10–11),[58] again with Hos 11:8–9 as

56. On the likelihood that "house of Arbel" (בֵּית אַרְבֵאל) actually refers to a city called "Beth-Arbel" in the Transjordanian region of Gilead, see Dearman, *Hosea*, 273, 373–74.

57. E.g., "Song of Songs" (שִׁיר הַשִּׁירִים) as "the *greatest* Song," "holy of holies" (קֹדֶשׁ הַקֳּדָשִׁים) as "the *most Holy* Place."

58. Silva Retamales, "Tradición del 'Éxodo' en Oseas," 151–52. However, I reject his adoption of the commonly proposed emendation of 11:5a from "he will *not* [לֹא] return to Egypt" (i.e., the MT reading) to "he shall return to Egypt" (i.e., eliminating the usual negative sense of לֹא by taking it as

a pivot. However, neither a chronological nor a geographical outline accounts completely for the fits and starts in an emotionally charged passage where YHWH pours out his longsuffering heart for his people.[59]

Overall, Hos 11 offers a classic case of a "lyrical plot"[60] that subordinates time and geography to a nonlinear development of estrangement, judgment, and reconciliation as themes in YHWH's dealings with Israel. Therefore, the commentary below will make a provisional attempt to trace the majestic speech of the incomparable God of Israel. Since YHWH himself declares at the climax of this passage, "For I am God and [I am] not a man" (11:9c–d), human concepts and categories are forever inadequate to describe him completely.

a. The Events of Salvation History (11:1–2)

YHWH begins the present cycle about salvation history (cf. 9:10, 15) by recounting a stark contrast between Israel's adoption and Israel's apostasy. Although Israel received grace in the exodus (11:1), this blessed nation consistently repaid YHWH with ingratitude and disobedience (11:2). This recital of historical events sets the stage for the emotionally charged metaphors of salvation history that follow (11:3–4).

(1) Adoption in the Exodus (11:1)

The exodus from Egypt initiated the process in which Israel became a member of YHWH's household: "Because/when [כִּי] Israel was a child, I loved him, and from Egypt I called my son" (11:1). Although numbered as a new chapter in our Bibles, Hos 11 opens with a conjunction כִּי ("when, because, for"; 11:1aα) that links the present passage with the conclusion of chapter 10. The conjunction could exhibit senses of both "because" and "when" in this literary context. On the one hand, the future certainty of judgment (10:9–15) meets YHWH's assertion that this judgment is tragically necessary *because* Israel is his son (v. 1aα). At the same time, the unchangeable *when* of God's love for his son in the exodus (v.1aα) grounds the theological truth that reconciliation will eventually triumph over estrangement (vv. 1aβ–11).[61] In fact, the emotional intensity of this passage suggests that כִּי also slows the discourse as a deictic interjection—"Look!"—that focuses attention on YHWH's personal involvement in salvation history.[62]

Hosea 11:1 also heralds this turn from estrangement to reconciliation with the return of first-person address (cf. 10:12–15). In a poignant declaration, the God of Israel states that "love" (אהב; cf. 3:1) was his heart's motivation that powerfully transformed his people from a generic "child" (נַעַר; 11:1a) to the privileged status of "my son" (בְּנִי; 11:1b). The נַעַר is the impressionable and sometimes addled youth (e.g., Prov 1:4; Isa 3:4; Jer 1:6),[63] a fitting description of Israel's plight before the exodus. For YHWH to "call [קרא] my son" (11:1b) is to extend an ancient formula for adoption to his

emphatic). Some translations reflect this emendation (e.g., NRSV), while others accept the MT reading but take the entire clause as a question rather than a statement (e.g., NIV). In contrast, the commentary below will argue for the coherence of MT Hos 11:5 in the present context as a statement.

59. Matthieu Richelle, "La structure et l'interprétation d'Osée 11," *RHPR* 88 (2008): 233–35.

60. See n. 4 above.

61. Mark S. Gignilliat, "For Israel Was A Child: A Case for the Causal Sense of כי in Hosea 11,1," *ZAW* 121 (2009): 277–80.

62. On this discourse function for כִּי, see Carl M. Follingstad, *Deictic Viewpoint in Biblical Hebrew Text: A Syntagmatic and Paradigmatic Analysis of the Particle* כִּי *(Kî)* (Dallas: SIL International, 2001), 53.

63. Though by no means poor or underprivileged in any way, since OT references to נַעַר clearly denote someone of relatively high birth (as shown by John MacDonald, "The Status and Role of the *Naʿar* in Israelite Society," *JNES* 35 [1976]: 147–70).

assumption of parental responsibility for an entire nation (cf. Exod 4:22; Deut 14:1).[64] Other peoples of the ancient Near East typically viewed kings as the exclusive son of a patron deity, making YHWH's adoption of a whole people unique in its cultural context.[65] This portrait of covenant as kinship also redirects the attention in YHWH's household from marital betrayal in the recent past (Hos 1–3) to that of a parent's love for their child from the very beginning of their relationship. YHWH has now become the parent of Israel rather than just the human patriarch whose apostate descendants the book had previously named as "the children of Israel" (e.g., 2:1–2[1:10–11]; 3:4–5).

(2) Apostasy in the Land (11:2)

Other voices besides YHWH's (cf. 11:1b) also "call" (קרא) to and from Israel, as Hos 9–10 records about the troubled family history of Israel (and chapters 12–13 explore further). Following the exodus from Egypt (11:1), apostate voices that sought to sway Israel toward political sins came quickly: "They [Israel] called to them [to Egypt], then they [Israel] went away from them [toward Assyria]" (11:2a–b; cf. 7:11). This awkward rendering accepts the MT's shift from first-person (11:1) to third-person plural forms (11:2) as well as the various ambiguities of third-person plural "they" and "them." Most English versions (with the notable exceptions of the NKJV and NASB) rely on the ancient witnesses in emending Hos 11:2 to first-person verbs or changing to the passive voice to resolve these issues.[66]

However, the same pair of plural verbs, קָרְאוּ ("they called"; 11:2a) and הָלְכוּ ("they went"; 11:2b) in the MT matches those in the earlier exposé of how Israel "called" (קָרָאוּ; 7:11c) for Egypt and "went" (הָלָכוּ; 7:11d) toward Assyria.[67] The broader context of Hos 11 also suggests a skittish reaction to imperialism through the mention of Egypt (11:1b) and YHWH's claim to be the only one who can "heal" Israel (11:3), over and against the mistaken notion that Assyria was able or willing to "heal" (5:13; 7:1). Hosea thereby contrasts between the exodus as YHWH's deliverance from imperialism (11:1) and Israel's irrational desire for an anti-exodus that gravitates toward the power politics of the nations (11:2a–b).

In addition to the realm of politics (cf. 11:2a–b), Israel also expressed its syncretism in cultic worship: "To the Baals they kept sacrificing, and to idols they kept offering incense" (11:2c–d). Earlier passages in Hosea have identified plural "Baals" and other idols as visible signs of a holistic system that includes economics, politics, and religion (e.g., 2:10[8], 15[13]). It is also possible that Baal deities function as an elliptical and delayed referent for "they" earlier in the verse, especially since such a referent would contrast starkly between YHWH who "calls" Israel in one direction (11:1b) even as the Baals "call" in another (11:2a). Given the messiness of Israel's entanglements in syncretism,

64. Janet L. R. Melnyk, "'When Israel Was a Child': Ancient Near Eastern Adoption Formulas and the Relationship between God and Israel," in *History and Interpretation: Essays in Honour of John H. Hayes*, ed. M. Patrick Graham, William P. Brown, and Jeffrey K. Kuan, JSOTSup 173 (Sheffield: JSOT Press, 1993), 251.

65. See discussion of "The Portrayal of YHWH as Israel's Kin in Hosea" in the introduction to Hosea, pp. 37–41. Cf. Richard D. Patterson, "Parental Love as a Metaphor for Divine-Human Love," *JETS* 46 (2003): 206–8.

66. E.g., NRSV/NLT: "The more *I* called them/him, the more/farther they/he went/moved from me"; NIV/ESV: "The more they *were* called, the more they went away from me." Similar renderings are offered by Dearman, *Hosea*, 275; Stuart, *Hosea–Jonah*, 174; Jörg Jeremias, *Der Prophet Hosea*, ATD 24/1 (Göttingen: Vandenhoeck & Ruprecht, 1983), 138.

67. Macintosh, *Hosea*, 439; Andersen and Freedman, *Hosea*, 578.

the precise identity of "they" is clearly a pagan influence and becomes somewhat moot.

Hosea 11:1–2 and the following verses serve as the OT framework for how Hos 11:1 is famously applied to Jesus Christ as a prophecy of his own exodus from Egypt: "He remained there until the death of Herod. This was to fulfill what had been spoken by the Lord through the prophet: 'Out of Egypt I called my son'" (Matt 2:15). Rather than being a direct prophecy of the Messiah, the reuse of Hos 11:1 in Matt 2:15 envisages Jesus as the overcomer of Israel's penchant for choosing the historical paradigm of exile rather than exodus, as described in the rest of Hos 11.

In indirect prophetic typology such as this, the interpreter must consider carefully the literary flow of the entire OT passage that stands in the background, despite the fact that the NT quotation only cites a single verse.[68] We will discuss Matthew's use of this passage later under "Canonical and Theological Significance," after we have explored the message of Hos 11 in its original context.

b. The Metaphors of Salvation History (11:3–4)

The emotional stakes of the passage ratchet up considerably as Hosea moves from the events of salvation history (11:1–2) to the heartfelt metaphors associated with it. In the space of just two verses, the prophet's kaleidoscope moves quickly through three metaphors in the familial realm—the tenderness of YHWH as parent (11:3a–b), the ignorance of Israel as child (11:3c–d), and YHWH's provision of guidance as both parent and shepherd (11:4).

(1) A Parent's Tenderness (11:3a–b)

The series of familial metaphors begins with the musings of Israel's divine parent. Although his son has continually wandered away and is now far from him (cf. 11:2), YHWH reminisces about a more innocent time when the child was taking his first steps: "As for me [וְאָנֹכִי], I taught Ephraim to walk" (11:3a). The tender וְאָנֹכִי ("as for me" or "on my part") is not grammatically necessary and pauses the discourse to emphasize YHWH's hands-on involvement in the parental action of "teaching to walk" (רגל *tiphel*; 11:3a). This is apparently a rare causative form of a verb that derives from the noun "feet" (רֶגֶל).[69] The nurturing picture continues with YHWH breaking the toddler's fall by "taking them by their arms" (11:3b), an expression that recalls two related episodes from Israel's past—YHWH's deliverance from Egypt by his mighty "arm" (e.g., Exod 6:6; 15:6) as well as his guidance in Israel's journeys through the wilderness and into Canaan (e.g., Deut 11:2; 26:8). The events of salvation history (Hos 11:1–2) evoke its metaphors (vv. 3–4) and vice versa.

(2) A Child's Ignorance (11:3c–d)

However, Israel has been ignorant of YHWH's care. This motif comes to the fore when YHWH temporarily assumes the persona of a doctor who confronts a patient in denial: "But they have not known [לֹא ידע] that I healed [רפא] them" (11:3c–d). To the mounting distress of YHWH and his prophet, the objects of "not-knowing" (לֹא ידע) and "lack of knowledge" (אֵין־דַּעַת) on Israel's part have been troublingly broad in the book of Hosea—both divine provision in creation (2:10[8]) and the

68. G. K. Beale, *Handbook on the New Testament Use of the Old Testament: Exegesis and Interpretation* (Grand Rapids: Baker Academic, 2012), 44.

69. GKC §55h. Macintosh (*Hosea*, 442–43) provides a full history of interpretation for this difficult verbal form, with most interpreters suggesting that it refers to guidance and education by a parent. Contrast the detailed philological argument of Jeremy M. Hutton and Safwat Marzouk, "The Morphology of the tG-Stem in Hebrew and *Tirgaltî* in Hos 11:3," *JHebS* 12 (2009): 1–42, who deny that Hos 11:3a contains the *tiphel* causative stem but offer no constructive alternative.

stipulations of the Decalogue (4:1). Such ignorance of God and his ways is reflected in spiritual harlotry (5:4), confusing YHWH with Baal (6:3), misunderstanding worship of YHWH to be a multitude of sacrifices (6:6), and syncretism that results in the nations coming to deport oblivious Israel (7:9).

Each kind of not-knowing symptomizes the deeper sickness of apostasy that YHWH has sought to "heal" (רפא; cf. 6:1; 7:1; 14:5[4]).[70] But once again, the bungling patient named "Ephraim/double fruitfulness" (אֶפְרַיִם; 11:3a) ignores YHWH's offer to "heal" (רפא; 11:3d). This pun mocks the object by reversing the first three Hebrew letters of this alternative epithet for Israel (cf. 8:9).

(3) A Parent's/Farmer's Provision (11:4)

Verse 4 interposes the depiction of YHWH's unrequited care between the metaphors of parenthood and animal husbandry. Scholars debate how these spheres overlap,[71] because the "cords of a man" (חַבְלֵי אָדָם; 11:4a) and "bands of love" (בַּעֲבֹתוֹת אַהֲבָה; 11:4a) seem to work across both.[72] Favoring a parental interpretation is the fact that "[covenantal] love" (אהב) characterizes these fetters, since Hosea's other references to this verbal root clearly belong to the familial realm (e.g., 3:1). But the metaphorical frame may also shift to a husbanding picture since "cords" and "bonds" are the farmer's usual tools for tying domestic animals, as when the same terms function figuratively in YHWH's condemnation of the unjust as "those who drag iniquity with the cords of [חַבְלֵי] falsehood, and sin like bonds of [עֲבֹת] an ox-cart" (Isa 5:18). The English term "harness" would be an appropriate way of bridging these spheres since such an object serves as a safety restraint for both toddlers and domestic animals.

Indeed, YHWH appears to have intentionally mixed metaphors of domestic relations when he characterizes himself among "those who lift the yoke [עֹל] from their jaws" (11:4b).[73] Hosea has twice described Israel as a bovine creature—both a stubborn heifer (4:16) as well as a trained heifer (10:11). Reversal of judgment fits well within this conceptual world of animals as the lifting of the "yoke" or moving it to a less uncomfortable position (11:4b).[74] At the same time, the "yoke" in other OT passages can denote the heavy burden of exile that YHWH has leveled upon his people but will someday break (cf. Lev 26:13), both in prophecies contemporaneous with Hosea (e.g., Isa 9:3[4]; 10:27) as well as in Jeremiah and Ezekiel, the earliest interpreters of Hosea's prophetic oracles (e.g., Jer 27:8; 30:8; Ezek 34:27).[75]

Indeed the closing picture of YHWH as one who will "bend down to them, I will feed [them]" (11:4c–d) is equally at home in the parental and animal domains. Whether as wandering child or animal (and likely some kaleidoscopic combination of both), Israel has continually rejected YHWH (11:2–3) despite his tender leading since the days of the exodus (11:1, 4). YHWH has truly been a pastor of his wayward people/sheep in every sense of this rich biblical metaphor (e.g., Pss 23:1; 80:1; Ezek 34:12–16).

70. Cf. D. F. O'Kennedy, "Healing As/Or Forgiveness? The Use of the Term רפא in the Book of Hosea," *OTE* 14 (2001): 458–74, who argues that the concept of forgiveness subsumes the metaphor of healing.

71. See overview of possibilities in Eidevall, *Grapes in the Desert*, 172–74.

72. Joy Philip Kakkanattu, *God's Enduring Love in the Book of Hosea: A Synchronic and Diachronic Analysis of Hosea 11,1–11*, FAT 14 (Tübingen: Mohr Siebeck, 2006), 58–63.

73. McConville, "Language about God in Hosea," 188–89.

74. Kathryn Chapman, "Hosea 11:1–4—Images of a Loving Parent," *RevExp* 90 (1993): 266.

75. Thus, a human/compassionate side to the metaphor does not require revocalizing Hos 11:4b from "yoke" (עֹל) to "infant/child" (עֻל), a move that yields a Hebrew text with an adorable picture but no support in the ancient witnesses. Several English versions reflect this unfounded text-critical decision: "I was to them like those who lift *infants* to their cheeks" (NRSV); "To them I was like one who lifts a *little child* to the cheek" (NIV).

c. The Reversals of Salvation History (11:5–7)

The picture of a meandering journey continues in vv. 5–7 with a portrayal of Israel on the move from its own land. Salvation history will come to an end when the people's lot changes from exodus to exile: "He will not return [שׁוּב] to the land of Egypt; but Assyria will be his king, since they refused to repent [שׁוּב]" (11:5). The two senses of the root שׁוּב as "return" (11:5a) and "repent" (11:5c) are both present and frame YHWH's countercultural message about empire in this verse.[76]

(1) The Journey of Exile: From Exodus to Anti-Exodus (11:5)

As noted above, some translations revise Hos 11:5a to speak positively of Egypt in a manner resembling other passages about Israel's return *to* Egypt (8:13; 9:3) or eventual restoration *from* Egypt (11:11). Since taking the MT at face value seems at first to contravene these passages, it is understandable that the NIV, among other translations, offers a compromise by rendering these clauses as ambiguous rhetorical questions. The following rendering emphasizes the certainty of exile while leaving open the issue of Israel's destination: "Will they not return to Egypt and will not Assyria rule over them because they refuse to repent?" (11:5 NIV).[77]

Although this verse is difficult, the anti-imperial opening to the chapter supports the MT; YHWH hereby denies Israel the escapism of Egypt as a refuge (cf. 7:11; 2 Kgs 17:4).[78] Rather than contradicting his predictions of a return to Egypt,[79] we need to see Hosea's references to places of nonpunishment as part of a delicate balance in a biblical theology of the nations, especially as presented in passages such as 5:8–7:16. The prophet forbids Israel from trusting in powerful empires such as Egypt and Assyria while describing them as YHWH's designated instruments of poetic justice when Israel persists in trusting them.

These complementary aspects to Hosea's presentation of empire have played out sequentially in the history of Israel. In Hos 11:5 the apostasy of God's people running to a minor empire (i.e., Egypt) can only be cured by the homeopathic remedy of suffering under an even greater, crueler empire (i.e., Assyria; cf. 8:7–9; 9:3; 10:6). And broadening this picture to the bigger storyline of Israel's history, exile to Assyria represents an anti-exodus to Mesopotamia that overturns the ancient exodus that Abraham once experienced when YHWH brought him from Ur to Canaan (Gen 15:7; Neh 9:7).

Two features of Hos 11:5 foreground the idea that YHWH sovereignly uses power politics to accomplish his purposes. First, he characterizes Assyria's relationship to Israel as "his king" (מַלְכּוֹ; 11:5b)—the imperial despot to whom Israel has chosen to offer loyalty, only to receive destruction in return! To suffer domination under a foreign king is a fitting punishment for Israel's syncretism with ancient Near Eastern kingship, as Hosea emphasizes in his portrayal of pagan models of leadership

76. LeCureux, *The Thematic Unity of the Book of the Twelve*, 75.

77. On the possibility of rendering the initial לֹא as the introduction to a negative rhetorical question, see Hos 10:9c and n45 above. The NIV rendering also harmonizes the inconsistency between singular (11:5a–b) and plural (11:5c) masculine pronouns in a manner similar to the NASB, ESV, NLT, and NRSV.

78. Mignon R. Jacobs, "YHWH's Call for Israel's 'Return': Command, Invitation, or Threat," *HBT* 32 (2010): 19–20; Macintosh, *Hosea*, 451.

79. This inconsistency explains NRSV's rendering of the particle לֹא with an asseverative force (i.e., "shall, surely") rather its usual meaning of negation (i.e., "not"). Although Andersen and Freedman (*Hosea*, 583–84) agree with this rendering, Macintosh (*Hosea*, 451) notes that the contradiction disappears upon realizing that the return and nonreturn to Egypt passages in Hosea (i.e., 7:11; 8:13; 9:3; 11:5) address different historical situations in Israel's fickle-relationship with empire.

as their own downfall (e.g., 7:5–7; 8:4–8). Israel has suffered a demotion from YHWH's beloved child (11:1) to the subject of an uncaring foreign ruler.

Second, Hosea depicts Assyria's rule over Israel as a direct consequence of a refusal to "repent" (שׁוּב; 11:5c). This statement plays on the verb שׁוּב, which the verse's opening clause (11:5a) employs in the sense of repentance as a figurative "return." The wordplay underscores that Israel's physical inability to return to Egypt (11:5a) results from the deeper spiritual problem of refusing to return to YHWH (11:5c). The determination to pursue strength like the nations weakens Israel because of increasing estrangement from YHWH.

(2) The Punishment of Exile: Two Kinds of Ruin (11:6–7)

Israel's obsession with its national security will ironically result in two kinds of ruin. The first will be the physical ruin that results from a military invasion: "So a sword will twirl in their cities, and will put an end to their gate-bars, and will consume because of their plans" (11:6). Earlier in Hos 8:14, the book had described the destruction of Israel's fortified cities. The present verse adds the disquieting picture that the enemy's "sword" (חֶרֶב; 11:6a, cf. 7:16; 14:1[13:16]) will "twirl/whirl" (חול; 11:6a) like a dancer (e.g., Judg 21:21, 23; cf. Jer 23:19) before "exterminating" (כלה *piel*; 11:6b) and finally "consuming/eating" (אכל; 11:6c). These personifications of weaponry reinforce the image of Assyria's armies as ruthless—a brutality well attested in the historical record.[80]

Israel cannot ultimately blame the awfulness of such a fate on YHWH or his human agents. Instead, Hosea asserts that all this happens because of "their plans" (11:6c). Along with its synonym עֵצָה from the same root יעץ ("to advise, counsel"), the term מוֹעֵצָה ("counsel, plan, strategy") refers to the mistaken political advice that the two kingdoms of Israel should trust in the empires of the eighth century BCE rather than in YHWH's incomparable power (e.g., Hos 10:6; Isa 30:1; 36:5). However, by choosing realpolitik over faith in YHWH during the Assyrian crises of the eighth century BCE, this pragmatic people will eventually be shattered by the very empires they have sought for help.

To his verdict of physical ruin (11:6) YHWH adds the dimension of spiritual ruin: "But as for my people, they are stuck on apostasy [מְשׁוּבָה] from me" (11:7a). מְשׁוּבָה ("apostasy, unfaithfulness"; cf. 14:5[4]) is a nominal derivative of the root שׁוב ("to return, repent"), which occurs twice in v. 5. The inability of Israel to "return" to both Egypt and YHWH (11:5) despite the chastisement of exile (11:6) symptomizes a deep-seated intransigence on Israel's part. YHWH pointedly observes how they remain "*my* people" but are set on "apostasy from *me*." These first-person pronouns embody the agonizing theological tension between estrangement and reconciliation that characterizes both this chapter and the entire book.[81]

Because this apostate people are in limbo between estrangement and reconciliation, their prayers will be ineffective: "Although to one above they will call [קרא] together, he will not lift [רום] them up" (11:7b–c). The verbs in brackets specify the nature of Israel's apostasy (cf. 11:7a), as well as having already appeared in Hos 11. The first, קרא ("to call"), denotes Israel's rejection of YHWH's

80. In one version of Shalmaneser III's annals, for example, this Assyrian king boasts of his exploits against an enemy city: "I decisively defeated them. I felled with the sword their fighting men. Like Adad, I rained down upon them a devastating flood. I piled them in ditches [and] filled the extensive plain with the corpses of their warriors. Like wool, I dyed the mountain with their blood. I took away from them . . . numerous chariots [and] teams of horses. I made a pile of heads in front of his city. I razed, destroyed [and] burned his cities" ("Shalmaneser III: Kurkh Monolith," trans. K. Lawson Younger, Jr. [*COS* 2.113A:262]).

81. Wolff, *Hosea*, 201.

gracious "call" (11:1) in favor of a "call" in the opposite direction to empires and their Baalized worship (11:2). Their present attempt to "call" (קרא; 11:7b) will fail since they are caught in syncretism, though it is unclear whether "one above" (עַל) to whom the people pray refers to YHWH or perhaps is a mockery of Baal deities (i.e., בַּעַל from v. 2, which rhymes in Hebrew with עַל).

Whichever deity is in view, Israel's supplications are futile because their object will not "lift" (רום) them, the second verb that the chapter repeats. Earlier, YHWH had graciously promised to "lift" (רום) the yoke from Israel and care for his people (11:4). But punishment becomes unavoidable when "one above" (11:7b) refuses to "raise [up]" (רום) Israel from a lowly position (11:7c). Conjoining the images of 11:4 and 11:7, Israel is a child or animal that is finally left to go its own way by a deity who has distanced himself. In fact, even the grammatical level of this verse reflects the ambiguity of whom Israel seeks in prayer, for YHWH's speech withdraws from the intimacy of first-person address (11:7a) to speaking of the functional deity of Israel in the third person (11:7b–c), whether himself or a rival like Baal. As elsewhere (e.g., 5:8–7:16; 8:1–9:9), Hosea signals the growing distance between YHWH and Israel through a change to impersonal address. What will happen to Israel now that YHWH is no longer on speaking terms with his people?

d. A New Beginning to Salvation History: The Rekindling of YHWH's Compassion (11:8–11)

Without warning and just as estrangement seems to have the last word, YHWH's personal speech reappears in the next section to offer Israel a new beginning. YHWH's return to speaking as first-person "I" (11:8–9) is the key that makes reconciliation possible in salvation history (cf. 2:21–25[19–23]; 14:6[5]). Indeed, YHWH promises to give Israel a new salvation history by gathering his people whom the exile had scattered from the west to the east, from Egypt all the way to Assyria (11:10–11).

(1) YHWH's Turn from Anger to Compassion (11:8–9)

The sudden divine monologue begins with four introspective, piercing questions in vv. 8–9. YHWH's questions are not directed at himself but are utterances for "you" to overhear so that Hosea's prodigal audience might grasp the enormous pain that they have inflicted on their God.[82]

The first two questions in the series reflect the testing of YHWH's resolve to destroy Israel. He declares his unwillingness to put an end to his people: "How could I give you over, O Ephraim? [How could] I hand you up, O Israel?" (11:8a–b).[83] The last two questions voice YHWH's determination to treat his people differently from other peoples, notwithstanding the fact that they deserve the same judgment: "How could I give you over like [at] Admah? [How could] I make you like [at] Zeboiim?" (11:8c–d). Admah and Zeboiim were cities in the vicinity of Sodom and Gomorrah (Deut 29:22[23]; cf. Gen 10:19), the two wicked cities of the Transjordan (Gen 13:10–13) whose destruction became proverbial OT examples of how the God of all nations must punish evil (e.g., Deut 32:32; Isa 13:19; Zeph 2:9).[84]

YHWH's heart then turns—the implicit answer to his musing over whether to destroy Israel is, "I could never!" Although Israel has often acted like

82. Dearman, *Hosea*, 287.

83. In this poetic technique called ellipsis, the interrogative in Hos 11:8a ("How?") does double duty as the interrogative for Hos 11:8b as well.

84. Christopher J. H. Wright, *The Mission of God's People: A Biblical Theology of the Church's Mission* (Grand Rapids: Zondervan, 2010), 84–86.

Sodom and Gomorrah (e.g., Isa 1:9–10), YHWH will not "overthrow" (הפך) his guilty people, as he had those cities (cf. Gen 19:21, 25, 29), but rather the dispositions of his inner life: "My heart is overthrown [הפך *niphal*] within me" (11:8e; cf. Jer 31:20). Whereas הפך describes the violent "overthrow" of Sodom and Gomorrah, it would be a grave mistake to understand Hos 11:8 to be YHWH's conflicted self-depiction as "a recovering God of violence."[85]

Instead it is the "heart/mind" (לֵב; 11:8e) of YHWH that is in anguish due to love and wrath simultaneously welling up toward his estranged people.[86] לֵב (along with its by-form לֵבָב) in Hebrew denotes the inner seat of feeling and thought in humans.[87] But it is theologically hazardous to apply the same concept to divinity in claiming without qualification that "[a] war is taking place within the battlefield of God's heart [לֵב]."[88]

All anthropopathic expressions (as in Hos 11:8) remain limited in their ability to portray an infinitely holy God (11:9).[89] While human language and imagery can never portray God exhaustively, it is equally impossible to speak about God meaningfully without some appeal to human experience.[90] So following Thomas Weinandy's thoughtful analysis of Abraham Heschel, it is more appropriate to interpret Hos 11:8–9 with the caution that "[s]tatements of divine pathos must not be lowered to the human level, but raised to the 'superhuman' level."[91]

We must neither deny nor exaggerate the significance of describing struggle or change in YHWH's emotional life, as when the last clause of the verse shifts the image from pain (11:8e) to that of heat: "My compassions [נִחֻמִים] are kindled to warmth [כמר]" (11:8f). כמר ("to be/become warm") can refer to heat generated by an "oven" (תַּנּוּר; Lam 5:10). Earlier Hosea had used the latter term three times as a figure for Ephraim's bloodlust (7:4), the physical warmth of drunkenness (7:6), and an assassin's smoldering excitement (7:7). But in Hos 11:8–9, the domain of heat loses these base associations by joining the relational domain of נִחֻמִים ("compassions"), a term of others-centeredness that can also mean "comfort" (e.g., Isa 57:18; Zech 1:13).

Hosea 11:9 expounds on this change in YHWH's emotions. Although YHWH referred vehemently in an earlier passage to "my anger" (אַפִּי; 8:5; cf. 14:5[4]), his wrath will no longer burn as before since "I will not carry out my fiery anger [אַפִּי], nor will I return to destroy Ephraim" (11:9a–b). As divine anger is thus extinguished, what bursts into flame is instead the pathos of YHWH—his "divine relatedness to humanity"[92]—which necessitates a reversal from wrath to mercy. Again, here we should be cautious about speaking too readily about YHWH as changing his mind or vacillating between anger and compassion.[93] How an

85. This is the terminology of Brueggemann, "Recovering God of Hosea," 19.

86. Kitamori, *Theology of the Pain of God*, 21: "The 'pain' of God reflects his will to love the object of his wrath."

87. Mark S. Smith, "The Heart and Innards in Israelite Emotional Expressions: Notes from Anthropology and Psychobiology," *JBL* 117 (1998): 431–32.

88. Barbara M. Leung Lai, "Hearing God's Bitter Cries (Hosea 11:1–9): Reading, Emotive-Experiencing, Appropriation," *HBT* 26 (2004): 33.

89. Cf. Frederik Lindström, "'I Am God and Not Human' (Hos 11,9): Can Divine Compassion Overcome Our Anthropomorphisms?," *SJOT* 29 (2015): 135–51.

90. Soskice, *Metaphor and Religious Language*, 142–53.

91. Weinandy, *Does God Suffer?*, 66.

92. Dennis Ngien, "'The Most Moved Mover': Abraham Heschel's Theology of Divine Pathos in Response to the 'Unmoved Mover' of Traditional Theism," *ERT* 25 (2001): 138.

93. Contrast, for example, Geir Hoaas, "Passion and Compassion of God in the Old Testament: A Theological Survey of Hos 11,8–9; Jer 31,20, and Isa 63,9+15," *SJOT* 11 (1997): 148–49; J. Gerald Janzen, "Metaphor and Reality in Hosea 11," *Semeia* 24 (1982): 18, 36; Andersen and Freedman, *Hosea*, 588.

indescribable God reveals himself through human categories involves a certain mystery, as the next two clauses show.

The people of YHWH cannot impute their own experience of the disjunction between anger and compassion to their God. YHWH reasons that he is in a class by himself: "For I am God and [I am] not a man, [I am] a Holy One in your midst" (11:9c–e). Both in the OT and in this passage, the divine attribute of holiness is less about inscrutable otherness and more about the intensity of his presence "in your midst" (בְּקִרְבְּךָ; 11:9e).[94] This prepositional phrase recalls the powerful yet intimate manifestation of YHWH's presence in Israel as his people journeyed from Egypt to Canaan (e.g., Deut 6:15; 7:21).

The common tendency to equate the theological categories of transcendence and immanence straightforwardly with YHWH's distance and nearness, respectively,[95] cannot do justice to the mystery of a holy God who yearns, even to the point of pain, to remain among his sinful people.[96] The covenantal background to Hos 11 means that the "not-returning" statements of YHWH in Hos 11:9 entail only the intensely relational manner of God's presence rather than his absence.[97] It is precisely the attribute of holiness that leads YHWH to offer Israel a new future characterized by salvation rather than destruction.[98] This moving monologue by YHWH therefore offers compelling reasons for Israel to return to YHWH—the Holy One is not as remote or imposing as he might seem.

(2) Israel's New Salvation History (11:10–11)

A new chapter will dawn in salvation history when Israel heeds this call to return. The first step is that a lion will summon the people from exile: "They will follow after YHWH. Like a lion he will roar. When on his part, he roars, then children will tremble from the west . . ." (11:10). Most significantly, the anticipated return of Israel is firstly *to* YHWH himself (11:10a–c), and only secondarily a return *from* faraway places of exile (11:10d). Earlier Hosea had linked the spiritual and geographical dimensions of apostasy through the description of Israel's wayward act of "going away" (הלך; 11:2), especially in rejecting YHWH's "call" (קרא; 11:1b) to follow the nations' "call" (קרא; 11:2a). Since Israel has been ignorant of YHWH's tender care (11:3–4) and refuses to repent (11:5–7), the fierceness of a lion's roar against Israel (11:10) now supersedes the gentleness of his divine parent's call (11:1).

The fact is that YHWH has already asserted his dominant presence "in your midst" (11:9e). This indicates that this divine lion's "roar" (שאג; 11:10b–c) serves both to keep order in the pride and protect Israel from enemies on the journey.[99] Leonine imagery in this passage serves a different purpose from Hosea's portrayal of YHWH elsewhere as predator (5:14; 13:7–8) and Amos's and

94. Kakkanattu, *God's Enduring Love*, 91.

95. As initially suggested in the chapter title, "God's Nearness and Distance: Immanence and Transcendence," in Millard J. Erickson, *Christian Theology*, 3rd ed. (Grand Rapids: Baker Books, 2013), 272–90. Erickson discusses both spatial and nonspatial understandings of these categories.

96. Terence E. Fretheim, *The Suffering of God: An Old Testament Perspective*, OBT (Philadelphia: Fortress, 1984), 70–71. It is critically significant that both a passibilist (Fretheim) and impassibilist (Weinandy) hold that transcendence and immanence are complementary rather than incompatible.

97. One could also render the MT for Hos 11:9f as "I will not into city" (KJV) or "I will not come against their cities" (NIV). As Lindström ("I Am God and Not Human," 144–45) notes, this would translate the theological contrast between Israel and Admah/Zeboiim in v. 8 into the spatial terms of YHWH declining to come and destroy "a city" in v. 9. That is, YHWH may be personifying Israel as a city that will not suffer destruction.

98. Kakkanattu, *God's Enduring Love*, 92–93.

99. Cf. Jacobs ("YHWH's Call," 23), who sees the lion's roar as a threat to overcome the reluctance of Israel to return.

Joel's portrayal of YHWH's "roar" (שׁאג) as a threat (Amos 1:2; 3:8; Joel 4[3]:16).[100]

Following this depiction of YHWH as an animal, the prodigal child who joins up with the divine lion then becomes an animal himself (cf. 10:11). Like the use of a creaturely image to describe YHWH (11:10b–c), the human children who "tremble [חרד] from the west" (11:10d) also become creatures who "will tremble [חרד] like birds from Egypt, and like doves from the land of Assyria" (11:11a). The root חרד denotes trembling and occurs twice in this passage's human (11:10d) and animal (11:11a) pictures of Israel. Compared to Hosea's earlier word picture, the objects of Israel's fear have changed from Egypt and Assyria to the God who is able to make his people return from these superpowers that Israel stupidly pursued like "dove" and "birds" (7:11–12; cf. 11:2).

This yields another creative reconfiguration of the animal world, reversing the fight-or-flight reflex so that edgy birds (i.e., Israel) draw near rather than bolting at the roar of a lion (i.e., YHWH). This divine lion is by turns more dangerous (5:13–15) and approachable (11:10–11a) than the ancient Near Eastern empires that purported to offer shelter to Israel. To summarize, the oddness of these creaturely pictures emphasizes the sheer uniqueness of the lionhearted God of Israel—not only the raw power needed to dislodge his weak people from the strong grip of empires but also the tremendous emotional cost to YHWH in journeying with his people from adoption to estrangement and then all the way back to reconciliation (11:1–9).

Following this potpourri of images, Hosea's characterization of YHWH and Israel becomes more conventional in the conclusion to this section. Spiritual restoration through repentance (11:10) means that physical restoration can also take place for Israel (11:11). These prophecies of return from exile look beyond the Assyrian threats against the kingdoms of Israel that culminated in 722 BCE with the deportation of the Northern Kingdom of Samaria. Although greatly weakened, the Southern Kingdom of Judah would survive until the Babylonians sacked Jerusalem in 587 BCE.

Now the prophet Hosea sees beyond the immediate future to a new salvation history even later than the "latter days" (3:5) mentioned earlier. In chapter 3 YHWH warned that Israel would "dwell" (ישׁב) in exile without its religious, political, and social institutions (3:4) so that chastened hearts would "tremble [פחד] before YHWH and his goodness" (3:5). But since that passage nowhere mentions a return to the land, chapter 11 completes the portrait of restoration by describing Israel not only as children/birds who "tremble" (חרד)[101] in repentance before YHWH (11:10d–11a) but also as people to whom YHWH has given back the land: "So I shall make them dwell [ישׁב] in their homes" (11:11b).

By this regathering of his people, YHWH will have fulfilled his covenant promise that the children of Abraham would dwell forever in the land of Canaan (Gen 13:14–17; cf. 15:18–21). From the perspective of the prophet and his audience who remain in the land at this precarious moment in the eighth century BCE, the final cycle of salvation history still lies far off. Exile is still an imminent threat rather than a foregone conclusion, much less restoration from exile in the distant future.[102] But YHWH shows his sovereignty over the cycles of salvation history—both by warning his people far in advance about what their apostasy will reap as well as by assuring Israel of reconciliation with him even as the consequences of estrangement are still unfolding in history. The prophet reasserts the divine origin of this utterance by stamping it with the divine *imprimatur*: "The Declaration of YHWH" (11:11c; cf. 2:15[13]f, 18[16]a, 23[21]b).

100. Strawn, *What Is Stronger than a Lion?*, 272–73.

101. The verbs פחד and חרד are synonyms for "trembling," as suggested by their parallelism in Isa 19:16.

102. Stuart, *Hosea-Jonah*, 182.

Canonical and Theological Significance

1. Word Pictures and God's Mission

More than any other prophet, Hosea employs the word pictures of metaphor and simile to describe covenant relationship between YHWH and Israel. In 9:10–11:11 alone, YHWH is portrayed as farmer (10:11c–d), parent (11:1, 3a–b, 4a), doctor (11:3d), and lion (11:10). The variety of images for Israel is even greater; in this passage he usually calls the nation "Ephraim" (meaning "double fruitfulness"), and whom he consequently describes in the natural terms of grapes (9:10a), figs (9:10b), infertile woman (9:11c), flourishing plant (9:13), dried plant (9:16a–c), bereaved parent (9:16d–e), fruitful vine (10:1), female cow (10:11a–b), son/children (11:1, 10d), and birds (11:11a). Other passages in the book also have clusters of natural word pictures (e.g., 5:12–15; 7:4–7; 8:8–9), but Hos 9:10–11:11 contains the highest concentration of them.

Why should Hosea speak so imaginatively of God and his people using categories from nature? At first the prophet's strategy seems counterintuitive, since it was precisely this realm that posed a problem in Israel's syncretistic nature religion. As seen elsewhere in the book, Israel brought the venerated fertility deities of the land alongside YHWH (e.g., 2:10[8]; 7:14; 13:1) and sometimes confused YHWH with Baal (e.g., 2: 18–19[16–17]). In mimetic rituals directed at Baal in particular, sexual activity in the human realm would call forth this Canaanite god of the storm to inseminate the world with rain and bring forth the harvest.

The sacralization of sex was a common feature of ancient Near Eastern worldviews in which the human body stood in a close analogy with the earth. This link led to birth in one realm becoming a reflection of birth in the other.[103] But far from making sex more sacred, Israel's adoption of the Canaanite expression of this worldview led to a ritual system of rape of younger women by older men (see 4:13–14 and commentary). Already in the eighth century BCE, Israel's cultic worship was "hyper-sexualized," with younger women being treated as sexual objects.[104] Then as now, sexual "liberation" became the cruelest master of all, especially for vulnerable young girls who tend to suffer the most.

Given the dangers of Canaanized religion, the Creator's homeopathic rather than antipathic posture toward his sexually confused creatures in this passage (by contrast with Hos 3) is surprising.[105] In this vein, Hos 1–3 portrays covenant as a

103. Simkins, *Creator and Creation*, 75–81.

104. On "hyper-sexualization" of preteen girls in the modern West, see Abigail Jones, "Sex and the Single Tween," *Newsweek*, January 24, 2014, www.newsweek.com/2014/01/24/sex-and-single-tween-245090.html.

105. As first noted by Jacob, "L'Héritage cananéen dans le livre du prophète Osée," 250–59.

marriage relationship to undo from within ancient Near Eastern worldviews centered on sacred marriages between the gods and their people. Hosea 9:10–11:11 similarly portrays the same creation that Israel sought to manipulate through nature rituals becoming YHWH's agent of judgment. Irony abounds when attempts to multiply fertility yield infertility (9:10–17), while veneration of animal images only debases worshipers from humans into the beasts that Israel venerated as icons (10:5, 11).[106] By flying close to the flame of sinful humanity, YHWH shows himself a missionary God who takes the risk of contextualizing his message in the indigenous language of earthiness that people living in Canaan would understand.

YHWH could have restricted his message to the supernatural category of salvation history, where he alone is the sovereign mover (e.g., 9:10; 12:10[9]; 13:4), to preempt all possibility of syncretism.[107] But YHWH does not take this safer approach to human culture, just as wise missionaries know from experience that the danger of *not* attempting to contextualize can be even greater than the risk of syncretism. Those who never hear God's timeless truth translated into their language and culture will either fail to understand it or reject a distortion of it,[108] while those who do believe will experience only superficial conversion rather than a deeper transformation of their worldview.[109] Many Westerners disparage homeopathy by labeling it as "alternative medicine," but this was Hosea's primary method for curing Israel of syncretism with Canaanite nature religion and replacing this with a biblical worldview of creation.[110] Analogously, the God who became incarnate in Jesus calls his people to pursue every form of cultural engagement, short of sin, in order to transform pagan worldviews from the inside out.[111] To do any less is to shrink the scope of what Jesus meant in the Great Commission when he directed his disciples to teach *all* the nations *all* that he had commanded to new disciples (Matt 28:19–20).

106. This subversive element in Hosea is well recognized by Sherwood (*The Prostitute and the Prophet*, 214–35), though she concludes needlessly that the book deconstructs itself rather than being homeopathic in its approach to Canaanized religion.

107. Numerous commentators observe Hosea's unique presentation of salvation history but assume without argument that this emphasis overrules the theme of creation despite the latter's equal prominence in the book (e.g., Wolff, *Hosea*, xxvi).

108. A humorous and perhaps apocryphal anecdote from missiology illustrates the essential role that contextualization plays in spiritual understanding and conversion. In southeast Asia, a well-meaning missionary employed the distinctive idiom of revivalist preaching to communicate the gospel to Buddhists. The language barrier was bridged by the help of a skilled interpreter. But upon hearing the missionary's invitation to be "born again by believing in Jesus," the Buddhist audience gasped and concluded that Christ was their worst nightmare. All their life they had been seeking to escape the endless cycle of being "born again"—the fearful prospect of reincarnation. Thus, the task of translation goes beyond language to include culture and worldview.

109. For more discussion of Hosea's relevance to contextualization, nominalism, and syncretism, see the "Canonical and Theological Significance" section on Hos 5:8–7:16.

110. Interestingly, Westerners' skepticism toward homeopathic medicine mirrors the longstanding preference among OT theologians for the theological category of salvation "history" over creation "myths" (on which see "Hosea's Distinctive Theology in Its Cultural Context" in the introduction to Hosea, pp. 31–37).

111. Paul G. Hiebert, *Transforming Worldviews: An Anthropological Understanding of How People Change* (Grand Rapids: Baker Academic, 2008).

2. Word Pictures and God's Nature

Conventional wisdom says that books with pictures are childish, but books with words are for adults. But what about a book with word pictures such as metaphors and similes, as is Hosea? And how adequately can word pictures describe a God who has forbidden attempts to represent him with physical images that can be seen and touched (Exod 20:4; Deut 4:15–19; 5:8)? The book of Hosea dares even to apply creational images to the Creator himself. To see why this is a risk worth taking, let us explore how the homeopathic remedy of linking human and animal pictures to YHWH succeeds in purifying Israel's tainted faith rather than worsening the ailment of syncretism.

The use of word pictures is characteristic not only of Hosea but also of Hebrew poetry in general. The unique combination of vividness and terseness in poetry (both of which characterize the prophecy of Hosea) invites new ways of thinking about God and his relationship to people.[112] In the act of reading, experiencing new connections between the mundane and the sublime requires the reader's active participation in entering fully the world of the text, or as Paul Ricoeur summarized in his famous maxim, "The symbol gives rise to thought."[113]

Psalm 18 provides a simple illustration. The psalmist's declaration that "YHWH is my rock and my fortress and my deliverer" (Ps 18:3[2]) requires only four Hebrew words (יְהוָה סַלְעִי וּמְצוּדָתִי וּמְפַלְטִי) to confess faith in YHWH from three different perspectives—nature ("rock"), secure dwelling ("fortress"), and champion in war ("deliverer"). Far from reducing the awesome to the mundane, the impossibility of simultaneous equivalence with YHWH in all three areas works in the opposite direction by kindling the reader's wonder about how YHWH could possess features of all three objects. Add to this the personalization of faith in this verse's threefold "my" pronominal suffixes in Hebrew, and these word pictures combine forces to inspire devotion to God far out of proportion to these brief words.

Images in the book of Hosea function the same way, but with greater variety that expresses the dynamism of Israel's God in his acts of judgment and salvation. Especially in Hos 11, poetic word pictures express the incomparability of YHWH as both sovereign and relatable. This chapter draws the audience back into the familial realm after an extended section that used the legal language of the courtroom and creational disorder (chs. 4–10). But the kinship metaphor of husband and wife (cf. chs. 1–3) has now become parent and child (11:1–4), the former a breakable relationship, the latter unbreakable.

112. Patrick D. Miller, "The Theological Significance of Biblical Poetry," in *Israelite Religion and Biblical Theology: Collected Essays*, LHBOTS 267 (Sheffield: Sheffield Academic, 2000), 248–49.

113. Paul Ricoeur, *The Symbolism of Evil*, trans. Emerson Buchanan (Boston: Beacon, 1969), 347.

The picture of YHWH as judge reappears briefly when capital punishment becomes the only verdict appropriate to this grown son's behavior (11:5–6). But just as final destruction looms and Israel's prayers seem most futile (11:7), the entire scene pivots dramatically from the courtroom back to the living room, so to speak, for legal verdict of exile could never supersede the covenantal love of God. The same parent who proclaimed that "when Israel was a child, I loved him" (11:1) voices the pain of losing his son through four piercing rhetorical questions that begin with "How?" (11:8a–d). Like an angry parent whose tenderness comes flooding back after discipline has achieved its desired effect, the God of Israel declares that his desire for his children was never to destroy but to restore them.

Strictly speaking, these metaphors and similes in Hos 11 are mutually incompatible, but together in poetry they express the inscrutable nature of YHWH. Rather than portraying fickleness or indecisiveness,[114] this kaleidoscope of images confronts the audience with a picture of YHWH who simultaneously possesses love to reconcile, holiness to judge, and power to save. For the incomparable God of Israel, as Paul Fiddes observes,

> Neither wrath nor restoration are a mechanical process of causation, but are to do with personal relations, and so both mean pain for God. There is then no *conflict* of love and wrath within God; *both* mean suffering for him, in an intricate double movement of pain, a complex experience that can be described poetically but not literally as a struggle with himself.[115]

The fullness of God's heart in both love and wrath finds perfect consistency in his insistence that "I am God and [I am] not a man. [I am] a Holy One in your midst" (11:9). This use of word pictures expresses the mystery that his emotions of love, pain, and anger are like ours in their genuineness while surpassing ours in their lack of ambivalence. Characterization of God using the aniconic means of metaphor and simile therefore articulates God's dwelling among his people without reducing his presence to physical categories, in contrast to the limitations imposed by visual or physical representations of deity.[116]

Finally, Hosea's magnificent presentation of Israel's God would simply would not be the same if cast in prose rather than poetry. This is not to say that prose in the Bible is unnecessary or inferior, for the historical books of the OT narrate the exile to Assyria that must and did occur in 722 BCE as a vindication of divine justice (2 Kgs 17). But poetry remains the primary medium to paint "a new world where destruction is a challenge, death an opportunity, and ends are beginnings and places

114. Cf. Brueggemann, "Recovering God of Hosea."

115. Fiddes, "The Cross of Hosea Revisited," 185–86, emphasis original.

116. Middlemas, "Aniconism and Multiple Imaging in the Prophets," 203–5; McConville, "Language about God in Hosea," 186–87.

of hope. . . . Israel's future is grounded in this new world. All unknowing, Hosea is glimpsing the Father not only of Israel but of the one who could say, 'I am the resurrection and the life.'"[117] Through Hosea's fascinating word pictures we can see, first dimly but then clearly with the NT's help, the matchless nature of a God who blends perfect love and perfect justice in history through the cross of Jesus Christ.

117. Beeby, *Hosea*, 149.

CHAPTER 9

Hosea 12:1–14:1[11:12–13:16]

E. Israel's Disobedience toward YHWH: Specific Verdicts from History and Creation

Main Idea of the Passage

The people of Israel bear a troubling family resemblance to Jacob, the patriarch whose life often exhibited treachery, materialism, and struggle with God. Hosea's audience is a new "Jacob" that must turn instead toward Moses, lest they repeat the wrong kind of history and sow the seeds of their own death—an ironic verdict for the Northern Kingdom that is also known as "double fruitfulness" (i.e., "Ephraim").

Literary Context

Following the signatory formula, "The Declaration of YHWH" (11:11), that closes the previous section (i.e., chapters 4–11), Hos 12:1–14:1[11:12–13:16] is the fifth and final covenant discourse in the book. After the general series of covenant lawsuits of Hos 4–11, the prophet now delves into a more specific exploration of how the motif of creation is interwoven with that history. Hosea 12:1–14:1[11:12–13:16] also goes further into Israel's past than the exodus traditions mentioned in previous passages (e.g., 4:1–3) by drawing upon traditions about Jacob, the eponymous ancestor of both kingdoms of Israel.

The positive and negative aspects of this patriarch's life in Genesis both feature in the comparison to "Jacob" in the present. Hosea's hearers have a brief opportunity to repent as Jacob did (12:5–7[4–6]), but they ultimately go the way of Moses's generation in becoming proud of their self-sufficiency in the land and forgetting YHWH (13:6). Therefore, the exile threatened by the sermons of Moses in Deut 27–28, from which Hos 13:12–16 borrows, must come. The lesser "east wind" (Hos 12:2[1]) of imperial power that Israel pursues for safety will give way to the greater "east wind" of YHWH's spirit, who buffets his people with drought-causing gales in creation and exile in history (13:15–14:1[13:16]).

Following the present section, the book ends with a penitential prayer by Hosea that renounces trust in Assyria and man-made gods (14:2–4[1–3]). YHWH responds that he will reverse the curses described in Hos 13–14:1[13:16] and again become the sustainer of Israel's fertility (14:5–9[4–8]). The prophecy of Hosea does not merely look to a future of inevitable judgment followed by salvation for God's people, for its timeless conclusion about walking in YHWH's ways is also intended for all who are wise and discerning (14:10[9]).

Translation and Exegetical Outline

(See pages 280–84.)

Structure and Literary Form

Hosea 12:1–14:1[11:12–13:16] contains many literary and discourse features from elsewhere in the book. Most notably, this section begins with a "quarrel/lawsuit" (רִיב; 12:3[2]) that accuses the people of YHWH of violating his covenantal stipulations. As in Hosea's previous references to רִיב (2:4[2]; 4:1), this passage is less a dispassionate legal case and more the emotionally charged orations of a God who yearns for his estranged people.

In presenting YHWH's רִיב as a family quarrel, Hos 12:1–14:1[11:12–13:16] seeks to move its audience using poignant communicative devices that appear in other passages: wordplays on Israel's various names (e.g., 12:3–4[2–3]; cf. 8:9),[1]

1. This is the discourse element of changed reference (*LDHB* §2.6) in which Hosea varies the title for the audience (e.g., "Ephraim" vs. "Jacob") as a way of reconfiguring YHWH's relationship with them.

Hosea 12:1[11:12]–14:1[13:16]

			E. Israel's Disobedience toward YHWH: Specific Verdicts from History and Creation (12:1[11:12]–14:1[13:16])
			1. A Summary Accusation of Ephraim and Judah (12:1–2[11:12–12:1])
12:1[11:12]a	סְבָבֻנִי בְכַחַשׁ אֶפְרַיִם	"Ephraim has encircled me with deception;	a. Spiritual Treachery (12:1[11:12])
12:1[11:12]b	וּבְמִרְמָה בֵּית יִשְׂרָאֵל	the household of Israel [has surrounded me] with treachery.	
12:1[11:12]c	וִיהוּדָה עֹד רָד עִם־אֵל	Judah is also roaming against El,	
	וְעִם־קְדוֹשִׁים נֶאֱמָן׃	even against the faithful Holy One.	
12:2[1]a	אֶפְרַיִם רֹעֶה רוּחַ	Ephraim is grazing on wind	b. International Intrigue (12:2[1]a–b)
2[1]b	וְרֹדֵף קָדִים כָּל־הַיּוֹם	and pursuing an east wind all the day.	
2[1]c	כָּזָב וָשֹׁד יַרְבֶּה	Falsehood and violence he multiplies.	(1) Syncretistic Politics (12:2[1]c–d)
2[1]d	וּבְרִית עִם־אַשּׁוּר יִכְרֹתוּ	They make a covenant with Assyria,	
2[1]e	וְשֶׁמֶן לְמִצְרַיִם יוּבָל׃	and olive oil is carried to Egypt.	(2) Syncretistic Economics (12:2[1]e)
			2. Judah and Israel as a New "Jacob" (12:3–9[2–8])
3[2]a	וְרִיב לַיהוָה עִם־יְהוּדָה	YHWH also has a quarrel with Judah	a. Treacherous "Jacob" Past and Present (12:3–5[2–4])
3[2]b	וְלִפְקֹד עַל־יַעֲקֹב כִּדְרָכָיו	to repay Jacob according to his ways.	
3[2]c	כְּמַעֲלָלָיו יָשִׁיב לוֹ׃	According to his deeds he (YHWH) will recompense him.	(1) Jacob's Opposition to Esau and God (3–4[2–3])
4[3]a	בַּבֶּטֶן עָקַב אֶת־אָחִיו	In the womb he grasped his brother,	
4[3]b	וּבְאוֹנוֹ שָׂרָה אֶת־אֱלֹהִים׃	and in his vigor he strove with God.	
5[4]a	וַיָּשַׂר אֶל־מַלְאָךְ	He strove with the angel	(2) Jacob's Melodramatic Turn (12:5[4]a–d)
5[4]b	וַיֻּכָל	and prevailed.	
5[4]c	בָּכָה	He wept	
5[4]d	וַיִּתְחַנֶּן־לוֹ	and was shown favor.	
5[4]e	בֵּית־אֵל יִמְצָאֶנּוּ	At Bethel he (God) finds him (Jacob),	(3) YHWH's Mercy to "Jacob" Past and Present (12:5[4]e–f)
5[4]f	וְשָׁם יְדַבֵּר עִמָּנוּ׃	and there he speaks with us.	
6[5]	וַיהוָה אֱלֹהֵי הַצְּבָאוֹת	As for YHWH God of Hosts,	b. An Invitation to Repentance (12:6–7[5–6])
	יְהוָה זִכְרוֹ׃	YHWH is his memorial name.	(1) The Background to Repentance: God's Deeds in the Exodus (12:6[5])

Verse	Hebrew	Translation	Outline
7[6]a	וְאַתָּה	But as for you,	(2) The Means of Repentance: God's Help
	בֵּאלֹהֶיךָ תָשׁוּב	by your God you shall return.	(12:7[6]a)
7[6]b	חֶסֶד וּמִשְׁפָּט שְׁמֹר	Keep mercy and justice,	(3) The Actions of Repentance: Covenant
7[6]c	וְקַוֵּה אֶל־אֱלֹהֶיךָ תָּמִיד׃	and wait for your God continually.	Fidelity (12:7[6]b–c)
8[7]	כְּנַעַן	[As a] merchant,	c. Ephraim's Unrepentance as "Canaan"
	בְּיָדוֹ מֹאזְנֵי מִרְמָה	in whose hand are scales of deception,	(12:8–9[7–8])
	לַעֲשֹׁק אָהֵב׃	he loves to oppress.[1]	(1) Social Injustices (12:8[7])
9[8]a	וַיֹּאמֶר אֶפְרַיִם	So Ephraim says,	(2) Materialistic Boasting (12:9[8])
9[8]b	אַךְ עָשַׁרְתִּי	'Surely, I have become rich;	(a) Strength (12:9[8]a–c)
9[8]c	מָצָאתִי אוֹן לִי	I have found vigor for myself.	
9[8]d	כָּל־יְגִיעַי לֹא יִמְצְאוּ־לִי עָוֺן	All my labors will not find in me any iniquity—	(b) Impunity (12:9[8]d)
	אֲשֶׁר־חֵטְא׃	which is sin.'	
10[9]a	וְאָנֹכִי יְהוָה אֱלֹהֶיךָ מֵאֶרֶץ מִצְרָיִם	But I am YHWH your God from the land of Egypt,	3. YHWH's Self-Reintroduction as God of the Exodus
			(12:10–14[9–13])
10[9]b	עֹד אוֹשִׁיבְךָ בָאֳהָלִים כִּימֵי מוֹעֵד׃	again I shall make you dwell in tents, as in the days of assembly.	a. The Promise of Another Wilderness (12:10[9]a–b)
11[10]a	וְדִבַּרְתִּי עַל־הַנְּבִיאִים	I shall speak by means of the prophets.	b. The Authority of the Prophetic Word
11[10]b	וְאָנֹכִי חָזוֹן הִרְבֵּיתִי	For on my part, I will multiply a vision,	(12:11[10]a–b)
11[10]c	וּבְיַד הַנְּבִיאִים אֲדַמֶּה׃	and by the hand of the prophets I speak similes:	c. The Power of Prophetic Stories (12:11[10]c–14[13])
12[11]a	אִם־גִּלְעָד אָוֶן	'If Gilead [has] wickedness/iniquity,	(1) The Futility of Wealth (12:12[11]a–b)
12[11]b	אַךְ־שָׁוְא הָיוּ	then they are vanity.	
12[11]c	בַּגִּלְגָּל שְׁוָרִים זִבֵּחוּ	In Gilgal they sacrifice bulls,	(2) The Futility of Nature Rituals
12[11]d	גַּם מִזְבְּחוֹתָם כְּגַלִּים עַל תַּלְמֵי שָׂדָי׃	but their altars are like heaps on the furrows of the field.'	(12:12[11]c–d)
13[12]a	וַיִּבְרַח יַעֲקֹב שְׂדֵה אֲרָם	Then Jacob fled to the field of Aram,	(3) "Jacob" vs. the Prophet (Moses)
13[12]b	וַיַּעֲבֹד יִשְׂרָאֵל בְּאִשָּׁה	and Israel served for a wife;	(12:13–14[12–13])
13[12]c	וּבְאִשָּׁה שָׁמָר׃	for a wife he guarded [sheep].	
14[13]a	וּבְנָבִיא הֶעֱלָה יְהוָה אֶת־יִשְׂרָאֵל מִמִּצְרָיִם	But by a prophet YHWH brought Israel up from Egypt,	
14[13]b	וּבְנָבִיא נִשְׁמָר׃	and by a prophet he was kept watch.'"	

Continued on next page.

1. Here and similarly to Hos 9:13a, dotted lines in the synopsis are used to link a predicate phrase ("[he] loves to oppress") back to its suspended subject ("[As a] merchant"). An intervening adverbial clause ("in whose hands are scales of deception") has separated them. This convention with dotted lines differs from the use of solid lines to mark clausal subordination.

Continued from previous page.

Verse	Hebrew	Translation	Outline
			4. Hosea's Lament for Ephraim (12:15[14])
15[14]a	הִכְעִיס אֶפְרַיִם תַּמְרוּרִים	"Ephraim has provoked to bitter anger,	a. The Inescapable Consequences of Sin
15[14]b	וְדָמָיו עָלָיו יִטּוֹשׁ	so his bloodguilt will be left upon him,	(12:15[14]a–b)
15[14]c	וְחֶרְפָּתוֹ יָשִׁיב לוֹ אֲדֹנָיו׃	and his Lord will bring his reproach back to him!"	b. YHWH's Poetic Justice (12:15[14]c)
13:1a	➝ כְּדַבֵּר אֶפְרַיִם	➝ "As soon as Ephraim spoke—	5. A Reflection on Exodus and Wilderness History
	רְתֵת	[there was] trembling!	(13:1–3)
1b	נָשָׂא הוּא בְּיִשְׂרָאֵל	He exalted himself in Israel.	a. Israel's Past Harlotry with Baal (13:1)
1c	וַיֶּאְשַׁם בַּבַּעַל	Then he became guilty by Baal	
1d	וַיָּמֹת׃	and he died.	
2a	וְעַתָּה יוֹסִפוּ לַחֲטֹא	But now they continue to sin:	b. Israel's Present Harlotry of "Baalism" (13:2)
2b	וַיַּעֲשׂוּ לָהֶם מַסֵּכָה	They make for themselves a graven image—	(1) The Crafting of Images: Metalwork
	מִכַּסְפָּם כִּתְבוּנָם עֲצַבִּים	idols from their silver according to their skill,	(13:2a–b)
	מַעֲשֵׂה חָרָשִׁים כֻּלֹּה	all of it craftsmen's work.	
2c	לָהֶם הֵם אֹמְרִים	To themselves they are saying,	(2) The Identity of Idols: Baal and Molech
2d	➝ זֹבְחֵי אָדָם	➝ 'As for those who sacrifice people,	(13:2c–d)
	עֲגָלִים יִשָּׁקוּן׃	they kiss calves!'	
3a	לָכֵן יִהְיוּ כַּעֲנַן־בֹּקֶר	Therefore they will be like a cloud of the morning,	c. Israel's Resulting Dissipation: Four Similes
3b	וְכַטַּל מַשְׁכִּים הֹלֵךְ	like dew of daybreak going away,	(13:3)
3c	כְּמֹץ יְסֹעֵר מִגֹּרֶן	like chaff blown from the threshing floor,	
3d	וּכְעָשָׁן מֵאֲרֻבָּה׃	and like smoke from a chimney.	
4a	וְאָנֹכִי יְהוָה אֱלֹהֶיךָ מֵאֶרֶץ מִצְרָיִם	But I am YHWH your God from the land of Egypt.	6. YHWH's Vindication in Salvation History (13:4)
4b	וֵאלֹהִים זוּלָתִי לֹא תֵדָע	You shall know no god besides me,	a. Israel's Responsibility to Know God (13:4a–c)
4c	וּמוֹשִׁיעַ אַיִן בִּלְתִּי׃	since there is no other deliverer.	
5	אֲנִי יְדַעְתִּיךָ בַּמִּדְבָּר	On my part, I have known you in the wilderness,	b. YHWH's Provision in Knowing Israel (13:5)
	בְּאֶרֶץ תַּלְאֻבוֹת׃	in the land of droughts.	

Verse	Hebrew	Translation	Outline
6a	כְּמַרְעִיתָם וַיִּשְׂבָּעוּ	According to their pasturage they were satisfied.	c. Israel's Complacent Forgetfulness of YHWH (13:6)
6b	שָׂבְעוּ	They were satisfied	
6c	וַיָּרָם לִבָּם	and their heart became prideful.	
6d	עַל־כֵּן שְׁכֵחוּנִי׃	As a result they forgot me.	
			d. YHWH's Danger to Israel: Five More Similes (13:7–8)
7a	וָאֱהִי לָהֶם כְּמוֹ־שָׁחַל	So I will be like a lion to them,	(1) Fierce Lion (13:7a)
7b	כְּנָמֵר עַל־דֶּרֶךְ אָשׁוּר׃	like a leopard I will pounce on the way.	(2) Pouncing Leopard (13:7b)
8a	אֶפְגְּשֵׁם כְּדֹב שַׁכּוּל	I will encounter them like a bereaved mother-bear,	(3) Bereaved Mother-Bear (13:8a–b)
8b	וְאֶקְרַע סְגוֹר לִבָּם	and I will tear open their chest cavity.	
8c	וְאֹכְלֵם שָׁם כְּלָבִיא	I will devour them there like a lioness,	(4) Devouring Lioness (13:8c)
8d	חַיַּת הַשָּׂדֶה תְּבַקְּעֵם׃	a beast of the field will tear them to pieces.	(5) Ferocious Beast (13:8d)
			7. YHWH's Taunt Against Israel (13:9–11)
9a	שִׁחֶתְךָ יִשְׂרָאֵל	[It is] your destruction,[2] O Israel,	a. Israel's Opposition to God's Help (13:9)
9b	כִּי־בִי בְעֶזְרֶךָ׃	for [you are] against me—against your helper!	
10a	אֱהִי מַלְכְּךָ אֵפוֹא	Where then is your king,	b. Loss of Military Leaders (13:10a–b)
10b	וְיוֹשִׁיעֲךָ בְּכָל־עָרֶיךָ	and [where is] your deliverer in all of your cities?	
10c	וְשֹׁפְטֶיךָ	And [where are] your judges	c. Loss of Political Leaders (13:10c–e)
10d	אֲשֶׁר אָמַרְתָּ	of whom you said,	
10e	תְּנָה־לִּי מֶלֶךְ וְשָׂרִים׃	'Give me a king and princes'?	
11a	אֶתֶּן־לְךָ מֶלֶךְ בְּאַפִּי	I would give you a king in my anger,	d. Israel's Kings as God's Poetic Justice (13:11)
11b	וְאֶקַּח בְּעֶבְרָתִי׃	but would take [him] in my wrath.	
12a	צָרוּר עֲוֹן אֶפְרָיִם	The iniquity of Ephraim is wrapped up,	8. Israel's Unavoidable Demise (13:12–16)
12b	צְפוּנָה חַטָּאתוֹ׃	his sin is preserved.	a. A Son Unready for Birth (13:12–13)
13a	חֶבְלֵי יוֹלֵדָה יָבֹאוּ לוֹ	The pangs of childbirth will come in for him.	
13b	הוּא־בֵן לֹא חָכָם	He is an unwise son,	
13c	כִּי־עֵת לֹא־יַעֲמֹד בְּמִשְׁבַּר בָּנִים׃	because at the proper time he does not appear in the birth canal.	

Continued on next page.

2. Following LXX and Vulgate, the *BHQ* commentary on the critical apparatus notes that שִׁחֶתְךָ (Hos 13:9a) should be understood as a nominal form of שחת (i.e., "your destruction" [NASB]) rather than a verbal form ("you are destroyed" [NIV], "I will destroy you" [NRSV, NET]).

Continued from previous page.

14a	מִיַּד שְׁאוֹל אֶפְדֵּם	Will I ransom them from the hand of Sheol?	b. A Buried People (13:14)
14b	מִמָּוֶת אֶגְאָלֵם	Will I redeem them from death?	(1) A Further Invitation to Death and Sheol (13:14a–d)
14c	אֱהִי דְבָרֶיךָ מָוֶת	Where are your plagues, O Death?	
14d	אֱהִי קָטָבְךָ שְׁאוֹל	Where is your pestilence, O Sheol?	
14e	נֹחַם יִסָּתֵר מֵעֵינָי׃	Pity will be hidden from my eyes.	(2) The Hiding of Divine Compassion (13:14e)
15a	כִּי הוּא בֵּן אַחִים יַפְרִיא ↓	↓ Although on his part he hopes to flourish among allies,	c. A Fountain and Treasury Stripped by the Wind/Spirit (13:15)
15b	יָבוֹא קָדִים	an east wind will come,	(1) The Wind/Spirit's Arrival (13:15a–c)
15c	רוּחַ יְהוָה מִמִּדְבָּר עֹלֶה	the Spirit of YHWH coming up from the wilderness.	
15d	וְיֵבוֹשׁ מְקוֹרוֹ	His fountain will dry up,	(2) The Wind/Spirit's Effects (13:15d–f)
15e	וְיֶחֱרַב מַעְיָנוֹ	his spring will run dry.	
15f	הוּא יִשְׁסֶה אוֹצַר כָּל־כְּלִי חֶמְדָּה׃	It will plunder his treasury of every precious vessel.	
14:1[13:16]a	תֶּאְשַׁם שֹׁמְרוֹן	Samaria must bear her guilt,	d. A Slain City (14:1[13:16])
1[13:16]b	כִּי מָרְתָה בֵּאלֹהֶיהָ	for she has rebelled against her God.	(1) The Cause of Death (13:16a–b)
1[13:16]c	בַּחֶרֶב יִפֹּלוּ	By the sword they will fall,	(2) The Cruelty of Death (13:16c–e)
1[13:16]d	עֹלְלֵיהֶם יְרֻטָּשׁוּ	their children will be dashed to pieces,	
1[13:16]e	וְהָרִיּוֹתָיו יְבֻקָּעוּ׃	their pregnant women will be ripped open."	

sudden changes in grammatical number and person (e.g., 12:7–8[6–7]; cf. 8:13–14),[2] flashbacks to the past with ethical implications for the present (e.g., 12:13–15[12–14]; cf. 9:10–11), and the use of terrifying natural images to emphasize how the Creator is sovereign over Israel's history (e.g., 13:7–8; cf. 5:14).

However, what makes Hos 12:1–14:1[11:12–13:16] unique among the covenant discourses of the book is its exposition of Israel's history as a seesaw quarrel between dueling "I"-voices. On the one hand, the long-running syncretism of Israel comes to its most blasphemous expression in a monologue of self-sufficiency: "Surely, I have become rich; I have found vigor for myself. All my labors will not find in me any iniquity—which is sin" (12:9[8]). Against such brashness by "double fertility" (i.e., the original meaning of "Ephraim"), the faithful God of the exodus counters immediately that it was his mighty act that brought Israel into existence: "I am YHWH your God from the land of Egypt" (12:10[9]; 13:4).[3] For YHWH to describe himself as "*your* God" (12:10[9]) who is always with his people highlights the massive void in Israel's self-understanding when attributing success to "*my* labors" (12:9[8]). These dueling pronouns are emblematic of the relational conflict that pervades Hos 12:1–14:1[11:12–13:16].

Because of Israel's persistently apostate speech, the covenant-keeping God, who has revealed himself as "I am/will be" (Exod 3:12, 14), must introduce a different predication of himself. He will make himself known in Israel's experience as an opponent like a ferocious animal: "I will be [אֱהִי] like a lion to them" (13:7). The conflict between estrangement and reconciliation raised by this wordplay is sharpened further by an אֱהִי homonym that means "where?," used three times in YHWH's soliloquies to ask whether any future remains for Israel: "Where [אֱהִי] then is your king?" (13:10); and "Where [אֱהִי] are your plagues, O Death? Where [אֱהִי] is your pestilence, O Sheol?" (13:14).[4] As will be discussed under "Canonical and Theological Significance," these questions receive their ultimate answer when the reign of Jesus Christ will reverse a summons for death to come (Hos 13:14) into a victory cry celebrating the death of death itself (1 Cor 15:53–57).

2. This is an additional use of changed reference (see n. 1) that employs shifts in grammatical relationships (e.g., from "you" to "him") as a discourse marker for the changing posture of YHWH toward Israel (e.g., from invitation to rebuke).

3. From a discourse perspective, the contention between different referents for "I" reflects a combination of changed reference (*LDHB* §2.6) and topical frames (*LDHB* §5.1). YHWH usurps the the "I"-pronoun in Israel's selfish monologue to introduce the topic that "I AM" is the real deliverer in Israel's history.

4. As with Hosea's other puns, we might consider these shifts on אֱהִי to be special cases of changed reference (*LDHB* §2.6). Yet in this passage, Hosea not only varies the terms and descriptors for participants in the discourse (nn. 1–3) but even changes the grammatical part of speech for אֱהִי from a nominal identifier for YHWH ("I am") into an interrogative pronoun ("Where?"). The semantic shifts for Hebrew terms that are "I"-pronouns, or resemble them, provide major turning points in the argument of Hos 12:1–13:16[11:12–13:16].

Explanation of the Text

1. A Summary Accusation of Ephraim and Judah (12:1–2[11:12–12:1])

The last verse of Hos 11 in English Bibles belongs with the following passage.[5] Hosea 11:1–11 had culminated with a prediction of Israel's return from exile, a fitting conclusion to "The Declaration of YHWH" (11:11c). This literary marker pairs with the first instance of this signatory formula (4:1) to enclose Hos 4:1–11:11 as another major section in Hosea. However, in Hos 12:1[11:12], the speech of YHWH returns from the eschatological future to the eighth century BCE by initiating the final cycle of covenant contentions in the book.

a. Spiritual Treachery (12:1[11:12])

Instead of opening this contention with a summons to the offending party (cf. 2:4[2]; 4:1), YHWH bypasses this decorum to accuse his people bluntly: "Ephraim has encircled me with deception [כַּחַשׁ], the household of Israel [has surrounded me] with treachery [מִרְמָה]" (12:1[11:12]a–b).[6] The first term used to describe spiritual treachery, כַּחַשׁ (12:1[11:12]a), recalls various kinds of betrayal mentioned earlier, such as Israel's "deception" in violating the Decalogue (4:2) as well as "lying" in the political realm through a coup d'état (7:3) and pursuing imperial power (10:13).

The second and similar term מִרְמָה (12:1[11:12] b) reappears later to describe social injustice by way of "scales of deception [מִרְמָה]" (12:8[7]). Israel's vices of deception and injustice are so pervasive that YHWH alludes to the Psalms in characterizing them as an army of opponents who "encircle" him (12:1[11:12]a; cf. Pss 22:13[12]; 59:14). Earlier in Hosea, only the sins of Israel were said to "surround" (סבב) the people (7:2), but now these sins have become so pervasive that Hos 12 portrays them as "surrounding" (סבב) YHWH as well.

To these accusations against "Ephraim," an often pejorative term for the Northern Kingdom (e.g., 4:17; 5:9; 10:11), Hosea adds the first of two surprising statements in this section about Judah (12:1[11:12]c; 12:3[2]a). Although translations render the ambiguity of the Southern Kingdom's figurative "roaming" (a participle of the rare root רוד; 12:1[11:12]c) both positively (e.g., "Judah still walks with God," ESV) and negatively (e.g., "Judah is unruly against God," NIV), the poetic parallelism with YHWH's accusations against Ephraim (12:1[11:12]a–b; 12:2[1]) and YHWH's later "dispute/quarrel" (ריב) with Judah (12:3[2]) suggest an apostate journey of some kind.

On this note, the passage modulates the grammatical person to reflect a growing relational distance between YHWH and Judah. While YHWH speaks directly using the first-person "I" to Ephraim (12:1[11:12]a–b), the sense of estrangement from his people grows palpably when addressing Judah in the third person from the vantage point of a more remote identification of himself as "El, even . . . the faithful Holy One" (12:1[11:12]c). The appellation "El" (אֵל) is a generic term for "God" (e.g., Hos 11:9; Mic 7:18) that contrasts with the personal

5. As correctly reflected in the Hebrew versification for Hos 12.

6. As often occurs in Hebrew poetry, the verb of Hos 12:1[11:12]a (סבב, "to encircle, surround") performs double duty as the implied verb of Hos 12:1[11:12]b.

name YHWH. Although the character of Judah's "roaming" (12:1[11:12]c) is unclear, the people of this kingdom are clearly going away from YHWH.

b. International Intrigue (12:2[1]a–b)

YHWH's contention becomes more pointed as he exposes his people's futile attempts at international intrigue. Shifting from the Southern Kingdom (cf. 12:1[11:12]c) back to the Northern Kingdom, the passage calls creation as a witness to testify of Ephraim's self-deception in "grazing [רעה] on wind and pursuing [רדף] an east wind all the day" (12:2[1]a–b). The pastoral verb רעה (12:2[1]a) could denote the domestic animal's act of feeding (e.g., Isa 5:17) or the shepherd's act of pasturing its flock (e.g., Mic 5:3[4]). Both tasks are equally ridiculous when taking "wind" (רוּחַ) as their object.

Likewise, Ephraim not only stupidly chases the "wind" (12:2[1]a) but also turns foolishly toward an "east wind" (קָדִים; 12:[2]1b). This is a scorching desert gale that blows in from the east (e.g., Jonah 4:8) with the power to uproot and kill (e.g., Jer 18:17). The act of pursuing rather than fleeing from a strong wind is a potent symbol for the folly of international intrigue.

(1) Syncretistic Politics (12:2[1]c–d)

In exposing Ephraim's idiocy, Hosea takes particular aim at foreign alliances that offer the Faustian bargain of protection by imperial power in exchange for vassalage. For Ephraim to reject YHWH as exclusive guardian leaves political intrigue on the world stage as the only means of survival: "Falsehood [כָּזָב] and violence [שֹׁד] he multiplies. They make a covenant with Assyria" (12:2[1]c–d). כָּזָב refers to political scheming (7:13) and is a synonym of the nouns for deceit mentioned in Hos 12:1[11:12], while שֹׁד denotes violent behavior as well as the violent demise for those who embrace the brutality of imperialism (e.g., 7:13; 9:6; 10:14).

Ephraim's sly pragmatism takes the form of a "covenant" (בְּרִית; 12:2[1]d) that is not merely political and economic but also religious in its posture toward empire. Israel's agreements with foreign powers all entailed the concession that their gods, whom these suzerain-vassal treaties listed as witnesses, were real deities with real power. Throughout the multiple Assyrian crises of the eighth century BCE, the divided kingdoms of Israel felt pressure to align with Assyria in treaty agreements that granted the theopolitical claim that Assur, the national god of Assyria, was the preeminent deity in the ancient Near East.[7] Given their apparent willingness to trust in Assyria and Ashur (e.g., Hos 14:4[3]), the people of Ephraim were all too eager to abandon their God.

(2) Syncretistic Economics (12:2[1]e)

The only remaining option for a people estranged from YHWH was to appeal to Egypt, the other traditional superpower in the ancient Near East (e.g., Hos 7:11; Isa 20:1–6). This fickleness of the Northern Kingdom—as a vulnerable people caught between the stronger empire of Assyria and the weaker, though no less ambitious, empire of Egypt—lies behind Hosea's cryptic statement that "olive oil [שֶׁמֶן] is carried to Egypt" (12:2[1]e).

Olive oil (שֶׁמֶן), a signature product of Canaan, was greatly prized by the Egyptian elite.[8] This suggests

7. See the discussion on theopolitics in the ancient Near East in the introduction to Hosea, pp. 28–31.

8. William A. Ward, "Trade, Foreign," in *Encyclopedia of the Archaeology of Ancient Egypt*, ed. Kathryn A. Bard (London: Routledge, 1999), 843.

that Hos 12:2[1] pictures this agricultural export greasing the palms of Egypt, so to speak, to join the fray and oppose Assyrian imperialism in the eastern Mediterranean.[9] In the latter eighth century BCE, such a diplomatic scenario could well describe the attempt of Hoshea king of Samaria to procure Egypt as an alliance partner against Shalmaneser king of Assyria (2 Kgs 17:4).[10]

2. Judah and Israel as a New "Jacob" (12:3–9[2–8])

However, the temptation to seek Egypt's help against Assyria could apply equally to the Southern Kingdom. King Hezekiah would face similar straits about three decades later than the time of King Hoshea (2 Kgs 18:21–24). More important than fixing a reference to a particular historical circumstance, the vulnerability of Israel's location sandwiched between ancient Near Eastern superpowers raised the constant temptation to ally with one side or the other.

The timeless constancy of this syncretism in politics and economics explains the accusation of the Southern Kingdom of Judah being just as guilty as Ephraim: "YHWH also has a quarrel [רִיב] with Judah" (12:3[2]a).[11] The last occurrence of רִיב was in Hos 4:1, which speaks broadly of YHWH's covenant household as "the children of Israel" (בְּנֵי יִשְׂרָאֵל) as well as the universal consequences of their sins for "the inhabitants of the land/earth" (יוֹשְׁבֵי הָאָרֶץ). Similarly, Hos 12 emphasizes that the apostasy of Israel is not confined to one black sheep among the twelve tribes, as one might initially conclude from the eponymous references to Ephraim (12:1[11:12]a; 12:2[1]a) or Judah (12:1[11:12]c; 12:3[2]a).

a. Treacherous "Jacob" Past and Present (12:3–5[2–4])

(1) Jacob's Opposition to Esau and to God (12:3–4[4–5])

Instead, waywardness among the people of God dates to the time of treacherous "Jacob," the common ancestor of the two kingdoms of Israel. Given the apostasies that date from centuries before Hosea, YHWH has long needed "to repay Jacob according to his ways. According to his deeds he (YHWH) will recompense him" (12:3[2]b–c). Because Jacob was the progenitor of both Ephraim and Judah, the invocation of the patriarch's name brings all his descendants into the same family tree.

For both old and new "Jacob," YHWH threatens that creation will "repay" (פקד; 12:3[2]b) and "recompense/bring back" (שׁוב *hiphil*; 12:3[2]c) sinful deeds with their own consequences. In two other passages (e.g., 4:9; 8:13), this pair of verbs points more to recompense from the intrinsic moral order of creation than to a legal act of retribution on YHWH's part.[12] To illustrate how poetic justice serves as repayment for treachery, Hosea then recalls three episodes from the patriarch's life.

From his birth as "Jacob" (יַעֲקֹב; Gen 25:26; 27:36) through his renaming as "Israel" (יִשְׂרָאֵל;

9. Cf. K. Deller, "*šmn bll* (Hosea 12,2). Additional Evidence," *Bib* 46 (1965): 349–52; Dennis J. McCarthy, "Hosea XII 2: Covenant by Oil," *VT* 14 (1964): 215–21. These scholars overlook the special significance of imported olive oil in Egypt and thereby propose that making a covenant (Hos 12:2[1]d) and a ceremony with oil (12:2[1]e) are synonymously parallel.

10. Macintosh, *Hosea*, 479.

11. The common tendency to emend "Judah" to "Israel" (e.g., Emmerson, *Hosea*, 63–65) reflects the assumption that references to the Southern Kingdom must be secondary in a northern prophecy. This proposal for Hos 12:3[2]a, however, overlooks the geographical reality that Canaan's inhabitants were always pawns in larger regional conflicts between Egypt and Mesopotamia.

12. Miller, *Sin and Judgment in the Prophets*, 122.

Gen 32:29[28]), the patriarch had lived up (or rather down) to his unflattering names: "In the womb he grasped [עקב] his brother, and in his vigor he strove [שׂרה] with God" (12:4[3]). These wordplays allude to Jacob's machinations as narrated in Genesis. Moreover, Hosea attributes to Jacob a youthful "vigor" (און; 12:4[3]), a Hebrew term that resembles two words for "iniquity" (אָוֶן, עָוֹן) that occur later in the passage (vv. 9[8], 12[11]). Jacob's seminal misuse of his און will blossom as the rotten fruit of אָוֶן and עָוֹן among his descendants.[13]

(2) Jacob's Melodramatic Turn (12:5[4]a–d)

The family resemblance between past and present "Jacob" grows stronger in v. 5[4]a–d through a dense cluster of references to the patriarch's life. This verse's rapid-fire allusions to events in the Jacob narrative cycle (Gen 28–35) each have Bethel as their setting—certainly no coincidence given that this town was where the northern kings of Israel established one of their syncretistic cult centers (1 Kgs 12:28–33; cf. Hos 10:5, 15; Amos 3:14; 5:5–6). Hosea recounts that headstrong Jacob began a transformation there from his rebellion as one who "strove with the angel and prevailed" (Hos 12:5[4]a–b; cf. Gen 32:29[28])[14] to his melodramatic turn as one who "wept [with his brother?] and was shown favor" (Hos 12:5[4]c–d; cf. Gen 33:4–5).[15] Hosea's interest in recalling Genesis is hardly simply historical, for the following clauses show that the patriarch's descendants are repeating history in surprising ways.

(3) YHWH's Mercy to "Jacob" Past and Present (12:5[4]e–f)

Hosea's audience is a new "Jacob" that now faces a similar moment of decision at the same place where their patriarch first encountered YHWH: "At Bethel he finds him (Jacob), and there he speaks with us" (12:5[4]e–f). These pregnant clauses join "Jacob" past (12:5[4]e) and present (12:5[4]f) by means of a striking ambiguity in the Hebrew object pronouns "him" and "us," both of which take the form of *-nû* pronominal suffixes. The first clause seems to refer to Jacob himself: "at Bethel he (God) finds *him* [יִמְצָאֶנּוּ]" (12:5[4]e). Reusing the *-nû* suffix, the second clause shifts the pronoun's sense from "him" to "us," that is, from Jacob the patriarch to his descendants: "and there he speaks with *us* [עִמָּנוּ]" (12:5[4]f). William Holladay observes that the flexible meaning of these *-nû* object pronouns conveys an important rhetorical surprise: "The assonance has been used to bring us an entirely unexpected conclusion: God is addressing us!"[16]

The God who speaks to Hosea's audience is therefore the same deity who showed mercy to a young Jacob and called an older, wealthy, but wayward Jacob back to Bethel. This was the place where he had once vowed to worship YHWH alone (Gen 28). But after the young Jacob had successfully resolved matters with Esau and experienced blessings on his journey, he grew complacent (Gen 29–34) and needed to renounce the materialism and syncretism that had led to his troubles (Gen 35). Just as Bethel furnished bookends in Jacob's

13. Morris, *Prophecy, Poetry and Hosea*, 122.

14. The assertion that Jacob "strove" (שׂרה) with the angel (12:5[4]a) picks up the previous clause's statement that he "strove" (שׂרה) with God (12:4[3]b). This is an instance of tail-head linkage (*LDHB* §1.6), which slows the discourse and reinforces the wordplay on Jacob's name as "Israel" (יִשְׂרָאֵל). Other examples of this discourse feature include Hos 2:23–24[21–22]; 4:5–6; 8:10.

15. The reference to Jacob "weeping" (בכה) alludes to the narrative of his cathartic encounter with Esau (Gen 33:4–5), but the ambiguous third-person masculine pronouns of Hos 12:5[4]c–d leave open the possibility that Jacob wept before the angel of YHWH. Nevertheless, the overall thrust remains clear: "Hosea has constructed a paradigm of repentance using the important figure of Jacob as an archetype" (Lyle M. Eslinger, "Hosea 12:5a and Genesis 32:29: A Study in Inner Biblical Exegesis," *JSOT* 18 [1980]: 94).

16. William L. Holladay, "Chiasmus, the Key to Hosea XII 3–6," *VT* 16 (1966): 62.

spiritual pilgrimage, his descendants—the audience of Hosea identified as "us"—must hear YHWH speaking again from the "house of God" (בֵּית־אֵל; Hos 12:5[4]e–f). Responding to this merciful God will involve a new "Jacob" renouncing Bethel's more recent association with syncretism as the "house of wickedness/iniquity" (בֵּית אָוֶן; Hos 4:15; 10:5).

b. An Invitation to Repentance (12:6–7[5–6])

The urgency of hearing YHWH's voice derives from more than YHWH's role as the ancestral family deity of Jacob and the local "God of Bethel" (Gen 31:13). In what follows, the exodus also looms large in this reactualization of saving history. Once again, YHWH reveals himself to Israel as a cosmically powerful God whom his people must never forget.

(1) The Background of Repentance: God's Deeds in the Exodus (12:6[5])

In verse 6[5] YHWH reintroduces himself as the sovereign deity of creation and history: "As for YHWH God of hosts, YHWH is his memorial name" (12:6[5]).[17] For YHWH to possess the quasi-military title "God of hosts" (אֱלֹהֵי הַצְּבָאוֹת; 12:6[5] α) is also to proclaim his rule as the Creator of all heavenly and earthly "hosts" (צְבָאוֹת; e.g., Gen 2:1; Ps 89:9–14[8–13]). YHWH has always been both a warrior God of history who fights for his people as well as the God who created all things.[18] Additionally, the description of the Tetragrammaton—the four Hebrew letters YHWH/יהוה—as his "memorial name" (זֵכֶר; Hos 12:6[5]) recalls the pivotal moment when this "God of your fathers" (Exod 3:15) showed himself incomparably great in the exodus and in the aftermath of the fiasco with the golden calf at Sinai.[19] The personal name YHWH is thus closely associated with defeating Egypt's gods and saving Israel from oppression (e.g., Exod 9:16; 12:12; 20:3).

(2) The Means of Repentance: God's Help (12:7[6]a)

Given YHWH's mercies despite the treachery of old Jacob (12:4–5[3–4]) and his powerful introduction to the exodus generation of Jacob's descendants (Hos 12:6[5]), the only act left for new "Jacob" (i.e., the conflicted audience of Hosea's prophecy) is to return wholeheartedly to YHWH. However, this repentance can only occur with help from God: "But as for you, by your God you shall return" (12:7[6]a).[20] As in the previous references to YHWH in the third person (v. 6[5]), Hosea is probably the speaker of the present invitation to return to "your God." Here the prophet strikes a delicate theological balance in stating that the *responsibility* to return is clearly Israel's (וְאַתָּה, "But as for you"), even as the *enablement* to do so comes "by your God" (בֵּאלֹהֶיךָ).[21] For YHWH to grant his people the ability to obey him (cf. Hos 10:12; 14:2[1]) upends the earlier description of Israel as unable or unwilling to "return/repent" (שׁוּב; 5:4; 7:10).

17. The foregrounded position of "YHWH God of Hosts" (12:6[5]α) slows the discourse, focuses attention on this God's unique identity, and paves the way for the invitation to repentance that follows (vv. 6–8[5–7]).

18. Cf. Shawn W. Flynn, *YHWH Is King: The Development of Divine Kingship in Ancient Israel*, VTSup 159 (Leiden: Brill, 2014), who proposes that these aspects of YHWH's royal identity developed in different historical periods.

19. On which see Austin Surls, *Making Sense of the Divine Name in the Book of Exodus: From Etymology to Literary Onomastics*, BBRSup 17 (Winona Lake, IN: Eisenbrauns, 2017).

20. The pleonastic pronoun וְאַתָּה ("but as for you"; 12:7[6] α) parallels the fronted clause in the previous verse, ("as for YHWH God of Hosts; 12:6[5]α), thereby highlighting the two main actors in this discourse who are at odds but need to be reconciled.

21. Wolff, *Hosea*, 214. With the exception of the ESV's rendering of 12:7[6]a ("by the help of your God"), the English versions tend not to translate the בְּ-preposition of agency (*IBHS* §11.2.5d) which identifies God as the means of Israel's repentance.

(3) The Actions of Repentance: Covenant Fidelity (12:7[6]b–c)

Divine enablement means that Israel possesses the ability to obey. Thus, the prophet issues two commands through which Israel can demonstrate its sincerity in keeping the covenant: "Keep mercy [חֶסֶד] and justice [מִשְׁפָּט], and wait for your God continually" (12:7[6]b–c). The terms חֶסֶד and מִשְׁפָּט are grouped among the covenant virtues that describe YHWH's own faithfulness to his people (Hos 2:21[19]; cf. Pss 33:5; 89:15[14]), as well as denoting the relational fidelity that YHWH seeks from them (Hos 6:6; 10:12) but that is sadly lacking (4:1; 6:4).[22]

Another way of describing the others-centeredness required in YHWH's household is given in the final command to "wait [קוה] for your God continually" (12:7[6]c). In the Psalms, the frequent exhortation for the worshiper to "wait" (קוה) upon God refers to trusting him for provision or deliverance rather than taking matters into one's own, helpless hands (e.g., Pss 25:3; 37:9; 130:5).

c. Ephraim's Unrepentance as "Canaan" (12:8–9[7–8])

However, as noted earlier for Hos 12:1[11:12], the people of YHWH resemble the enemies in the Psalms more closely than the worshipers described there. Since Israel apparently fails to heed the ensuing invitation to repentance (vv. 6–7[5–6]), their identity crisis as a new "Jacob" deepens in the following verses through a biting pun on "Canaan" as one who is guilty of both social injustices (v. 8[7]) and materialistic boasting (v. 9[8]).

(1) Social Injustices (12:8[7])

Hosea first insults the chosen but oppressive people of YHWH using the eponym for their ancient enemy: "[As a] merchant [כְּנַעַן], in whose hand are scales of deception, he loves to oppress" (12:8[7]). The original inhabitants of the land of "Canaan" (כְּנַעַן) were also seafaring "merchants" (כְּנַעַן; e.g., Isa 23:8) renowned for their shrewdness.[23] But here Israel proves to be the enemy of YHWH for being just as twisted as those they displaced (cf. Deut 9:4–5). The many injustices in Israel during the eighth century BCE have featured as a major theme in the book (e.g., 4:2; 5:10; 6:7–10).

Hosea reinforces the economic syncretism associated with כְּנַעַן using two Hebrew terms that point to oppression of the marginalized in Israel. The first is the mention of deceptive "scales" (מֹאזְנַיִם; 12:8[7]), a seller's tool that could be manipulated against a buyer by using doctored weights on one side of its balance (e.g., Amos 8:5; Prov 20:23). The second is Israel's determination to "oppress" (עשק; 12:8[7]), a term that other eighth-century prophets employ to describe the rich and powerful taking advantage of the poor and weak in Israel (e.g., Amos 4:1; Mic 2:2). In both kinds of economic sins, the "haves" of Israelite society seek what belongs rightfully to the "have-nots," most notably in confiscating the land and its produce that YHWH has given to all his people as an inheritance (Isa 3:13–15; Amos 5:11; cf. Deut 26:10–13).

(2) Materialistic Boasting (12:9[8])

Further evidence of Israel's social injustices comes from the boastful lips of the people themselves. Returning to the disputation form (cf. 6:1–6; 10:3–4), Hosea quotes his audience's conceited speech (12:9[8]a) as evidence that they are indeed a people like "Ephraim" (אֶפְרַיִם, "double fertility"; 12:9[8]a), the alternate name for the Northern Kingdom that recalls numerous puns about

22. See the detailed discussion of חֶסֶד and מִשְׁפָּט in the commentary on the passages listed above.

23. Kenton L. Sparks, *Ethnicity and Identity in Ancient Israel: Prolegomena to the Study of Ethnic Sentiments and Their Expression in the Hebrew Bible* (Winona Lake, IN: Eisenbrauns, 1998), 135–36.

syncretism with Canaanite nature religion (e.g., 8:9; 9:16).

Ephraim's first of two boasts in Hos 12:9[8] ("so Ephraim says"; 12:9[8]a) echoes the earlier description of Jacob as a strong young man: "Surely, I have become rich; I have found vigor [אוֹן] for myself" (12:9[8]b–c). The patriarch Jacob had similarly used his youthful "vigor" (אוֹן) to struggle against God (12:4[3]). Similarly, Ephraim's persistence in seeking his own blessing reveals a penchant for retracing Jacob's unreliable footsteps toward syncretism (12:5[4]) rather than his journey back to Bethel, the place where YHWH "finds [מצא]" and speaks with him/us (12:6[5]).

However, Ephraim not only selfishly asserts that he has "found [מצא] vigor for myself" (12:9[8]c),[24] but the second boast in Hos 12:9[8] also reuses the root מצא ("to find") in a negative construction that expresses the impunity of materialism: "All my labors will not find [מצא] in me any iniquity [עָוֹן]—which is sin" (12:9[8] d). Taking this verse as a whole, Ephraim arrogates to himself the discovery of economic אוֹן ("vigor"; 12:9[8]c) but not the moral corruption of עָוֹן ("iniquity"; 12:9[8]d). The nearly identical sound of these Hebrew words (along with אָוֶן, a similar term that means "wickedness, iniquity, trouble"; cf. 6:8; 10:5, 8) suggests that where obsession with economic power is, the sin of materialism cannot be far behind.[25] Indeed, the five first-person references to "I/myself" in this verse recall Israel's errant monologue that Moses anticipated would come upon experiencing Canaan's prosperity: "*My* power and the strength of *my* hand made *for myself* this wealth" (Deut 8:17).

3. YHWH's Self-Reintroduction as God of the Exodus (12:10–14[9–13])

Although the "I"-voice of Ephraim (12:9[8]) is selfish and brash, a stronger "I"-voice that has always provided a better foundation for Israel's identity rises to challenge it: "But I am YHWH your God from the land of Egypt" (12:10[9]a). This declaration of YHWH as the unique God of deliverance employs the "recognition formula" that is common in the book of Exodus. Throughout the narrative of Israel's deliverance from Egypt, YHWH desires for those on both sides of the struggle to "know that I am YHWH" (e.g., Exod 6:7; 7:5).[26] The climactic and fullest instance of YHWH's self-introduction occurs in the prologue to the Decalogue, "I am YHWH your God who brought you out of the land of Egypt, out of a house of bondage" (Exod 20:2).

Israel's self-worth as a nation must not derive from occupying Canaan as a prosperous nation (as in Hos 12:9[8]), but rather from YHWH's powerful "I"-speech and the gracious intervention associated with his name (Hos 12:10[9]a). But since Israel has exchanged the fullness of YHWH's revelation (cf. 4:1–2; 8:1) for the empty "I"-speech of self-actualization, YHWH responds in what follows with several "I"-proclamations that aim to reconstitute Israel as an exodus-shaped people.

a. The Promise of Another Wilderness (12:10[9]a–b)

The authoritative "I"-voice of YHWH (12:10[9]a) asserts first that Israel will experience another stint in the wilderness: "Again I shall make you dwell in tents, as in the days of assembly" (12:10[9]b). Although some interpret this description of "unlanded"

24. The centripetal dative "for myself" (לִי) adds a touch of chutzpah to Israel's selfishness. On this construction in Hebrew (e.g., Gen 12:1; Deut 4:23), see Takamitsu Muraoka, "On the So-Called *Dativus Ethicus* in Hebrew," *JTS* 29 (1978): 495–98.

25. R. B. Coote, "Hosea XII," *VT* 21 (1971): 393–94.

26. For more on the "recognition formula" in Exodus, see the Introduction to Hosea, pp. 41–45.

existence as a negative reference to punishment,[27] Hosea's generally nostalgic view of the wilderness as the honeymoon of YHWH's relationship with Israel (e.g., 2:17–18[15–16]; 9:10a–b) points in another direction.[28] Living in tents recalls a simpler time when Israel needed to depend fully on YHWH's provision in the wilderness. The faith lessons of this transient lifestyle were reenacted each year during the Feast of Tabernacles (Lev 23:34; Deut 16:13), a seven-day pause in which Israel returned to living in tents, commemorating the journey from the privation of the wilderness to the abundance of Canaan.

The chronological reference to "the days of assembly [מוֹעֵד]" also favors this festal, positive reading of Hos 12:10[9]b. The מוֹעֵד was both the occasion and place associated with the "Tent of Meeting" (אֹהֶל מוֹעֵד) where Israel repeatedly encountered YHWH in the wilderness (e.g., Exod 40:35; Lev 6:9[16]; Num 10:3). For Israel then and now, life in a desolate place is formative for faith despite originally being a punishment for rejecting YHWH (Hos 3:4–5; cf. Deut 8:15–20).

b. The Authority of the Prophetic Word (12:11[10]a–b)

The next reconfiguration of Israel's identity comes through the ministry of prophets. Rather than listening to its own "I"-voice, Israel should listen to the authorized messengers who convey the "I"-voice of YHWH: "I shall speak by means of the prophets" (12:11[10]a). The human representatives of YHWH "speak" (דבר) on behalf of this God who has already begun to "speak" (דבר) to Israel as to father Jacob at Bethel (12:5[4]). The authoritative role of the prophetic office in Israel dates to the time of Moses, who had promised that "YHWH your God will raise up for you a prophet like me from among you, from your brothers; it is to him you shall listen" (Deut 18:15).[29] This prediction of an unbroken line of prophets was first fulfilled in Joshua as successor to Moses and then in figures such as Elijah and Elisha. The latter two were particularly entrusted with a job description that lasts into Hosea's times—speaking hard truths as whistleblowers to the kings of Israel.

Prophets were also among the privileged few to whom YHWH would "multiply [רבה] a vision [חָזוֹן]" (Hos 12:11[10]b). Two Hebrew terms in this clause deserve comment for their links to other passages. The first is רבה, a verb that outlines the stark gap in Hos 12 between YHWH's intention to "multiply" his revelation to his people and Ephraim's desire to "multiply" violence and deceitful speech (12:2[1]). The second is חָזוֹן, a term for the prophet's experience of the heavenly realm (e.g., Hab 2:2–3; Dan 8:15) but that ultimately comes to God's people in earthly form as a spoken word (e.g., 1 Sam 3:1) or a prophetic book (e.g., Isa 1:1; Obad 1). This emphasis on the prophet's authority to speak for YHWH paves the way for the telling of prophetic stories that follows (12:11c–14[10c–13]).

c. The Power of Prophetic Stories (12:11c–14[10c–13])

In light of the emphasis on God's word through prophets in Hos 12:11[10]a–b, some combination of oral and tactile storytelling seems to underlie YHWH's somewhat puzzling statement, "By the hand [יָד] of the prophets I speak similes [דמה]" (12:11[10]c). Use of the "hand" (יָד) may refer

27. E.g., Stuart, *Hosea-Jonah*, 193–94.

28. Jeremias, *Hosea*, 156.

29. On which, see Daniel I. Block, "A Prophet Like Moses: Another Look at Deuteronomy 18:9–22," in *The Triumph of Grace: Literary and Theological Studies in Deuteronomy and Deuteronomic Themes* (Eugene, OR: Wipf & Stock, 2017), 349–73; idem, "A Prophet Like Moses? Who or Why?," in *Distinctions with a Difference: Essays on Myth, History, and Scripture in Honor of John N. Oswalt* (Wilmore, KY: First Fruits, 2017), 19–38.

figuratively to speaking "through" the involvement of the prophets (e.g., 1 Sam 28:15; Ezra 9:11) or literally to the role of their hand movements in acting out YHWH's message (e.g., Ezek 12:7).

For YHWH to "speak similes" (דמה I) puns upon a homonym that refers to Israel's tendency to "destroy" (דמה II) itself through ignorance or disobedience (Hos 4:5–6; 10:7, 15). To reach self-destructive people who are impervious to traditional methods of communication, the use of a simile or parable by a creative messenger can place the truth in a new light that is more easily received (e.g., 2 Sam 12:1–12). The goal of the three historical retrospectives that follow (vv. 12–14[11–13]) is to disarm the hearers.

(1) The Futility of Wealth (12:11[10]c–12[11]b)

YHWH's choice of prophets who tell stories (12:11[10]c) is followed by the first story, a brief if-then scenario: "If Gilead [has] wickedness/iniquity [אָוֶן], then they are vanity [שָׁוְא]" (12:12[11] a–b).[30] The if-clause ascribes to Gilead the trait of אָוֶן ("wickedness, iniquity, trouble"), much like an earlier passage in Hosea condemned the violent inhabitants of this Israelite city in the Transjordan as "doers of iniquity [אָוֶן]" (6:8). This Hebrew term renders the if-clause (12:12[11]a) momentarily ambiguous for sounding like both אוֹן ("vigor") and עָוֹן ("iniquity"), as in the wordplay of Hos 12:9[8].

Connotations of both "vigor" and "iniquity" may be present, since אָוֶן also evokes the calf image at בֵּית אָוֶן ("house of wickedness"). This is a pejorative name for Bethel (e.g., 10:5, 8) as host of a golden bovine cult whose image is as costly as it is evil. But the then-clause (12:12[11]b) resolves the suspense by unequivocally declaring that iniquity/calf image is "vanity" (שָׁוְא). שָׁוְא is a general term for "worthlessness" that occurs in the Decalogue with reference to false witness against a neighbor (Exod 20:7; Deut 5:11), as well as being applicable to any kind of empty or deceptive speech (e.g., Prov 30:8; Hos 10:4).

(2) The Futility of Nature Rituals (12:12[11]c–d)

Besides linking to the Decalogue (cf. Hos 4:2; 8:1), the frequent connection of שָׁוְא with syncretistic worship (e.g., Isa 1:13; Jer 18:15) may link this statement to the next story. Returning from the Transjordan (12:12[11]a–b) back to Israel proper, Hosea's discourse adds nature rituals to the long list of futile instruments in which Israel had trusted: "In Gilgal they sacrifice bulls, but their altars are like heaps on the furrows of the field" (12:12[11] c–d). Hosea's last mention of Gilgal, the site of the first Yahwistic shrine after Israel crossed the Jordan (Josh 4:19–20; 5:9–10), was a paradigmatic example of Israel's evil (9:15–17).

Nevertheless, this passage mentions Gilgal for specific cultic practices with "bulls" (12:12[11]c) and "altars" (12:12[11]d) that fall under YHWH's condemnation. Whatever the historical background for Hosea's shift in gender reference from female "heifer[s]" (עֶגְלוֹת; 10:5a) to male "bulls" (שְׁוָרִים; 12:12[11]c) as instruments of worship, the verdict of YHWH is that bovine rituals will backfire for Israel. The altars of "Gilgal" (גִּלְגָּל; 12:12[11]c) will become "heaps [גַּלִּים] on the furrows of the field" (12:12[11] d), a notable phrase since "furrows of the field" (תַּלְמֵי שָׂדָי) is exactly the metaphorical description of Israel's orderly but self-poisoning theopolitics given earlier (10:4). In sum, the syncretistic efforts of Israel to guarantee safety and fertility will only lead to danger and barrenness (cf. 9:1–2).[31]

30. This rendering of Hos 12:12[11]a takes אִם to be a conditional marker (ESV, so also GKC §159v), in contrast to an interrogative (NIV, NASB) or emphatic particle (NRSV, Andersen and Freedman, *Hosea*, 594, 619).

31. Morris, *Prophecy, Poetry and Hosea*, 59–60.

(3) "Jacob" vs. the Prophet (Moses) (12:13–14[12–13])

The third prophetic story told by Hosea returns to the enigmatic figure of Jacob. Compared to the earlier depiction of him as strong-willed but ultimately beaten (12:3–5[2–4]), Jacob now comes across as fickle and opportunistic: "Then Jacob fled to the field of Aram, and Israel served for a wife; for a wife he guarded [sheep]" (12:13[12]a–c). The narrative sequence of Jacob's sojourn in Aram (Gen 28–31) falls in the period covered in Hos 12:3–5[2–4], between the episodes of Jacob's treachery toward Esau (12:4[3]a; cf. Gen 27–33) and his return to Bethel (12:5[4]e; cf. Gen 35). The characterization of Jacob as fixated on working "for a wife [בְּאִשָּׁה]", a phrase that occurs twice (12:14[12]b, c), is more important than precise chronology. This double mention of Jacob's loves humorously echoes the depth of his romantic obsession in working double-time to gain Rachel as his wife (cf. Gen 29:15–29).

The comparatively petty vocation of Jacob emerges in another series of repetitions, this time of the noun נָבִיא ("prophet"; cf. 12:14[13]) and the verb שׁמר ("to guard, keep watch"). Whereas Jacob/Israel "guarded [שׁמר *qal*]" (12:13[12]c) the livestock of his uncle for his own sake, an unnamed prophet of YHWH undertook a far more noble and difficult task: "But by a prophet [נָבִיא] YHWH brought Israel up from Egypt, and by a prophet [נָבִיא] he was kept watch [שׁמר *niphal*]" (12:14[13]). This unusual passive construction clearly alludes to the vigilance of Moses and his pivotal role in preserving Israel during the exodus events (cf. Deut 34:12). But to describe him anonymously as a "prophet" validates the authority of the prophetic office just mentioned (12:11[10]) and the ministry of Hosea in particular. In the latter part of the eighth century BCE, however, both kingdoms of Israel contained false prophets who opposed YHWH's true prophets and led the people into apostasy (Hos 4:5; 9:7; Isa 3:2; 28:7; Mic 3:5–6).

4. Hosea's Lament for Ephraim (12:15[14])

An unidentified speaker responds to YHWH's "I"-speech (12:10–14[9–13]) with a heartfelt lament for the people: "Ephraim has provoked to bitter anger, so his bloodguilt will be left upon him, and his Lord will bring his reproach back to him!" (12:15[14]). Although not explicitly marked, the final clause's oblique third-person reference to Ephraim's God as "his Lord" (12:15[14]c) suggests that Hosea is the one lamenting. The title אָדוֹן ("lord/Lord, master") occurs nowhere else in the book, and this oddly detached way of referring to deity by title rather than by name reinforces the sense of estrangement hinted in the first clause when Ephraim is said to "provoke to bitter anger" (12:15[14]a).

Another sign of estrangement is that Hos 12:15[14]a seems directed at nobody in particular—a highly unusual feature for a causative verb of emotion (כעס *hiphil*; "to provoke/irritate [someone]") which, by definition, needs to take a person as its direct object.[32] YHWH has become so remote that he is absent even at the level of the sentence.[33] In sum, the broken grammar that opens this verse illustrates how deeply broken is the relationship between YHWH and his people.

At the same time, estrangement in this verse does not lack for emotion. The hidden God of

32. With only one exception (2 Kgs 23:19) besides Hos 12:15[14], the OT's other forty-five instances of כעס *hiphil* take a direct object, usually YHWH (e.g., Deut 9:18; Judg 2:12; 1 Kgs 14:9; Jer 7:18).

33. Cf. Mays, *Hosea*, 169.

Israel feels "bitter anger" (תַּמְרוּרִים; 12:15[14]a) in conjunction with his prophet who laments in solidarity with him.[34] To attribute the emotion of anger to YHWH may conjure up images of a "capriciously malevolent bully,"[35] as skeptics of every age have tended to caricature the God of the OT. But as Abraham Heschel famously notes, the righteousness of divine wrath makes it rather different from the whimsical nature of human anger:

> The prophets never thought that God's anger is something that cannot be accounted for, unpredictable, irrational. It is never a spontaneous outburst, but a reaction occasioned by the conduct of man. Indeed, it is the major task of the prophet to set forth the facts that account for it, to insist that the anger of God is not a blind, explosive force, operating without reference to the behavior of man, but rather voluntary and purposeful, motivated by concern for right and wrong.[36]

This passage vindicates the moral rightness of YHWH's anger by leaving Ephraim's sins to bear their own consequences. Following the lament that opens the verse (12:15[14]a), Hosea explains the verdict of "bloodguilt" (דָּמִים; 12:15[14]b) of Ephraim both as the transgression itself and the consequence of ritual defilement that unavoidably results (cf. 1:4; 4:2). By the same token, for YHWH to bring back "reproach" (חֶרְפָּה; 12:15[14]c) levels poetic justice against Ephraim in that "the 'reproach'-sin becomes the 'reproach'-punishment."[37] The former term דָּמִים comes from creation's intrinsic link between seed and harvest, while the latter term חֶרְפָּה from the ancient Near Eastern societal values of honor and shame.

Together, these clauses present a picture of divine wrath (12:15[14]a) as less destructive than purifying in intent—YHWH's anger seeks ultimately to revive the conscience of a people who have become numb to their self-imposed predicament.[38] In this regard, YHWH is utterly unique among the gods of the ancient world for seeking reconciliation after his people have estranged themselves from him. Divine initiative as the next chapter in a covenant story is notably absent from other ancient Near Eastern accounts of "divine abandonment" after people have offended and driven off their patron deities.[39]

5. A Reflection on Exodus and Wilderness History (13:1–3)

Hosea now recalls a different period in Israel's past (13:1) to compare and contrast with the present (13:2). Much like the wordplays on Israel's ancestors in what precedes (12:2[1], 4[3], 9[8]), the name "Ephraim" will provide a theological bridge

34. Wolff (*Hosea*, 207–8) and Andersen and Freedman (*Hosea*, 595–96) observe that Hosea's reference to תַּמְרוּרִים ("bitterness"; 12:14a) sounds like YHWH's earlier accusations of מִרְמָה ("treachery"; 12:1[11:12]; 12:8[7]).

35. In the influential terms of Richard Dawkins, *The God Delusion* (London: Black Swan, 2007), 51.

36. Heschel, *The Prophets*, 2:62.

37. Samantha Joo, *Provocation and Punishment: The Anger of God in the Book of Jeremiah and Deuteronomistic Theology*, BZAW 361 (Berlin: de Gruyter, 2006), 123.

38. Heschel, *The Prophets*, 2:72: "The secret of anger is God's care. There is nothing greater than the certainty of His care. Anger brings about destruction and distress, but not despair. The prophet's response is not only acceptance, but also gratitude. This is the climax of faith."

39. On the similarities and differences between Israel's literature and the ancient Near Eastern literary motif of "divine abandonment," see Daniel I. Block, *The Gods of the Nations: Studies in Ancient Near Eastern National Theology*, 2nd ed., ETSS (Grand Rapids: Baker Books, 2000), 113–53; idem, "Divine Abandonment: Ezekiel's Adaptation of an Ancient Near Eastern Motif," in *Perspectives on Ezekiel: Theology and Anthropology*, edited by M. S. Odell and J. T. Strong, SBL Symposium Series 9 (Atlanta, Scholars, 2000), 15–42; reprinted in *By the River Chebar: Historical and Theological Studies in the Book of Ezekiel* (Eugene, OR: Cascade, 2013), 73–99.

between an ancestor of Israel and his eponymous descendant. The first verse about "double fruitfulness" outlines the historical sins of Israel with Baal (13:1), while the second verse contemporizes the past by showing that "Baalism" remains a problem in Israel (13:2).

a. Israel's Past Harlotry with Baal (13:1)

Hosea introduces the historical transgressions of Ephraim once again (cf. 6:1–3; 10:3) as brazen speech against God: "As soon as Ephraim spoke, [there was] trembling! He exalted himself in Israel. Then he became guilty by Baal and he died" (13:1).[40] In context, this allusion may refer either to the previous chapter's smug monologue of materialism (12:9[8]) or the next verse's mention of Ephraim exulting over human sacrifices and making idols (13:2). Both kinds of sin are emblematic of the pride by which Ephraim "was exalted" (NIV) or "exalted himself" (NASB).[41]

The second half of 13:1 records how pride undermined itself in Israel's history. By veneration of Baal, the Canaanite god whom Israel wrongly thought to bring rain and ensure fertility (cf. Hos 2:10–11[8–9]; 1 Kgs 18), desecration rather than flourishing came upon the land as Ephraim became "guilty" (אשׁם; 13:1c). The verbal root אשׁם ("to become guilty") refers to ritual defilement of YHWH's holy space that Israel must atone for by means of the אָשָׁם (i.e., "guilt offering"; see Lev 5:14–19). It is deeply ironic that Ephraim's guilt with Baal results in death (13:1d), for this people named "double fruitfulness" fail to follow in Baal's footsteps by rising again like Baal did after his annual death to secure the cycles of nature.[42] The events of Hos 13:1 allude to an unspecified episode when apostasy with Baal(s) led to death, perhaps the plague leveled as punishment for Israel's spiritual harlotry at Baal-Peor (Num 25) or the historical pattern of defeat in battle whenever Israel worshiped Baal and similar deities (Judg 2:11–15).

b. Israel's Present Harlotry with "Baalism" (13:2)

Centuries later, the shadow of Baal continues to bring death rather than life. Even after the formal cult of Baal worship was brutally destroyed by King Jehu in the ninth century BCE (2 Kgs 10:18–28; cf. Hos 1:4–5), Canaanite influences upon Yahwism have been repackaged in the eighth century BCE under other guises that fall under the rubric of "Baal(s)."[43]

(1) The Crafting of Images: Metalwork (13:2a–b)

The shift from past to present occurs in the assertion that Israel is still involved in manufacturing idols: "But now [וְעַתָּה] they continue [יסף] to sin: They make for themselves a graven image—idols from their silver according to their skill, all of it craftsmen's work" (13:2a–b). The adverbial conjunction וְעַתָּה indicates a temporal shift from the past to the present that underscores Israel's failure

40. Temporal clauses with the כְּ-preposition convey a specific and immediate point in time (*BHRG* §39.10.4), in contrast to how the בְּ-preposition denotes a general time frame for subsequent ideas (*BHRG* §39.6.2). This indicates that Hos 13:1 envisions a particular episode in Israel's past harlotry with Baal.

41. As reflected in the different renderings, scholars differ over whether the unusual construction נָשָׂא הוּא (13:1b; cf. Mic 4:1) should be rendered reflexively/passively as a revocalized *niphal* (e.g., *BHS*; Wolff, *Hosea*, 219; Mays, *Hosea*, 171) or whether the pronoun הוּא ("he, it") is pleonastic and נָשָׂא needs an elliptical, implicit object such as "his voice" (e.g., Dearman, *Hosea*, 316n2; Andersen and Freedman, *Hosea*, 629–30). In either case the sense of Israel's self-promotion comes through clearly.

42. John Day, "Hosea and the Baal Cult," 218–19.

43. Graham I. Davies, *Hosea*, Old Testament Guides (Sheffield: Sheffield Academic, 1998), 41; Jeremias, "Der Begriff 'Baal' im Hoseabuch und seine Wirkungsgeschichte," 441–62.

to learn its lesson[44]—to "continue" (יסף; 13:2a) in sin means that the guilt of venerating Baal (13:1) remains through Ephraim's syncretism of crafting a "graven image" (מַסֵּכָה) and various "idols" (עֲצַבִּים).

The מַסֵּכָה ("graven image"; 13:2b) probably alludes to the golden calf of Israel's first days outside Egypt (Exod 32:4, 8), which then became the template for King Jeroboam's calf cult in Dan and Bethel (1 Kgs 12:28–33). Hosea has similarly linked עֲצַבִּים ("idols"; 13:2b) to drunken fertility rituals (4:17–18) and the golden calf at Bethel (8:4–5). As we observed earlier, the silver and gold for manufacturing images came from the international trade of Israel's agricultural commodities (e.g., Hos 2:10[8]; 8:4–10; 12:2[1]) since these precious metals were not native to Canaan.[45] Idolatry in the service of a calf cult linked to "Baal" therefore has broad implications for economics and politics as well.

(2) The Identity of Idols: Baal and Molech (13:2c–d)

The character of Ephraim's idolatry may also broaden beyond Baal (13:1) with an allusion to Molech, a Syro-Palestinian deity of the underworld. The prophet quotes a boastful liturgy of the people that involves some sort of ritual with sacrifice and bovine images: "To themselves they are saying, 'As for those who sacrifice people, they kiss calves'" (13:2c–d). Translations differ on whether the unparalleled construct phrase זֹבְחֵי אָדָם (13:2d) should be rendered objectively as people being sacrificed (NIV, ESV) or subjectively as people offering sacrifices (NASB, NRSV).

This commentary opts for the former interpretation since the OT records some kings of Israel and Judah practicing ritual human sacrifice during the time of the divided monarchy (e.g., 2 Kgs 16:3; 17:17; 21:6), likely as part of their veneration of the Ammonite god Molech/Milcom (e.g., Lev 18:21; 20:2–5).[46] Veneration of עֲגָלִים ("calves"; 13:2d), on the other hand, points to images that symbolize the presence of Baal rather than El, the father of Baal who is instead represented by a bull.[47] Nevertheless, some link between Molech and Baal remains since high places for the latter deity had become sites of child sacrifice for the former by the time of Jeremiah (Jer 32:35), the prophet who draws upon Hosea more than any other.

c. Israel's Resulting Dissipation: Four Similes (13:3)

Ironically, as elsewhere in the book (e.g., 6:4–6; 9:7–9), in Hos 13:3 syncretism with nature deities will cause this apostate people named "double fruitfulness" to dissipate rather than flourish in YHWH's world. This verse contains four similes that illustrate the verdict (לָכֵן, "therefore"; 13:3a) that Canaanized rituals lead to premature death.[48]

The first two of these similes assert that Ephraim will soon fade away: "Therefore they will be like a cloud of the morning, like dew of daybreak going away" (13:3a–b). In Hos 6:4 the twin similes "like a cloud of the morning" and "like dew of daybreak

44. In this context, עַתָּה functions more as a temporal adverb that pivots to the speaker's present (*BHRG* §40.39.2) than a discourse marker that links act with consequence (*BHRG* §40.39.1), as in Hos 5:3. In fact, punishment for sin (13:1d) has led to more sin in Israel (13:2a)—the opposite of the intended consequence.

45. Holladay, Jr., "The Kingdoms of Israel and Judah," 382.

46. G. Heider, "Molech," *DDD* 583–85; cf. John Day, *Molech: A God of Human Sacrifice in the Old Testament*, UCOP 41 (Cambridge: Cambridge University Press, 1989), who argues that Jerusalem was the only location of the Molech cult and hence does not see a reference to human sacrifice in Hos 13:2 (77n12).

47. Richter, "Eighth-Century Issues," 327n24.

48. In Hos 13:3a the conjunction לָכֵן is familiar from Hos 2 for introducing a verdict of judgment (e.g., vv. 8[6], 11[9]; cf. the rhetorical surprise of betrothal in v. 16[14]).

going away" were used to condemn the fickleness of Israel's devotion to YHWH. But the same similes recur in Hos 13:3 to characterize the demise of the people themselves!

Two more similes of fading creation follow the two that precede, though this time from the realm of man-made things that are fleeting "like chaff blown from the threshing floor, and like smoke from a chimney" (13:3c–d). "Cloud" and "dew" (13:3a–b) are both elements of God's creation that fade, while "chaff" and "smoke" (13:3c–d) both represent expendable waste from human activities. Taken together, these four elements offer a comprehensive picture of how ephemeral and unrooted Ephraim's future is, especially before the face of the unforgiving "wind" that will soon roar through the land (12:2[1]; 13:15).

6. YHWH's Vindication in Salvation History (13:4–8)

The passage returns from the past (13:1–3) to the present with YHWH's resounding "I"-speech of his saving acts: "But I am YHWH your God from the land of Egypt" (13:4a). This self-introduction from salvation history repeats verbatim the declaration of Hos 12:10[9] that served as rebuttal to Ephraim's self-aggrandizing "I"-voice. The exodus and wilderness traditions just mentioned in vv. 1–3 hereby regain a contemporary significance that opposes nominal Israel's tendency to consider them historical relics.

a. Israel's Responsibility to Know God (13:4a–c)

In the present literary context, the assertion that YHWH revealed himself in the exodus (13:4a) also highlights his incomparability. Much like the Decalogue, here YHWH declares to Israel "You shall know no god besides me, since there is no other deliverer" (13:4b–c; cf. Exod 20:2–4). This contrasts with Israel's lip-service claim to "know" YHWH (8:2; cf. 6:3), for to truly "know" (ידע) YHWH in Hosea's theology joins cognitive knowledge with experiential commitment to the covenant God who has been the provider, protector, and lawgiver for his people (e.g., 2:10[8], 22[20]; 4:6).

b. YHWH's Provision in Knowing Israel (13:5)

As important as it is for Israel to "know" YHWH (13:4), it is even more significant that Israel is "known" by YHWH (cf. Gal 4:9). The verb ידע ("to know") from Hos 13:4 appears in the next verse with a reversal of subject and object: "On my part [אֲנִי], I have known [ידע] you in the wilderness, in the land of droughts" (13:5). This poignant statement of Israel's divine election draws upon Deut 8, a chapter that explains how the "wilderness" (מִדְבָּר) was not merely a place of punishment (cf. Deut 1–2) but also where YHWH formed the faith of his people by providing for their needs.

YHWH is thus the Creator who provides for his children both in Canaan (Hos 2:10[8]; Deut 8:7–9) as well as the far more desolate wilderness (Hos 13:5; Deut 8:2–4).[49] The domain of YHWH also transcends the spheres of creation or history, for his unique sovereignty always includes all of these locations and realms.

c. Israel's Complacent Forgetfulness of YHWH (13:6)

Hosea 13 quotes from Deut 8 in warning Israel that the lavishness of creation's gifts can often become the greatest hindrance to remembering the Creator.[50] Like their ancestors who conquered Canaan, prosperous Ephraim in Hosea's time suffers

49. Vall, "An Epistemology of Faith," 32.

50. For a detailed study of the dependence of Hos 13:4–6 on Deut 8:12–14 in particular, see Carsten Vang, "When a Prophet Quotes Moses," 288–92.

from spiritual amnesia about both salvation history and creational blessings: "According to their pasturage they were satisfied. They were satisfied, and their heart became prideful. As a result they forgot me" (13:6). A sudden chill has descended upon the divine-human relationship through the change of YHWH's intimate address to "you" (13:4–5) into an aloof reference to "they" (13:6). This echoes other passages where changes in grammatical number indicate relational proximity or distance (e.g., 5:1–3). The conjunction עַל־כֵּן ("as a result"; cf. 4:3, 13; 6:5) indicates that it is Israel's experience of prosperity (13:6a–b) that leads directly to pride and forgetfulness (13:6c–d).

To be specific, the term "pasture/pasturage" (מַרְעִית; 13:6a) refers to grasslands where livestock will feed until they are "satisfied" (שׂבע; 2x in 13:6a, b). But unlike references to "pasture/pasturage" in Psalms that picture Israel as a glad flock led by YHWH (e.g., Pss 79:13; 95:7; 100:3), these figurative sheep do not rest contentedly in the shepherd's presence after grazing (cf. Ps 23:2) but take on the human foibles of arrogance (רום + לֵבָב; 13:6c) and a distressing tendency to "forget" (שׁכח; 13:6d). Moses had feared that satiety (שׂבע; 2x in Deut 8:10–12) in the land would lead Israel to become prideful (רום + לֵבָב; Deut 8:14) and forgetful (שׁכח; Deut 8:11, 14, 19) toward YHWH. Exactly such a tragic day has come in the eighth century BCE when Israel/Ephraim fails to "know [ידע] that man does not live by bread alone, but on everything that proceeds out of YHWH's mouth" (Deut 8:3; cf. Hos 13:5–6).

d. YHWH's Danger to Israel: Five More Similes (13:7–8)

In Hos 13:7 the prophet again takes up his role as purveyor of word pictures (12:11[10]) to communicate with a resistant people. But unlike the similes of Hos 13:3, which portrayed the dissipation of Ephraim as airborne phenomena, the creaturely images in vv. 7–8 pack much greater punch for comparing the Creator's arrival to a dangerous animal predator. In a manner anticipating the otherworldly creatures of OT apocalyptic literature (e.g., Dan 7:4–6), this passage describes Israel being attacked by the likenesses of five different creatures: (1) fierce lion (13:7a); (2) pouncing leopard (13:7b); (3) bereaved mother-bear (13:8a); (4) devouring lioness (13:8c); and (5) ferocious beast (13:8d).

The first two similes in the series draw on the feline family: "So I will be like a lion to them, like a leopard I will pounce on the way" (13:7a–b). Hosea previously mentioned that a lion would "tear" (טרף) Israel (5:14), and such a creature reappears in this passage (13:7a) alongside the leopard (13:7b). Taken together, these cats of renowned quickness and hunting instincts are a natural bridge to the third simile about a bear, a creature that shares the cats' ability to kill.[51] Hosea not only alludes to the fabled strength of the ursine but also mentions the particular rage of "a bereaved mother-bear" that will "tear open their chest cavity" (13:8a–b) and thereby inflict a fatal wound. The fierceness of such a mother-bear was proverbial for anger in the ancient world (e.g., Prov 17:12).

Continuing the progression beyond hunting (13:7a–b) and killing (13:8a–b), the cat family briefly reappears (13:8c; cf. 13:7a) as the eater of the prey as well as being combined with an unidentified predator (13:8d) to finish this composite picture of Israel's nemesis: "I will devour them there like a lioness, a beast of the field will tear them to pieces" (13:8c–d). Adding to the devastating power of these similes is the fact that the series of five begins

51. Strawn, *What Is Stronger than a Lion?*, 58.

with the verbal clause, "I will be . . . to them" (אֱהִי לָהֶם; 13:7a). This is normally the start of a promise by YHWH to protect and provide for his people (cf. Jer 24:7; 32:38; Ezek 11:20) but here becomes a vow to destroy them.

What are we to make of these terrifying depictions of the God of Israel? Some who downplay the book's many positive portrayals of YHWH label him as a "*recovering agent of violence*"[52] or "*an irresistible force meeting an infinitely moveable and impressionable object*."[53] These categorical statements neglect how vv. 7–8 go to great lengths to combine four instances of equivocation (כְּ/כְּמוֹ, "like/as") with the biological impossibility of any creature being any literal combination of lion, leopard, bear, lioness, and beast. The prevalence and creativity of images for YHWH in the book should not cause the reader to miss that "the prophet Hosea famously refrains from the strict metaphor form (A is B) in descriptions of the deity."[54]

Instead, the provocative word pictures of Hosea's prophecy expose the limitations of all human language and concepts even as they use familiar categories to express something true about God. Word pictures for YHWH move fluidly in the book between the human realm and the animal realm (e.g., 5:14–15),[55] thus demonstrating that no single image is ever adequate to capture the many roles and dispositions of Israel's God. Later I will address in detail the canonical and theological significance of divine violence, the nature of God, and the relationship between sin and judgment. What becomes unmistakable in the next verse of Hos 13 is that Israel has chosen this masochistic path for itself rather than YHWH leveling a punishment that is disproportionate or unreasonable (cf. Lev 26:22; Deut 32:24).

7. YHWH's Taunt against Israel (13:9–11)

The previous chapter concluded with Hosea's lament (12:15[14]) in response to the presentation of divine judgment. But in Hos 13, YHWH himself becomes the one lamenting the destruction of his people: "[It is] your destruction [שַׁחַת], O Israel, for [you are] against me—against your helper!" (13:9). The verbal root שׁחת ("to be[come] corrupt, destroy") earlier portrays the depths of how Israel had "become corrupt" (9:9) as well as YHWH's determination never to "destroy" his people again (11:9). Among this book's references to שׁחת, this passage is unique for using a nominal form to describe Israel's ruin as a case of self-destruction (13:9b–11). What ensues is a description of four ways in which Israel has ruined itself.

a. Israel's Opposition to God's Help (13:9)

The first kind of self-destruction involves Israel's willful act of turning "against me (YHWH)—against your helper" (13:9b).[56] To confess YHWH as "help/helper" (עֵזֶר) against foes is one of most cherished assertions of Israel's hymnody (e.g., Pss 33:20; 115:9–11; 121:1–2). By contrast, the act of forsaking YHWH (13:9) not only turns a helper

52. Brueggemann, "Recovering God of Hosea," 19, emphasis original.

53. Yvonne Sherwood, "'Tongue-Lashing' or a Prophetic Aesthetics of Violation: An Analysis of Prophetic Structures That Reverberate Beyond the Biblical World," in *The Aesthetics of Violence in the Prophets*, ed. Julia M. O'Brien and Chris Franke, LHBOTS 517 (New York: T&T Clark, 2010), 108, emphasis original.

54. Middlemas, "Aniconism and Multiple Imaging in the Prophets," 204.

55. McConville, "Language about God in Hosea," 187.

56. The preceding verses described Israel dispassionately as "them" (vv. 6–8). But with YHWH's self-identification as "*your* helper" (13:9b), emotional intensity increases markedly through the discourse feature of changed reference (*LDHB* §2.6). That is, YHWH shifts from indirect speech *about* Israel to direct speech *to* Israel.

into an enemy (13:7–8)—the following verses also assert that Israel must confront the painful reality that all other helpers are useless (13:10–11).

b. Loss of Military Leaders (13:10a–b)

In the first two clauses of v. 10, the lament for Israel's self-destruction (cf. 13:9) turns to open mockery by YHWH against those whom the people fancy to be the real leaders of their nation: "Where then is your king, and [where is] your deliverer in all of your cities?" (13:10a–b). In the opening clause, the sarcastic interrogative "Where?" (אֱהִי) is a homonym of the earlier verbal expression "I will be" (אֱהִי; 13:7).[57] This wordplay links YHWH's declaration about his destroying ways (13:7–8) to Israel's future in exile without human leaders (13:10–11; cf. 3:4–5).

The first kind of leaders whom Israel will lack are military leaders such as "king" (13:10a) and "deliverer" (13:10b), both of whom YHWH exposes for their futility to protect Israel from enemies. The ominous mention of "all of your cities" (13:10b) being vulnerable suggests that the massive threat posed by the revitalized Assyrian Empire stands directly in the background to Hosea's prophecy (cf. 8:14; 11:6, 9). Although Israel first sought kings mainly for military purposes (1 Sam 8:20), these "impotentates" will be helpless against the "great king" (Hos 5:13; cf. Isa 36:4, 13) of Assyria.

c. Loss of Political Leaders (13:10c–e)

YHWH continues the rhetorical question of "Where?" against political rather than military leaders: "And [where are] your judges of whom you said, 'Give me a king and princes'?" (13:10c–e). In this allusion to Israel's original request in the time of Samuel, the "judges" (שֹׁפְטִים) were the magistrates originally appointed by Samuel (1 Sam 8:1–2; cf. Hos 13:10c) but whom Israel rejected so as to request instead a "king [מֶלֶךְ] like all the nations" (1 Sam 8:5).

Among the many items this greedy monarch would confiscate from Israel (1 Sam 8:11–17) were the firstborn sons of the people (1 Sam 8:11–12) to be his "commanders/princes" (שָׂרִים; Hos 13:10e). This administrative role in Israel appears elsewhere in Hosea to describe officials of the royal court who share the king's guilt and also deserve YHWH's wrath (e.g., Hos 5:10; 9:15). In sum, the leaders of both kingdoms of Israel are corrupt (cf. 13:9) in the time of Hosea, following a historical pattern that goes back to the beginning.

d. Israel's Kings as God's Poetic Justice (13:11)

But why would YHWH grant the sinful desire of Israel for leadership like the nations? Although 1 Sam 8 at first appears to proscribe kingship, YHWH permitted this institution to exist with major restrictions to ensure Israel's uniqueness among the nations as a hierarchy-less people (Deut 17:14–20).[58] The overall history of the monarchy in Israel exposes the kings' blatant disregard for these restrictions (e.g., 1 Kgs 12) as well as a tendency for these kings to compete directly with YHWH's kingship over the people (e.g., Hos 10:3).

In the face of YHWH's mysterious allowances for a historically sinful institution, the final verse of YHWH's lament (Hos 13:9–11) offers a partial answer through another allusion to 1 Sam 8: "I would give you a king in my anger, but would take [him] in my wrath" (13:11). With regard to kingship, the interplay of the contrasting roots נתן ("to give") and לקח ("to take") with reference to kingship is already ironic in 1 Sam 8, for Israel's request that YHWH should "give" (1 Sam 8:6) a king meets the sobering

57. Macintosh, *Hosea*, 537–38.

58. Berman, *Created Equal*, 53, 60–64.

realization that this ruler will "take" (1 Sam 8:11, 13, 14, 15) all of Israel's best things and "give" them to his own servants (1 Sam 8:14).[59]

It is fitting that Hosea should take Israel's original request for a king in 1 Sam 8 and turn it on its head—kingship is the insatiable gift that keeps on taking! The original wordplay on נתן and לקח reappears in summarizing Israel's entire history with kingship through the imperfective first-person verbs אֶתֶּן ("I would be/kept giving"; 13:11a) and אֶקַּח ("I would be/kept taking"; 13:11b). These forms are difficult to render into idiomatic English, but they express the iterative notion that kings were repeatedly given and taken as YHWH's way of disciplining his people.[60] In other words, YHWH is like a wise parent who gives and takes precisely what his children want, at what may feel to them like inopportune times, to expose the folly of their desires.

8. Israel's Unavoidable Demise (13:12–16)

The next section indicates that Israel's window for repentance has closed irreversibly at this moment in the eighth century BCE. Four images from the spheres of creation and history declare the inevitability of Israel's death in exile—a son unready for birth (13:13), a people consigned to the grave (13:14), a fountain dried up by gale-force winds (13:15), and a slain city (14:1[13:16]).

a. A Son Unready for Birth (13:13)

But before introducing this fourfold series of images, Hosea draws upon the ancient Near Eastern legal practice of sealing evidence for an upcoming trial: "The iniquity [עָוֹן] of Ephraim is wrapped up, his sin is preserved" (13:12). The term עָוֹן ("iniquity/guilt; 13:15a) denotes inner waywardness and twistedness that renders a person culpable before God (e.g., 4:8; 7:1; cf. Isa 13:11), while its synonym חַטָּאת ("sin"; 13:15b) refers to an individual's failure to meet an objective and/or external standard (e.g., Judg 20:16; Prov 8:36). Together, these terms comprehensively describe Israel's accumulation of guilt that YHWH has noted and stored up in a package to be unwrapped on the day of punishment (Hos 13:12a; cf. Job 14:17; Deut 32:34–35).[61]

Following the legal procedure to preserve evidence described in Hos 13:12, v. 13 contains a surprising exposition of this figurative package's contents rather than a sealed indictment in which the accused is ignorant of the charges. The first element in the package is an obstetric image that describes Ephraim as both an expectant mother and her son to be born: "The pangs of childbirth will come in for him. He is an unwise son, because at the proper time he does not appear in the birth canal" (13:13).

Oddly enough, Hosea asserts that the motherly "pangs of childbirth" (Hos 13:13a) take hold "for *him*" (לוֹ). The metaphor of labor pains broadens here to include both the woman and her son in a striking way. Before birth, this son is already "unwise" (לֹא חָכָם; 13:13b) for being a breech baby (13:13c), an especially life-threatening predicament in an age before Caesarean sections were commonplace. The accusation that the people named "double fruitfulness" endanger themselves, both as suffering mother and unwise baby, offers a preemptive negative answer to the closing question of the

59. On these ironies in 1 Sam 8, see Jerry Hwang, "Yahweh's Poetic *Mishpat* in Israel's Kingship: A Reassessment of 1 Samuel 8–12," *WTJ* 73 (2011): 345–49.

60. Machinist, "Hosea and the Ambiguity of Kingship in Ancient Israel," 167.

61. Shalom E. Holtz, "Why Are the Sins of Ephraim (Hos 13,12) and Job (Job 14,17) Bundled?," *Bib* 93 (2012): 107–15.

book of Hosea: "Who is wise?" (מִי חָכָם; 14:10[9]). Certainly not foolish Ephraim!

b. A Buried People (13:14)

From the realm of birth and life (13:13), the second element of Ephraim's guilt moves to the realm of death and dying (13:14). The first two of four rhetorical questions concern the impossibility of deliverance and therefore expect "No!" for an answer: "Will I ransom [פדה] them from the hand of Sheol? Will I redeem [גאל] them from death?" (13:14a–b). The verbs פדה ("to ransom, pay a ransom") and גאל ("to redeem, save") both occur in the book of Exodus as descriptions of Israel's deliverance from Egypt (Exod 6:6; 13:13, 15; 15:13; cf. 34:20).

These echoes of Israel's foundational history render Hos 13:14a–b particularly grating. Glorious verbs of YHWH's salvation reappear in unthinkable questions about the nondeliverance of Ephraim from "Sheol" (שְׁאוֹל; 13:14a) and "death" (מָוֶת; 13:14b). Hosea expresses the historical finality of exile by combining a figurative term for the underworld (e.g., 1 Kgs 2:9; Ps 6:6[5]) with a literal term for natural death (e.g., 2 Sam 22:5; Ps 13:4[3]).

As if this verdict were not enough, Hosea personifies the just-mentioned realms of darkness of Sheol and death (13:14a–b) in an invitation for them to act as YHWH's agents and inflict even more torment upon the deceased: "Where are your plagues, O Death? Where is your pestilence, O Sheol?" (13:14c–d). The arrival of "plague" (דֶּבֶר; 13:14c) and "pestilence" (קֶטֶב; 13:14d) completes this verse's figurative journey of reversing the exodus—the same kinds of judgment signs that were inflicted on Egypt to enable deliverance (cf. 13:14a–b; cf. Exod 9:3, 15) have now been turned against Israel in an anti-exodus of sorts. Not only this, but Qeteb and Deber were forces of death that ancient Near Eastern peoples perceived as midday and nocturnal demons, respectively (cf. Ps 91:6).[62] But here YHWH has summoned these feared agents of destruction against his own people!

While the ringing tones of Hos 13:14c–d are familiar for their triumphant reuse in 1 Cor 15:55 as a statement of the death of death itself, this transformation of Hosea's negative rhetorical questions must await the advent of Jesus Christ (see discussion of "Canonical and Theological Significance" below). Before restoration and salvation can come, YHWH declares that the discipline wrought by suffering in exile must run its course since his compassion will no longer be available to Israel: "Pity will be hidden from my eyes" (13:14e). These people to be exiled are as good as deceased and buried (cf. 9:6–7).

c. A Fountain and Treasury Stripped by the Wind/Spirit (13:15)

The third element of Ephraim's guilt (cf. 13:12) appears to involve a futile attempt to stave off exile. In another wordplay on the name "Ephraim" (cf., e.g., 5:9; 8:11), Hos 13:15 begins with a concessive clause (כִּי, here with meaning "although")[63] that exposes the folly of relying on allies and paramours: "Although on his part he hopes to flourish [פרא] among allies [אַחִים] . . ." (13:15a).[64] The background to this clause comes from Hos 8:9, in

62. G. del Olmo Lete, "Deber," *DDD* 231–32; G. J. Riley, "Midday Demon," *DDD* 572–73; N. Wyatt, "Qeteb," *DDD* 673–74; Andersen and Freedman, *Hosea*, 640.

63. On the concessive use of כִּי as a synonym to אִם, see *BHRG* §§40.11.1b; 40.29.1.

64. The pleonastic pronoun "on his part" (הוּא) foregrounds Ephraim's desire for foreign help (13:15a) to maximize tension with YHWH's assertion that it is precisely this wish that will soon be thwarted (13:15b–f).

which אֶפְרַיִם ("double fruitfulness") is mocked as a wandering "donkey" (פֶּרֶא) looking for help from Assyria. In Hos 13:15, the use of the verbal root פרא ("to flourish") picks up both animal and political associations by describing Ephraim's desire to "flourish" like a stream (13:15a) among "allies" (אַחִים, lit. "brothers"; 1 Kgs 9:13).[65]

These verbs likely refer to alliance partners whom Hosea has described earlier in similarly figurative terms as "lovers" (8:9), rather than to the eponymous tribes of Israel.[66] Going the way of imperialism will therefore bring neither creational flourishing nor military security. In place of the threat of Assyria, the empire with which Hosea opened this section by describing as an "east wind" (קָדִים; 12:2[1]), there will rage an even greater "east wind" (קָדִים; 13:15b) that is "the wind/Spirit of YHWH" (רוּחַ יְהוָה; 13:15c). The fact that this creational wonder arrives from the "wilderness" (מִדְבָּר; 13:15c) shifts Hosea's emphasis on this place as an unlikely honeymoon with YHWH (2:16[14]; 9:10; 13:5; cf. Deut 8:1–5) back to the geographical reality of desolation (2:5[3]; cf. Deut 1:19).

The arrival of the wind/Spirit of YHWH (13:15b–c) will bring devastating effects. More than just drying up the figurative water of Ephraim's life (13:15d–e), the wind/Spirit of YHWH also "will plunder his (Ephraim's) treasury of every precious vessel" (13:15f). Even heavy or concealed objects stored in the "treasury" (אוֹצָר; cf. Isa 2:7; 2 Kgs 14:14) will be powerless to resist this force, which in Hos 12–13 symbolizes both Assyria as exile's human agent (12:2[1]d) as well as YHWH himself as the ultimate cause of Ephraim's death (13:15). Even so, the present chapter in Hosea has already emphasized that culpability for exile lies with Ephraim rather than any other entity (13:9).

d. A Slain City (14:1[13:16])

The fourth and final aspect of Ephraim's destruction shifts from the realm of creation (13:15) back to the realm of history. Instead of riding in on the wind (13:15b–f), divine justice is already present in the city of YHWH's people when "Samaria must bear her guilt" (14:1[13:16]a). To "bear guilt" (אשם; 14:1[13:16]a) more commonly denotes an individual accepting and receiving punishment for sin (e.g., Lev 4:22; 5:2; Num 5:6–7), making it likely that "Samaria" in this verse refers more to the Northern Kingdom's capital city that must die than to its inhabitants.

Hosea had previously referred to Samaria as a place of violence (7:1) and host of a golden-calf cult (8:5–6; cf. 10:5). These sins furnish the background to the summary statement that "she has rebelled [מרה] against her God" (14:1[13:16]b). The root מרה ("to be rebellious, defy") carries the connotation of irrational and stubborn betrayal against a higher authority (e.g., Deut 9:7, 24; 21:18). In this case the authority is the gracious God who rescued Israel from oppression in the exodus (Hos 12:10[9]; 13:4).

Besides emphasizing the cause of Samaria's demise (14:1[13:16]a–b), this passage also highlights the cruelty of Samaria's punishment for its rebellion against YHWH. The allusiveness of earlier predictions of exile (e.g., Hos 13:13–15) becomes explicit and violent descriptions of death: "By the sword they will fall, their children will be dashed to pieces, their pregnant women will be ripped

65. Stuart A. Irvine, "Relating Prophets and History: An Example from Hosea 13," in *Israel's Prophets and Israel's Past: Essays on the Relationship of Prophetic Texts and Israelite History in Honor of John H. Hayes*, ed. Brad E. Kelle and Megan Bishop Moore, LHBOTS 446 (New York: T&T Clark, 2006), 162.

66. Cf. Dearman, *Hosea*, 331; Macintosh, *Hosea*, 552.

open" (14:1[13:16]c–e).[67] We must understand this terrifying trio of ruthlessness against the backdrop of the Assyrian war machine's bombastic threats of violence against those who failed to comply with its treaty stipulations.[68] Prophesying in the same era of Assyrian imperialism and propaganda, Hosea echoes this well-known language of curses and imprecations to show that Samaria's Faustian desire to live by the Assyrian sword entails rejecting YHWH's help (13:9) and death by the same Assyrian sword (14:1[13:16]c).

The following statements reflect the tragic reality that children (14:1[13:16]d) and pregnant women (14:1[13:16]e) suffer disproportionately in war. But more than being literal accounts of Assyrian cruelty toward Israel, the stock nature of such terminology (cf. 2 Kgs 8:12; Isa 13:15–16) conjures up the figurative totality of the theological, military, economic, and political crisis that exile would bring.[69] In the final chapter of Hosea, the beginnings of penitence from a people who realize the folly of trusting Assyria (14:4[3]) will mean that death and the grave will not have the last word (cf. Hos 13:14).

Canonical and Theological Significance

1. Monologue and Identity

The act of talking to oneself is a feature of everyday life. Far from being a sign of immaturity or insanity, psychologists observe that self-conversation is an important way that people make sense of their world and place themselves in a bigger story. Although the "external processing" of children speaking aloud to themselves tends to become the adult's "internal processing" of unspoken thoughts and feelings, the constitutive function of the "I"-voice to shape personal identity never leaves us.[70] To this end, the monologue in William Ernest Henley's poem "Invictus" exemplifies the pinnacle of self-actualization. His meditation on the "unconquerable soul" within him ends with the defiant statement, "I am the master of my fate: I am the captain of my soul."[71]

Keeping in mind that any psychological study of the "I"-voice must remain grounded in the biblical text,[72] Hos 11:12–13:16 records YHWH's pointed first-person response to such "I"-voices of self-actualization. Elsewhere the Hebrew Bible

67. All three clauses in this verse employ marked word order in Hebrew to convey a bitter nuance: "by the sword" (14:1[13:16]c), "their children" (14:1[13:16]d), and "their pregnant women" (14:1[13:16]e) each precede the verbal clause they modify, thereby foregrounding the violent means (14:1[13:16]c) and helpless parties (14:1[13:16]d–e) in Israel's impending death.

68. This characteristic facet of neo-Assyria's tradition of treaty curses has been aptly described as "moral terrorism" (Kitchen and Lawrence, *Treaty, Law, and Covenant in the Ancient Near East*, 3:223).

69. Lim and Castelo, *Hosea*, 64.

70. On this function of self-conversation in children and adults, respectively, see Jerome S. Bruner and Joan Lucariello, "Monologue as Narrative Recreation of the World," in *Narratives from the Crib*, ed. Katherine Nelson and Jerome S. Bruner (Cambridge: Harvard University Press, 2006), 73–97; and James A. Blachowicz, "The Dialogue of the Soul with Itself," *Journal of Consciousness Studies* 4 (1997): 485–508.

71. William Ernest Henley, "Invictus," in *The Oxford Book of English Verse: 1250–1900*, ed. Arthur Thomas Quiller-Thomas (Oxford: Clarendon, 1918), 1019.

72. Barbara M. Leung Lai, *Through the "I"-Window: The Inner Life of Characters in the Hebrew Bible*, Hebrew Bible Monographs 35 (Sheffield: Sheffield Phoenix, 2011), 11.

typically employs monologue to allow characters to introduce themselves or voice aloud their thoughts (e.g., Gen 27:41; 1 Sam 27:1; Esth 6:6). Even when this sort of monologue involves a dialogue within a divided self (e.g., Pss 42–43), the speaker remains in control of the message.[73] However, this section of Hosea is unusual in that YHWH quotes Ephraim's monologues (e.g., 12:9[8]) for the purpose of replacing them with his own, definitive "I"-voice (e.g., 12:10[9]). Brazen speech that previously expressed a desire for self-actualization has been neutralized by YHWH's stronger "I"-voice as the sovereign God of history and creation.[74]

For YHWH to hear such musings of the heart shows that he is an omniscient God (1 Sam 16:7; Prov 5:21; 15:3).[75] Not only this, the act of exposing his people's private pride through public display in Hosea's prophecies is an act of shaming—the unspoken "I"-voice of Ephraim represents human hubris at its ugliest extreme precisely because it was never meant to be heard by others. In a collectivist culture as represented by the Bible,[76] unveiling Israel's sin in this embarrassing way is the painful first step to reshaping Israel's identity around YHWH's own, better "I"-voice.[77] The "false self" of misplaced ego needs to be purged to make way for a "true self" characterized by God-centeredness—humanity's journey of identity from the deserved shame of estrangement to the restored honor of reconciliation with God lies at the heart of the Bible's bigger storyline.

To reconstruct Israel's identity on a better foundation, Hosea recalls the association of YHWH's "I"-voice with the great acts of Israel's past, such as the promises to the patriarchs, the exodus from Egypt, and the revelation at Sinai. The distinctive history of Israel should have given birth to a unique people of "missional magnetism"[78] who served an incomparable God among the nations. On the opposite side of this divine grace stands the present ingratitude embodied in Israel's first-person speech, those sins of injustice, imperialism, and immorality that represent different manifestations of idolatry in the eighth century BCE. The existential crisis confronting the audience of Hosea is therefore the question of which "I" will be the primary mover in history—Ephraim or YHWH?

---

73. Luis Alonso Schökel, *A Manual of Hebrew Poetics*, SubBi 11 (Rome: Pontifical Biblical Institute, 1988), 178–79.

74. Meir Sternberg, "The World from the Addressee's Viewpoint: Reception as Representation, Dialogue As Monologue," *Style* 20 (1986): 295–318, notes that direct speech in the Hebrew Bible is often modified by its addressee in the process of being heard.

75. Although not explicitly stated, it is probable that Ephraim's monologue was unspoken rather than spoken. The Deuteronomic monologues of satiation upon which Hosea depends (Deut 8:17–18; cf. 7:17–19, 21; 9:4–7; 15:9; 18:21) are private soliloquies since Israel's speech is described in each instance as "in your heart" (בִּלְבָבְךָ).

76. For a good introduction to the Bible's culture as collectivist in orientation, see E. Randolph Richards and Brandon J. O'Brien, *Misreading Scripture with Western Eyes: Removing Cultural Blinders to Better Understand the Bible* (Downers Grove, IL: InterVarsity Press, 2012), 113–36.

77. Jacqueline E. Lapsley observes the similar cultural dynamics that are at work in Ezekiel ("Shame and Self-Knowledge: The Positive Role of Shame in Ezekiel's View of the Moral Self," in *The Book of Ezekiel: Theological and Anthropological Perspectives*, ed. Margaret S. Odell and John T. Strong, SBLMS 9 [Atlanta: SBL Press, 2000], 143–73), a prophetic book that has been deeply influenced by Hosea.

78. Wright, *The Mission of God's People*, 129.

The stories we tell about the past also reveal for the present whether God has been a minor character in our quest for self-actualization or whether we are actors in his larger drama of redemption as recorded in Scripture.[79] For the people called "double fruitfulness" (i.e., the meaning of "Ephraim"), the declaration of independence that "I have become rich, I have found vigor for myself" (12:9[8]b–c; cf. Dan 4:27[30]) could only lead to the delusion that "all my labors will not find in me any iniquity—which is sin" (12:9[8]d; cf. Obad 3).

Stories about lesser human characters such as Ephraim pale in comparison to the story of Israel's God. His mighty acts proved that "I am YHWH your God from the land of Egypt" (12:10[9]; 13:4; cf. 12:6[5]). In both Testaments, the identity of God's people derives from being a distinctive community that has been saved by grace through faith in the "I AM" (Exod 3:14; 20:2; John 8:58) rather than in their own works (cf. Eph 2:8–9). Indeed, the main subject of our monologues—whether us or God—determines the whole course of our lives.

The Divine Lion—Not Safe and/but/or Good?

However, the "I AM" of Israel's history responds fiercely to being spurned. As the commentary noted above, the picture of YHWH as the "I AM" of salvation history (Hos 12:10[9]; 13:4–5) joins with the fearsome introduction that "I AM [or "I am"] for them like [אֱהִי לָהֶם כְּמוֹ]" a multifaceted animal who will rip Israel to shreds (13:7–8; cf. 5:14). The lion is the dominant creature in these verses with both male (13:7a) and female (13:8c) making an appearance.

The divine brutality that Hosea describes recalls the moral dilemma of Canaanite genocide in Joshua and Deuteronomy. The "new atheist" Richard Dawkins has memorably objected, "The God of the Old Testament is . . . a vindictive, bloodthirsty ethnic cleanser; a misogynistic, homophobic, racist, infanticidal, genocidal, filicidal, pestilential, megalomaniacal, sadomasochistic, capriciously malevolent bully."[80] Although the issues are complex, the troubled reader of the OT will benefit greatly from scholars who respond to "new atheism" and have provided thoughtful answers on the ethical problem of Canaanite genocide.[81]

79. On the proper relation between our story and God's story, see Craig G. Bartholomew and Michael W. Goheen, *The Drama of Scripture: Finding Our Place in the Biblical Story*, 2nd ed. (Grand Rapids: Baker Academic, 2014).

80. Dawkins, *The God Delusion*, 31.

81. E.g., Daniel I. Block, "How Can We Bless YHWH? Wrestling with Divine Violence in Deuteronomy," in *Wrestling with the Violence of God: Soundings in the Old Testament*, ed. M. Daniel Carroll R. and J. Blair Wilgus, *BBRSup* 10 (Winona Lake, IN: Eisenbrauns, 2015), 31–50; Paul Copan and Matthew Flannagan, *Did God Really Command Genocide?: Coming to Terms with the Justice of God* (Grand Rapids: Baker Books, 2014); Heath Thomas, Jeremy A. Evans, and Paul Copan, eds., *Holy War in the Bible: Christian Morality and an Old Testament Problem* (Downers Grove, IL: InterVarsity Press, 2013); Christopher J. H. Wright, *The God I Don't Understand: Reflections on Tough Questions of Faith* (Grand Rapids: Zondervan, 2008), 76–108. Compare the presentation of different Christian approaches found in C. S. Cowles et al., *Show Them No Mercy: Four Views on God and Canaanite Genocide* (Grand Rapids: Zondervan, 2003).

Nonetheless, the theological issue in Hos 13–14:1[13:16] is actually more severe than Canaanite genocide—what of violence directed by God against his own people as described in these leonine images of attack? Or of the terror of siege's aftermath when Israelite infants are smashed and expectant mothers are disemboweled? The very character of Israel's God comes into question, for would YHWH not be complicit in the same war crimes that he condemns in another eighth-century-BCE prophecy (Amos 1:13)?

One common approach to the OT's leonine images of God has been to appeal to C. S. Lewis's depiction of Aslan the (divine) lion in *The Lion, the Witch, and the Wardrobe*.[82] Mr. Beaver describes the nature of Aslan in replying to a question by Susan as follows: "Who said anything about safe? 'Course he isn't safe. But he's good. He's the King, I tell you."[83] The picture of YHWH in Hos 13–14:1[13:16] certainly "isn't safe," but in what sense can we also describe this lion as "good"? Truly, to explain later in the book that Aslan is "good and terrible at the same time"[84] is a paradox not only in Narnia. Outside this mythical world, readers of Hosea experience this tension when the book describes God as a lion who dismembers his prey (5:14; 13:7–8). Or to restate the obvious, C. S. Lewis never portrays Aslan as an enemy who attacks and mutilates the Pevensie children.

I acknowledge that these issues are difficult, and many have concluded that the broad cultural gap between us and the OT makes a resolution impossible.[85] But in seeking to honor the Bible as the final authority, the problem seems to lie in understanding Mr. Beaver's theological categories of "safe" and "good" as timeless "Western" abstractions about God's nature that are detached from the more "Eastern" history of Israel with YHWH as a story unfolding in space and time.[86]

Along these lines, writing as a bicultural Chinese-American who was educated in the United States but teaches in Singapore (and perhaps not representing any of these cultures well!), we must openly acknowledge the predominance of individualist orientation in the West as a preliminary step to understanding the collectivist orientation that underlies an ancient Near Eastern text like Hos 13–14:1[13:16]. This recognition of a cultural difference is not the anachronism of distinguishing sharply between "primitive" societies that supposedly think only in groups and "developed"

82. E.g., Elmer A. Martens, *God's Design: A Focus on Old Testament Theology*, 4th ed. (Eugene, OR: Wipf & Stock, 2015), 60.

83. C. S. Lewis, *The Lion, The Witch and the Wardrobe* (London: Scholastic, 1987), 76.

84. Ibid., 123.

85. E.g., Cyril S. Rodd, *Glimpses of a Strange Land: Studies in Old Testament Ethics*, OTS (Edinburgh: T&T Clark, 2001), 185–206.

86. I am mindful that the labels "Western" and "Eastern" are themselves problematic for overgeneralized associations, respectively, with supposedly "Greek" and "Hebraic" ways of thinking. The dynamic hybridity of Western and Eastern cultures in dialogue has always been the norm, but especially so in a globalizing/globalized world (Jan Nederveen Pieterse, "Globalization Goes in Circles: Hybridities East-West," in *Hybridising East and West: Tales Beyond Westernisation. Empirical Contributions to the Debates on Hybridity*, ed. Dominique Schirmer, Gernot Saalmann, and Christl Kessler, Southeast Asian Modernities 2 [Berlin: LIT, 2006], 21–32).

societies with individuals who have found their own "I"-voice.[87] Against such caricatures, cultural anthropologists now recognize that all societies of every era contain a mixture of collective and individual elements of consciousness, even to the point of variations within subgroups.[88]

Instead, I refer to how individuals in Israel who suffered as part of a national judgment were generally more concerned for the survival of the nation than themselves (without denying that their own pain was genuine and worthy of expression). An illustration from 1 Sam 4:19–22, a passage about the dying wife of Phinehas, illustrates the priority given to national disaster over individual disaster (again, a matter of emphasis rather than a strict dichotomy). In this text, Phinehas's wife has just received word of both a national disaster and a disaster closer to home—the plunder of the ark of the covenant by the Philistines and the untimely deaths of Eli her father-in-law as well as of her husband.

This news sends her into the shock of premature labor and her life ebbs away (1 Sam 4:19–20). Even as the midwives try to assure her that her newborn son is healthy (v. 20), this dying widow's focus in naming her son remains on the nation rather than herself: "She named the boy Ichabod, saying, 'The Glory has departed from Israel'—because of the capture of the ark of God and the deaths of her father-in-law and her husband. She said, 'The Glory has departed from Israel, for the ark of God has been captured'" (vv. 20–21, NIV). In short, the reproach of losing the "Glory" (i.e., YHWH's divine presence in the ark; cf. 1 Sam 15:29) frames her speech twice and outweighs the tragedy in her family, to say nothing (literally) of her own death.

Modern individualist interpreters struggle to hear the words of Phinehas's wife without feeling that the narrator has effaced her identity from the story.[89] However, reading 1 Sam 4:19–22 more sympathetically helps us understand the culture of ancient Israel. Using primarily national categories, her mourning for this confluence of tragedies means that we should also interpret the references to brutality in Hos 13–14:1[13:16] in primarily national rather than individual terms. Our empathy for the individual infants and women suffering the consequences of a breached city (14:1) is vitally necessary in a modern world where such atrocities still occur.[90] But the

87. Note the repeated use of "primitive" in a colonialist manner throughout the seminal but flawed work of H. W. Robinson, *Corporate Personality in Ancient Israel*, rev. ed. (Philadelphia: Fortress, 1980). See the important critiques of Robinson's view of "corporate personality" by J. W. Rogerson, "The Hebrew Conception of Corporate Personality: A Re-Examination," *JTS* 21 (1970): 1–16. Nearer our time, the pejorative connotations of the English term "groupthink" (from George Orwell's novel, *1984*) continue to reflect a bias in favor of individualism.

88. Following the pioneering study of "grid-group" cultural theory by Mary Douglas, *Natural Symbols: Explorations in Cosmology* (London: Barrie and Jenkins, 1973), 77–92.

89. E.g., Danna Nolan Fewell and D. M. Gunn, *Gender, Power, and Promise: The Subject of the Bible's First Story* (Nashville: Abingdon, 1993), 69–70.

90. The history of the twentieth century is littered with such wartime horrors against women and children, such as the Kosovo War (1998–1999), the Rwandan genocide (1994), the Bangladeshi war of independence (1971), and the "Rape of Nanking" (1937). As of this writing, the Rohingya refugee crisis in Myanmar furnishes yet another example.

example of Phinehas's wife suggests that the victims described in Hos 14:1[13:16] inhabited a cultural matrix different from ours, in which women themselves would have interpreted their personal tragedy as part of, but less significant than, the national tragedy of Israel's death.[91]

The invitation for personified Death and Sheol to come and do their work (13:14) therefore represents the most devastating catastrophe of all. Hosea goes on to introduce Death (13:15–14:1[13:16]) using the kind of conventional language found in ancient Near Eastern treaty-curses for the death of nations (e.g., devouring animals, loss of fertility, ravishing of women, eating one's children).[92] These atrocities are not less than literal in that the Assyrian Empire inflicts them upon individuals, but they are also figurative pointers to the greater collective reality that Israel's future is being systematically extinguished. When we understand that the mindset of the nation is in view more than that of its individual members, we can join Hosea's generation in asking the question that would have burned in their consciousness even as their demise drew near—what hope remains for Israel beyond our own death?

Indeed, hope from YHWH persists beyond Hos 13–14:1[13:16]. The prophet has already foretold a day when YHWH will restore Israel after the judgment of exile (e.g., 2:4–25[2–23]; 3:3–5), and this hope comes to full expression in chapter 14. Far from being cold comfort to those yet to be judged, the faithfulness of their God beyond the grave would have assured Israelites that death would not be the final verdict for their nation.[93] Hosea's link between promise and fulfillment also explains Paul's easy transformation of a summons to death (Hos 13:14) into a victory cry over death itself (1 Cor 15:55). The apostle is not misreading the OT text but pushing it along the theological arc that already exists in its original context—the temporary death of exile (Hos 13–14:1[13:16]) as the seed of Israel's eventual resurrection (Hos 14:2[1]–10[9]). This same movement from death to life applies to believers who, along with the nation of Israel, are part of God's people.

Mr. Beaver's comments about Aslan as "good" now take on a new light. Although individual Israelites may languish in exile and never see restoration during their lifetime, the God of Israel will only allow his corporate "son" (11:1) to suffer temporary

91. A similar cultural dynamic is at work in Jer 45. When Baruch laments about his pain in ministering alongside Jeremiah the prophet (Jer 45:3), YHWH responds by redirecting his attention to Judah's judgment and restoration to come (45:4). Focusing on his own struggle more than the nation's would be an example of seeking "great things for yourself" (45:5). The underlying assumption is that Baruch's priorities should have been like those of Phinehas's wife.

92. Delbert R. Hillers, *Treaty-Curses and the Old Testament Prophets*, BibOr 16 (Rome: Pontifical Biblical Institute, 1964), 43–79.

93. The priority of Israel's corporate consciousness through its history suggests that historical criticism has been mistaken in viewing prophetic oracles of salvation as irrelevant to an audience about to undergo judgment. Scholars have tended to ascribe such passages to a later hand since their optimism would supposedly be irrelevant until judgment was past (e.g., Clements, "Understanding the Book of Hosea," 407), but this reflects a modern bias toward individual consciousness.

death before raising him up. This act of focusing on Israel in the singular finds its ultimate fulfillment in the person of Jesus Christ (Matt 2:15; Gal 3:16), the new Israel who will succeed everywhere that old Israel failed.[94] The "I AM" of Hos 12–13 both "isn't safe" and "is good" because his corporate son in both Testaments experiences an ignominious defeat as a precursor to final victory.

94. Other OT Prophets, most notably Isaiah, chart a different trajectory toward Jesus Christ with their focus on the Messiah as the son of David. Although Hos 3:5 does mention David briefly, the book of Hosea's emphases on Israel as individual children and the corporate child of YHWH suggest an alternative theological bridge to the NT. For more discussion of how the NT portrays Jesus as the culmination of Israel's story, see Christopher J. H. Wright, *Knowing Jesus through the Old Testament*, 2nd ed. (Downers Grove, IL: InterVarsity Press, 2014).

CHAPTER 10

Hosea 14:2–10[1–9]

Main Idea of the Passage

The repetition of the Hebrew root שׁוּב ("to turn, return, repent") and its derivative מְשׁוּבָה ("apostasy") signals the interplay between repentance and restoration as the theme of Hosea's concluding chapter. As Israel heeds the call to "return" to YHWH and receives healing from "apostasy," YHWH "turns" away his fierce anger and restores all the creational blessings that his people wrongly sought from nature gods and goddesses.

Literary Context

Following the horrendous picture of destruction with which Hos 13–14:1[13:6] concludes, Hos 14:2–10[1–9] provides a double ending in summarizing both the previous literary section of 12:1–14:1[11:12–13:16] as well as the entire book. In the immediate context, Hosea transforms four gruesome images of death (Hos 13:13–14:1[13:16]) into a portrayal of new life for Israel as a repentant people in a restored land (14:2–8[1–7]). And at the level of Hosea as a whole, this picturesque description of Israel's flourishing represents the endpoint of the book's creational storyline that "the land commits heinous harlotry in walking away from YHWH" (1:2) and "as a result, the land is mourning" (4:3). In response to apostasy, "God will sow" (i.e., "Jezreel"; 1:3–5, 11) a great day of salvation on which all heaven and earth "will answer Jezreel" (2:24[22]).[1] One could therefore summarize Hosea's prophecy as a salvation history of estrangement and reconciliation, not merely for the people of Israel but also for the land in which they dwell. People and land are partners in a covenantal relationship with YHWH so that the obedience of the former directly affects the welfare of the latter. This organic link between people and land means that Hosea often expresses YHWH's historical judgments against his people (e.g., exile) in creational categories (e.g., drought, infertility).

1. Braaten, "Hosea's Land Theme," 104–25.

Chapter 14:2–10[1–9] also points beyond the horizon of the eighth century BCE as the boundary between Hosea and the rest of the Book of the Twelve. As the first entry of this literary collection that spans the eighth–fifth centuries BCE, Hosea's closing call for the Northern Kingdom to "return/repent" (שׁוּב; 14:2–3[1–2]; cf. Amos 4:6–11) also beckons to the Southern Kingdom of Judah (e.g., Joel 2:12–13) as well as to its remnant that returns to the land after the destruction of Jerusalem (e.g., Zech 1:3–4; Mal 3:7).[2] The eventual failure of Judah, the secondary audience of Hosea's prophecy (1:1b), to return to YHWH means that Hosea's exposition of repentance and restoration ultimately points to the eschatological realm rather than the historical period of the Babylonian exile.

Three centuries after Hosea, the recalcitrant audience of Malachi would reject YHWH's plea for repentance by feigning ignorance about what repentance entailed: "How shall we return to you?" (3:7). The prophecy of Hosea had anticipated this question with a sapiential question that sets forth Hosea's theology of repentance and restoration as an abiding model for those who are "wise" (Hos 14:10[9]). The audience of the Twelve Prophets in Malachi's time and beyond ought to gain insight about repentance as set forth in Hosea, the opening book of the collection.

I. Superscription: YHWH's Word to Hosea (1:1)
II. Hosea's Family as Prophetic Sign-Act (1:2–3:5)
III. YHWH's Contentions with Israel (4:1–14:1[13:16])
➡ **IV. An Epilogue on Repentance and Restoration (14:2–10[1–9])**

Translation and Exegetical Outline

(See pages 316–17.)

Structure and Literary Form

The body of chapter 14:2–9[1–8] falls into three main parts: (1) Hosea's summons to corporate repentance and the penitent words that he urges Israel to offer to YHWH (14:2–4[1–3]); (2) YHWH's loving response of restoring Israel as land and people (14:5–9[4–8]), and (3) a final exhortation about the audience's need for wisdom (14:10[9]). Surprisingly, Israel is never said to speak Hosea's suggested

2. An argument developed at length by LeCureux, *The Thematic Unity of the Book of the Twelve*, 77–80

words (part 1) before YHWH responds affirmatively (part 2). This omission does not necessarily indicate that judgment and salvation are inevitable. Nor does it mean that Israel remained unrepentant and was thereby a passive observer in the prophet's recitation of a penitential liturgy.[3]

Instead, the gap between parts (1) and (2) highlights the prophet's mediatory role and YHWH's relenting from judgment. Hosea 14:2–9[1–8] is similar in this regard to Joel 2:12–18, but different from other passages in the Book of the Twelve that provide an explicit description of the audience's repentance as a link between the prophet's summons and YHWH's relenting from judgment (e.g., Jon 3:1–10; Hag 1:10–15; Mal 3:13–18). The literary flexibility in these portrayals of repentance illustrates the relational dynamism of estrangement and reconciliation under YHWH's covenant, since repentance in the Bible is relational rather than formulaic or mechanical at its core.[4]

Following the words of Hosea and YHWH (14:2–9[1–8]), part (3) is an anonymous sage's coda (v. 10[9]) to the eighth-century prophecy of Hosea that broadens its message into an enduring revelation about YHWH's dealings with his apostate people.[5] This concluding verse of the book recalls the wisdom literature of the OT with the assertion "that the ways of YHWH are upright. The righteous will walk in them, but the rebellious will stumble in them" (14:10[9]). Here the terminology of the "ways of YHWH" evokes the binary image of righteous and wicked journeys in Ps 1 and the book of Proverbs. These closing words indicate that Hosea's distinctive covenantal ethos of "knowledge of God" (4:1, 4, 6:6) stands close in content and form to OT wisdom traditions, especially in their exposition of creation as humanity's partner in covenant with YHWH.[6]

In sum, Hos 14:2–10[1–9] contains at least three speakers in an impassioned trialogue with overtones of liturgical worship—a spiritual leader of Israel (or two), Israel as the contrite people of God, and the welcoming voice of YHWH himself. This combination of liturgical and wisdom elements offers an apt conclusion to Hosea by mirroring the rest of the book. Besides the use of שׁוב ("to repent, return"), the wisdom motif of journey appears twice to describe how Israel has "stumbled" (כשׁל; 14:2[1], 10[9]; cf. 5:5[2x]) into sin and away from YHWH. Hosea also describes apostasy as sickness that YHWH alone can "heal" (רפא; 14:5[4]; cf. 5:13; 6:1; 7:1; 11:3), in particular, the syncretistic disease of trusting Assyria and its imperialistic worldview (14:4[3], 9[8]; cf. 7:11; 8:9). While Hos 14:2–10[1–9] does not describe the consequences of forsaking YHWH as creational chaos (cf. 9:16; 13:3), this chapter's

3. Cf. Wolff, *Hosea*, 233–34.

4. For a comprehensive discussion of repentance, see Mark J. Boda, *"Return to Me": A Biblical Theology of Repentance*, NSBT 35 (Leicester: Apollos, 2015).

5. The sage may be Hosea himself, the Hezekian scribes who compiled prophetic books from the same period (i.e., Isaiah, Amos, Hosea, Micah), or the authoritative editor of the Twelve Prophets. See the Introduction to Hosea for further discussion on oral, written, and edited stages of Hosea's prophecy.

6. Dell, "Hosea, Creation, and Wisdom," 409–24.

Hosea 14:2–10[1–9]

Verse	Hebrew	Translation	Outline
			IV. An Epilogue on Repentance and Restoration (14:2–10[1–9])
			A. Hosea's Summons to Repentance (14:2–4[1–3])
14:2[1]a	שׁוּבָה יִשְׂרָאֵל עַד יְהוָה אֱלֹהֶיךָ	"Do return, O Israel, to YHWH your God,	1. The Corporate Need for Repentance: Israel's Iniquity (14:2[1])
2[1]b	כִּי כָשַׁלְתָּ בַּעֲוֺנֶךָ׃	for you have stumbled in your iniquity.	
3[2]a	קְחוּ עִמָּכֶם דְּבָרִים	Take vows with you,	2. The Individual Means of Repentance: Israel's Vows
3[2]b	וְשׁוּבוּ אֶל־יְהוָה	and return to YHWH.	(14:3–4[2–3])
3[2]c	אִמְרוּ אֵלָיו	Speak to him,	a. Embracing Forgiveness (14:3[2]c–e)
3[2]d	כָּל־תִּשָּׂא עָוֺן	'Every iniquity you will forgive.	
3[2]e	וְקַח־טוֹב	Accept a good thing.'	
3[2]f	וּנְשַׁלְּמָה פָרִים שְׂפָתֵינוּ׃	Let us repay as bulls[1] our lips:	b. Renouncing Syncretism (14:3[2]f–14:4[3])
4[3]a	אַשּׁוּר לֹא יוֹשִׁיעֵנוּ	'Assyria will not deliver us;	(1) Renouncing Imperialism (14:3[2]f–14:4[3]b)
4[3]b	עַל־סוּס לֹא נִרְכָּב	upon horses we will not ride.'	
4[3]c	וְלֹא־נֹאמַר עוֹד אֱלֹהֵינוּ	And let us not say again, 'Our gods,'	(2) Renouncing Idolatry (14:4[3]c–d)
4[3]d	לְמַעֲשֵׂה יָדֵינוּ	to the work of our hands,	
4[3]e	אֲשֶׁר־בְּךָ יְרֻחַם יָתוֹם׃	for in you the orphan will be shown mercy."	(3) Recognizing YHWH's Uniqueness (14:4[3]e)
			B. The Restorative Love of YHWH (14:5–9[4–8])
5[4]a	אֶרְפָּא מְשׁוּבָתָם	"I will heal their apostasy,	1. YHWH's Abundant Love (14:5[4])
5[4]b	אֹהֲבֵם נְדָבָה	I will love them with abandon,	
5[4]c	כִּי שָׁב אַפִּי מִמֶּנּוּ׃	for my anger has turned away from him.	
6[5]a	אֶהְיֶה כַטַּל לְיִשְׂרָאֵל	I shall be like the dew for Israel.	2. YHWH's Restoration of Creation (14:6–8[5–7])
			a. The Gift: Moisturizing Life (14:6[5]a)
6[5]b	יִפְרַח כַּשּׁוֹשַׁנָּה	He will bud like a lily,	b. The Result: Israel's Flourishing—Land and People
6[5]c	וְיַךְ שָׁרָשָׁיו כַּלְּבָנוֹן׃	and his root will strike like [the cedars of] Lebanon.	(14:6[5]b–8[7])
			(1) Israel as a Hybrid Plant (14:6[5]b–c)
7[6]a	יֵלְכוּ יֹנְקוֹתָיו	His shoots will sprout forth,	(2) Israel as an Olive Tree (14:7[6])
7[6]b	וִיהִי כַזַּיִת הוֹדוֹ	his splendor will be like the olive tree,	
7[6]c	וְרֵיחַ לוֹ כַּלְּבָנוֹן׃	and his fragrance like [the cedars of] Lebanon.	

Verse	Hebrew	Translation	Outline
8[7]a	יָשֻׁבוּ יֹשְׁבֵי בְצִלּוֹ יְחַיּוּ דָגָן	Those who dwell in his shadow shall again revive grain,	(3) YHWH as the Ultimate Nature Deity (14:8[7])
8[7]b	וְיִפְרְחוּ כַגָּפֶן	they shall sprout forth like the vine.	
8[7]c	זִכְרוֹ כְּיֵין לְבָנוֹן׃	His remembrance will be like the wine of Lebanon.	
9[8]a	אֶפְרַיִם מַה־לִּי עוֹד לָעֲצַבִּים	O Ephraim, what do I still have to do with idols?	3. YHWH's Superiority to Other Deities (14:9[8])
9[8]b	אֲנִי עָנִיתִי	As for me, I have answered,	a. YHWH as Husband (14:9[8]a–b)
9[8]c	וַאֲשׁוּרֶנּוּ	and I have watched over him.	b. YHWH as Protector (14:9[8]c)
9[8]d	אֲנִי כִּבְרוֹשׁ רַעֲנָן	I am like a sprawling cypress tree;	c. YHWH as Tree (14:9[8]d–e)
9[8]e	מִמֶּנִּי פֶּרְיְךָ נִמְצָא׃	from me your fruit is found."	
			C. The Audience's Urgent Need for Wisdom (14:10[9])
10[9]a	מִי חָכָם	"Who is wise?	1. A Summons to the Wise (14:10[9]a–d)
10[9]b	וְיָבֵן אֵלֶּה	Then let him understand these things.	
10[9]c	נָבוֹן	[Who is] a discerning person?	
10[9]d	וְיֵדָעֵם	And may he know them!	
10[9]e	כִּי־יְשָׁרִים דַּרְכֵי יְהוָה	That the ways of YHWH are upright.	2. The Knowledge Needed by the Wise (14:10[9]e–g)
10[9]f	וְצַדִּקִים יֵלְכוּ בָם	The righteous will walk in them,	
10[9]g	וּפֹשְׁעִים יִכָּשְׁלוּ בָם׃	but the rebellious will stumble in them."	

1. Following Thomas E. McComiskey ("Hosea," in *The Minor Prophets: An Exegetical and Expository Commentary*, ed. Thomas E. McComiskey [Grand Rapids: Baker Books, 1992], 229–30), it seems best to take פָּרִים as an adverbial accusative, namely, "as bulls."

portrayal of restoration as cosmic in scope (vv. 6–8[5–7]) mirrors the fecundity to come that the rest of the book heralds (e.g., 2:23–25[21–23]).[7] Finally, the motif of Israel's penitent speech (14:3–4[2–3]) offers a reversal of the many occasions when Israel has spoken wrongly, as in literary contexts of liturgy (e.g., 6:1–3) or in disputations that cite the people's monologues of pride and self-sufficiency (e.g., 10:3; 12:9[8]).

Explanation of the Text

A. Hosea's Summons to Repentance (14:2–4[1–3])

The epilogue of Hosea's prophecy begins with a combination of corporate and individual summons to prodigal Israel. The corporate call (v. 2[1]) emphasizes the need for repentance due to Israel's sinfulness, whereas the call for individuals (v. 3[2]a–c) prescribes speaking vows to YHWH as the means of repentance. The penitential content of these vows reflects Israel's determination to trust only in YHWH rather than the syncretism of Canaanized worship and Assyrian power politics (v. 4[3]).

1. The Corporate Need for Repentance: Israel's Iniquity (14:2[1])

The initial command to "return" (14:2[1]a) is a singular imperative that addresses Israel as a corporate people. Here the prophet enjoins the heartfelt repentance that he earlier predicted of Israel's last days (3:5). Prior occurrences of the root שׁוּב ("to repent, return") with Israel as subject tended to express the people's inability to repent (e.g., 5:4) or their unwillingness to do so (e.g., 7:10), even to the point of Israel voicing insincere penitence (e.g., 6:1) or turning away from YHWH toward apostasy (e.g., 7:16). In addition to these figurative and relational uses of שׁוּב, this root also signifies literal motion in describing the people's waywardness as a "return" to Egypt/Assyria (8:13; 9:3; cf. 11:5). In short, the prophet's plea in v. 2[1] calls for a comprehensive turnaround in the nation's errant journeys—both physical and spiritual dimensions of repentance must be included in changing direction and moving toward YHWH.

The emphatic form of the singular imperative (שׁוּבָה, with an insistent paragogic ה, "*Do* return") underscores that repentance remains a genuine possibility for Hosea's audience.[8] Repentance only becomes an eschatological matter in a later era when the two kingdoms of Israel continue in apostasy and the judgment of exile(s) becomes unavoidable.[9] The audience must therefore respond to the urgent invitation that opens this chapter. The present path has already led them to "have stumbled [כשׁל] in . . . iniquity [עָוֹן]" (14:2[1]b), an allusion to the instances when Hosea says that Israel "stumbled" (כשׁל; 4:5; 5:5; cf. 14:10[9]). Similarly, Hosea has identified Israel's "iniquity, guilt, crookedness" (עָוֹן) as cultic transgressions (4:8),

7. Cf. Marlow, *Biblical Prophets and Contemporary Environmental Ethics*, 158–59.

8. Sweeney, *The Twelve Prophets, Volume 1*, 136–37. On the use of this "long imperative" form in beckoning the hearer to approach the speaker, see Ronald S. Hendel and Jan Joosten, *How Old Is the Hebrew Bible? A Linguistic, Textual, and Historical Study*, The Anchor Yale Bible Reference Library (New Haven: Yale University Press, 2018), 89–90.

9. Cf. Stuart, *Hosea–Jonah*, 7–8.

spiritual pride (5:5), violent political scheming (7:1), materialism (12:9[8]), and ungodly leadership (13:12). This variety befits the status of עָוֹן as one of Hebrew's most general words for sin. In addition, the consequences of these sins have already begun for Israel in the eighth century BCE, even as the present summons to corporate repentance (14:2[1]) suggests a fleeting hope of restoration.

2. The Individual Means of Repentance: Israel's Vows (14:3–4[2–3)

Hosea's metaphor of journey continues in the call for individuals within Israel to repent (v. 3[2]). Stumbling in sin (14:2[1]) is not fatal as long as a person quickly regains their footing and moves in the opposite direction from the community at large (14:3[2]). Moving to plural address, Hosea exhorts every Israelite with a series of three imperatives, beginning with "[you all] take vows with you" (14:3[2]a).[10] In contrast to sacrifices, which must be presented to YHWH at authorized sites by cultic personnel, any Israelite can offer "vows" (lit. "words," דְּבָרִים) to YHWH in any place. The accessibility of YHWH makes Hosea's second imperative, the plea to "return" (14:2[1]b), an urgent but realizable possibility.

a. Embracing Forgiveness (14:3[2]c–e)

The passage specifies the means of such repentance as verbal vows (14:3[2]a–b). As for the content of those vows, penitent Israelites are urged to "speak to him" (14:3[2]c) and be confident in YHWH's mercy: "Every iniquity you will forgive" (14:3[2]d). For YHWH to "forgive/take away" involves a figurative extension of the root meaning of נשׂא ("to lift, bear, remove"). In this case the object to remove is the "iniquity" (עָוֹן) that was Israel's obstacle to stumble over and thereby hinder repentance (14:2[1]).

Strikingly, no priest, ritual, and altar are necessary to claim the promise of sin's forgiveness—hardly small omissions given Samaria's efforts to recreate the sacrificial system available to Judah in Jerusalem following the division of the kingdoms (cf. 1 Kgs 12). In emphasizing the priority of sincere words over ritual observance, Hos 14:2–3[1–2] seems to envision a historical context prior to a time when the eschatological removal of the sacrificial system has been reversed (cf. 3:4–5).

Having reentered the figurative sanctuary by expressing trust in YHWH (14:3[2]c–d), worshipers may proceed by requesting that YHWH "accept a good thing" (14:3[2]e). Urging YHWH to "accept" (לקח; 14:3[2]e) such an offering parallels his people taking the first step to "take" (לקח) vows to him (14:3[2]a) as a sign of their contrite hearts. The "good thing" (טוֹב; 14:3[2]e) to be presented to YHWH emphasizes the holy character of their vows, for the OT frequently predicates the virtues of being "good" (טוֹב) or "goodness" (טוּב) of YHWH himself (e.g., Hos 3:5; Pss 25:8; 136:1). Similarly, for Israel to embrace the "good" is to cease from rejecting YHWH and the "good" that he demands in holy living (cf. Hos 8:3).

b. Renouncing Syncretism (14:3[2]f–4[3])

The final clause of Hos 14:3[2] introduces the content of the vows to be spoken before YHWH—a string of corporate confessions by "us," either by the people themselves or the prophet speaking on their behalf (both options are possible). With this change to first-person address ("us"; 14:3[2]f–4[3])

10. This is an instance of changed reference (*LDHB* §2.6), in which the new description of an existing participant shifts their position in the discourse. In the case of the move to plural address in Hos 14:3[2], YHWH is summoning the attention of every individual in the audience.

from the second-person address that precedes ("you"/"you all"; 14:2[1]–3[2]e),[11] the community unites in urging itself to give worshipful words as an offering to YHWH: "Let us repay as bulls our lips" (14:3[2]f). The book has often condemned bovine images (e.g., 8:5–6; 10:5; 13:2), but the present reference to "bulls" (פָּרִים) plays upon ritual language to depict "our lips" (שְׂפָתֵינוּ) as the sacrifices YHWH truly desired.

Therefore, Hos 14:3[2]f involves a double use of the literary device of *metonymy*—the reference to "bulls" evokes Israel's cultic worship that is inferior to "lips," which in turn is a metonym for the rueful confessions that Israel will speak in the next verse. The comparison between sacrifices and speech in v. 3[2] highlights the eternal truth that the heart and life of the worshiper are always more important than the form of cultic worship. In OT wisdom literature and especially in Proverbs, the words that fall from one's "lips" (שְׂפָתַיִם) reflect the true thoughts and feelings of the "heart/mind" (לֵב), whether for good or for ill (e.g., Prov 10:8, 13; 15:7; 26:23).

(1) Renouncing Imperialism (14:3[2]f–4[3]b)

Following this positive vow (14:3[2]f), two negative vows renounce Israel's longstanding courtship of imperial power. The first negative vow, "Assyria will not deliver [ישׁע] us" (14:4[3]a), disowns Israel's foolhardy reliance upon this empire as well as the inclination throughout history to seek alternatives to YHWH's unique power to "deliver/save" (ישׁע; cf. Ps 27:1; 1 Sam 2:1). It is also intriguing that this verb's subject is the proper noun אַשּׁוּר, the shared name of the Assyrian Empire, Assur its capital city, and Assur its national god.[12]

The multiple meanings of אַשּׁוּר impart additional nuance to Israel's renunciation of both an empire and its patron deity in favor of trusting YHWH, who had been their "savior" (מוֹשִׁיעַ, also from the root ישׁע; 13:4) from the exodus (e.g., Exod 14:30; 15:2). The fact that savvy Assyrian propagandists later in the eighth century BCE could offer their culture's vision of "Assyrianism" (on which see Hos 5:8–7:16 and commentary there) as a superior alternative to Yahwism, as if the former could fulfill all the covenant promises of the latter (2 Kgs 18:17–35 // Isa 36:2–20),[13] presumes that the Israelite kingdoms felt deeply torn between these worldviews.

The second vow not to ride upon horses (14:4[3]b) represents a similar turn away from Egypt, the main supplier of horses for chariots and cavalry in the Israelite kingdoms' wars of survival in the eighth century BCE (Isa 31:1–3; 36:8). Much like nuclear arms or aircraft carriers today, in the ancient world horses were the signature weapon of superpowers or states striving to achieve this status.[14] To forsake the imperialism of both Assyria (14:4[3]a) and Egypt (14:4[3]b) is then an inescapably religious matter of trusting that YHWH's power is able to protect his people in a land sandwiched between stronger empires (cf. Pss 20:8[7]; 33:17).

11. This mirrors the changed reference (*LDHB* §2.6) of the previous verse's shift from singular to plural address. The tone changes markedly in vv. 2–4[1–3] as the speaker moves from *exhorting* "you" to repentance (14:2[1]–3[2]e) to *joining* the community in repentance as one of "us" (14:3[2]f–4[3]).

12. A. Livingstone, "Assur," *DDD* 108, observes that this lexical coincidence often led to equating the city and god with each other.

13. Dominic Rudman ("Is the Rabshakeh Also Among the Prophets? A Rhetorical Study of 2 Kings XVIII 17–35," *VT* 50 [2000]: 106–8) shows how the Assyrian envoy to Hezekiah's Jerusalem under siege (ca. 701 BC) presents his master's plan for Judah as a better way to receive YHWH's covenant blessings, such as a "new exodus" to the abundant land of Assyria ("a land like your own land" [2 Kgs 18:32]) and a deliverer more powerful than Hezekiah and YHWH ("Who among the all the gods of the lands have delivered their land from my hand, that YHWH should deliver Jerusalem from my hand?" [2 Kgs 18:35]).

14. John Oswalt, *The Book of Isaiah, Chapters 1–39*, NICOT (Grand Rapids: Eerdmans, 1986), 570.

(2) Renouncing Idolatry (14:4[3]c–d)

Following these vows to abandon imperialism (14:4[3]a–b), the worship leader enjoins a more explicit repudiation of idolatry (cf. 14:3[2]f). Again, it is hardly surprising to find a quick shift from one sphere of sin to another due to the synergism that operates between them (cf. Isa 2:7): "And let us not say again, 'our gods,' to the work of our hands" (14:4[3]c–d). The offering of penitent and trusting speech to YHWH (14:3[2]) involves a corresponding repudiation of faith in false deities (14:4[3]).

In the polytheistic world inhabited by Israel, the deities formerly called "our gods" (אֱלֹהֵינוּ, probably plural rather than singular "our God") could denote manifestations of YHWH venerated through the calf cult(s) of Samaria (e.g., 8:5–6; 10:5; 13:2), Baal and other Canaanite nature deities (e.g., 2:10[8]; 7:14; 13:1), or the gods of Assyria and Egypt for whose sake these empires undertook their military conquests (e.g., Isa 36:19–20). Israel's syncretism suggests some combination of these options. Whatever the character of false worship, Hos 14:4[3]d stresses the impotence of Israel's deities in describing them as "the work of our hands" (מַעֲשֵׂה יָדֵינוּ).[15] Man-made gods and goddesses are useless and can never be worthy of worship (cf. Deut 4:28; Isa 2:8; Mic 5:12[13]; Ps 115).

(3) Recognizing YHWH's Uniqueness (14:4[3]e)

The final clause of Hos 14:4[3] contrasts between YHWH and other ancient Near Eastern deities by looking ahead to the declaration of YHWH's superiority to other deities in v. 9[8]. While peoples who had suffered defeat in battle were shamefully abandoned by their patron deities,[16] the opposite is true for Israel as a distinctive people whom YHWH has chastened temporarily to renew the covenant rather than bring it to an end. Thus the poignant confession that "in you the orphan will be shown mercy" (14:4[3]e) is less about social justice in this context (cf. Deut 10:18; 16:11; 24:17) and more about Israel as a subject/son who rejected his divine patron/parent (cf. 11:1–2). As a figurative "orphan" (יָתוֹם) Israel is far more pathetic than the regular orphan who, along with the widow, is truly a victim and on whose behalf YHWH issued special protections in OT law (e.g., Exod 22:21[22]; Deut 24:17–22). Israel has orphaned and victimized itself by rejecting YHWH (11:2; 13:9).

But with devotion in the face of betrayal that a Mediterranean society would find unthinkable (cf. Luke 15:20), YHWH persists in offering this prodigal people the gift of his "mercy" (רחם; cf. Exod 34:6).[17] The appeal to such countercultural "mercy" on YHWH's part reverses the sign-act of Hosea and Gomer's second child. YHWH will one day transform her name from Lo-Ruhamah (לֹא רֻחָמָה, "Not-Shown-Mercy"; 1:6) to Ruhamah (רֻחָמָה, "Shown-Mercy; 2:3[1]) as a symbol of the turn from estrangement to reconciliation. The consummate renewal associated with that eschatological day draws near with the merciful Creator's arrival in the following verses.

15. On biblical "monotheism" as the functional matter of YHWH's incomparable power vis-à-vis other deities more than the ontological question of how many deities exist, see Bauckham, "Biblical Theology and the Problems of Monotheism," 187–217.

16. Lyn M. Bechtel, "The Perception of Shame within the Divine-Human Relationship in Biblical Israel," in *Uncovering Ancient Stones: Essays in Memory of H. Neil Richardson*, ed. H. Neil Richardson and Lewis M. Hopfe (Winona Lake, IN: Eisenbrauns, 1994), 82–83.

17. Along these lines, the Israeli Bible Society's version of the prodigal-son parable in modern Hebrew rightly uses the root רחם to record the climactic moment of the father's "mercies" (רַחֲמִים; Luke 15:20) toward his stunned son returning from a faraway land.

B. The Restorative Love of YHWH (14:5–9[4–8])

In response to the faithful vows of his people (vv. 3–4[2–3]), YHWH vindicates Israel's hope of reconciliation by coming to his orphaned people with a flurry of first-person verbs (14:5–9[4–8]). The first section of YHWH's reassurances emphasizes the fullness of his love (v. 5[4]), the second highlights his reversal of creational curses (vv. 6–8[5–7]), while the third asserts his superiority to other deities (v. 9[8]).

1. YHWH's Abundant Love (14:5[4])

In two "I"-declarations, YHWH introduces himself both as the doctor who "will heal [רפא] their apostasy" (14:5[4]a) and the spouse or parent who "will love [אהב] them with abandon" (14:5[4]b).[18] Prior references to the verb רפא ("to heal") highlighted Israel's misguided pursuit of the Assyrian Empire to "heal" its political and military wounds (e.g., 5:13) as well as an unrecognizable YHWH who supposedly promises to "heal" (6:1) without discipline or pain. YHWH corrects these misconceptions by declaring that he alone will "heal" (14:5[4]a) the deeper wound of "apostasy" (מְשׁוּבָה). This heart condition of defiance has plagued Israel from its beginnings in the exodus (Deut 9:6–7; cf. Hos 11:2–7) but will now be resolved once for all. Earlier in Hosea's prophecy, Israel had squandered its last of many opportunities to return to YHWH (cf. 10:12; 12:7[6];14:2[1]), so excising Israel's sick heart of its unhealthy influences (cf. 3:4) is necessary before healing can proceed.

The covenantal devotion with which YHWH will "love" (אהב; 14:5[4]b) his people is even stronger than a medical metaphor for reconciliation (14:5[4]a). The adverb נְדָבָה ("with abandon") highlights the relentlessness of this love in a marked contrast to the tit-for-tat pragmatism of Israel's relationship with "lovers" (e.g., 2:7[5], 9[7]; 8:9). These paramours were the alliance partners and other gods of the ancient Near East that offered benefits on a strictly conditional basis in return for Israel's devotion. As the inferior party, Israel constantly faced the uncertainty of knowing that such arrangements were subject to the whims of a patron empire or deity.

YHWH differs radically from these coldly transactional partners (cf. Lam 1:2) since Israel will instead be loved effusively and in an unrepayable manner (14:5[4]b). The reason (כִּי) for this new beginning is that divine wrath has already run its course: "For [כִּי] my anger has turned away from him" (14:5[4]c; cf. Isa 40:2). In the chapter's final use of שׁוּב ("turn, repent, return") found here, the decisive "turn" in restoring a long-broken relationship has already been taken by the receding anger of YHWH.

2. YHWH's Restoration of Creation (14:6–8[5–7])

Similarly to 2:21–25[19–23], Hos 14:6–8[5–7] declares that YHWH will reverse the creational consequences wrought by estrangement from him as the Creator. As in other prophetic books, Hosea has flexibly described the desolation of the created order as the cause (e.g., 1:4), means (e.g., 2:14[12]), and result (e.g., 9:6) of Israel's historical punishment in exile. Reconciliation to YHWH, then, also brings the full renewal of Israel as a land and not merely as a people returning from exile.[19]

18. Cf. Bernhard Oestreich, *Metaphors and Similes for Yahweh in Hosea 14:2-9 (1-8): A Study of Hoseanic Pictorial Language*, Friedensauer Schriftenreihe Bd. 1 (Bern: Lang, 1998), 69–70, who collapses these disparate images under a single root metaphor of YHWH as father/king.

19. Terence E. Fretheim (*God and World in the Old Testa-*

In the process the triangular covenant relationship among God, people, and land that sin had ruptured (cf. 1:2; 4:1–3) comes back together.[20]

a. The Gift: Moisturizing Life (14:6[5]a)

The first creational element to return is the "dew" (טַל), formerly a metaphor of Israel's fleeting devotion to YHWH (6:4) and ensuing dissipation in exile (13:3). Following reconciliation to YHWH the Creator, this cool watery vapor becomes a symbol of his gift of moisturizing life: "I will be like the dew [טַל] for Israel" (14:6[5]a). The provision of nighttime dew was essential to keep crops alive when Canaan's rains ceased during the summer. This dry and hot season fell between the early rains of spring when crops were planted and the late rains of autumn when they grew to maturity for harvest.[21]

However, this climatological given of Canaan is not as striking as two new developments that spring from YHWH's promise of being "dew" to Israel. The first is that YHWH's declaration, "I am/will be" (אֶהְיֶה; Hos 14:6[5]a), regains its connotations of identifying a covenantal God (cf. Exod 3:14) who is protector rather than opponent to an estranged people, as when YHWH threatened that "*I will be* like a lion to them, like a leopard I will pounce on the way" (13:7; cf. 5:14).[22] The second development is that YHWH's attribution of "dew" (טַל) to himself usurps the domain of Tallayu, a Canaanite goddess of dew. As one of Baal's daughters, Tallayu sometimes had the epithet "disperser of showers."[23]

Together, these two breakthroughs effect Israel's renewed knowledge of YHWH as both a reconciling covenant God and a restoring, creator God. This unparalleled combination of divine attributes sets YHWH apart from the other gods and goddesses of the ANE. More instances of polemics will follow against Canaan's deities of the botanic realm—YHWH's homeopathic posture toward idols in which "everything you can do I can do better."[24]

b. The Result: Israel's Flourishing—Land and People (14:6[5]b–8[7])

YHWH's gift of moisture (14:6[5]a) brings a massive transformation in an otherwise arid land. His victory over Canaan's deities gains momentum in the following verses as Israel—both the land and its inhabitants—regains its creation vitality (14:6[5]b–c). Indeed, Hosea depicts YHWH as the ultimate nature deity for Israel (14:8[7]) in the process of reconstructing the tripartite relationship among God, people, and land.

(1) Israel as a Hybrid Plant (14:6[5]b–c)

Before undercutting idols again in vv. 8–9[7–8], YHWH asserts that restoration of dew (14:5a) will lead to a resurgence of botanic life (14:6[5]b–7[6]). He personifies his revitalized people/land as a fragrant lily blooming outward (14:6[5]b) and a towering cedar of Lebanon taking root downward (14:6[5]c)—a hybrid plant with an impressive mixture of scent and strength. The "lily" (שׁוֹשַׁנָּה, perhaps the Madonna white lily common in Palestine,

ment: A Relational Theology of Creation [Nashville: Abingdon, 2005], 157–98) has influentially observed the integral connections that the OT Prophets make between creation on the one hand, and the historical verdicts of judgment and salvation on the other.

20. On this feature of Israel's covenant worldview, see Wright, *Old Testament Ethics for the People of God*, 76–99; Block, *The Gods of the Nations*, 93–111.

21. Oestreich, *Metaphors and Similes for Yahweh in Hosea 14*, 157–60.

22. YHWH's self-identification in Hos 13:7 uses אֱהִי rather than אֶהְיֶה, but both verbal forms mean "I will be."

23. Aicha Rahmouni, *Divine Epithets in the Ugaritic Alphabetic Texts*, trans. J. N. Ford, Handbook of Oriental Studies. Section One, The Near and Middle East 93 (Leiden: Brill, 2008), 129–31; Frédéric Gangloff, "Yhwh ou les déeses-arbres? (Osée XIV 6–8)," *VT* 49 (1999): 37.

24. To quote the famous Irving Berlin song from the Broadway musical, *Annie Get Your Gun* (1946).

lilium candium) contains an oil often used in perfume, while the passage's first of three references to (the) "Lebanon" (לְבָנוֹן; vv. 6[5]c, 7[6]c, 8[7]c) is not to a country but rather to a wooded region's cedars (*cedrus libani*) that were prized for their height and resistance to rot.[25]

(2) Israel as an Olive Tree (14:7[6])

The plants then shift species in the metaphor to an olive tree with young shoots (14:7[6]a). The trunk and branches of this tree are covered with "splendor" (הוֹד; 14:7[6]b)—a description of Israel's fruitfulness that uses a term for the opulent majesty of kings, whether God or his human representatives (cf. Pss 8:2[1]; 21:6[5]; 1 Chr 29:11). But where the smell of an olive tree (cf. 14:6[5]c) is localized due to its short and gnarled branches (and therefore fruit that is easy to pick), the next clause describes Israel emitting far and wide a balsamic "fragrance" (רֵיחַ; Hos 14:7[6]c) like the "fragrance" (רֵיחַ) of Lebanon's expansive cedars (Song 4:11). In sum, the remarkable combination of water and plant images in Hos 14:6–7[5–6] recalls the garden of Eden (Gen 2:9–10) and similar allusions to a creational paradise in Israel's wisdom traditions (Ps 1:3; Prov 3:18–20).

(3) YHWH as the Ultimate Nature Deity (14:8[7])

To this point the imagery from the realm of creation has symbolized Israel as either land or people (and both to a degree). However, in v. 8[7] the cedar of Lebanon just mentioned (v. 7[6]c) appears to become a figure for YHWH himself as the guardian of Israel, since his people will become "those who dwell in his shadow [i.e., YHWH/the tree]" and receive his power to "again revive" (שׁוּב) agricultural production (14:8[7]a; cf. Ezek 17:23–24).[26] In addition, the restoration of "grain" (דָּגָן) in Hos 14:8[7]a plays upon Canaanite nature-deity traditions of both Baal, who underwent an annual cycle of death and resurrection, as well as Dagon (דָּגוֹן), the Phoenician god of "grain" (דָּגָן) who was also the national god of the Philistines (cf. 1 Sam 5:1–5).[27] Under the watchful eye of one of the tallest trees native to Palestine, the land and its people will "sprout forth like the vine" (14:8[7]b). Fruitfulness of this sort represents a return to Israel's early days with YHWH as a lush "vine" (גֶּפֶן; 10:1, cf. 9:10), the same term used in Hos 14:8[7]b.

In the process of taking all the functions of Canaan's nature deities for himself, the fame of this creator and sustainer God will disperse far and wide like his fragrant people when "his remembrance will be like the wine of Lebanon" (14:8[7]c). This passage's fluidity of metaphor in moving from people as fragrant Mediterranean plants (14:6[5]b, 7[6]c) to YHWH as aromatic Lebanese wine (14:8[7]c) underscores the close identification among YHWH, people, and land in this chapter's description of restoration as cosmic in scope. The "remembrance/memorial" (זֵכֶר; 14:8[7]c) that properly belongs to YHWH as the sole Creator who nourishes his creation (cf. 14:6[5]a, 8[7]b) also alludes to Hosea 2—YHWH succeeds fully in his determination to ensure that the names of nature deities in whom Israel trusted will no longer "be remembered" (זכר *niphal*; 2:19[17]).

25. *Fauna and Flora of the Bible*, 2nd ed., Helps for Translators (London: United Bible Societies, 1980), 108, 134–36.

26. Macintosh (*Hosea*, 573) notes that here the root שׁוב (usually "to return, repent," e.g., 14:2[1]) should instead be rendered as an auxiliary of repetition, viz., "again revive."

27. The lack of a definite article enhances the pregnant nature of the construction, as in the juxtaposition of asyndetic דָּגָן ("grain") with תִּירוֹשׁ ("new wine") in Hos 7:14. Both agricultural products are also Semitic names for nature deities, making a polemical reference likely (J. F. Healey, "Dagon," *DDD* 217–18).

Also in this clause Hosea reinforces the homeopathic character of YHWH's victory over foreign gods by comparing his unparalleled honor among them with the scent of "wine" (יָיִן; 14:8[7]c). This beverage is not merely one of Canaan's prized commodities (cf. 4:11) but also the demythologized name of Yayin, one of Ugarit's gods of wine.[28] In short, Hos 14:8[7] asserts that YHWH is better than the male nature deities of Baal, Dagon, and Yayin; v. 6[5]a has already undermined Tallayu, a female deity.[29] These subtle wordplays on natural elements to undermine nature deities will climax in the next verse's explicit condemnation of idols, the last instance of first-person divine speech in Hosea's prophecy.

3. YHWH's Superiority to Other Deities (14:9[8])

Hosea 14:9[8] completes YHWH's polemic with the assertion that no other god can compare with him. The God of Israel distinguishes himself from lifeless idols (14:9[8]a) in three word pictures that allude to earlier passages: (1) YHWH as Husband (14:9[8]a–b; cf. Hos 1–3); (2) YHWH as Protector (14:9[8]c; cf. 12:10[9]; 13:4); and (3) YHWH as Tree (14:9[8]d; cf. 14:8[7]a).

The indirect references to other deities in YHWH's speech (vv. 6[5]a, 8[7]a, 8[7]c) culminate in an exasperating condemnation of Israel's devotion to them and the agricultural products they supposedly provide. YHWH the Creator asserts that he has nothing in common with other deities: "O Ephraim, what do I still have to do with idols?" (14:9[8]a). Here the topic of fertility returns to the foreground in how YHWH addresses his people not as "Israel" (14:2[1]a) but by the pointed vocative, "O Ephraim" (14:9[8]a; cf. 6:4). This is an alternative name for YHWH's people that means "double fruitfulness" (cf. Gen 41:52) and that Hosea often uses to polemicize against nature religion (e.g., 8:11; 9:11).

YHWH's irritation is also on display in this verse's rhetorical question that communicates relational distance (Judg 11:12; 1 Kgs 17:18; cf. John 2:4) and invariably expects a negative answer (i.e., "What do I have to do with *x?* [Nothing!]"). YHWH directs his disdain particularly against "idols" (עֲצַבִּים; 14:9[8]a), a general term for forbidden images that the OT always uses in a disparaging manner (cf. Hos 4:17; 8:4; Isa 10:11). YHWH is a sovereign Creator with the ability to provide his people with the very same things that other deities supposedly do (vv. 6–8[5–7]). However, this must not result in syncretism that views him as merely a minor god of nature whom people can easily placate or manipulate (cf. 4:17; 6:1–3; 8:4). The ever-present temptation to misidentify YHWH with other gods of the natural realm lies behind the use of the adverb עוֹד ("still, again") in Hos 14:9[8]a to express YHWH's continual vexation.

a. YHWH as Husband (14:9[8]a–b)

Despite the constant danger of syncretism, YHWH is forthright in reintroducing himself as the ultimate God of creation who has married Israel in a covenant.[30] The pleonastic declaration that "*as for me*, I have answered" (14:9[8]b)

28. Morris, *Prophecy, Poetry and Hosea*, 129.

29. Frédéric Gangloff ("La religion chez Osée. Du combat des dieux au retour des déesses: un bref état de la question," in *Bible et Terre Sainte: mélanges Marcel Beaudry*, ed. José Enrique Aguilar Chiu et al. [New York: Lang, 2008], 167–77) rightly observes the need to recognize how Hosea polemicizes against both male and female deities, rather than limiting the scope of the comparison to YHWH and Baal.

30. Katharine J. Dell, "Covenant and Creation in Relationship," in *Covenant as Context: Essays in Honour of E. W. Nicholson*, ed. A. D. H. Mayes and Robert B. Salters (Oxford: Oxford University Press, 2003), 114–16.

momentarily slows the discourse while repeating YHWH's promise in chapter 2 that he will "answer" (ענה) his people's renewed marriage vows to him with overflowing creational blessings as the second part of his "answer" to them (2:23–25[21–23]). Hosea 2 had described the "answer" that leads to flourishing of people and land as a future event (i.e., imperfective forms of ענה), but for Hos 14:9[8] to depict YHWH's "answer" (v. 9[8]a) in the past tense (i.e., a perfective form of ענה) means that the promised renovation of creation has already begun (cf. 14:6–8[5–7]). In the context of this chapter, the event that precipitates the affirmative "answer" (14:9[8]a) of YHWH is the penitent speech offered by Israel (vv. 3–4[2–3]).

b. YHWH as Protector (14:9[8]c)

The declaration that "I have watched over him" (14:9[8]c) similarly transforms an earlier use of the verb שׁוּר ("to watch over, gaze on). Hosea 13:7 used the same verb to describe YHWH eyeing his apostate people like a hungry leopard lying in wait. But the negative image of impending judgment here becomes a positive image of שׁוּר as protection (cf. Num 23:9). What is more, YHWH's promise that "I have watched over him" (אֲשׁוּרֶנּוּ) sounds nearly identical to the Hebrew term for Assyria/Assur (אַשּׁוּר), the empire/deity that Israel has just renounced as unable to save (14:4[3]a).[31] This pun is difficult to reproduce in English (perhaps "YHWH will be Israel's *assurance* rather than *Assur*"), but it underscores YHWH's incomparability from other gods, even as he invades their turf and defeats them at their own game of ensuring the worshiper's fertility and security.

As if this wordplay were not enough, there may be a further pun on foreign deities in that the phrases "I have answered" (עָנִיתִי/ʿānîṯî 14:9[8]b) and "I have watched over him" (אֲשׁוּרֶנּוּ/ʾăšûrennû 14:9[8]c) sound respectively in Hebrew like the Canaanite goddesses Anat and Asherah, the two consorts of Baal. This phonological similarity even led Julius Wellhausen to emend the text of Hos 14:9[8]b–c to uncover a polemic against these goddesses that was supposedly too sensitive for Israelite scribes to let remain.[32] Although the number of emendations required and lack of manuscript evidence make this text-critical proposal unlikely, Morris rightly notes that the names of other deities need not actually be present for the text to make allusive jests of this sort against them.[33]

c. YHWH as Tree (14:9[8]d–e)

Most provocatively of all, YHWH introduces himself as a creature of the same type that had often ensnared Israel: "I am like a sprawling cypress tree. From me your fruit will be found" (14:9[8]d–e). The comparison between Israel's deity and a "cypress [?]" (בְּרוֹשׁ) employs a generic term for conifer trees such as fir, cypress, and juniper.[34] At the same time, the fact that this tree produces fruit (14:9[8]e) makes it unlikely to be an ordinary conifer (cf. Ezek 17:22–23 for the same attribution of fruit to a cedar). Indeed, this use of a non-specific word for tall trees allows an assortment of possibilities, notably among them the trio of oak, poplar, and

31. McComiskey, "Hosea," in *The Minor Prophets*, 236.

32. For the most recent discussion and critique of Wellhausen's proposal, see Youn Ho Chung, *The Sin of the Calf: The Rise of the Bible's Negative Attitude toward the Golden Calf*, LHBOTS 523 (New York: T&T Clark, 2010), 170–71.

33. Morris, *Prophecy, Poetry and Hosea*, 130: "What is too audacious for the God which this amazing prophet proclaims? Israel would not let God remove the Not-Gods from their mouth. They returned to sin even after God negated the Not-Gods by declaring himself God and Not-Man. So God gives Israel a final chance. If Israel must worship the gods of Canaan, then 'I Will Be' will become the gods of Canaan."

34. *Fauna and Flora of the Bible*, 115–16.

terebinth that were likely the sites for Israelite participation in sexual rituals (Deut 12:2; 2 Kgs 17:10).

Furthermore, while these sacred trees offered "shade" (צֵל; Hos 4:13) that protected those engaging in orgies below, "shade" is the very thing that YHWH ascribes to himself as a tall tree for Israel (14:8[7]a)! Thus, it is not exactly correct that Hos 14:9[8] is the only place in which YHWH compares himself to a tree,[35] for such a statement is already found in the previous verse (see also Ezek 17:22–24, in which the tree appears to be a messianic figure with close ties to YHWH himself). The fact that Deut 12:2 commands Israel to destroy "every sprawling [רַעֲנָן] tree" upon entering Canaan makes it all the more amazing that YHWH's polemic against Canaanite deities would portray himself as a "sprawling" (רַעֲנָן; 14:9[8]d) tree.

What is more, the final clause of Hos 14:9[8] transforms the often-mocked name of "Ephraim" (e.g., 5:9; 9:11; 10:11) and turns it into a promise of YHWH's bounty: "From me your fruit will be found" (14:9[8]e). This verse opened with YHWH's frustration toward "double fruitfulness" (אֶפְרַיִם; 14:9[8]a) but concludes with the promise of "fruit" (פְּרִי; 14:9[8]e). Many Hosean passages have punned upon the assortment of verbal roots that involve the semantic domain of fertility (פרה, "to bear fruit; רבב, "to be abundant") in exposing Ephraim's futile attempts to bless itself (e.g., 8:11; 10:1; 12:2[1]). Yet in this passage, YHWH goes even further in the daring promise that "double fruitfulness" will find its true identity in him as the only deity who can give "fruit"—not in the supposedly sacred trees or impotent deities of Canaanite nature religion.

C. The Audience's Urgent Need for Wisdom (14:10[9])

The fourteen chapters of Hosea outline the many ways in which Israel has repeatedly failed to grasp that YHWH is the supreme God of both creation and history. Future generations, by contrast, can learn from Israel's negative example and make better choices. For this reason the book of Hosea concludes in v. 10[9] with a *metacomment*. This is a feature in which a discourse steps outside its frame of reference to expound on its own significance.[36] To this end, a sage confronts Hosea's audience with a timeless question that doubles as an invitation to the naive: "Who is wise? Then let him understand these things. [Who is] a discerning person? And may he know them!" (14:10[9]a–c). Here the "Who?" question about wisdom (v. 10[9]a) follows a "What?" question about idolatry (v. 9[8]). Since Hosea is clearly the source of the "What?" question, the use of a similar "Who?" question in the following verse suggests by extension that the latter also has Hosea as its source. The contrast between wisdom and foolishness found throughout the book also supports the case for the prophet as the speaker of Hos 14:10[9].[37]

On the other hand, it remains possible that the men of Hezekiah added the present verse to Hosea's prophecy (cf. Prov 25:1). This group of royally trained scribes appears to have collected the eighth-century prophetic books and left a common editorial imprint upon them (Hos 1:2; Isa 1:1; Amos 1:1; Mic 1:1).[38] Another possibility is that scribes added a second ending in 14:10[9] to

35. Cf. Philip J. King, "Hosea's Message of Hope," *BTB* 12 (1982): 95.

36. See *LDHB* §1.3.

37. Cf. C. L. Seow ("Hosea 14:10 and the Foolish People Motif," *CBQ* 44 [1982]: 212–24), who catalogues the wisdom themes that find their natural conclusion in Hos 14:10[9]. He is perhaps too cautious when he speaks of "the 'Hoseanic composer' or an editor" (223) who was responsible for the book.

38. Freedman, "Headings in the Books of the Eighth-Century Prophets," 9–26.

Hosea's prophecy when it became part of the larger collection of the Twelve Prophets, some time in the Persian period.

1. A Summons to the Wise (14:10[9]a–d)

In any case, the previous chapter has asserted that Israel is "not wise" (לֹא חָכָם; 13:13b) as a preliminary answer to the question about the identity of the "wise" (חָכָם; 14:10[9]a). In contrast to the fool who refuses to forsake his folly (cf. Prov 13:16; 15:5), the wise in Israel (Hos 14:10[9]a) are those who possess the humble desire to "understand/discern" (בין; 14:10[9]b) and "know" (ידע; 14:10[9]d). Hosea uses both these verbal roots elsewhere to describe his unresponsive audience as people who lack "understanding/discernment" and "knowledge of God" (e.g., 4:1, 6, 14), even as they insist that they "know YHWH" (e.g., 6:3; 8:2). Deuteronomy similarly uses the verb ידע ("to know, acknowledge") to summarize the entirety of the covenantal ethos demanded by YHWH (e.g., Deut 4:35, 39; 7:9).

2. The Knowledge Needed by the Wise (14:10[9]e–g)

Living proof of knowing God (14:10[9]d) is always more than intellectual assent to propositional truths, for truly Godward knowledge involves the conviction "that the ways of YHWH are upright. The righteous will walk in them" (Hos 14:10[9] e–f). This metaphor of life as a journey, whether to walk in YHWH's "way/ways" (דְּרָכִים/דֶּרֶךְ) or in those of the wicked, is at home in both the covenantal traditions of Deuteronomy (e.g., 6:7; 8:2, 6) and the sage's creational thrust in Proverbs (e.g., 1:15; 4:26; 12:15).

Hosea's closing exhortation to "walk" (הלך; 14:10[9]f) in YHWH's ways, lest one "stumble" (כשׁל; 14:10[9]g) in life, is reminiscent of the Bible's many similar extensions of the journey metaphor. In anticipating the NT's description of discipleship as a pilgrimage with Jesus,[39] the book of Hosea closes by reminding the audience that to stay on YHWH's journey is to "walk in" (הלך בְּ־) his ways (e.g., Deut 10:12; 11:22). This journey involves walking in straight paths rather than straying "to the right and to the left" (יָמִין וּשְׂמֹאל; e.g., Prov 4:27; Deut 5:32).

With all these allusions to prior OT traditions, Hosea has clearly recontextualized older traditions of covenant and creation for a new audience in the eighth century BCE. New generations of hearers can find further wisdom for upright living in the original sources of such teaching in Deuteronomy and Proverbs. The rest of the Twelve Prophets illustrate how the choice between walking with the righteous (Hos 14:10[9]f) or stumbling in the company of the rebellious (14:10[9]g) is literally a matter of life and death (Joel 2:12–17; Zeph 2:3; Mal 3:18; cf. Ps 1:5–6).

Canonical and Theological Significance

1. Repentance

Calls to repentance are ubiquitous in the Bible (e.g., Jer 3:12; Joel 2:12; Matt 3:2; Acts 2:38). In Hos 14:2–10[1–9], the list of sins that Israel must forsake may appear

39. C. Spicq, *Vie chrétienne et pérégrination selon le nouveau testament*, LD 71 (Paris: Cerf, 1972).

to be a random assortment—wrong speech, Assyrian imperialism, battle horses, and graven images (vv. 3–4[2–3]). Is there any thread tying these political, military, and religious themes together? Or is Hosea referring to syncretism in the truest sense of the word, as an eclectic combination of issues? Since repentance involves a comprehensive turn from sin and return to God,[40] Hosea 14:2–10[1–9] speaks incisively into its cultural context by describing both kinds of movement in this journey.

The commonness of repentance in the Bible can obscure the fact that this theological idea takes a very different shape outside the Judeo-Christian tradition, if it is found at all. The OT shares with its context a "common theology of the ancient Near East" in which the gods levy punishment against humans for their sins,[41] an idea known as the *retribution principle*.[42] Outside the Bible, the suffering that ensues from retribution is addressed in two kinds of Mesopotamian literature that stand in the background of Hosea. Both genres differ from the intensely personal nature of penitence as outlined in Hos 14:2–10[1–9] and other passages. The first is the *lament prayer* that is familiar from the lament psalms and the book of Lamentations. But in the rest of the ancient Near East, this literary genre adds the cruel twists that the supplicant often does not know what sin has been committed, is uncertain about which of several possible deities has been offended, and consequently has no way to even begin atoning for their sins.[43]

In the polytheistic world around Israel, lament prayers naturally recorded the desperate sufferer engaging either in speculation about the offenses committed and deities involved (via superstition or divination) or "covering all the bases" with a general prayer for forgiveness. The plea for relief would go to all corners, rendering the oft-used label of "penitential" for these prayers a misnomer for implying that the supplicant turns from something and returns to someone.[44] By contrast, repentance in Hos 14:2–10[1–9] operates within a theological framework of knowing a personal God and his expectations as well as how to reconcile with him. Only the worldview of biblical monotheism, with a God both holy and gracious at the center, holds out the possibility that punishment for sin as not merely a moral necessity but also a loving form of discipline. The Bible is therefore unique for asserting that human pain can be both a problem and a gift from a covenantal God.[45]

The ancient Near East supplies the flip side of the retribution principle in other

40. Boda, *Return to Me*, 31 et passim.

41. Morton Smith, "The Common Theology of the Ancient Near East," *JBL* 71 (1952): 135–47.

42. J. H. Walton, *Ancient Israelite Literature in Its Cultural Context: A Survey of Parallels between Biblical and Ancient Near Eastern Texts*, Library of Biblical Interpretation (Grand Rapids: Zondervan, 1989), 179–80.

43. See, for example, the theme of the supplicant's helplessness in "Dingirhadibbas to Personal Deities" and "Erashaḫunga to Every God." The most recent translations and commentary are provided in Alan Lenzi, ed., *Reading Akkadian Prayers and Hymns: An Introduction*, SBLANEM 3 (Atlanta: SBL Press, 2011), 431–64.

44. Cf. ibid., 40–46.

45. Cf. Philip Yancey and Paul Brand, *The Gift of Pain: Why We Hurt And What We Can Do About It* (Grand Rapids: Zondervan, 1997).

literary genres that deal with human suffering, the *royally sponsored monuments and annals* of the Assyrian Empire that date from Hosea's time. In these skewed retellings of history, divine sanctions guarantee that those with power (i.e., Assyria) will inflict terror in Assur's name on those who are weak (i.e., Assyria's enemies). Victory over the deities of other lands and peoples then fuels propaganda about the worldwide fame of "Assur" (the high god's name, but conveniently also that of his capital city and empire).

The foreshadowing of modern spinmeisters is evident in the "Tiglath-pileser principle," so named after the great Neo-Assyrian ruler of Hosea's time who was prone to making grandiose claims for both the empire and Assur its national god—on a thin or nonexistent factual basis.[46] The Tiglath-pileser principle lives on beyond the time of Hosea through modern-day narcissists who shade the truth and project a larger-than-life persona to deceive others. However, the façade of success projected by such "Assyrianism" can scarcely hide the fact, then and now, that the prideful are just as insecure and fragile as anyone else.

Prophesying in the heyday of "Assyrianism," Hosea cuts a sharp course for the biblical model of repentance between his cultural milieu's extremes of desperate shame (i.e., the lament prayer) and vacuous honor (i.e., Assyrian royal propaganda). Both responses to the problem of suffering are wrongheaded for their failure to grasp that our identity must find roots in the loving nature of God who has made us in his image and chooses to participate emotionally in the life of his children (see Hos 11:8–9 and commentary there). Introspection and vanity might seem like opposites, but in reality share an obsession with staying in control that Larry Crabb has strikingly labeled "the problem of demandingness."[47]

Although Crabb speaks mainly of the book of Job, his description of the people of God seeking to take matters into their own hands is equally at home in Israel's disputations with YHWH recorded in the eighth century BCE (e.g., Hos 8:2; 12:9[8]), not to mention our prayers in the twenty-first century CE. He writes,

> We pray, asking God to hear our cry, pleading with Him to let nothing else go wrong. I wonder if sometimes the passion in our prayers reflects more of a demand than a petition. Frustration is excellent soil for growing a demanding spirit. It is therefore important that we handle difficulties well, allowing them to mature us rather than to push us toward demandingness.[48]

46. Baruch Halpern wittily describes, "In Assyrian royal inscriptions, then, the torching of a grain field is the conquest of a whole territory beyond it. A looting raid becomes a claim of perpetual sovereignty. But this does not mean that campaigns can be confected. The technique is that of putting extreme spin on real events. Interpreting such literature demands only a simple rule, the Tiglath-pileser principle. The question is, what is the minimum the king might have done to lay claim to the achievements he publishes? . . . *Each small mark of prestige becomes the evidence for grand triumph*" (*David's Secret Demons: Messiah, Murderer, Traitor, King* [Grand Rapids: Eerdmans, 2001], 126; emphasis added).

47. Larry Crabb, *Inside Out*, Rev. ed. (Colorado Springs, CO: NavPress, 1998), 143.

48. Ibid., 148.

Ironically, then, Israel's skittish reactions to its Assyrian crises tended toward the very same worldview of "Assyrianism" that posed a threat in the first place. This is the "problem of demandingness" that contrasts with the freedom of "repentance and rest . . . quietness and trust" (Isa 30:15) that Yahwism promises in the face of crisis.

Crabb rightly also links sowing and reaping in the manner that Hosea so often uses to describe the sometimes counterintuitive nature of faith in YHWH. The desire to remain in charge wherever possible—to trust in illusory human strength that is actually weakness instead of in YHWH's apparent weakness that is actually strength—is the tie that binds together the seemingly unrelated sins to be renounced in Hos 14:4[3]. Imperialism is the attempt to overcome frailty by accumulating more power (14:4[3]a–b), while idolatry represents a similar desire to manipulate one's existence toward greater prosperity (14:4[3]c–d).

Both imperialism and idolatry are sins that seek to usurp the authority of a sovereign God who has invited his people to "wait for your God continually" (12:7[6]). Turning from the false promises of human power involves a corresponding turn to God as the physician who can "heal" (cf. 5:13; 6:1; 7:1) from the gangrenous diseases of misplaced faith (14:5[4]). Following their return to God, the Creator himself turns from his anger (14:5[4]) and surprises his chastened people with all the wonderful gifts of creation that he had previously taken away (14:6–9[5–8]).

2. Monotheism

Hosea 14:6–9[5–8] offers a portrait of Israel's God unlike any other in the OT. While the prophet has often emphasized the importance of salvation history, this passage describes the relationship between Creator and creation in a manner unparalleled before or since. Simply put, it transforms the very creatures that so enticed Israel to syncretism with nature religion into descriptions of YHWH himself! This goes much further than Israel's testimony in other passages that all creation belongs to God (cf. Pss 24:1; 50:12; 95:4–7) or that creation shows forth his power (cf. Pss 104; 148).

This passage not only attributes natural images such as moisture and sacred trees to the Creator (Hos 14:6–8[5–7], 9[8]d–e), YHWH seems even to whisper the names of several nature deities (i.e., Anat, Asherah, Yayin, Tirosh, Dagan, Deber) on the way to asserting his superiority to them and absorbing all their power and prerogatives. This creative use of polemic reminds us that the missiological methods of *contextualization* are not just for "application" after the process of "interpretation" is complete but are rather an essential part of how the Bible itself sifts through what to reject, keep, and transform from its cultural milieu in the course of communicating its timeless message.[49]

Hosea's remarkable act of contextualization also means that YHWH theoretically

49. See the discussion of "Hosea's Distinctive Theology in its Cultural Context" in the introduction to Hosea.

has the ability to answer his own question—"What do I still have to do with idols?" (14:9[8]a)—rather differently from how he expresses his revulsion for Israel's syncretistic worship. Whereas the people of YHWH must answer "No!" to the mistake of believing that he is a nature deity, his own response can be "Yes!" to all the risks he takes. YHWH dares to portray himself as the ultimate nature deity who puts all lesser ones to shame[50] yet without opening himself to manipulation through the rituals that Israel attempted when confusing YHWH with other gods and goddesses.

The refusal to reduce the bountifulness of creation to a transaction with YHWH is the defining feature of Israel's covenantal worldview, rather than bracketing out the realm of creation and its associated spiritual powers from him in the first place.[51] Monotheism as the Bible defines it is not so much the denial that other deities exist but more the attribution of all the functions of divinity to Israel's God. Richard Bauckham rightly summarizes: "Though called gods, the other gods do not really deserve the term, because they are not effective divinities, acting with power in the world. YHWH alone is the God with supreme power."[52] The doctrine of monotheism is therefore not designed to minimize the possibilities in Israel's faith but to describe the maximalist way in which the Bible depicts YHWH as incomparable within any pantheon of gods (Exod 15:11; Deut 4:35; 39).

On this note, the fact that YHWH is one YHWH (Deut 6:4) has sometimes led to the conclusion that "[s]carcity is encoded in the Bible as a principle of Oneness (one land, one people, one nation) and in monotheistic thinking (one Deity), [and] it becomes a demand of exclusive allegiance that threatens with the violence of exclusion."[53] It is sadly true that professing monotheists have sometimes acted to exclude others. Behind the error of equating monotheism with narrowness, however, lies the failure to understand that the Creator is generous rather than stingy—he whose very nature is "goodness" (Hos 3:5) and who made everything "very good" (Gen 1:31) only denies empty things to people because they are a poor substitute for satisfying their God-given desires.[54] And since every generation of God's people faces the temptation to live unwisely and forget this truth, it is essential to remember that Hosea's call to repentance and YHWH's proclamation of monotheism in this chapter are two sides of the same coin of filling us with the best things, first of all in himself, and then in the gifts he lavishes. In this respect, St. Augustine could easily have been speaking of Hos 14:2–10[1–9] in his famous introduction to the *Confessions*: "Thou hast made us for thyself and restless is our heart until it comes to rest in thee."[55]

50. Cf. Andersen and Freedman, *Hosea*, 242.

51. Klaus Koch, *The Prophets*, trans. Margaret Kohl, 2 vols. (Philadelphia: Fortress, 1983), 1:89–90.

52. Bauckham, "Biblical Theology and the Problems of Monotheism," 196.

53. Regina M. Schwartz, *The Curse of Cain: The Violent Legacy of Monotheism* (Chicago: University of Chicago Press, 1998), xi.

54. Timothy Keller, *Counterfeit Gods: When the Empty Promises of Love, Money and Power Let You Down* (London: Hodder & Stoughton, 2010).

55. Book 1, Chapter 1. Online at http://www.ccel.org/a/augustine/confessions/.

Scripture Index

Genesis

Exodus

Leviticus

Numbers

Deuteronomy

Joshua

Judges

Ruth

1 Samuel

2 Samuel

1 Kings

2 Kings

1 Chronicles

Proverbs

Song of Songs

Isaiah

Jeremiah

Lamentations

Ezekiel

Daniel

Hosea

Joel

Amos

Obadiah

Jonah

Micah

Nahum

Habakkuk

Zephaniah

Haggai

Zechariah

Malachi

Matthew

Luke

John

Subject Index

Author Index